Business Logistics/ Supply Chain Management

Planning, Organizing, and Controlling the Supply Chain

FIFTH EDITION

Ronald H. Ballou

Weatherhead School of Management
Case Western Reserve University

PEARSON

Prentice
Hall

Pearson Education International

Acquisitions Editor: Wendy Craven
Editor-in-Chief: Jeff Shelstad
Assistant Editor: Melissa Pellerano
Editorial Assistant: Danielle Serra
Media Project Manager: Anthony Palmiotto
Marketing Manager: Michelle O'Brien
Marketing Assistant: Amanda Fisher
Managing Editor (Production): John Roberts
Production Editor: Maureen Wilson
Permissions Supervisor: Suzanne Grappi
Manufacturing Buyer: Michelle Klein
Cover Design: Lisa Boylan
Cover Illustration/Photo: Felix Clouzot/Getty Images Inc.—Image Bank
Composition/Full-Service Project Management: Progressive Publishing
Alternatives

Credits and acknowledgments borrowed from other sources and reproduced, with permission, in this textbook appear on appropriate page within text.

If you purchased this book within the United States or Canada you should be aware that it has been wrongfully imported without the approval of the Publisher or the Author.

Pearson Education LTD.
Pearson Education Singapore, Pte. Ltd
Pearson Education, Canada, Ltd
Pearson Education–Japan
Pearson Education Australia PTY, Limited

Pearson Education North Asia Ltd
Pearson Educación de Mexico, S.A. de C.V.
Pearson Education Malaysia, Pte. Ltd
Pearson Education Upper Saddle River, New Jersey

10 9 8
ISBN 0-13-123010-7

Business Logistics/
Supply Chain Management

For logistics/supply chain managers everywhere:

I have heard of you . . . that light and understanding and excellent wisdom are found in you . . . I have heard that you give interpretations and solve problems . . . you shall be clothed with purple and have a chain of gold about your neck.

—DANIEL 5:14

BRIEF CONTENTS

CONTENTS

PREFACE

—THOMAS CARLYLE

This book is about the vital subject of business logistics/supply chain—an area of management that has been observed to absorb as much as 60 to 80 percent of a firm's sales dollar and that can be essential to a firm's competitive strategy and revenue generation. This management area has been described by many names, including physical distribution, materials management, transportation management, logistics, and now supply chain management. The business activities of concern may include all or part of the following: transportation, inventory maintenance, order processing, purchasing, warehousing, materials handling, packaging, customer service standards, and production.

The focus of this book is on the planning, organizing, and controlling of these activities—key elements for successful management in any organization. Special emphasis is given to strategic planning and decision making as perhaps the most important parts of the management process. The mission of this managerial effort is to set the level of the logistics activities so as to make products and services available to customers at the time, place, and in the condition and form desired, in the most profitable or cost-effective way.

Because logistics activities have always been vital to companies and organizations, the field of business logistics/supply chain management represents a synthesis of many concepts, principles, and methods from the more traditional areas of marketing, production, accounting, purchasing, and transportation, as well as from the disciplines of applied mathematics, organizational behavior, and economics. This book attempts to unify these into a logical body of thought that can lead to the effective management of the supply chain.

As with any field of management, there are frequently changing terms to capture the methods and concepts of business logistics/supply chain. An attempt has been made to resist following the popular press and fads, and to present the ideas, principles, and techniques that are fundamental to good business logistics practice, now and in the near future. In this spirit, the fifth edition is organized around two themes. First, the basic activities of management, namely, planning, organizing, and controlling, provide the overarching theme for the book. Second, a triangle of interrelated transportation, inventory, and location strategies are at the heart of good logistics planning and decision making. This triangle is emphasized through the text.

Several trends have been noted that affect the scope and practice of business logistics/supply chain. These have been integrated into the body of the text as application illustrations of the fundamental ideas being presented. First, emphasis is placed on logistics/supply chain in a worldwide setting to reflect the growing internationalization and globalization of business in general. Second, the shifting toward more service-oriented economies by industrialized nations is emphasized by showing how logistics concepts and principles are equally applicable to service-producing firms as they are to product-producing ones. Third, attention is given to the integrated management of supply chain activities, as well as managing these activities among the other functional areas of business as well as across multiple enterprises. Fourth, many practical examples are given to show the applicability of the material. Fifth, computer software is provided to assist in solving logistics/supply chain problems reflecting the growing use of computer technology in managerial decision making.

Over the years, so many people and companies have contributed to the ideas embodied in this fifth edition that a list of acknowledgments would be far too long to print. However, to all those students and professors around the world who were willing to comment on the previous editions, to those businesspeople who were willing to try the ideas embodied in them, and to all others who made comments of praise as well as criticism—my heartfelt thanks. A special note of gratitude goes to my wife, Carolyn, for editorial assistance and encouragement throughout this revision. Considering all of this help, any shortcomings and errors that remain must be mine.

R. H. BALLOU
Weatherhead School of Management
Cleveland, Ohio

Business Logistics/
Supply Chain Management

Chapter 1

Business Logistics/Supply Chain—A Vital Subject

> *Physical distribution is simply another way of saying "the whole process of business"*[1]
>
> —PETER DRUCKER, 1969

INTRODUCTION

*A*s far back as history records, the goods that people wanted were not produced where they wanted to consume them, or these goods were not accessible when people wanted to consume them. Food and other commodities were widely dispersed and were only available in abundance at certain times of the year. Early peoples had the choice of consuming goods at their immediate location or moving the goods to a preferred site and storing them for later use. However, because no well-developed transportation and storage systems yet existed, the movement of goods was limited to what an individual could personally move, and storage of perishable commodities was possible for only a short time. This limited movement-storage system generally constrained people to live close to the sources of production and to consume a rather narrow range of goods.

Even today, in some areas of the world consumption and production take place only within a very limited geographic region. Striking examples can still be observed in the developing nations of Asia, South America, Australia, and Africa, where some of the population live in small, self-sufficient villages, and most of the goods needed by the

---

[1]Peter F. Drucker, "Physical Distribution: The Frontier of Modern Management," in Donald J. Bowersox, Bernard J. LaLonde, and Edward Smykay (eds.), *Readings in Physical Distribution Management* (New York: Macmillan, 1969), p. 4.

residents are produced or acquired in the immediate vicinity. Few goods are imported from other areas. Therefore, production efficiency and the economic standard of living are generally low. In this type of economy, a well-developed and inexpensive logistics system would encourage an exchange of goods with other producing areas of the country, or even the world.

Example

Suppose that consumers in the United States and South Korea buy DVD recorders and computer software. In the coming year, about the same number of consumers will purchase a word processing program and a television set. Because of the differences in local labor costs, tariffs, transportation, and product quality, the effective price to the consumers differs, as shown in Table 1-1. A consumer in South Korea and one in the United States (in this case, the economy of both countries) must pay a total of $1,450.00 to fill their needs.

Now, if each economy trades with the other those goods with which it has a cost advantage, both consumers and their economies will be better off. South Korea has low labor costs for making DVD recorders, whereas the United States has an advantage in producing low-cost, high-quality software. With the availability of inexpensive and reliable transportation, there is an economic advantage to specializing in the product that can be produced most cheaply and buying the remaining product from the other country. With reasonable transportation costs, South Korea can place DVD recorders in the United States at a price below the locally produced and locally transported product. Conversely, the United States has the design and production cost advantage for software and can incur a reasonable transportation charge to place software in South Korea and at a price below what is available locally. The revised economic picture can be seen in Table 1-2. Both consumers in the countries save $1,450 − 1,200 = $250. Expensive transportation would preclude the countries from trading with each other and realizing their comparative economic advantages by making the landed price of imported products higher than those available locally.

As logistics systems improved, consumption and production began to separate geographically. Regions would specialize in those commodities that could be produced most efficiently. Excess production could be shipped economically to other producing (or consuming) areas, and

Table 1-1
Consumer Prices to Buy Only Locally Produced Products

CONSUMER IN	DVD RECORDER	WORD PROCESSING SOFTWARE	TOTAL
South Korea	$250.00	$500.00	$ 750.00
United States	400.00	300.00	700.00
The economies			$1,450.00

Table 1-2

The Benefits of
Trading Products
When Transportation
Is Inexpensive

CONSUMER IN	DVD RECORDER	WORD PROCESSING SOFTWARE	TOTAL
South Korea	$250.00	$350.00[a]	$ 600.00
United States	300.00[b]	300.00	600.00
The economies			$1,200.00

[a] Imports from the United States
[b] Imports from South Korea

needed goods not produced locally were imported. This exchange process follows the *principle of comparative advantage*.

This same principle, when applied to world markets, helps to explain the high level of international trade that takes place today. Efficient logistics systems allow world businesses to take advantage of the fact that lands, and the people who occupy them, are not equally productive. Logistics is the very essence of trade. It contributes to a higher economic standard of living for us all.

To the individual firm operating in a high-level economy, good management of logistics activities is vital. Markets are often national or international in scope, whereas production may be concentrated at relatively few points. Logistics activities provide the bridge between production and market locations that are separated by time and distance. Effective management of these activities is the major concern of this book.

BUSINESS LOGISTICS DEFINED

Business logistics is a relatively new field of integrated management study in comparison with the traditional fields of finance, marketing, and production. As previously noted, logistics activities have been carried out by individuals for many years. Businesses also have continually engaged in move-store (transportation-inventory) activities. The newness of the field results from the concept of *coordinated* management of the related activities, rather than the historical practice of managing them separately, and the concept that logistics adds value to products or services that are essential to customer satisfaction and sales. Although coordinated logistics management has not been generally practiced until recently, the idea of coordinated management can be traced back to at least 1844. In the writings of Jules Dupuit, a French engineer, the idea of trading one cost for another (transportation costs for inventory costs) was evident in the selection between road and water transport:

> The fact is that carriage by road being quicker, more reliable and less subject
> to loss or damage, it possesses advantage to which businessmen often
> attach a considerable value. However, it may well be that the saving of

0 fr.87 induces the merchant to use the canal; he can buy warehouses and increase his floating capital in order to have a sufficient supply of goods on hand to protect himself against slowness and irregularity of the canal, and if all told the saving of 0 fr.87 in transport gives him an advantage of a few centimes, he will decide in favor of the new route . . .[2]

The first textbook to suggest the benefits of coordinated logistics management appeared around 1961,[3] in part explaining why a generally accepted definition of business logistics is still emerging. Therefore, it is worthwhile to explore several definitions for the scope and content of the subject.

A dictionary definition of the term *logistics* is:

The branch of military science having to do with procuring, maintaining, and transporting materiel, personnel, and facilities.[4]

This definition puts logistics into a military context. To the extent that business objectives and activities differ from those of the military, this definition does not capture the essence of business logistics management. A better representation of the field may be reflected in the definition promulgated by the Council of Logistics Management (CLM), a professional organization of logistics managers, educators, and practitioners formed in 1962 for the purposes of continuing education and fostering the interchange of ideas. Its definition:

Logistics is that part of the supply chain process that plans, implements, and controls the efficient, effective flow and storage of goods, services, and related information from the point of origin to the point of consumption in order to meet customers' requirements.[5]

This is an excellent definition, conveying the idea that product flows are to be managed from the point where they exist as raw materials to the point where they are finally discarded. Logistics is also concerned with the flow of services as well as physical goods, an area of growing opportunity for improvement. It also suggests that logistics is a *process*, meaning that it includes all the activities that have an impact on making goods and services available to customers when and where they wish to acquire them. However, the definition implies that logistics is part of the supply chain process, not the entire process. So, what is the supply chain process or, more popularly, supply chain management?

Supply chain management (SCM) is a term that has emerged in recent years that captures the essence of integrated logistics and even goes beyond it. Supply chain

---

[2]Jules Dupuit, "On the Measurement of the Utility of Public Works," reprinted in *International Economic Papers*, No. 2, translated from the French by R. H. Barback (London: Macmillan and Co., Ltd., 1952), p. 100.
[3]Edward W. Smykay, Donald J. Bowersox, and Frank H. Mossman, *Physical Distribution Management: Logistics Problems of the Firm* (New York: Macmillan, 1961).
[4]*Webster's New Encyclopedic Dictionary* (New York: Black Dog & Leventhal Publishers, 1993), p. 590.
[5]From the by laws of the *Council of Logistics Management*, accessed at CLM's Web site http://www.clm1.org.

management emphasizes the logistics interactions that take place *among* the functions of marketing, logistics, and production within a firm and those interactions that take place between the legally separate firms within the product-flow channel. Opportunities for cost or customer service improvement are achieved through *coordination* and *collaboration* among the channel members where some essential supply chain activities may not be under the direct control of the logistician. Although early definitions such as physical distribution, materials management, industrial logistics, channel management, and even rhocrematics, all terms used to describe logistics, have promoted this broad scope for logistics, there was little attempt to implement logistics beyond a company's own enterprise boundaries, or even beyond its own internal logistics function. Now, retail firms are showing success in sharing information with suppliers, which in turn agree to maintain and manage inventories on retailers' shelves. Channel inventories and product stockouts are lower. Manufacturing firms operating under just-in-time production scheduling build relationships with suppliers for the benefit of both companies by reducing inventories. Definitions of the supply chain and supply chain management reflecting this broader scope are:

> The *supply chain (SC)* encompasses all activities associated with the flow and transformation of goods from the raw materials stage (extraction), through to the end user, as well as the associated information flows. Materials and information flow both up and down the supply chain.
>   *Supply chain management (SCM)* is the integration of these activities, through improved supply chain relationships, to achieve a sustainable competitive advantage.[6]

After careful study of the various definitions being offered, Mentzer et al. propose the broad and rather general definition as follows:

> Supply chain management is defined as the systematic, strategic coordination of the traditional business functions and the tactics across these business functions within a particular company and across businesses within the supply chain, for the purposes of improving the long-term performance of the individual companies and the supply chain as a whole.[7]

The supply chain management model in Figure 1-1 viewed as a pipeline shows the scope of this definition. It is important to note that supply chain management is about the coordination of product flows across functions and across companies to achieve competitive advantage and profitability for the individual companies in the supply chain and the supply chain members collectively.

---

[6]Robert B. Handfield and Ernest L. Nichols Jr., *Introduction to Supply Chain Management* (Upper Saddle River, NJ: Prentice-Hall, 1999), p. 2.
[7]John T. Mentzer, William DeWitt, James S. Keebler, Soonhong Min, Nancy W. Nix, Carlo D. Smith, and Zach G. Zacharia, "Defining Supply Chain Management," *Journal of Business Logistics*, Vol. 22, No. 2 (2001), pp. 1–25.

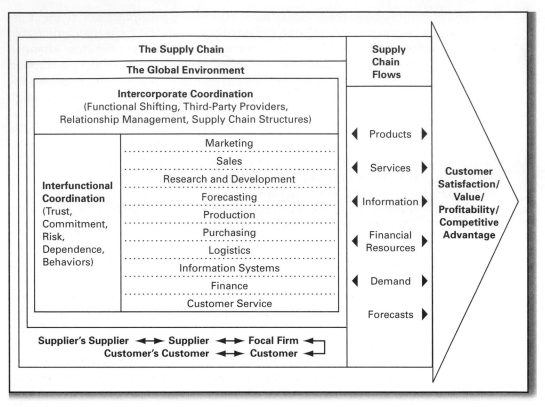

Figure 1-1 A Model of Supply Chain Management

Source: Mentzer et al., "Defining Supply Chain Management," *Journal of Business Logistics*, Vol. 22, No. 2 (2001), p. 19. Reproduced with permission of the Council of Logistics Management.

It is difficult, in a practical way, to separate business logistics management from supply chain management. In so many respects, they promote the same mission:

> To get the right goods or services to the right place, at the right time, and in the desired condition, while making the greatest contribution to the firm.

Some claim that supply chain management is just another name for integrated business logistics management (IBLM) and that the broad scope of supply chain management has been promoted over the years. Conversely, others say that logistics is a subset of SCM, where SCM considers additional issues beyond those of product flow. For example, SCM may be concerned with product pricing and manufacturing quality. Although SCM promotes viewing the supply channel with the broadest scope, the reality is that firms do not practice this ideal. Fawcett and Magan found that companies that do practice supply chain integration limit their scope to one tier upstream and one tier downstream.[8] The focus seems to be concerned with creating

---

[8]Stanley E. Fawcett and Gregory M. Magan, "The Rhetoric and Reality of Supply Chain Integration," *International Journal of Physical Distribution & Logistics Management*, Vol. 32, No. 5 (2002), pp. 339–361.

seamless processes within their own companies and applying new information technologies to improve the quality of information and speed of its exchange among channel members. The boundary between the logistics and supply chain management terms is fuzzy. For the purposes of this text, integrated business logistics management and SCM will be referred to interchangeably. The focus will be on managing the product and service flows in the most efficient and effective manner, regardless of descriptive title. This includes integrating and coordinating with other channel members and service providers to improve supply chain performance when practical to do so.

THE SUPPLY CHAIN

Logistics/SC is a collection of functional activities (transportation, inventory control, etc.), which are repeated many times throughout the channel through which raw materials are converted into finished products and consumer value is added. Because raw material sources, plants, and selling points are not typically located at the same places and the channel represents a sequence of manufacturing steps, logistics activities recur many times before a product arrives in the marketplace. Even then, logistics activities are repeated once again as used products are recycled upstream in the logistics channel.

A single firm generally is not able to control its entire product flow channel from raw material source to points of the final consumption, although this is an emerging opportunity. For practical purposes, the business logistics for the individual firm has a narrower scope. Usually, the maximal managerial control that can be expected is over the immediate physical supply and physical distribution channels, as shown in Figure 1-2. The *physical supply channel* refers to the time and space gap between a firm's immediate material sources and its processing points. Similarly, the *physical distribution channel* refers to the time and space gap between the firm's processing points and its customers. Due to the similarities in the activities between the two channels, physical supply (more commonly referred to as materials management) and physical distribution comprise those activities that are integrated into business logistics. Business logistics management is now popularly referred to as supply chain management.[9] Others have used terms such as *value nets, value stream*, and *lean logistics* to describe a similar scope and purpose. The evolution of the management of product flows toward SCM is captured in Figure 1-3.

Although it is easy to think of logistics as managing the flow of products from the points of raw material acquisition to end customers, for many firms there is a *reverse logistics channel* that must be managed as well. The life of a product, from a logistics viewpoint, does not end with delivery to the customer. Products become obsolete, damaged, or nonfunctioning and are returned to their source points for repair or disposition. Packaging materials may be returned to the shipper due to

---

[9]Some proponents of supply chain management include pricing within its scope. Business logistics management rarely does this.

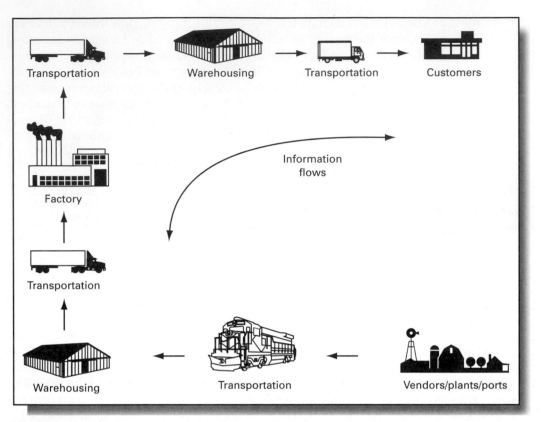

Figure 1-2 The Immediate Supply Chain for an Individual Firm

environmental regulations or because it makes good economic sense to reuse them. The reverse logistics channel may utilize all or a portion of the forward logistics channel or it may require a separate design. The supply chain terminates with the final disposition of a product. The reverse channel must be considered to be within the scope of logistics planning and control.

Example

The reverse logistics channel comes into play when a customer buys a toaster from a retailer. The customer takes the toaster home and finds it defective. The customer returns it to the retailer, who gladly refunds the purchase price. The retailer now has a defective toaster in in-store inventory. The retailer sends it to a central return center. Upon receipt, the toaster's Universal Product Code (UPC) is scanned for identification in the return center's database. The database determines that the toaster has a return-to-vendor disposition. The database credits the store inventory for the toaster and creates a charge back to the manufacturer for the cost of the toaster. The toaster is shipped back to the manufacturer. The retailer has made a cost recovery for this

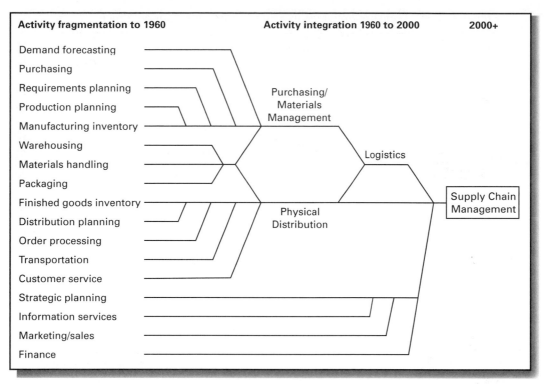

Figure 1-3 Evolution of Logistics Toward Supply Chain

Source: John Yuva, "Collaborative Logistics: Building a United Network," *Inside Supply Management*, Vol. 13, No. 5 (May 2002), p. 50 (with modification).

defective asset. The toaster is received at the manufacturer's return center. The manufacturer scans the toaster into its database and determines that it has a refurbish disposition. The toaster is repaired and sent for resale on the secondary market. The manufacturer has now gained value for this defective asset.[10]

THE ACTIVITY MIX

The activities to be managed that make up business logistics (supply chain process) vary from firm to firm, depending on a firm's particular organizational structure, management's honest differences of opinion about what constitutes the supply chain for its business, and the importance of individual activities to its operations. Follow

[10]Jerry A. Davis, Jerome G. Lawrence, Peter Rector, and Herbert S. Shear, "Reverse Logistics Pipeline," *Annual Conference Proceedings* (San Diego, CA: Council of Logistics Management, October 8–11, 1995), p. 427.

Figure 1-4 Logistics Activities in a Firm's Immediate Supply Chain

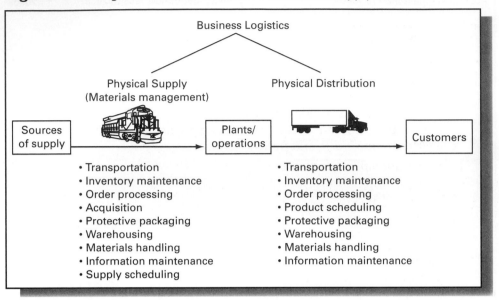

along the supply chain as shown in Figure 1-2 and note the important activities that take place. Again, according to the CLM:

> The components of a typical logistics system are: customer service, demand forecasting, distribution communications, inventory control, material handling, order processing, parts and service support, plant and warehouse site selection (location analysis), purchasing, packaging, return goods handling, salvage and scrap disposal, traffic and transportation, and warehousing and storage.[11]

Figure 1-4 organizes these components, or activities, according to where they are most likely to take place in the supply channel. The list is further divided into key and support activities, along with some of the decisions associated with each activity.

Key Activities

1. Customer service standards cooperate with marketing to:
   a. Determine customer needs and wants for logistics customer service
   b. Determine customer response to service
   c. Set customer service levels

2. Transportation
   a. Mode and transport service selection
   b. Freight consolidation
   c. Carrier routing

---

[11]*Careers in Logistics* (Oak Brook, IL: Council of Logistics Management), p. 3.

d. Vehicle scheduling
e. Equipment selection
f. Claims processing
g. Rate auditing

3. Inventory management

a. Raw materials and finished goods stocking policies
b. Short-term sales forecasting
c. Product mix at stocking points
d. Number, size, and location of stocking points
e. Just-in-time, push, and pull strategies

4. Information flows and order processing

a. Sales order-inventory interface procedures
b. Order information transmittal methods
c. Ordering rules

Support Activities

1. Warehousing

a. Space determination
b. Stock layout and dock design
c. Warehouse configuration
d. Stock placement

2. Materials handling

a. Equipment selection
b. Equipment replacement policies
c. Order-picking procedures
d. Stock storage and retrieval

3. Purchasing

a. Supply source selection
b. Purchase timing
c. Purchase quantities

4. Protective packaging designed for:

a. Handling
b. Storage
c. Protection from loss and damage

5. Cooperate with production/operations to:

a. Specify aggregate quantities
b. Sequence and time production output
c. Schedule supplies for production/operations

6. Information maintenance

a. Information collection, storage, and manipulation
b. Data analysis
c. Control procedures

Figure 1-5
The Critical
Customer Service
Loop

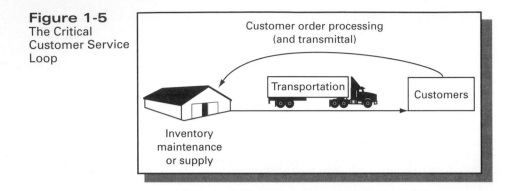

Key and support activities are separated because certain activities will generally take place in every logistics channel, whereas others will take place, depending on the circumstances, within a particular firm. The key activities are on the "critical" loop within a firm's immediate physical distribution channel, as shown in Figure 1-5. They contribute most to the total cost of logistics or they are essential to the effective coordination and completion of the logistics task.

Customer service standards set the level of output and degree of readiness to which the logistics system must respond. Logistics costs increase in proportion to the level of customer service provided, such that setting the standards for service also affects the logistics costs to support that level of service. Setting very high service requirements can force logistics costs to exceedingly high levels.

Transportation and inventorys maintenance are the primary cost-absorbing logistics activities. Experience has shown that each will represent one-half to two-thirds of total logistics costs. Transportation adds *place* value to products and services, whereas inventorys maintenance adds *time* value.

Transportation is essential because no modern firm can operate without providing for the movement of its raw materials or its finished products. This importance is underscored by the financial strains placed on many firms by such disasters as a national railroad strike or independent truckers' refusal to move goods because of rate disputes. In these circumstances, markets cannot be served, and products back up in the logistics pipeline to deteriorate or become obsolete.

Inventories are also essential to logistics management because it is usually not possible or practical to provide instant production or ensure delivery times to customers. They serve as buffers between supply and demand so that needed product availability may be maintained for customers while providing flexibility for production and logistics in seeking efficient methods for manufacture and distribution of the product.

Order processing is the final key activity. Its costs usually are minor compared to transportation or inventory maintenance costs. Nevertheless, order processing is an important element in the total time that it takes for a customer to receive goods or services. It is the activity triggering product movement and service delivery.

Although support activities may be as critical as the key activities in any particular circumstance, they are considered here as contributing to the logistics mission. In addition, one or more of the support activities may not be a part of the logistics activity mix for every firm. For example, products such as finished automobiles or commodities such as coal, iron ore, or gravel not needing the weather and security protection of warehousing will not require the warehousing activity, even though inventories are maintained. However, warehousing and materials handling are typically conducted wherever products are temporarily halted in their movement to the marketplace.

Protective packaging is a support activity of transportation and inventory maintenance as well as of warehousing and materials handling because it contributes to the efficiency with which these other activities are carried out. Purchasing and product scheduling often may be considered more a concern of production than of logistics. However, they also affect the overall logistics effort, and specifically they affect the efficiency of transportation and inventory management. Finally, information maintenance supports all other logistics activities in that it provides the needed information for planning and control.

The *extended supply chain* refers to those members of the supply channel beyond the firm's immediate suppliers or customers. They may be suppliers to the immediate suppliers or customers of the immediate customers and so on until raw material source points or end customers are reached. It is important to plan and control the previously noted activities and information flows if they affect the logistics customer service that can be provided and the costs of supplying this service. Management of the extended supply chain has the potential of improving logistics performance beyond that of just managing the activities within the immediate supply chain.

IMPORTANCE OF LOGISTICS/ SUPPLY CHAIN

Logistics is about creating *value*—value for customers and suppliers of the firm, and value for the firm's stakeholders. Value in logistics is primarily expressed in terms of time and place. Products and services have no value unless they are in the possession of the customers when (time) and where (place) they wish to consume them. For example, concessions at a sports event have no value to consumers if they are not available at the time and place that the event is occurring, or if inadequate inventories don't meet the demands of the sports fans. Good logistics management views each activity in the supply chain as contributing to the process of adding value. If little value can be added, it is questionable whether the activity should exist. However, value is added when customers are willing to pay more for a product or service than the cost to place it in their hands. To many firms throughout the world, logistics has become an increasingly important value-adding process for a number of reasons.

Costs Are Significant

Over the years, several studies have been conducted to determine the costs of logistics for the whole economy and for the individual firm. There are widely varying estimates of the cost levels. According to the International Monetary Fund (IMF),

Table 1-3

Recent Average
Physical Distribution
Costs in Percent of
Sales and $/cwt.[a]

CATEGORY	PERCENT OF SALES	$/CWT.
Transportation	3.34%	$26.52
Warehousing	2.02	18.06
Customer service/order entry	0.43	4.58
Administration	0.41	2.79
Inventory carrying cost @ 18%/year.	1.72	22.25
Total distribution cost[b]	7.65%	$67.71

[a] The statistics are for all firm types; however, they most closely represent manufacturing firms since they dominate the database.

[b] The authors of this survey claim the totals do not match the sum of the individual statistics due to a different number of data entries in each category.

Source: Herbert W. Davis and William H. Drumm, "Logistics Costs and Service Database—2002," *Annual Conference Proceedings* (San Francisco, CA: Council of Logistics Management, 2002) at www.clm1.org.

logistics costs average about 12 percent of the world's gross domestic product. Robert Delaney, who has tracked logistics costs for more than two decades, estimates that logistics costs for the U.S. economy are 9.9 percent of the U.S. gross domestic product (GOP), or $921 billion.[12] For the firm, logistics costs have ranged from 4 percent to over 30 percent of sales.[13] The results from a cost survey of individual firms are shown in Table 1-3. Although the results show physical distribution costs at about 8 percent of sales, this survey does not include physical supply costs. Probably another one-third may be added to this total to represent average logistics costs for the firm at about 11 percent of sales. Over the last decade, physical distribution costs have ranged between 7 percent and 9 percent of sales. There may be a trend of increasing costs for individual firms, although Wilson and Delaney show over the same period that logistics costs as a percent of U.S. GDP have declined by about 10 percent.[14] Logistics costs, substantial for most firms, rank second only to the cost of goods sold (purchase costs) that are about 50 percent to 60 percent of sales for the average manufacturing firm. Value is added by minimizing these costs and by passing the benefits on to customers and to the firm's shareholders.

Logistics Customer Service Expectations Are Increasing

The Internet, just-in-time operating procedures, and continuous replenishment of inventories have all contributed to customers expecting rapid processing of their

---

[12]Rosalyn Wilson and Robert V. Delaney, "11th Annual State of Logistics Report," *Cass Information Systems and ProLogis* (Washington, DC: National Press Club, June 5, 2000).
[13]For a history of these costs estimates, see Bernard J. LaLonde and Paul H. Zinszer, *Customer Service: Meaning and Measurement* (Chicago: National Council of Physical Distribution Management, 1976); Richard E. Snyder, "Physical Distribution Costs: A Two-Year Analysis," *Distribution Age* Vol. 62 (January 1963), pp. 50–51; and Wendall M. Stewart, "Physical Distribution: Key to Improved Volume and Profits," *Journal of Marketing* Vol. 29 (January 1965), p. 67.
[14]Wilson and Delaney, op. cit.

STANDARD PRODUCT MEASURES		1992	1993	1994	1995	1996	1997	1998	1999	2000	2001	2002
Total order cycle												
Time, days		8	7	7	6	9	8	7	8	8	7	8
Product availability	percent orders	84	84	86	87	87	87	85	85	86	87	88
	percent line items	92	92	92	92	94	94	93	90	92	93	95

Source: Herbert W. Davis and William H. Drumm, "Logistics Costs and Service Database—2002," *Annual Conference Proceedings* (San Francisco, CA: Council of Logistics Management, 2002) at www.clml.org.

Table 1-4 Average Customer Service Performance Measures for All Firms, Survey Years 1992–2002

requests, quick delivery, and a high degree of product availability. According to the Davis survey of hundreds of companies over the last decade, world-class competitors have average order cycle times (the time between when an order is placed and when it is received) of seven to eight days and line item fill rates of 90 percent to 94 percent.[15] LogFac summarizes world-class logistics performance for domestic companies as:

- Error rates of less than one per 1,000 orders shipped
- Logistics costs of well under 5 percent of sales
- Finished goods inventory turnover of 20 or more times per year
- Total order cycle time of five working days
- Transportation cost of one percent of sales revenue or less, if products sold are over $5 per pound[16]

As might be expected, the average company performs below these cost and customer service benchmarks, when compared with the statistics in Tables 1-3 and 1-4.

Supply and Distribution Lines Are Lengthening with Greater Complexity

The trend is toward an integrated world economy. Firms are seeking, or have developed, global strategies by designing their products for a world market and producing them wherever the low-cost raw materials, components, and labor can be found (e.g., Ford's Focus automobile), or they simply produce locally and sell internationally. In either case, supply and distribution lines are stretched, as compared with the producer who wishes to manufacture and sell only locally. Not only has the trend occurred naturally by firms seeking to cut costs or expand markets, but it is also being encouraged by political arrangements that promote trade. Examples of the latter are the European Union, the North America Free Trade Agreement (NAFTA)

---

[15]Herbert W. Davis and William H. Drumm, "Logistics Costs and Service 2001," *Annual Conference Proceedings*, (Kansas City, MO: Council of Logistics Management, 2001).
[16]"Logistics Rules of Thumb III," *LogFac*, www.logfac.com (2001).

Figure 1-6
Economic Benefit of
Sourcing from Low-
Cost Offshore
Locations Rather
Than from Higher-
Cost Local Suppliers

Source: "International
Logistics: Battleground
of the '90s" (Chicago: A.
T. Kearney, 1988).

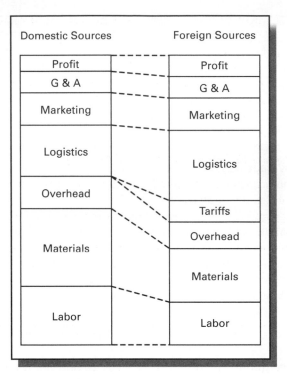

between Canada, the United States, and Mexico, and the economic trade agreement among several countries of South America (MERCOSUR).

Globalization and internationalization of industries everywhere will depend heavily on logistics performance and costs, as companies take more of a worldview of their operations. As this happens, logistics takes on increased importance within the firm since its costs, especially transportation, become a larger part of the total cost structure. For example, if a firm seeks foreign suppliers for the raw materials that make up its final product or foreign locations to build its product, the motivation is to increase profit. Material and labor costs may be reduced, but logistics costs are likely to increase due to increased transportation and inventory costs. The tradeoff, as shown in Figure 1-6, may lead to higher profit by reducing materials, labor, and overhead costs at the expense of logistics costs and tariffs. Outsourcing adds value, but it requires careful management of logistics costs and product-flow times in the supply channel.

Example

Toyota has 35 manufacturing plants in 25 countries (excluding Japan) at which it produces nearly 900,000 vehicles annually. While exports were down by 9 percent in 1993, overseas production was up by 16 percent. In the case of Georgetown, Kentucky, where Camrys are built, Toyota uses the just-in-time concept to supply parts from across the Pacific. The parts are loaded into ocean containers in Japan, shipped across the Pacific, and transferred to trains on the West Coast of the United States for relay to Georgetown, where they feed an assembly line that turns out 1,000 Camrys a day. Deliveries are scheduled to the minute in order to keep inventories low. Due to the long supply lines and the associated uncertainties, supply channels must be more carefully managed than if all production were local.[17]

Logistics/SC Is Important to Strategy

Firms spend a great deal of time finding ways to differentiate their product offerings from those of their competitors. When management recognizes that logistics/SC affects a significant portion of a firm's costs and that the result of decisions made about the supply chain processes yields different levels of customer service, it is in a position to use this effectively to penetrate new markets, to increase market share, and to increase profits. That is, good supply chain management can generate sales, not just reduce costs. Consider how Wal-Mart used logistics as the core of its competitive strategy to become the world's number one merchandise retailer.

Example

Wal-Mart Wins with Logistics Kmart and Wal-Mart are two retail merchandise chains that, a few years back, looked alike, sold the same products, sought the same customers, and even had similar names. When the race began, people were quite familiar with the "big red K," whose stores dotted metropolitan areas, but few had heard of Wal-Mart, whose stores were in rural settings. Considering the similarity of the stores and their mission, analysts attribute the fates of the two chains primarily to differing management philosophies.

In 1987, Kmart was far ahead, with twice as many stores and sales of $26 billion, compared to $16 billion for Wal-Mart. With its urban presence and a focus on advertising, Kmart had more visibility. In contrast, Wal-Mart began in stand-alone stores outside small towns, luring customers away from the mom-and-pop stores in aging downtowns. But so rapidly did Wal-Mart multiply over the rural landscape that an invasion of urban America—and a confrontation with Kmart—was inevitable.

Kmart executives focused on marketing and merchandising, even using Hollywood star Jaclyn Smith to promote her clothing line. By contrast, Sam Walton, Wal-Mart's founder, was obsessed with operations. He invested millions of dollars in a company-wide computer system linking cash registers to headquarters, enabling him to quickly restock goods. He also invested heavily in trucks and modern distribution centers. Besides enhancing his control of the supply chain, these moves sharply reduced costs. While Kmart tried to improve its image and cultivate store loyalty,

---

[17]Joseph Bonney, "Toyota's Global Conveyor Belts," *American Shipper* (September 1994), pp. 50–58.

Walton kept lowering costs, betting that price would prove more important than any other factor in attracting customers. Wal-Mart's incredibly sophisticated distribution, inventory, and scanner systems meant that customers almost never encountered depleted shelves or price-check delays.

Meanwhile, Kmart's woes mounted, as distribution horror stories abounded. Employees lacked the training and skill to plan and control inventory properly, and Kmart's cash registers often did not have up-to-date information and would scan items and enter incorrect prices. This led to a lawsuit in California, and Kmart settled for $985,000 for overcharging its customers.

Over the years, it has been Wal-Mart's focus on logistical matters that enables it to keep its prices low and its customers happy and returning often. Today, Wal-Mart is nearly six times the size of Kmart![18]

Kmart continued its focus on ad circulars and promotional pricing into the twenty-first century, whereas Wal-Mart continued to focus more on supply chain efficiencies and less on advertising, with the results that selling, administrative, and overhead costs were 17.3 percent for Wal-Mart and Kmart's were 22.7 percent. Wal-Mart was able to achieve prices that average 3.8 percent below Kmart's and even 3.2 percent below Target's. In 2002, Kmart went into bankruptcy and reorganization.[19]

Logistics/SC Adds Significant Customer Value

A product, or service, is of little value if it is not available to customers at the time and place that they wish to consume it. When a firm incurs the cost of moving the product toward the customer or making an inventory available in a timely manner, for the customer value has been created that was not there previously. It is value as surely as that created through the production of a quality product or through a low price.

It is generally recognized that business creates four types of value in products or services. These are: form, time, place, and possession. Logistics creates two out of these four values. Manufacturing creates *form* value as inputs are converted to outputs, that is raw materials are transformed into finished goods. Logistics controls the *time* and *place* values in products, mainly through transportation, information flows, and inventories. *Possession* value is often considered the responsibility of marketing, engineering, and finance, where the value is created by helping customers acquire the product through such mechanisms as advertising (information), technical support, and terms of sale (pricing and credit availability). To the extent that SCM includes production, three out of the four values may be the responsibility of the logistics/supply chain manager.

---

[18]"Loss Leader: How Wal-Mart Outdid a Once-Touted Kmart in Discount Store Race," *Wall Street Journal*, March 24, 1995, and revenue data for 2000 from Wal-Mart and Kmart financial reports found online at http://finance.yahoo.com
[19]Amy Merrick, "Expensive Ad Circulars Help Precipitate Kmart President's Departure," *Wall Street Journal*, January 18, 2002, B1ff.

Example

When discount houses selling computer software through Web sites, catalogs, and magazine advertisements wished to compete with local retailers, they had a price advantage due to the economies of scale that they could achieve. Operations were centralized at one location where lower-cost warehouse space rather than higher-cost retail space could be used. Their staff was predominately telephone order takers and warehouse order-fillers and packagers. Inventories were minimized relative to sales through centralization, but these discount operations also offered substantial variety and high levels of product availability. Conversely, retailers had the advantage of immediate availability for the anxious customer that would offset any price disadvantage of the local retailer. To counter this possible delivery advantage of retailers in their local markets, the discount houses made sure that customer orders could be placed using toll-free telephone numbers or through a Web site, that these orders were filled the *same day*, and that they were shipped overnight using priority air delivery. Many customers find this nearly as fast and, in many cases, a lot more convenient than traditional shopping! Value has been created for the busy customer through logistics.

Customers Increasingly Want Quick, Customized Response

Fast food retailers, automatic teller machines, overnight package delivery, and electronic mail on the Internet have led us as consumers to expect that products and services can be made available in increasingly shorter times. In addition, improved information systems and flexible manufacturing processes have led the marketplace toward mass customization. Rather than consumers having to accept the "one size fits all" philosophy in their purchases, suppliers are increasingly offering products that meet individual customer needs.

Observations

- Dell, a desktop computer company, will configure a PC to a customer's exact hardware requirements, and even install requested software.
- L. L. Bean sells clothes and other items through its catalog and Web site. In addition, some of the clothes may be altered to a customer's exact measurements. Moreover, L. L. Bean will ensure fast delivery by shipping via Federal Express at no additional charge (if the customer charges the order to an L. L. Bean Visa charge card).
- National Bicycle Industrial Co., a subsidiary of the Japanese electronics giant Matsushita, builds bicycles using *flexible* manufacturing techniques, those that allow switching from the production of one product to another with minimal setup cost. Rather than mass-producing in standard sizes and building inventories for retail sales, National Bicycle builds the bicycles to precise customer

specifications in over 11 million variations on 18 models of road, racing, and mountain bikes. Although it takes three hours to produce a bicycle using flexible manufacturing as compared to 90 minutes for mass production, the company is able to charge more than twice the price by pleasing customers with unique bikes built to their individual specifications.

Companies too have been applying the concept of quick response to their internal operations in order to meet the service requirements of their own marketing efforts. The quick response philosophy has been used to create a marketing advantage. Saks Fifth Avenue applied it, even though big profits are made through big margins and not on cost reductions that might be achieved from good logistics management. Supply chain costs may even rise, although the advantage is to more than cover these costs through increased profits.

Application

Retailers go out of business at an alarming rate. To Saks Fifth Avenue, this fear alone may have been adequate motivation for management to integrate merchandising and logistics. The benefits are obvious when merchandising relies on manufacturers that might cut cloth in Bangladesh and finish garments in Italy before shipping them to a ritzy selling floor in the United States. The difference between profit and loss on hot-selling items may be as little as seven to ten days, so good logistics performance requires that such items be on the selling floor *precisely* when needed most. How does Saks do it?

The company's 69 stores are served by just two distribution centers. One is in Yonkers, New York, close by Saks' flagship store on New York City's 5th Avenue. The second is in Ontario, California, well situated to serve the trendy southern California market. Rapid movement through the supply channel is key to profitability. Items are processed by the centers in a 24-hour turnaround. About 80 percent of Saks' imported items arrive by airfreight—those from Europe are handled by Yonkers and those from the Far East by Ontario. Items are exchanged between the centers by airfreight, with a dedicated flight between New York and Los Angeles every business day. Distribution centers then serve their local stores with a combination of airfreight and trucking.[20]

Logistics/SC in Nonmanufacturing Areas

It is perhaps easiest to think of logistics/SC in terms of moving and storing a physical product in a manufacturing setting. This is too narrow a view and can lead to many missed business opportunities. The logistics/SC principles and concepts

---

[20]Bruce Vail, "Logistics, Fifth Avenue Style," *American Shipper* (August 1994), pp. 49–51.

learned over the years can be applied to such areas as service industries, the military, and even environment management.

Service Industry

The service sector of industrialized countries is large and growing. In the United States, over 70 percent of all jobs are in what the federal government classifies as the service sector. The size of this sector alone forces us to ask if logistics concepts are not equally applicable here as they are to the manufacturing sector. If they are, there is a tremendous untapped opportunity yet to be fulfilled.

Many companies designated as service firms in fact produce a product. Examples include: McDonald's Corporation (fast foods); Dow Jones & Co., Inc. (newspaper publishing); and Sears, Roebuck and Co. (merchandise retailing). These companies carry out all the typical supply chain activities of any manufacturing firm. However, for service companies such as Bank One (retail banking), Marriott Corporation (lodging), and Consolidated Edison (electric power), supply chain activities, especially those associated with physical distribution, are not as obvious.

Even though many service-oriented companies may be distributing an intangible, nonphysical product, they do engage in many physical distribution activities and decisions. A hospital may want to extend emergency medical care throughout the community and must make decisions as to the locations of the centers. United Parcel Service and Federal Express must locate terminals and route pickup and delivery trucks. The East Ohio Gas Company inventories natural gas in underground wells during the off-season in the region where demand will occur. Bank One must locate and have cash inventory on hand for its ATMs. The Federal Reserve Bank must select the methods of transportation to move canceled checks among member banks. The Catholic Church must decide the number, location, and size of the churches needed to meet shifts in size and location of congregations, as well as to plan the inventory of its pastoral staff. Xerox's repair service for copying equipment is also a good example of the logistics decisions encountered in a service operation.

Examples

- Promise Keepers is a Christian men's ministry that conducts 23 major events around the United States—with attendance ranging from 50 to 80,000. Promise Keepers must rely on good logistics management to assure that their crusades can be conducted on time. The operation is large enough to involve a major motor carrier that handles the event logistics. Using the concept of *time definite delivery*, the carrier coordinates the receipt of supplies such as Bibles from Chicago, hats from Kansas City, in addition to trailer loads of stage equipment. The materials must be assembled and delivered to an event site and delivered precisely on time. Since events are held at stadiums, speedways, and the like, there are other events (ball games, races, etc.) also scheduled on the same weekend. There may be as many as 30 truckloads that must be coordinated to arrive precisely on time and leave just as precisely to avoid congestion with the logistics of the other events. Computer technology is used to track trailer movements and ensure that the extremely close coordination can be achieved.[21]

- During the time span of one week, there were three major stories that drew the largest TV audience in history: England's Princess Diana was killed in an automobile crash in Paris, India's Mother Teresa died of heart failure in Calcutta, and there was a major bombing incident in Jerusalem. Suddenly, the media had major logistical problems with covering three major news stories in three corners of the world. For example, CNN diverted a reporter from Paris to the Middle East, while other networks sent their Hong Kong correspondents to Calcutta. Then, there were the logistical problems of allocating airtime to the three stories.[22]

The techniques, concepts, and methods discussed throughout this text should be as applicable to the service sector as they are to the manufacturing sector. The key, according to Theodore Levitt, may be in transforming an intangible service into a tangible product.[23] Problems will remain in carefully identifying the costs associated with the distribution of an intangible product. Perhaps because of this, few service firms or organizations have a physical distribution manager on their staff, although they frequently do have a materials manager to handle supply matters. However, managing logistics in service industries does represent a new direction for the future development of logistics practice.

Military

Before businesses showed much interest in coordinating supply chain processes, the military was well organized to carry out logistics activities. More than a decade before business logistics' developmental period, the military carried out what was called the most complex, best-planned logistics operation of that time—the invasion of Europe during World War II.

Although the problems of the military, with its extremely high customer service requirements, were not identical with those of business, the similarities were great enough to provide a valuable experience base during the developmental years of logistics. For example, the military alone maintained inventories valued at about one-third of those held by all U.S. manufacturers. In addition to the management experience that such large-scale operations provide, the military sponsored, and continues to sponsor, research in the logistics area through such organizations as the RAND Corporation and the Office of Naval Research. With this background, the field of business logistics began to grow. Even the term *logistics* seems to have had its origins in the military.

---

[21]Roger Morton, "Direct Response Shipping," *Transportation & Distribution* (April 1996), pp. 32–36.
[22]Kyle Pope, "For the Media, Diana's Funeral Prompts Debate," *Wall Street Journal* September 8, 1997, B1.
[23]Theodore Levitt, *The Marketing Imagination* (New York: The Free Press, 1983), pp. 108–110.

The most recent example of military logistics on a large scale was the conflict between the United States and Iraq over Iraq's invasion of the small country of Kuwait. This invasion has been described as the largest military logistics operation in history.[24] The logistics support in that war is yet another illustration of what world-class companies have always known: Good logistics can be a source of competitive advantage. Lieutenant General William Pagonis, who was in charge of logistics support for Desert Storm, observed:

> When the Middle East started heating up, it seemed like a good time to pull out some history books on desert warfare in this region. . . . But there was nothing on logistics. Logistics is not a best seller. In a couple of his diaries, Rommel talked about logistics. He thought the Germans lost the battle not because they didn't have great soldiers or equipment—in fact, the German tanks outfought ours almost throughout World War II—but because the British had better logistics.[25]

Good logistics performance was obvious. The first wave of 200,000 troops and their equipment was deployed in a month and a half, whereas troop deployment took nine months in the Vietnam conflict. In addition, the application of many good logistics concepts was evident. Take customer service, for example:

> We believed that if we took care of our troops, the objectives would be accomplished no matter whatever else happened. The soldiers are our customers. It is no different than a determined, single focus on customers that many successful businesses have. Now, you take care of your soldiers not only by providing them cold sodas, and burgers, and good food: you make sure they have the ammunition on the front line, so that when they go fight the war they know they have what they need.[26]

This meant that when 120 mm guns rather than 105 mm guns were desired on tanks, they were changed. When brown vehicles were preferred over the traditional camouflage green, they were repainted at the rate of 7,000 per month.

Environment

Population growth and resultant economic development have heightened our awareness of environmental issues. Whether it is recycling, packaging materials, transporting hazardous materials or refurbishing products for resale, logisticians are involved in a major way. After all, the United States alone produces more than 160 million tons of waste each year, enough for a convoy of 10-ton garbage trucks reaching halfway to the moon.[27] In many cases, planning for logistics in an environmental setting is no different from that in manufacturing or service sectors. However,

---

[24]*Business Week*, March 4, 1991, pp. 42–43.
[25]Graham Sharman, "Good Logistics Is Combat Power," *McKinsey Quarterly*, No. 3 (1991), pp. 3–21.
[26]Ibid.
[27]E. J. Muller, "The Greening of Logistics," *Distribution* (January 1991), p. 32.

in a few cases additional complications arise, such as governmental regulations that make the logistics for a product more costly by extending the distribution channel.

Example

In Germany, the government requires retail grocers to collect cereal boxes at the point of sale. Typically, consumers pay for the product, then open the box and empty the contents into containers they brought from home, and put the empty boxes into collection bins. The seller has the responsibility either for recovery of the spent materials and their repackaging and reuse, or for their disposal.[28]

BUSINESS LOGISTICS/SC IN THE FIRM

It has been the tradition in many firms to organize around marketing and production functions. Typically, marketing means selling something and production means making something. Although few business people would agree that their organization is so simple, the fact remains that many businesses emphasize these functions while treating other activities, such as traffic, purchasing, accounting, and engineering, as support areas. Such an attitude is justified to a degree, because if a firm's products cannot be produced and sold, little else matters. However, such a pattern is dangerously simple for many firms to follow in that it fails to recognize the importance of the activities that must take place between points and times of production or purchase and the points and times of demand. These are the logistics activities, and they affect the efficiency and effectiveness of both marketing and production.

Example

General Motors (GM) hopes improving customer service will boost sales of Cadillacs, which have been squeezed as buyers shift to other U.S. cars as well as to imports. Cadillac loses substantial sales when customers are put off by lengthy delivery times. Research shows that 10 percent to 11 percent of sales are lost simply because the cars are not available in a timely manner.

A production and distribution program was tested in Florida, a major market for Cadillacs. Under the program, about 1,500 Cadillacs were sent to a regional distribution center in Orlando, Florida, where they would be delivered to dealers state-wide within 24 hours. In some areas of Florida, many buyers wait two days for popularly equipped cars. Additionally, GM's Cadillac factory in Detroit increased production of specially ordered Cadillacs as well as reducing shipping time. Custom Cadillacs

---

[28]"European Logistics Changes Sharply," *American Shipper* (May 1993), p. 66.

arrived at dealerships in about three weeks, compared with the usual 8 to 12 weeks. Under this program, GM expected dealership inventories to decline by about 50 percent.[29]

Scholars and practitioners of both marketing and production have not neglected the importance of logistics. In fact, each area considers logistics within its scope of action. For example, the following definition of marketing management includes physical distribution:

> Marketing (management) is the process of planning and executing the conception, pricing, promotion, and distribution of ideas, goods, and services to create exchanges with target groups that satisfy individual and organizational objectives.[30]

Marketing's concern is to place its products or services in convenient distribution channels to facilitate the exchange process. The concept of production/operations management often includes logistics activities. For example, "operations management has the responsibility for the production and delivery of physical goods and services."[31] Production/operations, on the other hand, is likely to be most interested in those activities that directly affect manufacturing and its primary objective of producing at the lowest unit cost. Now, viewing product flow activities as a process to be coordinated, product flow aspects within marketing, production, and logistics are collectively managed to achieve customer service objectives.

The difference in operating objectives (maximize revenue versus minimize cost) for marketing and production/operations may lead to a fragmentation of interest in, and responsibility for, logistics activities, as well as a lack of coordination among logistics activities as a whole. This, in turn, may lead to lower customer service levels or higher total logistics costs than are necessary. Business logistics represents a regrouping, either by formal organizational structure or conceptually in the minds of management, of the move-store activities that historically may have been partially under the control of marketing and production/operations.

If logistics activities are looked upon as a separate area of managerial action, the relationship of logistics activities to those of marketing and production/operations would be as shown in Figure 1-7. Marketing would be primarily responsible for market research, promotion, sales-force management, and the product mix, which create possession value in the product. Production/operations would be concerned with the creation of the product or service, which creates form value in the product. Key responsibilities would be quality control, production planning and scheduling, job

---

[29]*Wall Street Journal*, August 16, 1994, A5.

[30]Definition approved by the American Marketing Association as paraphrased in Philip Kotler, *Marketing Management: Planning, Analysis, Implementation, and Control*, 10th ed. (Upper Saddle River, NJ: Prentice-Hall, 2000), p. 13.

[31]John O. McClain and L. Joseph Thomas, *Operations Management: Production of Goods and Services*, 2nd ed. (Upper Saddle River, NJ: Prentice-Hall, 1985), p. 14.

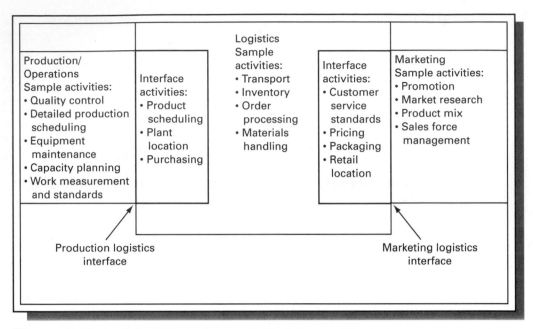

Figure 1-7 Logistics/SC Interfaces with Marketing and Production

design, capacity planning, maintenance, and work measurement and standards. Logistics would be concerned with those activities (previously defined) that give a product or service time and place value. This separation of the activities of the firm into three groupings rather than two is not always necessary or advisable to achieve the coordination of logistics activities that is sought. Marketing and production/operations, when broadly conceived and coordinated, can do an effective job of managing logistics activities without creating an additional organizational entity. Even if a separate functional area is created for logistics within the firm so as to achieve effective control of the firm's immediate logistics activities, logisticians will need to view their responsibility as one of coordinating the entire supply chain process rather than being just a local logistics activity administrator. To do otherwise may miss substantial opportunities for cost reduction and logistics customer service improvement.

Figure 1-7 also shows activities that are at the interface of marketing and logistics and production/operations and logistics within the immediate firm. An interface activity is one that cannot be managed effectively within one functional area. The interface is created by the arbitrary separation of a firm's activities into a limited number of functional areas. Managing the interface activities by one function alone can lead to suboptimal performance for the firm by subordinating broader company goals to individual functional goals—a potential danger resulting from the departmental form of organizational structure so common in companies today. To achieve interfunctional coordination, some measurement system and incentives for cooperation among the

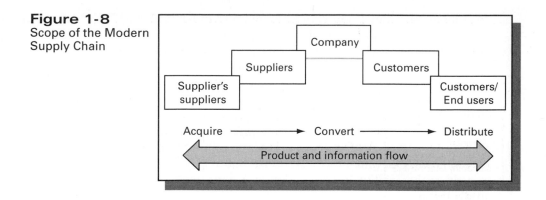

Figure 1-8
Scope of the Modern
Supply Chain

Company

Suppliers   Customers

Supplier's
suppliers

Customers/
End users

Acquire ⟶ Convert ⟶ Distribute

Product and information flow

functions involved need to be established. This is equally true of the interorganizational coordination required to manage product flows across company boundaries.

It is important to note, however, that establishing a third functional group is not without its disadvantages. Two functional interfaces now exist where only one between marketing and production/operations previously existed. Some of the most difficult administrative problems arise from the interfunctional conflicts that occur when one is attempting to manage interface activities. Some of this potential conflict may be dissipated if a new organizational arrangement is created whereby production/operations and logistics are merged into one group called supply chain.

Just as managers are beginning to understand the benefits of interfunctional logistics management, interorganizational management is being encouraged. Supply chain management proponents who view the area more broadly than some logisticians have been strongly promoting the need for collaboration among supply channel members that are outside the immediate control of a company's logistician, that is members who are legally separate companies. Collaboration among the channel members that are linked through buyer-seller relationships is essential to achieving cost-service benefits unable to be realized by managers with strictly an internal view of their responsibilities. Supply chain managers consider themselves to have responsibility for the entire supply channel of the scope as illustrated in Figure 1-8. Managing in this broader environment is the new challenge for the contemporary logistician.

OBJECTIVES OF BUSINESS LOGISTICS/SC

Within the broader objectives of the firm, the business logistician seeks to achieve supply channel process goals that will move the firm toward its overall objectives. Specifically, the desire is to develop a logistics activity mix that will result in the highest possible return on investment over time. There are two dimensions to this goal: (1) the impact of the logistics system design on the revenue contribution, and (2) the operating cost and capital requirements of the design.

Ideally, the logistician should know how much additional revenue would be generated through incremental improvements in the quality of customer service provided. However, such revenue is not generally known with great accuracy. Often, the customer service level is set at a target value, usually one that is acceptable to customers, the sales function, or other concerned parties. At this point, the logistics objective may become one of minimizing costs subject to meeting the desired service level rather than profit maximization or return on investment.

Unlike revenue, logistics costs usually can be determined as accurately as accounting practice will allow and are generally of two types: operating costs and capital costs. Operating costs are those that recur periodically or those that vary directly with variation in activity levels. Wages, public warehousing expenses, and administrative and certain other overhead expenses are examples of operating costs. Capital costs are the one-time expenses that do not change with normal variations in activity levels. Examples here are the investment in a private trucking fleet, the construction cost of a company warehouse, and the purchase of materials-handling equipment.

If it is assumed that there is knowledge of the effect of logistics activity levels on revenues of the firm, a workable financial objective for logistics can be expressed in the ratio known as *ROLA* (*return on logistics assets*). ROLA is defined as

$$\text{ROLA} = \frac{\text{Contribution to revenue} - \text{logistics operating costs}}{\text{Logistics assets}}$$

The contribution to revenue refers to the sales resulting from the logistics system design. Logistics operating costs are the expenses incurred to provide the level of logistics customer service needed to generate sales. Logistics assets are the capital investments made in the logistics system. ROLA is to be maximized over time.

If the value of money is high, maximizing the present value of cash flows or maximizing the internal rate of return is a more appropriate statement of the objective. Maximizing the cumulative return on investment over time is the single most important objective to ensure the long-run survival of the firm.

APPROACH TO THE STUDY OF LOGISTICS/SC

Now that a background of definition and significance has been provided, we can begin our study of the management of logistics in a systematic way. Two themes are used in this text; they follow what management does and the skills needed to perform in a technically complex world. First, the work of management can be looked upon as performing the tasks of planning, organizing, and controlling to achieve the objectives of the firm. *Planning* refers to deciding on the goals for the firm, *organizing* refers to collecting and positioning the resources of firm to accomplish the company goals, and *controlling* refers to measuring company performance and taking corrective action when performance is not in line with goals. Because these are central to what management does, each will be discussed within the various chapters of this book.

Second, managers, whether at entry level or top level, spend a great deal of time in the planning activity. To do effective planning, it is useful to have a vision of the goals of the firm, to have concepts and principles for guidance on how to get there, and to have tools that help to sort among alternative courses of action. Specifically for logistics management, planning follows a primary decision triangle of location, inventory, and transportation, with customer service being the result of these decisions (see Figure 1-9). Although the logistics' planning triangle is the primary organizational theme for this book, additional topics that relate to it will also be discussed. We begin with, an overview of a strategy for logistics planning and the information systems and technology that support the strategy. A chapter follows on the customer, who drives all logistics decision making. Chapters covering transportation, location, and inventory, which form the cornerstones of the logistics' planning triangle, are all included. Finally, chapters on organization and control round out the planning, organizing, and control theme. Contemporary issues such as global logistics, service industry logistics, quality, collaborative logistics, and reverse logistics are important, but are recognized as extensions of the basic ideas presented in the text. Therefore, their discussion is integrated throughout the text. Numerous examples are given to illustrate how the concepts and tools for good logistics/supply chain management apply to the problems actually encountered in the real world.

From just about every standpoint—whether cost, value to customers, or strategic importance to a firm's mission—logistics/SC is vital. However, only in recent years have businesses on a broad scale begun to manage supply chain activities in an

Figure 1-9 The Planning Triangle in Relation to the Principal Activities of Logistics/Supply Chain Management

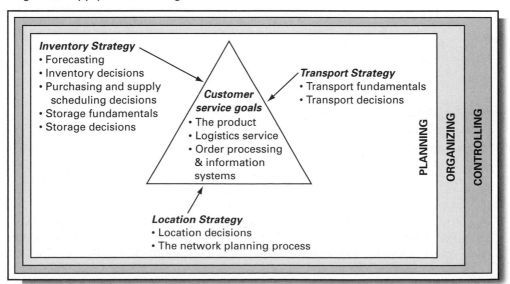

integrated way—that is, to think about products and services flowing seamlessly from the sources of raw materials to the final consumers. Moreover, in recent times that flow must include backward movement in the supply channel, or reverse logistics. The economic forces—mainly increased worldwide deregulation of business, proliferation of free trade agreements, increased foreign competition, increased globalization of industries, and increased requirements for faster and more certain logistics performance—have all been instrumental in elevating logistics to a high level of importance in many firms. New opportunities for logistics management, brought about by growth in the service sector, environmental issues, and information technology, will continue to support the vital nature of logistics for many years to come.

The primary emphasis of this text is directed toward dealing effectively with the managerial problems associated with moving and storing goods throughout the supply chain by business firms. These firms may be producing either goods or services and will have profit-making objectives.

This text is organized around the three primary tasks of management: planning, organizing, and controlling. Usually, the most difficult of these is planning, that is, the identification of, and selection among, alternative courses of action. Therefore, major emphasis will be given to this phase of management. It is the approach of this text to describe logistics problems as simply as possible and to apply definitive methodology in solving them that has proven to be of practical value in real applications. It is a decision-making approach.

QUESTIONS AND PROBLEMS

1. What is supply chain management? Contrast it with business logistics management.
2. Describe business logistics, as you would expect it to be practiced in the following countries or regions:
   a. United States
   b. Japan
   c. European Union
   d. Australia
   e. South Africa
   f. China
   g. Brazil
3. Summarize the factors and forces that give logistics importance among other functional areas (marketing, finance, production) of a firm.
4. Discuss the similarities and differences between logistics management of a manufacturing firm and
   a. a service firm (bank, hospital, etc.)
   b. a nonprofit organization (symphony orchestra, art museum, etc.)
   c. the military
   d. a retailing firm (general merchandise, fast food, etc.)
5. Discuss the role that efficient and effective logistics systems play in encouraging a high level of foreign trade.

6. Why is it that both marketing and production may claim some or all of logistics activities as part of their area of responsibility?
7. What are the key activities of the business logistics function? Discuss their existence and importance to the management of
   a. a TV manufacturer (Sony)
   b. a touring musical group (Berlin Philharmonic)
   c. a hospital (Massachusetts General)
   d. a city government (New York City)
   e. a fast-food chain (McDonald's)
8. How do you think international logistics differs from logistics for a firm with global operations?
9. Suggest some products that benefit significantly from increased time and place value.
10. Establishing logistics as a separate area for management within a business firm creates an additional set of interface activities. What are interface activities? Why would the creation of an additional set of interface activities cause concern in most companies?
11. The political and economic barriers are continuing to come down among the several countries of the European Union. If you are a manager of physical distribution for a multinational company that sells finished consumer goods (e.g., Procter & Gamble of Italy) within your own country, what distribution decisions are facing you in the future?
12. Suppose that a manufacturer of men's shirts can produce a dress shirt in its Houston, Texas plant for $8 per shirt (including the cost of raw materials). Chicago is a major market for 100,000 shirts per year. The shirt is priced at $15 at the Houston plant. Transportation and storage charges from Houston to Chicago amount to $5 per hundredweight (cwt.). Each packaged shirt weighs 1 pound.

    As an alternative, the company can have the shirts produced in Taiwan for $4 per shirt (including the cost of raw materials). The raw materials, weighing about 1 pound per shirt, would be shipped from Houston to Taiwan at a cost of $2 per cwt. When the shirts are completed, they are to be shipped directly to Chicago at a transportation and storage cost of $6 per cwt. An import duty of $0.50 per shirt is assessed.
    a. From a logistics-production cost standpoint, should the shirts be produced in Taiwan?
    b. What additional considerations, other than economic ones, might be considered before making a final decision?
13. Use the following form as part of an in-class exercise. Be prepared to discuss your choices and to contrast them with others in the class. Identify the common elements making some companies successful logistically and the elements that are missing among others leading to logistics/SC failures.

Examples of Good Logistics/ Supply Chain Strategy, or Lack Thereof

Many firms use logistics/supply chain strategy as a central element in their corporate strategy. You are asked to identify those firms that have been successful because of their logistics/supply chain strategy execution and to note why you consider the execution outstanding (Hall of Famers). Conversely, identify those firms that suffer from poor execution of an important logistics/supply chain strategy (Hall of Shamers).

1. **Hall of Famers.** Identify three firms that use a logistics/supply chain strategy as an important element of their overall business strategy.

Hall of Famers	Logistics/Supply Chain Elements Well Executed

2. **Hall of Shamers.** Identify three firms that have failed in the execution of a logistics/supply chain strategy important to their overall strategy.

Hall of Shamers	Logistics/Supply Chain Elements That Failed

3. From a logistics/supply chain viewpoint, what distinguishes the Hall of Famers from the Hall of Shamers?

Distinguishing Features

Chapter 2

Logistics/Supply Chain Strategy and Planning

> *While in the past physical distribution (logistics) has been referred to as the last frontier of cost economies,[1] it is now the new frontier of the demand generation.*

*I*n *Alice's Adventures in Wonderland*, Alice asks the Cheshire Cat, "Would you tell me, please, which way I ought to go from here?" "That depends a good deal on where you want to get to," said the Cat.[2] Deciding a company's strategic direction in order to meet its financial, growth, market share, and other objectives is an important first consideration for management. This is a creative, visionary process, usually conducted by top management, whereby a firm's overall direction is outlined and translated into a corporate action plan.

For the functional areas of the firm, the corporate plan is then divided into subplans, such as marketing, production, and logistics. These subplans require making many specific decisions. Regarding the supply chain, these decisions include locating warehouses, setting inventory policies, designing order-entry systems, and selecting transportation modes. Many of these may be aided by the application of various concepts for logistics and decision-making techniques available to the supply chain manager.

This chapter focuses on the planning process, first from the corporate-wide perspective and then from the logistics function viewpoint. A framework is set for planning that will form the basis for later chapters. This chapter, as well as much of this book, will be focused on

---

[1]Peter F. Drucker, "The Economy's Dark Continent," *Fortune* (April 1962), pp. 103, 265–270.
[2]Lewis Carroll, *Alice's Adventures in Wonderland* (New York: Knopf, 1983), p. 72.

planning and the decision making that leads to good logistics/SC plans that contribute to a firm's financial goals.

CORPORATE STRATEGY

Corporate strategy creation begins with a clear expression of the firm's objectives. Whether the company is to seek profit, survival, social, return on investment, market share, or growth goals should be well understood. Next, a process of *visioning* is likely to take place where unconventional, unheard of, and even counterintuitive strategies are considered. This requires addressing the four components of good strategy: *customers, suppliers, competitors,* and the *company* itself. Assessing the needs, strengths, weaknesses, orientations, and perspectives of each of these components is a beginning.[3] Then, brainstorming about what may be possible as a niche strategy is the output of this visioning process. The following are examples of such visions:

- General Electric's vision is to be number one or two in each market that it serves; it will get out of any market in which it cannot maintain that standard.
- Hewlett-Packard envisions serving the scientific community.
- IBM constantly reshapes itself to remain an effective competitor.[4]

Next, the broad, general visioning strategies need to be converted into plans that are more definitive. With a clear understanding of the firm's costs, financial strengths and weaknesses, market share position, asset base and deployment, external environment, competitive forces, and employee skills, a selection is made from alternative strategies that evolve from the threats and opportunities facing the firm. These strategies now become specific directions for how the vision will be made reality.

Examples

- Xerox's copier patents were running out, meaning the company would no longer have a differentiated product in the marketplace. Therefore, it adopted the strategy to be number one in field service.
- StarKist Foods adopted a supply-side strategy of buying and packing all the tuna that its own fleet and its contracted fleets could catch. This would help it to be the dominant packer in the tuna business.

The corporate strategy drives the functional strategies because they are contained within the former, as shown in Figure 2-1. The corporate strategy is realized as manufacturing, marketing, finance, and logistics shape their plans to meet it. When StarKist Foods decided on a supply-side strategy, marketing and logistics responded

---

[3]Roger Kallock, "Develop a Strategic Outlook," *Transportation and Distribution* (January 1989), pp. 16–18.
[4]Kenneth R. Ernst, "Visioning: Key to Effective Strategic Planning," *Annual Conference Proceedings*, volume 1 (Boston: Council of Logistics Management, 1988), pp. 153–165.

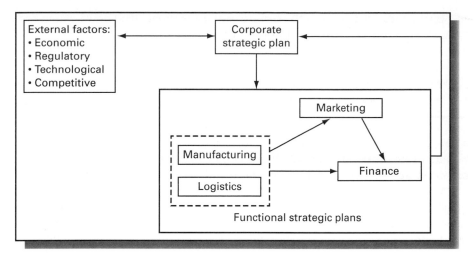

Figure 2-1 Overview of Corporate Strategic Planning to Functional Strategic Planning

Source: William Copacino and Donald B. Rosenfield, "Analytic Tools for Strategic Planning," *International Journal of Physical Distribution and Materials Management*, Vol. 15, No. 3 (1985), p. 48.

with their plan to control the potential excess inventories that would result. This plan was to place tuna on sale to reduce inventories when necessary. The plan works because tuna is in such demand that consumers often stock up when it is on sale. Let's now turn to the specific way logistics strategies are developed.

Logistics/SC Strategy

Selecting a good logistics/SC strategy requires much of the same creative processes as developing a good corporate strategy. Innovative approaches to logistics/SC strategy can give a competitive advantage.

Examples

- An office machine company took a bold step to save on valuable machine repair time. Traditionally, repair technicians were sent by a central service center to the customer repair site. These highly trained and highly paid personnel spent a fair amount of their time traveling to and from these sites. The company redesigned its logistics system so that inventories of on-loan and replacement machines were placed at service centers around the country. When a machine broke down, a replacement machine would be sent to the customer, and the broken machine sent to the service center for repair. The new system not only saved on repair costs, but improved customer service as well.

- American Hospital Supply developed an efficient purchasing system for its customers by putting terminals in each of its customers' offices. The system simplified and facilitated the ordering process for its customers, and guaranteed a higher proportion of orders for American Hospital Supply.[5]

It has been suggested that a logistics strategy has three objectives: cost reduction, capital reduction, and service improvement.

Cost reduction is strategy directed toward minimizing the variable costs associated with movement and storage. The best strategy is usually formulated by evaluating alternative courses of action, such as choosing among different warehouse locations or selecting among alternative transport modes. Service levels are typically held constant while the minimum cost alternatives are being found. Profit maximization is the prime goal.

Capital reduction is strategy directed toward minimizing the level of investment in the logistics system. Maximizing the return on logistics assets is the motivation for this strategy. Shipping direct to customers to avoid warehousing, choosing public warehouses over privately owned warehouses, selecting a just-in-time supply approach rather than stocking to inventory, or using third-party providers of logistics services are examples. These strategies may result in higher variable costs than strategies requiring a higher level of investment; however, the return on investment may be increased.

Service improvement strategies usually recognize that revenues depend on the level of logistics service provided. Although costs increase rapidly with increased levels of logistics customer service, the increased revenues may offset the higher costs. To be effective, the service strategy is developed in contrast with that provided by the competition.

Example

Parker Hannifin, a maker of seals and O-rings, won sales with superior logistics customer service. A customer's purchasing agent showed the Parker Hannifin salesperson two invoices for the same product, one from a competitor and one from Parker Hannifin. The competitor's price was 8 percent lower. However, if Parker Hannifin would maintain a service center (an inventory stocking point with additional value-added services) for the customer, then Parker Hannifin stood to gain over a million dollars of business at the higher price. Parker Hannifin complied and established the

---

[5]William Copacino and Donald B. Rosenfield, "Analytic Tools for Strategic Planning," *International Journal of Physical Distribution and Materials Management*, Vol. 15, No. 3 (1985), pp. 47–61.

center, getting the contract. The customer was satisfied and Parker Hannifin made a profit, since operating the service center cost 3.5 percent of the sale!

A proactive logistics strategy often begins with the business goals and customer service requirements. These have been referred to as "attack" strategies to meet competition. The remainder of the logistics system design can then be derived from these attack strategies.

Examples

- Nabisco comfortably reigned as king of steak sauces with its A-1 brand. Then Kraft came out with a spicier version called Bulls Eye. This competitive move by Kraft threatened Nabisco's franchise. Nabisco responded with A-1 Bold, throwing its supply chain into overdrive and putting Bold on the store shelves in a matter of months. Nabisco succeeded in knocking Bulls Eye off the market. Without Nabisco's fast-response supply chain, Bulls Eye, which was a very good product, would have had time to take market share.[6]
- Domino Pizza is just one of many in the pizza market, serviced by competitors such as Pizza Hut as well as an army of independent retail operations. It has now become America's second-largest pizza chain by promising customers a $3 discount on any pie not delivered within 30 minutes from the time it's ordered.[7]
- Frito-Lay developed a strategic advantage with its direct-to-store delivery system, and Atlas Door recognized that no company in the industrial door business could get a door to a customer in less than three months. Atlas stepped in and developed a strategy based on delivering a door in much less time, and it now enjoys a major share of the market.[8]

Each link in the logistics system is planned and balanced with each other in an integrated logistics planning process (see Figure 2-2). Design of the management and control systems completes the planning cycle.

Designing effective logistics customer service strategies requires no particular program or technique. It is simply the product of a sharp mind. Once the logistics service strategy is formulated, the task is then to meet it. This involves selecting among alternative courses of action. Such selection is amenable to various concepts and techniques for analysis. The next section sets the stage for such evaluation. A recurrent theme throughout this book is understanding the logistical alternatives open to the supply chain manager and how they can be evaluated.

---

[6]J. Robert Hall, "Supply Chain Management from a CEO's Perspective," *Proceedings of the Council of Logistics Management* (San Diego, CA: October 8–11, 1995), p. 164.
[7]"How Managers Can Succeed Through SPEED," *Fortune* (February 13, 1989), pp. 54–59.
[8]Ernst, "Visioning," pp. 153–165.

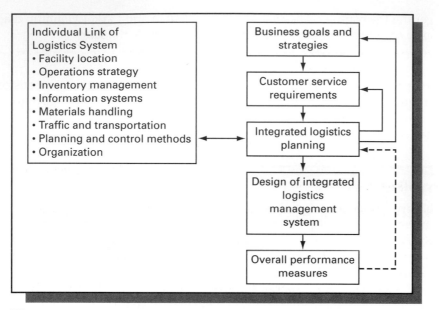

Figure 2-2 Flow of Logistics Planning

Source: William Copacino and Donald B. Rosenfield, "Analytic Tools for Strategic Planning," *International Journal of Physical Distribution and Materials Management*, Vol. 15, No. 3 (1985), p. 49.

LOGISTICS/SC PLANNING

Levels of Planning

Logistics planning attempts to answer the questions of what, when, and how, and it takes place at three levels: strategic, tactical, and operational. The major difference between them is the time horizon for the planning. *Strategic planning* is considered long-range, where the time horizon is longer than one year. *Tactical planning* involves an intermediate time horizon, usually less than a year. *Operational planning* is short-range decision making, with decisions frequently made on an hourly or daily basis. The concern is how to move the product effectively and efficiently through the strategically planned logistics channel. Selected examples of typical problems with these various planning time horizons are shown in Table 2-1.

Each planning level requires a different perspective. Because of its long time horizon, strategic planning works with data that are often incomplete and imprecise. Data may be averaged, and plans are usually considered good enough if they are reasonably close to optimum. At the other end of the spectrum, operational planning works with very accurate data, and the methods for planning should be able to handle a great deal of these data and still find reasonable plans. For example, we may strategically plan *all* company inventories not to exceed a certain dollar limit or to

	LEVEL OF DECISION		
DECISION AREA	STRATEGIC	TACTICAL	OPERATIONAL
Facility location	Number, size, and location of warehouses, plants, and terminals		
Inventories	Stocking locations and control policies	Safety stock levels	Replenishment quantities and timing
Transportation	Mode selection	Seasonal equipment leasing	Routing, dispatching
Order processing	Order entry, transmittal, and processing system design		Processing orders, filling back orders
Customer service	Setting standards	Priority rules for customer orders	Expediting deliveries
Warehousing	Handling equipment selection, layout design	Seasonal space choices and private space utilization	Order picking and restocking
Purchasing	Development of supplier-buyer relationships	Contracting, vendor selection, forward buying	Order releasing and expediting supplies

Table 2-1   Examples of Strategic, Tactical, and Operational Decision Making

achieve a certain inventory turnover ratio.[9] On the other hand, an operational plan for inventories requires that each item be managed individually.

Much of our attention will be directed toward strategic logistics planning, since it can be discussed using a general approach. Operational and tactical planning often requires an intimate knowledge of the particular problem, and specific approaches must be customized. Because of this, we begin with what is the major logistics planning problem, which is designing the overall logistics system.

Major Planning Areas

Logistics planning tackles four major problem areas: customer service levels, facility location, inventory decisions, and transportation decisions, as shown in Figure 2-3. Except for setting a desired customer service level (customer service is a resultant of the strategies formulated in the other three areas), logistics planning may be referred to as a triangle of logistics decision making. These problem areas are interrelated and should be planned as a unit, although it is common to plan them separately. Each has an important impact on system design.

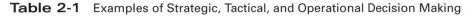

[9]Inventory turnover ratio is defined as the ratio of annual sales to the average inventory level for the same annual period, usually in dollar units.

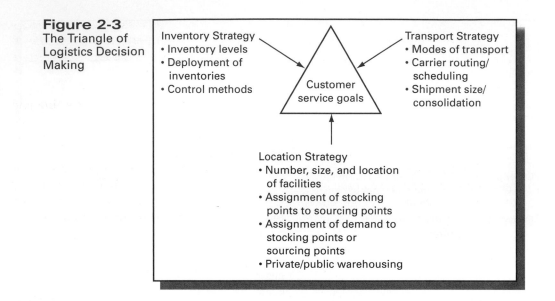

Figure 2-3
The Triangle of Logistics Decision Making

Inventory Strategy
• Inventory levels
• Deployment of inventories
• Control methods

Transport Strategy
• Modes of transport
• Carrier routing/ scheduling
• Shipment size/ consolidation

Customer service goals

Location Strategy
• Number, size, and location of facilities
• Assignment of stocking points to sourcing points
• Assignment of demand to stocking points or sourcing points
• Private/public warehousing

Customer Service Goals

More than any other factor, the level of logistics customer service provided dramatically affects system design. Low levels of service allow centralized inventories at few locations and the use of less expensive forms of transportation. High service levels generally require just the opposite. However, when service levels are pressed to their upper limits, logistics costs will rise at a rate disproportionate to the service level. Therefore, the first concern in logistics strategic planning must be the proper setting of customer service levels.

Facility Location Strategy

The geographic placement of the stocking points and their sourcing points creates an outline for the logistics plan. Fixing the number, location, and size of the facilities and assigning market demand to them determines the paths through which products are directed to the marketplace. The proper scope for the facility location problem is to include all product movements and associated costs as they take place from plant, vendor, or port locations through the intermediate stocking points, and on to customer locations. Assigning customer demand to be served directly from plants, vendors, or ports, or directing it through selected stocking points, affects total distribution costs. Finding the lowest cost assignments, or alternatively the maximum profit assignments, is the essence of facility location strategy.

Inventory Decisions

Inventory decisions refer to the manner in which inventories are managed. Allocating (pushing) inventories to the stocking points versus pulling them into stocking points through inventory replenishment rules represent two strategies. Selective location of various items in the product line in plant, regional, or field warehouses or managing inventory levels by various methods of perpetual inventory control are others. The particular policy used by the firm affects the facility location decision and, therefore, the policy should be considered in the logistics strategy.

Transport Strategy

Transport decisions can involve mode selection, shipment size, and routing and scheduling. These decisions are influenced by the proximity of warehouses to customers and plants, which, in turn, influence warehouse location. Inventory levels also respond to transport decisions through shipment size.

Customer service levels, facility location, inventory, and transportation are major planning areas because of the impact that decisions in these areas have on the firm's profitability, cash flow, and return on investment. Each decision area is interrelated and transport strategy should be planned with at least some consideration of the trade-off effect.

Conceptualizing the Logistics/SC Planning Problem

Another way to look at the logistics planning problem is to view it in the abstract as a network of *links* and *nodes*, as shown in Figure 2-4. The links of the network represent the movement of goods between various inventory storage points. These storage points—retail stores, warehouses, factories, or vendors—are the nodes. There may be several links between any pair of nodes, to represent alternate forms of transportation service, different routes, and different products. Nodes represent points

Figure 2-4 An Abbreviated Network Diagram for a Logistics System

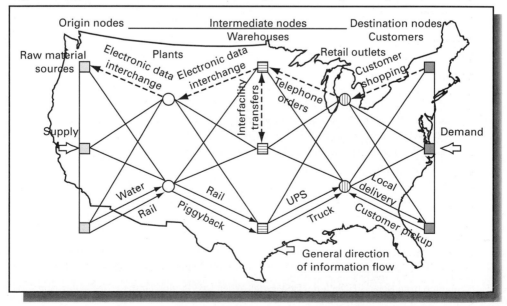

where the flow of inventory is temporarily stopped—for example, at a warehouse—before moving on to a retail store and on to the final consumer.

These move-store activities for inventory flows are only one part of the total logistics system. In addition, there is a network of information flows. Information is derived from sales revenues, product costs, inventory levels, warehouse utilization, forecasts, transportation rates, and the like. Links in the information network usually consist of the mail or electronic methods for transmitting information from one geographic point to another. Nodes are the various data collection and processing points, such as a clerk who handles order processing and prepares bills of lading[10] or a computer that updates inventory records.

In concept, the information network is much like the product flow network in that both can be viewed as a collection of links and nodes. However, a major difference in the networks is that product mainly flows "down" the distribution channel (toward the final consumer), whereas information mainly, but not entirely, flows "up" the channel (toward raw material sources).

The product flow network and the information network combine to form a logistics system. The networks are combined, since designing each separately can lead to a suboptimal design for the entire system. Thus, the networks are dependent. For example, the design of the information network influences the order-cycle times for the system. Order-cycle times, in turn, affect the inventory levels that must be maintained at the nodes in the product network. The availability of inventory affects customer service levels, and customer service levels, in turn, affect order-cycle times and the information network design. In addition, still other interdependencies require viewing the logistics system as a whole rather than by its parts.

Logistics planning is a design problem. The network is to be constructed as a configuration of warehouses, retail outlets, factories, deployed inventories, transportation services, and information processing systems that will achieve an optimum balance between the revenues resulting from the level of customer service established by the network design and the costs associated with the creation and operation of the network.

When to Plan[11]

In the planning process, when the network should be planned or planned again is the first consideration. If no logistics system currently exists, as in the case of a new firm or of new items within an existing product line, the need for planning a logistics network is obvious. However, in most cases in which a logistics network is already in place, a decision must be made either to modify the existing network or to allow it to continue to operate, even though it may not be an optimal design. A definitive answer to this question cannot be given without doing the actual planning. However, general guidelines for network appraisal and audit can be offered in the five key areas of demand, customer service, product characteristics, logistics costs, and pricing policy.

---

[10]A bill of lading is a contractual agreement between the shipper and carrier setting forth the conditions under which the freight will be moved.
[11]Adapted from Ronald H. Ballou, "How to Tell When Distribution Strategy Needs Revision," *Marketing News*, May 1, 1982, Sec. 2, p. 12.

Demand

Both the level of demand and its geographic dispersion greatly influence the configuration of logistics networks. Firms often experience disproportionate growth or decline in one region of the country compared with others. Although only expansion or reduction at current facilities may be required, substantial shifting of demand patterns may require that new warehouses or plants be located in rapidly growing areas while facilities in slow growth or declining markets need to be closed. Such disproportionate growth of only a few percentage points a year often is sufficient to justify network replanning.

Customer Service

Customer service broadly includes inventory availability, speed of delivery, and order filling speed and accuracy. The costs associated with these factors increase at a higher rate as the customer service level is raised. Therefore, distribution costs will be quite sensitive to the level of customer service provided, especially if it is already high.

Reformulating the logistics strategy is usually needed when service levels are changed due to competitive forces, policy revisions, or arbitrary service goals different from those on which the logistics strategy originally was based. However, minor changes in service levels, when they already are low, are not likely to trigger the need for replanning.

Product Characteristics

Logistics costs are sensitive to such characteristics as product weight, volume (cube), value, and risk. In the logistics channel, these characteristics can be altered through package design or finished state of the product during shipment and storage. For example, shipping a product in a knocked-down form can considerably affect the weight-bulk ratio of the product and the associated transportation and storage rates. Because altering a product's characteristics can substantially change one cost element in the logistics mix with little change to the others, this creates a new cost balance point for the logistics system. Thus, when substantial changes are made in the product characteristics, replanning the logistics system could be beneficial.

Logistics Costs

The costs that a firm incurs for physical supply and physical distribution often determine how frequently its logistics system should be replanned. All other factors being equal, a firm producing high-valued goods (such as machine tools or computers); with logistics costs being a small portion of total costs, will likely give little attention to the optimality of logistics strategy. However, when logistics costs are high, as they can be in the case of packaged industrial chemicals and food products, logistics strategy is a key concern. With high logistics costs, even the small improvements brought about by frequent replanning can result in substantial cost reductions.

Pricing Policy

Changes in the pricing policy under which goods are purchased or sold will affect logistics strategy, mainly because it defines responsibility for certain logistics activities. A supplier that switches from an f.o.b. factory price (transportation costs not included) to a delivered price (transportation costs included) will usually relieve the buying firm of the responsibility for providing or arranging for the inbound transportation. Similarly, price policy affects the transfer of title to goods and the responsibility for transportation in the distribution channel as well.

Although costs are transferable through the logistics channel regardless of how they are assigned by the pricing mechanism, some firms plan their logistics system based on the costs for which they are directly responsible. If a firm has a price policy where the customer pays for the delivery of goods, the resulting strategy is likely to be one where there are few stocking points, unless customer service restrictions force these to be increased. Due to the importance of transportation costs in total logistics costs, shifts in price policy will usually trigger strategy reformulation.

When changes have occurred in one or several of these areas, replanning the logistics strategy should be considered. Next, let us consider some of the logistics principles and concepts that are useful for strategy formulation.

Guidelines for Strategy Formulation

Many of the principles and concepts that guide logistics planning are derived from the unique nature of logistics activities, especially transportation. Others are a result of general economic and market phenomena. All give insight as to what the logistics strategy might be and set the stage for more detailed analysis. Several of these will now be outlined and illustrated.

Total Cost Concept

Central to the scope and design of the logistics system is trade-off analysis, which, in turn, leads to the total cost concept. The cost trade-off is the recognition that cost patterns of various activities of the firm frequently display characteristics that put them in conflict with one another. This conflict is managed by balancing the activities so that they are collectively optimized. For example, Figure 2-5 shows that when a transportation service is being selected, the direct cost of the transport service and the indirect cost effect on inventory levels in the logistics channel due to different delivery performance of carriers are said to be in cost conflict with each other. The best economic choice occurs at the point where the sum of both costs is lowest, as indicated by the dashed line in Figure 2-5.

Choosing a transportation service based on lowest rates or fastest service may not be the best method. Therefore, the basic problem in logistics is one of cost conflict management. Wherever there are substantial cost conflicts among activities, they should be managed in a coordinated manner. The network, as previously described, incorporates most of the potential cost conflicts relevant to logistics.

The total cost concept applies to more than the problem of selecting transportation service. Additional examples of logistics problems, where a trade-off of costs is indicated, are shown in Figure 2-6. Figure 2-6(a) illustrates the problem of setting the customer service level. As customers receive a higher level of service, fewer of them are lost because of out-of-stock situations, slow and unreliable deliveries, and inaccurate order filling. The cost of lost sales decreases with improved service. Counterbalancing the lost sales cost is the cost of maintaining the level of service.

Figure 2-5
Generalized Cost
Conflict Between
Transportation and
Inventory Costs
As a Function of
Transportation
Service
Characteristics

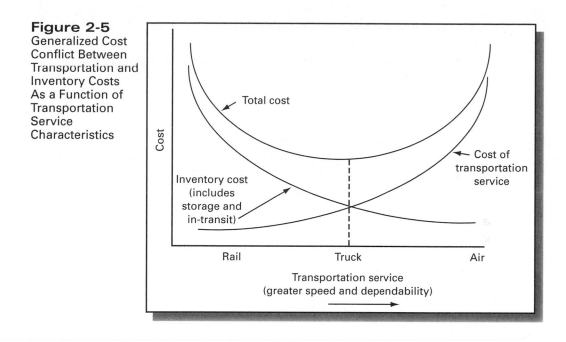

Improved service usually means that more must be paid for transportation, order processing, and inventories. The best trade-off occurs at a point below 100 percent (perfect) customer service.

Figure 2-6(b) shows the basic economic considerations in determining the number of stocking points in a logistics network. When customers purchase in small quantities and stocking points are replenished in large quantities, the cost of transportation from the stocking points exceeds the inbound costs so that transportation costs decline when the number of stocking points is increased. However, as the number of stocking points increases, the inventory level for the entire network increases and inventory costs rise. In addition, the customer service level is affected by this decision. The problem is one of balancing the combined inventory-transportation costs against the contribution to revenues from the customer service level provided.

Figure 2-6(c) illustrates the problem of setting the safety stock level for inventories. Because safety stock increases the average level of inventories and affects the customer service level through the availability of stock when an order is placed, the cost of lost sales declines. Increasing the average level of inventories will increase the inventory carrying cost. Transportation costs remain relatively unaffected. Again, a balance is sought between these opposing costs.

Finally, Figure 2-6(d) shows the basic features of a multiproduct scheduling problem. Production costs are affected by the sequence in which the products are produced and the length of production runs. As the production sequence is changed, inventory costs will increase, because orders will not necessarily be received at the optimum time to replenish depleted stocks. The effect is to raise the average inventory level. The best production sequence and run length to produce the products are found where the combined production and inventory costs are minimized.

Figure 2-6 Additional Generalized Logistics System Trade-Offs

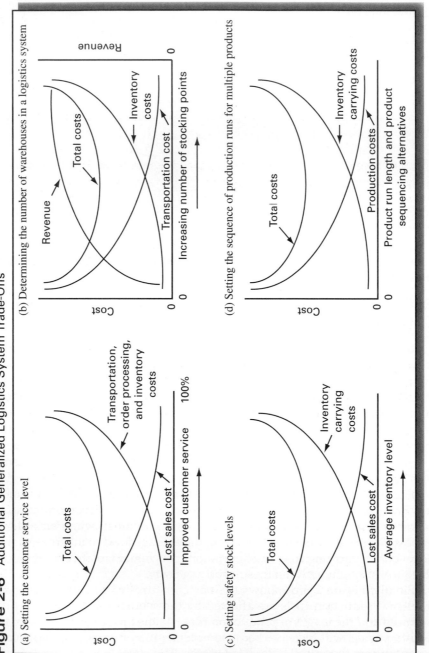

(a) Setting the customer service level

(b) Determining the number of warehouses in a logistics system

(c) Setting safety stock levels

(d) Setting the sequence of production runs for multiple products

These examples illustrate the total cost concept as applied to the internal problems of the firm and specifically to logistics problems. However, at times, decisions made by a firm in a channel of distribution affect the logistics costs of another firm. For example, the inventory policies of a buyer affect both the inventory costs of the shipper and the operating costs of the carrier. In this case, it is necessary to extend the boundaries of the system beyond either the logistics function or the firm, possibly to include several firms. Thus, the total cost equation would be expanded, and the scope of managerial decision making would extend beyond the legal limits of the firm.

The point is that the total cost, or alternately the total system, concept is a concept without clear boundaries. Although one might argue that in some way all activities of the entire economy are economically related to the logistics problem of the firm, to attempt to assess all the various cost trade-offs that might relate to any decision problem is folly. It is left to managerial judgment to decide the factors considered relevant and to include them in the analysis. This defines whether the total cost analysis will include only factors within the logistics function as we have defined it, or whether the analysis should be extended to include other factors under the control of the firm and even some beyond the immediate control of the firm, as in the entire supply chain. *The total cost concept is the trade-off of all costs that are in cost conflict with each other and that can affect the outcome of a particular logistics decision.*

Application

A large manufacturer of marine products was constructing a warehouse in St. Louis. The choice of location was based on minimizing transportation costs. A follow-up study that included the effect of inventory consolidation on transportation costs showed that the warehouse was best located in Chicago. The more comprehensive analysis resulted in cost differences that were so dramatic that the company sold the partially constructed warehouse and moved the inventory to Chicago.

Differentiated Distribution

Not all products should be provided the same level of customer service. This is a fundamental principle for logistics planning. Different customer service requirements, different product characteristics, and different sales levels among the multiple items that the typical firm distributes suggest that multiple distribution strategies should be provided within the product line. Managers have made use of this principle when they broadly classify their products into a limited number of groups, such as high, medium, and low sales volume, and then apply a different stocking level to each. To a lesser extent, the principle is also applied to inventory location. When a firm stocks all products at all warehouse locations, it may do so to simplify administration, but this strategy denies the inherent differences between products and their costs, and it leads to higher than necessary distribution costs.

An improved strategy might be first to differentiate those products that should move through the warehouse from products that should be shipped directly to customers from plant, vendors, or other source points. Because the transportation rate structure encourages shipments in vehicle-load volumes, the products might first be divided according to shipment size. Those customers ordering in high-volume quantities would be served direct, while all others would be served from warehouses.

Of the sales volume remaining, the products should be differentiated by location. That is, the fast-moving items should be placed in the field warehouses with the most forward locations in the distribution channel. Medium-volume items should be placed in fewer regional locations. The slow-moving items should be located only at centralized stocking points such as plants. As a result, each stocking point may contain a different product mix.

Application

A small specialty chemical company manufactured a variety of products for coating metals for corrosion prevention. All products were produced at a single location. A study of the distribution network recommended distribution patterns somewhat different from those historically used by the company. That is, all shipments that could be made in full truckload quantities were to be shipped direct from plant to customers. All large customer orders, the top ten percent of the company's volume, were also to be shipped direct to customers from the plant. The remainder of the product line, with its small shipment sizes, was to be shipped out of two strategically located warehouses as well as from the plant. This differentiated distribution strategy saved the company 20 percent of its distribution costs while preserving the existing level of logistics customer service.

Differentiated distribution may be applied to factors other than volume. That is, separate distribution channels may be established for regular customer orders and back orders. The regular distribution channel might be to fill orders from warehouses. When an out-of-stock situation occurs, a backup distribution system may come into play that fills the order from secondary stocking points and uses premium transportation to overcome the disadvantage of increased delivery distances. Similarly, many other examples can be offered where multiple distribution channels give lower overall distribution costs than a single channel design.

Mixed Strategy
The concept of a mixed strategy is similar to that of differentiated distribution. The concept is: *A mixed distribution strategy will have lower costs than a pure, or single strategy.* Although single strategies may benefit from economies of scale and administrative simplicity, they are at an economic disadvantage when the product line varies substantially in terms of cube, weight, order size, sales volume, and customer service requirements. A mixed strategy allows an optimal strategy to be established for separate product groups. This often has lower costs than a single, global strategy that must be averaged across all product groups.

Application

One retailer of prescription drugs and sundry products was faced with expanding its distribution system to meet rapidly increasing sales brought about by a program of retail store acquisitions. A configuration of six warehouses was used to service about one thousand stores throughout the United States. The company's strategy was to use only privately owned warehouses and trucks to provide high levels of service to the stores. Expansion plans called for the construction of a new $7 million facility. The warehouse was to supplement an overloaded facility that served a primary market area around Pittsburgh and to lower costs by using up-to-date handling and storage equipment and procedures. Management was committed to this strategy and had begun searching for a site for the new building.

At this time, a network planning study was conducted. The results showed that while the Pittsburgh facility was expensive to operate, the savings generated by the new warehouse could not justify the $7 million investment. Although this was informative, it did not solve the company's need for additional space.

A mixed strategy was suggested to the vice president of distribution (see Figure 2-7). The use of some public (for rent) warehouse space along with the company-owned space could offer lower total costs than the all-private strategy. The company was able to move the high-cube products into a nearby public warehouse, install new equipment, and recover enough space to meet foreseeable needs. The costs were about $200,000 for the new equipment and about $100,000 for additional annual transport expense for serving the stores from both facilities. Thus, the company was successfully able to avoid the $7 million that it had already agreed to spend if a single, or pure, distribution strategy were pursued.

Figure 2-7
A Total Cost Curve
for Single and Mixed
Warehousing
Strategies

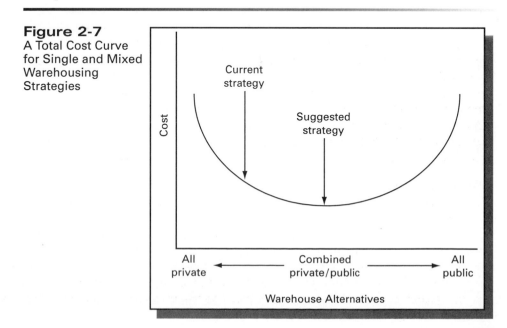

Postponement

The principle of postponement can be stated as follows: *The time of shipment and the location of final product processing in the distribution of a product should be delayed until a customer order is received.*[12] The idea is to avoid shipping goods in anticipation of when demand will occur (time postponement) and to avoid creating the form of the final product in anticipation of that form (form postponement).

Examples

- JCPenney regularly practices time postponement in its retail catalog operations by filling orders on demand from relatively few warehouse locations.
- Dell Computer, a manufacturer of mail-order personal computers, practices form postponement by configuring microcomputer systems to customer order from available options.
- Sherwin-Williams retail paint stores create an endless variety of colors for customers by mixing pigments in relatively few base colors, rather than stocking all colors ready mixed (form postponement).
- Steel service centers cut standard shapes and sizes of steel products into custom products for customers (form postponement).
- Postponement was used by Hewlett-Packard as a critical element in DeskJet Plus product design—the relationship between design and the eventual customization, distribution, and delivery of the product to multiple market segments.[13]
- SW, a manufacturer of graphical software, developed its products at its U.S. headquarters. To save on transportation and inventory costs, it shipped master copies of the software to Europe for duplication and final customization for that market.[14]

Specifically, consider how StarKist Foods reworked its distribution strategy using the principle of postponement.

Application

StarKist Foods, a canner of tuna products, changed its distribution strategy to take advantage of the postponement principle and lower inventory levels. Historically, the company packed fish in its California cannery for both company-label and

---

[12]Walter Zinn and Donald J. Bowersox, "Planning Physical Distribution with the Principle of Postponement," *Journal of Business Logistics*, Vol. 9, No. 2 (1988), pp. 117–136.

[13]Hau Lee, Corey Billington, and Brent Carter, "Hewlett-Packard Gains Control of Inventory and Service Through Design for Localization," *Interfaces*, Vol. 23, No. 4 (July/August 1993), pp. 1–11.

[14]Remko I. van Hoek, Harry R. Commandeur, and Bart Vos, "Reconfiguring Logistics Systems Through Postponement Strategies," *Planning for Virtual Response, Proceedings of the Twenty-Fifth Annual Transportation and Logistics Educators Conference* (Orlando, FL: The Transportation and Logistics Research Fund, 1996), pp. 53–81.

private-label markets. The end products were shipped to field warehouses for storage. A decision had to be made at the time of canning as to what proportion of the catch would be committed to the two end products, since there was too little capacity to store fish as a raw material. There was no difference in the quality of the final product under the two labels.

The company established a forward labeling operation on the East Coast to serve the eastern markets. The fish was packed in unlabeled cans called "brights" and shipped to the East Coast warehouse. As the market developed for the end products, the "brights" were labeled and shipped to customers. Inventories were lowered through avoiding the costs associated with having too little or too much of the product with a particular label.

Zinn and Bowersox classify five types of postponement and give suggestions as to the firms that might be interested in applying the principle. Form postponement can take four forms: labeling, packaging, assembly, and manufacturing; the fifth type is time postponement. Their suggestions are summarized in Table 2-2. Postponement is favored when the following characteristics appear to be present.

Table 2-2 Types of Firms Potentially Interested in Using the Postponement Principle

POSTPONEMENT TYPE	POTENTIALLY INTERESTED FIRMS
Labeling[a]	Firms selling a product under several brand names Firms with high unit value products Firms with high product value fluctuations
Packaging[a]	Firms selling a product under several package sizes Firms with high unit value products Firms with high product sales fluctuations
Assembly[a]	Firms selling products with several versions Firms selling a product whose cube is greatly reduced if shipped unassembled Firms with high unit value products Firms with high product sales fluctuations
Manufacturing[a]	Firms selling products with a high proportion of ubiquitous materials Firms with high unit value products Firms with high product sales fluctuations
Time[b]	Firms with high unit value products Firms with a large number of distribution warehouses Firms with high product sales fluctuations

[a]A type of form postponement
[b]Time postponement
Source: Adapted from Walter Zinn and Donald J. Bowersox, "Planning Physical Distribution with the Principle of Postponement," *Journal of Business Logistics*, Vol. 9, No. 2 (1988), p. 133.

Technology and Process Characteristics

- Feasible to decouple primary and postponed operations
- Limited complexity of customizing
- Modular product design
- Sourcing from multiple locations

Product Characteristics

- High commonality of modules
- Specific formulation of products
- Specific peripherals
- High value density of products
- Product cube and/or weight increases through customization

Market Characteristics

- Short product life cycles
- High sales fluctuations
- Short and reliable lead times
- Price competition
- Varied markets and customers[15]

Consolidation

Creating large shipments from small ones (consolidation) is a powerful economic force in strategic planning. It results from the substantial economies of scale that are present in the transport cost-rate structure. Managers can use this concept to improve strategy. For example, customer orders arriving at a warehouse might be combined with orders received later. This would increase the size of the average shipment, which in turn would lower average per-unit shipping costs. Potentially reduced customer service resulting from increased delivery time must be balanced with the cost benefits of order consolidation.

Application

A firm had a master warehouse in the Rochester, New York, area to serve a number of general merchandise stores in the eastern United States. The merchandise consisted of many items purchased in small quantities from thousands of vendors. To reduce inbound transportation costs, the company established consolidation terminals in major vendor regions. Vendors were instructed to ship the purchased quantities into the consolidation terminal. When full truckload quantities were accumulated, the company's own trucks moved the merchandise from the consolidation terminal to its master warehouse. This avoided shipping small quantities over long distances to the master warehouse, at very high per-unit transport rates.

---

[15]Ibid.

In general, the concept of consolidation will be most useful in strategy formulation when quantities shipped are small. That is, *the smaller the shipment size, the disproportionately greater the benefits of consolidation.*

Standardization

Variety exacts its price in the logistics channel. Proliferation of product variety can increase inventories and decrease shipment sizes. Just adding a new item to the product line that is similar to an existing one can increase the combined inventory levels of both items by 40 percent or more, even though total demand does not increase. The key question in strategy formulation is how to provide the variety in the marketplace that customers desire without dramatically increasing logistics costs. The use of the concepts of standardization and postponement in combination is often effective for this problem.

Standardization in production is created through interchangeable parts, modularizing products, and labeling the same products under different brand names. This effectively controls the variety of parts, supplies, and materials that must be handled in the supply channel. The disadvantages of product variety are controlled in the distribution channel through postponement. For example, automakers create endless product variety without increasing inventories by adding or substituting options at the point of sale and creating multiple brands from the same basic components. Clothing manufacturers do not attempt to stock exact sizes that many customers require, but alter standard sizes to fit.

SELECTING THE PROPER CHANNEL STRATEGY[16]

Selecting the proper channel design greatly affects the efficiency and effectiveness of the supply chain. Fundamentally, two strategies are significant—*supply-to-stock* and *supply-to-order*. These are the end points in a mixture of alternative strategies blended to meet a variety of product and demand characteristics.

A supply-to-stock strategy is one where the supply channel is set up for maximum *efficiency*. That is, inventories are used to achieve good economies by allowing economical production runs, purchasing in quantity, batch order processing, and transporting in large shipment sizes. Safety stocks are maintained to realize high levels of product availability. Demand is usually met from inventories, but careful control holds inventory levels to a minimum. In contrast, a supply-to-order strategy is one where the supply channel is set up for maximum *responsiveness*. The channel characteristics are excess capacity, quick changeovers, short lead times, flexible processing, premium transportation, and single order processing. Postponement strategies are used to delay the creation of product variety as long and as far down the supply channel as possible. The costs associated with responsiveness are offset by

---

[16]Based on Marshall L. Fisher, "What Is the Right Supply Chain for Your Product?" *Harvard Business Review*, Vol. 75, No. 2 (March/April 1997), pp. 105–116.

Figure 2-8
Characteristics of
Supply-to-Stock and
Supply-to-Order
Supply Chains

Supply Chain Type	Channel Design Characteristics
Efficient supply chain *Supply-to-Stock*	• Economical production runs • Finished goods inventories • Economical buy quantities • Large shipment sizes • Batch order processing
Responsive supply chain *Supply-to-Order*	• Excess capacity • Quick changeovers • Short lead times • Flexible processing • Premium transportation • Single order processing

the minimization of finished goods inventories. A summary of the differences between the two approaches is given in Figure 2-8.

The predictability of demand and the profit margin of products are the primary determinants of supply channel choice. When products have a stable demand pattern and are therefore reasonably predictable, planning their supply is reasonably easy. Many products that have a stable demand pattern also have a mature characteristic where competition is keen and profit margins are low. These characteristics lead the logistician to design a supply channel to be as low cost as possible consistent with meeting customer service goals. Typical products that might be in the predictable category are shown in Table 2-3.

On the other hand, products that are highly unpredictable frequently carry a higher profit margin than unpredictable ones. See examples in Table 2-3. They are often innovative, are new product developments, and incorporate new technology; therefore, they command a higher return. There is less of an historical basis for estimating their sales level. Even some products that have been in product lines for

Table 2-3
Classification of
Products

PREDICTABLE/MATURE PRODUCTS	UNPREDICTABLE/INTRODUCTORY PRODUCTS
• Gelatin desserts	• New CDs
• Corn flakes	• New computer games
• Lawn fertilizer	• High-fashion clothes
• Ballpoint pens	• Artwork
• Lightbulbs	• Movies
• Auto replacement tires	• Consulting services
• Some industrial chemicals	• New product offerings of existing product lines
• Tomato soup	

Figure 2-9
Actions for
Misclassified
Products

Supply Chain Design Type	Product Characteristic	
	Predictable/Mature	*Unpredictable/Introductory*
Supply-to-Stock/ Efficient	Tomato soup	If product is here
Supply-to-Order/ Responsive	If product is here	Personal computer models

many years display demand that is highly variable, or lumpy. Low volume items are typical of these. Unless the products are low valued, there is an economic disincentive to maintain inventories of these products to meet the uncertain demand. The better strategy is to respond quickly to demand at the time that it occurs, not from inventories but from production processes or from vendors. Applying the supply-to-stock design to the unpredictable product class results in excessive finished goods inventories needed to maintain adequate product availability levels, increased product cycle times resulting from batch production or quantity purchasing, and slow deliveries resulting from shipment consolidation. A responsive design avoids the long delivery times and/or excessive inventories by meeting demand as it occurs.

In fashioning the right strategy, it is necessary to categorize correctly existing items in a product line. Once this has been done, they should be matched to their supply chain design as shown in Figure 2-9. When there is a mismatch, two options are available. First, an attempt can be made to change the product characteristics. For an unpredictable product, an improved forecast method may be sought so that a supply-to-stock design is appropriate. Second, the type of supply chain design may be changed. A supply-to-stock design used for an unpredictable product may be changed to a supply-to-order, or responsive, design. On the other hand, a product categorized as predictable but being supplied under a responsive design can be changed to the efficient design. It is doubtful that a predictable product would be moved to the unpredictable category.

General guidelines have been provided to select the proper supply chain design; however, some mismatching of product characteristics to design type may be tolerated. Some products may have highly unpredictable demand, but their low value and low margin suggests that holding extra inventory resulting from poor forecasting, or highly variable replenishment lead times, is justified. Responsive design requiring careful management is not warranted. Similarly, products with predictable demand do not need to be moved from a responsive to an efficient design if there is no benefit from lower channel costs or higher customer service.

Consider how Benetton, an Italian clothing manufacturer and retailer best known for its colorful sweaters, introduced a supply-to-order strategy at its stores in a traditional supply-to-stock retail environment to reduce inventory obsolescence and increase sales. Sweater sales have been unpredictable, but because of long lead times from manufacturers, retailers took their best guess at sales and stocked accordingly. The principle of postponement plays an important role in the supply-to-order strategy whereby yarns and often sweaters are made up in a "gray" state ready for final knitting and dying to the finished color.

Example

Benetton, the Italian sportswear company, has knitting as its core. Located in Ponzano, Italy, Benetton makes and distributes 50 million pieces of clothing world-wide each year. They produce mostly sweaters, slacks, and dresses.

Benetton, found that the fastest way to run a distribution system is to create an electronic loop linking sales agent, factory, and warehouse, as illustrated in Figure 2-10. If, say, a salesperson in one of Benetton's Los Angeles shops finds that she is starting to run out of a best-selling red sweater in early October, she calls one of Benetton's 80 sales agents, who enters the order in his personal computer, which sends it to a mainframe in Italy. Because the red sweater was originally created on a computer-aided design system, the mainframe has all its measurements on hand in digital code, which can be transmitted to a knitting machine. The machine makes the sweaters, which factory workers put in a box with a bar code label containing the address of the Los Angeles store, and the box goes into the warehouse. That's right—one warehouse serves Benetton's 5,000 stores in 60 countries around the world. It cost $30 million, but this distribution center, run by only eight people, moves 230,000 pieces of clothing a day.

Once the red sweaters are sitting snugly in one of 300,000 slots in the warehouse, a computer sends a robot flying. By reading the bar codes, the robot finds the right box and any other boxes being shipped to the Los Angeles store, picks them up, and loads them onto a truck. Including manufacturing time, Benetton can get the order to Los Angeles in four weeks. If the warehouse already has red sweaters in stock, it takes one week. That's quite a performance in the notoriously slow garment industry, where hardly anyone else will even bother with reorders. And if Benetton suddenly realizes that it didn't make any, say, black cardigans and purple blouses this

Figure 2-10 Benetton's Delivery Channel

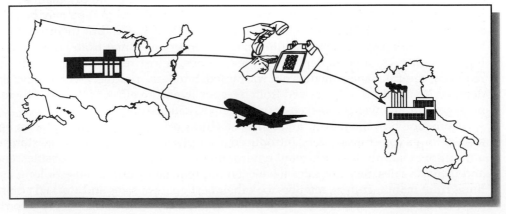

year and they're hot, it can manufacture and ship a "flash collection" of black cardigans and purple blouses in huge quantities in a few weeks.[17]

MEASURING STRATEGY PERFORMANCE

Once supply chain strategies are planned and implemented, managers want to know if they are working. Three measures are useful to monitor this: cash flow, savings, and return on investment. If all are positive and substantial, the strategies are probably working well. These financial measures are of particular interest to top management.

Cash Flow

Cash flow is the money that a strategy generates. For example, if the strategy is to decrease the amount of inventory in a supply channel, then the money released from the inventory carried as an asset is turned into cash. This cash can then be used to pay salaries or dividends, or can be invested in other areas of the business.

Savings

Savings refer to the change in all relevant costs associated with a strategy. These savings contribute to period profits of the business. A strategy that changes the number and location of the warehouses in a logistics network will affect transportation, inventory carrying, warehousing, and production/purchase costs. A good network design strategy will produce a significant annual costs savings (or, alternately, a customer improvement that contributes to revenue growth). These savings appear as a profit improvement on a business's profit and loss statement.

Return on Investment

Return on investment is the ratio of the annual savings from the strategy to the investment required by the strategy. It indicates the efficiency with which capital is being used. Good strategies should show a return greater than or equal to the expected return on a company's projects.

Application

A company was looking to consolidate its warehouses from 19 to four locations. The current system of warehouses had grown due to the company's aggressive merger program, resulting in warehouses not suited to the revised geographic demand

---

[17]"How Managers Can Succeed Through SPEED," *Fortune*, February 13, 1989, pp. 54–59. © 1989 The Time Inc. Magazine Company. All rights reserved.

profile. In addition, improvements in transportation allowed carriers to deliver products at farther distances in shorter time. As a result, fewer warehouses might save costs while preserving customer service.

Analysis of the four-warehouse strategy revealed substantial improvement in the three performance measures. It was reported to top management that cash flow would increase by $59 million, mainly due to inventory reduction. Profits would improve since a reduction in distribution costs would annually save $20 million dollars. Finally, because only one new warehouse was required and little moving expense was anticipated, the projected return on investment was 374 percent. Top management was pleased and the strategy was implemented.

CONCLUDING COMMENTS

This chapter has attempted to lay down a framework for planning the logistics network. The plan begins with a vision of where the company as a whole wishes to go and an outline of its competitive strategy. This vision is converted into specific plans for the functional areas of the firm, of which logistics is one.

Logistics strategy is typically formed around three goals: cost reduction, capital reduction, and service improvement. Depending on problem type, strategies may range from long to short time periods. Planning usually takes place around four key areas: customer service, location, inventories, and transportation. The network of links and nodes serves as an abstract representation of the planning problem.

Suggestions were given as to when the planning should be undertaken. Several principles and concepts were laid down that can prove useful to formulating effective logistics strategies. Finally, guidelines for selecting the right supply chain design were discussed.

QUESTIONS

1. You plan to start a company that will produce household furniture (sofas, chairs, tables, and the like). Outline a corporate strategy for competing in the marketplace. What logistics strategy might you derive from your corporate one?
2. Suppose in your company that you are responsible for distributing Taiwanese beer throughout the European Union. Suggest a distribution network that meets the three individual goals of cost reduction, capital reduction, and service improvement. Contrast each of these designs and suggest what you think would be a good balanced design.
3. Sketch a network diagram of the logistics systems you think would be appropriate for the following companies:
   a. A steel company supplying sheet steel to auto manufacturers.
   b. An oil company supplying heating fuel to the northeastern United States.
   c. A food company distributing canned goods to a domestic market.
   d. A Japanese electronics firm distributing television sets in Europe.

4. Consider the problem of locating a company-owned warehouse that will serve as a regional distribution point for its line of housewares.
   a. Describe the planning process that the logistician might follow to decide where to locate the warehouse.
   b. Which environmental factors are most important in this decision?
   c. What should the goals be for this problem—cost minimization, capital minimization, or service maximization?
   d. How should the logistician proceed with implementing the chosen plan, and how should the performance of the plan be controlled once it has been implemented?
5. Explain the meaning of strategic planning for a logistics system. Selecting several companies of your choice, discuss which activities should be included and why. How would you distinguish tactical and operational planning from strategic planning?
6. Describe as many cost trade-offs as you can that a logistics manager might encounter in strategic planning.
7. Describe the principle of differentiated distribution. Explain how it is illustrated in the following situations:
   a. Total distribution costs are minimized if back orders on field warehouse inventories are filled from plant inventories. Premium transportation is used to ship back orders directly from plant to customers.
   b. The product items stocked in a warehouse are grouped so that different stock availability levels are set for each of the groups.
   c. All products are grouped according to an *ABC* classification scheme, where *A* items have high sales volume, *B* items have moderate sales volume, and *C* items have low sales volume. *A* items are stocked in field warehouses, *B* items are stocked in regional warehouses, and *C* items are stocked only at plant locations.
8. The Savemore Grocery Company is a chain of 150 supermarkets. The stores in the chain are supplied from a central distribution center. The company uses only privately owned trucks to make these deliveries. How is this possibly a violation of the principle of mixed strategy?
9. Explain how the following situations illustrate the principle of postponement.
   a. Toothpaste is shipped in bulk quantities to warehouses close to markets where sales in the area determine the package size of the final product.
   b. A paint manufacturer ships "brights," or unlabeled product, into its warehouses. Labeling equipment in the warehouse commits the product to the final brand.
10. Describe how automakers routinely practice standardization in their distribution channels.
11. What economic facts form the basis for the principle of consolidation? As shipment sizes become smaller, why is this principle more effectively applied? Describe a situation where consolidation has substantial economic benefits.
12. A battery manufacturer ships unmarked product from its factory to a warehouse along with labels and cartons. As customer orders are received for private-label or company-label batteries, the warehouse places the appropriate labels on the

products and ships them in the proper cartons. What concept is the battery manufacturer applying, and what advantages is he likely to realize?

13. The traffic manager of the Monarch Electric Company has just received a rate-reduction offer from a trucking company for the shipment of fractional horse-power motors to the company's field warehouse. The proposal is a rate of $3 per hundredweight (cwt.) if a minimum of 40,000 pounds is moved in each shipment. Currently, shipments of 20,000 pounds or more are moved at a rate of $5 per cwt. If the shipment size falls below 20,000 pounds, a rate of $9 per cwt. applies.

To help the traffic manager make a decision, the following additional information has been gathered:

Annual demand on warehouse	5,000 motors per year
Warehouse replenishment orders	43 orders per year
Weight of each motor, crated	175 lb per motor
Standard cost of motor in warehouse	$200 per motor
Stock replenishment order handling costs	$15 per order
Inventory carrying costs as a percentage of average value of inventory on hand for a year	25 percent per year
Handling cost at warehouse	$0.30 per cwt.
Warehouse space	unlimited

Should the company implement the new rate?

14. What are the differences between a supply-to-stock and a supply-to-order supply channel design? When is the use of each appropriate?

15. Describe why you think the sales of the following products are predictable or unpredictable.
    a. Coca-Cola
    b. A music compact disc release of a new artist
    c. Lightbulbs
    d. Custom-fitted bicycles

Discuss what the supply channel characteristics should be for each product in terms of production processes, transportation services, inventory levels, order processing, and vendor responsiveness.

16. What differences are there, if any, between logistics management and supply chain management?

17. You are planning to start a mail-order business that will sell moderately priced clothing for short men and petite women. Local clothing stores, your major competition, carry a limited selection of sizes for this market, and have little opportunity to obtain items not in their immediate stock. Some customers appreciate the chance to try on clothes and listen to the advice of the salespeople, but are often frustrated by the limited selection. You feel that you have a price advantage because of low overhead (only order takers and order fillers make up the staff, and the warehouse is in a low rent district).

What strategy can you formulate that will allow you to compete effectively with local retailers?

18. Storck is a German producer of candies, of which the best-known brand names are Werther's, Riesen, and Golden Best. All production takes place in Europe; in

fact, Storck is the largest consumer of sugar in Europe. Storck USA imports its candy products to the United States through an East Coast port and distributes them to retail and distribution outlets such as Wal-Mart, CVS Pharmacy, McLane, Target, Tri-Cor Distributors, and Winn-Dixie. Sales in the United States are about $100 million. Distribution currently takes place through a few public warehouses and some pool points. Consolidation among the retailers and a repositioning of their warehouses, shifts in demand levels, and the need to correct some customer degradation in order to protect market share have led to reevaluating the U.S. distribution system.

Considering common logistics strategies that might maximize return on logistics assets (ROLA), what distribution system design can you propose that will generally meet each of this goal?

Chapter 3

The Logistics/Supply Chain Product

> *. . . the first rule in dealing with other people's cultures and customs is that you must follow them no matter what your role in the foreign land may be.*

—LIEUTENANT GENERAL WILLIAM PAGONIS

*T*he logistics/SC product is a collection of characteristics that can be manipulated by the logistician. To the extent that product characteristics can be shaped and reshaped to better position them for the marketplace, a competitive advantage can be created. Customers respond with their patronage.

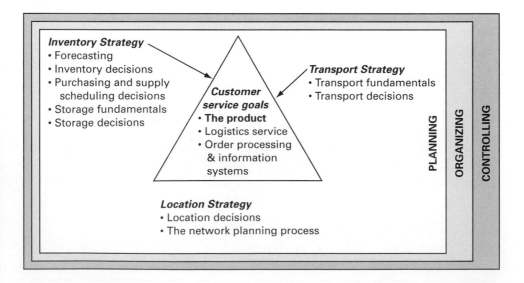

Inventory Strategy
• Forecasting
• Inventory decisions
• Purchasing and supply scheduling decisions
• Storage fundamentals
• Storage decisions

Customer service goals
• **The product**
• Logistics service
• Order processing & information systems

Transport Strategy
• Transport fundamentals
• Transport decisions

Location Strategy
• Location decisions
• The network planning process

PLANNING ORGANIZING CONTROLLING

The product is the center of focus in logistics system design because it is the object of flow in the supply chain, and, in its economic form, it generates the firm's revenues. A clear understanding of this basic element is essential to formulating good logistics system designs. It is the reason for exploring the product's basic dimensions, as represented by its characteristics, package, and price, as an element of customer service in the design of logistics systems.

NATURE OF THE LOGISTICS/SC PRODUCT

According to Juran, a product is the outcome, or result, of any activity or process.[1] The product is composed of a physical part and an intangible part which together make up what is called a company's total product offering. The physical portion of the product offering is composed of characteristics such as weight, volume, and shape as well as features, performance, and durability. The intangible part of the product offering may be after-sales support, company reputation, communication to provide correct and timely information (e.g., shipment tracking), flexibility to meet an individual customers needs, and recovery to rectify mistakes.[2] Any company's total product offering will be a mixture of both physical and service characteristics.

Classifying Products

Depending on who will use the product, the logistics system design should reflect the different use patterns. Broad product classifications are valuable for suggesting logistics strategy and, in many cases, for understanding why products are supplied and distributed in the manner that they are. One traditional classification is to divide goods and services into consumer products and industrial products.

Consumer Products

Consumer products are those that are directed to ultimate consumers. Marketing people have long recognized the basic differences in the way consumers go about selecting goods and services, and where they buy them. A threefold consumer products classification has been suggested: convenience products, shopping products, and specialty products.

Convenience products are those goods and services that consumers purchase frequently, immediately, and with little comparative shopping. Typical products are banking services, tobacco items, and many foodstuffs. These products generally

---

[1]Joseph M. Juran, *Juran on Leadership for Quality* (New York: The Free Press, 1989).
[2]Tommy Carlsson and Anders Ljundberg, "Measuring Service and Quality in the Order Process," *Proceedings of the Council of Logistics Management* (San Diego; Council of Logistics Management, 1995), pp. 315–331.

require wide distribution through many outlets. Distribution costs are typically high but are more than justified by the increased sales potential that is brought about by this wide and extensive distribution. Customer service levels, as expressed in terms of product availability and accessibility, must be high to encourage any reasonable degree of customer patronage for the products.

Example

PepsiCo and Coca-Cola recognize that their soft drink products are convenience goods. Therefore, one channel of distribution is through vending machines located just about anywhere people may congregate.

As a result, public telephones are located widely and conveniently throughout the land as are cellular telephone towers, which are now replacing many of the public telephone sites.

Shopping products are those for which consumers are willing to seek and compare: shopping many locations; comparing price, quality, and performance; and making a purchase only after careful deliberation. Typical products in this category are high-fashion clothes, automobiles, home furnishings, and medical care. Because of the customer's willingness to shop around, the number of stocking points is substantially reduced as compared with convenience goods and services. An individual supplier may stock goods or offer services in only a few outlets in a given market area. Distribution costs for such suppliers are somewhat lower than for convenience products, and product distribution need not be as widespread.

Example

High-level, specialized medical care is concentrated in relatively few university hospitals, clinics, and privately owned hospitals, due to the high costs of facilities, equipment, and highly trained personnel. Because patients often want the very best care possible, they are willing to seek out and travel to such places, often bypassing intervening health care providers that may be located closer to them.

Specialty products are those for which buyers are willing to expend a substantial effort and often to wait a significant amount of time in order to acquire them; examples range from fine foods to custom-made automobiles, or services such as management consulting advice. Because buyers insist on particular brands, distribution is centralized and customer service levels are not as high as those for convenience and shopping products. Physical distribution costs can be the lowest of any product category. Because of this, many firms will attempt to create brand preference for their product line.

Example

Many professional musicians will go to almost any length to find the right equipment to perform their very best. For example, a clarinetist requires a reed, which is a small piece of cane that is the tone generator for the clarinet. This capricious piece of dried grass can make or break a professional musician, or so he or she thinks. One brand of reed is particularly sought. It is grown in the south of France and distributed through only one retail outlet in the United States. According to the store owner, one professional clarinetist regularly drives over 600 miles to his store to acquire a supply of this specialty good.

Industrial Products

Industrial goods and services are those that are directed to individuals or organizations that use them to produce other goods or services. Their classification is quite different from consumer products. Because vendors typically seek the buyers, a classification based on shopping patterns would not be relevant.

Traditionally, industrial goods and services have been classified according to the extent to which they enter the production process. For example, there are goods that are part of the finished product, such as raw materials and component parts; there are goods that are used in the manufacturing process, such as buildings and equipment; and there are goods that do not enter the process directly, such as supplies and business services. Although this classification is valuable in preparing a selling strategy, it is not clear that it is useful in planning a physical distribution strategy. Industrial buyers do not seem to show preferences for different service levels for different product classes. This simply means that traditional product classifications for industrial products may not be as useful for identifying typical logistics channels as is the classification of consumer products.

The Product Life Cycle

Another traditional concept familiar to marketers is that of the product life cycle. Products do not generate their maximum sales volume immediately after being introduced, nor do they maintain their peak sales volume indefinitely. Characteristically, products follow a sales volume pattern over time, going through four stages: introduction, growth, maturity, and decline (see Figure 3-1). The physical distribution strategy differs for each stage.

The introductory stage occurs just after a new product is introduced into the marketplace. Sales are not at a high level because there is not yet wide acceptance of the product. The typical physical distribution strategy is a cautious one, with stocking restricted to relatively few locations. Product availability is limited.

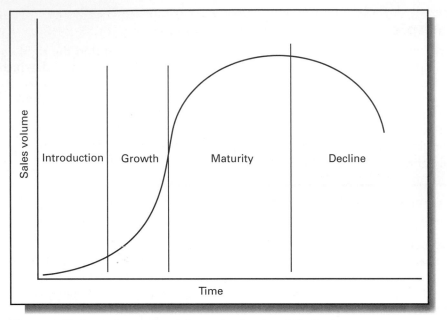

Figure 3-1 A Generalized Curve for Product Life Cycle

Example

When a young college graduate developed the popular board game Pictionary, a version of charades, no established manufacturing or distribution system existed. He borrowed $35,000 (from his parents) and had a limited supply of the game produced. To distribute Pictionary in this start-up phase, he hired teenagers to play the game in shopping malls and then sold them right there, to the interested passersby.

If the product receives market acceptance, sales are likely to increase rapidly. Physical distribution planning is particularly difficult in this stage. Often there is not much of a sales history to guide inventory levels at stocking points or even the number of stocking points to use. Distribution is frequently under managerial judgment and control during this expansion stage. However, product availability is also increasing rapidly over a wide geographic area in support of the growing customer interest in the product.

Example

An executive at the company distributing the Trivial Pursuit game purchased a copy of Pictionary and had his daughter and her friends play the game. Fascinated with their acceptance of the game, he arranged for the rights to its manufacture and sale. This was a wise move, as Trivial Pursuit was in the declining stage of its life cycle.

Pictionary was distributed through the channels already established for Trivial Pursuit. Pictionary, in its growth stage, increased sales rapidly, becoming the best-selling board game of its time.

The growth stage may be fairly short, followed by a longer stage called maturity. Sales growth is slow or stabilized at a peak level. The product volume is no longer undergoing rapid change and, therefore, can be assimilated into the distribution patterns of similar, existing products. At this time, the product has its widest distribution. Many stocking points are used with good control over product availability throughout the marketplace.

Example

The original Coca-Cola beverage, formulated by a pharmacist before the turn of the twentieth century, has been in the mature phase of its life cycle longer than about any other product. Distribution is worldwide, extending even to countries not usually considered to be open to free trade.

Eventually, the sales volume declines for most products as a result of technological change, competition, or waning consumer interest. To maintain efficient distribution, patterns of product movement and inventory deployment may have to be adjusted. The number of stocking points is likely to be decreased and the product stocking reduced to fewer, more centralized locations.

Examples

The Barnum and Bailey Circus once played in many cities across the nation. With changing interest patterns and competing entertainment options, demand for the circus has fallen from its previous levels. In the declining stage of its life cycle, the circus is now booked into only a few major population centers each year so that large enough crowds can be drawn to cover costs.

The turntable, once a major piece of hardware in audio systems to play recorded music, is now taking a backseat to the compact disk player. The market has declined to sales limited to collectors and audiophiles.

The product life cycle phenomenon has an influence on distribution strategy. The logistician needs to be continually aware of a product's life cycle stage so that distribution patterns may be adjusted for maximum efficiency in that stage. The life cycle phenomenon in products allows the logistician to anticipate distribution needs and plan for them well in advance. Because a firm's different products are typically in different stages of their life cycles, the product life cycle serves as a basis for the 80-20 curve.

THE 80-20 CURVE

The logistics problem of any firm is the total of the individual product problems. The product line of the typical firm is made up of individual products at different stages of their respective life cycles and with different degrees of sales success. At any point in time, this creates a product phenomenon known as the 80-20 curve, a particularly valuable concept for logistics planning.

The 80-20 concept is derived after observation of product patterns in many firms, from the fact that the bulk of the sales is generated from relatively few products in the product line and from the principle known as Pareto's law.[3] That is, 80 percent of a firm's sales are generated by 20 percent of the product line items. An exact 80-20 ratio is rarely observed, but the disproportionality between sales and the number of items is generally true.

To illustrate, consider 14 products of a small chemical company. These products are ranked according to their sales volume, as shown in Table 3-1. A cumula-

Table 3-1 ABC Classification of 14 Products of a Chemical Company

PRODUCT NUMBER	PRODUCT RANK BY SALES[a]	MONTHLY SALES (000s)	CUMULATIVE PERCENT OF TOTAL SALES[b]	CUMULATIVE PERCENT OF TOTAL ITEMS[c]	AN ABC CLASSIFICATION
D-204	1	$ 5,056	36.2%	7.1%	
D-212	2	3,424	60.7	14.3	A
D-185-0	3	1,052	68.3	21.4	
D-191	4	893	74.6	28.6	
D-192	5	843	80.7	35.7	B
D-193	6	727	85.7	42.9	
D-179-0	7	451	89.1	50.0	
D-195	8	412	91.9	57.1	
D-196	9	214	93.6	64.3	
D-186-0	10	205	95.1	71.4	
D-198-0	11	188	96.4	78.6	C
D-199	12	172	97.6	85.7	
D-200	13	170	98.7	92.9	
D-205	14	159	100.0	100.0	
		$13,966			

[a] Ranked according to sales volume
[b] Sum of item sales ÷ total sales, e.g., (5,056 + 3,424) ÷ 13,966 = 0.607
[c] Item rank ÷ total number of items, e.g., 6 ÷ 14 = 0.429

---

[3] The 80-20 curve was first observed by Vilfredo Pareto in 1897 during a study of the distribution of income and wealth in Italy. He concluded that a large percentage of the total income was concentrated in the hands of a small percentage of the population in a proportion of roughly 80 percent to 20 percent, respectively. The general idea has found wide application in business.

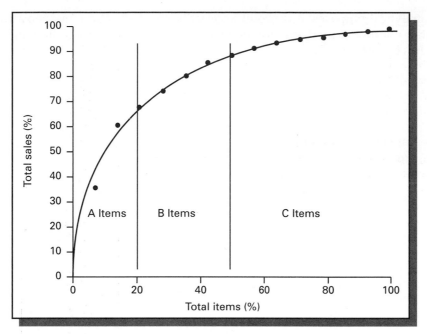

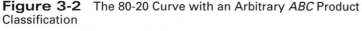

Figure 3-2 The 80-20 Curve with an Arbitrary *ABC* Product Classification

Source: Chemical company data from Table 3-1.

tive percentage of total dollar sales and of total number of items is computed. These percentages are then plotted, as in Figure 3-2, which exhibits the characteristic 80-20 curve. However, in this particular case, about 35 percent of the items account for 80 percent of the sales.

The 80-20 concept is particularly useful in distribution planning when the products are grouped or classified by their sales activity. The top 20 percent might be called *A* items, the next 30 percent *B* items, and the remainder *C* items. Each category of items could be distributed differently. For example, *A* items might receive wide geographic distribution through many warehouses with high levels of stock availability, whereas *C* items might be distributed from a single, central stocking point (e.g., a plant) with lower total stocking levels than for the *A* items. *B* items would have an intermediate distribution strategy where few regional warehouses are used.

Another frequent use of the 80-20 concept and an *ABC* classification is to group the products in a warehouse, or other stocking point, in a limited number of categories where they are then managed with different levels of stock availability. The product classifications are arbitrary. The point is that not all product items should receive equal logistics treatment. The 80-20 concept with a resulting product classification provides a scheme, based on sales activity, to determine the products that will receive various levels of logistics treatment.

For analytical purposes, it is useful to describe the 80-20 curve mathematically. Although a number of mathematical equations might be used, the following relationship has been suggested.[4]

$$Y = \frac{(1+A)X}{A+X} \qquad \text{(3-1)}$$

where

Y = cumulative fraction of sales
X = cumulative fraction of items
A = a constant to be determined

The constant A may be found by manipulating Equation (3-1) to give

$$A = \frac{X(1-Y)}{Y-X} \qquad \text{(3-2)}$$

where the relationship between Y and X is known. For example, if 25 percent of the items represent 70 percent of the sales, then, from Equation (3-2)

$$A = \frac{0.25(1-0.70)}{0.70-0.25}$$
$$= 0.1667$$

Equation (3-1) can be used to determine the relationship between various percentages of items and sales.

Example

Consider how the 80-20 rule is useful in estimating inventory levels. Suppose that a certain warehouse is to store 11 of the 14 items shown in Table 3-1. The same general relationship is expected to hold, that is, $X = 0.21$ and $Y = 0.68$, or 21 percent of the items result in 68 percent of the sales. Solving Equation (3-2) yields $A = 0.143$. A different inventory policy is maintained for different product groups. The turnover ratio (that is, annual sales/average inventory) for A items is 7 to 1, for B items 5 to 1, and for C items 3 to 1. If the annual sales through the warehouse are forecast to be $25,000, how much inventory investment in the warehouse can be expected?

---

[4]Paul S. Bender, "Mathematical Modeling of the 20/80 Rule: Theory and Practice," *Journal of Business Logistics*, Vol. 2, No. 2 (1981), pp. 139–157.

If the relationship is to be established on actual sales item data, the constant A can be found by using the least squares curve fitting procedure. This means solving the following expression:

$$\sum_{i}^{N} \frac{Y_iX_i - Y_iX_i^2}{(A+X_i)^2} - \sum_{i}^{N} \frac{(1+A)(X_i^2 - X_i^3)}{(A+X_i)^3} = 0$$

where Y_i and X_i are individual data pairs in a total sample size of N. The value for A is then determined through successive approximations. Constructing a small computer program to do these computations works nicely. When this technique was applied to the data in Table 3-1, an A value was found to be 0.143.

The items stocked at the warehouse are shown in Table 3-2. They are the same as those in Table 3-1 except for items 5, 8, and 9, which were selected to not be included. The remaining items are ranked according to their relative sales level, highest to lowest. The cumulative item proportion is determined from $1/N$ for the first item, $2(1/N)$ for the second, $3(1/N)$ for the third, and so on. The constant (A) is found from Equation (3-2), or $A = [0.21(1 - 0.68)]\,[0.68 - 0.21] = 0.143$. The cumulative sales proportion is found by applying Equation (3-1), using $A = 0.143$. The sales for the first item would be

$$Y = \frac{(1 + 0.143)(0.0909)}{(0.143 + 0.0909)}$$
$$= 0.4442,$$

which is the fraction of total warehouse sales represented by the first item, that is, $(0.4442 \times \$25,000) = \$11,105$. The procedure is repeated for each item in the list. The projected item sales is the difference between cumulative sales for successive items.

Average inventory value is then found by dividing the projected item sales by the turnover ratio for the item. The sum of the item inventory values is $4,401, which is the investment expected in the warehouse inventory.

Table 3-2 Warehouse Inventory Investment Estimation Using the 80-20 Curve

PRODUCT		ITEM NO.	CUMULATIVE ITEM PROPORTION (X)	CUMULATIVE SALES (Y)	PROJECTED ITEM SALES	TURNOVER RATIO	AVERAGE INVENTORY
D-204	A	1	0.0909[a]	$11,105	$11,105	7	
D-212		2	0.1818	15,994	4,889	7	
					$15,994		$2,285[c]
D-185-0		3	0.2727	18,745	2,751[b]	5	
D-192	B	4	0.3636	20,509[d]	1,764	5	
D-193		5	0.4545	21,736	1,227	5	
D-179-0		6	0.5454	22,639	903	5	
					$ 6,645		$1,329
D-195		7	0.6363	23,332	693	3	
D-198-0		8	0.7272	23,879	547	3	
D-199	C	9	0.8181	24,323	444	3	
D-200		10	0.9090	24,691	368	3	
D-205		11	1.0000	25,000	309	3	
					$ 2,361		$ 787
					$25,000		$4,401

[a] $1/N = 1/11 = 0.0909$
[b] $18,745 - 15,994 = 2,751$
[c] $\$15,994/7 = \$2,285$
[d] $[(1 + 0.143)(0.3636)/(0.143 + 0.3636)] \times [25,000] = \$20,509$

PRODUCT CHARACTERISTICS

The most important characteristics of the product that influence logistics strategy are the attributes of the product itself—weight, volume, value, perishability, flammability, and substitutability. When observed in various combinations, these characteristics are an indication of the need for warehousing, inventories, transportation, materials handling, and order processing. These attributes can best be discussed in four categories: weight-bulk ratio, value-weight ratio, substitutability, and risk characteristics.

Weight-Bulk Ratio

The ratio of product weight to bulk (volume) is a particularly meaningful measure, as transportation and storage costs are directly related to them. Products that are dense, that is, have a high weight-bulk ratio (e.g., rolled steel, printed materials, and canned foods), show good utilization of transportation equipment and storage facilities, with the costs of both tending to be low. However, for products with low density (e.g., inflated beach balls, boats, potato chips, and lamp shades), the bulk capacity of transportation equipment is fully utilized before the weight-carrying limit is reached. Also, the handling and space costs, which are weight-based, tend to be high relative to the product's sales price.

The effect of varying weight-bulk ratios on logistics costs is shown in Figure 3-3. As the product density increases, both storage and transportation costs decline as a percentage of the sales price. Although price may also be reduced by lower storage and transportation costs, they are just two cost factors among many that make up price. Therefore, total logistics costs can decline faster than price.

Figure 3-3 Generalized Effect of Product Density on Logistics Costs

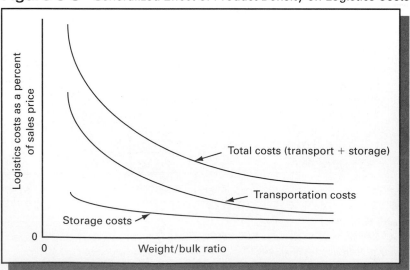

Figure 3-4
Generalized Effect of
Product Dollar
Density of Logistics
Costs

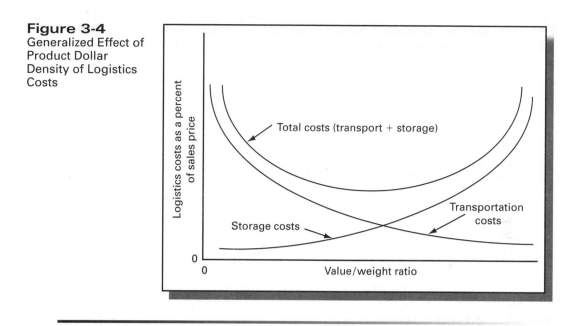

Examples

J. C. Penney ships catalog furniture items in a knocked-down condition to reduce the packaged product bulk and lower transportation costs, but this practice forces assembly on the customer.

A steel storage rack manufacturer ships knocked-down racks to a forward assembly point in the distribution channel, where cross members are welded onto the frame and the product bulk is increased as close to the marketplace as possible. Again, transportation costs are reduced through controlling the weight-bulk ratio in this manner.

Value-Weight Ratio

The dollar value of the product being moved and stored is important to storage costs since those costs are particularly sensitive to it. When product value is expressed as a ratio to weight, some obvious cost trade-offs emerge that are useful in planning the logistics system. Figure 3-4 shows the trade-off.

Products that have low value-weight ratios (e.g., coal, iron ore, bauxite, and sand) also have low storage costs but high movement costs as a percentage of their sales price. Inventory carrying costs are computed as a fraction of the product's value. Low product value means low storage cost, since inventory-carrying cost is the dominant factor in storage cost. Transport cost, on the other hand, are pegged to weight. When the value of the product is low, transport costs represent a high proportion of the sales price.

High value-weight ratio products (e.g., electronic equipment, jewelry, and musical instruments) show the opposite pattern, with higher storage and lower transport costs. This results in a U-shaped total logistics cost curve. Hence, firms dealing with low value-weight ratio products frequently try to negotiate more favorable transportation rates (rates are generally lower for raw materials than for finished products of the same weight). If the product has a high value-weight ratio, minimizing the amount of inventory maintained is a typical reaction. Of course, some firms attempt to adjust an unfavorable value-weight ratio by changing accounting procedures to alter value or by changing packaging requirements to alter weight.

Substitutability

When customers find little or no difference between a firm's product and those of competing suppliers, the products are said to be highly substitutable. That is, the customer is readily willing to take a second-choice brand when the first is not immediately available. Many food and drug products have a highly substitutable characteristic. As might be expected, suppliers spend great sums of money attempting to convince customers that such generic products as aspirin tablets and laundry soaps are not all alike. Distribution managers try to provide product availability at a level so that customers will not have to consider a substitute product.

In large part, the logistician has no control over a product's substitutability, yet he or she must plan for the distribution of products with varying degrees of substitutability. Substitutability can be viewed in terms of lost sales to the supplier. Higher substitutability usually means a greater chance for a customer to select a competing product, thus resulting in a lost sale for the supplier. The logistician generally deals with lost sales through transportation choices, storage choices, or both. To illustrate, consider Figure 3-5.

Figure 3-5(a) shows that improved transportation can be used to reduce lost sales. For a given average inventory level, a supplier can increase the speed and dependability of product deliveries and lower the incidence of loss and damage. The product becomes more readily available to the customer, and fewer product substitutions by the customer are likely to occur. Of course, the higher cost of premium transportation is in trade-off with the cost of lost sales. Figure 3-5(b) shows the same type of cost trade-off, except that the stock availability to the customer is controlled through the inventory level, with the transportation choice remaining constant.

In either case, the logistician is in a prime position to control the impact of product substitutability on the firm's profits.

Risk Characteristics

Product risk characteristics refer to features such as perishability, flammability, value, tendency to explode, and ease of being stolen. When a product shows high risk in one or more of these features, it simply forces certain restrictions on the distribution system. Both transport and storage costs are higher in absolute dollars and as a percentage of the sales price, as shown in Figure 3-6.

Figure 3-5
Generalized Effect of Transportation Service and Average Inventory Level on Logistics Costs for a Product with a Given Degree of Substitutability

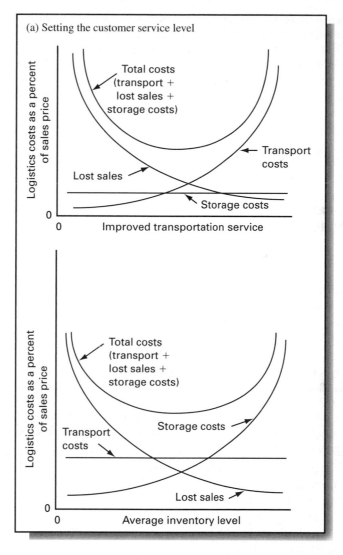

Consider products, such as pens, watches, or cigarettes, that have a high risk of being stolen. Special care must be taken in their handling and transport. Inside warehouses, special fenced-in and locked areas are set up to handle these and similar products. Highly perishable products (e.g., fresh fruits and whole blood) require refrigerated storage and transportation, and products that may have a tendency to contaminate fresh food products, such as automobile tires, cannot be stored near them in a warehouse. Whether in transportation, storage, or packaging, special treatment adds to the cost of distribution.

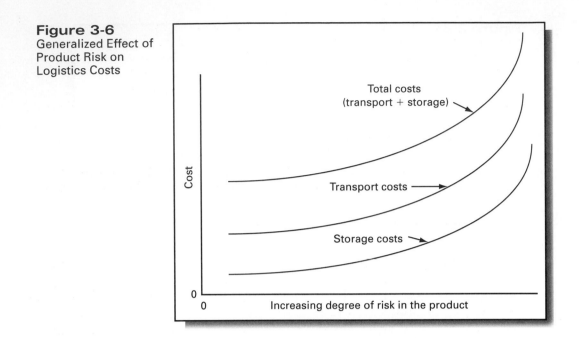

Figure 3-6
Generalized Effect of
Product Risk on
Logistics Costs

Cost

Total costs
(transport + storage)

Transport costs

Storage costs

0

0   Increasing degree of risk in the product

PRODUCT PACKAGING

With the exception of a limited number of items, such as raw materials in bulk, auto-mobiles, and furniture items, most products are distributed in some kind of packag-ing. There are a number of reasons why a packaging expense is incurred. The reason may be to:

- Facilitate storage and handling
- Promote better utilization of transport equipment
- Provide product protection
- Promote the sale of the product
- Change the product density
- Facilitate the use of the product
- Provide reuse value for the customer[5]

Not all of these objectives can be met through logistics management. However, changing product density and protective packaging are of concern in this area. The need for changing product density to achieve more favorable logistics costs has already been discussed (recall Figure 3-3).

Protective packaging is a particularly important dimension of the product for logistics planning. In many respects, it is the package that must be the focus of plan-ning, with the product itself of secondary concern. It is the package that has shape, vol-

---

[5]Adapted from Theodore N. Beckman, and William R. Davidson, *Marketing*, 8th ed. (New York: Ronald Press, 1967), p. 444.

ume, and weight. The product may not have the same characteristics. The point is that if a television set were removed from its shipping carton and replaced with shock-testing equipment, as is frequently done to test for damage during rough handling, the logistician would not treat the shipment differently, assuming that the change was not known. The package gives a revised set of characteristics to the product.

The protective package is an added expense that is counterbalanced with lower transportation and storage rates as well as fewer and less extensive damage claims. The logistician brings these costs into balance while working closely with sales and engineering to achieve the overall objectives for packaging.

Logistical considerations in package design can be important for marketing to achieve its objectives. Controlling product density can be critical to the success of a product.

Example

Johnson & Johnson identified a significant market among women for a product to handle incontinence. Using the technology developed for diapers, Johnson & Johnson created Serenity, a boat-shaped, cuplike product, packaged 12 or 24 to the box. When marketing personnel reviewed the product, the concern was that its bulky nature would limit sales. The product would have to compete for restricted shelf space in retail stores, causing frequent stockouts, thus limiting its exposure to customers. The logistics staff came through with the answer: *Change the product density*. By folding the product in half and further collapsing it in a pouch package, the size of the resulting box was less than one-half of its former dimensions. Not only did this satisfy marketing's shelf-space concern, it also saved on storage, transportation, and packaging costs.

PRODUCT PRICING

Along with quality and service, price also represents the product to the customer. Although the logistician is usually not directly responsible for setting price policy, he or she does have influence on pricing decisions. This is because product price often has a relationship to geography and because incentive prices often are pegged to transportation rate structures.

Pricing is a complex decision-making problem involving economic theory, buyer behavior theory, and theory of competition, among others. The discussion here is limited to methods of pricing that are geographically related and to incentive pricing arrangements that are derived from logistics costs.

Geographic Pricing Methods

Customers are not concentrated at a single point for most suppliers, but are usually dispersed over wide areas. This means that the total cost to distribute to them varies with their location. Pricing should be simple then? Not so! Companies can have customers numbering in the hundreds of thousands. Administering separate prices becomes overly burdensome as well as costly. Choice of a pricing method depends in part on balancing the detail in the pricing structure with the costs of managing it. There are a limited number of categories that define most geographic pricing methods. These pricing categories are f.o.b., zone, single or uniform, freight equalization, and basing point.

F.O.B. Pricing

To understand geographic pricing, it is best to begin by considering the f.o.b. pricing options. In a dictionary sense, f.o.b. stands for "free on board." In a practical sense, this policy simply denotes the location at which the price is effective. F.o.b. factory means that the price is quoted at the factory location. F.o.b. destination means that the price is quoted at the customer's location or in the vicinity. It is also implied that the customer takes title to the goods at the point designated. There are a great many alternatives under f.o.b. pricing. F.o.b. factory and f.o.b. destination are the most popular.

The *f.o.b. factory price* is a single price established at the factory location (shipment origin). Customers take ownership of the goods at this point and are responsible for transportation beyond this point. As a practical matter, the customers may have the suppliers make the shipping arrangements simply because the supplier may be better equipped and more skilled at it, or may be able to obtain lower shipping costs by combining the orders of several customers. Customers are then billed for the actual transportation costs.

Example

Automobiles are price-quoted at the factory or port of entry with a destination (transportation) charge in an amount depending on where the customer (automobile dealer) is located.

The *f.o.b. destination*, or *delivered price* is the price to the customer's location or in the general vicinity. Under this policy, transportation costs are already included in the price. It is expected that the supplier will make all of the transport arrangements. This policy recognizes that the supplier may be in a position to handle transportation more economically than the customer, or that the customer does not possess the desire or expertise to make such arrangements. There may be a net transportation cost advantage to the buyer if the buyer has insufficient shipping volume to secure transportation rates as low as those available to the supplier.

Example

Burger King prices its fast foods to the customer at the point of retail sale. All transportation charges for acquiring the products' raw materials are already included in the prices.

Many combinations of f.o.b. factory and destination pricing are possible, depending on how freight charges are paid. A variety of these arrangements is shown in Figure 3-7.

Zone Pricing

For those companies that must deal with thousands of customers, it is not necessarily the wisest policy to establish a different price for each customer. Suppliers of finished goods often cannot afford the administrative complexity of individual prices. Also, prices overall may have to be somewhat higher to support the cost of the complex administrative structure.

Zone pricing reduces administrative complexity by establishing a single price within a wide geographic area. Any number of areas may be defined, depending on the degree to which a company may want geographic price differences. For example, the Ball Corporation, a manufacturer of home canning equipment, created 89 geographic pricing zones throughout the country.

To illustrate zone pricing on a less grand scale, consider the pricing policy of Colonial Originals,[6] a manufacturer of colonial furniture in kit and finished form sold through a catalog and a Web site. The company is located in Boston. The furniture items are priced at Boston with a shipping charge added. This is a form of f.o.b. factory pricing, with the supplier arranging transportation. The variation is that the country is divided into eight zones according to postal zip code designations to achieve gradations in transportation costs. The prices effective for various zones throughout the country for a tavern table weighing 30 pounds and priced at $129.95 at the factory can be derived from Table 3-3. This table gives the shipping rates for each zone, by weight, for United Parcel Service's ground residential delivery service. The customer has a choice. Note that UPS has no zone 1. Using the table, the effective zone prices across the country may be developed for the tavern table (Figure 3-8).

Single, or Uniform, Pricing

The ultimate in pricing simplicity would be to have a single price for all customers, regardless of their location. This pricing method is used for many fair-trade items, first-class mail, and books. There is a certain appeal to customers in knowing that the same price for a product is charged everywhere. However, such a pricing policy masks the differences in costs of distributing to different customers. Such costs must be averaged.

Freight Equalization Pricing

The practical concerns of competition have an impact on pricing strategy. If two firms have equal efficiency in producing and selling, which results in the same product cost at the factory locations, then competitive pricing is a matter of transportation costs. If the markets are not equidistant from each factory location, the firm farthest from the marketplace may wish to absorb enough of the freight charges to meet the price competition. This practice is referred to as *freight equalization* and results in dif-

---

[6]A disguised name.

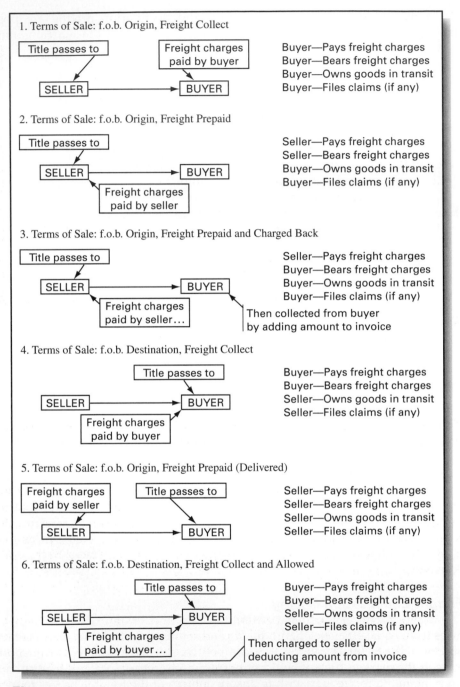

Figure 3-7 The Variety of F.O.B. Pricing Arrangements

Source: Edward J. Marien, "Making Sense of Freight Terms of Sale," *Transportation & Distribution* (September 1996), pp. 84–86.

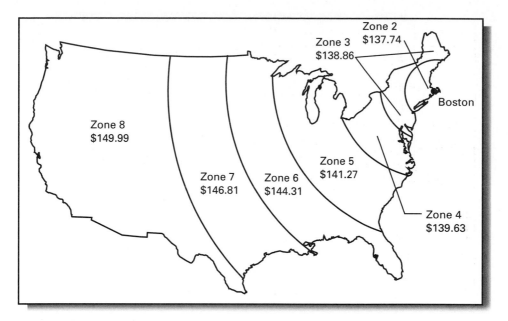

Figure 3-8 Zone Prices for a Tavern Table Shipped from Boston
Source: Table 3-3 and f.o.b. Boston table price.

ferent net returns for the firm engaging in it. Transportation as well as production costs across a number of producing locations are averaged.

Basing Point Pricing

As with freight equalization, the motives behind basing point pricing are competitive. Basing point pricing establishes some point other than the one from which the product is actually delivered as the point from which to compute price. Price is computed as if the product were delivered from the basing point. If the location chosen is the location of a major competitor, prices can be forced to be similar to the competitor's at every geographic customer location. This new location for price computation is referred to as a *basing point*. Firms may use single or multiple basing points.

The steel and cement industries were early leaders in the use of the basing point pricing method. This is understandable because basing point pricing is attractive when (1) the product has a high transportation cost relative to its overall value; (2) there is little preference among buyers as to the supplier of the product; and (3) there are relatively few suppliers and any price cutting leads to retaliation by rival firms. From the customer's perspective, the industries are located at the same points. Because this is in fact not true, the actual cost of supplying a given customer by each firm is different. Then how can a firm charge the same prices?

Table 3-3 Zone Shipping Rates from Boston (Zip Code 010) for United Parcel Service Residential Ground Service

Shipping Charges—To find shipping charges, first find in the Zone Chart the zone number that corresponds to the delivery destination zip code. Then, for the weight of the shipment, in the Shipping Charges chart find the charges that correspond to the zone number.

ZONE CHART

FIRST 3 DIGITS OF ZIP CODE	ZONE NO.	FIRST 3 DIGITS OF ZIP CODE	ZONE NO.	FIRST 3 DIGITS OF ZIP CODE	ZONE NO.
004–005	2	300–322	5	550–555	6
010–041	2	323–325	6	556–559	5
042–046	3	326	5	560–576	6
047	4	327–339	6	577	7
048–049	3	341–342	6	580–585	6
050–079	2	344	5	586–593	7
080–086	3	346–349	6	594–599	8
087–128	2	350–353	5	600–634	5
129–132	3	354	6	635	6
133–135	2	355–362	5	636–639	5
136	3	363–367	6	640–676	6
137–139	2	368	5	677–679	7
140–142	3	369	6	680–689	6
143	4	370–374	5	690–693	7
144–146	3	375	6	700–729	6
147	4	376–379	5	730–736	7

SHIPPING CHARGES

WEIGHT NOT TO EXCEED	ZONE 2	ZONE 3	ZONE 4	ZONE 5	ZONE 6	ZONE 7	ZONE 8
1 lb.	$4.16	$4.27	$4.50	$4.56	$4.75	$4.79	$4.90
2 lb.	4.23	4.43	4.77	4.88	5.17	5.27	5.53
3 lb.	4.32	4.59	4.98	5.14	5.44	5.59	6.01
4 lb.	4.44	4.74	5.19	5.41	5.71	5.85	6.33
5 lb.	4.58	4.88	5.38	5.62	5.92	6.12	6.65
6 lb.	4.73	5.01	5.53	5.83	6.13	6.39	6.92
7 lb.	4.88	5.13	5.64	5.99	6.34	6.60	7.18
8 lb.	5.02	5.26	5.75	6.10	6.50	6.86	7.61
9 lb.	5.15	5.39	5.85	6.21	6.66	7.18	8.03
10 lb.	5.29	5.50	5.96	6.37	6.88	7.61	8.51
11 lb.	5.43	5.63	6.07	6.52	7.14	8.09	9.04
12 lb.	5.57	5.77	6.17	6.68	7.41	8.57	9.63
13 lb.	5.70	5.92	6.27	6.79	7.72	9.04	10.22
14 lb.	5.81	6.07	6.37	6.90	8.10	9.52	10.79
15 lb.	5.92	6.23	6.46	7.06	8.47	10.00	11.38
16 lb.	6.01	6.40	6.62	7.27	8.85	10.47	11.97

						Weight							
148–149	3	380–381	6	737	6	17 lb.	6.10	6.58	6.78	7.53	9.25	10.96	12.56
150–165	4	382–385	5	738–739	7	18 lb.	6.19	6.77	6.99	7.85	9.64	11.43	13.13
166–179	3	386–397	6	740–749	6	19 lb.	6.30	6.96	7.21	8.17	10.03	11.92	13.72
180–181	2	399	5	750–754	7	20 lb.	6.42	7.15	7.42	8.49	10.42	12.34	14.31
182	3	400–410	5	755–757	6	21 lb.	6.55	7.34	7.64	8.81	10.81	12.76	14.89
183	2	411–412	4	758–797	7	22 lb.	6.68	7.53	7.86	9.13	11.22	13.18	15.47
184–187	3	413–427	5	798–799	8	23 lb.	6.82	7.72	8.09	9.39	11.61	13.67	16.06
188	2	430–449	4	800–812	7	24 lb.	6.96	7.91	8.31	9.66	12.00	14.14	16.64
189–199	3	450–454	5	813–815	8	25 lb.	7.10	8.07	8.54	9.93	12.39	14.63	17.23
200–205	4	455–458	4	816–820	7	26 lb.	7.24	8.24	8.75	10.19	12.78	15.05	17.76
206–208	3	459–479	5	821	8	27 lb.	7.37	8.39	8.99	10.46	13.17	15.47	18.29
209	4	480–489	4	822–828	7	28 lb.	7.51	8.56	9.23	10.74	13.58	15.90	18.88
210–214	3	490–491	5	829–874	8	29 lb.	7.65	8.72	9.46	11.03	13.97	16.38	19.46
215	4	492	4	875–877	7	30 lb.	7.79	8.91	9.68	11.32	14.36	16.86	20.04
216–219	3	493–499	5	878–880	8	40 lb.	9.07	10.71	11.97	14.23	18.09	21.64	25.72
220–241	4	500–505	6	881	7	50 lb.	10.05	12.36	13.99	17.00	21.10	26.05	30.73
242	5	506–507	5	882–883	8	60 lb.	10.91	13.42	15.47	18.98	23.44	28.18	33.38
243–279	4	508–516	6	884	7	75 lb.	27.43	29.26	31.13	31.90	33.93	36.68	39.76
280–282	5	520–539	5	885–898	8	100 lb.	40.88	42.39	42.76	44.01	46.58	47.90	50.50
283–285	4	540	6	900–961	8	125 lb.	50.02	51.69	52.33	53.05	56.40	58.26	60.86
286–299	5	541–549	5	970–994	8	150 lb.	59.05	60.99	61.89	62.09	66.24	68.62	71.23

Source: Zones and shipping charges from Internet Web site for United Parcel Service, http://www.ups.com.

Some Legal Concerns

Whenever a pricing method generates prices that are not in line with the cost of producing, selling, and distributing the product, certain legal considerations result. For the logistician, unless actual transportation costs are reflected in the product to each customer, there is a degree of price discrimination. Single, zone, freight equalization, and basing point pricing methods are inherently discriminatory. For example, if the same price is charged throughout a zone, those customers nearest the point from where the goods are being delivered absorb more than their share of the transportation costs, or they are paying for some "phantom" freight. Those customers in the farthest reaches of the zone are subsidized. The extent of the freight subsidizing depends on zone size.

Although some methods of geographic pricing can be discriminatory, some discrimination can benefit all customers even though the benefits may not be uniform. The reduced costs associated with administering fewer prices may be enough to offset the phantom freight charges to the least favorably located customer.

The Federal Trade Commission has challenged some delivered pricing policies and freight absorption policies. However, such policies are not necessarily illegal as long as the seller is willing to sell on an f.o.b. basis at the purchaser's request; the seller maintains uniformity of price at all delivered points, as in the case of a single national price policy; the price after freight absorption is higher than that of a competitor; and the buyers and/or their customers are noncompetitive.

INCENTIVE PRICING ARRANGEMENTS

Logistics costs are often a driving force behind price incentives. Two common types of price incentives are the quantity discount and the "deal."

Quantity Discounts

Economic theory teaches that the more goods that are handled during a single transaction, the lower the cost on a per-unit basis. The principle is known as *economies of scale*, where fixed costs spread over an increasing number of units reduce per-unit costs. This idea has led many firms to use purchase volume as a way of offering lower prices to buyers and increasing the supplier sales. The buyer benefits from a lower price if the larger purchase can be absorbed, and the supplier benefits through increased profits.

Legal restrictions have complicated the use of quantity discounts as a sales stimulant. Some firms are discouraged from using them altogether. The thrust of the Robinson-Patman Act, directed at competitive practices, is that it is unlawful to discriminate in price between different buyers if the effect is to lessen competition or to create a monopoly. Quantity discounts potentially create this discrimination but can be justified in terms of the cost savings obtained in the manufacturing, selling, and

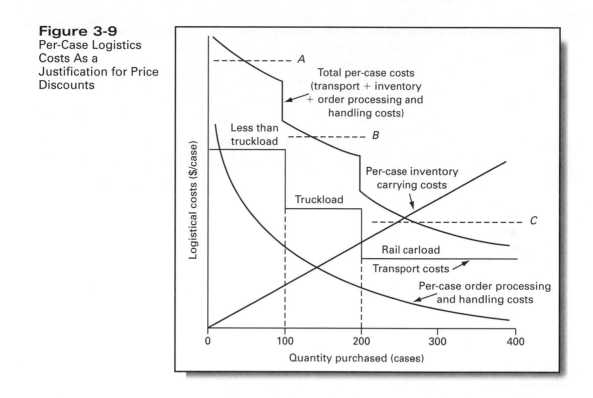

Figure 3-9
Per-Case Logistics Costs As a Justification for Price Discounts

delivery activities. In practice, it is difficult to argue convincingly that cost savings in manufacture and sale in fact take place on a by-sale basis. Logistics costs, on the other hand, which are largely composed of transportation costs, have well-known volume-cost breaks. If transportation is purchased outside a company, documentation of the cost savings is readily available in public records. Hence, logistics costs become a key factor in support of a discount schedule, as can be illustrated in the following example for a manufacturer of glass products.

Example

Glass jars used for home canning are sold primarily through distributors. These distributors may purchase in various case quantities. The component costs of total logistics costs for the manufacturer are shown as they vary with the quantity purchased in Figure 3-9. Transportation costs are the key to determining at what quantity the price break will occur and how large the price break will be.

If fewer than 100 cases are purchased at any one time, the order must be shipped at less-than-truckload rates. With the addition of inventory-carrying costs needed to support an order of that size and the per-unit costs of handling the order, the total per-unit costs would average out to be *A* in Figure 3-9. Purchasing in quantities ranging from 100 to 199 cases allows for truckload rates and a total average per-unit cost of B. Purchasing in quantities of 200 cases or more up to a practical limit of 400 cases has an average total cost of C. Therefore, if price were brought in line with costs, no price discounts would be offered for a purchase order of 0–99 cases. The maximum discount for the purchase of 100–199 cases would be $(A - B)/A$. If A is $2.20/case and B is $2.00/case, the transportation costs could be reduced by $(2.20 - 2.00)/2.20 = .09$, or 9 percent. For the range of 200 to 400 cases, with an average cost of C or $1.70/case, the discount on transportation costs could be as much as $(A - C)/A$, or $(2.20 - 1.70)/2.20 = .23$, or 23 percent. If the remaining manufacturing and sales costs, including markup, of $10 per case are now added to logistics costs, the price to the purchaser would be

Quantity Cases	Purchase Price, $/case	Price Discount; %
0–99	$12.20	0%
100–199	12.00	1.6[a]
Over 200	11.70	4.1

[a]$(12.20 - 12.00)/12.20 = 0.016$, or 1.6%

THE DEAL

Occasionally, some companies offer reduced product prices for a short time in exchange for larger than normal purchase quantities from its customers. A selling company may wish to reduce its inventories, maintain output levels, or encourage sales as the motivation for lowering price. From the buyer's perspective, whether to accept purchases under the price incentive and how much to buy if it does requires trading off the benefit of the price reduction with costs that it incurs, which are generally logistical in nature. The buyer must weigh the effect of a larger than normal buying quantity with its benefit of lower price against common logistics costs of transportation, inventory carrying, and storage. Determining the size of the special buying quantity is discussed in Chapter 10.

CONCLUDING COMMENTS

Understanding the nature of a product, whether it is a good or a service, in its economic environment provides useful insights for logisticians planning a strategy for supply and distribution. Therefore, this chapter has examined such important concepts as product classification, product life cycle, the 80-20 curve, and a set of product characteristics.

Product classification helps to group products according to how customers behave toward them. Customers of finished goods require different logistics services than do industrial customers. Even customers within the same customer class have marked differences in service needs. Often, a good distribution strategy can be obvious from a careful identification and classification of the product.

The product life cycle describes the sales activity level that most products achieve over time. The four life cycle stages—introduction, growth, maturity, and decline—are well documented. Each stage may require a different distribution strategy.

The 80-20 curve expresses the relationship that 80 percent of a firm's sales are derived from 20 percent of its product items. This curve is simply a result of the products being in different stages of their life cycles. This disproportionality between sales and the number of products becomes very useful when deciding where to locate products within the distribution system and which products should be inventoried at any given stocking point.

The product characteristics focus on certain physical and economic features of the product that influence logistics system design to a substantial extent. These characteristics are weight-bulk ratio, value-weight ratio, substitutability, and risk.

Two additional dimensions of the product have been discussed: (1) the package, which can alter a product's physical characteristics and, therefore, the requirements for a distribution system and (2) with customers dispersed geographically and costs varying on a geographic basis, certain pricing aspects of the product are of concern to the logistician. Although the logistician normally might not be concerned with pricing matters, the fact that incentive pricing is perhaps more easily justified on the grounds of logistics cost than any other forces him or her into the pricing arena.

QUESTIONS

1. Indicate whether you think the following types of firms handle convenience, shopping, or specialty goods.
   a. Jack Spratt's Woodwind Shop sells musical instruments and supplies nationwide, to professional woodwind musicians.
   b. Hart, Schaffner, and Marx produces and sells, nationally, top-of-the-line, ready-to-wear men's suits.
   c. Edward's Bakery produces and sells, regionally, a line of baked goods, mainly bread. Distribution is primarily through food retail chain stores.
   Describe what you think an efficient distribution system should be in each case, as might be dictated by the product characteristics in each situation.
2. Contrast the product life cycle of a brand of laundry detergent with that of the works of a contemporary artist. Suggest how the physical distribution of these might be handled at each stage of their life cycles.
3. A drug retailer has two ways that he can replenish his shelf merchandise: directly from vendors or through the company's warehouse. Items with high sales volume and high replenishment quantity usually have a cost advantage if they can be purchased directly from vendors because no extra warehouse storage and handling are required. The remaining items are more efficiently handled through warehousing. The retailer has heard of the 80-20 principle and thinks that it might be a useful way of separating the product line into high and low volume groups to achieve the greatest supply economies.

There are 12 items in a particular drug class. Annual sales data have been collected as noted here.

Product Code	Dollar Sales
10732	$ 56,000
11693	51,000
09721	10,000
14217	9,000
10614	46,000
08776	71,000
12121	63,000
11007	4,000
07071	22,000
06692	14,000
12077	27,000
10542	18,000
Total	$391,000

If the order size closely follows sales level, use the 80-20 principle to determine the items that should be purchased directly from vendors. Use 20 percent of the items as the break point.

4. Identify several products that have extreme characteristics as to weight-bulk ratio, value-weight ratio, substitutability, and risk. Some suggestions are assembled bicycles, sand for glassmaking, and prescription drugs sold at retail, but you should choose different examples. Explain how knowledge of the product's characteristics can be used to specify or alter the way in which the products are distributed.

5. Explain the role the product package plays in the design of a supply or distribution strategy.

6. Suppose that a customer were to purchase from Colonial Originals a furniture kit that has a catalog price of $99.95 and a shipping weight of 26.5 pounds.
   a. Using Table 3-3, determine the total cost of the kit if delivery is to be made by UPS residential ground service to one of the following zip code areas in the United States:
   (i) 11101, (ii) 42117, (iii) 74001, (iv) 59615
   b. What can you say about the fairness and efficiency of this pricing arrangement?

7. What is the motivation of a basic steel products manufacturer to use the freight equalization pricing method?

8. Why are uniform and zone pricing schemes fair for customers on the whole but discriminatory and unfair for a great many of them individually?

9. Why are logistics costs, and especially transportation costs, so important in developing incentive pricing arrangements?

10. Describe how transportation charges are paid under the following terms of sale:
    a. F.o.b. destination, freight prepaid
    b. F.o.b. origin, freight prepaid

c. F.o.b. destination, freight collect and allowed
d. F.o.b. origin, freight prepaid and charged back
e. F.o.b. origin, freight collect

If the pricing policy is such that a firm's customers pay for the freight, should the supplying firm consider such costs in making warehouse location, transportation service selection, and similar decisions?

11. Davis Steel Distributors is planning to set up an additional warehouse in its distribution network. Analysis of item-sales data for its other warehouses shows that 25 percent of the items represent 75 percent of the sales volume. The company also has an inventory policy that varies with the items in the warehouse. That is, the first 20 percent of the items are the A items and are to be stocked with an inventory turnover ratio of 8. The next 30 percent of the items, or B items, are to have a turnover ratio of 6. The remaining C items are to have a turnover ratio of 4. There are to be 20 products held at the warehouse with sales on the warehouse forecasted to be $2.6 million annually. What dollar value of average inventory would you estimate for the warehouse?

12. Beta Products is planning to add another warehouse. Ten products from the entire line are to be stored in the new warehouse. These products will be the A and B items. All C items are to be served out of the plant. Forecasts of annual sales that are expected in the region of the new facility are 3 million cases (A, B, and C items). Historical data show that 30 percent of the items account for 70 percent of the sales. The first 20 percent of the entire line are designated as A items, the next 30 percent as B items, and the remaining 50 percent as C items. Inventory turnover ratios in the new warehouse are projected to be 9 for A items and 5 for B items. Each inventory item, on the average, requires 1.5 cubic feet of space. Product is stacked 16 feet high in the warehouse.

What effective storage space is needed in square feet excluding aisle, office, and other space requirements?

13. An analysis of the product line items in the retail stores of the Save-More Drug chain shows that 20 percent of the items stocked account for 65 percent of the dollar sales. A typical store carries 5,000 items. The items accounting for the top 75 percent of the sales are replenished from warehouse stocks. The remainder is shipped directly to stores from manufacturers or jobbers. How many items are represented in the top 75 percent of sales?

14. The costs associated with producing, distributing, and selling a domestically produced automotive component to Honda in Japan can be summarized as follows:

Cost Type	Cost per Unit, $
Purchased materials	25
Manufacturing labor	10
Overhead	5
Transportation	Varies by shipment size
Sales	8
Profit	5

Transportation costs vary as follows. If the purchase (shipping) quantity is 1,000 units or less, the transportation cost is $5 per unit. For more than 1,000 units but less than or equal to 2,000 units, the transportation cost is $4.00 per unit. For more than 2,000, the transportation cost is $3.00 per unit.

Construct a price schedule, assuming the vendor would like to pass the transportation economies on to the customer. Indicate the discount percentage the customer will receive through buying at various quantities.

Chapter 4

Logistics/Supply Chain Customer Service

Anyone who thinks the customer isn't important should try doing without him for a period of ninety days.

—ANONYMOUS

*C*ustomers view the offerings of any company in terms of price, quality, and service, and respond accordingly with their patronage or lack of it. Service, or customer service, is a broad term that may include many elements ranging from product availability to after-sale maintenance. From a logistics perspective, customer service is the outcome of all logistics activities or supply chain processes. Therefore, the design

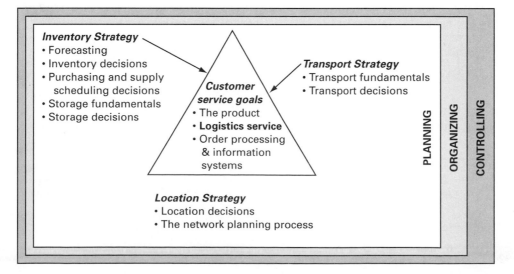

Inventory Strategy
- Forecasting
- Inventory decisions
- Purchasing and supply scheduling decisions
- Storage fundamentals
- Storage decisions

Customer service goals
- The product
- **Logistics service**
- Order processing & information systems

Transport Strategy
- Transport fundamentals
- Transport decisions

Location Strategy
- Location decisions
- The network planning process

PLANNING

ORGANIZING

CONTROLLING

of the logistics system sets the level of customer service to be offered. Revenues generated from customer sales and the costs associated with the system design establish the profits to be realized by the firm. Deciding the level of customer service to offer customers is essential to meeting a firm's profit objectives.

In this chapter, we will explore the meaning of customer service to the firm as a whole and to logistics specifically. The important elements of service will be identified. Methods will be suggested as to how the relationship between sales and the level of service can be determined, and how they might be used to find the optimal logistics customer service level. Finally, planning for service contingencies will be discussed.

CUSTOMER SERVICE DEFINED

Since logistics customer service is necessarily a part of a firm's overall service offering, we will begin with service from the firm's perspective and then distill out those elements that are specific to logistics. Kyj and Kyj observed that

> . . . customer service, when utilized effectively, is a prime variable that can have a significant impact on creating demand and retaining customer loyalty.[1]

To another customer service expert, customer service

> . . . refers specifically to the chain of sales-satisfying activities which usually begins with order entry and ends with delivery of product to customers, in some cases continuing on as equipment service or maintenance or other technical support.[2]

More simply, Heskett states that logistics customer service for many firms is

> . . . the speed and dependability with which items ordered (by customers) can be made available . . .[3]

More recently, customer service has been referred to in terms of a *fulfillment process*, which has been described as

> . . . the entire process of filling the customer's order. This process includes the receipt of the order (either manual or electronic), managing the payment, picking and packing the goods, shipping the package, delivering the

---

[1]Larissa S. Kyj and Myroslaw J. Kyj, "Customer Service: Differentiation in International Markets," *International Journal of Physical Distribution & Logistics Management,*" Vol. 24, No. 4 (1994), p. 41.
[2]Warren Blanding, *11 Hidden Costs of Customer Service Management* (Washington, DC: Marketing Publications, 1974), p. 3.
[3]James L. Heskett, "Controlling Customer Logistics Service," *International Journal of Physical Distribution & Logistics Management,* Vol. 24, No. 4 (1994), p. 4.

package, providing customer service for the end user and handling the possible return of the goods.[4]

These definitions and descriptions of customer service are broad and need further refinement if we are to use them effectively.

Customer Service Elements

From a corporate-wide perspective, customer service has been viewed as an essential ingredient in marketing strategy. Marketing has often been described in terms of an activity mix of four Ps—*product, price, promotion,* and *place,* where place best represents physical distribution. Which elements constitute customer service and just how they impact on buyer behavior has been the focus of much research throughout the years.[5] Because customers cannot easily identify what motivates their behavior, precisely defining customer service will remain elusive. However, some insight can be gained through several customer surveys.

A comprehensive study of customer service, sponsored by the National Council of Physical Distribution Management,[6] identified the elements of customer service according to when the transaction between the supplier and customer took place.[7] These elements, listed in Figure 4-1, are grouped into pretransaction, transaction, and posttransaction categories.

Pretransaction elements establish a climate for good customer service. Providing a written statement of customer service policy, such as when goods will be delivered after an order is placed, the procedure for handling returns and back orders, and methods of shipment, let customers know what kind of service to expect. Establishing contingency plans for times when labor strikes or natural disasters affect normal service, creating organizational structures to implement customer service policy, and providing technical training and manuals for customers also contribute to good buyer-supplier relations.

Transaction elements are those that directly result in the delivery of the product to the customer. Setting stock levels, selecting transportation modes, and establishing order-processing procedures are examples. These elements, in turn, affect delivery times, accuracy of order filling, condition of goods on receipt, and stock availability.

Posttransaction elements represent the array of services needed to support the product in the field; to protect consumers from defective products; to provide for the return of packages (returnable bottles, reusable cameras, pallets, etc.); and to handle claims, complaints, and returns. These take place after the sale of the product, but they must be planned for in the pretransaction and transaction stages.

---

[4]James E. Doctker, "Basics of Fulfillment," *Proceedings of the Council of Logistics Management* (New Orleans, LA: Council of Logistics Management, Sept. 24–27, 2000), p. 356.
[5]Francis G. Tucker, "Creative Customer Service Management," *International Journal of Physical Distribution & Logistics Management,* Vol. 24, No. 4 (1994), pp. 32–40.
[6]Renamed the Council of Logistics Management.
[7]Bernard J. LaLonde and Paul H. Zinszer, *Customer Service: Meaning and Measurement* (Chicago: National Council of Physical Distribution Management, 1976).

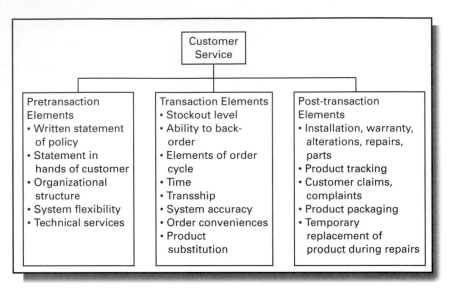

Figure 4-1 Elements of Customer Service

Source: Adapted from Bernard J. LaLonde and Paul H. Zinszer, "Customer Service As a Component of the Distribution System," Working Paper Series WPS 75-4 (Columbus, OH: The Ohio State University, College of Administrative Science, February 1975).

Corporate customer service is the sum of all these elements because customers react to the total mix. Of course, some elements are more important than others. Given this, which of the elements would seem most important to manage? Research has shown some interesting results.

Relative Importance of Service Elements

Sterling and Lambert studied the office systems and furniture industry and the plastic industry in some depth. From a large number of variables (99 and 112, respectively) representing product, price, promotion, and physical distribution, they were able to determine those that were most important to the buyers, customers, and influencers of purchases from these industries. Based on mean scores of importance, as indicated by respondents on a one to seven point scale, they rank ordered the service elements in each of these industries, as shown in Table 4-1. For the office systems and furniture industry, they concluded the following:

> The research showed that physical distribution (PD/customer service) is an integral and necessary component of the marketing mix, and that it offers a significant opportunity for firms to gain differential advantage in the marketplace. Evaluation of the 16 variables rated as most important by dealers, end users, and architectural and design firms disclosed that at least one-half were physical distribution/customer service variables.[8]

---

[8]Jay U. Sterling and Douglas M. Lambert, "Customer Service Research: Past, Present, and Future," *International Journal of Physical Distribution & Materials Management*, Vol. 19, No. 2 (1989), p. 17.

Table 4-1 Customer Service Variables Ranked by Order of Importance for Two Industries

OFFICE SYSTEMS AND FURNITURE INDUSTRY			PLASTICS INDUSTRY		
MEAN/STD. DEV.[a]	MARKETING MIX COMPONENT	DESCRIPTION	MEAN/STD. DEV.[a]	MARKETING MIX COMPONENT	DESCRIPTION
6.5/.8	Logistics	Ability of manufacturer to meet promised delivery date	6.6/.6	Product	Supplier's resins are of consistent quality
6.3/.8	Logistics	Accuracy in filling orders	6.5/.8	Promotion	Quality of sales force—honesty
6.2/.9	Product	Overall manufacturing and design quality relative to price	6.4/.8	Logistics	Accuracy in filling orders (correct product is shipped)
6.1/1.0	Price	Competitiveness of price	6.4/.9	Price	Competitiveness of price
6.1/1.0	Logistics	Advance notice on shipping delays	6.4/.9	Product	Processability of resin
6.1/.9	Promotion	Timely response to requests for assistance from manufacturer's representatives	6.3/1.0	Product	Supplier's resins are of consistent color
6.0/1.0	Logistics	Action on customer service complaints	6.3/.8	Logistics	Consistent lead times (vendor consistently meets expected delivery date)
5.9/1.1	Logistics	Order cycle consistency (small variability)	6.3/.9	Product	Supplier's resins are of consistent melt flow
5.9/1.0	Logistics	Accuracy of manufacturer in forecasting estimated ship dates	6.3/.9	Logistics	Ability to expedite emergency orders in a fast responsive manner
5.9/.9	Product	Overall aesthetics and finish	6.2/.9	Logistics	Information provided when order is placed—projected shipping date
5.9/1.0	Product	Continuity (nonobsolescence of products)	6.2/1.0	Logistics	Advance notice of shipping delays
5.9/1.0	Logistics	Manufacturer's willingness to accept returns of damaged products	6.1/1.0	Price	Adequate quality of resin relative to price
5.8/1.2	Logistics	Length of promised lead time for quick-ship orders	6.1/1.1	Product	Overall quality of resin relative to price
5.8/1.1	Logistics	Completeness of contract orders	6.1/1.1	Logistics	Information provided when order is placed—projected delivery date
5.8/1.1	Logistics	Completeness of quick-ship orders	6.1/1.0	Logistics	Actions on complaints (e.g., order servicing, shipping, product, etc.)
5.8/1.1	Price	Realistic, consistent pricing policy	6.1/1.0	Logistics	Length of promised lead times (from order submission to delivery—in-stock products)
			6.1/1.0	Promotion	Quality of sales force—prompt follow-up
			6.0/1.2	Logistics	Information provided when order is placed—inventory availability

[a]Scored on a scale of 1 to 7.

Source: Douglas M. Lambert and Thomas C. Harrington, "Establishing Customer Service Strategies Within the Marketing Mix: More Empirical Evidence," *Journal of Business Logistics,* Vol. 10, No. 2 (1989), p. 50.

For the plastics industry, nine of the 18 variables rated as most important were related to logistics. Of the remaining variables, five related to product quality, two to price, and two to the sales force.[9]

The Sterling-Lambert research certainly suggests that logistics customer service is dominant in the minds of customers in the office systems and furniture industry and the plastics industry. Although such a small sample of industries may not be overly convincing, others have observed the same phenomenon. In a similar study of the auto glass after market, Innis and LaLonde found that six out of the top ten customer service attributes were logistical in nature.[10] Notably, high *fill rates, frequency of delivery*, and information on *inventory availability*, projected *shipping date*, and projected *delivery date* at the time of order placement received high ratings among the retail customer base. Further, LaLonde and Zinszer found that *product availability* (order completeness, order accuracy, and stocking levels) and *order-cycle time* (order-transit time and time for assembly and shipping) were dominant in the minds of users, being most important to 63 percent of the respondents in their study.[11] Marr also surveyed a number of firms with the following conclusions:

1. Only one respondent mentioned cost of service.
2. Of the top seven elements, only one was outside the control of distribution management.
3. The most important service element was speed of delivery.[12]

Shycon Associates surveyed purchasing and distribution executives across a large cross section of American industry, asking them to rate their suppliers.[13] Figure 4-2 shows what the respondents felt were the most common service failures. Late delivery, a logistics customer service variable, accounted for nearly half of the mentioned service infractions, while product quality mistakes represented about a third.

Jackson, Keith, and Burdick were able to show how service elements take on different degrees of importance, depending on the product type being purchased.[14] They surveyed 254 purchasing agents in 25 companies about the importance of 6 physical distribution service elements. Their results are shown in Table 4-2. Again, note the relative importance of lead-time and delivery time consistency.

---

[9]Thomas C. Harrington and Douglas M. Lambert, "Establishing Customer Service Strategies Within the Marketing Mix: More Empirical Evidence," *Journal of Business Logistics*, Vol. 10, No. 2 (1989), pp. 44–60.
[10]Daniel E. Innis and Bernard J. LaLonde, "Customer Service: The Key to Customer Satisfaction, Customer Loyalty, and Market Share," *Journal of Business Logistics*, Vol. 15, No. 1 (1994), pp. 1–27.
[11]LaLonde and Zinszer, "Customer Service: Meaning and Measurement."
[12]Norman E. Marr, "Do Managers Really Know What Service Their Customers Require?," *International Journal of Physical Distribution & Logistics Management*," Vol. 24, No. 4 (1994), pp. 24–31.
[13]Steven G. Baritz and Lorin Zissman, "Researching Customer Service: The Right Way," *Proceedings of The National Council of Physical Distribution Management*, Vol. II (New Orleans, LA: October 25, 1983), pp. 608–619.
[14]Donald W. Jackson, Janet E. Keith, and Richard K. Burdick, "Examining the Relative Importance of Physical Distribution Service Elements," *Journal of Business Logistics*, Vol. 7, No. 2 (1986), pp. 14–32.

Figure 4-2
Common Customer
Service Complaints

Source: Steven G. Baritz
and Lorin Zissman,
"Researching Customer
Service: The Right Way,"
*Proceedings of the National
Council of Physical
Distribution Management,*
Vol. II (New Orleans, LA:
October 25, 1983), p. 611.

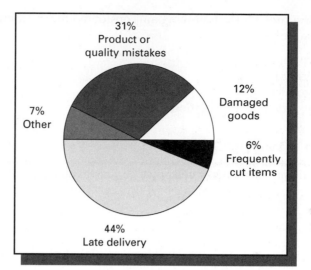

Table 4-2 Ranking of Six Physical Distribution Service Elements by Product Type
(1 = Most Important)

	PRODUCT TYPE				
	MAJOR CAPITAL[a]	MINOR CAPITAL[b]	MATERIALS[c]	COMPONENT PARTS[d]	SUPPLIES[e]
In-stock performance	2	1	3	3	1
Lead time	3	3	2	2	3
Consistency of delivery	1	2	1	1	2
Order progress information	4	5	5	5	5
Protective packaging	6	6	6	6	6
Cooperation in handling shipping problems	5	4	4	4	4

[a]Major capital items are goods that have a useful life of more than one year, do not become part of the firm's final product, and cost more than $10,000 per unit.
[b]Minor capital items are goods that have a useful life of more than one year, do not become part of the firm's final product, and cost between $1,000 and $10,000 per unit.
[c]Materials are goods that become part of the final product, but need further processing before they do.
[d]Component parts are goods that become part of the final product without further processing.
[e]Supplies are goods that do not become part of the final product, but are used to support their creation.

Source: Adapted from Donald W. Jackson, Janet E. Keith, and Richard K. Burdick, "Examining the Relative Importance of Physical Distribution Service Elements," *Journal of Business Logistics*, Vol. 7, No. 2 (1986), p. 23.

In summary, the following are considered the most important logistics customer service elements.

- On-time delivery
- Order fill rate
- Product condition
- Accurate documentation[15]

ORDER CYCLE TIME

The primary elements of customer service that the logistician can control are captured within the concept of order (or service) cycle time. *Order cycle time* can be defined as

> the elapsed time between when a customer order, purchase order, or service request is placed and when the product or service is received by the customer.

The order cycle contains all the time-related events that make up the total time required for a customer to receive an order. An illustration of the components that make up a typical order cycle is presented in Figure 4-3. Note that individual order cycle time elements are order transmittal time, order processing time, order assembly time, stock availability, production time, and delivery time. These elements are directly or indirectly controlled through choice and design of order transmittal methods, inventory-stocking policies, order processing procedures, transport modes, and scheduling methods.

The order transmittal time may be composed of several time elements, depending on the method used for communicating orders. A salesperson–electronic communication system would have an order transmittal time composed of the length of time the salesperson and the sales office retain the order before transmitting it, and the length of time the order is in the transmission channel. A customer-prepared order plus electronic transmission would have a total transmittal time essentially of a telephone call, facsimile, electronic data interchange, or Web site use. At times, it may be important to factor into order cycle time the customer's time for filling out an order or the time between salespersons' visits.

Another major component of order cycle time is the time for order processing and assembly. Order processing involves such activities as preparing shipping documents, updating inventory records, coordinating credit clearance, checking the order for errors, communicating with customers and interested parties within the company on the status of orders, and disseminating order information to sales, production, and accounting. Order assembly includes the time required to make the shipment ready for delivery after the order has been received and the order information has been made available to the warehouse or shipping department. It involves picking the order from stock, moving the order to the outbound point in the warehouse, any necessary packaging or light manufacturing, and consolidation with other orders moving

---

[15]James E. Keebler and Karl B. Manrodt, "The State of Logistics Performance Measurement," *Proceedings of the Council of Logistics Management* (New Orleans, LA: Council of Logistics Management, Sept. 24–27, 2002), pp. 275–281; and Robert Miller, Logistics Tip of the Week, Tips@logfac.com (January 8, 2002).

in the same direction. If no inventories are available, then processing may include manufacturing.

To a degree, order processing and assembly take place concurrently, so the total time expended for both activities is not the sum of the times required by each. Rather, both activities overlap, with order processing taking place slightly ahead of order assembly, due to error checking and initial handling of the paperwork. Shipping document preparation and inventory updating can be carried out while assembly operations occur.

Stock availability has a dramatic effect on total order cycle time because it often forces product and information flows to move out of the established channel. A normal channel may be to supply customers through a warehouse, as shown in Figure 4-3. When stock is not available in warehouse inventories, a second, or

Figure 4-3 Components of a Customer Order Cycle

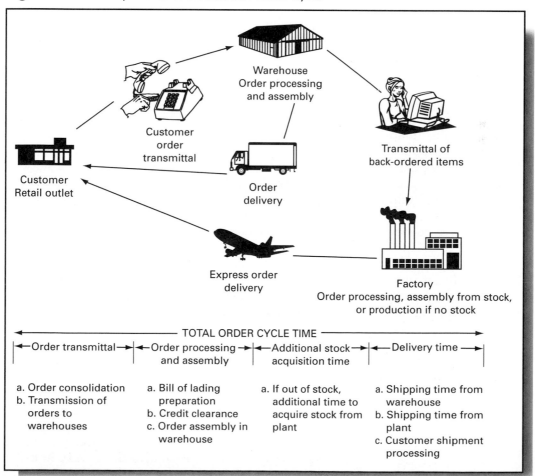

Figure 4-4
Frequency
Distribution for Total
Order Cycle Time
When Out-of-Stock
Situations Occur

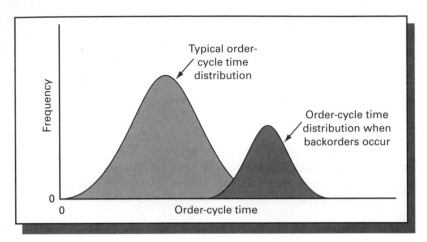

backup, distribution channel may be used. For example, a back order for the out-of-stock item would be transmitted to the plant to be filled from plant stocks. If there is no plant stock available, a production order is prepared and stock is produced. Delivery is then made directly from the plant to the customer. Other possible backup systems are transshipping back-ordered goods from a secondary warehouse or simply holding back orders at the primary stocking point. The backup scheme shown in Figure 4-3 is for a specialty chemical company selling highly substitutable products.

The final primary element in the order cycle over which the logistician has direct control is the delivery time—the time required to move the order from the stocking point to the customer location. It may also include the time for loading at the origin point and unloading at the destination point.

For any one customer, the time to receive an order is expressed in terms of a bimodal frequency distribution, as shown in Figure 4-4. The frequency distribution is a result of the individual distributions for each of the order cycle elements. The second hump in the distribution reflects the longer order cycle time that can result when a significant number of out-of-stock situations occur. Order cycle time may be expressed quantitatively in such usual statistical terms as the mean, the standard deviation, and the frequency distribution form.

Example

A firm produces a product in the United States and delivers it to a stocking point in Sao Paulo, Brazil, for supplying the local customers. Order filling requires order processing, product manufacture or order filling from warehouse stocks, shipment consolidation, inland transport, ocean transport, and customs clearance. Tracing the total order cycle from stock replenishment order placement to delivery in Brazil shows the following cycle time elements and their estimated times. Constructing the order cycle in this manner reveals that order entry and order filling at plants and warehouses are consuming the majority (50 percent) of the order cycle time and should be the target for significant order cycle time reduction.

	Time in Days		
Distribution Time Elements	Min.	Max.	Avg.
Order entry and production/warehouse processing	1	86[a]	36
Transport to consolidation point	1	5	2
Freight consolidation	2	14	7
Freight pickup	0	1	1
Transport to port	1	2	1
Vessel waiting	1	4	2
Ocean transit	17	20	18
Deconsolidation	3	4	4
Customs clearance	1	4	2
Inland transport to inventory point	0	2	1
Totals	27	142	74

[a] 90th percentile

Adjustments to Order Cycle Time

Until this point in the discussion, it has been assumed that the elements of the order cycle have been operating without constraint. At times, however, customer service policies will distort the normal order cycle time patterns. Several of these policies relate to order processing priorities, order condition, and order size constraints.

Order Processing Priorities

Order cycle time for an individual customer may vary greatly from the company standard, depending on the priority rules, or lack of them, that have been established for processing incoming orders. Distinguishing one customer from another may be necessary when backlogs occur.

Example

In processing orders from its industrial customers, a medium-size paper manufacturer noted that when order backlogs occurred and pressure was applied to reduce them, order-processing personnel had a tendency to process the smaller and less-complicated orders first. This relegated the orders from the larger and more-valued customers to a time later than they normally would have been handled. The company was increasing its order cycle time to its larger customers during periods of order backlog because arbitrary priority rules for processing orders were unconsciously being applied.

Order Condition Standards

What is a normal order cycle time can be substantially altered if the products ordered arrive at the customer location in a damaged or unusable state. Most firms do not wish to absorb the high cost, nor customers the high price, to eliminate the chance of a damaged or inaccurate order. Standards set for package design, procedures for returning and replacing incorrect or damaged goods, and standards set for monitoring order quality will establish how much the order cycle time will be increased on the average.

Order Constraints

Under some circumstances, the logistician may find it desirable to impose a minimum order size, to have orders placed according to a preset schedule, or to have order forms prepared by the customer that conform to preset specifications. These constraints permit important economies to be achieved in product distribution. For example, a minimum order size and precise scheduling of product movements often result in lower transportation costs and increased delivery speed. For some customers, the effective order-cycle time may be lengthened by such a practice. On the other hand, this practice may allow service to be provided to some low-volume markets that might not otherwise be served very frequently or reliably.

IMPORTANCE OF LOGISTICS/SC CUSTOMER SERVICE

Logistics managers may be tempted to dismiss customer service as a marketing or sales department responsibility. We have already noted that buyers do recognize logistics customer service elements as important, often ranking these ahead of product price, product quality, and other marketing, finance, and production-related elements. The key concern at this point is whether it makes a difference to the selling firm in any way that can affect its profitability. How service affects sales and how service affects customer loyalty are questions that need to be explored.

Service Effects on Sales

Logisticians have long believed that sales are affected to some degree by the level of logistics customer service provided. The fact is that logistics customer service represents an element within total customer service, sales cannot be precisely measured against the of levels logistics customer service, and buyers themselves do not always accurately express their desires for service and consistently respond to service offerings. This typically leads logisticians to preset customer service levels and then to design the supply channel around them. Of course, this approach is not ideal, but it is practical.

There is now more definitive evidence that logistics customer service does affect sales. In the careful customer service study by Sterling and Lambert, they were able to conclude that marketing services do affect market share and that the marketing mix components of product, price, promotion, and physical distribution do not contribute equally to market share.[16] Recall that Sterling and Lambert also found that the elements of customer service most important to customers were logistical in nature. Krenn and Shycon were able to conclude from their in-depth interviews of 300 GTE/Sylvania customers that

> ... distribution, when it provides the proper levels of service to meet customer needs, can lead directly to increased sales, increased market share, and ultimately to increased profit contribution and growth.[17]

Observations[18]

- International Minerals & Chemicals Corporation, after instituting an extensive customer service program, reported a 20 percent increase in sales and a 21 percent increase in earnings.
- A manufacturer reallocated its plant territories and added to its warehouse facilities for an increase in logistics costs of $200,000, a reduction of production costs of $1,400,000, and a net profit increase of $500,000 from an increase in annual sales from $45 to $50 million.
- For a large retail chain with sales of over $1 billion, a consolidation of storage points at five distribution centers was estimated to produce a $9 million saving in cost of goods sold (including inbound freight costs), a $4 million saving in logistics costs, and an additional $10 million increase in net profit resulting from a $100 million increase in retail sales.

Baritz and Zissman were able to show that customers (purchasing and distribution executives) can perceive service differences among their "best" and their "average" suppliers.[19] More definitively, they observed that when service failures occur, buyers often impose penalizing action on the responsible supplier. These actions will affect the supplier's cost or revenues. The types of specific actions taken against suppliers are illustrated in Figure 4-5. The researchers were able to conclude with the following strong statement about service effects on sales:

> Differences in customer service performance have been quantified to account for five to six percent of the variations in a supplier's sales.[20]

[16]Sterling and Lambert, "Customer Service Research: Past, Present, and Future," pp. 14–17.
[17]John M. Krenn and Harvey N. Shycon, "Modeling Sales Response to Customer Service for More Effective Distribution," *Proceedings of the National Council of Physical Distribution Management,* Vol. I (New Orleans, LA: October 2–5, 1983), p. 593.
[18]Paraphrased in James L. Heskett, "Controlling Customer Logistics Service," *International Journal of Physical Distribution & Logistics Management,* Vol. 24, No. 4 (1994), p. 4–10.
[19]Baritz and Zissman, "Researching Customer Service: The Right Way," pp. 610–612.
[20]Ibid., p. 612.

Figure 4-5
Penalties for
Customer Service
Failures Imposed by
Purchasing Agents
Against Suppliers

Source: Steven G. Baritz
and Lorin Zissman,
"Researching Customer
Service: The Right Way,"
*Proceedings of the National
Council of Physical
Distribution Management,*
Vol. II (New Orleans, LA:
October 25, 1983), p. 611.

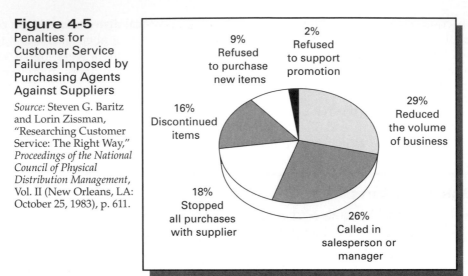

Similarly, Blanding makes the following statement:

> In industrial markets, a 5% decrease in service levels will result in a 24% drop in purchases by the existing customer base.[21]

Finally, a study by Singhal and Hendricks of 861 publicly held companies found that supply chain failures have an adverse effect on stock prices.[22] When a company announces a supply chain malfunction, such as a production or shipping delay, its stock price can immediately fall 9 percent and by as much as 20 percent over a six-month period. The six most common reasons for supply chain glitches were: parts shortages, changes requested by customers, new product ramp/rollouts, production problems, development problems, and quality problems.

Service Effects on Customer Patronage

Another way to look at the importance of customer service is through the costs associated with customer patronage. Logistics customer service plays a critical role in maintaining customer patronage and must be carefully set and consistently provided if customers are to remain loyal to their suppliers. When it is realized that 65 percent of a firm's business comes from its present customers,[23] we understand why it is so important to maintain the current customer base. As Bender observed,

> On the average it is approximately six times more expensive to develop a new customer than it is to keep a current customer. Thus, from a financial

---

[21]Warren Blanding, "Customer Service Logistics," *Proceedings of the Council of Logistics Management,* Vol. I (Anaheim, CA: October 5–8, 1986), p. 367.
[22]"Study Links Supply Chain Glitches with Falling Stock Prices," *OR/MS Today,* Vol. 28, No. 1 (February 2001), pp. 21ff.
[23]Ibid. p. 366.

104   Part II   Customer Service Goals

point of view, resources invested in customer service activities provide a substantially higher return than resources invested in promotion and other customer development activities.[24]

The chairman and chief executive officer of AT&T must believe this because when responding to communication price wars, he said:

> We've got to focus on rewarding and creating loyalty among existing customers rather than spending big to buy back defectors.[25]

DEFINING A SALES-SERVICE RELATIONSHIP

The importance of logistics customer service is now clear. However, logistics decision making would be enhanced if we knew more precisely how sales change with changes in logistics customer service levels. We would like to express this effect mathematically as a sales-service relationship. Consider the general nature of such a relationship.

From the available research findings and theories, it is possible to construct what the sales-logistics service relationship must look like, at least in a generalized form. This relationship, shown in Figure 4-6, indicates how sales are likely to change when

Figure 4-6
General Relationship of Sales to Customer Service

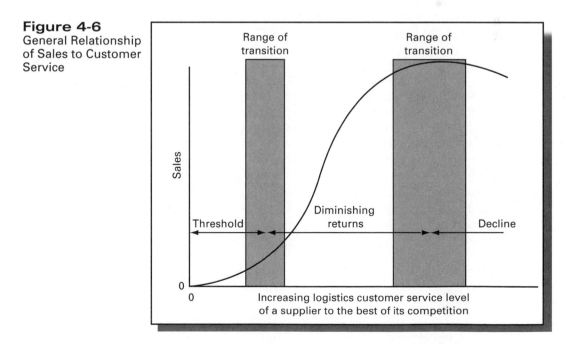

---

[24]Paul S. Bender, *Design and Operation of Customer Service Systems* (New York: AMACOM, 1976), p. 5.
[25]"The 'New' AT&T Faces Daunting Challenges," *Wall Street Journal*, September 19, 1996, B1.

service is improved above that offered by competing suppliers. Note the three distinct stages of the curve: threshold, diminishing returns, and decline. Each stage shows that equal increments of service improvements do not always bring equal gains in sales.

When no customer service exists between a buyer and a supplier, or when service is extremely poor, little or no sales are generated. Obviously, if a supplier offers no logistics customer service and the buyer isn't providing it, there is no way of overcoming the time and space gap between the two. No exchange, and thus no sales, can take place.

As service is increased to that approximating the offering by competition, little sales gain can be expected. Assuming that price and quality are equal, the firm is not, in effect, in business until its service level approximates that of the competition. This point is the threshold service level.

When a firm's service level reaches this threshold, further service improvement relative to competition can show good sales stimulation. Sales are captured from competing suppliers by creating a service differential. As the service is further improved, sales continue to increase, but at a slower rate. The region from the service level at threshold to the point of sales decline is referred to as one of diminishing returns. It is in this region that most firms operate their supply chains.

Why do sales increase with improvements in service? It has been observed that buyers are sensitive to the service that they receive from suppliers.[26] Improved service generally means lower inventory costs for the buyer, assuming that product quality and acquisition price remain unaffected by the improved service offering. Buyers are then motivated to shift their patronage to the supplier offering the best service.

The taper, or diminishing returns, in the curve has been observed in empirical studies.[27] It results both from the buyer's inability to benefit in the same degree from higher service levels as from lower ones, and of purchase policies that require more than one source of supply. The impact that service has on buyers' costs tends to diminish with increased service. Hence, patronage is likely to follow the same pattern. Also, the common purchase policy of maintaining multiple sources of supply puts limits on the degree of sales patronage that any buyer can offer to a supplier. When the policy is to spread purchases across many buyers, the effect is to produce the taper noted in Figure 4-6.

Finally, it is possible that service improvements can be carried too far, with a resulting decline in sales. Whereas improvements in inventory availability, order-cycle time, and condition of delivered goods carry no negative impact on sales, such

---

[26]Baritz and Zissman, "Researching Customer Service: The Right Way," pp. 610–612; and Ronald P. Willett and P. Ronald Stephenson, "Determinants of Buyer Response to Physical Distribution Service," *Journal of Marketing Research* (August 1969), pp. 279–283.

[27]Ronald H. Ballou, "Planning a Sales Strategy with Distribution Service," *Logistics and Transportation Review*, Vol. 9, No. 4 (1974), pp. 323–333; Willett and Stephenson, "Determinants of Buyer Response to Physical Distribution Service" Nicos Christofides and C. D. T. Watson-Gandy, "Improving Profits with Distribution Service," *International Journal of Physical Distribution & Materials Management*, Vol. 3 (Summer 1973), pp. 322–330; and Krenn and Shycon, "Modeling Sales Response to Customer Service for More Effective Distribution," pp. 581–601.

customer service factors as frequency of vendors' visits to examine buyers' stock levels and take orders, and the nature and frequency of order-progress reporting information may become excessive for some buyers. The buyers may see this as pestering and withdraw sales patronage from a supplier. However, such effects would likely take place only at extreme levels of service when customers become saturated with too much of a seemingly good thing.

MODELING THE SALES-SERVICE RELATIONSHIP

The sales-service relationship for a given product may deviate from the theoretical relationship shown in Figure 4-6. A number of methods for modeling the actual relationship might be used in specific cases. Four of these are the two-points method, before-after experiments, game playing, and buyer surveys.

Two-Points Method

The two-points method involves establishing two points on the diminishing return portion of the sales-service relationship through which a straight line can be drawn. This line is then used as an acceptable approximation to the curvilinear relationship, as shown in Figure 4-7. The method is based on the notion that multiple data points to accurately define the sales-service curve would be expensive or unrealistic to obtain, and if data were available, it is not usually possible to describe the relationship with a great deal of accuracy.

Figure 4-7
Approximation of a
Sales-Service
Relationship by the
Two-Points Method

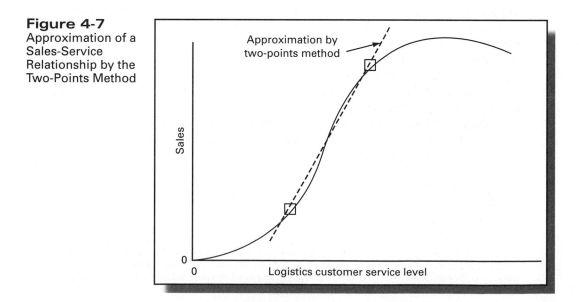

The method involves first setting logistics customer service at a high level for a particular product and observing the sales that can be achieved. Then the level is reduced to a low level and sales are again noted. Although the technique seems simple to execute, some methodological problems may limit its usefulness. First, it may not be practical to substantially change the service levels of currently selling products in order to collect the sales response information. Second, the length of time that the service change is in effect, the extent to which customers are informed of the change, and the extent to which other activities are operating that affect sales (promotions, price changes, and product quality changes) may introduce so much variability in the sales results as to render them meaningless. These limitations suggest that a careful selection of the situation to which it is to be applied must be made if reasonable results are to be obtained.

Before-After Experiments

Knowing the sales response to a particular change in service may be all that is needed to evaluate the effect on costs. Generating the sales-service curve over a wide range of service choices may be unnecessary and impractical. Thus, sales response may simply be determined either by inducing a service level change and monitoring the change in sales, or by observing the same effect from historical records when a service change occurred in the past. The service change needs to be great enough so that true sales differences are not masked by normal sales fluctuations or measurement errors.

Before-after experiments of this type are subject to the same methodological problems as the two-points method. However, these experiments may be easier to implement because the current service level serves as the "before" data point. Only the "after" data point is then needed.

Game Playing

One of the more serious problems in measuring the sales response to service changes is controlling the business environment so that only the effect of the logistics customer service level is determined. One approach is to set up a laboratory simulation, or gaming situation, where the participants make their decisions within a controlled environment. This environment attempts to replicate the elements of demand uncertainty, competition, logistics strategy, and others that may be relevant to the particular situation. The game involves decisions about logistics activity levels (and hence service levels) with the objective of generating sales consistent with the costs of producing them. By monitoring the game playing over time, extensive data can be obtained to generate a sales-service curve. Specialized games can be created for this purpose, or generalized logistics games that are available for teaching purposes can be considered.[28]

---

[28]Examples of these generalized logistics games are found in J. L. Heskett, Robert M. Ivie, and Nicholas A. Glaskowsky, Jr., *Business Logistics: Instructor's Supplement* (New York: Ronald Press, 1964), pp. 100–108; and "Simchip—A Logistical Game," in Donald J. Bowersox, *Logistical Management,* 2nd ed. (New York: Macmillan, 1978), pp. 465–478.

The artificiality of the gaming environment will always lead to questions about the relevance of the results to a particular firm or product situation. To the extent that the predictive value of the gaming process is established through validation procedures, the technique offers the advantage of being able to manipulate the problem elements and the environment without intruding on an ongoing process. In addition, the gaming process can be continued as long as needed to acquire the desired information, and replicated for further validation.

Buyer Surveys

The most popular method for gathering customer service information is to survey buyers or other persons who influence purchases. Mail questionnaires and personal interviews are frequently used because a large sample of information can be obtained at relatively low cost. Some questions in the survey may be designed to determine how buyers would change their patronage or purchase levels among suppliers if the customer service offered were changed to some degree. The composite responses from multiple buyers reacting to different proposed levels of logistics customer service provide the basic data for generating the sales-service curve.[29]

Survey methods, too, must be used with caution because biases can occur. A major bias is the fact that buyers are asked to indicate how they *would* respond to service changes and not how they *do* respond to them. In addition, the questions must be carefully designed so as not to lead the respondents or to bias their answers and yet capture the essence of service that the buyers find important.

COST VERSUS SERVICE

It was noted earlier that logistics customer service is a result of setting logistics activity levels. This implies that each level of service has an associated cost level. In fact, there are many logistics system cost alternatives for each service level, depending on the particular logistics activity mix. Once the sales-service relationship is generally known, it is then possible to match costs with service, as shown in Figure 4-8.

As activity levels are increased to meet higher customer service levels, costs increase at an increasing rate. This is a general phenomenon observed in most economic activities as they are forced beyond their point of maximum efficiency. The diminishing returns in the sales-service relationship and the increasing cost-service curve result in a profit curve of the form shown in Figure 4-8. The profit contribution curve results from the difference between revenue and costs at various service levels. Because there is a point on the profit contribution curve where profit is maximized, it is

---

[29]Examples of the use of this technique can be found in Ballou, "Planning a Sales Strategy with Distribution Service"; Perreault and Russ, "Physical Distribution Service in Industrial Purchase Decisions," *Journal of Marketing*, Vol. 10, No. 3 (1976), pp. 3–10; Willett and Stephenson, "Determinants of Buyer Response to Physical Distribution Service"; and Krenn and Shycon, "Modeling Sales Response to Customer Service for More Effective Distribution."

Figure 4-8
General Cost-
Revenue Trade-Offs
at Varying Levels of
Logistics Customer
Service

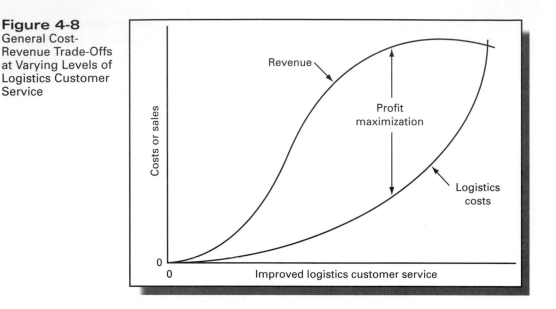

this ideal service level that is sought in planning the logistics system. This maximum profit point typically occurs between the extremes of low and high service levels.

DETERMINING OPTIMUM SERVICE LEVELS

Once the revenue and logistics cost for each service level are known, we can then determine the service level that will maximize the firm's profit contribution. The optimum profit point is found mathematically. We will consider the theory for doing this, and then look at an example of how the theory is applied in practice.

Theory

Suppose that the objective is to maximize the contribution to profit, that is, the difference between logistics-associated revenues and logistics costs. Mathematically, maximum profits are realized at the point where the change in revenue equals the change in cost, that is, marginal revenue equals marginal cost. For purposes of illustration, imagine that the sales-service (revenue) curve is given by $R = 0.5\sqrt{SL}$, where SL is the service level represented as the percentage of orders having a five-day order cycle time. The nature of this curve is shown in Figure 4-9. The corresponding cost curve is given by $C = 0.00055SL^2$. The expression to be optimized is revenue minus cost, or

$$P = 0.5\sqrt{SL} - 0.00055SL^2$$

(4-1)

where P = profit contribution in dollars.

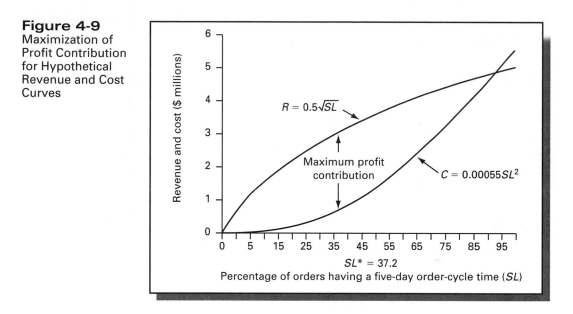

Figure 4-9
Maximization of
Profit Contribution
for Hypothetical
Revenue and Cost
Curves

Using differential calculus, Equation (4-1) can be optimized. The resulting expression for the service level (SL) to optimize profit contribution is[30]

$$SL^* = \left[\frac{0.5}{4(0.00055)} \right]^{2/3}$$

(4-2)

Therefore, $SL^* = 37.2$. That is, approximately 37 percent of the orders should have a five-day order cycle time, as shown in Figure 4-9.

Practice

Consider how the previous theory is applied to warehouse inventory service levels for a manufacturer of food products. One item is selected, but the methodology applies equally to each of the other items in the warehouse.

---

[30]The expression of SL^* is determined as follows:

$$P = 0.5\sqrt{SL} - 0.00055SL^2$$

To optimize P with respect to SL, take the first derivative of P with respect to SL and set the result equal to zero. That is,

$$dP/dSL = (1/2)(0.5)SL^{-1/2} - (2)(0.0055)SL = 0$$

Solve for SL^*.

$$SL^* = \left[\frac{0.5}{4(0.00055)} \right]^{2/3}$$

Example

Borden Foods holds a lemon juice product in one of its warehouses. The company holds so much inventory of this product that it would not run out of the product for as long as four years. The service level for the product was set in excess of 99 percent. Although this was one of the company's high-volume products, the question was whether the stock level needed to be set so high.

The general feeling in the company was that a 0.1 percent change in sales would occur for each 1 percent change in service level. The warehouse replenished retail stores on a weekly basis so that the customer service level could be defined as the probability of being in stock during the warehouse replenishment lead time. The trading margin (markup) was $0.55 per case with annual sales through the warehouse of 59,904 cases. The standard cost per case was $5.38 and the annual inventory carrying cost was estimated at 25 percent. The replenishment lead time was one week, with average weekly sales of 1,152 cases and a standard deviation of 350 cases.

The optimum service is found at the point where net profit at the warehouse is maximized, or $NP = P - C$. P is gross profit at the location of the warehouse in the supply channel and C is the safety stock cost in the warehouse. Optimality occurs where the change (Δ) in gross profit equals the change in safety stock costs; $\Delta P = \Delta C$. Because the sales response is constant for all levels of service, the change in gross profit is found from

$$\Delta P = \text{Trading margin (\$/case)} \times \text{Sales response (fractional change in sales/1\% change in service)} \times \text{Annual sales (cases/year)}$$
$$= 0.55 \times 0.001 \times 59,904$$
$$= \$32.95 \text{ per year per 1\% change in service level} \tag{4-3}$$

The change in cost is a result of the amount of safety stock that needs to be maintained at each service level. Safety stock is the extra inventory held as a hedge against demand and replenishment lead time variability.[31] This change in safety stock is given by

$$\Delta C = \text{Annual carrying cost (\%/year)} \times \text{Standard product cost (\$/case)} \times \text{Demand standard deviation during replenishment period (cases)} \times \Delta z \tag{4-4}$$

where z is a factor (called the normal deviate) from the normal distribution curve that is associated with the probability of being in stock during the lead time period. (The rationale for this equation is discussed in the chapter on inventory management.) The change in annual cost is

$$\Delta C = 0.25 \times 5.38 \times 350 \times \Delta z$$
$$= \$470.75 \times \Delta z \text{ per year}$$

for each Δz. The change in safety stock costs for various values for Δz are given in the following tabulation:

---

[31]See Chapter 9, "Inventory Policy Decisions," for more information on safety stock.

Change in Service Level (SL), %	Change in z (Δz)[a]	Change in Safety Stock Cost (ΔC), $/year
87–86	$1.125 - 1.08 = 0.045$	$ 21.18
88–87	$1.17 - 1.125 = 0.045$	21.18
89–88	$1.23 - 1.17 = 0.05$	23.54
90–89	$1.28 - 1.23 = 0.05$	23.54
91–90	$1.34 - 1.28 = 0.06$	28.25
92–91	$1.41 - 1.34 = 0.07$	32.95
93–92	$1.48 - 1.41 = 0.07$	32.95 ←
94–93	$1.55 - 1.48 = 0.07$	32.95
95–94	$1.65 - 1.55 = 0.10$	47.08
96–95	$1.75 - 1.65 = 0.10$	47.08
97–96	$1.88 - 1.75 = 0.13$	61.20
98–97	$2.05 - 1.88 = 0.17$	80.03
99–98	$2.33 - 2.05 = 0.28$	131.81

[a]These z values can be found in Appendix A.

Plotting the ΔP and ΔC values on a graph (see Figure 4-10) shows that the optimum service level (SL^*) is 92 to 93 percent. This is the point where the ΔP and C curves intersect.

Note: It is not necessary to account for changes in all product revenue and costs, only the relevant profit and inventory cost effects.

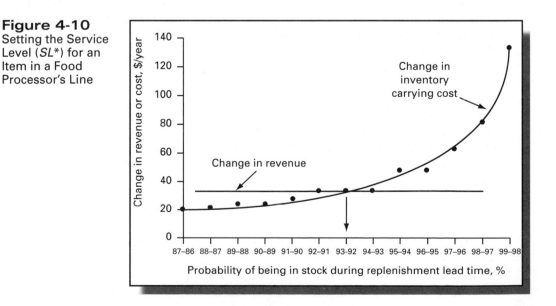

Figure 4-10
Setting the Service Level (SL^*) for an Item in a Food Processor's Line

Borden conducted a similar analysis for a large sample of the thousands of items inventoried in its multiple warehouses. Millions of dollars in inventory cost savings were projected due to stocking at higher levels than could be justified by the added profits to be realized from stocking above the optimum service levels.

SERVICE VARIABILITY

Customer service to this point in the discussion has referred to the average value of the variable representing customer service. However, *variability* in customer service performance is usually more important than average performance. Customers can plan for known and even marginal customer service performance, but variability in service performance is uncertainty. High degrees of service uncertainty cause the customer to incur high costs through elevated inventories, expedited transportation, and additional administrative costs. How much variability to allow is an economic issue. When variability cannot be controlled, information may be used to soften the uncertainty effects.

Loss Function

Just as product quality can be judged by its conformance to specifications, logistics customer service can be judged by the extent to which the supply chain processes meet target delivery dates, in-stock frequencies, order-filling accuracy rates, or other service variables. Quality and customer service are similar and, therefore, much of what has been said about product quality in the last 10 to 15 years applies to customer service as well. Genichi Taguchi's loss function is valuable to managing the processes that produce the customer service levels. Taguchi proposed that inconsistent quality in product and services results in expense, waste, loss of goodwill, and lost opportunity whenever the quality target value is not met exactly. Traditionally, quality was viewed to be satisfactory and without cost penalty as long as quality variation remained within the upper and lower limits of an acceptable range (see Figure 4-11). According to Taguchi, losses occur at an increasing rate as service (quality) deviates from its target value. This loss increases at an increasing rate according to the following formula:

$$L = k(y - m)^2 \tag{4-5}$$

where

L = loss in dollars per unit (cost penalty)
y = value of the quality variable
m = target value of the quality variable y
k = a constant that depends on the financial importance of the quality variable

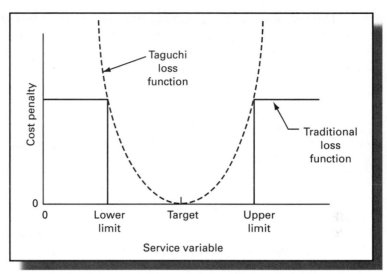

When the loss function is known, it places a value on not meeting customer service targets. Along with the cost of adjusting the process to achieve different levels of quality, the process can be optimized for the best level of variability in quality.

Example

Suppose that a package courier service promises to deliver to customers by 10:00 A.M. on the morning after pickup. Delivery later than two hours after the promised delivery time is unacceptable. The company is penalized $10.00 in the form of customer rebate for each late delivery. Converting the penalty to a loss function, the k value in the loss function of Equation (4-5) can now be found:

$$L = k(y - m)^2$$
$$10.00 = k(2 - 0)^2$$
$$k = \frac{10}{2^2} = \$2.5 \text{ per hour}^2$$

The value for m is set at 0 since only the deviation y from the target value is sought.

The cost per delivery for controlling the process declines as more deviation is allowed from the target delivery time. The company estimates that process costs are high when there is no deviation allowed from the target value but they decline in a linear fashion from the target value such that process cost $= A - B(y - m)$. The process cost is found to decline with increasing deviation from the target value as $PC = 20 - 5(y - m)$.

The total cost is the sum of the process cost (*PC*) and the penalty cost (*L*). The point $y - m$ where the marginal loss equals the marginal process cost is[32]

$$(y - m) = \frac{B}{2k} = \frac{5}{2(2.5)} = 1 \text{ hour}$$

Thus, the company should set its service process to allow no more than one-hour deviation from the target delivery time $m = 0$.

Information Substitution

At times, the uncertainty in customer service performance cannot be controlled to the level that might be desired by customers. In such cases, it may be possible to reduce the impact of the uncertainty by using information as a substitute. One obvious practice is to provide customers with information about their order progress. Order-tracking systems that provide information from the time of order entry until delivery are increasing in popularity. Their use in just-in-time systems is essential to managing the flow of product where little or no inventory is maintained. They are appearing in many retail systems as well. The benefit is that customers know the stage of their order and can anticipate its arrival rather than be in doubt about order progress and unable to plan accurately for delivery delays on inventory levels, production schedules, and the like. A well-designed tracking system should, in addition to providing order-tracking status, give the current estimate of completion times for each stage.

Observation

The Dell Corporation, a manufacturer of personal computers, provides customers using the Internet (and telephone customer service) with the capability to track orders through the *entire* order cycle. When an order is placed through the company's Web site or through a sales person, a tracking number is given to the customer. The customer may then find the order status hyperlink on Dell's Web site and see whether the order has passed the order entry stage, the production stage, or the shipping preparation stage. Order status is updated in real time. Once the order leaves the factory, an interface with UPS or other carrier is also provided on the Web page to track the order through the various stages of delivery to the customer's

---

[32]Alternately, using differential calculus, the optimal allowed deviation from the target value can be found as follows.

$$TC = A - B(y - m) + k(y - m)^2$$
$$\frac{dTC}{d(y - m)} = 0 - B + 2k(y - m) = 0$$
$$(y - m) = \frac{B}{2k}$$

location. The customer can anticipate within a narrow time window when the order will arrive and can make plans for its receipt.

SERVICE AS A CONSTRAINT

Customer service is often treated as a constraint on the logistics system when a sales-service relationship cannot be developed. In this case, a predetermined customer service level may be selected, and the logistics system is designed to meet this level with a minimum cost. The service level is often based on factors such as the service levels established by competitors, the opinions of salespersons, and tradition. There is no guarantee that a service level set in this manner will result in a logistics system design that is the best balance between revenues and logistics costs.

In order to move toward an optimum system design when service is treated as a constraint, sensitivity analysis can be used. In this case, sensitivity analysis involves changing the factors that make up service and then finding the new minimum-cost system design. If this type of analysis is repeated a number of times, an array of system costs for various service levels can be obtained, as illustrated in Table 4-3. Although it is not known how logistics system design and the resulting service level affect sales, it is possible to impute a worth to a service level. As shown in Table 4-3, by improving customer service from an 85 percent level to a 90 percent level, logistics

Table 4-3 Logistics System Design Costs As a Function of Various Customer Service Levels

ALTERNATIVE	LOGISTICS SYSTEM DESIGN[a]	ANNUAL LOGISTICS COSTS	CUSTOMER SERVICE LEVEL[b]
1	Mail-order transmittal, manual-order entry, water transportation, low inventory levels	$ 5,000,000	80%
2	Mail-order transmittal, manual-order entry, rail transportation, low inventory levels	7,000,000	85
3	Telephone order entry, truck transportation, low inventory levels	9,000,000	90
4	Telephone order entry, rail transportation, high inventory levels	12,000,000	93
5	Telephone order entry, truck transportation, high inventory levels	15,000,000	95
6	Web site order entry, airfreight, high inventory levels	16,000,000	96

[a]Minimum cost design to produce the stated customer service level.
[b]Percentage of customers receiving goods within five days.

costs will increase from $7 million to $9 million annually. The imputed worth of these five percentage points in customer service improvement is at an added cost of $2 million. Thus, enough of a sales increase from this service improvement must be realized to cover the added logistics costs. The final choice of a service level is left to managerial judgment, but information about the cost of various service levels facilitates the decision-making process.

MEASURING SERVICE

Finding a comprehensive measure to effectively assess logistics customer service performance is quite difficult, considering the many dimensions of service to customers. Total order-cycle time and its variability are probably the best single measures of logistics customer service since they embody so many of the variables that are considered important to customers. It can be represented statistically by mean and standard deviations (e.g., for the 95th percentile 10 ± 2 days), or alternatively as a percent of orders meeting target order cycle times.

Customer service may also be measured in terms of each logistics activity. Some common performance measures include the following:

Order Entry

- Minimum, maximum, and average time for order handling
- Percent of orders handled within target times

Order Documentation Accuracy

- Percent of order documents with errors

Transportation

- Percent of deliveries on time
- Percent of orders delivered by customer request date
- Damage and loss claims as a percent of freight costs

Inventory and Product Availability

- Stockout percentage
- Percent of orders filled complete
- Order fill rate and weighted average fill rate
- Average percent of items on backorder
- Item fill rate

Product Damage

- Number of returns to total orders
- Value of returns to total sales

Production/Warehousing Processing time

- Minimum, maximum, and average time to process orders

Many others measures can be used and they should be tailored to the design of the particular logistics system operated by a company.

There are two potential shortcomings to these service measures. First, they are internally oriented to the firm, probably because data are more readily available and control is easier compared to externally oriented measures. On the other hand, they do not promote coordination that is essential to good customer service performance involving multiple channel members. Good externally oriented service measures are yet to be developed.

Second, they may not focus on the needs of the customers. Too often, firms measure customer service in terms of those elements under their direct control. Narrow definitions and measures of customer service may lead a firm to believe that it is performing well, but customers may find the service does not include all the service factors important to them. This leaves the firm unknowingly vulnerable to competitors that recognize the total customer service need and manage service performance from the viewpoint of the customer.

Observation

A major producer of fluid motion control equipment (hoses, connectors, hydraulic cylinders, and control instrumentation) had a substantial market in Latin America. Customer service for the company was measured as the percent of orders shipped (from factory or warehouse) by the customer-requested date. Since customers selected their favorite freight forwarder for ocean transport to Caribbean and South American countries, it would appear that customers should be satisfied. However, the company placed 40 percent of total order cycle time in the hands of their customers. Customers selected the means of transportation from the factories because the company offered no alternatives. With its narrow definition of customer service, the company not only missed the opportunity to use its shipping volume to find lower cost/better ocean service alternatives (such as through a third party logistics provider or 3PL), than the customer could find acting alone, but left itself vulnerable to competitors who sought to manage the customers' entire order cycles.

SERVICE CONTINGENCIES

Much of the logistician's planning and control effort is directed toward running an efficient operation under normal conditions. At the same time, preparations must be made to handle those extraordinary circumstances that may shut down the system or drastically alter its operating characteristics in a short time period, such as labor strikes, fire, flood, or dangerous product defects. Two common contingencies are system breakdown and product recall.

System Breakdown

No logistics operating system will run perfectly all of the time. Some service interruptions are bound to occur, but we would not necessarily consider them significant enough to have special plans ready in case of their happening. Expediting a delayed purchase order, handling seasonal ordering peak loads, or having redundant equipment to meet breakdowns—none of these situations really require contingency plans since they are a normal part of business activity.

Example

Federal Express uses "sweep airplanes" to meet surges in volume, weather delays, and equipment failures. The company considers this redundancy a normal part of their highly service-oriented business.

Contingency planning is different and outside of the normal planning processes. Hale classifies the nature of the event to indicate when contingency planning should be undertaken:

- The probability of occurrence is considered lower than for events included in the regular planning process.
- The actual occurrence of such an event would cause serious damage, especially if not dealt with quickly.
- It deals with a subject about which the company can plan ahead to deal with swiftly if the event occurs.[33]

There are no special methods for contingency planning. It simply is a matter of asking what-if questions about critical elements of the logistics system and setting up appropriate courses of action, should an unexpected event occur to a vital part of the logistics system. Management's desire to ensure the target level of customer service heightens the need to undertake this type of planning.

Application

The West Coast warehouse of a well-known office copying equipment manufacturer burned extensively one Friday afternoon. The warehouse, containing replacement parts for office copiers and general supplies, served a substantial portion of the West Coast area. Considering the competitive nature of that business, the fire represented a potential disaster in lost sales. A portion of the distribution system had broken down.

Fortunately, the company's distribution staff had anticipated this possibility and had contingency plans for just such an event. By Monday, the company had shipped by airfreight enough stock into a public warehouse to be ready for business. Customer service was maintained so near to previous levels that many customers were unaware that the fire had taken place.

---

[33]Bernard J. Hale, "The Continuing Need for Contingency Planning by Logistics Managers," *Proceedings of Council of Logistics Management*, Vol. I (Atlanta, September 27–30, 1987), p. 93.

Martha and Subbakrishna recognize the particular vulnerability of supply chains due to their design based on speed and efficiency. Quick response, "lean" logistics, and just-in-time deliveries have been encouraged over the last 30 years as a way of reducing inventories, freeing capital, and improving quality. This logistics strategy heightens the risk and impact of disruptions since a continuous flow of product throughout the supply chain with precise timing is required. There are few or no inventories to relieve the shock of disruptions at various stages of the supply chain. The entire supply chain can be at risk of shutdown. The following actions have been suggested to lessen or avoid the impact of sudden supply chain interruptions:

- Insure the risk.
- Plan for alternate supply sources.
- Arrange alternate transportation.
- Shift demand.
- Build quick response to demand shifts.
- Set inventories for disruption possibilities.[34]

Insuring against financial loss is an obvious protection for service breakdowns. However, as insurance companies selectively exclude certain types of risks, such as terrorism, other steps need to be taken. These are generally directed at preserving service levels or keeping customers satisfied during service disruptions.

Maintaining multiple supply sources or planning for alternate suppliers may allow product flow during supply channel disruptions. Reliance on a single supplier source is the major risk. Maintaining a single supply source has been encouraged in recent years by the proponents of just-in-time systems.

Example

When Hurricane Mitch blew through Central America, flooding destroyed banana plantations, two major producers lost much of their area capacity. Dole lost 70 percent of its capacity there, or about one-quarter of its entire capacity. Because Dole had no alternate supply sources, the company experienced a 4 percent drop in revenue.

On the other hand, Chiquita Brands was able to maintain supply. It increased productivity at other locations, such as Panama, and made purchases from associated producers in the regions that were not damaged by the hurricane. As a result, Chiquita's revenues *increased* by 4 percent in the fourth quarter of 1998.

Transportation is a particularly vulnerable element in the supply channel. Arranging in advance for alternative modes of delivery is the obvious counterresponse to disruptions from strikes, natural disasters, and terrorism. Substituting one mode for another or using alternative routing offers the needed flexibility. Of course, there may be an added cost to keeping the supply chain operating.

---

[34]Joseph Martha and Sunil Subbakrishna, "Targeting a Just-in-Case Supply Chain for the Inevitable Next Disaster," *Supply Chain Review*, Vol. 6, No. 5 (2002), pp. 18–23.

Shifting demand is an indirect way to treat supply disruptions. This is the recognition that when one product cannot be made available, customers may be encouraged through incentives to select an alternative product. Sales may be maintained until supply chain performance can be restored.

Example

When an earthquake hit Taiwan in 1999, the supply of components to PC and laptop manufacturers was interrupted for two weeks. Apple Computer faced shortages of semiconductors and components for its popular products. Although attempts were made to ship slower-speed versions of these models, customers complained. Supply problems continued as product configurations were unable to be altered.

By contrast, Dell Computer fared better. Using its product selection Web site to promote special deals and price incentives, Dell was able to shift some demand to other products not affected by the shortages. Earnings actually improved 41 percent during the quarter affected by the supply disruptions.

When terrorists attacked the World Trade Center, the subsequent disruptions to travel suddenly shifted demand to other modes of transportation. When severe winter weather slowed truck travel in northern states, demand shifted to rail. When Russian grain purchases increased the demand for rail hopper cars, regular rail shippers encountered a hopper car shortage. Spikes in demand are frequently not easily absorbed within the normal operation of a supply channel. Planned flexibility is needed. Supply channels built around multiple suppliers or producing points, inventories, and mixed transport methods are best able to handle demand shocks. "Lean" logistics systems are not. Extra capacity and quick response systems may be needed to deal with such unexpected changes in demand levels, probably at additional cost.

Inventories have been a primary way in which companies have dealt with disruptions. They act as a safety net or buffer when demand and supply do not match. Just-in-time and "lean" logistics programs have minimized inventories and increased the negative effect of delays or temporary shutdowns of part of the supply channel. Establishing or increasing inventories at key points in the supply channel can significantly reduce the effects of some type of disruptions.

Actions taken to deal with the risks associated with system breakdowns due to various disruptions in general cause increased costs, unless service is allowed to deteriorate. Although a smoothly running supply chain is the ideal, the reality is that disasters do occur. Responsible managers will take time to anticipate the events that might occur and plan accordingly.

Sometimes, events occur that have such a low probability they are not anticipated at all. Contingency plans cannot be formulated because the events themselves cannot be adequately defined. In such cases, contingency planning may involve having a crisis team in place, ready to be activated when an emergency strikes. Being able to respond quickly and effectively to logistical alternatives as they unfold can be the key to maintaining operations when unforeseen disruptions do occur.

Example

Chrysler activated its logistical command center when terrorists attacked the World Trade Center in New York City, which resulted in the temporary shutdown of domestic air flights and delayed ground transportation at international borders when security was tightened. Chrysler, like other auto producers, was operating its plants under a just-in-time manufacturing system. Very low inventories were held at plants, which relied on a smoothly operating transportation system that can reliably ship small quantities of parts frequently. Even minor disruptions could cause plants to shut down for lack of parts.

The crisis-management team handled the crisis with the following actions:

- Shut the plants down for one day.
- With GM and Ford counterparts, lobby U.S. Customs officials to add more inspectors at the main truck link between Detroit and Ontario, Canada, to ease truck congestion.
- Send word electronically to 150 of its largest suppliers to ship an extra eight to 12 hours' worth of parts to the plants.
- When commercial flights were allowed to resume two days later, truckers en route were instructed to head for the nearest airport where a plane picked up the load and forwarded it to plants in the United States and Mexico.

The result was that plant operations were disrupted for only one day![35]

Product Recall

The rise of consumerism has focused the attention of many companies on the customer with an intensity not previously known. Spearheaded by Ralph Nader, the consumerism movement has increased the public's awareness of product offerings in general and of defective products in particular. In 1972, Congress passed the Consumer Product Safety Act, which allows the Consumer Product Safety Commission to set mandatory safety standards for products. Some of the awareness is forced. For example, the Consumer Product Safety Commission can require a manufacturer to recall a product to repair it, replace it, or destroy it. Failure to comply may mean civil penalties or imprisonment. These are just the overt, legal actions. Many companies see the failure to manage defective products as leading to the loss of customer goodwill and possible legal repercussions. The point is that the risks are higher than ever for the company that fails to anticipate a product recall possibility.

---

[35]Jeffrey Ball, "How Chrysler Averted Parts Crisis in the Logjam Following Attacks," *Wall Street Journal*, September 24, 2001.

Contingency planning for product recall involves nearly every function within a business. Those responsible for logistics matters are particularly affected. They are responsible for the logistics channel through which retromovement is likely to take place. Logisticians become involved in product recall in three ways: chairing a task force committee for recall, tracing the product, and designing the reverse logistics channel.

One of the first steps in planning for a future recall, or meeting one that has occurred, is to establish a task force committee to guide the recall efforts. Because the primary duty of such a committee is to pull the product back toward the manufacturer, it is likely that the distribution executive will be the task force chairperson. The committee may also be responsible for stopping production, starting recall action, and carrying out the necessary steps to comply with appropriate regulatory agencies.

Attempting to recall products that cannot be easily located within the distribution system can be a very expensive operation and an unnecessary one, if the recall could have been prevented. Two product-tracing methods seem popular. For years, firms have been coding products by manufacturing location. Because few firms have engaged in further coding as the product moves through various locations in the distribution channel, manufacturing coding can only approximate the final location of products. However, it is readily available.

The second tracing method uses warranty card information. This method has its faults as well. It is confined to those products that use such cards, and not all cards are returned by customers. For better tracing, one electronics equipment retailer requires all customers to fill out an identification card at the point of sale.

Product tracing is being improved markedly using computers. Consider some examples:

- With the use of bar codes, satellite communications, radio-dispatched trucks with on-board computers, and hand-held scanners, Federal Express's COSMOS package tracking system is able to locate a package anywhere in the system.
- Pillsbury, through its Product Control and Identification System, can locate products through the stages of production to retail inventories. It can trace 98 percent of its products within 24 hours, and 100 percent within days.
- Ford Motor Company uses an automated system called North American Vehicle Information System for product tracing. This system can identify each of a vehicle's 15,000 parts for approximately 4 million units sold per year.

The final product recall decision concerns how goods are to be moved back through the distribution channel, or reverse distribution system design. Depending on the nature of the product defect and how the company plans to handle it, all or a portion of the distribution channel may be used. Recalled autos are returned only to the dealers' service centers. On the other hand, many small appliances and electronic goods are returned to the factory or regional service centers for repair or replacement.

Example

When CVS Corporation, a leading U.S. retail chain and pharmacy dispenser, receives returned merchandise at a retail store or must recall a item, all merchandise is initially returned to the warehouse serving the store. The manufacturer informs CVS of the disposition of the product. Many manufacturers choose to give CVS credit for the item and have it destroyed on site rather than to pay the transportation and handling charges to have it returned to their factories.

Designing the channel for retromovement requires consideration of product, customer, middleman, and company characteristics, as well as the nature of the defect, market coverage, recall type, remedial program required, current distribution system, and financial capabilities of the company. Although on the surface it may seem the best strategy to recall products from distributors and customers through existing distribution channels, this may not be wise. One possible danger is contaminating the good product flowing in the channel with the recalled product. In such cases, the recalling firm may establish a separate channel (public warehousing and for-hire trucking, for example) to specifically handle the recall. There are as many variants for reverse logistics channel design as there are for product recall circumstances. The logistician should be aware of the variety of channel designs available and should not necessarily confine recalled products to the existing distribution channel.

Why has product recall been considered in a discussion of logistics customer service? Traditionally, goods were considered to flow from manufacturer to consumer. Customer service reflected the idea of supplying a customer, not servicing a customer. Now, however, the consumerism movement, as well as the recycling movement, has generated concern for customer service after the product sale. Thus, the logistician must be concerned with designing product flow channels to satisfy customer needs before and after purchase.

Examples

- When Xerox installs a new, large copier for a customer, the copier is shipped from a central warehouse to a staging location in the customer's area. A local installation crew picks up the copier from the staging facility, transports it to the customer site, and completes the setup. An existing machine, if there is one, is returned to the staging facility, ultimately to be sent to a renovation center in Arizona for refurbishing and resale. The logistician, when planning the staging facility locations, must be concerned with both the forward product movement to customers as well as the return movement of the used copiers. The best staging facility locations may be different when only forward product movement is considered as opposed to product movement in both forward and reserve directions.

- Retail merchants in the United States are often faced with returned items resulting from liberal store return policies and sometimes poor product performance. Since returned items frequently are missing parts or don't work, or the package is no longer presentable, retailers are faced with receiving manufacturer's credit for the item, reconditioning it, or marking it down as an opened item. As an alternative, large merchants such as Wal-Mart may be able to sell these items to Mexican firms that purchase them for a fraction of their retail value but for more than the discounted value that the item may bring on the retail shelf as a reconditioned or opened item. The items are shipped to a Mexican plant where they are refurbished, if practical, and sold as new in the Latin American marketplace. They often sell at a higher price than they commanded in the U.S. market.

CONCLUDING COMMENTS

Logistics customer service is the net result of executing all activities in the logistics mix. Although no general agreement exists as to the most appropriate definition of logistics customer service, research seems to indicate that order cycle time and the elements that compose it are among the most critical. Even for overall customer service, logistics components of customer service seem to play a dominant role.

Because customer service has a positive effect on sales, the most appropriate way to approach logistics planning is from a profit-maximization rather than a cost-minimization viewpoint. Determining how sales respond to service has proven to be quite difficult and of questionable accuracy at best. This has generally led to managers specifying a service level and planning to meet it in the most economical way possible. However, in those cases where demand seems particularly sensitive to service, the sales-service relationship may be determined by one or more of the following methods: two-points method, before-after experimental design, game playing, and buyer surveys. Once this relationship is known, costs may be balanced against revenues so that optimal service levels may be found and the return on logistics assets (ROLA) may be maximized.

Customer service concerns may extend beyond satisfying customers under normal operating conditions. Prudent managers may also plan for the rare case when the logistics system breaks down or a product must be recalled. Preplanned actions for contingent events may prevent a loss of customer goodwill that could take an extended time period to recover once good service performance under normal conditions has been restored. When it is impractical to provide customers with the level of service desired or there are temporary breakdowns in service performance, information in real time about service status may be used to reduce the negative effects of poor service performance.

QUESTIONS

1. Logistics customer service might be quantified in terms of average order cycle time and order cycle time variability. How satisfactory is this as a general statement of logistics customer service? Of customer service overall?
2. What factors make up order cycle time? How do these factors differ, whether orders are filled in a regular distribution channel or are filled through a backup channel when an out-of-stock situation occurs?

3. How is it that customer service results from managing all activities in the logistics mix?
4. What is a logistics sales-service relationship? How does one go about determining it for a particular product line? Of what value is the relationship once it is obtained?
5. How can information, such as an order tracking system, be a substitute for customer service performance?
6. The Cleanco Chemical Company sells cleaning compounds (dishwashing powders, floor cleaners, nonpetroleum lubricants) in a keenly competitive environment to restaurants, hospitals, and schools. Delivery time on orders determines whether a sale can be made. The distribution system can be designed to provide different average levels of delivery time through the number and location of warehousing points, stocking levels, and order processing procedures. The physical distribution manager has made the following estimates of how service affects sales and the cost of providing service levels:

	Percentage of Orders Delivered Within One Day						
	50	60	70	80	90	95	100
Estimated annual sales (millions of $)	4.0	8.0	10.0	11.0	11.5	11.8	12.0
Cost of distribution (millions of $)	5.8	6.0	6.5	7.0	8.1	9.0	14.0

a. What level of service should the company offer?
b. What effect would competition likely have on the service level decision?
7. Five years ago, Norton Valves, Inc., introduced and publicized a program in which 56 items in its hydraulic valve line would be made available on a 24-hour-delivery basis, instead of the normal 1- to 12-week delivery period. Quick order processing, stocking to anticipated demand, and using premium transportation services when necessary were elements of the 24-hour delivery program. Sales history was recorded for the five years before the service change as well as for a five-year period after the change. Because only a portion of the product family was subject to the service improvement, the remaining products (102 items) served as a control group. Statistics for one of the test product groups showing the before and after annual unit sales levels are given as follows:

Product Family	Sales Before Service Change		Sales After Service Change	
	5-Year Average	Standard Deviation[c]	5-Year Average	Standard Deviation[c]
Test group[a]	1,342	335	2,295	576
Control group[b]	185	61	224	76

[a]Products in the family with 24-hour delivery
[b]Products in the family with 1- to 12-week delivery
[c]For the individual sales

The average value of products in this family was $95 per unit. The incremental cost for the improved service was $2 per unit, but the company did not intend to pass along the costs as a price increase. Instead, it hoped that additional sales volume would more than offset the added costs. The profit margin on sales at the time was 40 percent.

a. Should the company continue the premium service policy?

b. Appraise the methodology as a way of accurately determining the sales-service effect.

8. A food company is attempting to set the customer service level (in-stock probability in its warehouse) for a particular product line item. Annual sales for the item are 100,000 boxes, or 3,846 boxes biweekly. The product cost in inventory is $10, to which $1 is added as profit margin. Stock replenishment is every two weeks and the demand during this time is assumed normally distributed with a standard deviation of 400 boxes. Inventory carrying costs are 30 percent per year of item value. Management estimates that a 0.15 percent change in total revenue would occur for each 1 percent change in the in-stock probability.

a. Based on this information, find the optimum in-stock probability for the item.

b. What is the weakest link in this methodology? Why?

9. An item in the product line for the food company discussed in question 8 has the following characteristics:

Sales response rate = 0.15% change in revenue for a 1% change in the service level

Trading margin = 0.75 per case

Annual sales through the warehouse = 80,000 cases

Annual carrying cost = 25%

Standard product cost = $10.00

Demand standard deviation = 500 cases per 1 week lead time

Lead time = 1 week

Find the optimum service level for this item.

10. A retailer has targeted a shelf item to be out of stock only 5 percent of the time (m). Customers have come to expect this level of product availability, so much so, that when the out-of-stock percentage increases, customers seek substitutes and lost sales occur. From market research studies, the retailer has determined that when the out-of-stock probability increases to the 10 percent level (y), sales and profit drop to one-half of those at the target level. Decreasing the out-of-stock percentage from the target level seems to have little impact on sales, but it does increase inventory-carrying costs substantially. The following data have been collected on the item:

Price	$5.95
Cost of item	4.25
Other expenses associated with stocking the item	$0.30
Annual items sold @ 95% in-stock	880

The retailer estimates that for every one percentage point that the in-stock probability is allowed to vary from the target level, the unit cost of supplying the item decreases according to $C = 1.00 - 0.10(y-m)$, where C is the cost per unit, y is the out-of-stock percentage, and m is the target out-of-stock percentage.

How much variability from the target stocking percentage should the retailer allow?

11. Appraise the various methods by which a logistics sales-service relationship might be determined. Under what circumstances do you suppose one method might be more appropriate than another? If no sales-service relationship can reasonably be established, how might the logistician still go about designing the logistics system?

12. Discuss the extent of the effect that each order cycle element will have on logistics system design.

13. Outline some of the actions that a logistician might take in the event of a logistics system breakdown caused by the following:
    a. A warehouse fire
    b. A trucker strike
    c. A worker shortage for order processing and order filling
    d. A shortage of a key raw material for manufacturing
    e. The Internet-based transport management system is inoperative

14. Suggest how a product might be traced and what methods might be used to move the product back up the distribution channel in the following product recall situations:
    a. A defective part on an automobile
    b. A defective 27-inch television set
    c. A defective part in a space shuttle
    d. A defective software program for a microcomputer
    e. Contaminated drugs on the retail shelf

Chapter 5

Order Processing and Information Systems

The difference between mediocre and excellent logistics is often the firm's logistics information technology capabilities.

—DALE S. ROGERS, RICHARD L. DAWE, AND PATRICK GUERRA[1]

*T*he time needed to complete the activities of the order cycle is at the very heart of customer service. It has been estimated that the

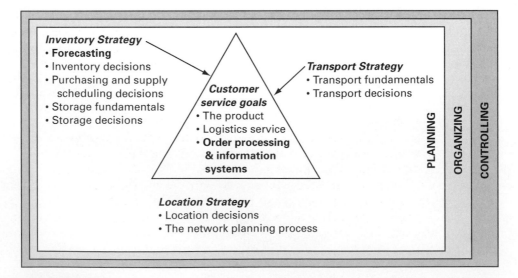

Inventory Strategy
• Forecasting
• Inventory decisions
• Purchasing and supply scheduling decisions
• Storage fundamentals
• Storage decisions

Customer service goals
• The product
• Logistics service
• Order processing & information systems

Transport Strategy
• Transport fundamentals
• Transport decisions

Location Strategy
• Location decisions
• The network planning process

PLANNING   ORGANIZING   CONTROLLING

[1]Dale S. Rogers, Richard L. Dawe, and Patrick Guerra, "Information Technology: Logistics Innovations for the 1990s," *Annual Conference Proceedings*, Vol. II (New Orleans, LA: Council of Logistics Management, 1991), p. 247.

activities associated with order preparation, transmittal, entry, and filling represent 50 to 70 percent of the total order cycle time in many industries.[2] Therefore, if a high level of customer service is to be provided through short and consistent order cycle times, it is essential that these order processing activities be carefully managed. Management begins with an understanding of the alternatives available for order processing.

Over the years, the cost of providing timely and accurate information throughout the supply chain has dropped dramatically, whereas the costs of labor and materials have risen. Because of this, there have been increasing efforts to substitute resources with information. For example, information has been used to replace inventories, thus reducing logistics costs. In addition to examining the management of order processing, we will explore logistics information systems, especially regarding how they have led to improved supply chain process management.

DEFINING ORDER PROCESSING

Order processing is represented by a number of the activities included in the customer order cycle (recall Figure 4-3). Specifically, they include order preparation, order transmittal, order entry, order filling, and order status reporting, as illustrated in Figure 5-1. The time required to complete each activity depends on the type of ordering involved. Order processing for a retail sale will likely be different from that of an industrial sale. We will build on knowledge developed in Chapter 4.

Order Preparation

Order preparation refers to the activities of gathering the information needed about the products and services desired and formally requesting the products to be purchased. It may involve determining an appropriate vendor, filling out an order form, determining stock availability, communicating order information by telephone to a sales clerk, or making selections from a Web site menu. This activity has benefited greatly from electronic technology, as illustrated next.

- We all are familiar with the bar code scanning of our grocery selections at the supermarket checkout. Such technology speeds order preparation by electronically gathering information about the requested item (size, quantity, and description) and presenting it to a computer for further processing.
- Many sellers now have Internet Web sites that provide extensive information about their products and even allow orders to be placed directly through the Web page. Products that are reasonably standardized (maintenance, repair, spare parts, etc.) are good candidates for ordering in this manner, but highly engineered products will eventually be ordered in this way as well.

---

[2]Bernard J. LaLonde and Paul H. Zinszer, *Customer Service: Meaning and Measurement* (Chicago: National Council of Physical Distribution Management, 1976), p. 119.

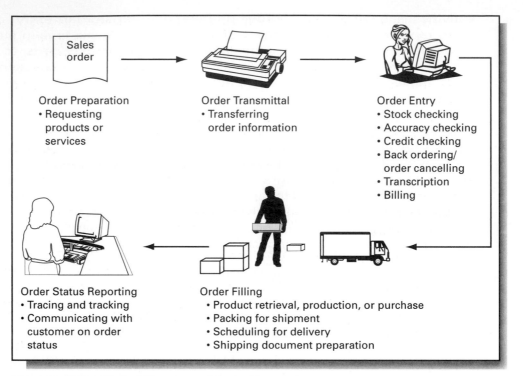

Figure 5-1 Typical Elements of Order Processing

- Some industrial purchase orders are generated directly by the company's computer, often in response to depleted inventory levels. By connecting buyer and seller computers through electronic data interchange (EDI) technology, paperless transactions are accomplished that lower order preparation costs and reduce order replenishment times.

Technology is eliminating the need to manually fill out order forms. Voice-actuated computers and wireless encoding of product information, called radio frequency and identification system (RF/ID), are new technologies that will further reduce the time for the order preparation phase of the customer's order cycle.

Order Transmittal

After order preparation, transmitting the order information is the next sequential activity of the order-processing cycle. It involves transferring the order request from its point of origin to the place where the order entry can be handled. Order transmission is accomplished in two fundamental ways: manually and electronically. Manual transmission can include the mailing of orders or the physical carrying of orders by the sales staff to the point of order entry.

Electronic transmission of orders is now very popular with the wide use of toll-free telephone numbers, data phones, Web sites on the Internet, EDI, facsimile machines, and satellite communications. This almost instantaneous transfer of order information, with its high degree of reliability and accuracy, increasing security, and ever decreasing cost, has nearly replaced manual order transmittal methods.

The time required to move order information in the order processing system can vary significantly, depending on the methods chosen. Sales personnel collection and drop-off of orders and mail transmission are perhaps the slowest methods. Electronic information transfer in its various forms, such as telephoning, electronic data interchange, and satellite communication, is the fastest. Speed, reliability, and accuracy are performance characteristics that should be balanced against the cost of any equipment and its operation. Determining the effects of performance on revenue remains the challenge here.

Observation

Currently, companies debate whether they should be using EDI or the Internet as the preferred method for managing order transmittal. EDI is the older of the two and refers to a dedicated electronic link between the computers of buyers and sellers. It is secure communication, but requires equipment and access to dedicated transmission lines. Transmission costs can be as high as $0.025 per 1,000 characters sent. By way of contrast, the Internet is a low-cost, widely available public forum that uses the standard network of the telephone system. Although improving, security can be an issue and should be the same at both ends of the transmission. There are no standards for the Internet as there can be for EDI. Message delivery is not guaranteed, and it can be longer than for EDI due to message routing protocols that cause delays. However, the modest cost for Internet communication comes from requiring only a local telephone call and the services of an Internet service provider, which can be as low a $10 per month. On balance, many companies have maintained and even expanded the use of EDI in light of the proliferation of Internet use. However, as the Internet technology improves and security is no longer a concern, EDI and Internet communications will merge and become indistinguishable.[3]

Order Entry

Order entry refers to many tasks that take place prior to the actual filling of an order. These include (1) checking the accuracy of the order information, such as item description and number, quantity, and price; (2) checking the availability of the requested items; (3) preparing back-order or cancellation documentation, if necessary; (4) checking the customer's credit status; (5) transcribing the order information as necessary; and (6) billing. These tasks are necessary because order request information is not always in the form needed for further processing, it may not be represented

---

[3]Stuart Sawabini, "EDI and the Internet," *Journal of Business Strategy* (January–February 2001), pp. 41–43; "EDI Delivers for USPS," *Traffic World* (January 11, 1999), p. 36; Tom Andel, "EDI Meets Internet. Now What?" *Transportation & Distribution* (June 1998), pp. 32–34, 38ff; and Curt Harler, "Logistics on the Internet: Freeway or Dead End?" *Transportation & Distribution* (April 1996), pp. 46–48.

| | METHOD OF DATA ENTRY | |
CHARACTERISTIC	KEYBOARD ENTRY	BAR CODE
Speed[a]	6 seconds	0.3 to 2 seconds
Substitution error rate	1 character error in 300 characters entered	1 character error in 15 thousand to 36 trillion characters entered
Encoding costs	High	Low
Reading costs	Low	Low
Advantages	Human	Low error rate
		Low cost
		High speed
		Can be read at a distance
Disadvantages	Human	Requires education of the user community
	High cost	Equipment cost
	High error rate	Dealing with missing or damaged images
	Low speed	

[a]Comparison of speed assumes encoding a 12-character field.
Source: Based on Craig Harmon, "Bar Code Technology As a Data Communications Medium," *Proceedings of the Council of Logistics Management*, Vol. I (St. Louis: October 27–30, 1985), p. 322.

Table 5-1 A Comparison of Data Entry Techniques

accurately, or additional preparation work may be needed before the order can be released for filling. Order entry may be accomplished by manually completing these tasks, or the steps may be fully automated.

Order entry has benefited greatly from technological improvements. Bar codes, optical scanners, and computers have substantially increased the productivity of this activity. Bar coding and scanning are especially important for entering order information accurately, quickly, and at low cost. In comparison with computer keyboard data entry, bar code scanning offers significant improvement (see Table 5-1). This likely explains the growing popularity of bar coding throughout retailing, manufacturing, and service industries.

Observation

Bar coding has been a key to controlling purchasing and inventory costs in large companies such as Wal-Mart and Home Depot. On the other hand, in the medical industry, where cost reduction is a prime concern and where $83 billion per year is spent on medical and surgical supplies, only one-half of all medical supplies are bar coded. It is estimated that $11 billion could be eliminated through improved supply chain practices.

Health care giants such as Columbia/HCA Healthcare and Kaiser Permanente have not been the leaders in bar coding. That distinction goes to St. Alexius Medical Center. Before St. Alexius installed its first scanners a decade ago, it couldn't account for as much as 20 percent of its supply costs. That figure has dropped to as low as 1 percent in some departments, and inventory costs have plummeted 48 percent, or a total of $2.2 million, over the past four years.[4]

Computers are also being used to an increasing extent in the order entry activity. They are replacing the manual stock and credit checking and transcription activities with more automated procedures. As a result, order entry takes only a fraction of the time to complete than it did only a few years ago.

Through the loading of the order-processing and -filling system, the method of order collection, restrictions on order size, and the timing of order entry affect order cycle time. Order design must be closely coordinated with sales order taking. For example, one order entry procedure might have sales personnel collecting orders while they check the trade. Order entry rules may require that the equivalent of a full truckload of order volume be collected by a salesperson before the order is forwarded to an order-processing point. Alternately, the procedures might be adjusted where the customer fills out a standard order form that is required to be mailed by a certain date in order to guarantee that the order will be delivered by a specified date. Further, a restriction might be imposed that only minimum order sizes will be accepted. This would ensure that very high transportation costs would not occur, especially if the supplying firm pays the freight. The revised order entry system might free up salespeople from a nonselling activity, allowing the orders from a large region to be consolidated for more efficient transport routing, and so improve the order-picking-loading patterns on the stocking facility.

Order entry might include the methods that are used to introduce the sales order into the order information system. The options might range from non-electronic transmission of the order information to electronic (computer) breakdown of the order information to ease order picking and processing.

Order Filling

Order filling is represented by the physical activities required to (1) acquire the items through stock retrieval, production, or purchasing; (2) pack the items for shipment; (3) schedule the shipment for delivery; and (4) prepare the shipping documentation. A number of these activities may take place in parallel with those of order entry, thus compressing processing time.

Setting order-filling priorities and the associated procedures affect the total order cycle time for individual orders. Too often, firms have not established any formalized rules by which orders are to be entered and dealt with during the initial stages of order filling. One company experienced significant delays in filling important customer orders when order clerks, during busy periods, would handle the less-complicated orders first. Priorities for processing orders may affect the speed with

---

[4]"Hospital Cost Cutters Push Use of Scanners to Track Inventories," *Wall Street Journal*, June 10, 1997, 1ff.

which all orders are processed or the speed with which the more important orders are handled. Some alternative priority rules might be the following:

1. First-received, first-processed
2. Shortest processing time
3. Specified priority number
4. Smaller, less-complicated orders first
5. Earliest promised delivery date
6. Orders having the least time before promised delivery date

Selection of a particular rule depends on such criteria as fairness to all customers, the differentiated importance among orders, and the overall speed of processing that can be achieved.

The process of order filling, either from available stock or from production, adds to the order cycle time in direct proportion to the time required for order picking, packing, or production. At times the order cycle time is extended by split-order processing or freight consolidation.

When product is not immediately available for order filling, a split order may occur. For stocked products, there is a reasonably high probability of incomplete order filling occurring, even when stocking levels are quite high. For example, if an order contains five items, each of which has as an in-stock probability of 0.90, the probability of filling the complete order (fill rate, FR) is

$$FR = (.90)(.90)(.90)(.90)(.90) = 0.59, \text{ or } 59\%$$

Therefore, partially filling the order from a backup source for the product is more likely than we might first think. As a result, additional order-processing time and procedures will be needed to complete the order.

Split deliveries and a large portion of any additional order information handling time can be avoided by simply holding the order until replenishment stocks for the out-of-stock items are available. This may adversely affect customer service to the point of being unacceptable. Therefore, the decision-making problem is one of trading off the added costs of the increased order information handling and the transportation costs with the benefits of maintaining the desired service level.

The decision to hold orders rather than fill and ship them immediately, for consolidating the order weight into larger but lower per-unit transport cost loads, does require more elaborate order-processing procedures. Increased complexity is a consequence since these procedures must be tied into delivery scheduling to achieve an overall improvement in order processing and delivery efficiency.

Order Status Reporting

This final order-processing activity ensures that good customer service is provided by keeping the customer informed of any delays in order processing or delivery of the order. Specifically, this includes (1) tracing and tracking the order throughout the entire order cycle; and (2) communicating with the customer about where the order may be in the order cycle and when it may be delivered. This monitoring activity does not affect the overall time to process an order.

Observation

Technology has played a major role in order status reporting. Companies such as FedEx and UPS have been leaders in being able to tell customers where their shipments are at any point between origin and destination. Laser-beam bar coding, a worldwide computer network, and specially designed software are key technological elements that drive their tracking systems. The information systems are so sophisticated that they can report who received the shipment and when and where. In addition to telephone support, shippers, armed with only the shipment number, can even track their shipments both nationally and internationally through the Internet.

Dell Computer uses and extends this technology to track an order for a computer from the time of order entry until it is received by the customer. Typical progress stages are order verification and credit checking, time waiting for components, manufacturing, staging for carrier pickup, and routing steps through the delivery process. Customers, knowing their order numbers, can check the order progress throughout the entire order cycle from the company's Web site, or call a customer service center via a toll-free telephone number.

ORDER PROCESSING EXAMPLES

The general activities involved in order processing have been identified, but they alone do not indicate how order processing works as a system. Such systems are illustrated through examples from a variety of settings.

Industrial Order Processing

A manual order-processing system is one that has a high component of human activity throughout the system. Some aspects of order processing may be automated or handled electronically, but manual activity will represent the largest portion of the order-processing cycle. Consider how a manufacturer selling to industrial customers designed its order-processing system.

Example

The Samson-Packard Company produces a full line of custom hose couplings, valves, and high-strength hose for industrial use. The company processes 50 orders per day on the average. The order-processing portion of the total order cycle time is 4 to 8 days out of 15 to 25 days. The total order cycle time is long, because orders are manufactured to customer specifications. The primary steps in the order-processing cycle, excluding the order filling activity, are the following:

1. Customer requests are entered into the order-processing system in two ways. First, salespeople collect orders from the field and mail or telephone them to

company headquarters. Second, customers take the initiative to mail or telephone their orders directly to headquarters. The customized nature of most customer orders precludes ordering through the company's Web site. Electronic data interchange (EDI) connection with most customers is not available.

2. Upon receipt of telephone orders, a customer service receptionist transcribes the order to an abbreviated order form. Along with the mailed-in orders, the orders accumulated for a given day are passed along to the senior customer service representative, who then tallies the information for the sales manager.

3. The sales manager reviews the order information to keep abreast of the sales activity. He also occasionally writes special notes of instruction on an order about the needs of a particular customer.

4. Next, the orders are sent to the order-preparation clerks, who transcribe the order information, along with special instructions, onto Samson-Packard's standard order form.

5. At this point, the orders are sent to the accounting department for credit checks. They are then forwarded to the sales department for price verification.

6. Next, the data processing department keys the order information into the computer to be used for transmission to the plant, for more convenient handling, and for easy tracing of the order once in process.

7. Finally, the senior customer service representative checks the order in its final form and transmits it via electronic transmission to the appropriate plant. In the same process, an order acknowledgment is prepared for the customer and e-mailed as order verification.

Retail Order Processing

Companies, such as retailers, that operate intermediate to vendors and customers frequently design their order-processing systems with at least a moderate degree of automation. Very quick order response time is usually not necessary, since there are inventories available for final consumers. These inventories act as a buffer against the indirect effects of the replenishment order cycle. However, replenishment order cycle times that help to maintain a fixed replenishment schedule are important.

Modern information systems have had the benefit of replacing many of the assets previously needed to run a business. Using the Internet, companies have been able to reduce warehouse space, lower inventory levels, reduce handling time, and better track order progress. Consider how a warehouse-free-distribution, direct-to-customer delivery system works.

Example

Finished goods distributors can use EDI to create a direct-from-supplier distribution system. The product does not need to be stored in a distributor's warehouse or on its shelves. Customers receive their goods directly from the supplier. As shown in Figure 5-2, the order information and products flow through the supply chain in the following way:

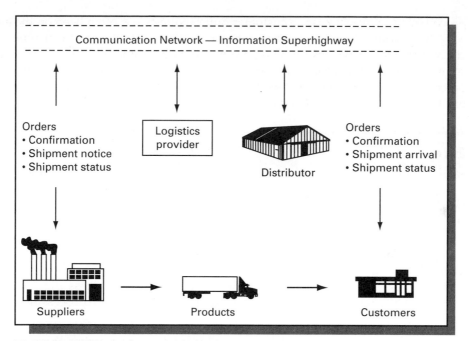

Figure 5-2 Direct-to-Customer Delivery Utilizing the Internet

1. The customers tell the distributor how much of which products are wanted and where via EDI.
2. The distributor tells the suppliers how much of which products must be shipped via EDI.
3. The distributor tells the logistics provider where to pick up product and how much via EDI.
4. The distributor tells the logistics provider how much of which products is to be delivered where and when via EDI.
5. The suppliers prepare the product for shipment.
6. The logistics provider picks up the product, and sorts and segregates the product to the distributor's specifications.
7. The logistics provider delivers the products to the customers.[5]

Customer Order Processing

Order-processing systems that are designed to interact directly with final consumers will be based on elevated levels of customer service. Meeting customer product requests from retail stocks provides almost instantaneous order processing. McDonald's has built a very successful food franchise business on fast order

---

[5]Information from http://www.skyway.com.

processing. Quick response to customer order requests has often been on the cutting edge of customer service for many companies that sell to the final consumer, especially when the products involved are highly substitutable. As the next example shows, some firms can provide quick response to customer orders even when their place of business is some distance from the customers who can acquire the same products from local retail outlets.

Example

Many remote discount computer hardware and software supply houses have sprung up as competitors to local retail stores. Traditionally, customers would drive to their local retail computer stores and purchase what they wanted on the spot, or, if out of stock, the retailers would in turn order the items from local distributors.

Computer supply houses located at one place in the country can offer customers low prices that result from low overhead and buying economies. However, overcoming location disadvantages is important if these discount houses are to be truly successful. Many have developed a strategy to compress the order cycle time, which usually involves the following steps in the order-processing chain of activities.

1. A customer calls in an order using a toll-free telephone number or enters the order through the company's Web site. Mail is also an option, but it substantially increases order transmittal time.
2. An order taker keys the order request into a computer terminal, or the customer has entered it electronically at the time of order placement. Inventory availability of the items is immediately checked from computerized inventory records, prices are found or calculated, and order charges are computed. If method of payment is by credit card, a credit check on the card is conducted electronically.
3. The order request is transmitted electronically to the warehouse to be filled, usually within the same day the order is received.
4. Normally, the order is shipped using UPS, FedEx, or another courier directly to the customer's home or place of business. Overnight delivery may be made for an increased charge, if requested by the customer.

The result is often a total order cycle time that is quicker *and* a price that is lower than what can be offered by local retailers.

Electronic commerce, once practiced by only a few firms such as Wal-Mart, General Motors, and Baxter International, is now becoming a reality for a great many companies. As the security issues are resolved on the Internet, the Internet becomes a driving force to eliminate much of the paperwork in order processing that occurs when one firm sells to another (B2B). E-commerce can reduce the cost of processing a purchase order by 80 percent. Figure 5-3 diagrams how a paperless order-processing system can work using the Internet as the point of order entry.

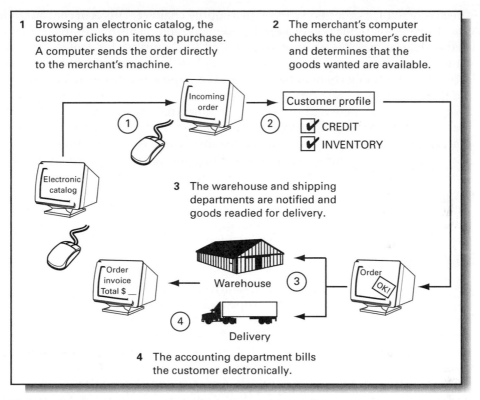

1 Browsing an electronic catalog, the customer clicks on items to purchase. A computer sends the order directly to the merchant's machine.

2 The merchant's computer checks the customer's credit and determines that the goods wanted are available.

Incoming order

Customer profile
☑ CREDIT
☑ INVENTORY

Electronic catalog

3 The warehouse and shipping departments are notified and goods readied for delivery.

Warehouse

Order invoice Total $ ___

Order OK!

Delivery

4 The accounting department bills the customer electronically.

Figure 5-3 Electronic Commerce Through the Internet

Source: "Invoice? What's an Invoice?" *Business Week*, June 10, 1996, pp. 110ff

Example

With its in-house computer expertise and a high-speed intranet, MIT has one of the most sophisticated purchasing systems anywhere. Staff can order pencils and test tubes by clicking through a Web-based catalog, which makes sure nobody spends more than they're authorized to spend. Payments are handled with purchasing cards through American Express. And MIT has contracted with two main suppliers— Office Depot, Inc., and VWR Corp.—to deliver most items within a day or two right to the purchaser's desk, not just a building's stockroom.[6]

Web-Based Channel Order Planning

The low cost of initiating and operating a Web site on the Internet makes it an attractive way for multiple parties to communicate with each other. The Web can be used

---

[6]"Invoice? What's an Invoice?" *Business Week*, June 10, 1996, p. 112.

effectively to plan order flows through a supply channel. This is in contrast to traditional supply planning where a product demand forecast is made, an efficient order size is determined, the order is transmitted to a supplier for replenishment, and after a lead-time period, inventories are replenished from which demand can be served. Each supply channel member (buyer, supplier, carrier, etc.) often operates independently by simply providing a portion of the information required for managing the product flow and responding to immediate requirements, such as filling the order, transporting it, or forecasting demand. If the Internet is integrated into the overall planning process, channel members can easily communicate with each other, share relevant information in real time, and respond quickly and often efficiently to shifts in demand, material shortages, transport delays, and order-filling inaccuracies. Order status is transparent, since all channel members can share a common database, which facilitates tracking and expediting. Low-cost access to the Internet encourages communication among channel partners, which further encourages coordination within the channel, leading to lower ordering costs and improved customer service.

The following example about McDonald's Japan is specific to a more formalized business model referred to as *CFPR®*, which stands for *collaborative planning, forecasting*, and *replenishment*. Under *CPFR*, supply channel members share information and comanage important business processes in their supply chains. By integrating demand and supply-side processes, *CPFR* will improve efficiencies, increase sales, reduce fixed assets and working capital, and reduce inventory for the entire supply chain, while at the same time satisfying consumer needs. *CPFR* promotes a holistic view of supply chain management. Impressive results from pilot studies on *CPFR* partnerships have been reported for Wal-Mart, Sara Lee, Branded Apparel, K-Mart, Kimberly Clark, Nabisco, Wegmans Supermarkets, Procter & Gamble, Hewlett Packard, and Heineken USA.[7]

Example

McDonald's Japan operates 3,800 restaurants, with annual sales of about $3.3 billion. More than 3 million customers visit the restaurants each day. There is substantial competition not only from other hamburger restaurants, but also from sushi and ramen (noodles) shops, as well as other sandwich places. The result is a downward pressure on prices and the implementation of many promotions. Traditional forecasting methods, such as time series forecasting, regression modeling, and focus forecasting, do not work well. McDonald's Japan had inventory excesses and shortages, high shipping costs from expedited and uneconomical order sizes, frequent order changes, and inefficient purchase quantities that were the result of poor forecasting of highly variable demand at the store level. As an alternative to store demand forecasting, McDonald's Japan established an information center built around the Internet, whereby stores, headquarters (marketing), distribution centers,

---

[7]Information found at www.cpfr.org; and Sam Dickey, "Forecasting and Ordering System Rides the 'Net,'" *Midrange Systems*, Vol. 10, No. 1 (January 17, 1997), p. 40.

Figure 5-4 Web-Based Order Processing at McDonald's Japan, Where Data Requirements and Order Planning Transcend Channel-Member Boundaries

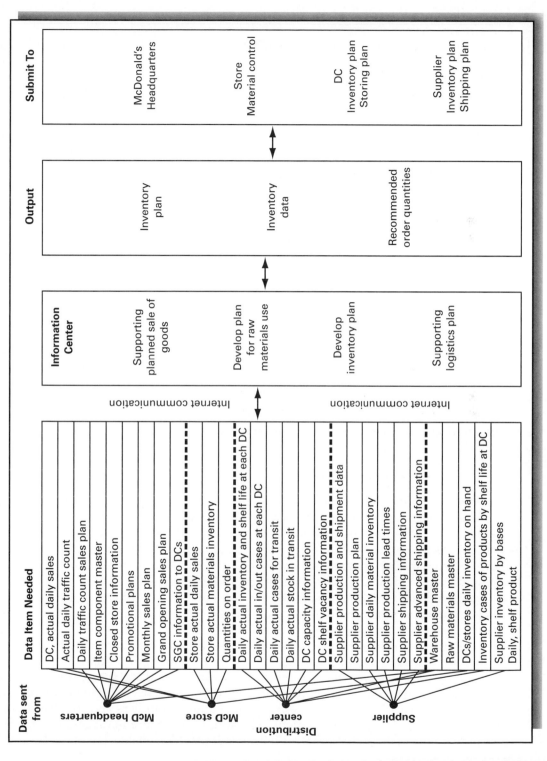

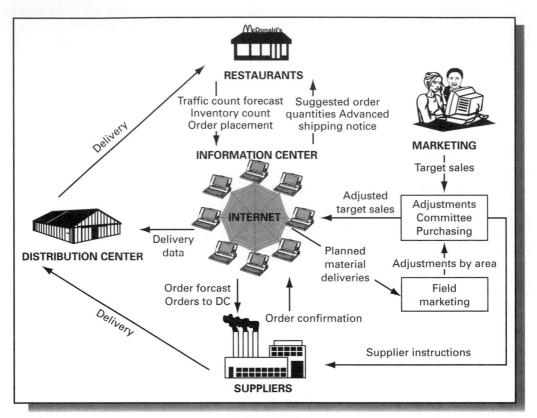

Figure 5-5 Web-Based Order Planning at McDonald's Japan

and suppliers would communicate and collaborate via the company's Web site to agree on expected sales quantities, order sizes, and supply replenishment delivery schedules.

Each channel member shares information to make the entire system operate smoothly and efficiently. As Figure 5-4 shows, the stores provide initial estimates of customer counts as well as actual sales, current inventory levels, and quantities on order. The distribution centers know quantities in transit, quantities on hand, shelf vacancy information, and the like. Suppliers provide information concerning production schedules, shipping schedules, and capacities. Finally, McDonald's marketing division offers the sales plan, timing of promotions, store expansions and closings, and the like. The information center acts as the hub for decision making, as shown in Figure 5-5.

The information center maintains the Internet servers and helps with the central planning of order quantities and their timing. However, online communication among all parties allows for quick response to unexpected changes in demand and supply, or to demand and supply that are inherently so variable that uncertainties must be countered with high inventory levels. This Web-based ordering system allows suppliers and the distribution centers to respond quickly and efficiently to store needs. Store managers can modify orders in real time up to a freeze date with the result that McDonald's Japan has been able to achieve a 50 percent reduction in the number of restaurant shipments and a 20 percent reduction in restaurant inventories. This may also mean that supplier production cost will be lowered as well. Improved communication in real time and the smoothing of product flow in the supply channel have been keys to these improvements.

OTHER FACTORS AFFECTING ORDER-PROCESSING TIME

Selection of the hardware and systems for order processing represent only part of the design considerations. There can be a number of factors to speed up or slow down processing time. These factors result from operating procedures, customer service policies, and transportation practices.

Processing Priorities

Some firms may prioritize their customer list as a way of allocating limited resources of time, capacity, and effort to the more profitable orders. In doing so, they will alter the order-processing times. High-priority orders may be given preferential processing, while low-priority orders may be held for later processing. In other firms, orders may be processed in the order in which they are received. Although the latter approach may seem fair to all customers, it is not necessarily so. It may result in longer processing times, on the average, for all customers as a class. Although there may not be stated order-processing priorities, tacit rules will always be in effect and may adversely affect order-processing times.

Example

A paper manufacturer had no stated priority in processing its orders from food chains for bags and wrapping papers; however, there was an implied order-processing priority. When the processing load became heavy, the order clerks would process the smaller, simpler orders first. The larger orders, which usually were the more profitable ones, were relegated to being processed last.

Parallel Versus Sequential Processing

In some cases, processing times may be significantly reduced by carefully arranging the order-processing tasks. The longest processing times can occur when all tasks are completed in sequence. By undertaking some tasks simultaneously, total processing time can be reduced. Recall the Samson-Packard Company illustration where all order-processing tasks were conducted *sequentially*. Just a simple change of creating multiple copies of an order so that the sales manager could review one copy while transcription and credit-checking activities were being completed on another would somewhat compress the order-processing time (*parallel* processing).

Order-Filling Accuracy

Being able to complete the order-processing cycle without introducing error into the customer's order request is likely to minimize processing time. It is probable that some errors will occur, but their numbers should be carefully controlled if order-processing time is a prime consideration in the company's operation.

Order Batching

Collecting orders from multiple customers into groups for batch processing may reduce processing costs. On the other hand, holding orders until the batch size is realized will likely add to processing time, especially for those orders entering the batch first.

Lot Sizing

A customer order may be too large to be filled from the stocks immediately on hand. Rather than waiting for the order to be completely produced, small lot sizes of the total order quantity may be produced and shipped. Rather than waiting for the complete order, the customer receives her order partially filled and has some of the ordered product available sooner. Although order-processing time may be improved for part of the order, transportation costs are likely to be higher due to shipping several orders of smaller size.

Shipment Consolidation

Much like order batching, orders may be held in order to create an economical shipment size. Consolidating several small orders to build a larger shipping volume reduces transportation costs. Processing time may be increased so that transportation cost may be decreased.

THE LOGISTICS INFORMATION SYSTEM

A logistics information system can be described in terms of its functionality and its internal operation.

Function

The major purpose for collecting, retaining, and manipulating data within a firm is to make decisions, ranging from strategic to operational, and to facilitate the transactions of the business. Larger computer memory space, faster computing, increased access to information throughout the organization from enterprise-wide information systems such as SAP, Oracle, Baan, PeopleSoft, and J. D. Edwards, and improved platforms for transmitting information such as EDI and the Internet have created the opportunity for firms to share information conveniently and inexpensively throughout the supply chain. More efficient logistics operations are possible from the benefits that timely and comprehensive information can provide within the firm, as well as from the benefits of sharing appropriate information among other channel members. This has led companies to think of information for logistics purposes as a logistics information system.

A logistics information system (LIS) can be represented as shown in Figure 5-6. The LIS should be comprehensive and capable enough to allow for communication not only between the functional areas of the firm (marketing, production, finance, logistics, etc.), but also between the members of the supply chain (vendors and customers). Sharing selected information about sales, shipments, production schedules, stock availability, order status, and the like with vendors and buyers has the value to reduce uncertainties throughout the supply chain as users find ways of benefiting from information availability. Of course, there will continue to be a reluctance to openly share information of a proprietary nature that may jeopardize a firm's competitive position. Even though the benefits of information sharing across enterprise boundaries are being recognized, there is likely to be a limit to how much information firms are willing to share with others outside of their control.

Figure 5-6
Overview of the Logistics Information System

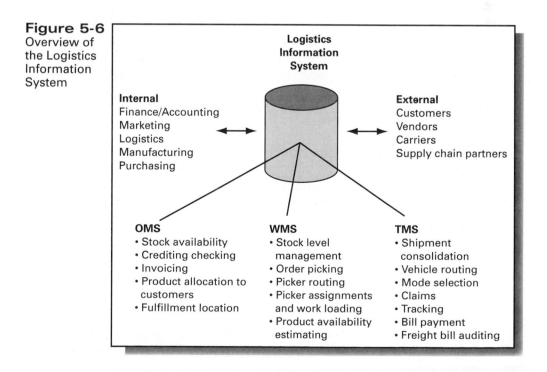

Logistics Information System

Internal
Finance/Accounting
Marketing
Logistics
Manufacturing
Purchasing

External
Customers
Vendors
Carriers
Supply chain partners

OMS
• Stock availability
• Crediting checking
• Invoicing
• Product allocation to customers
• Fulfillment location

WMS
• Stock level management
• Order picking
• Picker routing
• Picker assignments and work loading
• Product availability estimating

TMS
• Shipment consolidation
• Vehicle routing
• Mode selection
• Claims
• Tracking
• Bill payment
• Freight bill auditing

Within the LIS, the major subsystems are (1) an order management system (OMS), (2) a warehouse management system (WMS), and (3) a transportation management system (TMS). Each contains information for transactional purposes but also decision support tools that assist in planning the particular activity. Information flows between them as well as between the LIS and the firm's other information systems to create an integrated system. The information systems are typically expressed in the form of computer software packages.

The Order Management System

The order management subsystem (OMS) manages the initial contact with the customer at the time of product inquiries and order placement. It is the front-end system of the LIS. The OMS communicates with the warehouse management system to check product availability, either from inventories or from the production schedules. This provides information about the location of the product in the supply network, quantity available, and possibly the estimated time for delivery. Once product availability is acceptable to the customer, credit checking may occur whereby the OMS communicates with the company's financial information system to check customer status and verify credit standing. Once the order is accepted, the OMS will allocate the product to the customer order, assign it to a production location, decrement inventory, and when shipping has been confirmed, prepare an invoice.

The OMS does not stand in isolation from the other information systems of the firm. If the customer is to be served effectively, information must be shared. For example, if the OMS is to provide order tracking, the transportation management system will be interrogated. Communication compatibility is essential.

It should be noted that while the discussion has focused on the orders being received by a firm, there is a similar OMS for the purchase orders placed by the company. Whereas a customer-based OMS will maintain data oriented around the firm's customers, the purchase-based OMS will concentrate on the company's vendors, showing their delivery performance ratings, costs and terms of sale, capabilities, availabilities, and financial strength. Vendors are constantly monitored and reports prepared that assist in optimizing vendor selection.

The Warehouse Management System

The warehouse management system (WMS) may contain the OMS, or it may be treated as a separate entity within the LIS. The WMS must at least tie back to the OMS so the sales department knows what is available for sale. It is an information subsystem assisting in the management of product flowing through and stored in the facilities of the logistics network. The key elements can be identified as (1) receiving, (2) putaway, (3) inventory management, (4) order processing and retrieving, and (5) shipment preparation. All of these elements will appear in the WMS of a typical distribution warehouse, but some may not be present in warehouses used primarily for long-term storage or those having very high turnover.

Receiving. This is the entry or "check-in" point for information into the WMS. Product is off-loaded from the receiving carrier at the warehouse's inbound dock and identified by product code and quantity. Data about the product are entered into the

WMS using bar code scanners, radio frequency (RF) data communication terminals, or manual keyboards. Weight, cube, and package configuration of the product are known by matching the product code against an internal product file.

Putaway. The incoming product needs to be temporarily stored within the warehouse. The WMS retains the space layout within the building and the inventory stored in the locations. Based on available space and stock layout rules, the WMS assigns the incoming product to a specific location for later retrieval. If multiple products are to be stored in multiple locations on the same trip, the WMS can specify the putaway sequence and route to minimize travel time. The stock level at each affected location is incremented and the inventory location record is adjusted.

Inventory management. The WMS monitors the product levels at each stocking location in the warehouse. If inventory levels are under the local control of the warehouse, then the replenishment quantities and timing are suggested according to specified rules. The request for replenishment is transmitted to the purchasing department or directly to vendors or company plants through EDI or the Internet.

Order processing and retrieving. Planning for stock retrieval in the warehouse, that is, picking the items requested on an order, is perhaps the most valuable aspect of the WMS. Stock retrieval is the most labor intensive and usually the most expensive part of warehouse operations.

The WMS, with its internal decision rules, will, upon receiving an order, decompose the order into item groups that require different types of processing and picking. Items will be grouped according to the location where inventory is stored. Some items require picking in small, split case quantities, whereas others are picked in full-case or pallet-load quantities. Still others may be picked from separate, secured areas of the warehouse. Each area has different picking characteristics to the extent that it is inefficient to simply pick the order in its entirety in one pass through the warehouse. The WMS splits the order judiciously for efficient order picking and schedules the order flow through the various areas of the warehouse so that the items arrive at the shipping dock as a complete order and in the proper sequence with other orders to be loaded onto a truck or railcar for delivery.

In addition, the WMS subdivides the items within an order-picking area among the order pickers to balance picker workload. Then, items assigned to a particular worker are sequenced for picking to minimize distance traveled, bending and fatigue, and picking time.

Shipment preparation. Orders are often picked in waves through the warehouse, meaning that from among all orders, a subset will be processed at one time. The size of this order subset and the orders within it are selected based on shipment considerations. Orders for customers located within the same proximity are picked simultaneously to arrive at the shipping dock and truck stall at the same time. Estimates are made of cube and weight of the multiple customer orders to be placed on a truck, container, or rail car. Color-coding the merchandise flowing from the different areas of the warehouse aids in assembling the merchandise common to an order and sequencing it onto the delivery vehicle for most efficient routing. In the case of retail merchandise, price tags may be affixed so that the items may be placed on retail shelves without further handling.

Overall, the WMS aids managing warehouse operations in the form of labor planning, inventory-level planning, space utilization, and picker routing. The WMS shares information with the OMS and TMS to achieve integrated performance.

Example

A large drug store chain receives weekly orders from several hundred of its retail stores, or about 50 orders per day in a particular warehouse. A local warehouse supplies stores with general merchandise. Pharmaceuticals are supplied from a centralized warehouse. Upon receipt of the orders at company headquarters, the orders are split between the two product categories. Pharmaceutical orders are filled first and shipped to the local warehouse, to be merged with the general merchandise part of the order going to the same store. Then, at the local warehouse, orders are further split into items that are picked from split-case, full-case, bonded (secured), and bulk areas. Since about 8,000 of the 12,000 items stocked in the warehouse require picking from split-case areas, good management of this labor-intensive area is essential. To do this, the portion of the items in the split-case picking area is further subdivided for each order picker. The order picker processes only those items in his or her immediate zone. The picking sequence of the items is established from the routing rules within the WMS.

The WMS controls the timing for the start of picking in all the areas of the warehouse so that the elements of the order arrive at the shipping dock at approximately the same time. Identifying stickers are placed on the cartons and tote boxes so that the complete order may be assembled at the shipping dock for loading onto a delivery truck that will ultimately contain as many as five separate store orders.

Every time stock replenishment merchandise from vendors is received, information about the incoming products is then entered into the WMS. The WMS then assigns the product to storage locations and maintains a record of the age of the product to control retrieval sequencing.

The Transportation Management System

The transportation management system (TMS) focuses on the inbound and outbound transportation of a firm and is an integral part of the LIS, as shown in Figure 5-6. Like the WMS, it shares information with other LIS components, such as order content, item weight and cube, quantity, promised delivery date, and vendor shipping schedules. Its purpose is to assist in the planning and controlling of the firm's transportation activity. This involves (1) mode selection, (2) freight consolidation, (3) routing and scheduling shipments, (4) claims processing, (5) tracking shipments, (6) and freight bill payment and auditing. A particular firm's TMS may not contain all of these elements. Each activity will be discussed in light of informational requirements and decision assistance provided by the TMS.

Mode selection.   Many firms transport in multiple shipment sizes that result in multiple freight services to consider. Transport service choices typically range from small airfreight and ground package carriers to ocean container and rail carload movements. The TMS can match shipment size with transport service cost and performance requirements, especially where there are competing choices involved. A good TMS will store data on multiple modes, freight rates, expected shipment times, mode availability, and service frequency and will suggest the best carrier for each shipment.

Freight consolidation.   A very valuable function for the TMS is to suggest the patterns for consolidating small shipments into larger ones. Since a primary characteristic of freight rates is that unit shipping costs drop disproportionately as shipment size increases, shipment consolidation can result in substantial transport cost savings, especially when shipment sizes are small. The TMS can keep track of, in real time, shipment sizes, destinations, and promised delivery dates. From this information and using internal decision rules, economical loads can be built while considering delivery service goals.

Routing and scheduling shipments.   When a firm owns or leases a fleet of vehicles, careful management is required to ensure that the fleet is operated efficiently. With order information from the OMS and order-processing information from the WMS, the TMS assigns loads to vehicles and suggests the sequence in which the vehicle stops should be made. Time windows during which stop offs can be made, pickup of returning merchandise from the stop off points, planning for back hauls, driver restrictions on length of driving and rest breaks, and utilization of the fleet across multiple time periods all need to be considered. The TMS retains data on stop locations; vehicle type, number, and capacity; stop loading/unloading times; stop time windows; and other restrictions on the route. Given this background information, shipments to be made in the current period are planned using decision rules or algorithms imbedded in the TMS.

Claims processing.   It is inevitable in transportation that some shipments will be damaged. By retaining such information as shipment content, product value, carrier used, origin and destination, and liability limits, many claims can be processed automatically or with minimal human intervention.

Tracking shipments.   Information system technology has played a major role tracking the progress of shipments once they have been transferred to transport carriers. Bar coding, radio transmission en route, global positioning systems, and on-board computers are key information system elements that allow the location of shipments to be known in real time. Tracking information from the TMS can then be made available to the shipments' receivers through the Internet or other electronic means. Even estimates of arrival times can be calculated.

    The small-shipment carriers such as DHL, Airborne Express, FedEx and UPS are at the forefront in such information system development, since it is customer satisfaction that they sell. Guaranteed delivery service is often promised, and a sophisticated shipment tracking system helps fulfill the goal.

Application

Federal Express bar codes every shipping document with a unique number for easy and rapid identification of a package throughout its journey. The bar code is scanned at the point of entering the delivery system, at sorting, during delivery, and at the destination point. Installed in the delivery trucks are small computers that accept radio communications. This allows the trucks to be routed for pickups and deliveries, as well as to serve as a data input point for information about shipment and truck location. The delivery agent carries a handheld scanner that reads the shipment number at the time of pickup or delivery. The scanning device, with its coded information, can be plugged into the truck's on-board computer and read into the database of the company's transportation information system.

Satellite communication and global positioning systems represent the latest technologies to be integrated into tracking systems. In just-in-time systems, where uncertainties in shipment arrivals can cause serious consequences for production operations, navigational satellites are being used to identify the exact location of truckload shipments as they move through the distribution pipeline and to maintain real-time communication with drivers to report breakdowns and delays, and to estimate arrival times.

Application

A contract trucking company is now using a two-way mobile satellite communication and position-reporting system to monitor the location of its trucks in order to improve performance under just-in-time programs. The heart of the system is a small in-truck computer that is able to communicate with a navigational satellite. The satellite can pinpoint the geographical location of the truck anywhere. Messages between drivers and headquarters may be exchanged without the need of telephone communication.

Freight bill payment and auditing.   Determining the freight charges for shipments can be complicated because of the many exceptions that can be placed on freight rates. Since carriers charge only the lowest applicable rate, when a rating error occurs, the shipper can make a claim on the carrier for the difference between the actual charges and the lowest charges. It is the responsibility of the shipper (party purchasing the transportation service) to audit freight bills for these errors and apply for a rebate from the carrier. Freight bill auditing can be a labor-intensive activity due to the large number of routes and rate combinations. The computer-based TMS can quickly search for the minimum cost routing and compare the cost to that on the freight bill.

Freight bill payment can also be facilitated in the TMS. Rather than a decision-assisting use of the TMS, bill payment is a transactional activity. Here the TMS records that shipment has been made and requests the company's financial information system to execute payment to the carrier, often electronically.

Only a limited description of the LIS and its components can be provided since the features vary with the needs of a particular application. For example, some warehouse management systems might further include radio frequency control of all tasks, standards and performance measures, stock cycle counting, and dock scheduling, to name a few. The TMS might include mode selection, routing of full vehicle loads, and performance measurement of carriers. However, some of the fundamental capabilities of the LIS have been discussed that illustrate how information technology is having an impact on the planning and control of operations.

Internal Operation

From the viewpoint of internal operation, a logistics system can be represented schematically, as shown in Figure 5-7. Note three distinct elements that make up the system: (1) the input, (2) the database and its associated manipulation, and (3) the output. Figure 5-8 further highlights the data elements of the system.

Figure 5-7
Operating
Components of the
Logistics Information
System

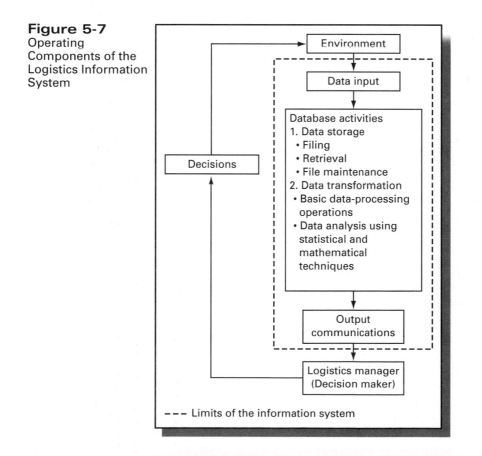

Environment

Data input

Database activities
1. Data storage
   • Filing
   • Retrieval
   • File maintenance
2. Data transformation
   • Basic data-processing
     operations
   • Data analysis using
     statistical and
     mathematical
     techniques

Decisions

Output
communications

Logistics manager
(Decision maker)

- - - Limits of the information system

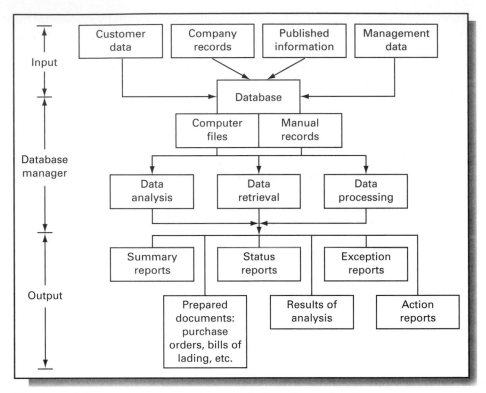

Figure 5-8 Exploded View of the Logistics Information System

The Input

The first activity associated with the information system is acquiring the data that will assist the decision-making process. After carefully identifying those data items needed for planning and operating the logistics system, the data can be obtained from many sources, notably, (1) customers, (2) company records, (3) published data, and (4) management. Customers, through their sales activity, indirectly provide much useful data for planning. During order entry, data are captured that are useful for forecasting and operating decisions, such as sales volume, and its timing, location of sales, and order size. Similarly, data about shipment sizes and transportation costs are obtained from deliveries made to customers. Freight bills, purchase orders, and invoices are additional sources of this type of primary data.

Company records, in the form of accounting reports, status reports, reports from internal and external studies, and various operating reports, provide a wealth of data. Data from these reports are usually not organized in any meaningful way for logistics decision-making purposes. Selected data items are captured by the information system to be manipulated in a later stage.

Published data from external sources represent a unique source of data. Much data are available from federally sponsored research, research sponsored by trade associations, data sharing through the Internet and EDI, and suppliers who will provide valuable data just for the goodwill that such sharing creates. Professional journals and trade magazines are additional examples. This type of external data tends to be broader and more generalized than internally generated data.

Company personnel can also be a valuable source of data. Predictions of future sales levels, actions of competition, and the availability of purchased materials are just a few of the examples. These types of data are not so much maintained in company files, computer records, or libraries as they are in the human mind. Company personnel such as management, internal consultants and planners, and activity specialists are close to data sources and become good data sources themselves.

Observation

The computer has brought about new sources of data not previously available and has led to significant improvements in operations. Sears, Roebuck & Co. is a significant retailer of major household appliances, of which it makes nearly 4 million home deliveries annually. Because customers may purchase such goods only every 10 to 15 years, delivery patterns rarely repeat. Historically, Sears' personnel would manually match customer addresses to geocodes. For example, for Ontario, California, the process would take two hours with a 55 percent "hit rate." Using address-matching computer software, the process there now takes 20 minutes with a "hit rate" of over 90 percent.[8]

Database Management

Converting data to information, portraying it in a manner useful for decision making, and interfacing the information with decision-assisting methods are often considered to be at the heart of an information system. Management of the database involves selection of the data to be stored and retrieved, choice of the methods of analysis to include, and choice of the basic data processing procedures to implement.

After determining the content of the database, the first concern in database design is to decide which data should be maintained in traditional hard copy form, the data to be retained in computer memory for quick access, and the data not to be retained on any regular basis. Data maintenance can be expensive and data retention in any form should be based on (1) how critical the information is for decision making; (2) the rapidity of information retrieval; (3) the frequency of data access; and (4) the effort required for manipulating the data into the form needed. Information needed for infrequent strategic planning often does not require immediate access. Information for more frequent operations planning has just the opposite characteristics. A traffic clerk who recalls a freight rate from the computer storage records, or the customer service representative who checks the status of an order through the firm's order-tracking system, takes advantage of these basic storage and online/real-time retrieval capabilities of the information system.

---

[8]"Logistics and Distribution Moves Toward 21st Century," *ARC News*, Vol. 18, No. 2 (Summer 1996), pp. 1–2.

Data processing is one of the oldest and most popular features of an information system. When computers were first introduced into the business community, it was for the purpose of reducing the burdens of computing invoices for thousands of customers and preparing accounting records. Now, preparation of purchase orders, bills of lading, and freight bills is a common data processing activity to aid the logistician in planning and controlling materials flow. Data processing, or transactional, activities represent relatively simple and straightforward conversion of the data in the files to some more useful form. This transactional activity was the dominant feature of the ERP (enterprise resource planning) software systems by SAP, i2, Oracle, and others so popular with companies over the past decade.

Data analysis is the most sophisticated and newest use made of the information system. The system may contain any number of mathematical and statistical models, both general and specific to the firm's particular logistics problems. Such models convert information into problem solutions that provide decision support. Planning picker routing in a high turnover warehouse, routing delivery trucks, and allocating customers to warehouses and plants are examples of decisions that can be assisted by the mathematical tools imbedded within the information system. What started as essentially transactional systems, the ERP software systems are now adding decision-support modules to enhance their capabilities.

The Output

The final element of the information system is the output segment. This is the interface with the user of the system. The output is generally of several types and transmitted in several forms. First, the most obvious output is some form of report such as (1) summary reports of cost or performance statistics; (2) status reports of inventories or order progress; (3) exception reports that compare desired performance with actual performance; and (4) reports (purchase orders or production orders) that initiate action. Second, the output may be in the form of prepared documents such as transportation bills of lading and freight bills. Finally, the output may be the result of data analysis from mathematical and statistical models.

The input, a database management capability, and the output are the key features of the internal operation of the LIS. In addition to basic transactional capabilities, the major purpose of the system is to be a decision-support tool for planning and operating the logistics system.

INFORMATION SYSTEM EXAMPLES

In practice, information systems to assist supply chain planning and operation appear within companies in a number of ways. Several examples will help to illustrate them.

A Retail System

Some firms with extensive retail operations have developed elaborate information systems to speed checkout (improve customer service) as well as to increase the efficiency of stocking and replenishing the many items typically offered customers (lower costs).

The high transaction volume routinely handled and the high inventory turnover that retailers like to achieve has led them to use computers and the latest order-handling technology to realize their goals.

Application

A major retailer of general merchandise sells through nearly 1,000 stores. The logistics system alone involves 200,000 items flowing from over 20,000 suppliers. The company strategy is to make every store a profit center. This means that stocking decisions from over 40,000 merchandising departments need to be made at the store level. At the same time, purchasing is centralized.

The information system designed to support this decentralized management philosophy involved installing registers in stores with optical scanning capability to read bar codes on merchandise tickets. With minicomputers at stores and mainframe computers at more centralized locations, store sales activity can be captured instantly. The system offers a number of benefits including faster checkouts, more optimal inventory control, faster credit checking, instant stock status reporting, and better planning of purchase quantities and their timing.

The operation of the system is schematically diagrammed in Figure 5-9. The first step is receipt of the product from the warehouse or supplier. Suppose that the product is a coffeemaker. An automatic ticket maker produces a ticket that indicates the coffeemaker's color, price, stock number, and the clerk's department number. When a customer takes the coffeemaker to the register, the clerk scans the ticket with a reading wand or keys product information into the register.

If the customer wants to pay with a credit card, the wand picks up a magnetic code and, in less than a second, clears the card through the store's minicomputer. The coffeemaker's data are stored in the minicomputer until the end of the business day. Then, they are automatically transferred to one of the company's 22 regional data centers, where larger mainframe computers process the information. There, the customer's credit account is charged, sales and tax figures are entered into the accounting department's records, and the sales clerk's commission record is sent to the payroll department.

Sales data also enter the coffeemaker department's inventory-management system. If the day's coffeemaker sales lower the department's inventory below a predetermined point, the computer automatically prints a purchase order, which is sent to the department manager the next morning. If the manager decides to buy more coffeemakers, the reorder goes by EDI to the supplier who fills it.

At the same time, the sales data are channeled through the regional data center to a central data processing station at company headquarters, where national unit-sale information is compiled.

Vendor-Managed Inventory

When retailers managed inventory, one of the methods for inventory control was to use some form of a trigger-point method replenishment program. That is, when an

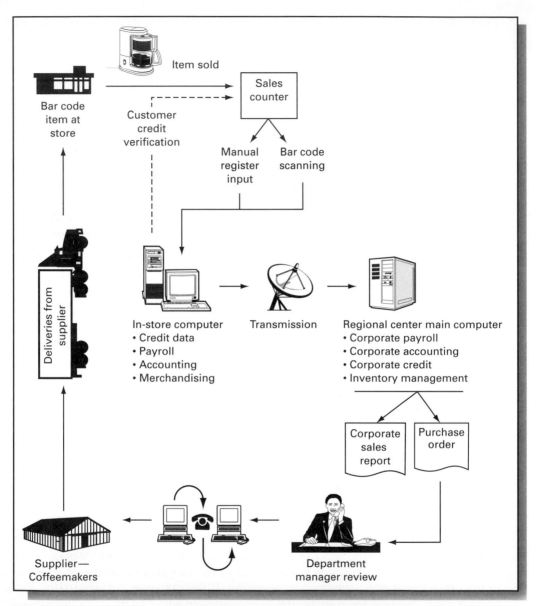

Figure 5-9 Information System for a Large Merchandise Retailer

item in stock is depleted to the level of the trigger-point quantity, a purchase order is placed on a vendor to replenish the item. In such systems, retailers make their own forecasts and inventory-control rules. Alternately, retailers will replenish on a fixed cycle (e.g., once per week) and order an amount to fill designated shelf space for an item. According to the International Mass Retail Association, over 60 percent of hard goods and almost 40 percent of soft goods are under replenishment programs managed by retailers.[9]

Although retailer-managed replenishment programs are expected to continue, there is also expected to be a substantial growth in vendor-managed inventories (VMI), that is, continuous replenishment. With electronic data interchange and point-of-sale data, vendors can be as aware of what is on the retailer's shelf as the retailer itself. Retailers such as Wal-Mart and Toys "Я" Us allow the vendors to be in charge of their own inventory, deciding what and when to ship. Ownership of the inventory generally shifts to the retailer once the product is received, although some retailers would like to reach the point where they don't even own the goods sitting on their shelves. The increased availability of information is permitting new alternatives for managing the flow of goods in the supply channel to emerge.

Vendors require that their customers supply them with information about product sales, current inventory levels, dates for receipt of goods, and dead stock and returns. Information flows to the vendor through an EDI or other electronic network so that it is up-to-date at all times. Vendors sometimes incur greater costs for VMI, for example, by absorbing the transportation costs, but feel that the additional costs are covered by increased sales that are realized from the use of VMI.

Application

Western Publishing is making VMI work in its Golden Book lines. Western, a publisher of children's books, develops a relationship with its retailers in which these retailers give Western point-of-sale data. The point-of-sale information provides the publisher with the remaining inventory at the retailer that is then compared with a fixed reorder point quantity. Inventory levels below the reorder point automatically trigger a replenishment order. Ownership of the inventory shifts to the retailer once the product is shipped. The sharing of point-of-sale information is the key to making continuous replenishment work in a timely and efficient manner.

E-Commerce

For many companies, e-commerce, which uses the Internet to facilitate business transactions, is an extension of the traditional way warehouses and retail stores conduct business. In contrast to start-up Web companies, which typically own no logistics infrastructure and ship directly from vendors using for-hire transportation, established companies have inventories, warehouse space, transportation capabilities, and logistics expertise. With the addition of a Web site for entering customer orders, established companies may append and integrate Web orders with their existing logistics operations. Others may separate the Web order operations from internal operations and even seek outside support of a third-party logistics provider, arguing that the customer requirements are sufficiently different to warrant such a

---

[9]Tom Andel, "Manage Inventory, Own Information," *Transportation and Distribution* (May 1996), p. 58.

separation. However, we can expect to see that whether orders enter through a Web site or through the sales desk, serving them logistically will not show the marked differences as seen in the past, when e-commerce was new and novel.

Application

Lowe's, the large do-it-yourself home improvement retailer, turned to NFI Interactive as a third-party provider to service its online customers when it began offering its products through the Internet. NFI uses the warehouse management system (WMS) software of All Points Systems to run operations for Lowe's in its 425,000-square-foot Atlanta, Georgia, warehouse, 205,000 square feet of which is being utilized by Lowe's.

Every 15 or 20 minutes, orders from the Web site are downloaded to the WMS. An inventory reserve is put on the ordered items until the customer's credit is verified. From there, the system chooses a parcel delivery method (FedEx, UPS, less-than-truckload, etc.) and orders are released to workers on the warehouse floor.

Product is scanned into and out of inventory using handheld and vehicle-mounted computers. Warehouse order picking is organized according to wave, postal code, order size, and ship-by date or time. Once orders are packed, boxes are conveyed to the Quantronix CubiScan system for sizing and weighing. Then, the appropriate shipping label is generated using Zebra Technologies' printers, and the goods head for their final destination.[10]

A Decision Support System

Dispatching trucks to replenish gasoline supplies at auto service stations is a logistics-planning problem that can be aided by a well-designed information system. Incorporating methods into the information system that can analyze data as well as organize and present it can support the user in making important decisions. Data analysis methods can take the form of optimizing procedures. In the well-designed information system, the user not only can call upon the system to provide an initial answer to the decision problem, but can also interact with the system to provide his or her inputs to realize a more practical solution to the problem than the optimizing procedures alone can offer.

Application

Every day throughout the country, a major oil company makes thousands of gasoline and diesel fuel deliveries. Each day's delivery problem is different as customer mix, volumes, and product mix change. The use of a mathematical programming model to help make the dispatching decisions reduces the number of trucks needed to make deliveries and the total miles traveled by them.

---

[10]Rick Gurin, "Lowe's Gets to Know Online Distribution," *Frontline Solutions*, Vol. 2, No. 3 (March 2001), p. 46.

The order information inputs to the TMS are not noteworthy since speed is not critical in this application. Once the order information is received from service stations, the order request information is directed to the regional distribution terminal that will fill the order and deliver it. It is first displayed on a computer screen for the dispatcher. He or she previews the orders and separates those having obvious delivery patterns due to large shipment volumes or special delivery requirements. Next, the remaining orders are submitted to the decision-assisting model within the TMS. The model provides an optimized route and schedule for each order and the truck on which it should travel. Finally, interacting with the displayed routes on the computer screen, the dispatcher reviews the schedule and adjusts it as necessary. The TMS then prepares a printed schedule for each driver.

CONCLUDING COMMENTS

Recall that the order cycle can be defined as the time elapsed between the point when the customer prepares an order to the point when the order is received. Order-processing activities can represent most of the time in the customer's total order cycle time. Therefore, managing the activities of the order-processing component of the total order cycle is critical to the level of customer service to be achieved. This is perhaps even more essential, considering customers' continuing desire to compress total order cycle time.

The five key elements of order processing include (1) order preparation; (2) order transmittal; (3) order entry; (4) order filling; and (5) order status reporting. The first three elements have been particularly subject to technological improvements, including bar code scanning, computerized order handling, and electronic communication. For firms using such technology, order preparation, transmittal, and entry can be reduced to almost an insignificant portion of the total order cycle time.

The logistics information system may be decomposed into the order management system (OMS), the warehouse management system (WMS), and the transportation management system (TMS). The transactions and planning decisions associated with each are generally supported with significant computer software programs that greatly assist in making the repetitive decisions required of daily operations. The OMS, WMS, and TMS, while focusing on different aspects of logistics operations, communicate with each other for better overall control of logistics processes. To the extent that timely information for logistics managers will continue to replace assets in the business, we can expect an expanding scope and increasing sophistication in the design of information systems. Logistics information systems show the benefits of the information technology revolution.

QUESTIONS

1. A manufacturer of men's and women's sportswear will distribute its Hong Kong–made products to markets in the United States and Europe. The primary outlets will be small retail stores and some department stores. Suggest several designs for handling order processing. What might be the relative costs and benefits of each?

2. What benefits are there to using bar codes and scanners for order entry as opposed to keyboard encoding into a computer database? Are there any disadvantages?

3. Review the Samson-Packard Company example given beginning on page 137, and suggest how you might compress the order processing time through the sequencing of the activities and the use of technology.

4. In the following situations, indicate the effect on order processing time of (1) processing priorities; (2) parallel versus sequential processing; (3) order-filling accuracy; (4) order batching; and (5) shipment consolidation:
   a. Patients seeking services at a medical clinic
   b. Purchasing sheet steel from a steel manufacturer for use in auto body manufacture
   c. Customers waiting in lunchtime lines at McDonald's restaurants
   d. A supermarket placing stock replenishment orders to their supplying warehouses

5. A logistics manager for a television producer in South Korea has been given the responsibility for setting up a logistics information system for his company. How would you answer his questions below?
   a. What types of information do I want from the information system? Where would I obtain the information?
   b. Which items in the information database should I retain in the computer for easy access? How should I handle the remainder?
   c. What types of decision problems would the information system help me address?
   d. What models for data analysis would be most useful in dealing with these problems?

6. For the following companies, suggest the types of data that should be collected to plan and control their supply chains:
   a. A hospital
   b. A city government
   c. A tire manufacturer
   d. A retailer of general merchandise
   e. An ore-mining company
   For each of these, what tools for information analysis do you think should be included in the logistics information system?

7. A toy manufacturer is planning a vendor-managed inventory program with one of its retailers, Toys "Я" Us. To operate such a program, what information should the retailer provide to the toy manufacturer? Describe how each information element will be used.

8. Discuss the impact that order-processing priority rules can have on total order-processing time. Under what circumstances would you prefer to process orders according to the first-received, first-processed versus shortest processing time rule?

9. Suppose that you work for a company that sells automotive repair parts and are put in charge of developing an e-commerce strategy for the firm. A Web site is prepared to promote and provide information about the product line, and to

accept orders online. How will you plan for order fulfillment, that is, order processing, inventory management, warehousing, shipment preparation, and delivery? What information systems technology might be useful for carrying out these activities?

10. The OMS, WMS, and TMS make up a logistics information system (LIS).
   a. Describe the data elements and decision-support tools that should be in the LIS for (i) a fast food retailer such as Burger King or Pizza Hut, (ii) an auto manufacturer such as General Motors, Toyota, or Fiat, and (iii) a service organization such as the Red Cross.
   b. To form an integrated LIS, what types of data should be shared among the OMS, WMS, and TMS to form an effective logistics information system?

11. A manufacturer of digital cameras and other photographic equipment sells these items through a network of retailers. Several plants located around the world produce the products that are shipped to warehouses, where the products are held as inventory used to supply the retailers. Products are scheduled to go to production based on orders from the warehouses. Warehouses stock products based on anticipated orders from retailers. Retailers reorder for their in-store inventories based on the sales forecasts for their local territories. Trucking is used to move products throughout the supply channel (plant-warehouse-retail store). Uncertainties in the supply channel result from missed forecasts, transport delays, changed production schedules, unanticipated product promotions, and inaccurate inventory counts.

Using the Internet and the company's Web site, design an ordering system that is an alternative to the current ordering approach. Suggest the type of information that each channel member should supply, how ordering decisions should be made, how uncertainties are to be handled, and what the overall advantages might be to Web-based ordering compared with the current ordering system.

Chapter 6

Transport Fundamentals

> *When the Chinese write the word crisis, they do so in two characters—one meaning danger, the other opportunity.*

> —ANONYMOUS

*T*ransportation usually represents the most important single element in logistics costs for most firms. Freight movement has been observed to absorb between one-third and two-thirds of total logistics costs.[1] Thus, the logistician needs a good understanding of transportation matters. Although a comprehensive discussion of transportation is not possible

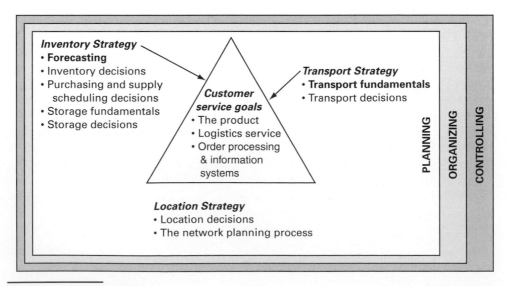

---
[1]Recall Table 1-3 on page 14.

within the scope of this text, this chapter highlights what is essential to the logistician for his or her managerial purposes.

The focus is on the facilities and services that make up the transportation system and on the rates (costs) and performance of the various transport services that a manager might select. Specifically, we wish to examine the characteristics of the transportation service alternatives that lead to optimal performance. It is performance that the user buys from the transportation system.

IMPORTANCE OF AN EFFECTIVE TRANSPORTATION SYSTEM

One needs only to contrast the economies of a "developed" nation with those of a "developing" one to see the part that transportation plays in creating a high level of economic activity. It is typical in the developing nation that production and consumption take place in close proximity, much of the labor force is engaged in agricultural production, and a low proportion of the total population lives in urban areas. With the advent of inexpensive and readily available transportation services, the entire structure of the economy changes toward that of developed nations. Large cities result from the migration of the population to urban centers, geographical areas limit production to a narrow range of products, and the economic standard of living for the average citizen usually rises. More specifically, an efficient and inexpensive transportation system contributes to greater competition in the marketplace, greater economies of scale in production, and reduced prices for goods.

Greater Competition

With a poorly developed transportation system, the extent of the market is limited to the areas immediately surrounding the point of production. Unless production costs are extremely low compared with those at a second production point—that is, the production cost difference offsets the transportation costs of serving the second market—not much competition is likely to take place. However, with improvements in the transportation system, the landed costs for products in distant markets can be competitive with other products selling in the same markets.

In addition to encouraging direct competition, inexpensive, high-quality transportation also encourages an indirect form of competition by making goods available to a market that normally could not withstand the cost of transportation. Sales can actually be increased through market penetration normally unavailable to certain products. The goods from outside a region have a stabilizing effect on prices of all similar goods in the marketplace.

Application

In many markets, fresh fruits, vegetables, and other perishable products can be available at only certain times of the year due to seasonal growing patterns and lack of good growing conditions. Yet, many such products are in season at any time during the year somewhere in the world. Rapid shipment at reasonable prices places these perishable products in markets that would not otherwise have the products available. Bananas from South America are available in New York in January, live New England lobsters are served in Kansas City restaurants throughout the year, and Hawaiian orchids are plentiful in the eastern United States in April. An efficient and effective transportation system makes this possible.

Economies of Scale

Wider markets can result in lower production costs. With the greater volume provided in these markets, more intense utilization can be made of production facilities and specialization of labor usually follows. In addition, inexpensive transportation also permits decoupling of markets and production sites. This provides a degree of freedom in selecting production sites so that production can be located where there is a geographic advantage.

Observation

Auto parts manufactured in such places as Taiwan, Indonesia, South Korea, and Mexico are used in assembly operations in the United States and are sold in the U.S. marketplace. Low labor costs and high-quality production are the attractions to manufacture in these foreign locations. However, without inexpensive and reliable transportation, the cost of placing parts throughout the United States would be too high to compete with domestic production.

Reduced Prices

Inexpensive transportation also contributes to reduced product prices. This occurs not only because of the increased competition in the marketplace but also because transportation is a component cost along with production, selling, and other distribution costs that make up the aggregate product cost. As transportation becomes more efficient, as well as offering improved performance, society benefits through a higher standard of living.

Observation

Crude oil can be obtained from domestic sources or it can be imported. Oil reserves in the Middle East are more accessible than they are domestically, and oil can be produced at a lower cost. With the use of large supertankers, oil can be transported to markets around the world and sold at lower prices than locally produced crude oil, if it is available at all.

SERVICE CHOICES AND THEIR CHARACTERISTICS

The user of transportation has a wide range of services at his or her disposal that revolve around the five basic modes: water, rail, truck, air, and pipeline. A transport service is a set of performance characteristics purchased at a given price. The variety of transport services is almost limitless. The five modes may be used in combination (e.g., piggyback or container movement); transportation agencies, shippers' associations, and brokers may be used to facilitate these services; small-shipment carriers (e.g., Federal Express and United Parcel Service) may be used for their efficiency in handling small packages; or a single transportation mode may be used exclusively. From among these service choices, the user selects a service or combination of services that provides the best balance between the quality of service offered and the cost of that service. The task of service-choice selection is not as forbidding as it first appears, because the circumstances surrounding a particular shipping situation often reduce the choice to only a few reasonable possibilities.

To aid in solving the problem of transportation service choice, transportation service may be viewed in terms of characteristics that are basic to all services: price, average transit time, transit time variability, and loss and damage. These factors seem to be the most important to decision makers (recall Table 4-2), as numerous studies over the years have revealed.[2] It is presumed that the service is available and can be supplied with a frequency that makes it attractive as a possible service choice.

Price

Price (cost) of transport service to a shipper is simply the line-haul rate for transporting goods and any accessorial or terminal charges for additional service provided. In the case of for-hire service, the rate charged for the movement of goods between two points plus any additional charges, such as for pickup at origin, delivery at destination, insurance, or preparing the goods for shipment, makes up the total cost of service. When the shipper owns the service (e.g., a fleet of trucks), the cost of service is an allocation of the relevant costs to a particular shipment. Relevant costs include items such as fuel, labor, maintenance, depreciation of equipment, and administrative costs.

Cost of service varies greatly from one type of transport service to another. Table 6-1 gives the approximate cost per ton-mile for the five modes of transportation. Notice that airfreight is the most expensive, and pipe and water carriage are the least costly. Trucking is about seven times more expensive than rail, and rail is about four times as expensive as water or pipeline movement. These figures are averages that result from the ratio of freight revenue generated by a mode to the total

---

[2]For results of these studies, see James R. Stock and Bernard J. LaLonde, "The Transportation Mode Decision Revisited," *Transportation Journal* (Winter 1977), p. 56; James E. Piercy and Ronald H. Ballou, "A Performance Evaluation of Freight Transport Modes," *Logistics and Transportation Review*, Vol. 14, No. 2 (1978), pp. 99–115; and Douglas M. Lambert and Thomas C. Harrington, "Establishing Customer Service Strategies Within the Marketing Mix: More Empirical Evidence," *Journal of Business Logistics*, Vol. 10, No. 2 (1989), p. 50.

Table 6-1
Average Freight
Ton-Mile
Transportation
Price by Mode

Mode	Price, ¢/ton-mile[a]
Rail	2.28[b]
Truck	26.19[c]
Water	0.74[d]
Pipe	1.46[e]
Air	61.20[f]

[a]Based on average per ton-mile
[b]Class 1
[c]Less than truckload
[d]Barge
[e]Oil pipeline
[f]Domestic
Source: Rosalyn A. Wilson, *Transportation in America 2000*, 18th ed. (Washington, DC: ENO Transportation Foundation, 2000), p. 19.

ton-miles shipped. While these average costs may be used for general comparisons, cost comparisons for the purpose of transport service selection should be made based on actual charges that reflect the commodity being shipped, the distance and direction of the movement, and any special handling required.

Transit Time and Variability

Repeated surveys have shown (recall Table 4-1) that average delivery time and delivery time variability rank at the top of the lists as important transportation performance characteristics. Delivery (transit) time is usually referred to as the average time it takes for a shipment to move from its point of origin to its destination. The different modes of transportation vary according to whether or not they provide direct connection between the origin and destination points. For example, shipments move on air carriers between airports or on water carriers between seaports. However, for purposes of comparing carrier performance, it is best to measure transit time door-to-door, even if more than one mode is involved. Although the major movement of a shipment may be by rail, local pickup and delivery are often made by truck if no rail sidings are available at the shipment origin and destination points.

Variability refers to the usual differences that occur between shipments by various modes. All shipments having the same origin and destination points and moving on the same mode are not necessarily in transit for the same length of time due to the effects of weather, traffic congestion, number of stop offs, and differences in time to consolidate shipments. Transit time variability is a measure of the uncertainty in carrier performance.

Statistics on carrier performance are not extensive, as no one business utilizes the total transportation system enough to provide worthwhile comparisons on a large scale. However, the military and government agencies use the domestic transportation system extensively for all kinds of commodity movements and maintain good records on delivery times. Where the data are available, selective cross-checking

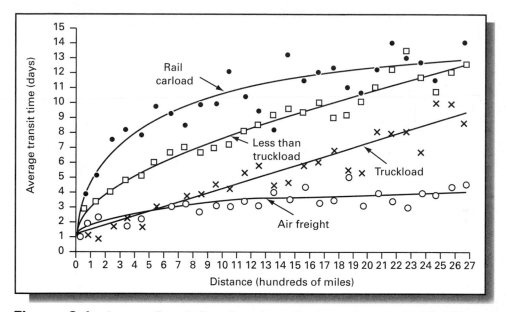

Figure 6-1 Average Transit-Time Experience for Approximately 16,000 Military and Industrial Shipments by Selected Transport Service

Source: James Piercy, "A Performance Profile of Several Transportation Freight Services," (Ph.D. diss., Case Western Reserve University unpublished, 1977).

against industrial shipments shows no significant differences between the data sources with regard to transit time variability.

One of the most extensive studies of carrier performance was carried out on more than 16,000 military and industrial shipments. Some of the results are summarized in Table 6-2 and Figure 6-1. Particularly note that over long distances, rail and air shipments approach constant average transit times, whereas truck transit times continue to increase. Of course, on the average, airfreight is the fastest mode for distances of more than 600 miles, with truckload, less than truckload, and rail following, respectively. For distances less than 600 miles, air and truck are comparable. For very short distances of less than 50 miles, the transit time is influenced more by the pickup and delivery operation than the line-haul transit time.

In terms of variability, the transport services can be roughly ranked as they were for average delivery time. That is, rail has the highest delivery time variability and air has the lowest, with truck service falling between these extremes. If variability is viewed relative to the average transit time for the transport service, air can be the least dependable and truckload the most dependable.

Loss and Damage

Because carriers differ in their ability to move freight without loss and damage, loss and damage experience becomes a factor in selecting a carrier. Product condition is a primary customer service consideration.

Table 6-2 A Comparison of Average Transit Time and Time Range for 95% of Shipments in Days by Various Transport Services for Selected Mileages

Selected Mileages	Railcarload		Less Than Truckload		Truckload		Airfreight		Air Express		Piggyback[a]	
	Avg.	95% Range	Avg.	95% Range	Avg.	95% Range	Avg.	95% Range	Avg.	95% Range	Avg.	95% Range
0–49	1.5	0[b]–3.5	1.7	0–5.1	0.8	0–3.2	—[c]	—[c]	—[c]	—[c]	—[c]	—[c]
100–199	5.2	0–11.9	3.4	0–7.7	2.0	0–5.6	2.3	0–7.7	1.9	0–5.1	3.8	0–7.4
300–399	8.3	1.4–15.2	5.0	0.4–9.6	1.9	0–4.7	1.8	0–5.9	2.1	0–5.7	4.4	1.7–7.1
500–599	9.8	2.5–17.1	6.0	0–12.0	2.7	0–6.4	3.1	1.1–6.0	1.6	0–4.1	6.6	0–13.7
700–799	8.6	0.6–16.6	7.1	0–14.5	4.1	0–8.9	3.2	0.1–6.3	2.3	0–6.1	6.2	1.0–11.4
1000–1099	12.2	2.9–21.5	7.4	1.3–13.5	4.0	1.1–6.9	3.0	0.2–5.9	1.4	0–3.7	6.1	1.5–10.7
1500–1599	11.1	5.6–16.6	8.9	0.7–17.2	5.3	0.8–9.9	4.6	0.7–9.9	1.5	0–4.9	4.6[d]	0–10.0[d]
2000–2099	11.5	1.4–21.5	11.1	3.2–18.9	8.0	0–16.1	4.0	0–9.0	1.8	0–4.6	5.1[d]	2.6–7.7[d]
2500–2599	12.4	8.3–16.6	12.3	6.7–17.9	8.8	3.3–14.3	4.4	0–10.1	3.4	0–9.6	6.7[d]	1.1–12.2[d]
3000–3099	10.6	1.5–19.7	12.9	3.8–22.0	10.4	5.9–14.9	3.2	0.7–7.0	6.0	0–23.3	5.6[d]	3.9–7.3[d]

[a]Trailer on flatcar

[b]Zero refers to shipment deliveries made in less than one day.

[c]Insufficient data

[d]DeHayes' data

Source: Adapted from James Piercy, "A Performance Profile of Several Transportation Freight Services," (Ph.D. diss., Case Western Reserve University unpublished, 1977); and Daniel DeHayes, Jr., "The General Nature of Transit Time Performance of Selected Transportation Modes in the Movement of Freight," (Ph.D. diss., Ohio State University, 1968): pp. 163–177.

Common carriers have an obligation to move freight with reasonable dispatch and to do so using reasonable care in order to avoid loss and damage. This responsibility is relieved if loss and damage result from an act of God, default by the shipper, or other causes not within control of the carrier. Although carriers, upon proper presentation of the facts by the shipper, incur the direct loss sustained by the shipper, there are certain imputed costs that the shipper should recognize before making a carrier selection.

Potentially the most serious loss that the shipper may sustain has to do with customer service. The shipment of goods may be for replenishing a customer's inventory or for immediate use. Delayed shipments or goods arriving in unusable condition means inconvenience for the customer or possibly higher inventory costs arising from a greater number of stockouts or back orders when anticipated replenishment stocks are not received as planned. The claims process takes time to gather pertinent facts about the claim, takes effort on the part of the shipper to prepare the proper claim form, ties up capital while claims are being processed, and sometimes involves a considerable expense if the claim can be resolved only through court action. Obviously, the fewer the claims against a carrier, the more favorable the service appears to the user. A common reaction of shippers to a high likelihood of damage is to provide increased protective packaging. This expense must ultimately be borne by the user as well.

SINGLE-SERVICE CHOICES

Each of the five basic transportation modes offers its services directly to users. This is in contrast to the use of a "transportation middleman," such as a freight forwarder, who sells transportation services but usually owns little or no line-haul movement capability. Single-mode service is also in contrast to those services involving two or more individual transportation modes.

Rail

The railroad is a long hauler and slow mover of raw materials (coal, lumber, and chemicals) and of low-valued manufactured products (food, paper, and wood products) and prefers to move shipment sizes of at least a full carload. In 1999, the average length of haul was 712 miles,[3] with an average train speed of 20 miles per hour.[4] Average car distance traveled was 64 miles per day in line-haul service.[5] This relatively slow speed and short car distance traveled in a day reflect the fact that the majority (86 percent) of freight car time is spent in loading and unloading operations, moving from place to place within terminals, classifying and assembling cars into trains, or standing idle during a seasonal slump in car demand.

---

[3]Rosalyn A. Wilson, *Transportation in America 2000*, 18th ed. (Washington, DC: ENO Transportation Foundation, 2000), p. 51.
[4]*Statistical Abstract of the U.S.: 2000*, p. 695.
[5]*Statistical Abstract of the U.S.: 1989*, p. 606.

Rail service exists in two legal forms, common carrier or privately owned. A common carrier sells its transportation services to all shippers and it is guided by the economic[6] and safety regulations of the appropriate government agencies. In contrast, private carriers are shipper owned with the usual intent of serving only the owner. Because of the limited scope of the private carrier's operations, no economic regulation is needed. Nearly all rail movement is of the common carrier type.

Common carrier line-haul rail service is primarily carload (CL). A carload quantity refers to a predetermined shipment size, usually approaching or exceeding the average capacity of a railcar to which a particular rate is applied. A multiple-carload quantity rate per hundredweight (cwt.) may be offered and is less than the less-than-carload (LCL) rate, which reflects the reduced handling time required for high-volume shipments. Nearly all rail freight today moves in carload quantities, a reflection of the trend toward volume movement. Larger freight cars are being used with an average freight car capacity of 83 tons, and single-commodity trains (called unit trains) of 100 or more cars per train are being used with rate reductions of 25 to 40 percent over single carloads.

Railroads offer a diversity of special services to the shipper, ranging from the movement of bulk commodities such as coal and grain to special cars for refrigerated products and new automobiles which require special equipment. Other offerings include expedited service to guarantee arrival within a certain number of hours; various stop-off privileges, which permit partial loading and unloading between origin and destination points; pickup and delivery; and diversion and reconsignment, which allow circuitous routing and changes in the final destination of a shipment while en route.

Truck

In contrast with rail, trucking is a transportation service of semifinished and finished products with an average length of freight haul of 717 miles for less than truckload (LTL) and 286 miles for truckload (TL).[7] In addition, trucking moves freight with smaller average shipment sizes than rail. More than half of the shipments by truck are less than 10,000 pounds, or LTL volume. The inherent advantages of trucking are its door-to-door service, involving no loading or unloading between origin and destination, as is often true of rail and air modes; its frequency and availability of service; and its door-to-door speed and convenience.

Truck and rail services show some distinct differences, even though they compete for many of the same product shipments. First, in addition to the common and private legal classification of carriers, trucking offers services as contract carriers as well. Contract carriers do not hire themselves out to service all shippers as do common carriers. Shippers enter into a contractual arrangement to obtain a service that better meets their particular needs without incurring the capital expense and administrative problems associated with private ownership of a trucking fleet.

---

[6]Little federal economic regulation remains since the passing of the Staggers Rail Act of 1980, which economically deregulated rail transportation. Some regulation remains at the state level.
[7]*Transportation in America 2000*, p. 51.

Second, trucks can be judged less capable of handling all types of freight than rail, mainly due to highway safety restrictions that limit the dimensions and weight of shipments. Most shipments must be shorter than the popular 40- to 53-foot trailer (unless a double or triple bottom) and less than 8 feet wide and 8 feet tall to ensure road clearance. Specially designed equipment can accept loads in different dimensions than these.

Third, trucking offers reasonably fast and dependable delivery for LTL shipments. The trucker needs to fill only one trailer before moving the shipment, whereas a railroad must be concerned with making up a train length of 50 cars or more. On balance, trucking has a service advantage in the small-shipment market.

Air

Air transportation is being considered by increasing numbers of shippers for regular service, even though airfreight rates exceed those of trucking by more than two times and those of rail by more than 16 times. The appeal of air transportation is its unmatched origin-destination speed, especially over long distances. The average length of a freight haul is 1,001 miles.[8] Commercial jets have cruising speeds between 545 and 585 miles per hour, although airport-to-airport average speed is somewhat less than cruising speed because of taxi and holding time at each airport and the time needed to ascend to and descend from cruising altitude. But this speed is not directly comparable with that of other modes because the times for pickup and delivery and for ground handling are not included. All these time elements must be combined to represent door-to-door air delivery time. Because surface freight handling and movement are the slowest elements of total door-to-door delivery time, overall delivery time may be so reduced that a well-managed truck and rail operation can match the schedule of air. Of course, this depends on individual cases.

Air-service dependability and availability can be rated as good under normal operating conditions. Delivery-time variability is low in absolute magnitude, even though air service is quite sensitive to mechanical breakdown, weather conditions, and traffic congestion. Variability, when compared with average delivery times, can rank air as one of the least reliable modes.

The capability of air has been greatly constrained by the physical dimensions of the cargo space in the aircraft and the aircraft's lifting capacity. This is becoming less of a constraint, however, as larger aircraft are put into service. For example, "jumbo" airplanes such as the Boeing 747 and Lockheed 500 (commercial version of the military's C5A) handle cargo of 125 to 150 tons. Door-to-door ton-mile costs are expected to drop to about one-half of the current cost levels through the benefits of new technology, deregulation, and productivity-improvement programs. This would make air a serious competitor with the more premium forms of surface-transport services.

Air transportation has a distinct advantage in terms of loss and damage. According to a classic study by Lewis, Culliton, and Steele,[9] the ratio of claim costs to

---

[8]Ibid.
[9]Howard T. Lewis, James W. Culliton, and Jack W. Steele, *The Role of Air Freight in Physical Distribution* (Boston: Division of Research, Graduate School of Business Administration, Harvard University, 1956), p. 82.

freight revenue was only about 60 percent of those for truck or rail. In general, less protective packaging is required for airfreight, if ground handling does not offer a higher exposure to damage than the en route phase of the movement and airport theft is not excessive.

Air transportation service exists in common, contract, and private legal forms. Direct air service is offered in seven types: (1) regular domestic truck-line carriers; (2) all-cargo carriers; (3) local-service airlines; (4) supplemental carriers; (5) air taxis; (6) commuter airlines; and (7) international carriers. About a dozen airlines operate currently over the most heavily traveled routes. These airlines offer cargo-carrying services in addition to their regularly scheduled passenger operations. All cargo carriers are common carriers of freight only. Service is concentrated at night, and rates average 30 percent less than those for domestic trunk-line carriers. Local-service airlines provide a "connecting" service with domestic trunk-line carriers for less populated centers. They provide both cargo and passenger service. Supplemental (charter) carriers operate much as do trunk-line carriers, except that they do not have regular schedules. Commuter airlines are like local-service carriers that "fill in" routes abandoned by trunk-line carriers since deregulation. In general, smaller aircraft are operated than those of trunk-line carriers. Air taxis are small aircraft, namely, helicopters and small fixed-wing aircraft, offering a shuttle service for passengers and cargo between downtown areas and airports. They often have only irregular service. International carriers transport freight and passengers beyond their domestic regions.

Water

Water transportation service is limited in scope for several reasons. Domestic water service is confined to the inland waterway system, which requires shippers to be located on the waterways or to use another transportation mode in combination with water. In addition, water service on the average is slower than rail. The average speed on the Mississippi water system is between five and nine miles per hour, depending on direction. The average length of a freight haul is 481 miles on rivers, 507 miles on the Great Lakes, and 1,648 miles along U.S. coasts.[10] Availability and dependability of water service are greatly influenced by the weather. Movement on the waterways in the northern part of the country during the winter is impossible, and floods and droughts may interrupt service at other times. There is tremendous capacity available in water carriers, with barge tows up to 40,000 tons, and there are individual barges with standardized dimensions 26 by 175 feet and 35 by 195 feet. Capability and handling are being increased as barge-carrying ships are being developed, and such improvements as satellite navigation with radar, refined depth finders, and auto piloting mean around-the-clock service.

Water services are provided in all legal forms, and most commodities shipped by water move free of economic regulation. In addition to unregulated private carriage, liquid cargoes in bulk moving in tank vessels and commodities in bulk such as coal,

---

[10]*Transportation in American 2000*, p. 51.

sand, and grain, which make up over 80 percent of the total annual ton-miles by water, are exempt. Outside of the handling of bulk commodities, water carriers, especially those in foreign service, do move some higher-valued commodities. This freight moves in containers[11] on containerized ships to reduce handling time, to affect intermodal transfer, and to reduce loss and damage.

Loss and damage costs resulting from transporting by water are considered low relative to other modes because damage is not much of a concern with low-valued bulk products, and losses due to delays are not serious (large inventories are often maintained by buyers). Claims involving transport of high-valued goods, as in ocean freight, are much higher (approximately 4 percent of ocean-ship revenues). Substantial packaging is needed to protect goods, mainly against rough handling during the loading and unloading operations.

Pipeline

To date, pipeline transportation offers a very limited range of services and capabilities. The most economically feasible products to move by pipeline are crude oil and refined petroleum products. However, there is some experimentation with moving solid products suspended in a liquid, referred to as a "slurry," or containing the solid products in cylinders that in turn move in a liquid within the pipe. If these innovations prove to be economical, pipeline service could be greatly expanded. Early experience with coal suspended in a liquid has not been favorable, because the pipes have eroded.

Product movement by pipeline is very slow, only about three to four miles per hour. This slowness is tempered by the fact that products move 24 hours a day, 7 days a week. This makes the effective speed much greater when compared with other modes. Pipeline capacity is high, considering that a 3-mph flow in a 12-in.-diameter pipe can move 89,000 gallons per hour.

Concerning transit time, pipeline service is the most dependable of all modes, because there are few interruptions to cause transit time variability. Weather is not a significant factor, and pumping equipment is highly reliable. In addition, the availability of pipeline capacity is limited only by the use that other shippers may be making of the facilities at the time capacity is desired.

Product loss and damage for pipelines is low because (1) liquids and gases are not subject to damage to the same degree as manufactured products; and (2) the number of dangers that can befall a pipeline operation is limited. There is liability for such loss and damage when it does occur because pipelines have the status of common carriers, even though many are private carriers in form.

To summarize the quality of the services offered by transportation industry, Table 6-3 shows a ranking of the various modes using the four cost and performance characteristics set forth at the beginning of this section. It should be recognized that under specific circumstances of product type, shipping distance, carrier management, user-carrier relationships, and weather conditions, these rankings may change, and the service of particular modes may not be available.

---

[11]Containers are standardized "boxes," usually $8 \times 8 \times 10$ ft, $8 \times 8 \times 20$ ft, or $8 \times 8 \times 40$ ft, in which freight is handled as a unit and which are easily transferred as a unit to other transportation modes.

	PERFORMANCE CHARACTERISTICS				
			DELIVERY-TIME VARIABILITY		
MODE OF TRANSPORTATION	COST[b] 1 = HIGHEST	AVERAGE DELIVERY TIME[c] 1 = FASTEST	ABSOLUTE 1 = LEAST	PERCENT[d] 1 = LEAST	LOSS AND DAMAGE 1 = LEAST
Rail	3	3	4	3	5
Truck	2	2	3	2	4
Water	5	5	5	4	2
Pipe	4	4	2	1	1
Air	1	1	1	5	3

[a] Service is assumed to be available
[b] Cost per ton-mile
[c] Door-to-door speed
[d] Ratio of absolute variation in delivery time to average delivery time
Source: Author's estimates for average performance over a variety of circumstances.

Table 6-3 Relative Rankings of Transportation Mode by Cost and Operating Performance Characteristics[a]

INTERMODAL SERVICES

In recent years, there has been an increase in shipping products using more than one transportation mode in the process. Beyond obvious economic benefits, increased international shipping has been a driving force. The major feature of intermodalism is the free exchange of equipment between modes. For example, the container portion of a truck trailer is carried aboard an airplane, or a railcar is hauled by a water carrier. Such equipment interchange creates transportation services that are not available to a shipper using a single-transportation mode. Coordinated services are usually a compromise between the services individually offered by the cooperating carriers. That is, cost and performance characteristics rank between those of the carriers separately.

There are ten possible intermodal service combinations: (1) rail-truck; (2) rail-water; (3) rail-air; (4) rail-pipeline; (5) truck-air; (6) truck-water; (7) truck-pipeline; (8) water-pipeline; (9) water-air; and (10) air-pipeline. Not all of these combinations are practical. Some that are feasible have gained little acceptance. Only rail-truck, called *piggyback*, has seen widespread use. Truck-water combinations, referred to as *fishyback*, are gaining acceptance, especially in the international movement of high-valued goods. To a much lesser extent, truck-air and rail-water combinations are feasible, but they have seen limited use.

Trailer on Flatcar

Trailer on flatcar (TOFC), or piggyback, refers to transporting truck trailers on railroad flatcars, usually over longer distances than trucks normally haul. TOFC is a blend of the convenience and flexibility of trucking and the long-haul economy of rail. The rate is usually less than for trucking alone and has permitted trucking to extend its economical range. Likewise, rail has been able to share in some traffic that normally would move by truck alone. The shipper benefits from the convenience of door-to-door service over long distances at reasonable rates. These features have made piggyback the most popular coordinated service. The number of railcars loaded with highway trailers and containers has shown a steady and dramatic increase from 554,000 in 1960 to 9,740,000 in 1996 (annualized), or 55 percent of rail-car loadings.[12]

Five different plans are offered for TOFC service, depending on who owns the highway equipment and rail equipment and on the rate structure established. These plans are as follows:

- *Plan I.* Railroads transport the trailers of highway common carriers. Billing is through the highway carriers, and the railroads charge a portion of the carriers' rate or a flat fee for moving the trailer.
- *Plan II.* Railroads use their own trailers and containers and transport these on their own flatcars to provide a door-to-door service. Railroads contract with local truckers to handle assembly at originating terminals and delivery from destination terminals. Shippers deal only with railroads and receive rates comparable to those of highway common carriers.
- *Plan II 1/4.* Similar to Plan II, except railroads provide either pickup or delivery, or both.
- *Plan II 1/2.* Railroads provide the trailers or containers and the shippers provide the service of moving these to and from the rail terminals.
- *Plan III.* Shippers or freight forwarders can place their own trailers or containers, empty or loaded, on railroad flatcars for a flat rate. The rate is for ramp-to-ramp; that is, pickup and delivery are the responsibility of the shippers.
- *Plan IV.* Shippers furnish not only the trailers or containers, but also the railroad equipment on which the trailers or containers move. The railroad charges a flat rate for moving the cars, empty or loaded. The payment to the railroad is for the rails and for pulling power.
- *Plan V.* Two or more rail and truck carriers quote jointly on TOFC service. Each carrier may solicit freight for the other, which has the effect of extending the territory of each into that served by the other.

Containerized Freight

Under a TOFC arrangement, the entire trailer is transported on a railroad flatcar. However, it is also possible to visualize the trailer in two ways, that is, (1) as a container or box in which the freight is packaged; and (2) as the trailer's chassis. In a truck-rail intermodal service, it is possible to haul only the container, thus saving the dead weight of the understructure and wheels. Such a service is called container-on-flatcar (COFC).

---

[12]"Intermodal Traffic Creeps Upward," *Daily Trucking and Transportation News* (July 24, 1996).

The standardized container is a piece of equipment that is transferable to all surface transportation modes with the exception of pipeline. Because containerized freight avoids costly rehandling of small shipment units at the point of intermodal transfer and offers a door-to-door service capability when combined with truck, water carriers use container ships so that combinations of water-truck service can be provided. This type of service is expanding, especially due to the increase in international trade. The container can also be used in combination services with air. The most promising to date is the air-truck combination. The container is important to air transportation because the high movement costs prohibit transporting the chassis of a highway trailer. The use of large containers in air transportation has been limited by the dimensions of the existing aircraft and the small shipment sizes that air transportation predominantly handles, but as air freight rates are reduced, possibly due to larger aircraft being put into service, coordinated air-truck service should expand.

The services of coordinated transportation services will hinge on the container size that is adopted as standard. A container that is too large for trucking or that is incompatible with trucking equipment will exclude trucking from participating. The same argument holds for the other modes. The typical container sizes are 8 by 8 by 20 feet and 8 by 8 by 40 feet. Both are compatible with the standard 40-foot highway trailer and with most other modes.

Observation

Containerized freight movement began in 1956 when Malcom McClean first moved freight in ocean-borne trailers on a World War II tanker that sailed from Newark, New Jersey, to Houston, Texas. Soon after this, a ship was specially converted to stack van-sized boxes on its deck. Containerized service spread from Puerto Rico to Europe to the Pacific. McClean's idea cut terminal handling time, stealing, and insurance costs. Now, 75 percent of the U.S. ocean merchandise trade with the rest of the world is hauled in big containers instead of the crates, tubs, sacks, and boxes previously used.[13]

AGENCIES AND SMALL SHIPMENT SERVICES

Agents

Several agencies exist that offer transportation services to shippers but own little or no line-haul equipment. Primarily, they handle numerous small shipments and consolidate them into vehicle-load quantities. Rates competitive with those for LTL are charged, and the agency, through its consolidation of the many small shipments it handles, can obtain vehicle-load rates. The freight-rate differential between large

---

[13]"McClean Makes Containers Shipshape, 1956," *Wall Street Journal*, November 29, 1989, B1.

and small shipments helps to offset operating expenses. In addition to consolidation, agencies provide pickup and delivery services to shippers. Transportation agencies include air and surface freight forwarders, shippers' associations, and transport brokers.

Freight forwarders are for-hire carriers of freight. They do own some equipment, but this is mainly for pickup and delivery operations. They purchase long-distance services from air, truck, rail, and water carriers. A major advantage of freight forwarders is that they can quote rates on shipments up to 30,000 pounds, while the average shipment weight handled is only about 300 pounds.

Shippers' associations are cooperative organizations operating on a nonprofit basis. Members belong to the association to realize lower shipping costs. The associations are designed to perform services similar to those of freight forwarders. They act as a single shipper in order to obtain volume rates. Each member shipper pays a portion of the total freight bill, based on the amount to be shipped.

Transport brokers are agents that bring shippers and carriers together by providing timely information about rates, routes, and capabilities. They may arrange for transportation, but assume no liability for it. They are especially valuable to carriers that use brokers to find business for them. Numerous Web sites have emerged that, for a fee, match shippers and carriers for better use of transportation equipment for carriers and lower rates for shippers.

Small-Shipment Services

Parcel post is a small-shipment delivery service offered by United States Postal Service. Shipments are limited in size and may weigh up to 70 pounds and be up to 130 inches in length,[14] and delivery is made to all points in the United States. Rates are based on the distance from the point of shipment origin to the point of delivery. Parcel post uses the service of line-haul carriers. United Parcel Service and Federal Express offer small-package services similar to parcel post, with competitive rates and performance levels. Pickup service is available and deliveries are made in all states and around the world. Premium air small-shipment services also are available that offer overnight and, in some cases, same-day delivery. Federal Express is the most popular service of this type, although UPS and United States Postal Service offer competing services.

In addition to agencies that specialize in small-shipment services, line-haul carriers also move small shipments. There is usually a flat charge when the shipment weight is below a certain minimum weight, generally 200 to 300 pounds for trucking. Service is often less favorable than for large shipments. Revenues among these services are distributed as follows: UPS truck—31.6 percent; LTL truck—39.6 percent; normal air—4.2 percent; special air[15]—24.6 percent; and rail and bus—negligible.[16]

---

[14]Size refers to the sum of the length (longest dimension) and girth (twice the width plus twice the depth). These limits are further reduced for first-class postal service.
[15]Federal Express, UPS, DHL, and Airborne Express.
[16]Rosalyn A. Wilson, *Transportation in America*, 17th ed. (Washington, DC: ENO Transportation Foundation, 1999), p. 19.

COMPANY-CONTROLLED TRANSPORTATION

An available alternative to outsourcing transport of goods is to provide transportation service through company ownership of equipment or contracting for transportation services. Ideally, the user hopes to gain better operating performance, greater availability and capacity of transportation service, and a lower cost. At the same time, a certain amount of financial flexibility is sacrificed because the company must invest in a transportation capability or must commit itself to a long-term contractual arrangement. If the shipping volume is high, it may be more economical to own the transportation service than to rent it. However, some companies are forced to own or contract for transportation even at higher costs because their special requirements for service cannot be adequately met through common carrier services. Such requirements might include (1) fast delivery with very high dependability; (2) special equipment not generally available; (3) special handling of the freight; and (4) a service that is available on demand. Common carriers serve many customers and cannot always meet the specific transportation requirements of individual users.

INTERNATIONAL TRANSPORTATION

The success of the transportation industry in developing a fast, reliable, and efficient transportation system has substantially contributed to the dramatically expanding level (24 times) of international trade occurring in the last 30 years (about a threefold increase in revenue for international air and water movements from 1980 to 1996 alone).[17] Inexpensive transportation has allowed domestic companies to take advantage of the differences in labor rates worldwide, to secure raw materials that are geographically dispersed, and to place goods competitively in markets far from their domestic borders. Thus, the logistician must be knowledgeable about the special requirements for moving goods internationally.

Overview

Water carriers dominate international transportation, with more than 50 percent of the trade volume in dollars and 99 percent by weight. Air moves 21 percent of the dollar trade volume, and the remainder is transported by truck, rail, and pipeline between bordering countries.

The dominance of particular transport modes is largely affected by the geography of the country and the proximity of major trading partners. Island countries, such as Japan and Australia, must use air and water modes extensively. However, many of the member countries of the European Union can make use of rail, truck, and pipeline modes.

Route choices become much more restricted than in domestic movement because goods must move through a limited number of ports and customs points in order to

---

[17]*Statistical Abstract of the U.S.: 1997*, p. 656.

leave or enter a country. Although this may make routing easier and more obvious as compared with domestic movements, the problems brought about by the legal requirements of moving goods between two or more countries and the more limited liability of international carriers as compared with domestic carriers can make international movement more complex. That is, international shipments must move under more documents than domestic shipments, are subject to delays brought about by the legal requirements for entering and exiting a country, and are subject to the routing restrictions of two or more countries. In addition, limited carrier liability (ocean carriers need only provide a seaworthy vessel as evidence of responsibility) results in increased protective packaging, and increased insurance and documentation costs as a hedge against potential loss. This helps to explain some of the popularity of containerization for moving high-valued goods in international markets.

Physical Plant

The physical plant for international transportation differs only in a few respects from the domestic system. The transportation equipment is of the same type except the size may differ somewhat. The physical routes are different because they cover different geographic territories than do domestic routes. However, a distinct difference is the foreign trade zone and the role that it plays in the routing of international shipments.

Customers' expenses, tariffs, duties, and taxes are assessments that governments place on imported goods. These often prove burdensome to the exporter. The exporter may find it a disadvantage to pay duties to the importing country at the time and in the form that goods are received for import, and/or the exporter might like to use the labor of the importing country or its strategic location for manufacturing and storage but finds it uneconomical because of the duties. Foreign trade zones, or free ports, eliminate this disadvantage, to the benefit of both the exporting and importing countries. There is no direct counterpart to the trade zone in domestic trade.

Trade zones are duty-free areas established at one or more entry points within a country, such as seaports and airports, where foreign goods may enter, be held or processed in some way, and be reshipped without incurring any duties. Figure 6-2 shows a diagram of how the trade zone operates. There are 225 general-purpose zones and 359 subzones located in the United States.[18] They can offer numerous advantages to the logistician responsible for international movement of goods. The important advantages of foreign trade zones can be summarized as follows:

1. Imported goods may be left at trade zones for storage, manipulation to change custom classification, assembly, exhibition, grading, cleaning, selling, mixing with foreign and domestic merchandise, repacking, destruction, sorting, and other services and then shipped out of the zone to another country without customs formalities or control.
2. Foreign governments pay duties on goods in the trade zone only when they enter the customer's territory of the importing country.

---

[18]Web site for the National Association of Foreign-Trade Zones, found at www.naftz.org.

3. Imported goods that are improperly marked for entry into the domestic market can be remarked at the trade zones, thus avoiding fines on the goods.

4. Goods may be repacked into smaller or larger quantities.

5. Goods that undergo shrinkage to spoilage, evaporation, or damage do not incur duties on the amount lost.

6. Savings sometimes can be realized through shipping goods unassembled to the zone and then assembling them.

7. The capital tied up in duties and bonds can be released for more profitable uses when products using duty-subject foreign materials are shipped to the trade zones to remain until foreign buyers are found or buyers are ready for delivery.

8. Importers may obtain privileged foreign trade status whereby duties are frozen against future increases.

9. Manufacturing conducted in trade zones incurs duties only on the imported materials and component parts in the finished product entering into the domestic market.

10. Tangible personal property is generally exempt from state and local taxes.

11. Customs security requirements provide protection against theft.

12. Merchandise may remain in a zone indefinitely.[19]

Figure 6-2 Operation of a Foreign (Free) Trade Zone

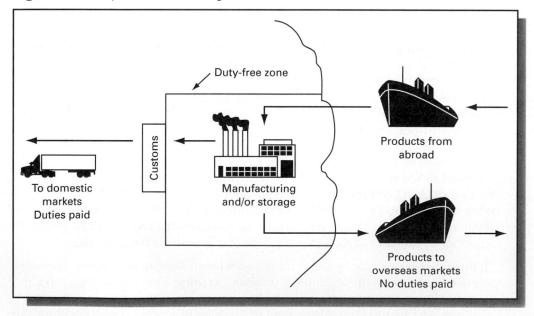

[19]Derived from an excellent discussion of trade zones by Gordon E. Miracle and Gerald S. Albaum, *International Marketing Management* (Homewood, IL: Richard D. Irwin, 1970), pp. 438–445; Pat J. Calabro, "Foreign Trade Zones—A Sleeping Giant in Distribution," *Journal of Business Logistics*, Vol. 4, No. 1 (1983), 51–64; Web site for the National Association of Foreign-Trade Zones, www.naftz.org; and Dick Morreale, "Logistics Rules of Thumb IV," www.logfac.com (August 2001).

Foreign (free) trade zones become forward bases for goods moving to or for goods received from foreign markets or suppliers. The advantages that they provide may well affect the routing of goods. Bonded warehouses, both public and private, can serve as foreign trade zones.

Application

Dorcy International Inc. is an assembler of flashlights and lanterns, the supplies for which are imported from China. Historically, Dorcy paid a 12.5 percent duty on parts as soon as they arrived on the West Coast. Now, yellow and black flashlights are freighted from China and shipped by rail to the abandoned Rickenbacker military base near Columbus, Ohio, which has become a foreign trade zone. By establishing the operation within the Rickenbacker trade zone, Dorcy has postponed duties until the goods are assembled, packed, and shipped to customers such as Sears, Wal-Mart, and Kmart—a process that can take 30 days. The delayed payment of duties can save Dorcy hundreds of thousands of dollars per year. And if the flashlights are assembled and exported to another country, no duties are paid at all. For tax purposes, it is as if the product never landed in the United States.[20]

Agencies and Services

Another distinguishing characteristic of international transportation is the number and variety of middlemen, or agents, that can assist the shipper or buyer engaged in international transportation. These include customhouse brokers, international freight forwarders, export merchants, export agents, export commission houses, import commission houses, wholesalers (or jobbers), brokers, international departments of banks, and the like. When agents are used, they provide more services than just transportation. They handle getting shipments across borders. This can include preparing paperwork for customs, coordinating customs inspections, shipment warehousing and consolidation, freight optimization, and shipment tracking. However, firms with significant international activity may establish special groups within their own traffic department to handle international transportation matters.

Example

The Parker-Hannifin Corporation is a world leader in the manufacture of hydraulic equipment such as hose, fittings, cylinders, seals, controls, and filters. Manufacturing takes place in the United States, Europe, and Asia with sales in nearly every country. International sales are handled in three ways. As shown in Figure 6-3, shipments may be handled through an agent (A). Product is trucked to a

---

[20]Clarke Ansberry, "For This Midwest City, Slow and Steady Wins Today's Economic Race," *The Wall Street Journal*, February 22, 2001, A1ff.

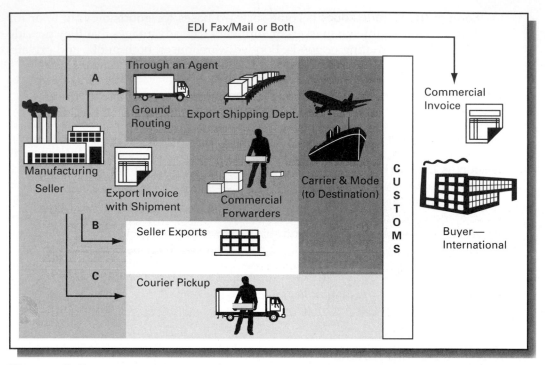

Figure 6-3 Alternative Shipping Methods for International Customers of the Parker-Hannifin Corporation

warehousing location where small shipments are consolidated into large ones. A freight forwarder, either an air or ocean carrier, is used to transport the goods to the final destination. The second alternative (B) is to ship directly with an air or ocean carrier where there is significant volume going to a particular region. This is a reasonable choice when shipments are larger than those in A. Finally, a courier service can be used (C) such as FedEx or UPS. This alternative is particularly attractive for rush orders. Air is the dominant mode used in this case. Using a variety of shipping methods allows Parker to carefully match shipping efficiency considerations with customer service needs.

TRANSPORT COST CHARACTERISTICS

The prices a logistician must pay for transportation services are keyed to the cost characteristics of each type of service. Just and reasonable transportation rates tend to follow the costs of producing the service. Because each service has different cost characteristics, under any given set of circumstances there will be potential rate advantages of one mode that cannot be effectively matched by other services.

Variable and Fixed Costs

A transportation service incurs a number of costs, such as labor, fuel, maintenance, terminal, roadway, administrative, and others. This cost mix can be arbitrarily divided into those costs that vary with services or volume (variable costs) and those that do not (fixed costs). Of course, all costs are variable if a long enough time and a great enough volume are considered. For purposes of transport pricing, however, it is useful to consider costs that are constant over the "normal" operating volume of the carrier as fixed. All other costs are treated as variable.

Specifically, fixed costs are those for roadway acquisition and maintenance, terminal facilities, transport equipment, and carrier administration. Variable costs usually include line-haul costs such as fuel and labor, equipment maintenance, handling, and pickup and delivery. This is not a precise allocation between fixed and variable costs, as there are significant cost differences between transportation modes, and there are different allocations depending on the dimension being examined. All costs are partly fixed and partly variable, and allocation of cost elements into one class or the other is a matter of individual perspective.

Line-haul transportation rates are based on two important dimensions: distance and shipper volume. In each case, fixed and variable costs are considered slightly different. To illustrate, consider the cost characteristics of a railroad. Total costs for service vary with the distance over which the freight must be transported, as shown in Figure 6-4(a). This is to be expected, because the amount of fuel used depends on distance, and the amount of labor for the haul is a function of distance (time). These are the variable costs. Fixed costs are substantial for rail because railroads own their roadways, terminals and switching yards, and equipment. These latter costs are treated as invariant with distance traveled. The sum of the fixed and variable cost elements gives the total cost.

In contrast, Figure 6-4(b) shows a railroad cost function based on the shipper's volume. In this case, line-haul labor is not variable, but handling costs are treated as variable. Significant reductions in the handling of shipments of at least carload quantities or trainload quantities cause discontinuities in the total cost curve such as occur between LTL, TL, and multiple-trailer shipment sizes. Volume rate reductions are usually pegged to these drops in costs.

Common or Joint Costs

It was mentioned previously that reasonable transport rates are those that follow the costs of producing the service. Beyond the problem of deciding whether a cost is fixed or variable, determining what the actual costs are for a particular shipment requires some arbitrary cost allocations, even though the total costs of operating may not be known. The reason is that many transportation costs are indivisible. Many shipments in different sizes and weights move jointly in the same haul. How much of the cost should be assigned to each shipment? Should the costs be assigned based on shipment weight to total load, on the proportion of total cubic footage used, or on some other basis? There is no simple formula for cost allocation, and production costs on a per-shipment basis remain a matter of judgment.

Figure 6-4
Generalized Railroad
Costs (and
Revenues) As
Functions of Volume
and Distance

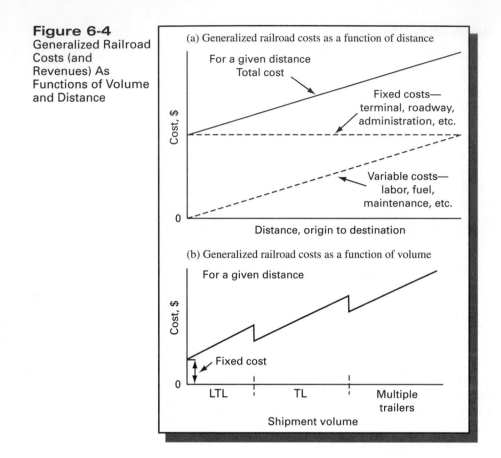

(a) Generalized railroad costs as a function of distance

For a given distance
Total cost

Fixed costs—
terminal, roadway,
administration, etc.

Variable costs—
labor, fuel,
maintenance, etc.

Cost, $

0

Distance, origin to destination

(b) Generalized railroad costs as a function of volume

For a given distance

Cost, $

Fixed cost

0

LTL   TL   Multiple
                   trailers

Shipment volume

The back haul that all carriers experience, with the exception of pipeline, is a case in point. Carriers rarely can perfectly balance the traffic between the forward movement and the return (back haul) movement. By definition, the forward haul is the heavy traffic direction and the back haul is the light traffic direction. Shipments in the back haul may be allocated their fair share of total costs of producing the back haul. This makes the cost per shipment high compared with the forward haul. The back haul may be treated as a byproduct of the forward haul because it results from producing the forward haul. All, or most of the costs, are then allocated to forward-haul shipments. Back-haul costs would be considered zero, or assigned only the direct costs to move a shipment in the back-haul direction.

There are several dangers in the latter approach. For one, rates on the forward haul may have to be set at a level that would restrict volume in this direction. In addition, back-haul rates could be set low to help cover some fixed expenses. The effect may be that the back haul gains significantly in volume and possibly surpasses the forward-haul volume. A carrier then may find itself not meeting its fixed expenses and facing rate adjustments that could greatly alter the traffic balance. The by-product has now become the main product. In addition, a significant difference in cost allocation and in rates that follow these costs may lead to questions of rate discrimination between forward-haul and back-haul shippers. The key to discrimination is whether the service in both directions is judged to be under essentially the same conditions and circumstances.

Cost Characteristics by Mode

The type of services that a carrier is likely to emphasize is indicated by the nature of the general cost function under which it operates and by the relationship of the function to those of other carriers.

Rail

As a transporter of freight and passengers, the railroad has high fixed costs and relatively low variable costs. Loading, unloading, billing and collecting, and yard switching of multiple-product, multiple-shipment trains contribute to high terminal costs for rail. Increased per-shipment volume and its effect on reducing terminal costs result in some substantial economies of scale, that is, lower per-unit costs for increased per-shipment volume. Roadway maintenance and depreciation, terminal facility depreciation, and administration expenses also add to the level of fixed cost. Railroad line-haul costs, or variable costs, typically include wages, fuel, oil, and maintenance. Variable costs by definition vary proportionately with distance and volume; however, a degree of indivisibility does exist in some variable costs (labor, for example), so variable costs per unit will decrease slightly. Traditionally, variable costs have been taken as one-half to one-third of total costs, although there is a great deal of controversy over the exact proportion.

The net effect of high fixed costs and relatively low variable costs is to create significant economies of scale in railroad costs. Distributing the fixed costs over greater volume generally reduces the per-unit costs, as shown in Figure 6-5. Similarly, rail ton-mile costs drop when fixed costs are allocated over increasing lengths of haul.

Figure 6-5
Generalized Surface Carrier Cost Structure Based on Shipment Size

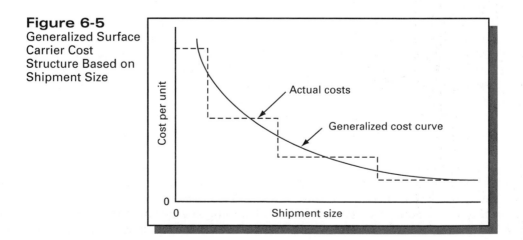

Highway

Motor carriers show contrasting cost characteristics with rail. Their fixed costs are the lowest of any carrier because motor carriers do not own the roadway over which they operate, the tractor-trailer represents a small economic unit, and terminal operations do not require expensive equipment. On the other hand, variable costs tend to be high because highway construction and maintenance costs are charged to the users in the form of fuel taxes, tolls, and weight-mile taxes.

Trucking costs are mainly broken down into terminal expenses and line-haul expenses. Terminal expenses, which include pickup and delivery, platform handling, and billing and collecting, are 15 to 25 percent of total trucking expenses. These expenses, on a dollar-per-ton basis, are highly sensitive to shipment sizes below 2,000 to 3,000 pounds. Terminal expenses for shipments larger than 3,000 pounds continue to drop as pickup and delivery and handling costs are spread over larger shipment sizes. However, the reduction is far less dramatic than for small shipment sizes. The costs as a function of shipment size follow the same general form as previously shown in Figure 6-5.

Line-haul trucking costs are 50 to 60 percent of total costs. It is not clear that per-unit, line-haul costs necessarily decrease with distance or volume. However, total-unit trucking costs do decrease with shipment size and distance as terminal costs and other fixed expenses are spread over more ton-miles, but not as dramatically as rail costs.

Water

The major capital investment that a water carrier makes is in transport equipment and, to some extent, terminal facilities. Waterways and harbors are publicly owned and operated. Little of this cost, especially for inland waterway operations, is charged back to water carriers. The predominant fixed costs in a water carrier's budget are associated with terminal operations. Terminal costs include the harbor fees, as the carrier enters a seaport, and the costs for loading and unloading cargo. Loading and unloading times are particularly slow for water carriers. High stevedoring costs make terminal costs almost prohibitive for all but bulk commodities and containerized freight where mechanized materials-handling equipment can be used effectively.

These typically high terminal costs are somewhat offset by very low line-haul costs. Without user charges for the waterways, variable costs include only those costs associated with operating the transport equipment. Operating costs (excluding labor) are particularly low because of the minimal drag to movement at slow speeds. With high terminal costs and low line-haul costs, ton-mile costs drop significantly with distance and shipment size. Thus, water is one of the least expensive carriers of bulk commodities over long distances and in substantial volume.

Air

Air transportation has many of the same cost characteristics as water and highway carriers. Airline companies generally do not own the air space nor the air terminals. Airlines purchase airport services as needed in the form of fuel, storage, space rental, and landing fees. If we include ground handling and pickup and delivery in the case of airfreight operations, these costs are the terminal costs for air transportation.

In addition, airlines own (or lease) their own equipment, which, when depreciated over its economic life, becomes an annual fixed expense. In the short run, airline variable expenses are influenced more by distance than by shipment size. Because an aircraft has its greatest inefficiency in the takeoff and landing phases of operation, variable costs are reduced by the length of haul. Volume has indirectly influenced variable costs as greater demand for air transportation services has brought about larger aircraft that have lower operating costs per available ton-mile.

Combined fixed and variable expenses generally make air transportation a premium service, especially for short distances; however, distribution of terminal expenses and other fixed charges over increased volume offers some reduction in per-unit costs. Substantial per-unit cost reductions come from operating aircraft over long distances.

Pipeline

Pipeline parallels the railroad in its cost characteristics. Pipeline companies, or the oil companies that own the pipelines, own the pipe, terminals, and pumping equipment. They may own or lease the right-of-way for the pipe. These fixed costs, with the addition of other costs, give pipeline the highest ratio of fixed cost to total cost of any mode. To be competitive, pipelines must work on high volume over which to spread these high fixed costs.

Variable costs mainly include power to move the product (usually crude oil or refined petroleum products) and costs associated with the operation of pumping stations. Power requirements vary markedly, depending on the line throughput and the diameter of the pipe. Larger pipes have disproportionately less circumference to cross-sectional area as compared with smaller pipes. Frictional losses, and therefore pumping power, increase with the pipe circumference, and volume increases with the cross-sectional area. As a result, costs per ton-mile decrease substantially with larger pipes, if there is sufficient throughput to justify the larger pipe. There are also diminishing returns to scale if too large a volume is forced through pipe of a given size. These general cost characteristics are shown in Figure 6-6.

Figure 6-6
Generalized Pipeline Costs As Functions of Pipe Diameter and Throughput Volume

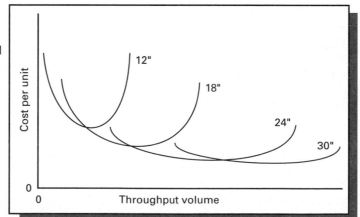

RATE PROFILES

Transportation rates are the prices that for-hire carriers charge for their services. Various criteria are used in developing rates under a variety of pricing situations. The most common rate structures are related to volume, distance, and demand.

Volume-Related Rates

The economies of the transportation industry show that costs of service are related to the shipment size. Rate structures in general reflect these economies, as shipments in consistently high volumes are transported at lower rates than smaller shipments. Volume is reflected in the rate structure in several ways. First, rates may be quoted directly on the quantity shipped. If the shipment is small and results in very low revenue for the carrier, the shipment will be assessed either a minimum charge or an any-quantity (AQ) rate. Larger shipments that result in charges greater than the minimum charge but are less than a full-vehicle-load quantity are charged at a less-than-vehicle load rate that varies with the particular volume. Large shipment sizes that equal or exceed the designated vehicle-load quantity are charged the vehicle-load rate.

Second, the system of freight classification permits some allowance for volume. High volume can be considered justification for quoting a shipper special rates on particular commodities. These special rates are considered deviations from the regular rates that apply to products shipped in lesser volume.

Volume-related rate structures are more complex than this discussion indicates. However, because much of the following section on transport rates is concerned with volume, further discussion is deferred until later in this chapter.

Distance-Related Rates

Rates, as a function of distance, range from being completely invariant with distance to varying directly with distance, with most rate structures lying between these extremes.

Uniform Rates

Simplicity can be a key factor in establishing a rate structure. The simplest of all is the uniform rate structure in which there is one transport rate for all origin-to-destination distances [Figure 6-7(a)]. An example is the first-class postage rates in the United States. The uniform rate structure for mail is justified because a large portion of the total cost for delivering mail is in handling. Handling costs are shipment, not distance, related. On the other hand, using a uniform rate structure for truck transportation, where line-haul costs are at least 50 percent of total cost, would raise serious questions of rate discrimination.[21]

---

[21]Discrimination is assumed to occur whenever rates do not follow the costs of producing the service in question.

Figure 6-7 Four Distance-Related Freight Rate Structures

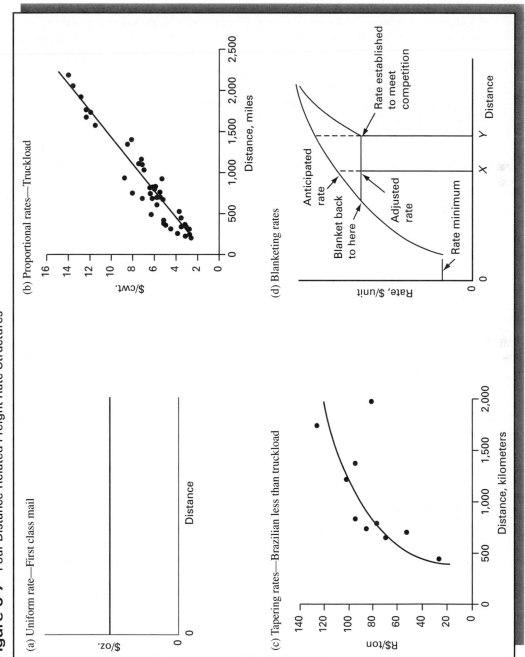

(a) Uniform rate—First class mail

(b) Proportional rates—Truckload

(c) Tapering rates—Brazilian less than truckload

(d) Blanketing rates

Proportional Rates

For those carriers with significant line-haul cost components (truck and, to a lesser extent, air), a compromise between rate structure simplicity and service costs is provided by the proportional rate structure [Figure 6-7(b)]. By knowing only two rates, one can determine all other rates for a commodity by straight-line extrapolation. Although there are some obvious advantages to this simple structure, it does adversely discriminate against the long-haul shipper in favor of the short-haul shipper. Terminal charges are not recovered on the short haul. Truckload rates can have this characteristic because handling costs are minimal.

Tapering Rates

A common rate structure is built upon the tapering principle. Because in the United States terminal charges are typically included in line-haul charges, a rate structure that follows costs will show rates increasing with distance but at a decreasing rate, as shown in Figure 6-7(c). A major reason for this shape is that with increased distance of the shipment, terminal costs and other fixed charges are distributed over more miles. The degree of taper will depend on the level of fixed costs that a carrier has and the extent of economies of scale in line-haul operations. Thus, if only economies dictate the rate structure, we logically would expect greater taper for rail, water, and pipe than for truck and air.

Blanket Rates

The desire to meet the competitors' rates and to simplify rate publications and administration led carriers to establish blanket rate structures. Blanket rates are merely single rates that cover a wide area at the origin, destination, or both. The resulting rate structure is illustrated in Figure 6-7(d), with the plateau as the area of rate grouping, or blanketing. Blanket rates are most common for products being hauled over long distances and whose producers or markets are grouped in certain areas. Such products include grain, coal, lumber, and produce from California that is sold in eastern markets. Even parcel post and UPS rates that are quoted for wide zones radiating from the origin are a form of blanket transportation rates.

Blanketing is a form of rate discrimination, but the benefits of rate simplification for both the carriers and shippers outweigh the disadvantages. In addition, it generally offers the users of transportation services a broader selection of carriers.

At times, competition forces rates along a route to be lower than would normally be predicted from the general rate structure and the cost profile. See point Y in Figure 6-7(d). To offer the lower rate at Y can create a situation where points ahead of Y, such as X, suffer from seemingly unfair rate treatment. Carriers may wish to eliminate this type of rate inequity by making the rate for X and for all other points ahead of Y that would have a rate greater than that of Y, equal to Y's rate. This process is called *blanketing back*.

Demand-Related Rates

Demand, or value of service, may also dictate rate levels bearing little resemblance to the costs of producing the transportation service. Recognized here is the fact that

Figure 6-8
Value of
Transportation
Service

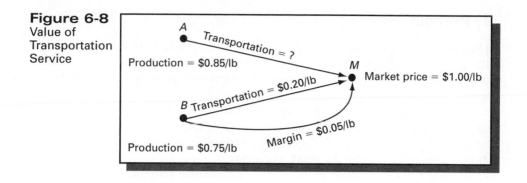

users view transportation as having only so much value to them. Thus, the rates cannot exceed an upper limit if the user is to hire the carrier in question. Two dimensions suggest the value of transportation service to a shipper: the shipper's own economic circumstances and available alternative transportation services.

Example

Producers A and B manufacture and promote a product that sells for $1 per pound in market M, as illustrated in Figure 6-8.

A's expenses, other than transportation costs, are 85¢ per pound and B's are 75¢ per pound. B can make a 5¢ per pound profit on the product selling for $1 per pound. Because B establishes the price, the maximum that A can reasonably pay for transportation is 15¢ per pound, at which rate there would be no profit. This is the maximum that transportation service is worth to A. If rates are set above this level, the product will not move.

The second dimension is seen in the two service alternatives available to B. If it is assumed that both alternatives have equal performance characteristics, the value of the service to B is the lower rate. The high-priced service would have to meet the 20¢ per pound rate to be competitive and move some of the product. Thus, demand, or competition, establishes the rate level. Competitive rates based on value of service tend to distort cost-oriented rate structures and increase the complexities of rate quotation, administration, and publication.

LINE-HAUL RATES

Transport prices can be classified as rates for line-haul services or special service charges. Line-haul rates refer to the charges incurred between origin and destination terminals, or door-to-door in the case of truckload motor carrier service. Special service charges are prices for additional services, such as terminal services, stop-off services, and detention of carrier equipment. Line-haul rates may be usefully classified by product, by shipment size, by route, or miscellaneous.

By Product

If an individual rate were quoted for each product item between all origin-destination point combinations for all transport services, an impractically large number of rates to be administered would result. To substantially reduce the number of rates needed, a product classification system was devised in which most product items are assigned to one of 31 classes ranging from class 13 to 400. Rates were quoted for class 100, and rates on products with different class ratings were generally found as a percentage of the class 100 rate. Currently, carriers do not follow this formula exactly and publish rates for specific product classes.

At one time, a number of product classification schemes existed that differed depending on the territory of the country to which it applied. Since the mid-1950s, many railroads, truckers, and water carriers have adopted a single classification code in the Uniform Freight Classification. Motor carriers also use a similar product classification scheme of the National Motor Freight Classification but with two important exceptions: (1) those products not expected to move by truck are excluded, and (2) there are 18 LTL classes ranging from 50 to 500. Water carriers either use a weight-space formula or base their rates on the rail and motor carrier product classifications. Freight forwarders use the rail-motor carrier classifications. The single-product nature of pipeline requires no classification. Classification of products moving by air is not widespread, with no national product classification system available. Table 6-4 shows a section of the National Motor Freight Classification.

As a practical matter, not all product items are separately listed in the classification or have a specific rating. Both rail and motor carrier classifications provide for this by collecting under one heading all products not separately described in the classifications and denoting these products as not otherwise indexed (NOI).[22] All NOI products have a single rating. Several examples of the NOI classification appear in Table 6-4.

Under certain circumstances, product ratings deviate from those listed in the classification and are referred to as "exceptions to the classification." These exceptions take precedence over the published ratings and are generally lower than the class rating. They are established to reflect special conditions, especially competition and operating conditions that cannot be realized under a classification that must provide an average rating for products shipped under average circumstances.

A number of factors based on *density, stowability, ease of handling,* and *liability* are taken into account in establishing a product rating. These factors can include the following:

- Weight per cubic foot as packed for shipment
- Value per pound as packed for shipment
- Liability to loss, damage, waste, or theft in transit
- Likelihood of injury to other freight with which it may come in contact
- Risks due to hazards of carriage
- Kind of container or package as bearing upon the matter of liability or risk

---

[22]NOI is specifically used in the National Motor Freight Classification. The Uniform Freight Classification uses NOIBN to mean the same thing, and is translated as "not otherwise indexed by name."

- Expense of, and care in, handling
- Ratings on analogous articles
- Fair relation of ratings between all articles
- Competition between articles of different description but largely used for similar purposes
- Commercial conditions and unit of sales
- Trade conditions
- Value of service
- Volume of movement for the entire country[23]

Implementation of provisions of the acts to deregulate transportation may lead to fewer factors being used for classification purposes.

Class Rates

A companion to the freight classification is a tariff, or transportation price list. Once a product has a class rating, then line-haul charges can be determined.

The class rate is a function of the distance between shipment origin and destination points as well as other factors. Shipping distances on which to base rates are found by using such standard distance tables as the *Household Goods Movers Guide, Rand-McNally Mileage Guide,* or other mileage guides that are acceptable to both shipper and carrier. In these guides, zip codes are frequently used to reference the location of origin and destination points. This allows clustering many addresses into a manageable number of reference points while providing acceptable accuracy representing distances. A rate table can then be constructed where rates vary by zip code (distance) and class rating, as shown in Table 6-5.

Shippers do not always pay the rates for the quantities exactly as shown in Table 6-4. That is, if a shipment were to be made up of 9,000 lb, the rate for the >5,000 lb weight break would not necessarily be used. Carriers allow the shipment size to be declared the next higher weight-break quantity and that rate used if the total charges are less than those for the straight calculation. Within every weight break, there is some quantity offering this advantage. The quantity at which the break occurs can be found by the formula

$$\text{Break weight} = \frac{Rate_{Next} \times Weight_{Next}}{Rate_{Current}} \qquad \textbf{(6-1)}$$

where

$$\begin{aligned}
\text{Break weight} &= \text{Weight above which the next higher weight break rate} \\
&\quad\;\; \text{should be used for lower transport costs} \\
Rate_{Next} &= \text{Rate for next higher weight break} \\
Weight_{Next} &= \text{Minimum weight of next higher weight break} \\
Rate_{Current} &= \text{Rate for true weight of shipment}
\end{aligned}$$

---

[23]Charles A. Taff, *Management of Physical Distribution and Transportation,* 6th ed. (Homewood, IL.: Richard D. Irwin, 1978), pp. 356–357.

Table 6-4 National Motor Freight Classification for Selected Products

ITEM NUMBER	DESCRIPTION	LESS-THAN TRUCKLOAD	TRUCKLOAD	MINIMUM WEIGHT, LB
	ABRASIVES GROUP:			
	Alundum, Corundum, Emery or other Natural or Synthetic Abrasive Material, consisting chiefly of aluminum oxide or silicon carbide:			
1070-00	Crude or lump, LTL, in bags, barrels or boxes: TL, loose or in packages	55	35	50,000
1090-00	Flour or grain, in packages	55	35	36,000
2010-00	Refuse, including broken wheels, wheel stubs or wheel grindings, in packages; also TL, loose	55	35	40,000
2030-00	Wheels, pulp grinding, on skids or in boxes or crates	55	40	30,000
2055-00	Cloth or Paper, abrasive, including Emery Cloth or Paper or Sandpaper, in packages	55	37.5	36,000
2070-00	Accessories or Furniture, cat or dog, in boxes and having a density on pounds per cubic foot of:			
2070-01	Less than 1	400	400	AQ[a]
2070-02	1 but less than 2	300	300	AQ[a]
2070-03	2 but less than 4	250	250	AQ[a]
2070-04	4 but less than 6	150	100	12,000
2070-05	6 but less than 8	125	85	15,000
2070-06	8 but less than 10	100	70	18,000
2070-07	10 but less than 12	92.5	65	20,000
2070-08	12 but less than 15	85	55	26,000
2070-09	15 or greater	70	40	36,000
	ADVERTISING GROUP:			
	Advertising Matter, NOI, prepaid, in packages			
4660-01	Cloth or oilcloth	85	55	24,000
4660-02	Paper or paperboard, other corrugated or fluted	70	40	30,000
4740-00	Almanacs, prepaid, in packages	77.5	55	24,000

Item Number	Description	Less-Than Truckload	Truckload	Minimum Weight, lb
4745-00	traveling bags, Gloves, Head Visors or Mats, cloth, printed with advertising, prepaid, in boxes	100	70	20,000
4800-00	Calendars, prepaid:			
4800-01	Cloth, in packages; or steel, celluloid covered, in boxes	85	55	24,000
4800-02	Paper or pulpboard, in packages	70	55	24,000
4850-00	Catalogs, prepaid; or Catalog Parts or Sections, paper, prepaid; in packages	60	35	40,000
4860-00	Circulars, Books, Booklets, Leaflets, Pamphlets, Sheets or Price Lists			
4860-01	Printed entirely on newsprint	60	35	30,000
4860-02	Not printed entirely on newsprint	77.5	55	24,000
4920-00	Displays, consisting of brick or tile facings, roofing, shingles, siding or tile; mounted on panels, prepaid, in boxes or crates	70	55	24,000
4960-00	Displays, dummy articles, such as imitation butter squares, fruits, vegetables or meats, prepaid, in boxes or crates	100	70	20,000
4980-00	Displays, Figures or Images, rubber, NOI, other than foam rubber, prepaid, in boxes or crates	100	70	20,000

[a]AQ refers to Any Quantity.

Source: Adapted from Southern Motor Carriers' PC FastClass Software.

Table 6-5 Nondiscounted, Less-Than-Truckload Rates for Class 100 Product Moving From New York City, NY, to Selected Zip Sectional Centers

Zip	Location	Min.[a]	<500[b]	≥500[c]	≥1,000[c]	≥2,000[c]	≥5,000[c]	≥10,000[c]	≥20,000[c]	≥30,000[c]	≥40,000[d]
021	Boston MA	9,768	5,877	4,636	3,474	3,075	2,444	1,742	1,009	733	687
029	Providence RI	9,351	5,401	4,276	3,203	2,866	2,271	1,592	882	662	601
041	Portland ME	8,460	5,854	4,597	3,441	3,206	2,537	2,269	1,321	965	931
122	Albany NY	12,838	6,665	5,288	4,038	3,459	2,971	2,218	1,315	1,022	980
152	Pittsburgh PA	13,263	6,957	5,246	4,015	3,446	2,976	2,215	1,265	970	945
194	Philadelphia PA	10,825	5,132	4,069	3,071	2,561	2,083	1,423	735	554	525
198	Wilmington DE	11,110	5,290	4,195	3,174	2,648	2,167	1,501	805	619	567
200	Washington DC	13,262	6,890	5,553	4,310	3,666	3,069	2,235	1,293	988	936
212	Baltimore MD	11,084	5,579	4,421	3,361	2,843	2,373	1,689	942	716	674
232	Richmond VA	11,296	6,158	4,899	3,744	3,218	2,756	2,021	1,154	875	860
282	Charlotte NC	12,973	6,502	5,992	4,873	3,867	3,082	2,521	1,217	979	876
292	Columbia SC	13,248	6,842	6,310	5,146	4,099	3,271	2,709	1,385	1,110	998
303	Atlanta GA	14,826	8,196	7,494	6,114	4,965	3,973	3,344	1,836	1,490	1,336
331	Miami FL	14,396	9,142	8,495	6,779	5,575	4,290	4,200	2,278	1,829	1,654
336	Tampa FL	14,081	8,664	8,046	6,416	5,232	4,037	3,948	2,131	1,708	1,545
379	Memphis TN	13,313	6,928	6,395	5,214	4,159	3,320	2,758	1,429	1,141	1,030
402	Louisville KY	12,787	7,474	6,425	4,787	4,323	3,546	2,784	1,905	1,625	1,422
432	Columbus OH	12,276	6,856	5,902	4,340	3,920	3,221	2,483	1,702	1,450	1,268
441	Cleveland OH	12,161	6,710	5,781	4,238	3,826	3,142	2,412	1,656	1,409	1,229
452	Cincinnati OH	12,504	7,112	6,118	4,525	4,085	3,354	2,608	1,784	1,526	1,330

Code	City										
462	Indianapolis IN	12,672	7,331	6,301	4,683	4,229	3,471	2,713	1,860	1,584	1,384
482	Detroit MI	14,808	8,639	7,418	5,598	5,017	4,143	3,308	2,411	2,069	1,805
532	Milwaukee WI	13,097	7,848	6,739	5,051	4,564	3,738	2,963	2,028	1,727	1,511
554	Minneapolis MN	14,165	9,043	7,754	5,901	5,339	4,334	3,520	2,414	2,059	1,807
606	Chicago IL	15,128	8,451	7,379	5,586	4,999	4,093	2,856	1,957	1,664	1,458
631	St. Louis MO	13,289	8,074	6,927	5,213	4,707	3,855	3,069	2,104	1,793	1,565
701	New Orleans LA	17,032	10,849	9,530	7,720	6,402	5,100	3,750	2,028	1,625	1,462
722	Little Rock AR	13,993	8,851	7,587	5,760	5,203	4,249	3,435	2,353	2,007	1,756
731	Oklahoma City OK	14,976	9,886	8,463	6,486	5,864	4,785	3,923	2,690	2,290	2,006
752	Dallas TX	17,353	10,775	9,226	7,114	6,414	5,221	4,011	2,748	2,343	2,052
782	San Antonio TX	17,313	11,882	10,139	7,863	7,095	5,799	4,831	3,380	2,895	2,534
802	Denver CO	16,345	11,830	9,543	7,949	6,895	6,072	4,685	4,140	3,602	3,367
850	Phoenix AZ	18,650	13,626	10,987	9,161	7,945	6,991	5,461	4,812	4,185	3,912
900	Los Angeles CA	20,614	14,954	12,094	10,092	8,727	7,672	6,065	5,365	4,660	4,341
921	San Diego CA	19,560	14,345	11,555	9,632	8,349	7,356	5,764	5,097	4,434	4,145
933	Bakersfield CA	18,778	13,803	11,094	9,274	8,033	7,091	5,541	4,893	4,247	3,992
946	Oakland CA	18,931	13,927	11,192	9,355	8,102	7,153	5,595	4,938	4,290	4,030
972	Portland OR	19,725	14,473	11,657	9,720	8,424	7,424	5,819	5,144	4,472	4,184
981	Seattle WA	18,896	14,173	11,389	9,519	8,247	7,286	5,709	5,031	4,376	4,115

[a]Minimum charge in cents (¢)

[b]Rates in cents per hundred pounds (¢/cwt.)

[c]When a charge computed at the true weight exceeds the charge computed on the next at the weight breakpoint, the lesser charge will apply.

[d]Charges will be the lowest that can be computed, either by using the applicable LTL rate at actual or estimated weight, or by using the TL rates.

Source: Published rates of the Yellow Freight System, Inc.

Example

Suppose 15,000 lb of aprons used as advertising material is to be shipped by truck from New York City to Detroit, Michigan. The class rating for this product (item 4745-01 in Table 6-4) is 100. From a trucker's rate list (Table 6-5), the class 100 tariff is found to be $33.08 per cwt. for shipments between 10,000 and 20,000 lb, and $24.11 per cwt. for shipments greater than 20,000 lb. The carrier offers a 60 percent discount from the rate list. Calculate the break weight as $(24.11 \times 20,000) \div 33.08 = 14,576$ lb. Since the shipment is greater than 14,576 lb, ship as if it is 20,000 lb using the $24.11/cwt. rate. Therefore, shipping charges are 24.11×200 cwt. $= \$4,822.00$. Taking the discount of $0.60 \times \$4,822.00 = \$2,893.20$. The net charge is $\$4,822.00 - 2,893.20 = \$1,928.80$.

Recall that the class tariff is similar to list prices found on many products. These rates are widely disseminated and generally known among shippers and carriers. They can be obtained from various carriers' Web sites or on disks that are supplied free of charge by the carriers. Among carriers, these list rates are quite similar and provide little basis for competition. Hence, it is a common practice for carriers to deeply discount from these rates in order to offer attractive rates to win a shipper's business. Discounts frequently range from 40 to 70 percent. The discount rate is negotiated between shipper and carrier.

Application

A chemical company produces and ships a high proportion of its paint and corrosion-prevention products from the Cleveland, Ohio, area to many points throughout the United States. Most shipments are small and at less-than-truckload weights. Any given shipment is not of sufficient weight nor are the shipments directed to a few enough points to justify its truckers offering it special rates. Instead, the truckers allow a 40 percent discount from the class tariff to retain this valued customer.

Contract Rates

Although the class rate structure provides a general way in which rates for a wide range of merchandise can be determined, many carriers are quoting special rates to shippers. These rates reflect a number of circumstances around an individual shipment or shipper, such as volume of the shipment(s), direction of the movement, and overall value as a customer. These rates may or may not be built on a systematic basis. Contract rates are meant to take precedence over the more general class rates. These may be special, one-of-a-kind rates reflecting individual shipping situations.

Before transportation deregulation, commodity rates were special rates quoted in the rate tariff to represent special shipping circumstances that were not covered by the general class rate structure. These rates were lower than class rates and took precedence over them. Since deregulation, commodity rates seem to be fading into the background in favor of the contract rate, which serves the same purpose.

The bulk of the total miles shipped in the economy use these specially quoted rates. However, most of the shipments that are small use the general class rates for rate quoting simplicity.

Freight-All-Kinds

When carriers quote single rates for a shipment regardless of the classification of the commodities that make up the shipment, the rate is referred to as a freight-all-kinds (FAK) rate or an all-commodity rate (ACR). Freight forwarders are frequent users of this type of rate because they primarily deal with mixed shipments. The rates follow the costs of providing the transportation service rather than the value of the service.

By Shipment Size

Rates and actual transportation charges vary depending on the quantity tendered, that is, on shipment size. Rates are quoted on a dollar-per-hundred-pound (cwt.) basis and can be different depending on where the shipment size falls in relation to prescribed minimum quantities established in the rate tariff. Any number of minimum quantities may appear in the tariff. There may be multiple minimum quantities, for example, 5,000-lb, 10,000-lb, 20,000-lb, and 30,000-lb minimums. There may be only a single rate for all quantities, which is referred to as an any-quantity (AQ) rate.

Railroads, truckers, and transportation brokers customarily have a lower quantity limit on which to base charges, or they have a flat minimum charge such that actual charges cannot drop below this minimum. It is common to find rates quoted by class rating and with a minimum charge. Because class ratings are for less-than-vehicle loads and vehicle loads with a single minimum vehicle-load quantity, then there also is a less-than-vehicle-load rate and a vehicle-load rate in addition to the minimum charge.

Some tariffs may highlight weight breaks instead of the class ratings. Table 6-6 shows a sample of a truck class 100 tariff with common weight breaks to 40,000 pounds.

Example

Suppose an item is rated at class 60, has a shipping weight of 1,000 pounds (10 cwt.), and is to move from Louisville, Kentucky, to Chicago, Illinois. Based on Table 6-6, the transportation charges would be $20.43/\text{cwt.} \times 10 \text{ cwt.} = \$204.30$.

Many carriers make their tariffs available on computer disks and distribute them to their customers for a nominal fee or free of charge. With this aid, shippers can easily rate their own shipments using five-level zip codes to identify shipment origin-destination points. The carriers can then negotiate with the shipper an appropriate discount from this general class tariff.

Table 6-6 Selected Class Truck Rates in $ per cwt. by Classification Number and Weight-Break Quantity in lb for Shipments from Louisville, Kentucky, to Chicago, Illinois

MCª $75.40 CLASS	<500	≥ 500	≥ 1,000	≥ 2,000	≥ 5,000	≥ 10,000	≥ 20,000	≥ 30,000	≥ 40,000
500	165.39	132.31	99.26	82.70	59.51	54.44	28.67	28.67	28.67
400	139.03	111.22	83.43	69.51	50.03	45.76	24.10	24.10	24.10
300	110.26	88.21	66.17	55.13	39.68	36.68	19.11	19.11	19.11
250	95.88	76.70	57.54	39.55	34.50	31.56	16.62	16.62	16.62
200	79.10	63.28	47.47	39.55	28.46	26.04	13.71	13.71	13.71
175	69.51	55.61	41.72	34.76	25.01	22.88	12.05	12.05	12.05
150	62.32	49.86	37.40	31.16	22.43	20.51	10.80	10.80	10.80
125	52.73	42.19	31.65	26.37	18.98	17.36	9.14	9.14	9.14
110	52.34	40.27	30.21	25.17	18.11	16.57	8.73	8.73	8.73
100	47.94	38.35	28.77	23.97	17.25	15.78	8.31	5.69	4.37
92.5	45.54	36.43	27.33	22.77	16.39	14.99	7.89	5.41	4.15
85	42.19	33.75	25.32	21.09	15.18	13.89	7.31	5.01	3.85
77.5	39.79	31.83	23.88	19.90	14.32	13.10	6.90	4.72	3.63
70	37.39	29.91	22.44	18.70	13.46	12.31	6.48	4.44	3.41
65	35.48	28.38	21.29	17.74	12.77	11.68	6.15	4.21	3.23
60	34.04	27.23	20.43	17.02	12.25	11.20	5.90	4.04	3.10
55	32.60	26.08	19.56	16.30	11.73	10.73	5.65	3.87	2.97
50	31.16	24.93	18.70	15.58	11.21	10.26	5.40	3.70	2.84

ª MC = minimum charge in $

Source: Southern Motor Carriers' CZAR-LITE software.

Further examples of how actual transportation charges are computed under various circumstances are shown in Table 6-7. Although truck rates are used in the examples, the methods of computation are generally applicable to the other transportation modes as well.

Other Incentive Rates

There are additional rates that act as incentives to ship in large quantities. One such rate is the in-excess rate (see Table 6-7, example H). In-excess rates are lower than vehicle-load rates and apply to only those quantities that exceed the vehicle-load minimums. This rate encourages shippers to increase shipment size and allows carriers to better utilize the capacity of their equipment.

Carriers further encourage shippers to ship in quantities greater than vehicle-load minimums through multiple-vehicle rates and even trainload rates. Carriers can effect economies of scale on larger loads and pass these economies along to shippers

Table 6-7 Examples of Transportation Charge Computations for Different Shipment Combinations of Class Ratings, Distances, and Shipment Weights

Example	Shipment Specifications	Calculation Rate, $/cwt.	Actual Freight of Charges	Charges	Comments
A	Item 2070-02; Louisville, KY, to Chicago, IL; Volume = 300 lb.	MC = $75.40, $110.26	$110.26 × 3 = $330.78	$330.78	Class = 300 from Table 6-4; Rate from Table 6-6
B	200 lb of paper calendars; Louisville, KY, to Chicago, IL	MC = $75.40, $37.39	37.39 × 2 = $74.78 Pay minimum charge	$75.40	Class = 70 for item 4800-02 in Table 6-4; Rate from Table 6-6
C	Cat furniture; New York, NY, to Portland, OR; Volume 15,000 lb at a density of 5 lb/cu. ft.	MC = $197.25, $58.19	$58.19 × 150 = $8,728.50 Break quantity is 17,680 lb[a]	$8,728.50	Class = 100 for item 2070-05 from Table 6-4; Rate from Table 6-5
D	150 lb of books printed on glossy paper; Louisville, KY, to Chicago, IL	MC = $75.40, $39.79	$39.79 × 1.5 = $59.69 Pay minimum charge	$75.40	Class = 77.5 for item 4860-02 from Table 6-4; Rate from Table 6-6
E	18,000 lb. of bags with advertising; Louisville, KY, to Chicago, IL	LTL: $15.78 @100 TL: $6.48 @70[b]	LTL: $15.78 × 180 = $2,840.40 TL: 6.48 × 200 = $1,296.00	$1,296.00 Ship TL at lower class and rate	Class = 100 LTL and 70 TL for item 4745-00 from Table 6-4; Rates from Table 6-6
F	Grain in packages; Louisville, KY, to Chicago, IL; Volume 27,000 lb	$5.65@20,000 $3.87 @30,000	$3.87 × 300 = $1,161.00 Break quantity is 20,549 lb	$1,161.00	Class = 55 for item 1090-00 from Table 6-4; Rates from Table 6-6
G	Class 100 item; New York, NY, to Little Rock, AR; Volume = 40,000 lb; 40% rate discount	$17.56 less 40% = $10.54	$10.54 × 400 = $4,216.00	$4,216.00	Rate from Table 6-5
H	40,000 lb of refuse; Louisville, KY, to Chicago, IL	TL Class = 35 Rate @35% of 4.37 = 1.52[c]	$1.52 × 400 = $608.00	$608.00	Class = 35 for item 2010-00 from Table 6-4; Base rate from Table 6-6
I	Class 100 item; New York, NY, to Dallas, TX; 45,000 lb; Minimum volume for truckload = 36,000 lb; in-excess rate offered = $15.00/cwt.[d]	TL: Rate = $20.52	TL: $20.52 × 360 = $7,387.20 EX: $15.00 × 90 = $1,350.00 Total $8,737.20	$8,737.20	Rate from Table 6-5

[a]Break quantity = (51.44 ÷ 58.19) × 20,000 = 17,680 lb
[b]Rate for class 70 and shipping weight of 20,000 lb
[c]Rate is approximate as a percent of class 100 rate. A truckload rate is likely to be quoted separately from the tabled rates.
[d]Rate applies to all weight in excess of the minimum volume. The minimum volume moves at the CL rate.

in the form of incentive rates. They are also a competitive weapon against competing carriers. The railroads have been very effective in meeting pipeline competition for the movement of coal by the use of single-commodity trains (unit trains) and train-load rates.

Some carriers have established time-volume rates. Reduced rates are offered if a minimum tonnage is moved within a specified period. Coal is frequently moved under this arrangement.

By Route

When shipments involve full-vehicle-load movements, carriers use a per-mile charge to compute total shipping expenses. For truckloads, rates between states are frequently quoted on a per-mile basis. When the vehicle is loaded with cargo destined for more than one stop, a stop-off charge may be added to the bill. The per-mile rate is determined by the location of the last point on the route.

Example

A truck shipment of 42,000 lb originates at Atlanta, Georgia, and makes three stops for delivery at Dallas, Texas, Oklahoma City, Oklahoma, and St. Louis, Missouri. A stop-off charge of $75 per stop is assessed. The distance from Atlanta to Dallas is 822 miles, from Dallas to Oklahoma City is 209 miles, and from Oklahoma City to St. Louis is 500 miles. The per-mile cost at St. Louis is $1.65. The trip cost would be $(822 + 209 + 500) \times \$1.65 = \$2,526.15$. Adding three stops at $75 each gives a total transport cost of $2,526.15 + 225 = $2,751.15.

Miscellaneous Rates

A number of rates do not fit into the preceding classifications, and they are simply collected under the heading "miscellaneous." The following discussion is selective of the many special rates offered.

Cube Rates
The class rating structure is an average of many different product characteristics. When articles are very light and bulky, class ratings do not fully compensate the carrier for the costs incurred for transporting these items, so cube rates are used. Cube rates are based on space occupied rather than weight.

Import or Export Rates
To encourage foreign trade, special rates, called import or export rates, are established on inland shipments originating from or destined to foreign points. Such shipments move over domestic transportation routes at lower rates than comparable shipments with origins and destinations inland. These rates take precedence over class or commodity rates applicable to shipments via the same route.

Deferred Rates

At times, the shipper is willing to accept the possibility of increased delay in delivery compared with regular service in exchange for lower rates. The shipper is promised that delivery will be made no later than a given date. Carriers use such freight to fill out available space. Deferred service is used most often in air and water transportation.

Released Value Rates

Common carriers are responsible for the value of the goods while in their keeping. If goods are lost or damaged, the shipper can claim up to the full value of the goods. Normally, rates are based on this unlimited liability. In contrast, common carriers are permitted to establish rates based on limited liability, called released value rates. Under released value rates, the carrier's liability is limited to some fixed figure. For example, movers of household goods commonly limit claims for loss and damage to a fixed dollar-per-pound figure. Released value rates are particularly useful when the actual value of the goods is difficult to estimate.

Ocean Freight Rates

Shipments moving internationally by water represent a substantial difference from the way goods are moved domestically. Rates do not closely follow the classification schemes of domestic carriers. They are quoted on either a space or a weight basis, at the carrier's option. Ocean carriers may belong to conferences for the purposes of collective rate making. Rates are stabilized within the conference, but they may vary from conference to conference. In addition to the basic freight rate, further fees and surcharges may be added to cover such items as tolls and handling.

SPECIAL SERVICE CHARGES

Carriers frequently provide special services for which extra charges are made. Although some of these charges may be included in the line-haul rates, they may be added to the freight bill over and above line-haul charges. These special services are classified as special line-haul services or as terminal services. Only the more frequently used services are discussed.

Special Line-Haul Services

These services refer to the line-haul portion of the movement and not to the terminal operation.

Diversion and Reconsignment

Diversion of a shipment refers to changing the destination of a shipment while en route. Reconsignment refers to changing the consignee of a shipment, usually after it has reached the original destination. In practice, however, no distinction is made between the terms.

Shippers have frequently used the diversion and reconsignment privilege in two ways. First, when the commodities are perishable, such as fruits and vegetables, the shipper may start a carload (or truckload) toward the general market area, and when the exact destination has been found or negotiated, the shipment will be diverted to that market. The shipper potentially can gain much from this privilege in terms of flexibility in meeting dynamic market conditions (both demand and price) at a nominal charge per carload.

Second, the carrier's equipment can be used as a warehouse. Through circuitous routing, the shipper may substantially increase the time in transit from that normally required. When a demand for the goods develops, the shipment can then be routed directly to the market. Because this practice, if abused, can greatly increase carrier costs, rail carriers especially have questioned its desirability.

Application

The Anchor-Hocking Glass Company manufactures dinnerware products at its plants located mainly east of the Mississippi River. Soda ash, a key ingredient in glassmaking, is mined only in the area of Green River, Wyoming. Rail shipments take at least seven days in transit to reach the plants. During one January day, the state of Ohio shut down all transit access due to a heavy snowfall. A shipment of soda ash that was already on its way from Wyoming and destined for the Ohio plant was diverted at St. Louis to the company's Houston plant. A later shipment that normally would have gone to Houston was diverted to the Ohio plant. The railroad's diversion and reconsignment privilege helped keep the glass plants operating during the unplanned event for just a small extra expense.

Transit Privileges

Rail carriers and, to a lesser extent, motor carriers have established a special service that permits shipments to be stored before moving to the final destination. A shipment, for rate purposes, is treated as if it moves directly from an origin point to a destination point, and the freight charge is composed of the through rate from origin to destination plus a small additional charge for the stop. Without such an in-transit privilege, shippers would pay the sum of the through rate from the origin to the stop-off point plus the through rate from the stop-off point to the *final* destination point, the sum of which is generally higher than the transit privilege rate. This privilege clearly reduces location disadvantages of processors and allows the carrier to better meet competition by committing the shipper to using the carrier for both segments of the haul. Grain is frequently processed (milled) and transported under this privilege.

A related service is the stop-off privilege to complete loading or to partially unload. To complete loading, a shipper may request that the carrier stop at an intermediate point between the origin and destination points, although the intermediate point need not necessarily be on a direct line between the two points. The advantage of this privilege is that the shipper can obtain a rate on the shipment as

Figure 6-9
Example of Stop-Off
Privilege to
Complete Loading

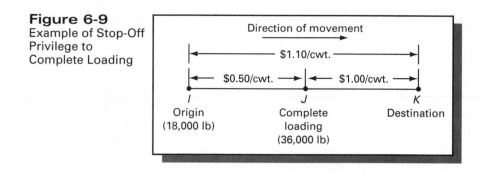

if it originated entirely from the starting point plus a nominal stop-off charge. This is usually less than the sum of individual rates.

Example

Consider the transportation problem shown in Figure 6-9. A shipment of 18,000 lb is originated at point *I*. An additional 36,000 lb is to be combined with it at point *J* and both shipments are to move on to point *K* for delivery. Rather than the shipper paying the individual rates between each point, the shipper may elect, where tariffs permit, to pay the rate from *I* to *K* on the entire shipment plus a stop-off charge. If the rate from stop-off point to the final destination is higher than the rate over the entire route, then the *J* to *K* rate would govern. Table 6-8 shows a comparison of the freight charges with and without a stop-off privilege.

The stop-off privilege applied to partial unloading is similar to that for complete loading. At times, it is cheaper for the shipper to consolidate several shipments moving to different destinations in order to take advantage of substantial volume rate breaks while only incurring modest stop-off charges. For partial unloading, stop offs are of two types. In the first type, all unloading is made from

Table 6-8 Freight Charges for Example Problem with and Without a Stop-Off Privilege

LOADING	ROUTE	RATE	CHARGES WITHOUT STOP-OFF PRIVILEGE	RATE	CHARGES WITH STOP-OFF PRIVILEGE
18,000 lb at *I*	*I* to *J*	$0.50/cwt.	$ 90.00	—	—
additional	*I* and *J*	$1.00/cwt.[a]	540.00	$1.10/cwt.[b]	$594.00
36,000 lb at *J*	to *K*	stop-off charge	—	stop-off charge	25.00
		Total charges	$630.00	Total charges	$619.00

[a]Based on the combined weight of 54,000 lb.
[b]Rate applies from point *I* on complete load.

the equipment in which the shipment was originally loaded [Figure 6-10(a)]. In the second type, transfer at a transloading point is made to different equipment before moving on to final the destination [Figure 6-10(b)]. Carriers do not charge for transloading; rather, the charges are made as if the partial unloading occurred entirely from the original equipment.

Rates for the stop-off privilege are based on the consolidated shipment weight moving to the final destination point. An additional charge is added for each stop made, which may or may not be based on the amount loaded or unloaded. When the stop-off privilege is used, carriers require that charges be collected at only one time. Commonly, up to three stops to unload are permitted, but some piggyback tariffs allow up to five stops. In general, the stop-off privilege will show an advantage over separately priced shipments when the greatest proportion of the total shipping occurs at points farthest from the origin point.

Figure 6-10
Examples of Stop-Off Privilege for Partial Unloading

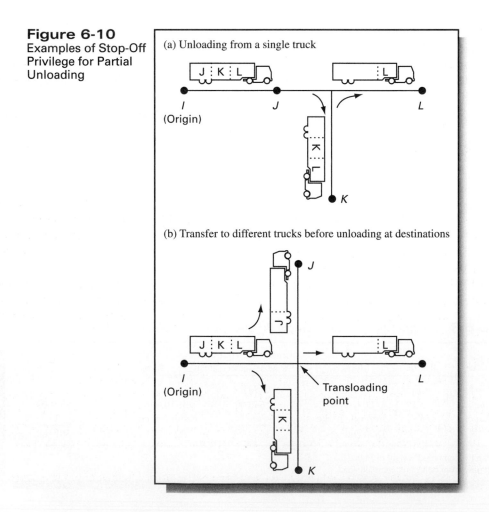

Table 6-9 A Comparison of Total Charges for Partial Unloading of Two Points With and Without a Stop-Off Privilege

	WITHOUT STOP-OFF PRIVILEGE				WITH STOP-OFF PRIVILEGE			
	LOAD, LB	POINTS	RATE, $/CWT.	FREIGHT CHARGES	LOAD, LB	POINTS	RATE $/CWT.	FREIGHT CHARGES
	8,000	I to J	3.05	$ 244.00	30,000	I to J	3.00	$900.00
	12,000	I to K	3.35	402.00			3 stops @ $15/stop[a]	45.00
	10,000	I to L	3.60	360.00				
Total	30,000		Total charges	$1,006.00			Total charges	$945.00

[a]The endpoint L also incurs the stop-off charge.

Example

To illustrate the differences in freight charges with and without a stop-off privilege, consider the example shown in Figure 6-10(a), where $J = 8,000$ lb, $K = 12,000$ lb, and $L = 10,000$ lb, with a 30,000-lb minimum quantity. Table 6-9 shows the cost comparisons. A savings of $1,006 - 945 = $61 can be realized by using a stop-off privilege rather than pricing each shipment separately.

Protection

Many articles, because of their particular physical characteristics, require some type of protection in transit in addition to that normally provided. Perishable commodities may need refrigeration, icing, ventilation, or heating. Fragile commodities may require extra packing, or dunnage.[24] In these cases, carriers may furnish special equipment such as damage-free cars, refrigerated cars, and heaters, as well as the necessary labor and materials needed to provide the protective service. Whereas the extra service for some commodities is reflected in the class rating for the commodities, carriers often add charges to the freight bill to reflect their increased costs.

Interlining

Not all carriers serve all regions. When this is the case, one carrier may pick up a shipment and then give it to another carrier that serves the destination region. In this case, the first carrier pays the second, but the shipper is billed by the first. The total shipment charge must reflect profit to be made by both carriers, and the rate may be higher than if one carrier could handle the shipment from origin to destination.

---

[24]*Dunnage* refers to the cross bracings in a railroad car that prevent the load from shifting during transit, which can damage the load.

Terminal Services

Additional charges may be made to the freight bill for services that take place around the terminal points in a carrier's routing network. Terminal services of major importance are pickup and delivery, switching, and demurrage and detention.

Pickup and Delivery

Many carriers provide pickup and delivery service as a part of their regular service offering and include the charges as part of the line-haul rates. However, this practice is not universal. Some carriers do not provide pickup and delivery—for example, some water carrier services. When they are provided, pickup and delivery may be offered at an extra charge (as in airfreight service). When the pickup and delivery service is "free," tariffs usually limit the service to the immediate area of the carrier's terminal, that is, within the city's corporation limits, or within a mile of the terminal where there is no town.

Switching

The "line haul" for a railroad involves the movement between terminals or stations. The movement of railroad cars from private sidings and junctions to rail terminals or stations, or vice versa, is referred to as *switching*. Switching is similar to pickup and delivery, except that only railroad cars are involved. Line-haul railroads do not always have tracks connecting directly to shippers and consignees and have worked out reciprocal switching agreements with other railroads serving these points. Many railroads absorb the switching charges and the shipper pays nothing above the line-haul rate, if the line-haul shipment produces a certain level of revenue. If the transportation charge is not sufficient to permit the carrier to absorb the switching charge, or if no reciprocal arrangements can be made to serve the siding or junction, the shipper or consignee (receiver of the goods) pays the switching charge on a flat-charge-per-car basis.

Demurrage and Detention

Demurrage and detention are equivalent terms referring to penalty charges imposed on the shipper or consignee for holding the carrier's equipment beyond an allowed free time that the carrier may hold a shipment. In the case of rail cars, 48 hours is the standard free time permitted for loading or unloading. If retention of the equipment is due to reasons under the shipper's or consignee's control, the railroad may impose a daily charge. Sundays and holidays are generally considered part of free time, but they may be charged for once demurrage charges begin. Detention of trucking equipment follows a similar plan, except that free time is much shorter. A graduated upward rate scale is typically used for longer equipment retention periods for both truck and rail.

Demurrage charges may be assessed in two ways. One is the straight plan, where each piece of equipment is treated individually for determining demurrage charges. Each piece of equipment is charged based on the length of time it is detained. In contrast, the average plan represents an agreement between the carrier and the shipper to average the shipper's detention performance over a monthly period and to charge accordingly. Under this plan, releasing a railcar within the first 24-hour period carries an allowance of one credit. For each day a car is retained after the free time period, one debit is assessed. If the sum of debits and credits at month end results in debits, the demurrage charge is applied according to an increasing scale. A net credit balance results in no demurrage charge.

PRIVATE CARRIER COSTING

The major reason that a company owns or leases transport equipment is to provide a level of customer service that is not always obtainable from for-hire carriers. According to a survey of 248 private trucking fleets, the reasons for having the fleets were (1) service reliability, (2) short order cycle times, (3) emergency response capability, and (4) improved customer contact.[25] Achieving a lower cost than for-hire carriage was not the motivating factor, although this may be realized if there is a sufficiently high utilization of the transport equipment.

Observation

For Domino's Pizza, Inc., the $2.6-billion-in-sales delivered pizza giant, running a private fleet is vital to the company's success. The reason why Domino's operates a private fleet is to provide customized food service deliveries to individual stores so the store managers can focus on selling pizza. When the owner opens his store each day for business, the food is there, put away and ready for use. All the owner has to do is make and sell pizza.

The fleet delivers to each store two to three times a week, making about 10,000 weekly deliveries nationwide. A total order cycle time of 48 hours is guaranteed from the time the order is placed to store delivery. No for-hire carrier with a profit motive can meet this service goal.[26]

The cost of operating privately controlled transport is determined in much the same way as with any asset. Whereas the for-hire carrier has summed up all the appropriate costs, allocated them among different hauls, and expressed them as a rate, the owner of privately controlled transportation must undertake this task if a comparison is to be made among alternative transport services. Customarily, such costs are represented on a per-mile basis. Consider a privately owned truck fleet. Costs are typically grouped into three broad categories: fixed costs, operator costs, and vehicle operating costs.

Fixed costs are those that do not vary with the distance that the vehicle travels over time. They include insurance on the vehicle, interest charges on the money tied up in the vehicles, licensing fees, equipment amortization, and expenses associated with housing the vehicles.

[25]Lisa H. Harrington, "Private Fleets: Finding Their Niche," *Transportation & Distribution* (September 1996), pp. 55–60.
[26]Ibid.

Operator costs result from driver compensation. Common expenses are wages; contributions to health and pension plans; per diem expenses while on the road, such as meals, hotel, and other living costs; contributions to Social Security, unemployment insurance, and workers' compensation; and miscellaneous expenses, such as telephone calls. A number of these costs are related to the time that the vehicle is on the road rather than the distance traveled.

Vehicle operating costs are those incurred in keeping the vehicle on the road. Typical expenses are fuel, tires, maintenance, and the like. These various costs are divided by the total fleet miles driven and then by the number of vehicles in the fleet to give an average cost per mile per vehicle. Because of the various fixed costs, the per-mile cost is sensitive to the routing and scheduling that affect the total miles driven. These per-mile costs multiplied by the distances between origin and destination points can then be compared with the rates offered by common or contract carriers. As a rule of thumb, privately owned trucks need to achieve about 80 percent of their miles loaded to be less expensive than for-hire carriers. Private trucking costs average $1.42 per mile, whereas for-hire truckload rates average about $1.33 per mile.[27]

DOCUMENTATION

The three basic document types in domestic freight transportation are the bill of lading, the freight bill, and the freight claim. International transportation has these and many more.

Bill of Lading

The bill of lading is the key document on which freight moves. It is a *legal contract* between the shipper and the carrier for the movement of designated freight with reasonable dispatch to a specified destination, arriving damage free. According to Taff, the bill of lading has the following three purposes:

1. It serves as a receipt for goods, subject to the classifications and tariffs that were in effect on the date that the bill of lading was issued. It certifies that the property described on the bill of lading was in apparent good order except as noted. The shipper and an agent for the carrier should both sign the bill of lading, but a carrier cannot avoid its liability because it does not issue a receipt or bill of lading.
2. It serves as a contract of carriage . . . [and] . . . identifies the contracting parties and prescribes the terms and conditions of the agreement.
3. It serves as documentary evidence of title. It is necessary, however, to qualify this statement. Although this is true of a negotiable bill of lading, in the case of the straight bill of lading, the person who has possession of a straight bill of lading may have title to the goods. That, however, depends upon the facts in the individual case. Such matters as the terms of sale have influence in establishing title to the goods covered by the straight bill of lading.[28]

---

[27]Ibid.
[28]Taff, *Management of Physical Distribution and Transportation*, pp. 516–517.

The straight bill of lading, as contrasted with the order bill of lading, is a non-negotiable legal document. Under the straight bill of lading, the goods are consigned only to the specific person noted in the document. This bill cannot be traded or sold. Under the order bill of lading, the goods are consigned to the order of a person. This instrument may be traded or sold by endorsing the order to another person other than the one specified in the original bill. Being able to change title allows the shipper to obtain payment for the goods before they reach their destination by endorsing the order bill of lading over to a bank and receiving payment. The bank, in turn, passes the document on to the consignee's bank, the consignee, and finally the carrier. The procedure works in much the same manner as bank drafts filter through the banking system.

Freight Bill

The bill of lading ordinarily does not contain information about the freight charges, although some altered forms do include these charges. More frequently, the charges appear on a separate document, commonly referred to as a *freight bill*. The freight bill (an invoice of carrier charges) contains, in addition to freight charges, much of the same information as a bill of lading, such as shipment origin and destination, quantity shipped, product, and the persons involved.

The freight charges may be prepaid by the shipper or billed collect from the consignee. Payments for rail service are made before delivery, except that credit is extended to financially responsible shippers. Credit terms vary, depending on the carrier involved. For example, users of rail services may be allowed up to 96 hours to make payment. Motor carriers must present shippers with freight bills within seven days, and shippers have seven days to pay after receiving the bill. Transportation agencies can extend credit up to seven days. Domestic water carriers generally allow credit to 48 hours and sometimes up to 96 hours.

Freight Claims

Generally, two types of claims are made against carriers. The first arises from the carrier's legal responsibilities as a common carrier, and the second because of overcharges.

Loss, Damage, and Delay Claims
A common carrier has the responsibility to move freight with "reasonable dispatch" and without loss or damage. The bill of lading specifically defines the limits of carrier responsibility.

Observation

A common carrier is not liable for loss, damage, or delay resulting from an act of God, negligence of the shipper, act of a public enemy, or legal action taken against the shipper of the goods. Otherwise, a carrier is liable for the full value of the goods that are lost or damaged, unless the extent of the carrier's liability is specifically limited by the bill of lading.

Losses due to "unreasonable" delay or failure to meet guaranteed schedules are recoverable to the extent of the value reduction resulting directly from the delay.

Overcharges

A claim against a carrier for overcharges results from some form of incorrect invoicing, such as application of incorrect classification, failure to use the correct rates, use of incorrect distances, simple arithmetic errors, duplicate collection of freight charges, errors in determining item weights, and differences in interpretations of rules and tariffs. Normal bill auditing may detect these errors before payment is made, and a corrected freight bill may be issued. Otherwise, up to three years is allowed for overcharge claims on interstate shipments.

INTERNATIONAL TRANSPORT DOCUMENTATION

A feature distinguishing international transportation from domestic movement is the amount of documentation required for imports and exports. A listing of the more popular documents and their purposes follows.

Exporting

- *Bill of lading.* Receipt for the cargo and a contract for transportation between the shipper and the carrier.
- *Dock receipt.* Used to transfer accountability for cargo between domestic and international carriers.
- *Delivery instructions.* Provides specific instructions to the inland carrier regarding delivery of the goods.
- *Export declaration.* Required by the U.S. Department of Commerce as a source document for export statistics.
- *Letter of credit.* Financial document guaranteeing payment to the shipper for the cargo being transported.
- *Consular invoice.* Used to control and identify goods shipped to particular countries.
- *Commercial invoice.* Bill for the goods from seller to the buyer.
- *Certificate of origin.* Used to assure the buying country precisely in which country the goods were produced.
- *Insurance certificate.* Assures the consignee that insurance is provided on goods while in transit.
- *Transmittal letter.* A list of the particulars of the shipment and a record of the documents being transmitted, together with instructions for disposition of the documents.

Importing

- *Arrival notice.* Informs as to the estimated arrival time of the shipment along with some details of the shipment.
- *Customs entries.* A number of documents describing the merchandise, its origin, and duties that aid in expediting clearance of the goods through customs, with or without the immediate payments of duties.
- *Carrier's certificate and release order.* Certifies to customs the owner or consignee of the cargo.
- *Delivery order.* Issued by the consignee to the ocean carrier as authority to release the cargo to the inland carrier.
- *Freight release.* Evidence that the freight charges for the cargo have been paid.
- *Special customs invoice.* An official form usually required by U.S. Customs if the rate of duty is based upon the value, and the value of the shipment exceeds a fixed dollar amount.

Many foreign trade specialists facilitate the paperwork preparation that can aid the shipper and receiver of goods moving internationally.

CONCLUDING COMMENTS

Transportation is a vital component in the design and management of logistics systems. It may account for one-third to two-thirds of total logistics costs. It has been the purpose of this chapter to describe the transportation system in terms of the choices available to the users. These choices typically include the five major transport modes—air, truck, rail, water, and pipe—and their combinations. Users may hire the services or own them.

Transport services are best described by their *cost* and *performance* characteristics. These distinguish one transport service from another, and it is what a user buys from the transportation system. The cost characteristics vary from one mode to another and give rise to their rate structures. Rates are based primarily on three factors— distance, shipment size, and competition. On the other hand, carrier performance is based on the extent of shipment handling at terminals and inherent speed of the carrier. It is adequately described in terms of average transit time, transit-time variability, and loss and damage.

International transportation is an area of growing interest and concern to the logistician. The transportation equipment is the same as that used domestically, with the exception that certain transportation system elements become more important. For example, containerization is popular in international movements. The transportation routes, of course, contrast with those used domestically. The user of the international transportation system may feel overwhelmed with the increased documentation, differences in carrier liability, by various customs procedures, and the use of foreign trade zones—all of which are made complex because two or more governments have jurisdiction over the move. Fortunately, there exists a plethora of middlemen, agents, freight forwarders, and brokers to assist the shipper with international movements.

QUESTIONS

1. Why is transportation considered so important to the U.S. economy? Why is it so important to an individual firm?
2. Broadly outline what a logistics manager needs to know about transportation facilities and services.
3. What is transportation service? Contrast the following in terms of speed, reliability, availability, loss and damage, and cost of service:
   a. A shipment of lettuce from California to New York by air, piggyback, rail, or truck.
   b. A shipment of personal computer monitors from South Korea to London by air or water.
   c. A shipment of auto parts from Detroit to Mexico City by air, rail, piggyback, water, or truck.
   d. A shipment of television sets from the port of Los Angeles to five distribution centers in California by for-hire truck or by privately owned truck.
4. Identify three of the product types that are primarily moved using the five modes of transportation. Why do you think that each mode has an advantage with its particular product group?
5. There are ten possible coordinated transportation service combinations. Speculate why only two of these have gained any significant popularity.
6. Referring to Figure 6-1, explain each of the following:
   a. Less-than-truckload shipments take longer on the average for all distances than truckload shipments.
   b. There is more taper in the rail-carload curve than in the truckload curve.
   c. Airfreight movements beyond 500 miles have the same average transit time regardless of distance.
   d. Rail-carload shipments show greater transit-time variability than any of the other transport services.
7. Construct a performance characteristics table like Table 6-3 for the five basic modes of transportation for distances of 80, 100, 500, 1,000, and 3,000 miles and for the following products:
   a. Electronic equipment such as CD players, VCRs, or TVs.
   b. Coal, sand, or gravel.
   c. Perishable foods such as oranges, grapes, or celery.
8. Why has containerization become such a popular packaging method in international transportation? Why is it not used more extensively for domestic movements?
9. For-hire carriers are required to move products with reasonable dispatch and care. In your judgment, should a for-hire carrier have to pay for the following claims?
   a. A shipment takes 30 days to arrive at its destination when the carrier normally takes two weeks for delivery.
   b. A shipment of furniture is extensively damaged in a derailment.
   c. A trucker accidentally rolls over his trailerload of oranges on an icy road. Most of the load is damaged or stolen by passersby and a guardrail is damaged.
   d. A truckload of television sets is stolen after the shipping contract is signed at the shipping point but before the shipment can be delivered.
   e. An air cargo shipment is lost when the aircraft carrying it is struck by lightning.
   f. A shipment of packaged foodstuffs shows external damage when the railcar is opened at the destination.

10. For the following shipping situations, rank the basic transport modes in terms of (1) availability of the service; (2) average transit time; (3) transit-time variability; (4) price of the service; and (5) loss and damage.
 a. A 10,000-lb shipment of hardware items moving from Dallas, Texas, to Boston, Massachusetts.
 b. A containerload of men's suits moving from Hong Kong to Los Angeles, California.
 c. A 70,000-lb shipment of paper products moving from Spokane, Washington, to Denver, Colorado.
 d. A 40,000-lb shipment of sheet steel moving from Chicago, Illinois, to Cincinnati, Ohio.
 e. A 5,000-lb shipment of fresh flowers from California to New York City.
11. What role do small shipment services and agencies play in the transportation system? What common types are there? What services do they provide?
12. When does privately owned transportation become a better choice than common carrier transportation? Discuss in terms of product characteristics, customer service, and costs.
13. Discuss how a foreign trade zone might be used for:
 a. computer monitors imported to the United States from Japan.
 b. importing wines to the United States from France.
 c. importing into Taiwan from South Korea computer components that are then assembled into personal computers and shipped to Europe.
 d. importing bananas into the United States from South America.
14. A power company in Missouri can buy coal for its generating plants from western mines in Utah or from eastern mines in Pennsylvania. The maximum purchase price for coal of $20 per ton at the Missouri plant is set according to the price of competing energy forms. The cost to mine coal in the West is $17 per ton and in the East is $15 per ton. Transportation cost from the eastern mines is $3 per ton. What is the value of transportation from the western mines?
15. Shipments for a certain product originate at point X and are to be sent to points Y and Z. Y is an intermediate point to X and Z. The rate to Y is $1.20 per cwt., but due to competitive conditions at Z, the rate to Z is $1.00 per cwt. Apply the principle of blanketing back, and explain how it eliminates rate discrimination.
16. Using Tables 6-4, 6-5, and 6-6, determine the freight charges for the following shipments:
 a. A 2,500-lb shipment of paper place mats with printed advertising moving from New York to Los Angeles.
 b. A 150-lb shipment of rubber displays for advertising purposes moving from New York to Providence, RI.
 c. A 27,000-lb shipment of emery cloth in packages moving from Louisville, Kentucky, to Chicago, Illinois. *Note:* For any product classification number below 50, use 50 in Table 6-6.
 d. A 30,000-lb shipment of cat accessories at a density of 10 lb per cubic foot moving between Louisville, Kentucky, and Chicago, Illinois.
 e. A 24,000-lb shipment of advertising circulars not printed on newsprint moving between Louisville, Kentucky, and Chicago, Illinois. A rate discount of 40 percent is offered.

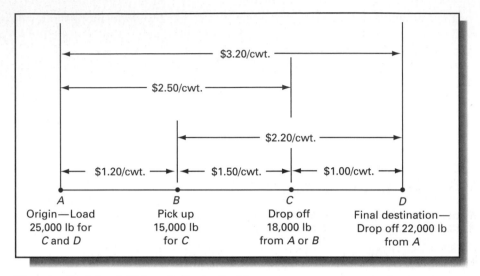

Figure 6-11   A Pickup-Delivery Problem

17. What is the difference between freight classification and class rates (tariff)? Explain the difference between a contract rate and a class rate.

18. Compare the cost structures of railroads with motor carriers and suggest how these might influence the rate structures of each.

19. A number of customers are to receive deliveries. These customers are based along a main route from a shipping point. A truck tariff has been written that allows for a stop-off privilege. What are the general characteristics of the customers in terms of their shipment weights and their locations relative to the shipment origin point that makes the stop-off privilege an attractive option?

20. Suggest the documents that might be needed for the following international movements:
    a. Importing autos from Japan destined for St. Louis, MO.
    b. Exporting computers from White Plains, New York, to Sydney, Australia.

21. A traffic manager has two options in scheduling a truck to make multiple pickups and deliveries. The pickup-delivery problem is shown pictorially in Figure 6-11. The traffic manager can ship the accumulated volumes as single shipments between the designated points or can use the stop-off privilege at $25 per stop for any or all portions of the trip. If the traffic manager wishes to minimize shipping costs, which alternative should be chosen? Assume that the final destination point incurs the stop-off charge.

22. Explain why transport rates typically vary with (a) the weight of a shipment; (b) the distance a shipment is transported; and (c) the value of the transport service.

Chapter 7

Transport Decisions

> If you are planning for one year, grow rice. If you are planning for 20 years, grow trees. If you are planning for centuries, grow men.

—A CHINESE PROVERB

*T*ransportation is a key decision area within the logistics mix. Except for the cost of purchased goods, transportation absorbs, on the average, a higher percentage of logistics costs than any other logistics activity. Although transport decisions express themselves in a variety of

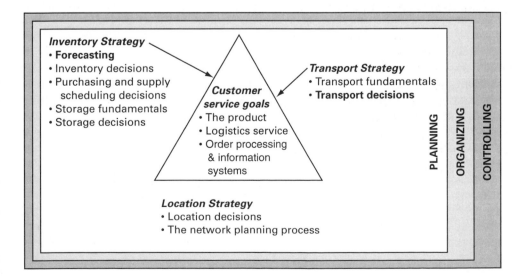

Inventory Strategy
• **Forecasting**
• Inventory decisions
• Purchasing and supply
   scheduling decisions
• Storage fundamentals
• Storage decisions

Customer service goals
• The product
• Logistics service
• Order processing
   & information
   systems

Transport Strategy
• Transport fundamentals
• **Transport decisions**

Location Strategy
• Location decisions
• The network planning process

PLANNING   ORGANIZING   CONTROLLING

219

forms, chief among these are mode selection, carrier routing, vehicle scheduling, and shipment consolidation. Methods for dealing with these important decisions will be illustrated in this chapter.

TRANSPORT SERVICE SELECTION

The selection of a mode of transportation or service offering within a mode of transportation depends on a variety of service characteristics. McGinnis found that six variables are key to transport service choice: (1) freight rates, (2) reliability, (3) transit time, (4) loss, damage, claims processing, and tracing, (5) shipper market considerations, and (6) carrier considerations.[1] Although freight rates are important and can be the determinant of choice in some situations, service remains more important overall. As Evers et al. note, "Timeliness and availability are quite important for each mode while firm contact, suitability, restitution, and cost are of lesser importance."[2] Other studies support the same idea.[3] Considering that transportation service cannot be selected if it is not available leaves transit time (speed) and transit time variability (dependability) as the key factors for service choice followed by cost. In the United States, shippers rank reliability ahead of cost and other service variables.[4]

Basic Cost Trade-Offs

When transportation service is not used to provide a competitive advantage, the best service choice is found by trading off the cost of using a particular transport service with the indirect cost of inventory associated with the performance of the selected mode. That is, speed and dependability affect both the shipper's and the buyer's inventory levels (both order quantity stock and safety stock) as well as the amount of inventory that is in transit between the shipper's and buyer's locations. As slower, less reliable services are selected, more inventory will appear in the channel. Inventory-carrying cost may be in trade-off with lower cost for the transportation service. Given alternatives, the favored service will be the one that offers the lowest total cost consistent with customer service goals while meeting customer service objectives.

The effects of transportation performance, similar to those on inventory, can be seen on production scheduling. Production systems operating with little or no raw material inventories are highly vulnerable to delays and shutdowns from transport performance variability.

---

[1]Michael A. McGinnis, "The Relative Importance of Cost and Service in Freight Transportation Choice: Before and After Deregulation," *Transportation Journal*, Vol. 30, No. 1 (Fall 1990), pp. 12–19.

[2]Philip F. Evers, Donald V. Harper, and Paul M. Needham, "The Determinants of Shipper Perceptions of Modes," *Transportation Journal*, Vol. 36, No. 2 (Winter 1996), pp. 13–25.

[3]Douglas M. Lambert, M. Christine Lewis, and James R. Stock, "How Shippers Select and Evaluate General Commodities LTL Motor Carriers," *Journal of Business Logistics*, Vol. 14, No. 1 (1993), pp. 131–143; and Paul R. Murphy and Patricia K. Hall, "The Relative Importance of Cost and Service in Freight Transportation Choice Before and After Deregulation: An Update," *Transportation Journal*, Vol. 35, No. 1 (1995), pp. 30–38.

[4]Murphy and Hall, op. cit.

Example

The Carry-All Luggage Company produces a line of luggage goods. The typical distribution plan is to produce a finished-goods inventory located at the plant site. Goods are then shipped to company-owned field warehouses by way of common carriers. Rail is currently used to ship between the East Coast plant and a West Coast warehouse. The average transit time for rail shipments is $T = 21$ days. At each stocking point, there is an average of 100,000 units of luggage having an average value of $C = \$30$ per unit. Inventory-carrying costs are $I = 30$ percent of unit inventory value per year.

The company wishes to select the mode of transportation that will minimize total costs. It is estimated that for every day that transit time can be reduced from the current 21 days, average inventory levels can be reduced by 1 percent, which represents a reduction in safety stock. There are $D = 700,000$ units sold per year out of the West Coast warehouse. The company can use the following transport services:

Transport Service	Rate, \$/Unit	Door-to-Door Transit Time, Days	No. of Shipments per Year
Rail	0.10	21	10
Piggyback	0.15	14	20
Truck	0.20	5	20
Air	1.40	2	40

Procurement costs and transit-time variability are assumed negligible.

A diagram of the company's current distribution system is shown in Figure 7-1. By selecting alternate modes of transportation, the length of time that inventory is in transit will be affected. The entire annual demand (D) spends some time in transit; this fraction of the year is represented by $T/365$ days, where T is the average transit time in days. The annual carrying cost of this in-transit inventory is $ICDT/365$.

The average inventory at both ends of the distribution channel can be approximated as $Q/2$, where Q is the shipment size. The holding cost per unit is $I \times C$, but the item value C must reflect *where* the inventory is in the channel. For example, the value of C at the plant is the price, but at the warehouse, it is the price *plus* the transportation rate.

Figure 7-1
Current Distribution for the Carry-All Luggage Company

East Coast Plant

Inventory = 100,000 units

21 days

West Coast Warehouse

Inventory = 100,000 units

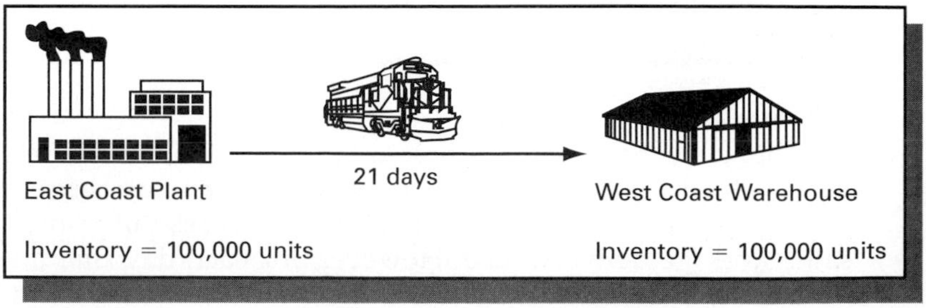

The transportation rate applies to the annual demand such that R × D represents the total annual transportation cost. Calculation of these four relevant costs for each transport choice is shown in Table 7-1. Trucking offers the lowest total cost, even though rail transport offers the lowest rate and air transport offers the lowest inventory cost. With trucking, transit time can be reduced to five days, and the inventory levels at each end of the channel can be reduced by 50 percent.

Competitive Considerations

The selection of a transport mode may be used to create a competitive service advantage. When a buyer in a supply channel purchases goods from more than one supplier, the logistics service offered, as well as price, influences supplier selection. Conversely, if the suppliers select the transport mode to be used in their respective channels, they can control this particular element of the logistics service offering and thus influence the buyer's patronage. To the buyer, better transport service (lower transit time and transit-time variability) means that lower inventory levels can be maintained and/or operating schedules can be met with greater certainty. In order to encourage choice of the most desirable transport service, and thereby lower its costs, the buyer offers to the supplier the only thing that it can—patronage. The buyer's action may be to shift its share of purchases toward the supplier offering the preferred transport service. The profit from this increased business may defray the cost associated with a more premium transport service and encourage a supplier to seek the transport service that is appealing to the buyer rather than simply the one offering the lowest cost.

When there is choice among supply sources in the distribution channel, transport service selection becomes a joint decision between supplier and buyer. The supplier competes for the buyer's patronage through the transport mode choice. A rational buyer responds to the choice by offering the supplier more business. How much more business a buyer should offer depends on the transport service differential created among competing suppliers. For a supplier to settle on a single transport service is difficult in a dynamic, competitive environment where suppliers can offer services to counter those of competing suppliers, and the relationship between transport service choice and the degree of patronage potentially offered by buyers is hard to estimate. A simple example is shown where there are no service countermoves made by a competing supplier, and the extent to which purchases are shifted to the supplier with the more favorable transport service is known.

Example

An appliance manufacturer located in Pittsburgh purchases 3,000 cases of plastic parts valued at $100 per case from two suppliers. Purchases are currently divided equally between the suppliers. Each supplier uses rail transport and achieves the same average delivery time. However, for each day that a supplier can reduce the average delivery time, the appliance manufacturer will shift 5 percent of its total

Table 7-1 Transport Choice Evaluation for the Carry-All Luggage Company

Cost Type	Method of Computation[a]	Modal Choice			
		Rail	Piggyback	Truck	Air
Transportation	$R \times D$	(0.10)(700,000) = 70,000	(0.15)(700,000) = 105,000	(0.20)(700,000) = 140,000	(1.40)(700,000) = 980,000
In-transit inventory	$\dfrac{ICQ}{365}$	[(0.30)(30)(700,000) × (21)]/365 = 363,465	[(0.30)(30)(700,000) × (14)]/365 = 241,644	[(0.30)(30)(700,000) × (5)]/365 = 86,301	[(0.30)(30)(700,000) × (2)]/365 = 34,521
Plant inventory	$ICQ/2$	[(0.30)(30)(100,000)][b] = 900,000	[(0.30)(30)(50,000)(0.93)[c]] = 418,500	[(0.30)(30)(50,000)(0.84)[c]] = 378,000	[(0.30)(30)(25,000)(0.80)[c]] = 182,250
Field inventory	$IC'Q/2$	[(0.30)(30.1)(100,000)] = 903,000	[(0.30)(30.15)(50,000)(0.93)[c]] = 420,593	[(0.30)(30.2)(50,000)(0.84)[c]] = 380,520	[(0.30)(30.4)(25,000)(0.80)[c]] = 190,755
	Totals	$2,236,465	$1,185,737	$984,821	$1,387,526

[a] R = transport rate; D = annual demand; I = carrying cost (%/yr.); C = product value at plant; C' = product value at warehouse (C + R); T = time in transit; and Q = shipment size.

[b] 120,000 is more than the shipping quantity/2 to account for safety stock.

[c] Accounts for improved transport service and the number of shipments per year.

purchases, or 150 cases, to the supplier offering the premium delivery service. A supplier earns a margin of 20 percent on each case before transportation charges.

Supplier A would like to consider whether it would be beneficial to switch from rail to air or truck modes. The following transportation rates per case and average delivery times are known for each mode:

Transport Mode	Transport Rate	Delivery Time
Rail	$ 2.50/case	7 days
Truck	6.00	4
Air	10.35	2

Supplier A's choice can simply be made based on the potential profits to be received. Table 7-2 shows the profits from supplier A's perspective for a transport modal choice.

If the appliance manufacturer remains true to its promise to increase its patronage to the supplier with the better delivery service, supplier A should switch to truck delivery. Of course, supplier A should be watchful of any countermoves by supplier B that may neutralize this advantage.

Appraisal of Selection Methods

The methods discussed for the transport service selection problem recognize the need to account for the indirect effect that transportation choice has on inventory costs and the patronage of the logistics channel member receiving the transportation mode performance offering. This is in addition to the direct cost of the service provided. However, there are often other factors to be considered, some of which are not under the control of the decision maker. First, effective cooperation between supplier and buyer is encouraged if a reasonable knowledge of each party's cost is available. If the supplier and the buyer are separate legal entities, it is doubtful that perfect cost information is possible unless some form of information exchange is worked out. In any case, sensitivity to the other party's reactions to a transport service choice or to the degree of patronage should indicate the direction of cooperation.

Table 7-2   A Profit Comparison for Supplier A's Transport Modal Choices

TRANSPORT MODE	CASES SOLD	GROSS PROFIT	−	TRANSPORT COST	=	NET PROFIT
Rail	1,500	$30,000.00	−	$ 3,750.00	=	$26,250.00
Truck	1,950	39,000.00	−	11,700.00	=	**27,300.00**
Air	2,250	45,000.00	−	23,287.50	=	21,712.50

Second, where there is a competing supplier in the distribution channel, the buyer and the supplier should act rationally to gain optimum cost-transport service trade-offs. Of course, rationality among the parties cannot be guaranteed.

Third, price effects have not been considered. If a supplier were to provide a higher quality transportation service than the competition, he might raise the product price to compensate, at least in part, for the added cost. The buyer should consider both price and transport performance when determining patronage.

Fourth, transport rate changes, changes in product mix, and inventory cost changes, as well as possible transport service retaliation by a competing supplier, add a dynamic element to the problem that is not directly considered.

Fifth, the indirect effects of transport choice on supplier inventories are not evaluated. Suppliers may experience increased or decreased inventory levels resulting from the shipment size associated with the transport choice, just as does the buyer. Suppliers may adjust price to reflect this, which, in turn, will affect transport choice.

VEHICLE ROUTING

Because transportation costs typically range between one-third and two-thirds of total logistics costs, improving efficiency through the maximum utilization of transportation equipment and personnel is a major concern. The length of time that goods are in transit reflects on the number of shipments that can be made with a vehicle within a given period and on the total transportation costs for all shipments. To reduce transportation costs and to improve customer service, finding the best paths that a vehicle should follow through a network of roads, rail lines, shipping lanes, or air navigational routes that will minimize time or distance is a frequent decision problem.

Although there are many variations of routing problems, we can reduce them to a few basic types. There is the problem of finding a path through a network where the origin point is different from the destination point. There is a similar problem where there are multiple origin and destination points. Moreover, there is the problem of routing when origin and destination points are the same. Consider how each type might be solved.

Separate and Single Origin and Destination Points

The problem of routing a vehicle through a network has been nicely solved by methods designed specifically for it. Perhaps the simplest and most straightforward technique is the *shortest route method*. The approach may be paraphrased as follows. We are given a network represented by links and nodes, where the nodes are connecting points between links, and the links are the costs (distances, times, or a combination of both formed as a weighted average of time and distance) to traverse between nodes. Initially, all nodes are considered unsolved, that is, they are not yet on a defined route. A solved node is on the route. Starting with the origin as a solved node, then:

- *Objective of the nth iteration.* Find the *n*th nearest node to the origin. Repeat for n = 1, 2, . . . until the nearest node is the destination.
- *Input for nth iteration.* $(n - 1)$ nearest nodes to the origin, solved for at previous iterations, including their shortest route and distance from the origin. These nodes, plus the origin, will be called *solved nodes*; the others are *unsolved nodes*.
- *Candidates for the nth nearest node.* Each solved node that is directly connected by a branch to one or more unsolved nodes provides one candidate—the unsolved node with the shortest connecting branch. Ties provide additional candidates.
- *Calculation of nth nearest node.* For each such solved node and its candidate, add the distance between them and the distance of the shortest route to this solved node from the origin. The candidate with the smallest such total distance is the *n*th nearest node (ties provide additional solved nodes), and its shortest route is the one generating this distance.

Although the procedure sounds somewhat complicated, an example can illustrate its simplicity. Relate the problem to the mapping and driving distance programs found on the Web, such as Mapquest.[5] The ROUTE module of LOGWARE can solve such problems quickly as problem size increases and where hand computation is not practical.

Example

Suppose that we have the problem shown in Figure 7-2. We seek a minimum-time route between Amarillo and Fort Worth, Texas. Each link has an associated driving time between nodes, and the nodes are road junctions.

Figure 7-2
A Schematic Representation of the Highway Network Between Amarillo and Fort Worth, Texas, with Driving Times

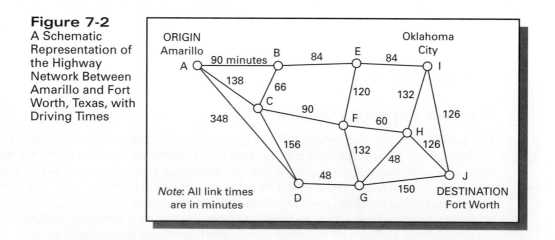

Note: All link times are in minutes

[5]www.mapquest.com

Step	Solved Nodes Directly Connected to Unsolved Nodes	Its Closest Connected Unsolved Node	Total Cost Involved	nth Nearest Node	Its Minimum Cost	Its Last Connection[a]
1	A	B	90	B	90	AB*
2	A	C	138	C	138	AC
	B	C	90 + 66 = 156			
3	A	D	348			
	B	E	90 + 84 = 174	E	174	BE*
	C	F	138 + 90 = 228			
4	A	D	348			
	C	F	138 + 90 = 228	F	228	CF
	E	I	174 + 84 = 258			
5	A	D	348			
	C	D	138 + 156 = 294			
	E	I	174 + 84 = 258	I	258	EI*
	F	H	228 + 60 = 288			
6	A	D	348			
	C	D	138 + 156 = 294			
	F	H	228 + 60 = 288	H	288	FH
	I	J	258 + 126 = 384			
7	A	D	348			
	C	D	138 + 156 = 294	D	294	CD
	F	G	288 + 132 = 360			
	H	G	288 + 48 = 336			
	I	J	258 + 126 = 384			
8	H	J	288 + 126 = 414			
	I	J	258 + 126 = 384	J	384	IJ*

[a] Asterisk (*) denotes minimum-cost route.

Table 7-3 Tabulation of Computational Steps for the Shortest Route Method

We begin with labeling a table, as shown in Table 7-3. The first point to be identified as a solved node is the origin, or A. The nodes directly connecting to A that are unsolved are B, C, and D. In step 1, we note that B is the nearest node to A and record the connection. Node B now takes on the status of a solved node since it is the only choice available.

Next, we note the nearest unsolved nodes from the solved nodes A and B. Listing only the closest connecting nodes from each solved node, we have $A \rightarrow C$ and $B \rightarrow C$. We list them as step 2. Note now that to reach a node through an already connected node requires that the minimum time to reach the solved node be added to the link time. That is, to reach C through B requires a total time of $AB + BC$, or $90 + 66 = 156$

minutes. Comparing the total times to reach the unsolved nodes in step 2 shows that the minimum time of 138 minutes is achieved by linking *A* and *C*. *C* is now a solved node.

The third iteration finds the nearest unsolved nodes that are connected to the solved nodes. As Table 7-3 shows, there are three of these. Summing all times from the origin to the unsolved nodes in question shows total times of 348, 174, and 228. The minimum time of 174 is associated with the link *BE*. It is now recorded as the result of step 3.

The procedure continues in this manner until the destination node *J* is reached, as shown in step 8. The minimum route time of 384 minutes is noted. The route is found by linking the portions of the route starting with the destination working back to the origin. These links are identified with an asterisk (*). The optimum route is $A \to B \to E \to I \to J$.

The various shortest route methods lend themselves nicely to computerized solution, where the network of links and nodes can be maintained in a database. By selecting particular origin and destination pairs, the shortest routes can be developed. Absolute shortest distance routes do not account for time to traverse the network, since the quality of the links is not taken into account. Therefore, a practical route may be generated where *both* travel time and distance are given weights.

Application

PC*Miler and IntelliRoute are examples of commercial software products available for finding the most desired routes through a network.[6] Suppose a truck is to be routed from Ashton, Iowa, to Des Moines, Iowa. The shortest practical route (a blend of distance and time) is the objective of route design. PC*Miler produces the trip report as shown in Figure 7-3, and a map as shown in Figure 7-4. Note that the driver can be given specific instructions for the exact roads to drive, the interchanges to take, and the distance and expected time that should be traveled on each leg of the journey. In this case, a practical route is 233 miles long with an expected driving time of 5 hours and 13 minutes.

In addition to finding the shortest routes, such software commonly include toll costs, up-to-date road construction, fuel tax reporting, GPS positioning, and distance traveled in each state. These expanded capabilities have led to reduced rate disputes, reduced fines, and improved audit efficiencies, which in turn result in improved customer service, delivery, reporting, asset utilization, and driver retention.

---

[6]Software products of ALK Associates, Inc. (www.alk.com and www.pcmiler.com) and Rand McNally (www.milemaker.com), respectively.

Miles: 233.0 Time: 5:13 Cost: 256.30

Practical Route, Borders Open

State/Country		Route	Miles	Hours	Interchange	Leg Miles	Leg Hours	Total Miles	Total Hours
Origin: 51232 Ashton, IA, Osceola				0:00	(On-duty) 0.00				
IA	S	IA-60	10.0	0:15	Sheldon, IA	10.0	0:15	10.0	0:15
IA	E	US-18	12.0	0:18	+US 18 US 59, IA	22.0	0:33	22.0	0:33
IA	S	US-59	32.0	0:48	+US 59 IA 3, IA	54.0	1:21	54.0	1:21
IA	E	IA-3	6.0	0:09	+IA 3 IA 7, IA	60.0	1:30	60.0	1:30
IA	E	IA-7	73.5	1:50	+US 169 IA 7, IA	133.5	3:20	133.5	3:20
IA	S	US-169	6.3	0:08	+US 20 US 169S, IA	139.8	3:28	139.8	3:28
IA	E	US-20	32.3	0:37	I 35 X142, IA	172.1	4:05	172.1	4:05
IA	S	I-35	56.0	1:01	+I 35 I 80N, IA	228.1	5:06	228.1	5:06
IA	W	I-235	4.3	0:06	+I 235 US 69, IA	232.4	5:11	232.4	5:11
IA		Local	0.6	0:01	Des Moines, IA	233.0	5:13	233.0	5:13
Arrive Loaded									
Dest: 50301 Des Moines, IA, Polk			0:00	(On-duty) 0.00		233.0	5:13	233.0	5:13

Figure 7-3 Route Plan for Truck Travel Between Ashton, Iowa, and Des Moines, Iowa, As Generated by PC*Miler

Figure 7-4 Map of Route Design

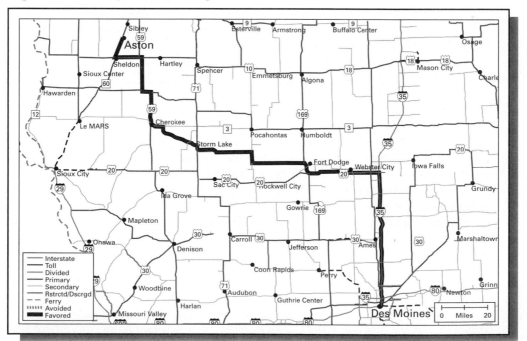

A novel approach to finding shortest routes is based on the collective behavior of ants. Dubbed "swarm intelligence," observing the self-organization, supervision-less work environment, and interaction among individual ants in a colony leads to efficient solutions to difficult routing problems. Consider how ants work in finding the shortest path to a food source by laying and following chemical trails. Simply, two ants leave the nest at the same time taking different trails to a food source laying down pheromones—a chemical substance that attracts other ants—as they go. The ant taking the shortest trail will return to the nest first, and this trail from nest to food and back will have twice as much scent on it compared to the trail taken by the second ant. The ants back at the nest will be attracted by the trail having the stronger scent. As more ants take the route, more pheromones are deposited, reinforcing the shortest route. Routes are determined by following two basic rules: Lay pheromone and follow the trail of others. The routing ideas from swarm intelligence have effectively been applied to routing problems in telecommunications, air cargo shipping, and truck routing.[7]

Multiple Origin and Destination Points

When there are multiple source points that may serve multiple destination points, there is a problem of assigning destinations to sources as well as finding the best routes between them. This problem commonly occurs when there is more than one vendor, plant, or warehouse to serve more than one customer for the same product. It is further complicated when the source points are restricted to the amount of the total customer demand that can be supplied from each location. A special class of the linear programming algorithm known as the *transportation method* is frequently applied to this problem type.

Example

Suppose that a glass manufacturer contracts with three soda ash (used in glassmaking) suppliers at various locations to supply three manufacturing facilities. The contract quantities are not to be exceeded, but the production requirements must be met. Figure 7-5 shows the problem along with the appropriate per-ton shipping rates. These rates are the result of finding the shortest route between each supplier and each plant. Supply and requirements are in tons.

Solving this problem with the use of the software module in LOGWARE called TRANLP gives the following results in its output file:

[7]For more information on swarm intelligence, see Eric Bonabeau and Christopher Meyer, "Swarm Intelligence: A Whole New Way to Think About Business," *Harvard Business Review*, Vol. 79, No. 5 (May 2001), pp. 106–114.

```
Optimum Supply Schedule
            TO:
        1     2     3
FROM:
  1    400     0     0
  2    200   200   300
  3      0   300     0
Total units transferred = 1400.
Minimum total cost = 6600.
```

The interpretation of this output is

Ship
400 tons from supplier A to plant 1
200 tons from supplier B to plant 1
200 tons from supplier B to plant 2
300 tons from supplier B to plant 3
300 tons from supplier C to plant 2

The minimum cost for this routing plan is $6,600.

Figure 7-5
Example of a
Multiple Origin-
Destination Routing
Problem

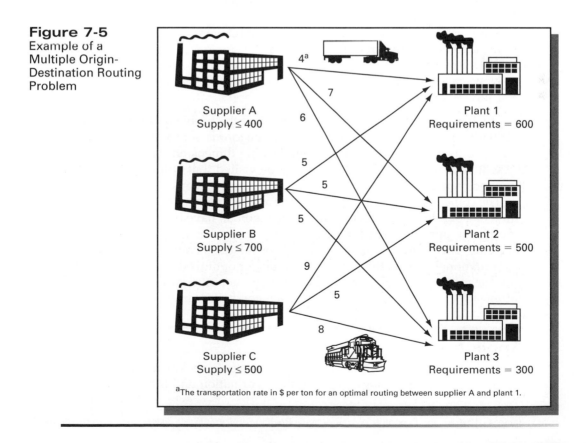

[a]The transportation rate in $ per ton for an optimal routing between supplier A and plant 1.

Coincident Origin and Destination Points

The logistician frequently encounters routing problems in which the origin point is the same as the destination point. This class of routing problem commonly occurs when transport vehicles are privately owned. Familiar examples include

- Beverage delivery to bars and restaurants
- Currency delivery and scheduling at ATM machines
- Dynamic sourcing and transport of fuels
- Grease pickups from restaurants
- Home appliance repair, service, and delivery
- Internet-based home grocery delivery
- Milk pickup and inventory management
- Pickup of charitable donations from homes
- Portable toilet delivery, pickup, and service
- Prisoner transportation between jails and courthouses
- Retrieval of dead and diseased animals from roadsides
- Snowplow and snow-removal routing
- Transport of test samples from medical offices to laboratories
- Transportation of disabled individuals by vans and taxis
- Trash pickup and trans-shipments
- Wholesale distribution from warehouses to retailers
- Postal delivery truck routing
- School bus routing
- Newspaper delivery
- Delivery of meals to shut-ins[8]

This type of routing problem is an extension of the problem of separate origin and destination points, but the requirement that the tour is not complete until the vehicle returns to its starting point adds a complicating dimension. The objective is to find the sequence in which the points should be visited that will minimize total travel time or distance.

The coincident origin and destination routing problem is generally known as the "traveling salesman" problem. Numerous methods have been proposed to solve it. Finding the optimal route for a particular problem has not been practical for such problems when they contain many points or require a solution to be found quickly. Computational time on the fastest computers for optimization methods has been too long for many practical problems. Cognitive, heuristic, or combination heuristic-optimization solution procedures have been good alternatives.

Application

The Central Valley School District located near Spokane, Washington, is leading the way in applying technology to managing information and carrying out its day-to-

---

[8]Janice G. Partyka and Randolph W. Hall, "On the Road to Service," *OR/MS Today* (August 2000), pp. 26–35.

day school bus routing tasks, all at a fraction of the time and cost of previous methods. For decades, Central Valley generated school bus routes using paper maps, pushpins, plastic transparencies, and colored pens. Addresses for every student had to be located on a paper map and marked by hand. Using their own judgment, the routers grouped the closest students, marked pickup points, and created the more than 250 bus runs for district students. After using customized routing software, the school district realized a full week's reduction in the time it took to create the state reports and a reduction of five to six routes, resulting in an additional $125,000 in savings.[9]

Points Are Spatially Related

Good solutions to traveling salesman problems of a realistic size can be found by using the pattern recognition capabilities of the human mind. We know that good stop sequences are formed when the paths of the route do not cross. In addition, the route shape will usually bulge, or form a teardrop shape, where possible. Good and poor route designs are illustrated in Figure 7-6. Based on this principle, an analyst can quickly sketch out a route plan that might require a computer many hours to find.

Alternatively, a computer model can be used to find the stop sequences on a route. This can be a better choice than cognition when the spatial relationship between stops does not represent their true travel time or distance. This may be the case when there are travel barriers, one-way streets, or traffic congestion present, all of which can distort the graphical representation of the problem. However, whenever possible, locating stops geographically, such as with coordinate points, can simplify the problem by reducing the amount of data that needs to be collected to

Figure 7-6
Examples of Poor and Good Stop Sequencing

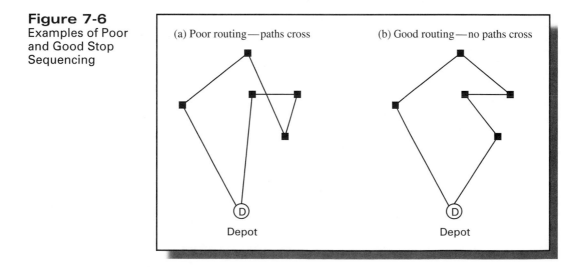

(a) Poor routing—paths cross

(b) Good routing—no paths cross

Depot

Depot

[9]"School Bus Routing Goes High-Tech," *ESRI ArcNews* (Winter 2000/2001), p. 1ff.

represent a problem. (There can be thousands of distances or times needed for even a relatively simple problem.) The computer is assigned the task of estimating the distances or times. Special computational procedures have been developed that rapidly solve the spatially represented problem and produce results that are close to optimum.

Example

The Anheuser-Busch Company uses route salespersons to sell beer and other beverages from a truck owned by the local distributor. The salesperson is paid on a commission and, like the distributor, does not wish to spend any more time or travel any greater distance than necessary to cover the accounts on a daily basis. Pins on a map are used to locate the current accounts for a particular salesperson. An example of this type of information for 20 rural accounts has been transferred to the grid-overlay map shown as Figure 7-7(a). The coordinates relate to distance. The truck is to start at the depot and return to the depot, visit all accounts, and travel the least distance possible.

Try the cognitive approach. Now compare your solution with the one generated by ROUTESEQ software (a module in LOGWARE) as shown in Figure 7-7(b). The total tour distance (cost) is 37.59 coordinate units. This is a good solution, but not necessarily an optimal one.

Points Are Not Spatially Related

Where it is not easy to establish the spatial relationship between stops on the tour, either by plotting them on a map or by identifying them with coordinate points, or

Figure 7-7
Stops on a Beer Truck Sales Route with Suggested Routing Pattern as Developed by ROUTESEQ Software

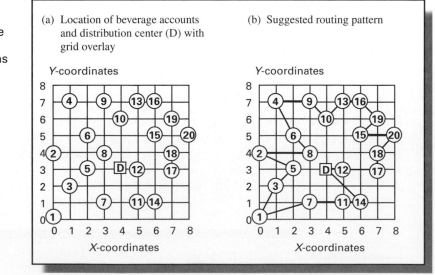

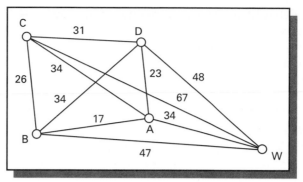

Figure 7-8
Example Delivery
Problem with Travel
Time in Minutes

where the spatial relationships become distorted for practical reasons as previously noted, exact distances, or times, should be specified between stop pairs. Cognitive procedures are less applicable, and we must resort to one of the many mathematical procedures suggested over the years to treat this problem. Although the interstop distances, or times, can be as exact as we wish to specify them, solution procedures tend to give approximate answers.

Example

A small delivery problem using a warehouse as a depot and having four stops is shown in Figure 7-8. Travel times between stops are found from first choosing the most appropriate route and then multiplying by the speed to find the time to traverse the distance. We assume the time to travel between stop pairs is the same in both directions.

Using the "traveling salesman" tour module of STORM,[10] a tour stop sequence of W → D → C → B → A → W is found. The total time to make the round-trip is 156 minutes.

VEHICLE ROUTING AND SCHEDULING

Vehicle routing and scheduling (VRP) is an extension of the basic vehicle routing ("traveling salesman") problem. Realistic restrictions are now included such as (1) each stop may have volume to be picked up as well as delivered; (2) multiple vehicles may be used having different capacity limitations to both weight and volume; (3) a maximum total driving time is allowed on a route before a rest period of at least ten hours (Department of Transportation safety restriction); (4) stops may permit pick-

---

[10]A collection of computer decision support tools by Hamilton Emmons, A. Dale Flowers, Chandrashekar M. Kott, and Kamlesh Mathur, *STORM 4.0 for WINDOWS: Quantitative Modeling for Decision Support* (Lakeshore Publishing, Cleveland, OH: 2001).

ups and deliveries only at certain times of the day (called *time windows*); (5) pickups may be permitted on a route only after deliveries are made; and (6) drivers may be allowed to take short rests or lunch breaks at certain times of the day. These restrictions add a great deal of complexity to the problem and frustrate our efforts to find an optimal solution. As Gendreau et al. point out ". . . to this day only relatively small VRP instances can be solved to optimality."[11] However, good solutions to such problems can be found by applying principles for good routing and scheduling or some logical heuristic procedures. Consider the routing and scheduling problem where trucks are to start at a central depot, visit multiple stops to make deliveries, and return to the depot in the same day.

Principles for Good Routing and Scheduling

Decision makers, such as truck dispatchers, can go a long way toward developing good truck routes and schedules by applying eight guideline principles. These are outlined as follows.

1. *Load trucks with stop volumes that are in the closest proximity to each other.* Truck routes should be formed around clusters of stops that are nearest each other in order to minimize the interstop travel between them. This also minimizes the total travel time on the route. Figure 7-9(a) shows the type of clustering for the purpose of truck loading that should be avoided. Figure 7-9(b) shows better clustering.

Figure 7-9
Clustering for Assigning Stop Volumes to Vehicles

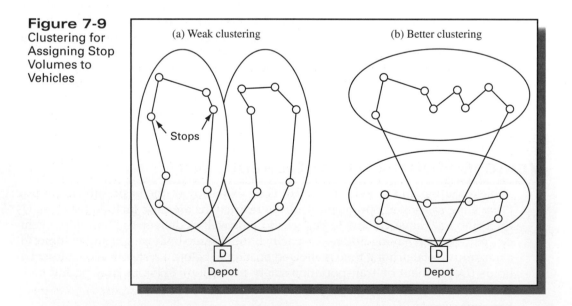

[11]Michel Gendreau, Alain Hertz, and Gilbert Laporte, "A Tabu Search Heuristic for the Vehicle Routing Problem," *Management Science*, Vol. 40, No. 10 (October 1994), p. 1276.

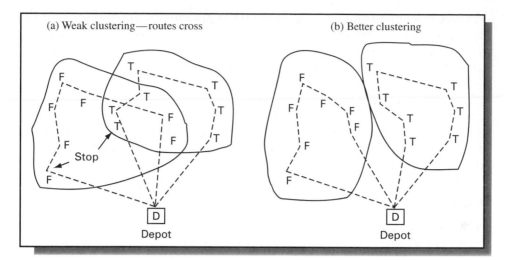

Figure 7-10 Clustering Stops by Day of the Week

2. *Stops on different days should be arranged to produce tight clusters.* When stops are to be served during different days of the week, the stops should be segmented into separate routing and scheduling problems for each day of the week. The daily segments for which routes and schedules are to be developed should avoid overlapping stop clusters. This will help to minimize the number of trucks needed to serve all stops as well as to minimize truck travel time and distance during the week. Figure 7-10 shows examples of good and bad clustering.

3. *Build routes beginning with the farthest stop from the depot.* Efficient routes can be developed through building stop clusters around the farthest stop from the depot and then working back toward the depot. Once the farthest stop is identified, selecting the volume from the tightest cluster of stops around this key stop should be used to fill out the assigned truck capacity. After the stop volumes have been assigned to the vehicle, select another vehicle and identify the farthest stop from the depot among the remaining stops not yet assigned to a vehicle. Proceed in this manner until all stop volumes have been assigned to vehicles.

4. *The sequence of stops on a truck route should form a teardrop pattern.* Stops should be sequenced so that no route paths cross, and the route appears to have a teardrop shape. Recall Figure 7-6. Time window restrictions and the forcing of stop pickups after deliveries may cause route paths to cross.

5. *The most efficient routes are built using the largest vehicles available.* Ideally, using a vehicle large enough to handle all stops in one route will minimize total distance, or time, traveled to serve the stops. Therefore, the largest vehicles among the multiple sizes in a fleet should be allocated first, providing that good utilization for them can be realized.

6. *Pickups should be mixed into delivery routes rather than assigned to the end of routes.* Pickups should be made, as much as possible, during the course of the

deliveries to minimize the amount of path crossing that can occur when such stops are served after all deliveries are made. The extent that this can be done will depend on the vehicle configuration, the size of the pickup volumes, and the degree to which they may block access to the delivery merchandise inside the vehicle.

7. *A stop that is greatly removed from a route cluster is a good candidate for an alternate means of delivery.* Stops that are isolated from the stop clusters, especially those with low volume, are served at great driver time and vehicle expense. Using small trucks to handle such stops may prove to be more economical, depending on the isolation of particular stops and their volumes. Also, using a for-hire transportation service would be a good alternative.

8. *Narrow stop time window restrictions should be avoided.* Time window restrictions on stops, where they are narrow, can force stop sequencing away from ideal patterns. Since time window restrictions are often not absolute, any stop(s) forced to be served in a less-than-desired routing pattern should have its time window limits renegotiated and hopefully widened.

Such principles as these can be easily taught to operating personnel to produce satisfactory, although not necessarily optimal, solutions to realistic routing and scheduling problems. They provide guidelines for good route design, yet operating personnel still have the latitude to deal with the restrictions not directly accounted for in the methodology or the exceptions (rush orders, road detours) that can occur in any truck operation. Route designs developed in this manner can offer substantial improvements over otherwise unschooled routing and scheduling methods.

Example

The Case Casket Company manufactures and distributes a complete line of burial caskets to funeral homes. Funeral homes maintain a small inventory of the more popular caskets, but often customers select a casket from a catalog. Typically, a funeral director will order caskets to replenish his or her inventory or to meet the particular needs of a family. Orders are usually in small quantities, frequently no more than one casket at a time. To serve this market, Case Casket has over 50 distribution warehouses located throughout the country. One such warehouse and its associated territory is shown in Figure 7-11. A representative week's order quantities and their locations are also shown. The warehouse operates two specially racked trucks that each haul a maximum of 18 caskets. Deliveries are made five days a week. We wish to develop a routing and scheduling plan for this territory.

Following the guidelines for good routing and scheduling, we begin by segmenting the territory into five daily customer clusters based on five delivery days per week. Using principle number 3, we recognize that customers should be clustered starting with the farthest customer and then adding customers by progressively moving toward the warehouse. Therefore, we construct four customer groups for outlying stops for the first four days of the week, and one group for the fifth day that serves stops close to the warehouse. Balancing the workload for each of the five

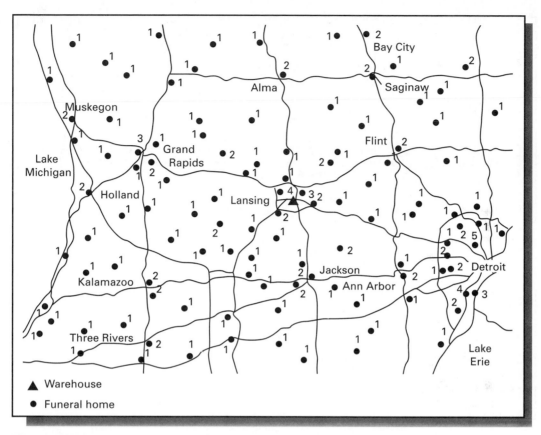

Figure 7-11 Funeral Home Locations and a Typical Week's Casket Orders from the Central Michigan Territory of the Case Casket Company

groups is desirable to avoid the need for more than two trucks. A third truck would be greatly underutilized on some days. We begin with an expanding square radiating out from the warehouse to capture enough stop volume to fill two trucks. Next, since Detroit is a dominant market point, we divide it over two days. Sweeping in both directions we capture approximately equal stop volume in each of the four stop clusters. These clusters are shown in Figure 7-12.

Next, we load the trucks and design the routing patterns. Each day is considered separately. Starting with the farthest stop, we cluster enough stops in close proximity to each other until the capacity of a truck is filled. Then we select the farthest stop from the remaining ones and repeat the process for loading the next truck. For the stops assigned to a truck, the stops are sequenced so that the paths within a route do not cross, and they bulge outward. The result is the route designs for each day of the week, as shown in Figure 7-13.

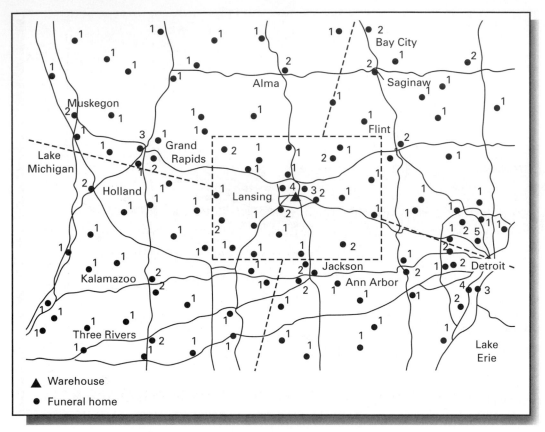

Figure 7-12 Division of Case Casket's Central Michigan Sales Territory into Customer Groups for Each Day of the Week

Methods for Routing and Scheduling

The problem of finding good solutions to the vehicle routing and scheduling problem becomes more difficult as additional constraints are placed on the problem. Time windows, multiple trucks with different capacities by weight and cube, maximum total driving time allowed on a route, different speeds within different zones, barriers to travel (lakes, detours, mountains), and break times for the driver are a few of the practical considerations that need to be given to route design. From among the many approaches that have been suggested to deal with such complex problems, we will examine two methods. One is simple (the "sweep" method), and the other is more complex, handling more practical considerations and producing higher-quality solutions under a broader range of circumstances (the "savings" method). A discussion of other solution procedures, classified as (1) constructive algorithms, (2) two-phase algorithms, (3) incomplete optimization algorithms, and (4) improvement methods, can be found in Gendreau et al.[12]

---

[12]Michel Gendreau, Alain Hertz, and Gilbert Laporte, op. cit., pp. 1276–1290.

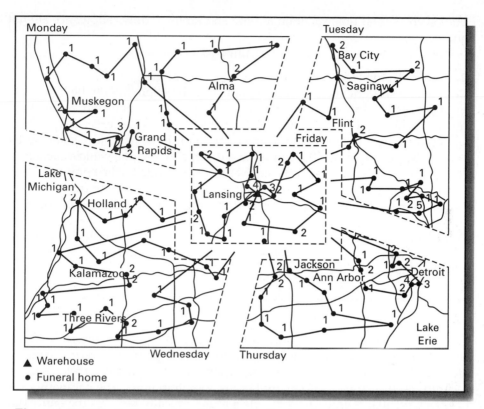

Figure 7-13 Daily Truck Delivery Route Design for the Case Casket Company

The "Sweep" Method

The "sweep" method for routing vehicles is simple enough to lend itself to hand calculation, even for large-size problems. When programmed into computer software, this method solves problems rapidly, without requiring enormous amounts of computer memory. For a variety of problems, the accuracy is projected to produce an average error rate of about 10 percent.[13] This level of computational error may be acceptable where results must be obtained in short order and good solutions are needed as opposed to optimal ones. Dispatchers are often faced with needing to generate routing patterns within one hour of receiving the final data on the stops to make and on their volumes.

The disadvantage of the method has to do with the way routes are formed. The process is two-staged, with stops being assigned to vehicles first. Then, the stop sequence on the routes is determined. Because of this two-staged process, timing

---

[13]Ronald H. Ballou and Yogesh K. Agarwal, "A Performance Comparison of Several Popular Algorithms for Vehicle Routing and Scheduling," *Journal of Business Logistics*, Vol. 9, No. 1 (1988), pp. 51–65.

issues such as total time spent on a route and time windows allowance are not well handled.

The "sweep" method may be paraphrased as follows:

1. Locate all stops including the depot on a map or grid.
2. Extend a straight line from the depot in any direction. Rotate the line clockwise, or counterclockwise, until it intersects a stop. Ask the question: If the inserted stop is included on the route, will the vehicle capacity be exceeded? If the answer is no, proceed with the line rotation until the next stop is intersected. Ask the question: Will the cumulative volume exceed the vehicle capacity? Use the largest vehicles first. If the answer is yes, exclude the last point and define the route. Continuing the line sweep, begin a new route with the last point that was excluded from the previous route. Continue with the sweep until all points have been assigned to routes.
3. Within each route, sequence the stops to minimize distance. The sequencing may be accomplished by applying the tear-drop method or by using any algorithm that solves the "traveling salesman" problem.

Example

The P.K. Smith Trucking Company uses vans to pick up merchandise from outlying customers. The merchandise is returned to a depot point, where it is consolidated into large loads to be moved over long distances. A typical day's pickups are shown in Figure 7-14(a). The pickup quantities are shown in units. The company uses vans that can haul 10,000 units. To complete a route typically requires the entire day. The

Figure 7-14 P. K. Smith Trucking Company Routing by the "Sweep" Method

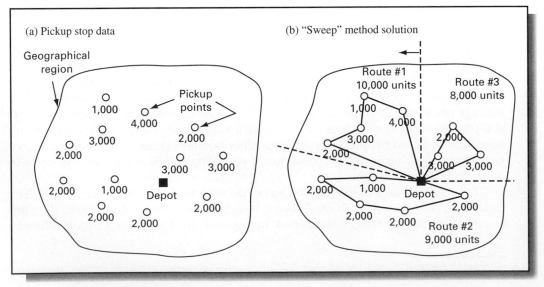

company wants to determine how many routes (trucks) are needed, which stops should be on the routes, and in which sequence the route truck should serve the stops.

Begin the sweep with a line drawn due north and a counterclockwise sweep. These are arbitrary. Swing the line counterclockwise picking up volume until a 10,000-unit truck is filled but not overflowing. Once the stop assignments to trucks are made, sequence the stops on each route using the "teardrop" method. The final route design is shown in Figures 7-14(b).

The "sweep" method has the potential of giving very good solutions when (1) each stop volume is a small fraction of the vehicle capacity, (2) all vehicles are the same size, and (3) there are no time restrictions on the routes.

The "Savings" Method

One method, the Clarke-Wright savings approach,[14] has stood out over the years as being flexible enough to handle a wide range of practical constraints, being relatively fast computationally for problems with a moderate number of stops, and capable of generating solutions that are nearly optimum. Comparisons with optimal results for small problems with a limited number of constraints have shown that the "savings" approach gives solutions that are, on the average, two percent over the optimum.[15] The method can handle many practical constraints, mainly because it is able to form routes and sequence stops on the routes simultaneously.

The objective of the savings method is to minimize the total distance traveled by all vehicles and to indirectly minimize the number of vehicles needed to serve all stops. The logic of the method is to begin with a dummy vehicle serving each stop and returning to the depot, as shown in Figure 7-15(a). This gives the maximum distance to be experienced in the routing problem. Next, two stops are combined together on the same route so that one vehicle can be eliminated and the travel distance reduced. To determine the stops to combine on a route, the distance *saved* is calculated before and after the combination. The distance saved by combining two points (*A* and *B*) otherwise not on a route with any other stops is found by algebraically subtracting the route distance shown in Figure 7-15(b) from that in Figure 7-15(a). The result is a savings value of $S = d_{0,A} + d_{B,0} - d_{A,B}$. This calculation is carried out for all stop pairs. The pair of stops with the largest savings value is selected for combination. The revised route is illustrated in Figure 7-15(b).

The combining process continues. In addition to combining single stops, the process may insert a stop into a route that contains more than one stop. For example, if a point is to be inserted between stops *A* and *B*, where *A* and *B* are on the same route, the savings value can be expressed as $S = d_{0,C} + d_{C,0} + d_{A,B} - d_{A,C} - d_{C,B}$. If stop *C* is to be inserted after the last stop (*B*) on a route as per Figure 7-15, the savings

[14]G. Clarke and J.W. Wright, "Scheduling of Vehicles from a Central Depot to a Number of Delivery Points," *Operations Research*, Vol. 11 (1963), pp. 568–581.
[15]Ballou and Agarwal, op. cit., pp. 51–65.

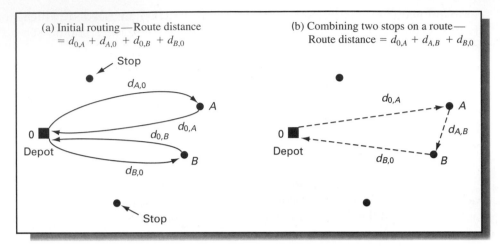

value would be $S = d_{B,0} - d_{B,C} + d_{0,C}$. Conversely, if the stop C is inserted *before* stop A, the savings value is $S = d_{C,0} - d_{C,A} + d_{A,0}$. The savings value calculations are repeated at each iteration. The largest savings value identifies the stop that should be considered for inclusion on a route. If that stop cannot be included due to restrictions such as the route would be too long, time windows cannot be met, or the capacity of a vehicle would be exceeded, the stop having the *next* largest savings value is considered for inclusion. The iterative process is continued until all stops are considered.

The robust nature of the savings approach allows it to include many restrictions that seem so important in realistic applications. The method's robustness comes from the ability to simultaneously assign a stop to a route and to place it in the proper sequence on the route. Therefore, before a stop is accepted for a route, the route with the new stop should be previewed. A number of questions can be asked about the projected route design, such as whether the route time exceeds its maximum allowed driving time, whether the time for a driver rest or lunch break has been reached, whether a vehicle large enough to accept the route volume is available, and whether the stop time window is met. Violations to such conditions can reject the stop from the route entirely or from that particular place in the stop sequence. The next stop can then be selected according to the largest savings value and the process of consideration repeated. The approach does not guarantee an optimal solution, but, considering the complex nature of the extended problem, a good solution can be found.

Example

Regal Metals manufactures steel lavatory partitions for commercial buildings. Once a week, orders ($X = 460$, $Y = 720$) are accumulated at the Toledo, Ohio, plant for delivery to construction sites. The firm owns five trucks with a hauling capacity of 40,000 lb each. For a particular week, the following deliveries are to be made:

Construction Site	X	Y	Order Size, lb
Milwaukee, WI	220	800	3,000
Chicago, IL	240	720	31,500
Detroit, MI	470	790	16,500
Buffalo, NY	670	860	6,000
Cleveland, OH	540	730	4,500
Pittsburgh, PA	630	680	6,750
Cincinnati, OH	420	570	3,750
Louisville, KY	370	490	6,000
St. Louis, MO	130	500	7,500
Memphis, TN	180	270	9,000
Knoxville, TN	480	360	5,250
Atlanta, GA	480	210	18,000
Columbia, SC	660	250	3,000
Raleigh, NC	760	390	6,750
Baltimore, MD	810	640	11,250
Total			138,750 lb

The trucks are to be scheduled in such a way that all orders for the week are to be shipped at one time beginning no earlier than 7:00 A.M. at Toledo, capacities of the trucks are not to be exceeded, and all trucks are to be returned to the Toledo plant when the route is completed. Additional restrictions are that all deliveries are to be made between 7:00 A.M. and 6:00 P.M., drivers are to take a one-hour lunch break after 12 noon and an overnight (12-hour) break after 7:00 P.M., and there is an imposed travel barrier in the Great Lakes region. Average driving speed is 50 miles per hour, and the time for unloading at a stop is 30 minutes per stop. Road distances are estimated to be 21 percent higher than straight line, coordinate-computed distances. Driver and truck costs are $1.30 per mile. When not traveling, drivers are assigned duties at the plant.

The ROUTER software in LOGWARE, which can handle the additional restrictions within the savings approach, generates the routing plan shown in Figure 7-16. A route summary is given in Table 7-4 and a time summary is shown in Table 7-5. The total cost for the deliveries is 5,776 miles × $1.30 per mile = $7,508.80.

Table 7-4 Route Summary for Regal Metals' Deliveries

		TIME				ROUTE	ROUTE	ROUTE	TRUCK
ROUTE	STOPS[a]	START	DAY	RETURN	DAY	DISTANCE, MI	TIME, (HR)	WEIGHT, (LB)	SIZE, LB
1	2,1	7:00 A.M.	1	1:44 P.M.	2	787	30.7	34,500	40,000
2	3,6	7:00 A.M.	1	9:11 A.M.	2	609	26.2	23,250	40,000
3	5,4,15,14	7:00 A.M.	1	5:03 P.M.	3	1,503	58.1	28,500	40,000
4	7,8,10,9	7:00 A.M.	1	3:22 P.M.	3	1,418	56.4	26,250	40,000
5	11,12,13	7:00 A.M.	1	3:40 P.M.	3	1,459	56.7	26,250	40,000
						5,776 mi.	228.1 hr.	138,750 lb	

[a] Stops in sequence of their delivery.

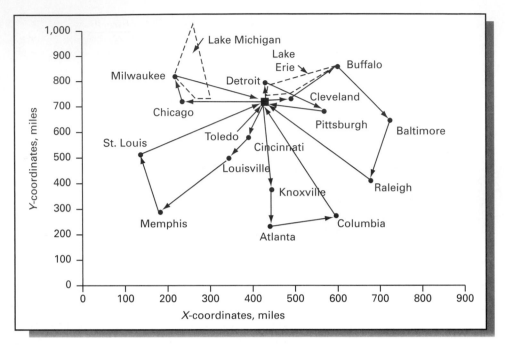

Figure 7-16 Routing Plan for Regal Metal's Deliveries As Generated by the "Savings" Method in ROUTER

Table 7-5 Arrival Time Summary for Regal Metals' Deliveries

STOP	ARRIVAL TIME	DAY	STOP	ARRIVAL TIME	DAY
Milwaukee	3:49 P.M.	1	St. Louis	5:16 P.M.	2
Chicago	1:19 P.M.	1	Memphis	9:28 A.M.	2
Detroit	8:47 A.M.	1	Knoxville	4:43 P.M.	1
Buffalo	3:17 P.M.	1	Atlanta	8:51 A.M.	2
Cleveland	8:57 A.M.	1	Columbia	2:49 P.M.	2
Pittsburgh	4:27 P.M.	1	Raleigh	5:46 P.M.	2
Cincinnati	10:45 A.M.	1	Baltimore	10:05 A.M.	2
Louisville	2:32 P.M.	1			

Application

Domino's Pizza, the $2.5-billion national pizza delivery chain, prides itself on getting its pies to customers' doors in a speedy manner; however, this logistical feat begins long before a customer receives his or her pizza. The company's 18 distribution sites must deliver fresh ingredients and supplies to 4,256 stores several times a week, which translates into annual transportation costs totaling $30 million, or 65 percent of Domino's entire budget. Transportation planning for its 160-truck private fleet was a big effort involving pushpins and huge wall maps as its routing tools. This manual routing was conducted about every year, but included nothing from a daily operational standpoint or in response to changing environments. Redoing the maze of threads and pins was not practical on a daily basis.

In response to an increasingly competitive marketplace, routing and scheduling software was installed. The results were dramatic. At the Company's Connecticut distribution center, one of Domino's largest, a new master schedule was developed in two days. That enabled the site to cut its average weekly miles driven by 7,000, a reduction of 21 percent, and scale down its trailer fleet from 22 to 16.

Across the entire distribution network, Domino's has slashed an estimated 1 million miles from its fleet travel, an average reduction of at least 10 percent for every DC. Transportation planning now takes place daily rather than annually, as under the previous manual system.[16]

Route Sequencing

The routes designed by the routing and scheduling methods that have previously been described assume that a route is assigned to a specific vehicle. If the route is of short duration, the vehicle is underutilized for the remainder of the time horizon. In practice, however, if another route begins after the first route is completed, the vehicle is available to be assigned to that second route. Therefore, the number of vehicles needed is determined by sequentially placing routes end-to-end so that the vehicle has a minimum slack time. Suppose that a truck routing problem, with the same-size trucks, produces the routes shown in Table 7-6.

Sequencing these routes over the period of one day to minimize truck downtime might lead to the plan shown in Figure 7-17. Sequencing in this manner minimizes the number of trucks required to serve all routes. Although the routes are sequenced

Table 7-6
Time Limits on Ten
Truck Routes

ROUTE	DEPARTURE TIME	RETURN TIME
1	8:00 A.M.	10:25 A.M.
2	9:30 A.M.	11:45 A.M.
3	2:00 P.M.	4:53 P.M.
4	11:31 A.M.	3:21 P.M.
5	8:12 A.M.	9:52 A.M.
6	3:03 P.M.	5:13 P.M.
7	12:24 P.M.	2:22 P.M.
8	1:33 P.M.	4:43 P.M.
9	8:00 A.M.	10:34 A.M.
10	10:56 A.M.	2:25 P.M.

[16]Kelly H. Madden, "Software Drives Down Transportation Costs," *Distribution* (February 1997), pp. 50–51.

Figure 7-17
Route
Sequencing
to Minimize
the Number
of Trucks

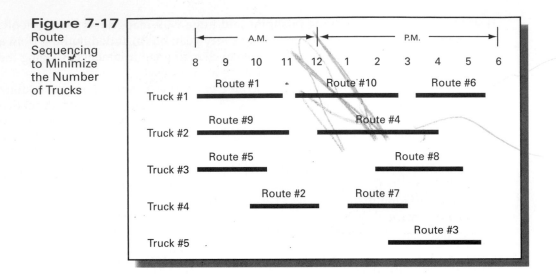

manually, a computer program can be written to do this and integrated with the routing and scheduling solution to provide an overall plan for the trucks.

A popular variant of this sequencing problem is for trucks to make deliveries to stops with different frequencies over an extended period. For example, trucks make weekly visits or biweekly visits to customers over the period of one month. The frequency is determined by customer volume. Those customers close to the depot may be served quickly, with the truck returning to the depot before the week is finished and becoming available for another route within the week. However, another issue arises: the particular weeks that the nonweekly customers should be assigned. Some customers may be delivered to in weeks 1 and 3, while others in weeks 2 and 4. Careful assignment of stops and loads to the week, thus balancing weekly loads, helps to minimize the number of trucks needed in the fleet.

Implementation of Vehicle Routing and Scheduling Methods

Vehicle routing and scheduling problems are rich in variety and endless in the number and types of restrictions that can be placed on them. The problems of moving less-than-truckload freight between a network of terminals (as in the case of Federal Express, United Parcel Service, or LTL common carrier) are quite different from routing school buses and individually responsive transport such as Dial-A-Ride. In addition, there are always exceptions to the typical problem that must be handled as a part of normal operations. Every vehicle routing and scheduling problem seems to require its own special approach to a solution. Even so, the resulting methods are not likely to handle the entirety of the problem. If they are to be used in practice, care must be taken in the manner in which they are implemented.

One practical approach to quantitative solution methodology implementation in an operating environment is the three-stage *preview-solve-review* technique. A model is constructed that will capture as much of the real problem as practical, given the need to solve it within a reasonable time and with a quality solution. Optimizing methods can often be used for this purpose, since the features that are most difficult to handle optimally are not included in the model formulation. Practical solutions to the real problems are developed in a three-step process. First, the analyst *previews* the problem for exceptions (deliveries requiring special handling) or deliveries and pickups that are obvious (full truckload movements). Next, usually with the aid of a computer, the reduced problem is *solved* and the solution made available to the analyst. Finally, the analyst *reviews* the mathematical solution and makes modifications to it as necessary to make it practical.

Application

A major oil company makes replenishment deliveries to service stations that request one or more grades of gasoline. Compartmentalized trucks are used that can hold varying numbers and quantities of gasoline grades, depending on the particular tank truck design. The truck dispatcher at a local distribution terminal receives the daily orders from local service stations in his territory. Order quantities and locations vary.

A mathematical programming model was developed to plan the routes for 20 to 50 stops. This model was designed to treat the problem in its most general form from a typical database of road distances, travel times, and truck and driver availability. However, the model could not hope to cope with all the intricacies of day-to-day routing.

Dispatchers do not rely entirely on the model to generate good route designs in all cases. They first preview the daily orders for special delivery requests and exceptions from normal patterns, ranging from emergency deliveries and full truckload quantities to special product blends that are not to be mixed with the regular products. These cases are manually routed, leaving the remainder of the orders to be submitted to the computer routing model. Although the computer routing model may guarantee an optimal solution to the mathematical problem of routing, the dispatcher uses it only as a guideline solution to the problem, which is further reviewed for functionality. Adjustments in the schedule may need to be made for reasons such as complying with union rules, routing around temporary road detours, and awaiting late-arriving orders. Thus, the dispatcher and a computer model work together to produce a good routing schedule that meets both customer service and cost-minimizing objectives, and to do it within reasonable parameters of time and effort.

Ship Routing and Scheduling

Much of the discussion about routing and scheduling to this point has related to over-the-road vehicles. In contrast, we will illustrate a routing and scheduling problem for ships sailing between different ports. Such a problem is characterized by the need to minimize the number of vessels required, due to high fixed costs, while meeting promised pickup and delivery dates at various ports. Transport capacity is assumed adequate for any movement between origin and destination ports, and the movement times between all points are known. This problem type can be formulated as a linear programming transportation problem.

Example[17]

A European petroleum refiner has three refineries (D_1, D_2, and D_3) along the European coastline. The company obtains oil from two ports (L_1 and L_2) in the Middle East. The crude oil is moved between the loading and discharge ports using tanker vessels. The sailing times in days between ports plus the time required for loading and unloading are summed in the following matrix:

SAILING PLUS LOADING TIMES

	Discharge Points		
	D_1	D_2	D_3
Loading L_1	21	19	13
Loading L_2	16	15	12

For simplicity, the times between ports, regardless of direction, are assumed the same, and the loading and unloading times are equal. Based on requirements over the next two months, the refineries need deliveries on the following days, counting from the present time:

From	L_2	L_1	L_1	L_2
To	D_3	D_1	D_2	D_3
On day	12	29	51	61

Due to loading and sailing time, it follows that loading needs to occur according to the following dates if the discharge dates are to be met:

LATEST LOADING TIMES

To	D_1	D_2	D_3
From L_1	8	32	—
From L_2	—	—	0 and 49

The company would like to know how many ships are needed to meet this schedule, and what the routing of each ship should be.

An initial transportation problem cost matrix can be developed, as shown in Figure 7-18. The rows represent the terminal states, and the columns are the initial states. The

---

[17]Based on the original example by George B. Danzig and D. R. Fulkerson, "Minimizing the Number of Tankers to Meet a Fixed Schedule," *Naval Research Logistics Quarterly*, Vol. 1, No. 3 (September 1954), pp. 217–222.

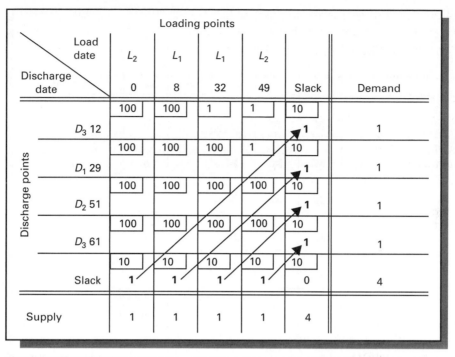

Figure 7-18 Transportation Problem Setup of the Ship Scheduling Problem with Initial Solution

demand values and supply values are the number of times each state occurs. In our case, all demand and supply rim values are 1. Next, we must recognize that only certain cells have feasible solution values. For example, the cell at row = 4, column = 2 cannot be feasible because a ship cannot be directed from unloading on day 61 to meet a loading date on day 8. All cells are examined in this manner, and those infeasible ones are given a very high cell cost, say 100 cost units, to lock them out of solution. Feasible cells are assigned arbitrarily low costs, say 1 cost unit. Slack cell costs should be moderately high to discourage assignment to them, say 10 cost units. An initial feasible solution to our problem can be achieved by making an initial assignment to the slack cells. Of course, this solution represents the maximal number of ships that might be needed.

Solving the cost matrix by any appropriate transportation method[18] yields the solution matrix shown in Figure 7-19. To read this solution, we start with the initial state at column = 1 and then find the cell solution value = 1 associated with the terminal state at row = 1. This cell is row = 1, column = 3. Next, we look for a cell solution value = 1 for row = 3, which is equal to the previous column number of 3. This is now a slack cell, and we stop. Repeat for the next available column value until no further 1s are available in the slack row. The first routing, as shown in Figure 7-19, is a connected path of $L_2, 0 \rightarrow D_3, 12 \rightarrow L_1, 32 \rightarrow D_2, 51$. Starting with the second initial

---

[18]TRANLP is the transportation method module in LOGWARE.

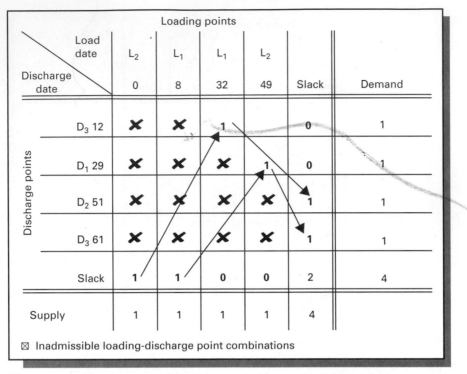

Discharge date	Load date	L_2 0	L_1 8	L_1 32	L_2 49	Slack	Demand
		Loading points					
D_3 12		✗	✗	1		0	1
D_1 29		✗	✗	✗	1	0	1
D_2 51		✗	✗	✗	✗	1	1
D_3 61		✗	✗	✗	✗	1	1
Slack		1	1	0	0	2	4
Supply		1	1	1	1	4	

⊠ Inadmissible loading-discharge point combinations

Figure 7-19   Solution Matrix for the Ship Scheduling Problem

state, we trace a similar path of $L_1,8 \rightarrow D_1, 29 \rightarrow L_2,49 \rightarrow D_3,61$. Since there are two distinct routes, two ships are required.

FREIGHT CONSOLIDATION

In transportation, the reduced rates with larger shipment sizes encourage managers to ship in large quantities. Consolidating small shipments into large ones is the primary way to achieve a lower transportation cost per unit of weight. Shipment consolidation is usually achieved in four ways. First, there is *inventory* consolidation. That is, an inventory of items is created from which demand is served. This allows large and even full vehicle-load shipments to be made into the inventory. This is a fundamental principle of inventory control and is discussed in Chapter 9 on inventory management.

Second, there is *vehicle* consolidation. In this case, where pickups and deliveries involve less than vehicle-load quantities, more than one pickup or delivery is placed on the same vehicle for more efficient transport. Vehicle routing and scheduling procedures exploit this type of economy. This phenomenon has been presented in this chapter.

Third, there is *warehouse* consolidation. The fundamental reason for warehousing is to allow the transportation of large shipment sizes over long distances and the transportation of small shipment sizes over short distances. A warehouse used in a break-bulk operation is an example. The economics of warehousing are discussed in Chapter 11 on storage.

Fourth, there is *temporal* consolidation. In this case, orders from customers are held so that a few larger shipments may be made at one time, rather than making many small shipments at various times. Economies in transportation are achieved through improved routing of the larger shipments as well as through lower per-unit rates. Of course, these costs are typically in trade-off with the effects of service deterioration that result from not shipping orders as soon as they are received and filled. The cost savings are obvious, but the effect on service may be difficult to estimate.

Example

The shipment (class 100, discount 40 percent) of distributor orders by a food products company from its plant in Fort Worth, Texas, to the Kansas sales territory can illustrate temporal consolidation. An analysis of past orders from three Kansas cities over a consecutive three-day period shows the following order volumes:

	From Fort Worth (76102)	Day 1	Day 2	Day 3
To	Topeka (66603)	5,000 lb	25,000 lb	18,000 lb
	Kansas City (66101)	7,000	12,000	21,000
	Wichita (67202)	42,000	38,000	61,000

The company typically has shipped orders the same day that they are received. Management is wondering whether a three-day consolidation of orders would be worth the reduction in service.

Given rates (in $/cwt.) as quoted by carriers operating in the region, the following costs are incurred if orders are shipped on the day they are received:

	Day 1 Rate × Volume = Cost	Day 2 Rate × Volume = Cost	Day 3 Rate Volume = Cost	Totals
Topeka	16.41 × 50 = $ 820.50	9.91 × 250 = $2,477.50	14.90 × 180 = $2,682.00	$ 5,980.00
Kansas City	15.87 × 70 = 1,110.90	14.38 × 120 = 1,725.60	9.55 × 210 = 2,005.50	4,842.00
Wichita	6.33 × 420 = 2,658.60	6.33 × 400[a] = 2,532.00	6.33 × 610 = 3,861.30	9,051.90
Total	$4,590.00	$6,735.10	$8,548.80	$19,873.90

[a] Ship 380 cwt. as if full truckload of 400 cwt.

If orders are held for three days and then shipped, the transport costs would be

Rate × Volume = Cost		
Topeka	$7.09 \times 480^a =$	$ 3,403.20
Kansas City	$6.83 \times 400 =$	2,732.00
Wichita	$6.33 \times 1410 =$	8,925.30
Total		$15,060.50

$^a480 = 50 + 250 + 180.$

The savings in transport cost of order consolidation would be $19,873.90 − 15,060.50 = $4,813.40. Now, either research must show the effect on revenues of a lengthened order cycle time for customers so that they can be compared with these costs, or management must decide whether $4,813.40 is enough of a savings to justify the reduced service level.

CONCLUDING COMMENTS

Transportation decisions are some of the most important decisions facing the logistician. In this chapter, the most frequently occurring transport problems are examined, including mode selection, carrier routing, vehicle routing and scheduling, and freight consolidation. Fortunately, these decision problems can be reasonably approached by mathematical analysis, and a number of these techniques have been illustrated.

QUESTIONS

1. A firm that manufactures medical research supplies delivers them to hospitals and medical centers around the country. The deliveries can be made using LTL truck, air express, private truck fleet, and UPS. What factors should be considered in selecting among these alternatives? Rank them in terms of their importance.
2. Explain why the performance of a transport service should be a consideration in its selection.
3. Suppose that you are to travel by car from New York City to Los Angeles. When selecting the roads that you will travel, how much weight will you give to routes that minimize travel *time* versus those that minimize travel *distance*? Should a trucking company use the same weights when delivering freight?
4. What are the similarities and differences between routing school buses and routing Federal Express local pickup and delivery trucks?
5. What are the differences between the problem of routing and that of vehicle routing and scheduling?
6. What are the characteristics of the savings approach to vehicle routing and scheduling that allow it to handle so many restrictions and realistic conditions?
7. Describe the *preview-solve-review* technique for implementing routing and scheduling computer models into the workplace. What are its advantages?
8. What measures would you take to help truck dispatchers accept and use the type of routing and scheduling technology described in this chapter?

9. Describe the four types of freight consolidation. In *temporal* freight consolidation, how would you propose finding the effect on revenues of holding orders for the purpose of reducing shipping costs?

PROBLEMS

A number of the problems and case studies in this chapter can be solved or partially solved with the aid of computer software. The software packages in LOGWARE that are most important in this chapter are TRANLP (*T*), ROUTE (*RO*), ROUTER (*R*), and ROUTESEQ (*RS*). The CD icon **R** will appear with the software package designation where the problem analysis is assisted by one of these software programs. A database may be prepared for the problem if extensive data input is required. Where the problem can be solved without the aid of the computer (by hand), the hand icon is shown. If no icon appears, hand calculation is assumed.

1. The Wagner Company supplies electric motors to Electronic Distributors, Inc. on a delivered-price basis. Wagner has the responsibility for providing transportation. The traffic manager has three transportation service choices for delivery—rail, piggyback, and truck. He has compiled the following information:

Transport Mode	Transit Time, Days	Rate, $/Unit	Shipment Size, Units
Rail	16	25.00	10,000
Piggyback	10	44.00	7,000
Truck	4	88.00	5,000

Electronic Distributors purchases 50,000 units per year at a delivered contract price of $500 per unit. Inventory-carrying cost for both companies is 25 percent per year. Which mode of transportation should Wagner select?

2. Suppose two truck services are being considered for deliveries from a company plant to one of its warehouses. Service *B* is cheaper but slower and less reliable than service *A*. The following information has been assembled:

Demand (known)	9,600 cwt./year
Order cost	$100/order
Product price, f.o.b. source	$50/cwt.
Shipping quantity	As per EOQ
In-transit carrying cost	20%/year
Inventory-carrying cost	30%/year
In-stock probability during the lead time	90%
Out-of-stock costs	Unknown
Selling days	365 days/year

	Service	
	--------------	--------------
	A	B
Transit time (*LT*)	4 days	5 days
Variability (std. dev., s_{LT})	1.5 days	1.8 days
Rate	$12.00/cwt.	$11.80/cwt.

A reorder point control method of inventory control is used at the warehouse. From the point of view of the inventory in the warehouse, which truck service should be selected? (*Note:* Refer to Chapter 9 on inventory management for discussion of the reorder point method of inventory control. *Hint:* The standard deviation of the demand-during-lead-time distribution is $s' = d(s_{LT})$, where s_{LT} is assumed the transit time variability and d is the daily demand rate.)

3. The Transcontinental Trucking Company wishes to route a shipment from Buffalo to Duluth over major highways. Because time and distance are closely related, the company dispatcher would like to find the shortest route. A schematic network of the major highway links and mileage between city pairs is shown in Figure 7-20. Find the shortest route through the network by using the shortest route method.

4. The U.S. Army Materiel Command was preparing final arrangements to move its M113 Full-Tracked Armored Personnel Carrier from various subcontractors'

Figure 7-20 Feasible Routes for Transcontinental Trucking Company Problem

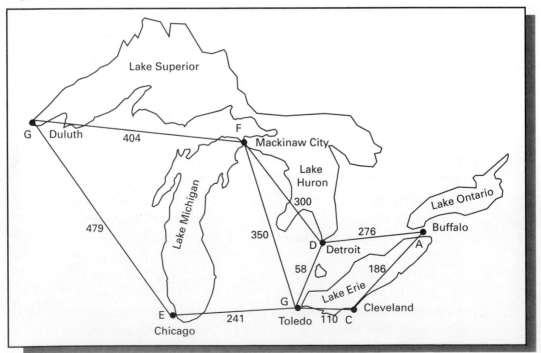

manufacturing facilities to intermediate storage facilities at Letterkenny, Pennsylvania, for those units destined for Europe and for several army bases within the United States. The production schedule for December plus the units on hand at the plant and the requirements for December are shown as follows:[19]

Production Schedule for December

Cleveland, OH	150 units plus 250
South Charleston, WV	150
San Jose, CA	150

Requirements for December

U.S. Army, Europe via Letterkenny, PA	300 units
Fort Hood, TX	100
Fort Riley, KS	100
Fort Carson, CO	100
Fort Benning, GA	100

Figure 7-21 shows the location of the supply and demand points as well as the per-unit transportation costs from supply to demand points.

Find the least-costly delivery plan for December to meet the requirements, but do not exceed the production schedule requirements.

Figure 7-21 Transportation Network with Associated Costs for U.S. Army Materiel Command Problem

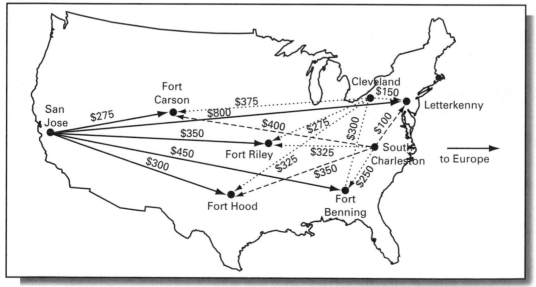

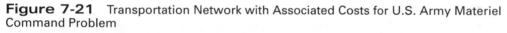

---

[19]This problem is adapted from a case study by Colonel James Piercy.

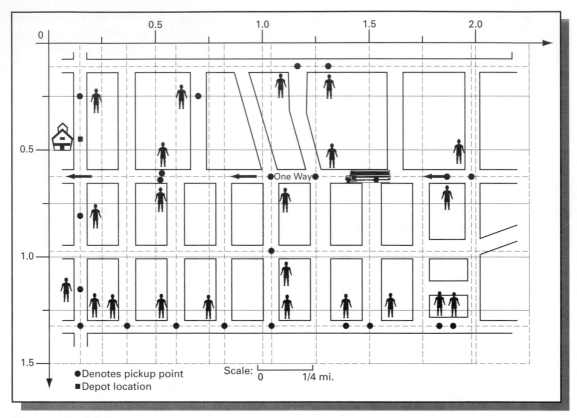

Figure 7-22 School Bus Routing Exercise

5. The Evansville Local School District provides bus transportation for its elementary schoolchildren. One bus has been assigned to the neighborhood, as defined in Figure 7-22. Each year there is a new roster of children, and the location of the stops for them can be plotted on a map. Sequencing the stops determines the time and distance required to complete the bus tour. Using your best cognitive skills, design the shortest bus tour possible given the following conditions:[20]

- Only one bus is to be used.
- The bus starts at the elementary school and returns to it.
- Each stop is to be visited.
- Children may be picked up or dropped off from either side of the street.
- A pickup or dropoff at a corner may be made from either adjacent street.
- No U-turns are permitted.
- The bus has adequate capacity to transport all the children on the route.

Use a ruler or the linear grid to determine the total distance for the bus tour.

---

[20]Adapted from a routing exercise by William L. Berry.

Figure 7-23
Store Accounts (X)
and Motel Locations
(M)

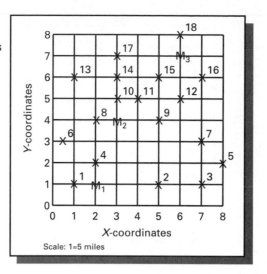

Y-coordinates

X-coordinates

Scale: 1=5 miles

6. Dan Pupp is a jewelry salesperson who calls on store accounts in the Midwest. One of his territories is shown in Figure 7-23. His mode of operation is to arrive at the territory the night before making his calls to stay at one of the local motels. He covers the region in two days and leaves the morning of the third day. Since he pays his own expenses, he would like to minimize his total costs for serving the accounts. Accounts 1 to 9 are covered the first day, and the remainder are visited the second day. He would like to compare two strategies:

Strategy 1. Stay at motel M_2 all three nights at $49.00 per night.

Strategy 2. Stay at motel M_1 to visit accounts 1 to 9, staying there two nights at $40.00 per night. Then, stay at motel M_3 one night at $45.00 per night to visit accounts 10 to 18. After visiting accounts 1 to 9, he returns to M_1 to stay overnight before moving to M_3. He then stays overnight at M_3 before moving on the next morning. The distance between M_1 and M_3 is 36 miles. Disregard any distance that he travels to and from the territory. Dan figures mileage costs at $0.30 per mile.

Which strategy seems best for Dan?

7. A bakery delivers daily to five large retail stores in a defined territory. The driver for the bakery loads goods at the bakery, makes deliveries to the retail stores, and returns to the bakery. A diagram of the territory is shown in Figure 7-24. The associated network travel times in minutes are

To →		B	1	2	3	4	5
	B	0	24	50	38	55	20
	1	22	0	32	23	45	18
From	2	47	35	0	15	21	60
	3	39	27	17	0	14	25
	4	57	42	18	16	0	42
	5	21	16	57	21	41	0

Figure 7-24
Bakery Routing
Territory Map

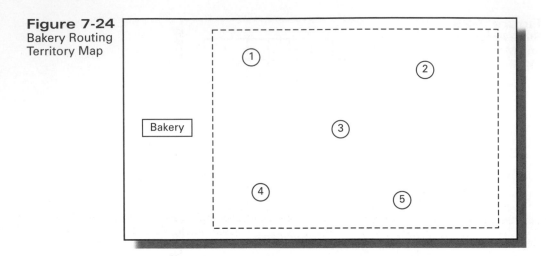

Note that because of one-way streets and detours, the travel times are slightly different, depending on the direction (asymmetrical).

a.   What is the best routing sequence for the delivery truck?

b.   If loading or unloading times are significant, how might they be included in the analysis?

c.   Retail store 3 is located in such a densely populated urban area that the travel times to and from this point may increase by as much as 50 percent, depending on the time of day. Travel times for the other points remain relatively unchanged. Would the solution in part (a) be sensitive to such variations?

8. Sima Donuts supplies its retail outlets with the ingredients for making fresh donuts. A central warehouse from which trucks are dispatched is located in Atlanta. Trucks can leave the Atlanta warehouse as early as 3 A.M. to make pallet-load deliveries to the Florida market and may return at any time. The trucks may also pick up empty containers and supplies from vendors in the general area. Pickups are allowed only after all deliveries on a route are made. A simple linear grid is placed over the Georgia–Florida area and grid coordinates found for warehouse, retail, and vendor sites. The 0, 0 coordinates are in the northeast corner. For example, the Atlanta warehouse is located at X = 2084, Y = 7260. The scaling factor on the map, including a road circuity factor, is 0.363. The total time on a route may be 40 hours and total route distance may be up to 1,400 miles. Team drivers are used so that no overnight breaks are required, but one-hour rest breaks are allowed at 12 noon and 8 P.M. each day. Average driving speed is taken to be 45 miles per hour. Additional data about the stops are as follows:

No.	Stop Location	Stop Type	Volume, Pallets	X-Coordinate	Y-Coordinate	Loading/ Unloading Time (Min.)	Time Window Open	Close
1	Tampa, FL	Delivery	20	1147	8197	15	6 A.M.	12 A.M.[a]
2	Clearwater, FL	Pickup	14	1206	8203	45	6 A.M.	12 A.M.
3	Daytona Beach, FL	Delivery	18	1052	7791	45	6 A.M.	12 A.M.
4	Fort Lauderdale, FL	Delivery	3	557	8282	45	3 A.M.	12 A.M.

5	North Miami, FL	Delivery	5	527	8341	45	6 A.M.	12 A.M.
6	Oakland Park, FL	Pickup	4	565	8273	45	3 A.M.	12 A.M.
7	Orlando, FL	Delivery	3	1031	7954	45	3 A.M.	12 A.M.
8	St Petersburg, FL	Pickup	3	1159	8224	45	3 A.M.	12 A.M.
9	Tallahassee, FL	Delivery	3	1716	7877	15	10 A.M.	12 A.M.
10	West Palm Beach, FL	Delivery	3	607	8166	45	6 A.M.	12 A.M.
11	Miami-Puerto Rico	Delivery	4	527	8351	45	6 A.M.	12 A.M.
			80					

[a]Midnight

There are three trucks with a 20-pallet capacity, one with a 25-pallet capacity, and one with a 30-pallet capacity. The cost for drivers and truck is $1.30 per mile.

Design the routes for this set of deliveries and pickups. Which trucks are to be assigned to which routes? What is the dispatch plan? What is the cost for the dispatch?

9. Queens Lines operates a fleet of tanker ships to transport crude oil world wide. One scheduling problem concerns the movement of oil from Middle East ports to four European ports in England, France, and Belgium. The sailing time in days between ports is

	European Discharge Ports			
Middle East ports	A	B	C	D
1	20	18	12	9
2	17	14	10	8

Within the next three months, deliveries are to be made according to the following schedule:

From loading port	1	2	1	2	1	2
At discharge port	D	C	A	B	C	A
Day	19	15	36	39	52	86

Assume that ships are available to start anywhere and can end up at any port.

How many ships are needed to meet the schedule, and how should they be deployed? (*Hint:* Requires solving the linear programming transportation problem.)

10. The Maxim Packing Company is considering a freight consolidation program for serving the Kansas market. The program would involve the small-volume customers located at Hays, Manhattan, Salina, and Great Bend. The proposal is to hold all orders from these areas for several weeks in order to realize lower transportation charges. Assume all orders are now shipped LTL directly from Fort Worth, Texas, to their destination in Kansas. Average biweekly orders from the Kansas territory are as follows:

Hays	200 cases
Manhattan	350
Salina	325
Great Bend	125

FROM FORT WORTH TO	RATES ($/CWT.)			
	TRUCK AQ[a]	≥ 10,000 LB	≥ 20,000 LB	≥ 40,000 LB
Hays	12.78	5.19	4.26	3.06
Manhattan	12.78	5.19	4.26	2.22
Salina	10.26	4.08	3.42	2.46
Great Bend	12.27	4.98	4.08	2.94

[a]Any quantity less than 10,000 lb

Table 7-7 Truck Rates Between Fort Worth Texas, and Selected Destination Points in Kansas

The average case weighs 40 pounds. Orders could be shipped in the biweekly period that they are received, held, and shipped after two biweekly order periods, or held and shipped after three biweekly order periods. The potential loss of sales has been estimated at $1.05 per case for each additional biweekly period that orders are held. Transportation rates to Kansas are given in Table 7-7.

Should the program be implemented? If so, how long should orders be held before shipment?

11. The Sunshine Bottling Company bottles soft drinks that it distributes to retail outlets from nine warehouses in the Michigan area. A single bottling plant is located in Flint, Michigan. The product is shipped from the plant to the nine warehouses in full truckload quantities. The typical plant-to-warehouse movement is to transport a trailer of palletized soft drink to the warehouse, drop off the loaded trailer, and bring a trailer of empty pallets back to the plant. The unloading and hitching of the trailer at the warehouse takes 15 minutes. Since the routes are traveled frequently, travel times, unloading times, and break times are known with a great deal of certainty. The number of trips needed to meet demand and the route times for a typical week are as follows:

Warehouse Location	Distance, Miles	Number of Weekly Trips	Driving Time, hr.[a]	Unloading Time, hr.	Break/Lunch Time, hr.	Total Route Time, hr.
Flint	20	43	1.00	0.25	0	1.25
Alpena	350	5	9.00	0.25	1.25	10.50
Saginaw	80	8	2.00	0.25	0	2.25
Lansing	118	21	3.25	0.25	0.25	3.75
Mt. Pleasant	185	12	4.50	0.25	0.75	5.50
W. Branch	210	5	5.00	0.25	0.75	6.00
Pontiac	90	43	2.50	0.25	0	2.75
Traverse City	376	6	9.00	0.25	1.25	10.50
Petoskey	428	5	10.00	0.25	1.50	11.75

[a]Round-trip time

Figure 7-25
Funeral Home
Locations for the
Nockem Dead
Casket Company
with the Number of
Caskets Ordered

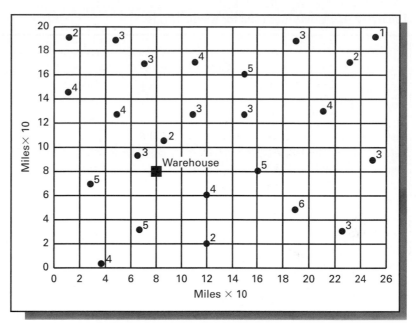

It is desirable to schedule trucks to leave the plant at or after 4:00 A.M. and to return no later than 11:00 P.M. the same day. Unloading can take place only when the warehouse is open, which is from 6:30 A.M. until 11:00 P.M.

By sequencing the routes to maximize truck utilization, determine the *minimum* number of trucks that is needed to serve all the routes. The company was using 10 trucks.

12. The Nockem Dead Casket Company supplies funeral homes with caskets throughout the state of California. The funeral homes for a particular warehouse territory are located as shown on the map in Figure 7-25.

   a. Suppose that the funeral home locations (•) and associated number of caskets for each funeral home represent a single, daily dispatch. If the company has six trucks with capacities of 20 caskets each, develop a routing plan using the "sweep" method. (Use a counterclockwise sweep with a due north start.) Place your design on the map. How many trucks are actually used and what is the total travel distance for the route design? You may scale distances from the diagram.

   b. Appraise the sweep method as a good method for truck routing and scheduling.

or

13. As an adjunct to its retail business, Medic Drugs fills prescriptions for outlying nursing homes, extended care facilities, rehabilitation centers, and retirement homes. Part of this service is to deliver the prescription order to the customer site. Station wagons having a capacity of 63 cartons are used for delivery. Customer locations are geocoded by a linear grid overlay with a map-scaling factor of 4.6 per coordinate unit. Customer data for a typical delivery day is given in Table 7-8. The 0,0 coordinates on the grid are in the southwest corner.

Table 7-8 Customer Data for Medic Drugs

CUSTOMER LOCATION	TYPE OF STOP	VOLUME, CARTONS	X COOR-DINATES	Y COOR-DINATES	UNLOADING TIME, MIN.	TIME WINDOW OPEN	TIME WINDOW CLOSE
Covington House	D	1	23.4	12.9	2	9 A.M.	5 P.M.
Cuyahoga Falls	D	9	13.4	13.4	18	9 A.M.	5 P.M.
Elyria	D	1	6.3	16.8	5	9 A.M.	5 P.M.
Euclid Manor	D	4	11.8	18.6	4	9 A.M.	5 P.M.
Ester Marie	D	3	19.4	23.4	3	9 A.M.	5 P.M.
Fairmount	D	4	13.6	21.1	5	9 A.M.	5 P.M.
Gables	D	1	18.3	22.8	2	9 A.M.	5 P.M.
Geneva Medicare	D	4	19.5	23.5	2	9 A.M.	5 P.M.
Heather Hill	D	7	16.5	20.0	11	9 A.M.	5 P.M.
Hill Haven	D	11	13.2	12.5	17	9 A.M.	5 P.M.
Homestead Genev	D	2	19.4	23.5	2	9 A.M.	5 P.M.
Inn Conneaut	D	6	23.8	25.6	8	9 A.M.	5 P.M.
Judson Park	D	2	11.7	18.3	5	9 A.M.	5 P.M.
Amer. Lakeshore	D	6	11.9	18.7	8	9 A.M.	5 P.M.
Con Lea	D	3	13.4	23.6	2	9 A.M.	5 P.M.
Villa Care Ctr	D	2	10.8	18.2	5	9 A.M.	5 P.M.
Madison Village	D	1	18.4	22.8	2	9 A.M.	5 P.M.
Manor House	D	1	23.2	12.7	2	9 A.M.	5 P.M.
Meadow Brk Mnr	D	2	23.9	12.7	5	9 A.M.	5 P.M.
Medicare	D	1	11.8	18.5	5	9 A.M.	5 P.M.
N Manor Center	D	2	23.2	12.8	5	9 A.M.	5 P.M.
O Extended Care	D	13	5.4	19.3	8	9 A.M.	5 P.M.
Oak Park	D	5	13.0	17.0	10	9 A.M.	5 P.M.
Ohio Pythian	D	3	9.0	13.2	4	9 A.M.	5 P.M.
Park Rehab	D	6	13.0	20.0	5	9 A.M.	5 P.M.
Patrician	D	5	10.6	15.9	4	9 A.M.	5 P.M.
Perry Ridge	D	1	17.3	22.7	2	9 A.M.	5 P.M.
Pine Valley	D	6	11.4	14.8	10	9 A.M.	5 P.M.
Royal View Manor	D	7	11.1	15.9	6	9 A.M.	5 P.M.
Shady Acres	D	8	18.3	22.9	8	9 A.M.	5 P.M.
St Augustine Mr	D	5	10.5	18.5	9	9 A.M.	5 P.M.
Shagri-La	D	5	9.1	13.3	5	9 A.M.	11 A.M.
Singleton	D	1	11.7	18.7	4	9 A.M.	5 P.M.
Stewart Lodge	D	1	18.4	22.8	2	9 A.M.	5 P.M.
Town Hall	D	2	19.7	19.3	3	9 A.M.	5 P.M.
Algart	D	1	10.5	18.5	4	9 A.M.	5 P.M.
Ambassador	D	7	12.3	19.8	5	9 A.M.	5 P.M.
Ashtabula	D	5	21.3	24.4	9	9 A.M.	5 P.M.
Austin Woods	D	4	21.7	12.7	3	9 A.M.	5 P.M.
Bolton	D	1	18.3	22.9	3	9 A.M.	5 P.M.
Broadway	D	4	11.6	19.5	2	9 A.M.	5 P.M.

Cle Golden Age	D	1	11.6	18.4	5	9 A.M.	5 P.M.
Villa Santa Ann	D	3	13.2	19.4	9	9 A.M.	5 P.M.
Wadsworth	D	5	10.7	11.5	3	9 A.M.	5 P.M.
Wickliffe Cntry	D	7	13.0	20.6	8	9 A.M.	5 P.M.
Westbay Manor	D	6	8.4	18.0	10	10:30 A.M.	11:30 A.M.
Westhaven	D	2	8.5	18.1	5	9 A.M.	5 P.M.
Broadfield Mnr	D	6	18.2	22.9	2	9 A.M.	5 P.M.
Total		193					

Deliveries may begin as early a 8 A.M. (drivers leave depot) and drivers are to return to the base pharmacy by 6 P.M. Average driving speed is 30 miles per hour. Drivers are allowed a one-hour lunch break after 12 noon. Most customers may receive their deliveries between 9 A.M. and 5 P.M., although there are a few exceptions. The base pharmacy is located at $X = 13.7$, $Y = 21.2$. If a driver returns early to the base pharmacy, the station wagon may be reloaded and sent on a second route.
a. Design a dispatch route plan that will minimize total distance traveled.

Figure 7-26 Five-day Demand Locations for Nockem Dead Casket Company

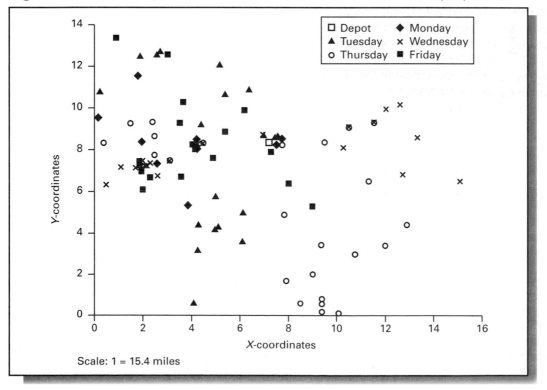

b. Can any routes be assigned to the same station wagon to reduce the total number of drivers and vehicles needed to service the customers? If not, is there anything that might be done to accomplish this?

14. The Nockem Dead Casket Company sells and distributes caskets to funeral homes in the Columbus, Ohio, region. Funeral homes place orders at a warehouse ($X = 7.2$, $Y = 8.4$) for delivery throughout the week. The funeral home locations and the weekdays for delivery are given in Figure 7-26. Number of caskets and the funeral home coordinates are given in Table 7-9. Deliveries are made using one 18-casket truck and one 27-casket truck. Trucks leave the warehouse to make deliveries and return the same day.

Using the *Principles for Good Routing and Scheduling*, develop a good routing plan for the company. Be creative.

Table 7-9 Funeral Home Locations and Number of Caskets to Be Delivered on Each Day of the Week

MONDAY			TUESDAY			WEDNESDAY			THURSDAY			FRIDAY		
X	Y	VOL.	X	Y	VOL.	X	Y	VOL.	X	Y	VOL.	X	Y	VOL.
4.9	7.6	2	5.4	10.7	1	12.7	6.8	1	7.8	4.9	5	4.9	7.6	1
4.3	8.1	1	6.4	10.8	1	13.3	8.6	1	7.9	1.7	3	4.1	8.3	1
4.3	8.2	1	5.2	12.2	3	12.6	10.2	3	9.0	2.0	2	4.4	8.3	1
4.3	8.3	1	2.7	12.7	1	12.0	10.5	1	9.4	0.6	5	4.2	8.1	1
4.2	8.4	1	2.6	12.6	1	11.5	9.3	1	9.4	0.7	1	2.0	7.0	1
3.1	7.5	1	1.9	12.5	1	10.5	9.1	3	8.5	0.6	1	1.9	7.3	1
2.5	7.8	1	0.9	13.4	1	10.3	8.1	2	9.4	0.2	4	1.9	7.4	3
0.1	9.6	2	0.1	10.8	2	4.5	8.4	1	10.2	0.1	1	2.3	6.7	1
1.8	11.6	1	4.4	9.2	3	2.1	7.2	1	10.7	3.0	3	5.4	8.9	1
1.9	8.4	1	5	5.8	2	2.2	7.3	4	9.4	3.4	2	2.0	6.1	1
2.5	7.4	1	4.3	4.4	2	3.1	7.5	1	4.3	8.2	2	9.0	5.3	2
2.4	6.7	1	5.1	4.3	2	2.3	7.4	1	4.5	8.4	1	3.6	6.7	1
3.9	5.3	3	5.0	4.2	1	2.1	7.1	2	4.2	8.1	4	5.4	8.9	2
7.6	8.6	1	4.3	3.2	1	2.0	7.4	3	2.5	7.8	1	3.5	9.3	3
7.6	8.3	1	4.1	3.6	1	2.6	6.8	1	0.4	8.4	1	3.7	10.3	1
7.7	8.5	2	6.1	5.0	2	5.4	8.9	1	1.5	9.3	1	3.0	12.6	2
			7.0	8.7	2	15.1	6.5	1	2.4	9.4	2	0.9	13.3	2
			7.5	8.6	2	0.5	6.4	1	2.5	8.7	3	6.2	9.9	1
			7.4	8.6	1	1.1	7.2	2	10.5	9.1	1	7.3	7.9	1
						1.7	7.2	2	9.5	8.4	1	8.0	6.4	1
						2.0	7.5	1	11.3	6.5	1			
						7.0	8.7	1	12.9	4.4	1			
						7.5	8.6	1	12.0	3.4	1			
									7.7	8.3	1			
									11.5	9.3	1			
Total		21	*Total*		30	*Total*		36	*Total*		49	*Total*		28

CASE STUDIES

Fowler Distributing Company[†]

Roy Fowler is the owner of the Fowler Distributing Company, a regional franchised distributor of beer and wine coolers for a large brewery Roy faces a major problem in the efficient transportation of the beer and wine products to customer accounts. Roy owns the delivery trucks, but union route drivers peddle store accounts by selling beer and wine from the inventory on the trucks. Drivers are interested in maximizing their incomes by maximizing their revenues. While Roy is pleased with the drivers' selling effort, he is also interested in minimizing the number of trucks needed to serve the accounts and the miles driven, since truck-operating expenses are charged to the company rather than against a driver's income.

BACKGROUND

Roy Fowler, a returning veteran of the Korean conflict, purchased two buses to provide transportation for the residents of his hometown. Roy struggled to make a living in this business, where he was both driver and maintenance man. To control expenses, Roy would purchase only one license plate for two buses, swapping them between the buses when one was out for repair or otherwise out of service. He was put out of business when the city set up its own transit system.

Roy's transportation experience led him to establish a beer distributorship and to peddle beer from a local warehouse to the various retail accounts in the region surrounding the warehouse. As the brewery became a dominant beer producer, Roy's distributorship thrived as well. Although he is the largest distributor in his area, controlling costs is essential to maintaining his competitive edge.

DELIVERY OPERATIONS

A regular route is an assignment of retail and other accounts to a particular driver and truck. Drivers are unionized and bid for these routes. They win the routes based on seniority, act as salespersons on the routes, and further develop accounts in order to increase their income. Drivers are paid on a commission basis and have been known to earn as much as $4,000 per week during a good selling period. As might be expected, drivers jealously guard their route composition and design. Roy must confront the union when attempting to reconfigure the routes.

There is another set of accounts known as pre-sell accounts, that are served on secondary routes. There is some opportunity for optimizing the secondary route design. Pre-sell accounts place an order in advance of delivery rather than wait for the route salesperson to drop by. The orders for these accounts can be put on trucks separate from those of the commission accounts and routed as desired without many restrictive union rules. No sales commission is paid, since no selling by the driver takes place.

A TYPICAL PROBLEM

On a typical day, the 21 pre-sell accounts might occur, as described in Table 1 and located in Figure 1. There are 250 operating days per year. Table 1 gives the number of cases demanded, the expected time (in minutes) to service the account, and time of day in which the account can be served, if restricted. Figure 1 gives a map of the location of each account (by number) and of the warehouse (*W*). The map is scaled with

---

[†]Adapted from a routing problem by William L. Berry.

Account Number	Coordinates		Cases Demanded	Delivery Time, Min.	Time Windows
	X	Y			
1	7.5	28.5	120	60	8:00 A.M.–5:00 P.M.
2	10.0	9.0	200	90	8:00 A.M.–10:30 A.M.
3	12.0	24.0	120	60	8:00 A.M.–5:00 P.M.
4	13.0	30.0	150	80	8:00 A.M.–5:00 P.M.
5	13.5	34.0	50	40	8:00 A.M.–5:00 P.M.
6	17.5	16.5	90	50	8:00 A.M.–5:00 P.M.
7	23.0	38.5	140	70	8:00 A.M.–8:30 A.M.
8	23.0	16.5	60	40	8:00 A.M.–5:00 P.M.
9	23.5	25.0	110	60	8:00 A.M.–5:00 P.M.
10	27.0	33.5	180	90	8:00 A.M.–10:45 A.M.
11	29.0	28.0	30	20	8–11 A.M. & 2–4 P.M.
12	11.0	40.0	90	50	8:00 A.M.–8:30 A.M.
13	32.0	40.0	80	50	8:00 A.M.–10:00 A.M.
14	7.5	18.0	50	30	12:30 P.M.–5:30 P.M.
15	5.0	13.5	160	90	8:00 A.M.–12:45 P.M.
16	23.0	8.0	100	60	8:00 A.M.–5:00 P.M.
17	27.0	8.0	140	60	8:00 A.M.–5:00 P.M.
18	36.0	8.0	50	30	8:00 A.M.–5:00 P.M.
19	32.0	4.0	90	50	12:00 P.M.–4:00 P.M.
20	32.5	22.0	150	70	8:00 A.M.–5:00 P.M.
21	31.5	13.0	80	40	8:00 A.M.–5:00 P.M.
		Total	2,240	1,190	
Warehouse	15.0	35.0			

Table 1 Account Data

the approximate number of miles to travel north and south or east and west on the grid. The area's road network is well developed, and there are no rivers, lakes, or other barriers to take into consideration. Distance and driving time are directly related by an average speed of 25 miles per hour.

The company currently has five delivery vehicles to handle the pre-sell accounts and an ample number of drivers for them (warehouse workers often double as pre-sell account drivers). Each truck has a capacity of 500 cases, a price of $20,000, and an operating cost of $0.90 per mile, which includes truck depreciation.

The trucks are three years old and have a useful life of seven years. They can be sold for 10 percent of their initial purchase price at the end of their useful life. Drivers are paid $13 per hour, which includes a 30 percent fringe benefits package.

The trucks must leave the warehouse between 6:30 A.M. and 8:00 A.M. to make deliveries. Drivers are paid double the standard rate of pay (no fringe benefits) for time on the route above eight hours per day, not including the lunch break. Roy abhors paying overtime. One half hour is allocated on the route for lunch, which must be taken between 11:30 A.M. and

Figure 1
Map of Accounts
and Warehouse
Location

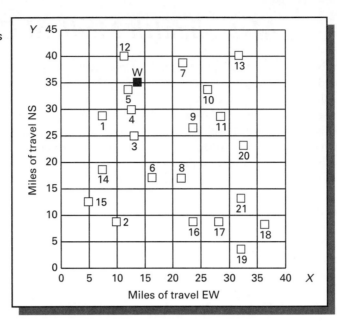

1:30 P.M. Several accounts require that delivery occur between specified time windows. The truck is not to make a delivery at a stop before the time window opens or after it closes, but these requirements are sometimes not met.

Current company dispatching gives a route design as follows:

Route	Start Time	Stop Sequence
1	7:45 A.M.	12,15,1,14,5
2	7:33 A.M.	2,3,4
3	7:22 A.M.	6,16,17,8,19
4	8:00 A.M.	11,20,18,21,9
5	7:39 A.M.	7,13,10

ASSIGNMENT

1. Determine the best number of trucks and routes, and the stop sequence on each route. Is it fair to compare this design with the current one?

2. What does it cost Roy Fowler to serve the restrictive time windows other than the 8:00 A.M. to 5:00 P.M. Time windows? Is there anything that he might do to reduce this cost?

3. If larger trucks, priced at $35,000 and having a capacity of 600 cases, are available, should they be purchased? They are expected to increase operating costs by $0.05 per mile.

4. If Roy can use an outside transport service to deliver to all accounts with demand of 50 cases or less for a price of $35.00 per account, should he do it?

5. The union is negotiating for a $7\frac{1}{2}$ hour workday, excluding lunchtime, before overtime begins. What implication does this have for route design and costs?

6. Roy would like to consider a more central location for the warehouse at coordinates $X = 20$, $Y = 25$. The lease cost for the building is the same as the current location, but the pre-sell demand portion of the one-time moving cost is $15,000. Is such a move economically attractive for pre-sell demand?

7. How would you go about implementing a computerized software package such as ROUTER for truck dispatching on a daily basis? What problems would you anticipate, and how would you deal with them?

Metrohealth Medical Center*

MetroHealth System is a municipal hospital network located in Cleveland, Ohio, consisting of multiple facilities providing an array of diagnostic and treatment services. It is the focal point for the Cuyahoga County hospital system. MetroHealth Medical Center (MMC) is the city's primary hospital and largest on the west side. The system provides for the health care needs of a sizable number of patients, including significant elderly and indigent populations.

The movement of patients, staff, and supplies must move fluidly between MetroHealth's primary hospital (769 beds), long-term care facility (172 beds), Cuyahoga County Women and Infant Care (WIC), Maternity and Infant Care (M&I), Clement Center, and outlying ambulatory clinics.

The medical center has a stated goal of "responding to community needs, improving the health status of the region, and controlling health care costs." MetroHealth Transportation/Logistics Services supports this goal with a mission "to increase access to health care in the region by providing safe, timely, and comfortable rides for the system's patients and to provide support for all customers and staff with the transport of personnel, supplies, and materials throughout the MetroHealth System." For the patient, this means that a high level of customer service is to be provided where patients are to be picked up and returned to their origins with a minimum of waiting, and to do this in the most cost-efficient manner possible.

The focus of this case study is on the movement of patients to and from the primary hospital and not on the movement of staff and materials. The patients involved cannot provide transportation for themselves. Since the expenses associated with their diagnosis and treatment are typically paid by a third party (e.g., Medicare or private insurance), the hospital can recover the costs for such services and does not charge patients for transportation. Although such services might normally be provided for benevolent reasons, the increased competition among hospitals for patients has led the hospital to use transportation/logistics services as a strategic weapon in its quest to cover all of its expenses. Revenues of about $230 per patient visit are generated whereas patient expenses are 90 percent of revenues including transportation. Transporting patients appears to be good business for the hospital.

TRANSPORT OPERATIONS

MMC's transportation service is offered to all those current and potential patients who cannot manage their own transportation to the hospital complex and want to use MMC services. A patient calls the Transport Services Department two or more days ahead of his or her scheduled appointment. After patient status verification, the appointment time and patient location are entered in to a computer database. A daily appointment list is prepared, showing the location and scheduled appointment time. Patients are expected to be ready for pickup two hours before their scheduled appointment time. Given the daily appointment list, the drivers divide the list between east and west collection zones and determine the routes that will best meet the appointment times. Figure 1 diagrams the information flow that produces the daily appointment list.

Throughout the day as patients finish with their visits, they move to a waiting, or staging, area. They are then picked up for their return trip home. A waiting time in the staging area of no more than 45 minutes is considered good

*This case was prepared with the assistance of Dominic Rinaldi, Manager, Transportation/Logistics' Services, MetroHealth Medical Center and Hena Montesinos-Bar, Weatherhead School of Management, Case Western Reserve University.

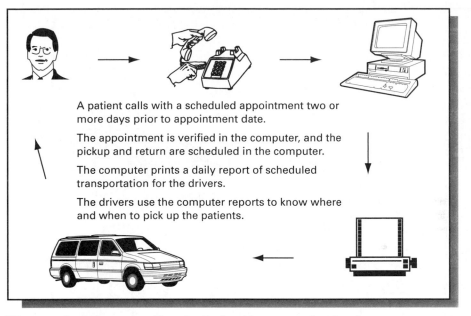

A patient calls with a scheduled appointment two or more days prior to appointment date.

The appointment is verified in the computer, and the pickup and return are scheduled in the computer.

The computer prints a daily report of scheduled transportation for the drivers.

The drivers use the computer reports to know where and when to pick up the patients.

Figure 1   Information Flow for Patient Transportation Service

customer service. Returning patients ride on the same vehicle that has been dispatched to pick up patients. Pickups and returns are serviced simultaneously on the same route. Vehicles circulate between the patient pickup zones and the MetroHealth Medical Center several times a day.

The service territory is divided between the east side and the west side of the city by zip code (see Figure 2). Transportation Services uses its own vehicles to serve the close-in patients. Two vehicles with 15-passenger capacity are generally both assigned to one side of town. Another six-passenger van is also available that represents spare capacity to meet schedule overload or to cover equipment breakdowns. A staff of one manager, seven drivers, and one clerk is employed with responsibilities for staff and materials transportation as well as for patient transportation. Transportation Services manages transportation for all zip codes within the county but provides service with its own vehicles only to the close-in zip codes, or the

crosshatched areas shown in Figure 2. Other zip codes within the county are outsourced to transportation providers. Those zip codes that represent distant locations or areas with a low patient density historically have been handled by taxicabs with a voucher arrangement. More recently, this type of patient transportation is provided under the hospital's ambulance contract. An ambulance service, such as Physicians Ambulance Service, bids on the lucrative ambulance business. In order to win the contract, it may also offer to provide patient transportation on a limited basis. The direct cost of this add-on service is often less than MMC's transport costs; however, not all patient transportation can be outsourced at such low rates without forcing a renegotiation of the ambulance contract with rates that are likely to be somewhere between MMC's costs and taxi costs.

TYPICAL DAILY SCHEDULES

A sample of daily transportation requests for a representative day is given in Table 1. This

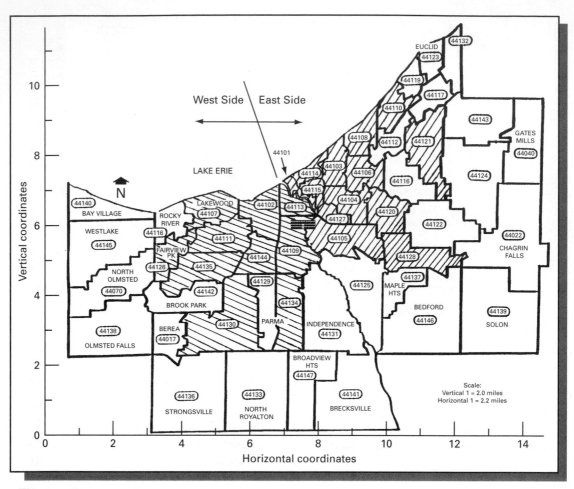

Figure 2 East Side and West Side Patient Collection Areas for MMC-Managed Transportation

daily period is considered typical of demand for transportation service throughout the year. The transportation service is offered 52 weeks of the year to an average of 64 patients per day. The appointment list is available at the beginning of the workday; however, adjustments to the list occur throughout the day in the form of cancellations, requests for pickups, or changes in appointment times. Such occurrences usually represent no more than two or three in a list of about 60 patients. Some patients simply do not show up when the van arrives. Not all patients need a return ride since some may have made other transportation arrangements. Arrival and departure times at MMC are known only for some patients. Figure 3 shows the distribution of pickups and deliveries in a typical week.

A report for November shows the number of patients picked up by zip code area. Many zip codes within the county have only a few patients that will ever use MMC transport services. Table 2 gives the number of patients originating from the various zip codes.

Table 1 A Representative Daily Patient Appointment List for MMC Transportation Services

No.	Appointment Time[a]	Patient Name	Pickup Zip Code[b]	Arrival Time[c]	Departure Time[d]
1	8:30 A.M.	Baker, Horace	44104E	—	—
2	8:30	Boyd, Jessie	44104E	—	9:50 A.M.
3	9:00	Carver, William	44128E	8:40 A.M.	
4	9:00	Ivey, Edna	44120E		12:09 P.M.
5	9:00	Rashed, Kareemah	44110E	7:40 A.M.	
6	9:00	Walsh, John	44126E	8:40	10:12 A.M.
7	9:30	Johnson, Fannie	44104E	8:40	1:25 P.M.
8	9:45	Burgess, David	44106E	8:57	
9	9:45	Delgado, Genoveva	44103E		
10	10:00	Fairrow, Annie	44106E	8:57	12:09
11	10:00	Middlebrooks, Sharon	44105E	9:40	
12	10:00	Suech, John	44107E		
13	10:30	Lawson, Linnette	44104E	9:40	12:09
14	10:30	Reed, William	44106E	10:10	11:00 A.M.
15	10:45	Bongiovanni, Anita	44105E	2:04	
16	11:00	Miller, Dawn	44105E	9:40	11:00 A.M.
17	11:30	Talley, Levannah	44120E		
18	11:45	Williams, Irelia	44115E	10:10	
19	12:30	Dumas, Tyere	44105E	10:50 A.M.	2:10 P.M.
20	12:45	Taylor, Frances	44120E		
21	1:00	Barker, Mary	44105E		
22	1:00	Lhota, Angelina	44127E	12:15 A.M.	
23	1:00	Manco, Alessandro	44110E		
24	1:00	Webb, Kimberly	44106E		
25	1:00	Wilson, Daryl	44105E	12:15 A.M.	2:10 P.M.
26	2:00	Arrington, Catherine	44120E		
27	2:00	Staunton, Gerald	44104E		
28	2:00	Wall, John	44105E		
29	2:00	Williams, Alberta	44103E		2:54
30	8:15	Caruso, Betty	44109W		
31	8:30	West, James	44102W		
32	9:00	Amaro, Antonia	44102W		2:15
33	9:00	Brown, Frances	44109W		
34	9:00	Ciesicki, Sophie	44129W		
35	9:00	Pinkevich, Galina	44109W		
36	9:00	Staufer, Kenneth	44102W		
37	9:00	Winterich, Susan	44109W		
38	9:15	Brown, Betsy	44135W		
39	9:30	Ball, Ruth	44102W		
40	9:30	Lanza, Santa	44102W		

Table 1 *(cont.)*

No.	Appointment Time[a]	Patient Name	Pickup Zip Code[b]	Arrival Time[c]	Departure Time[d]
41	9:30	Mayernik, Elaine	44113W		
42	9:45	Toyal, Todd	44107W		
43	10:00	Heffner, Betty	44135W		
44	10:00	Jarrell, Barbara	44107W		
45	10:00	Piatak, Robert	44134W		
46	10:00	Swaysland, Louise	44102W		
47	11:00	Baer, Barbara	44135W		
48	11:00	Wills, Elizabeth	44107W		
49	1:00	Fauber, Ann	44107W		
50	1:00	Mullins, Cheryl	44113W		
51	1:00	Pack, Mary	44144W		
52	1:15	Westerfield, Joann	44102W		2:15 P.M.
53	1:30	Lisiewski, Stella	44111W		2:15 P.M.
54	2:00	McPherson, Gary	44107W		
55	2:30	Mykytuk, Theresa	44102W		
56	3:00	Gutschmidt, Glenda	44102W		

[a]Time to arrive at MMC for medical appointment
[b]E and W refer to east and west pickup zones
[c]Actual arrival time at MMC
[d]Departure time from MMC for return trip

Figure 3 Appointment and Return Time Distributions

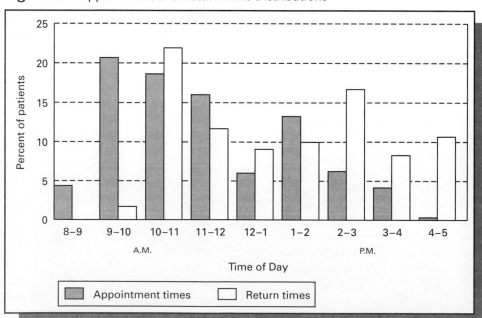

Table 2 Number of Patients Using MMC Transport Services by Zip Code

Zip Code	Number of Patients
44101	1
44102	154
44103	57
44104	73
44105	141
44106	70
44107	77
44108	42
44109	175
44110	56
44111	52
44112	1
44113	69
44114	7
44115	7
44120	51
44121	6
44126	19
44127	7
44128	29
44129	12
44130	4
44134	28
44135	115
44139	1
44142	1
44144	15
Total	1270

DRIVER AND VEHICLE COSTS

The fleet of vehicles at MMC dedicated to patient transportation currently consists of two large vans capable of handling up to 15 passengers and one small van that can handle six passengers. The large van has a purchase price of $23,000 and the smaller has a price of $19,000. Vans have a useful life of about four years and accumulate approximately 30,000 miles per year. Repair costs average $1,000 per year based on 30,000 miles driven per year, and there is no significant salvage value at the end of their useful lives. The MMC board of directors expects at least an eight percent annual rate of return on these vehicles, although the logistics manager feels that an 18 to 20 percent return is more realistic.

Drivers used for patient transportation are drawn from the pool of seven available drivers. Wages for a driver are $23,500 per year including benefits.

Transportation Services operates on all days except weekends and holidays. This represents about 20 days per month, or 240 days per year. It has been estimated that Transportation Services incurs a cost of $8 per patient trip, or $16 for a round-trip. By contrast, subcontracting the transportation service to outside providers is an alternate way of providing the patient service. Taxis have been used at an average cost of about $11 per transport. Historically, a taxi bill of approximately $10,000 per month was incurred. More recently, an ambulance service company has won a contract with MMC to transport patients for a low incremental cost of $4.33 per one-way transport. Because the service is provided as an add-on to the contract for ambulance service, a limit of 500 round-trips per month applies. If all transportation were to be subcontracted to the ambulance service, it is expected that the rate would likely increase to be in line with the taxi rate.

From surveys of the transport operation, it was found that the average loading time at each stop was six minutes. Driving speed was found to be 25 miles per hour on the east side of the city and 30 miles per hour on the west side. In city driving, both large and small vans average about 13 miles per gallon of fuel. Fuel cost averages $1 per gallon.

CUSTOMER SERVICE

Providing the patients with a high level of transport service is a goal of MMC. To look favorably toward MMC for their medical services, patients want prompt, courteous transportation. They prefer pickup close to their appointment times and a prompt return trip after their appointment. Physicians complain when patients are not available for their scheduled appointment times because of late arrivals. MMC management is cognizant that the revenue generated from the patients that choose MMC because of the transport service is quite high. For these reasons, customer service should be a top priority. ∎

QUESTIONS

1. Which vans from the current fleet should be used? To what extent should subcontracting be used?
2. How many subcontracted trips should MMC negotiate and at what price?

3. MMC is considering using only six-passenger vans. Would this be a good decision?

Orion Foods, Inc.

Anita Bailey is the newly appointed traffic manager for Orion Foods, a packer of a wide variety of fruits and vegetables sold throughout the United States. The first project given her by her boss, the director of operations, is to "clean up the distribution mess in the West." Compared with product distribution in other parts of the United States, the cost to distribute the product in the West Coast area is considered excessively high. Surely costs can be reduced, she thought.

CURRENT DISTRIBUTION

Orion packs throughout the United States its line of fruits and vegetables and even imports some of its product line from regions such as South America and Canada. In the western United States, as shown in Figure 1, Orion has established regional distribution centers at Fresno, California and Burns, Oregon. From these master warehouses, field, or local, warehouses are supplied that, in turn, ship to their immediate retail areas. There are seven of these field warehouses located at (1) Los Angeles,

California; (2) Phoenix, Arizona; (3) Salt Lake City, Utah; (4) San Francisco, California; (5) Portland, Oregon; (6) Butte, Montana; and (7) Seattle, Washington. Currently, the Burns regional distribution center serves Portland, Seattle, and Butte field warehouses. The Fresno distribution center supplies the remaining field warehouses. The capacities for the regional distribution centers are 50,000 cwt.[1] of inventory for Fresno and 15,000 cwt. of inventory for Burns. Each has a turnover ratio[2] of eight. The field warehouses have average annual throughput volumes as given in Table 1. Additional location data are given in Appendix A.

Orion contracts with trucking companies to move its products between regional and field warehouses. Its contract reads that it will pay its carriers $1.30 per mile for truckload quantities that average 30,000 lb, the typical shipment size. Anita understands that her predecessor had left the choice of the specific routes to travel to the individual carriers, assuming that they were in a better position to determine the best ones, even though Orion had the option of specifying

---

[1]Cwt. equals one hundred pounds.
[2]The ratio of annual warehouse throughput to average inventory.

Figure 1   Road Network for Orion's West Coast Distribution Area with Approximate Distances in Miles

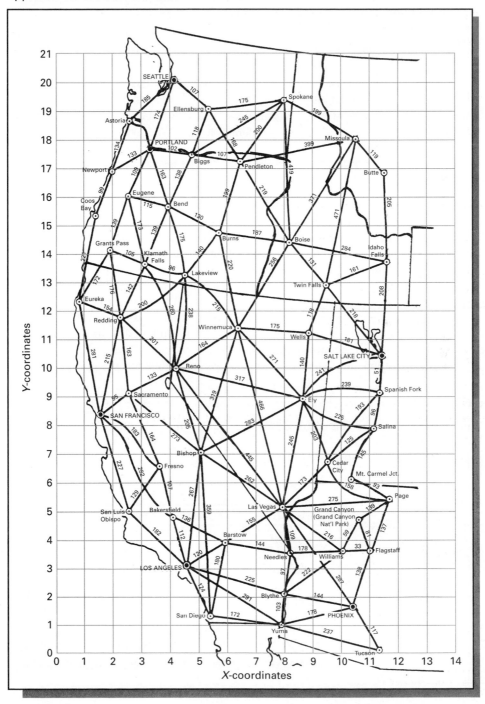

Table 1
Current-Year
Average Throughput
Volumes for the
Field Warehouses
with Transportation
Costs

FIELD WAREHOUSE	SERVED FROM	ANNUAL THROUGHPUT VOLUME, CWT.	ANNUAL TRANSPORTATION COSTS, $
Los Angeles, CA	Fresno, CA	110,000	104,485
Phoenix, AZ	Fresno, CA	60,000	163,280
Salt Lake City, UT	Fresno, CA	35,000	131,871
San Francisco, CA	Fresno, CA	84,000	66,612
Portland, OR	Burns, OR	43,000	54,470
Butte, MT	Burns, OR	5,000	15,846
Seattle, WA	Burns, OR	56,000	115,710
Totals		393,000	652,274

the roads to use. She does not know the routes that were currently being used by the carriers.

The Burns regional warehouse is currently operating near its capacity limit. If it were to be expanded, additional space in minimal increments of 10,000 cwt. of inventory could be acquired for $300,000 per increment.

Anita had seen the growth projections for the region and was surprised at the expected increases. The marketing department had developed sales projections for five years from now, as shown in Table 2. She had also heard that top management has been considering the possibility of consolidating the Fresno and Burns warehouses into a single warehouse located at Reno, NV. Although this would result in a net one-time cost of $2,000,000,[3] total inventory could be reduced as much as 40 percent through this consolidation. Inventory-carrying costs are estimated to be 35 percent per year before taxes, and the standard cost for 100 lb of average product mix is $60. ■

QUESTIONS

1. Can Anita improve upon the current distribution operations?
2. Is there any benefit to expanding the warehouse at Burns, OR?
3. Is there any merit to consolidating the regional warehousing operation at Reno, NV?

Table 2
Five-Year Projections
of Warehouse
Throughput

FIELD WAREHOUSE	ANNUAL THROUGHPUT VOLUME, CWT.
Los Angeles, CA	132,000
Phoenix, AZ	84,000
Salt Lake City, UT	56,000
San Francisco, CA	105,000
Portland, OR	57,000
Butte, MT	15,000
Seattle, WA	79,000
Total	528,000

---

[3]The cost to construct and equip the Reno warehouse, and to sell off Fresno and Burns warehouses.

Node Identification Data

Seq No.	Node no.	Node name	X-Coordinates	Y-Coordinates
1	1	Seattle WA	4.00	20.10
2	2	Ellenberg WA	5.40	19.00
3	3	Spokane WA	8.00	19.40
4	4	Astoria OR	2.60	18.70
5	5	Portland OR	3.30	17.70
6	6	Biggs OR	4.80	17.40
7	7	Pendleton OR	6.50	17.20
8	8	Missoula MT	10.50	18.00
9	9	Newport OR	2.00	16.90
10	10	Butte MT	11.60	16.80
11	11	Eugene OR	2.50	16.00
12	12	Bend OR	3.90	15.70
13	13	Coos Bay OR	1.40	15.30
14	14	Burns OR	5.70	14.70
15	15	Boise ID	8.20	14.30
16	16	Idaho Falls ID	11.70	13.70
17	17	Grants Pass OR	1.90	14.10
18	18	Klamath Fls OR	3.10	13.60
19	19	Lakeview OR	4.50	13.20
20	20	Twin Falls ID	9.50	12.90
21	21	Eureka CA	0.80	12.20
22	22	Redding CA	2.20	11.80
23	23	Winnemucca NV	6.40	11.30
24	24	Wells NV	8.90	11.20
25	25	S Lake City UT	11.50	10.40
26	26	Reno NV	4.20	9.90
27	27	Sacramento CA	2.50	9.10
28	28	Spanish Fork UT	11.40	9.10
29	29	Ely NV	8.70	8.90
30	30	S Francisco CA	1.60	8.30
31	31	Salina UT	11.10	7.90
32	32	Bishop CA	5.10	7.10
33	33	Cedar City UT	9.60	6.70
34	34	Fresno CA	3.70	6.60
35	35	Mt Carmel J. UT	10.30	6.10
36	36	S. L. Obispo CA	2.50	5.00
37	37	Bakersfield CA	4.10	4.80

Node Identification Data *(cont.)*

Seq No.	Node no.	Node name	X-Coordinates	Y-Coordinates
38	38	Las Vegas NV	7.90	5.10
39	39	Page AZ	11.70	5.40
40	40	Grd Canyon AZ	10.70	4.70
41	41	Barstow CA	5.90	3.90
42	42	Flagstaff AZ	11.00	3.60
43	43	Williams AZ	10.00	3.50
44	44	Needles CA	8.20	3.50
45	45	Los Angeles CA	4.50	3.10
46	46	Blythe CA	8.00	2.10
47	47	San Diego CA	5.30	1.30
48	48	Yuma CA	7.80	1.00
49	49	Phoenix AZ	10.40	1.60
50	50	Tucson AZ	11.30	0.10

R&T Wholesalers

R&T Wholesalers distributes general merchandise to retailers throughout India. There are numerous warehouses located all over the country that serve as stocking points and depots for delivery vehicles that serve retailers in the towns surrounding the warehouses. The warehouse serving the Prakasam, Guntur, Krishna, West Godavari, and East Godavari districts is located at Vijayawada. Trucks make deliveries every day of the week except Saturday and Sunday (24 days per month) and each town is visited either two or four times per month, that is, either weekly or biweekly. There is flexibility for a town visited twice a month to be on a cycle for either weeks 1 and 3 or 2 and 4. The day of the week for delivery to a town is set by the dispatcher. Similarly, a town can be assigned for delivery to any of the five days of the week. The logistics manager wishes to create efficient routes for the company's truck fleet that will minimize both the number of trucks needed throughout the month's planning cycle and the total distance traveled by the fleet. He feels that this will minimize the cost of drivers and truck operation.

Delivery volume is represented in terms of average sales activity per town visit, which aggregates the stops at a number of retailers within the town. From a map of the warehouse region (see Figure 1), linear coordinates are constructed for the warehouse and each town. The coordinates have a map scaling factor of 1 coordinate unit = 12.2 kilometers. The circuity factor that converts coordinate-computed distances to road distances is 1.12. Location data as well as stop unloading times are summarized in Table 1. Unloading times refer to the hours required to unload the merchandise from the truck to the retailer's dock. Since there may be more than one retailer in a town, the unloading times represent the total unloading time for *all* retailers in the town.

There are currently four T407 trucks for deliverys, each with a capacity of Rs 500,000 and four T310 trucks at Rs 350,000. Capacity is expressed in terms of sales in rupees (Rs). Trucks operate over the region at an average speed of 40 km/hr throughout the day on each day of the week. The T407 has an operating cost of Rs 13,500 per month with running cost of Rs 5

Figure 1   Delivery Territory of the Vijayawada Warehouse (map not to scale)

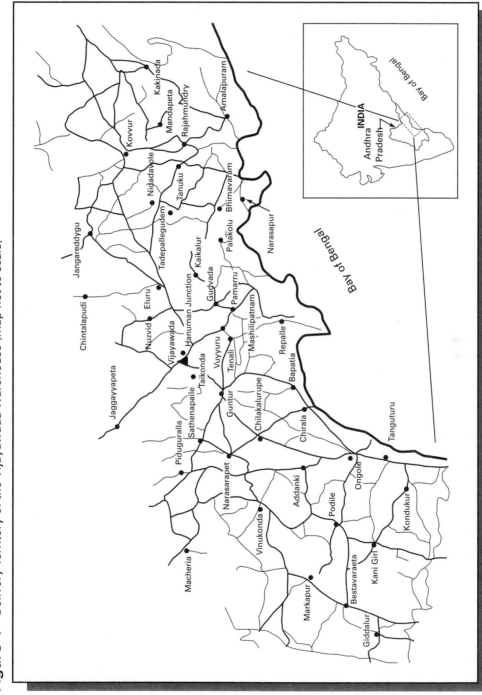

Table 1 Sales Activity and Point Coordinates for the Vijayawada Warehouse Region

No.	Town	Coordinates X	Coordinates Y	Sales per Visit, Rupees	Visits per Month	Hours per Town Visit
0	Vijayawada	19.4	15.1	Warehouse	—	—
1	Tanguturu	14.5	5.3	66,000	2	1.0
2	Podili	10.7	7.0	24,000	2	0.5
3	Ongole	14.5	6.2	305,000	4	2.5
4	Markapur	7.7	8.2	60,000	2	0.5
5	Kani Giri	9.6	5.1	24,000	2	2.5
6	Kondukur	13.2	3.5	90,000	2	1.0
7	Giddalur	3.8	5.0	25,000	2	1.0
8	Chirala	17.2	9.0	98,000	4	2.0
9	Bestavaipetta	6.3	6.3	25,000	2	0.5
10	Addanki	13.9	8.8	60,000	2	0.5
11	Chilakalurupet	15.4	11.4	92,000	2	1.0
12	Narasaraopet	14.5	12.5	100,000	4	1.0
13	Vinukonda	11.8	11.0	65,000	2	1.0
14	Tadikonda	18.1	14.3	60,000	2	1.0
15	Sattenapalle	15.2	14.0	45,000	2	1.0
16	Repalie	21.3	10.6	50,000	2	1.0
17	Guntur	18.0	13.0	450,000	4	3.0
18	Vuyyuru	21.3	13.6	39,000	4	1.0
19	Tenali	19.7	12.5	140,000	4	1.0
20	Pamarru	22.3	13.2	62,000	2	1.0
21	Nuzvid	21.3	17.5	37,000	2	0.5
22	Machilipatnam	23.8	12.0	108,000	4	1.0
23	Kaikalur	24.4	15.5	48,000	2	1.0
24	Jaggayyapeta	14.9	18.5	37,000	2	0.5
25	Hanuman Junction	19.5	15.2	50,000	2	1.0
26	Gudivada	22.7	14.3	180,000	2	1.0
27	Bapatia	18.2	9.7	82,000	2	1.0
28	Rajahmundry	29.5	19.6	470,000	4	3.5
29	Mandapeta	30.8	18.3	170,000	2	2.0
30	Narasapur	28.7	14.5	160,000	2	1.0
31	Amaiapuram	31.5	15.6	90,000	2	1.0
32	Kakinada	33.5	19.1	228,000	4	2.0
33	Kovvur	29.0	19.7	45,000	2	1.0
34	Tanuku	28.8	17.4	134,000	2	1.0
35	Nidadvole	28.5	18.7	50,000	2	1.0
36	Tadepallegudem	27.2	17.9	130,000	4	1.5
37	Eluru	23.6	17.0	198,000	4	2.0
38	Palakolu	25.9	15.7	180,000	4	1.0
39	Bhimavaram	27.3	15.3	148,000	4	1.5

40	Jangareddygudem	25.2	20.6	68,000	2	0.5
41	Chintalapudi	22.5	20.0	68,000	2	0.5
42	Macheria	9.1	14.7	150,000	2	2.0
43	Piduguralia	13.2	14.8	30,000	2	1.0

per kilometer and the T310 has an operating cost of Rs 7,000 with a running cost of Rs 3 per kilometer. Each truck has a crew of two, a driver, and a helper. The driver is paid Rs 2,200 per month and the helper is paid Rs 1,400 per month. Crews are hired in full-month increments. While on the road, each crew member is given an allowance of Rs 60 per day for meals and other expenses. Planned breaks for the crew members are at approximately 6 A.M., 12 noon, and 6 P.M. Breakfast and lunchtime breaks are 30 minutes each, while the dinner break is 60 minutes. Breaks do not necessarily have to be taken precisely at these times. Informal breaks can be taken throughout the day and are figured into driving speed and unloading times. Crew members are allowed at least an eight-hour overnight break before starting a route on the following day. No overtime is paid, and the company policy is to return the crews to the warehouse each day rather than plan for overnight layovers.

The normal operation is for trucks to make deliveries within towns from 9:00 A.M. until 6:00 P.M. Trucks return to the depot from a route, get loaded during the night, and leave the next morning on another route. The earliest starting time for trucks is 12 A.M. Monday morning and each day thereafter through Friday. Early start times may be necessary to arrive at distant towns and meet the restrictions of time windows, time on route, and so on. Trucks returning to the depot within the same day due to the shortness of the route may be sent on another route with the same crew after allowing two hours for reloading. Duplicate allowances are not paid when the multiple routes are completed using the same crews.

The company can contract the deliveries to a third-party carrier at an estimated rate of Rs 15 per kilometer one-way to the town. This rate applies as if single deliveries are made regardless of the shipment size or the number of stops actually handled in a particular delivery. A mixture of contract and private deliveries is possible.

Actual driving distances between all towns are given in Table 2. The distance is assumed the same regardless of direction traveled on the roads. ∎

QUESTIONS

Design the route for a typical month of operation showing
1. the number of trucks needed and their type
2. the truck routes with stop sequence
3. the days of a four-week month that a town is to be visited
4. the schedule of truck usage throughout the month
5. the schedule for using the crews.
   Minimizing total monthly costs for the trucks, crews, and allowances is the objective.

Table 2 Approximate Driving Distances Between Towns in Kilometers (see Table 1 for town numbers)

	0	1	2	3	4	5	6	7	8	9	10	11	12	13	14	15	16	17	18	19	20	21	22
0	0																						
1	150	0																					
2	162	76	0																				
3	139	29	47	0																			
4	186	138	45	92	0																		
5	191	64	29	76	64	0																	
6	180	14	79	43	124	50	0																
7	254	151	97	146	61	82	91	0															
8	89	79	97	50	142	126	93	194	0														
9	216	118	60	107	24	54	104	33	157	0													
10	114	65	51	36	96	80	79	144	86	111	0												
11	74	105	91	69	136	120	119	184	39	151	40	0											
12	76	126	112	90	157	141	140	205	60	172	61	21	0										
13	118	102	62	73	72	86	116	159	102	222	37	63	42	0									
14	21	155	141	119	186	170	169	234	89	201	90	50	49	91	0								
15	59	145	131	109	176	160	159	224	79	191	80	40	19	61	49	0							
16	67	137	155	108	127	184	151	254	58	215	134	85	84	126	65	84	0						
17	35	140	126	104	171	155	154	219	74	186	75	35	34	76	15	34	50	0					
18	33	202	188	166	233	217	216	281	78	248	137	97	96	138	52	96	97	62	0				
19	36	140	150	111	195	179	154	243	61	210	99	59	58	102	39	58	35	24	66	0			
20	47	217	203	181	248	232	231	296	93	263	152	112	111	153	67	111	112	77	15	81	0		
21	42	311	297	275	342	326	325	390	187	357	246	206	205	247	161	205	206	102	115	106	55	0	
22	74	241	227	205	272	256	255	320	117	287	176	136	135	177	91	135	136	101	39	105	24	74	0
23	68	240	226	204	271	255	254	319	116	286	175	135	134	176	90	134	135	100	63	104	48	72	66
24	77	205	191	169	236	220	219	284	139	251	140	100	79	121	109	60	144	94	103	109	118	94	142
25	2	172	158	136	203	187	186	251	48	218	107	67	66	108	22	66	67	32	30	36	45	70	69
26	47	208	194	172	239	223	222	287	84	254	143	103	102	144	58	102	103	68	22	72	15	45	34
27	76	92	110	63	155	139	106	209	13	170	99	52	73	115	63	93	45	48	62	48	125	150	149
28	151	297	283	261	328	312	311	376	173	343	232	192	191	233	147	191	192	157	135	161	140	112	197
29	162	342	328	306	373	357	356	421	218	388	277	237	236	278	192	236	237	202	175	206	160	142	148
30	127	303	289	267	334	318	317	382	179	349	238	198	197	239	153	197	198	163	126	167	111	135	129
31	165	328	314	292	359	343	342	407	204	374	263	223	222	264	178	222	223	188	151	192	136	160	154
32	200	388	374	352	419	403	402	467	264	434	323	283	282	324	238	282	283	248	221	252	206	188	194
33	146	307	293	271	338	322	321	386	183	353	242	202	201	243	157	201	202	167	130	171	135	107	148
34	132	302	288	266	333	317	316	381	178	348	237	197	196	238	152	196	197	162	135	166	120	102	108
35	134	324	310	288	355	339	338	403	200	370	259	219	218	260	174	218	219	184	157	188	142	124	130
36	113	250	236	214	281	265	264	329	126	296	185	145	144	186	100	144	145	110	73	114	78	50	89
37	63	235	221	199	266	250	249	314	111	281	170	130	129	171	85	129	130	95	58	99	63	35	74
38	85	258	244	222	289	273	272	337	134	304	193	153	152	194	108	152	153	118	81	122	66	90	84
39	108	276	262	240	307	291	290	355	152	322	211	171	170	212	126	170	171	136	99	140	84	108	102
40	109	290	276	254	321	305	304	369	166	336	225	185	184	226	140	184	185	150	113	154	118	90	129
41	80	282	268	246	313	297	296	361	158	328	217	177	176	218	132	176	177	142	105	146	110	82	121
42	141	188	140	159	95	159	219	156	130	119	123	91	70	76	119	82	154	104	166	128	181	206	205
43	85	143	129	114	137	158	157	220	80	187	78	71	50	65	80	31	115	65	127	89	142	167	166

	23	24	25	26	27	28	29	30	31	32	33	34	35	36	37	38	39	40	41	42	43
0																					
1																					
2																					
3																					
4																					
5																					
6																					
7																					
8																					
9																					
10																					
11																					
12																					
13																					
14																					
15																					
16																					
17																					
18																					
19																					
20																					
21																					
22																					
23	0																				
24	166	0																			
25	68	73	0																		
26	32	109	36	0																	
27	148	153	80	116	0																
28	131	198	125	117	205	0															
29	112	243	170	144	250	24	0														
30	63	229	131	95	211	80	60	0													
31	88	254	156	120	236	69	50	47	0												
32	158	289	216	190	296	56	46	102	55	0											
33	112	208	135	112	215	7	29	80	76	75	0										
34	72	203	130	104	210	40	40	40	52	86	40	0									
35	94	199	126	103	206	22	44	62	72	60	15	22	0								
36	85	151	78	55	158	62	107	63	119	36	57	50	48	0							
37	70	136	63	40	143	77	122	78	134	153	72	67	63	15	0						
38	18	184	86	50	166	113	94	45	70	90	90	54	76	50	69	0					
39	36	202	104	68	184	95	76	27	52	72	72	36	58	36	51	18	0				
40	125	191	118	95	198	65	115	115	127	30	50	75	53	42	55	91	73	0			
41	117	183	110	87	190	69	157	125	158	24	62	117	62	55	47	124	106	38	0		
42	204	142	136	172	152	261	306	267	292	352	271	266	262	214	199	222	240	254	246	0	
43	165	91	97	133	113	222	267	192	253	313	232	227	223	175	160	183	201	215	207	63	0

285

Chapter 8

Forecasting Supply Chain Requirements

> *Seven years of plenty will come through the land . . . but there will follow seven years of famine, and then all the plenty will be forgotten . . .*

—GENESIS 41:28–30

*P*lanning and controlling logistics/supply chain activities require accurate estimates of the product and service volumes to be handled by the supply chain. These estimates are typically in the form of

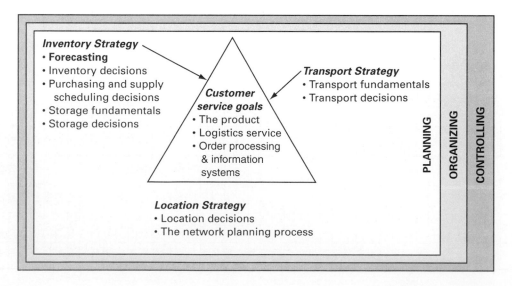

Inventory Strategy
- **Forecasting**
- Inventory decisions
- Purchasing and supply scheduling decisions
- Storage fundamentals
- Storage decisions

Customer service goals
- The product
- Logistics service
- Order processing & information systems

Transport Strategy
- Transport fundamentals
- Transport decisions

Location Strategy
- Location decisions
- The network planning process

PLANNING   ORGANIZING   CONTROLLING

forecasts and predictions. However, it is not usually the responsibility of the logistician alone to produce the general forecasts for the firm. More than likely this task will be assigned to marketing, economic planning, or a specially designated group. Under certain circumstances, especially short-term planning such as inventory control, order sizing, or transport scheduling, the logistician often finds it necessary to take it upon him or herself to produce this type of information. Therefore, this chapter is dedicated to an overview of those forecasting techniques most likely to be directly used for logistics planning and control.

The discussion is directed mainly at demand forecasting. The need for demand projections is a general need throughout the planning and control process. However, certain types of planning problems such as inventory control, economical purchasing, and cost control, forecasting lead times, prices, and costs may be needed as well. The forecasting techniques discussed in this chapter are equally applicable to these.

When the uncertainty of the predictive variable is so high that standard forecasting techniques and their use in supply chain planning lead to unsatisfactory results, other planning approaches are needed. Collaborative forecasting is a contemporary approach to demand prediction. These alternatives to traditional forecasting are discussed as well.

NATURE OF FORECASTING

Forecasting demand levels is vital to the firm as a whole, as it provides the basic inputs for the planning and control of all functional areas, including logistics, marketing, production, and finance. Demand levels and their timing greatly affect capacity levels, financial needs, and general structure of the business. Each functional area has its special forecasting problems. Logistics forecasting concerns the spatial as well as temporal nature of demand, the extent of its variability, and its degree of randomness.

Spatial versus Temporal Demand

Time, or temporal, concerns about demand levels are common in forecasting. Demand variation with time is a result of growth or decline in sales rates, seasonality in the demand pattern, and general fluctuations caused by a multitude of factors. Most short-term forecasting methods deal with this type of temporal variation, often referred to as a time series.

Logistics has both space and time dimensions. That is, the logistician must know *where* demand volume will take place as well as *when* it will take place. Spatial location of demand is needed to plan warehouse locations, balance inventory levels across the logistics network, and geographically allocate transportation resources. Forecasting techniques should be selected to reflect geographic differences that may affect demand patterns. Also, the techniques may differ depending on whether all demand is forecasted and then disaggregated by geographic location (top-down forecasting) or whether each geographic location is forecasted separately and aggregated if necessary (bottom-up forecasting).

Lumpy versus Regular Demand

Logisticians collect products into groups to differentiate service levels among them or simply to manage them differently. These groups and the individual items within them form various demand patterns over time. When demand is "regular," it will typically be represented by one of the general patterns shown in Figure 8–1. That is, demand patterns can usually be decomposed into trend, seasonal, and random components. As long as random variations are a small portion of the remaining variation in the time series, good forecasting success is usually obtained from popular forecasting procedures.

When demand for items is intermittent, because of low volume overall and a high degree of uncertainty as to when and at what level demand will occur, the time series is said to be lumpy, or irregular, as in Figure 8–2. This pattern is often found in products that are phasing in or out of the product line, demanded by relatively few customers, divided among many stocking locations so that demand at each location is low, or derived from the demand for other items. Such demand patterns are particularly difficult to forecast using the more popular techniques. However, because such items may represent as much as 50 percent of the products a firm handles, they represent a special demand-forecasting problem for the logistician.

Derived versus Independent Demand

The nature of demand can greatly differ, depending on the operation of the firm for which the logistician must plan. In one case, demand is generated from many customers, most of which individually purchase only a small fraction of the total volume distributed by the firm. Demand is said to be independent. In another, demand is derived from the requirements specified in a production schedule, and demand is said to be dependent. For example, the number of new tires to order from a supplier is a multiple of the number of new cars an automaker will build. This fundamental difference gives rise to alternate ways in which requirements are forecasted.

When demand is independent, statistical forecasting procedures work well. Most of the short-term forecasting models are based on conditions of independence and randomness in demand. In contrast, derived demand patterns are highly biased and not random. Understanding these biases replaces the need for forecasting, since demand is known for sure.

Requirements forecasting through the derived demand procedure results in perfect forecasts to the extent that end-product demand is known for sure. This type of procedure is a good example of how forecasting is improved by recognizing systematic biases, regularities, and patterns that occur in demand over time. When the causes for demand variation are unknown and result from many factors,

Figure 8-1 Some Typical "Regular" Demand Patterns

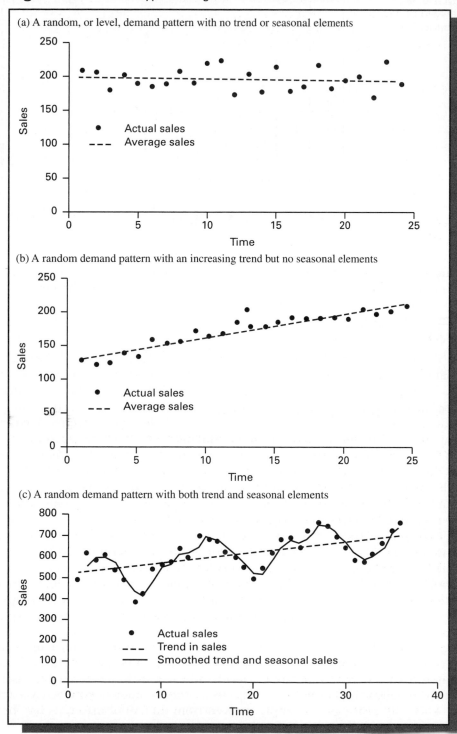

(a) A random, or level, demand pattern with no trend or seasonal elements

• Actual sales
- - - Average sales

(b) A random demand pattern with an increasing trend but no seasonal elements

• Actual sales
- - - Average sales

(c) A random demand pattern with both trend and seasonal elements

• Actual sales
- - - Trend in sales
—— Smoothed trend and seasonal sales

Figure 8-2
Example of a Lumpy
Demand Pattern

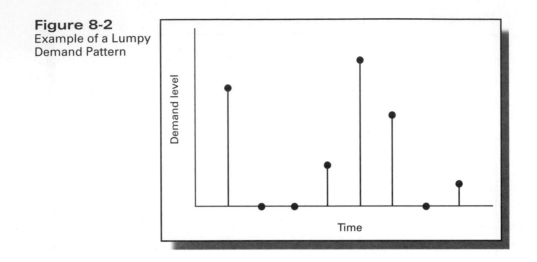

randomness exists. Statistically based forecasting procedures deal effectively with this latter case, and they will be the focus of the remainder of this chapter.

Example

The Power Equipment Division of a major manufacturer produced a line of fractional horsepower electric motors for industrial customers who, in turn, used them in finished products such as floor cleaners and polishers. Although not a particularly complex product, each motor could contain from 50 to 100 individual parts. Production schedules were developed from firm orders that were received by the company but were to be delivered at a future date, and from a forecast of the more standardized, "off-the-shelf" motors. Based on these requirements, a build schedule was developed for three months in advance of production that showed when a particular motor model would be produced and in what quantity. It was then the job of the materials manager to ensure that all subcomponents and materials were available for production when needed.

Two general approaches were used to determine the requirements for supply planning. For those materials used in most of the motors produced (copper wire, sheet steel, and paint), a forecast was made of the general usage rate. Then, purchases were made to support an inventory. Components that were of high value and custom-designed, the rotor shaft and bearings, were purchased according to the requirements in the production schedule. The requirements for purchasing these items were derived from the build schedule by "exploding" the bill of materials. For example, suppose that three motor models are to be built in a particular month. There are 200, 300, and 400 motors for each model to be produced. Each model requires the same rotor shaft, but models 1 and 2 require two ball bearings each and model 3 requires only one ball bearing. Hence, the requirements for 900 rotor shafts and 1,400 ball bearings are simply derived from the bill of materials list for each motor model and then combined by component type to form the total requirements for each part.

Note that the company is using a combination of statistical forecasting procedures and derived demand procedures to plan supply material flows. Statistical forecasting was effectively used on 20 percent of the raw materials. Planning to requirements was reserved for the remaining 10 percent that were high valued, critical, or custom to the end product.

FORECASTING METHODS

A number of standardized forecasting methods are available. These have been categorized into the three groups: qualitative, historical projection, and causal. Each group differs in terms of the relative accuracy in forecasting over the long run versus the short run, the level of quantitative sophistication used, and the logic base (historical data, expert opinion, or surveys) from which the forecast is derived. A summary and brief description of some popular forecasting techniques, including these popular methods, are given in Table 8-1.

Qualitative Methods

Qualitative methods are those that use judgment, intuition, surveys, or comparative techniques to produce quantitative estimates about the future. The information relating to the factors affecting the forecast are typically nonquantitative, soft, and subjective. Historical data may not be available or may be of little relevance to the forecast at hand. The nonscientific nature of the methods makes them difficult to standardize and validate for accuracy. However, these methods may be all that is available when trying to predict the success of new products, government policy changes, or the impact of new technology. They are likely to be methods of choice for medium- to long-range forecasting.

Historical Projection Methods

When a reasonable amount of historical data is available and the trend and seasonal variations in the time series are stable and well defined, projecting these data into the future can be an effective way of forecasting for the short term. The basic premise is that the future time pattern will be a replication of the past, at least in large part. The quantitative nature of the time series encourages the use of mathematical and statistical models as the primary forecasting tools. The accuracy that can be achieved for forecasted periods of less than six months is usually quite good. These models work well simply because of the inherent stability of the time series in the short run.

Time series models of the types noted in Table 8-1 are reactive in nature. These models track change by being updated as new data become available, a feature that allows them to adapt to changes in trend and seasonal patterns. However, if the change is rapid, the models do not signal the change until after it has occurred.

Table 8-1 Summary of Selected Forecasting Techniques[a]

Method	Description	Forecast Time Horizon[x]
Delphi[b]	A panel of experts is interrogated by a sequence of questionnaires in which the responses to one questionnaire are used to produce the next questionnaire. Any set of information available to some experts and not others is thus passed on to the others, enabling all experts to have access to all the information for forecasting. This technique eliminates the bandwagon effect of majority opinion.	Medium-Long
Market research[c]	The systematic, formal, and conscious procedure for evolving and testing hypotheses about real markets.	Medium-Long
Panel consensus	This technique is based on the assumption that several experts can arrive at a better forecast than just one person. There is no secrecy, and communication is encouraged. The forecasts are sometimes influenced by social factors and they may not reflect a true consensus. Solicitations of executive opinions fall into this class.	Medium-Long
Sales force estimates	Opinions of the sales force may be solicited since salespersons are close to customers and are in a good position to estimate their needs.	Short-Medium
Visionary forecast	A prophecy using personal insights, judgments, and, when possible, facts about different future scenarios. It is characterized by subjective guesswork and imagination; in general, the methods used are nonscientific.	Medium-Long
Historical analogy[d]	This is a comparative analysis of the introduction and growth of similar new products that bases the forecast on similarity patterns.	Medium-Long
Moving average[e]	Each point of a moving average of a time series is the arithmetic or weighted average of a number of consecutive points of the series, where the number of data points is chosen so that the effects of seasonality or irregularity are eliminated.	Short
Exponential smoothing[f]	This technique is similar to the moving average, except points that are more recent are given more weight. Descriptively, the new forecast is equal to the old one plus some portion of the past forecasting error. Double and triple exponential smoothing are complex versions of the basic model that account for trend and seasonal variation in the time series.	Short
Box-Jenkins[g]	A complex, computer-based iterative procedure that produces an autoregressive, integrated moving average model, adjusts for seasonal and trend factors, estimates appropriate weighting parameters, tests the model, and repeats the cycle as appropriate.	Short-Medium
Time series decomposition[h]	A method for decomposing a time series into seasonal, trend, and regular components. It is quite good at identifying turning points and an excellent forecasting tool for the medium-range time period, that is, three to 12 months.	Short-Medium

Method	Description	Horizon
Trend projections[i]	This technique fits a trend line using a mathematical equation and then projects it into the future by means of the equation. There are several variations: slope-characteristic method, polynomials, logarithms, and so on.	Short-Medium
Focus forecasting[j]	Tests a number of simple decision rules to see which is most accurate over a coming three-month period. Computer simulation is used to test the various strategies on past data.	Medium
Spectral analysis[k]	The method attempts to break down a time series into its fundamental components, called spectra. These components are represented by geometric sine-cosine curves. Reassembling these components produces a mathematical expression that can be used for forecasting.	Short-Medium
Regression model[l]	Relates demand to other variables that "cause" or explain its level. Variables are selected on the grounds of statistical significance. The general availability of powerful regression computer programs makes this a popular technique.	Short-Medium
Econometric model[m]	An econometric model is a system of interdependent regression equations that describes some sector of economic sales activity. The regression equation parameters are usually estimated simultaneously. As a rule, these models are relatively expensive to develop, however, due to the system of equations inherent in such models, they will better express the causalities involved than an ordinary regression equation and hence will predict turning points more accurately.	Short-Medium
Intention-to-buy and anticipation surveys[n]	These surveys of the public (a) determine intentions to buy certain products or (b) derive an index that measures the general feeling about the present and the future, and estimates how this feeling will affect buying habits. These approaches to forecasting are more useful for tracking and warning than forecasting. The basic problem in using them is that a turning point may be signaled incorrectly.	Medium
Input-output model[o]	A method of analysis concerned with the interindustry or interdepartmental flow of goods or services in the economy and its markets. It shows what flows of inputs must occur to obtain certain outputs. Considerable effort must be expended to use these models properly, and additional detail, not normally available, must be obtained if they are to be applied to specific businesses.	Medium
Economic input-output model[p]	Econometric models and input-output models are sometimes combined for forecasting. The input-output model is used to provide long-term trends for the econometric model. It also stabilizes the econometric model.	Medium
Leading indicators[q]	Forecasts generated from one or more preceding variables that are systematically related to the variable to be predicted.	Short-Medium
Life cycle analysis[r]	This is an analysis and forecasting of new-product growth based on S curves. The phases of the product acceptance by such various groups as innovators, early adopters, early majority, late majority, and laggards are central to the analysis.	Medium-Long

293

Table 8-1 *(cont.)*

METHOD	DESCRIPTION	FORECAST TIME HORIZON[x]
Adaptive filtering	A derivative of a weighted combination of actual and estimated outcomes, systematically altered to reflect data pattern changes.	Short-Medium
Dynamic simulation[s]	The method uses the computer to simulate over time the effect of end-product sales on requirements at various points in the distribution and supply channel. Requirements are indicated by inventory policies, production schedules, and purchasing policies.	Medium-Long
Accurate response[t]	A simultaneous process of improving forecasts while redesigning the planning processes to minimize the impact of inaccurate forecasts. Accurate response entails figuring out what forecasters can and cannot predict well, and then making the supply chain fast and flexible so that managers can postpone decisions about their most unpredictable items until they have some market signals, such as early sales results, to help correctly match supply with demand.	
Neural networks[u]	Mathematical models for forecasting that are inspired by the functioning of biological neurons. They are characterized by their ability to learn as new data arrive. Forecasting accuracy appears to be better than other time series methods when the time series is discontinuous.	Short
Collaborative forecasting[v]	Supply channel members jointly maintain and update a single forecasting process to produce a forecast that is more accurate than can be produced individually. Collaborative forecasting is likely to offer improved results over individual member-produced forecasts when each member brings something unique to the forecasting process.	Short
Rule-based forecasting[w]	The method uses an expert systems approach to forecasting. Through experience, if-then rules are developed that guide the handling of data issues and forecast model preparation. Forecasting expertise as expressed by the rule base and domain knowledge are used to produce forecasts according to features of the data.	Short-Long

| Random walk | The method uses the most recent observation as the forecast. It may be the method of choice when there is a high uncertainty and no trend in the time series. | Short |

[a] Updated and expanded from the original articles by John C. Chambers, Satinder K. Mulick, and Donald D. Smith. Reprinted by permission of the Harvard Business Review (An exhibit from "How to Choose the Right Forecasting Technique," by J. C. Chambers, S. K. Mulick, and D. D. Smith (July/August 1971). Copyright © 1971 by the President and Fellows of Harvard College; all rights reserved); and David M. Georgoff and Robert G. Murdick, "Manager's Guide to Forecasting," *Harvard Business Review*, Vol. 64 (January–February 1986), pp. 110–120.

[b] Harper Q. North and Donald L. Pyke, "Probes of the Technological Future," *Harvard Business Review* (May/June 1969), p. 68.

[c] Paul E. Green, Donald S. Tull, and Gerald Albaum, *Research for Marketing Decisions*, 5th ed. (Upper Saddle River, NJ: Prentice Hall, 1988).

[d] Milton Spencer, Colin Clark, and Peter Hoguet, *Business and Economic Forecasting* (Homewood, IL: Irwin, 1961).

[e] Richard B. Chase and Nicholas J. Aquilano, *Production and Operations Management* (Homewood, IL: Irwin, 1989), pp. 223–226.

[f] R. G. Brown, *Smoothing and Prediction of Discrete Time Series* (Upper Saddle River, NJ: Prentice Hall, 1963).

[g] E. P. Box and G. M. Jenkins, *Time Series Analysis, Forecasting and Control* (San Francisco: Holden-Day, 1970).

[h] Bruce L. Bowerman and Richard T. O'Connell, *Time Series Forecasting* (Boston: Duxbury Press, 1987), Sec. 5.6.

[i] John Neter, William Wasserman, and G. A. Whitmore, *Applied Statistics* (Boston: Allyn and Bacon, 1988), pp. 820–846.

[j] Bernard T. Smith and Oliver W. Wight, *Focus Forecasting: Computer Techniques for Inventory Control* (Boston: CBI Publishing, 1978).

[k] Hung Chan and Jack Hayya, "Spectral Analysis in Business Forecasting," *Decision Sciences*, Vol. 7 (1976), pp. 137–151.

[l] John Neter, William Wasserman, and Michael H. Kutner, *Applied Linear Regression Models* (Homewood, IL: Richard D. Irwin, 1983).

[m] J. Johnston, *Econometric Methods* (New York: McGraw-Hill, 1963); R. C. Clelland, J. S. deCani, F. E. Brown, J. P. Bursk, and D. S. Murray, *Basic Statistics with Business Applications* (New York: John Wiley, 1966), pp. 522–559.

[n] Publications of Survey Research Center, Institute for Social Research, University of Michigan; and U. S. Bureau of the Census.

[o] W. W. Leontief, *Input-Output Economic* (New York: Oxford University Press, 1966).

[p] Michael Evans, Discussion Paper #138, Wharton School of Finance and Commerce, University of Pennsylvania.

[q] Michael Evans, *Macro-Economic Activity: Theory, Forecasting and Control* (New York: Harper & Row, 1969).

[r] Philip Kotler, *Marketing Management*, 6th ed. (Upper Saddle River, NJ: Prentice Hall, 1988), pp. 421–425.

[s] Jay W. Forrester, "Industrial Dynamics: A Major Breakthrough for Decision Makers," *Harvard Business Review* (July/August 1958), pp. 37–66.

[t] Marshall L. Fisher, Janice H. Hammond, Walter R. Obermeyer, and Ananth Raman, "Making Supply Meet Demand in an Uncertain World," *Harvard Business Review*, Vol. 72 (May–June 1994), pp. 83–89+.

[u] Tim Hill, Marcus O'Conner and William Remus, "Neural Network Models for Time Series Forecasts," *Management Science*, Vol. 42, No. 7 (July 1996), pp. 1082–1092.

[v] Yossi Aviv, "The Effect of Collaborative Forecasting on Supply Chain Performance," *Management Science*, Vol. 47, No. 10 (October 2001), pp. 1326–1343; and www.cpfr.org.

[w] Fred Collopy and J. Scott Armstrong, "Rule-Based Forecasting; Development and Validation of an Expert Systems Approach to Combining Time Series Extrapolations," *Management Science*, Vol. 38, No. 10 (1992), pp. 1394–1414.

[x] *Short term* is less than six months; *medium term* is six months to several years; and *long term* is more than several years.

Because of this, projections by these models are said to lag fundamental changes in the time series and are weak in signaling turning points before they take place. This need not be a serious limitation when forecasts are made over short time horizons unless changes are particularly dramatic.

Causal Methods

The basic premise on which causal models for forecasting are built is that the level of the forecast variable is derived from the level of other related variables. For example, if customer service is known to have a positive effect on sales, then by knowing the level of customer service provided, the level of sales can be projected. We might say that service "causes" sales. To the extent that good cause-and-effect relationships can be described, causal models can be quite good at anticipating major changes in the time series and forecasting accurately over the medium- to long-range period.

Causal models come in a variety of forms: statistical, in the case of regression and econometric models; and descriptive, as in the case of input-output, life cycle, and computer simulation models. Each model derives its validity from historical data patterns that establish the association between the predicting variables and the variable to be forecasted.

A major problem with this class of forecasting model is that truly causal variables are often difficult to find. When they are found, their association with the variable to be forecasted is often disturbingly low. Causal variables that lead the forecasted variable in time are even more difficult to find. Too often, the time to acquire data for the leading variables uses up all or a substantial portion of the one to six months that such variables are found to be leading the forecast. Models based on regression and economic techniques may experience substantial forecasting error because of these problems.

USEFUL TECHNIQUES FOR LOGISTICIANS

Generally, the logistician need not be directly concerned with the broad spectrum of available forecasting and predicting techniques. Because various segments of the organization need forecasted information, especially the sales forecast, the forecasting activity is often centralized in the marketing, planning, or economic analysis area of the firm. Forecasts of medium- or long-term periods usually are provided to the logistician. Unless there is a need to develop specific long-term forecasts, the logistician's is limited to the short-term forecasts that assist in inventory control, shipment scheduling, warehouse load planning, and the like. Based on the degree of sophistication, potential usefulness, and likelihood of data availability, only a limited number of the methods outlined in Table 8-1 need be considered in detail. This is because numerous studies have shown the "simple" models of the time series variety often predict as well as or better than more sophisticated, complex versions. Time series models can be superior to causal models. In general, complexity in forecasting models does not increase predictive accuracy.[1] Therefore, the following discusses three basic time series forecasting methodologies: exponential smoothing, classic time series decomposition, and multiple regression analysis.

Exponential Smoothing

Probably the most useful technique for short-term forecasting is exponential smoothing. It is simple, requires a minimum amount of data to be retained for continued application, has been observed to be the most accurate among competing models in its class, and is self-adapting to fundamental changes in the forecasted data. It is a type of moving average, where the past observations are not given equal weight. Rather, observations that are more recent are weighted more heavily than older ones.

Such a geometric weighting scheme can be reduced to a simple expression involving only the forecast from the most recent period and the actual demand for the current period. Thus, the demand forecast for the next period is given by

$$\text{New forecast} = \alpha(\text{actual demand}) + (1 - \alpha)(\text{previous forecast}) \qquad \textbf{(8-1)}$$

where α is a weighting factor, commonly called the exponential smoothing constant, with values between 0 and 1. Note that the effect of all of history is included in the previous forecast so that only one number needs to be retained at any time to represent demand history.

Example

Suppose that a demand level of 1,000 units was forecasted for the current month. Actual demand for the current month is 950 units. The value of the smoothing constant is = 0.3. The expected value for demand next month, according to Equation (8-1), would be

$$\text{New forecast} = 0.3(950) + 0.7(1{,}000)$$
$$= 985 \text{ units}$$

This forecast becomes the previous forecast when the procedure is repeated one month from now. And so it goes.

For convenience, we can write this "level only" model as

$$F_{t+1} = \alpha A_t + (1 - \alpha)F_t \qquad \textbf{(8-2)}$$

---

[1]For a summary of these results, see Robin M. Hogarth and Spyros Makridakis, "Forecasting and Planning: An Evaluation," *Management Science*, Vol. 27, No. 2 (February 1981), pp. 115–138.

where

t = current time period

α = exponential smoothing constant

A_t = demand at period t

F_t = forecast for period t

F_{t+1} = forecast for period following t, or the next period

It is identical to Equation (8-1).

Example

The following quarterly data represent a demand time series for a product:

	QUARTER			
	1	2	3	4
Last year	1,200	700	900	1,100
This year	1,400	1,000	$F_3 = ?$	

We wish to forecast the demand for the third quarter of this year. We will assume that $\alpha = 0.2$ and the previous forecast is constructed from the average for the four quarters of last year. Hence, $F_0 = (1,200 + 700 + 900 + 1,100)/4 = 975.$ We begin forecasting the first quarter of this year and carry the computations forward until we reach the third quarter.

The forecast for the first quarter of this year is

$$F_1 = 0.2A_0 + (1 - 0.2)\ F_0$$
$$= 0.2(1,100) + 0.8(975)$$
$$= 1,000$$

The forecast for the second quarter of this year is

$$F_2 = 0.2A_1 + (1 - 0.2)F_1$$
$$= 0.2(1,400) + 0.8(1,000)$$
$$= 1,080$$

The forecast for the third quarter of this year is

$$F_3 = 0.2A_2 + (1 - 0.2)F_2$$
$$= 0.2(1,000) + 0.8(1,080)$$
$$= 1,064$$

Summarizing,

	QUARTER			
	1	2	3	4
Last year	1,200	700	900	1,100
This year	1,400	1,000		
Forecast	1,000	1,080	**1,064**	

Choosing the proper value for the exponential smoothing constant requires a degree of judgment. The higher the value of α, the greater is the weight placed on the more recent demand levels. This allows the model to respond more quickly to changes in the time series. However, too high an α value may make the forecast "nervous" and track random variations in the time series rather than the fundamental changes. The lower the α value, the greater is the weight given to demand history in forecasting future demand and the longer is the time lag in responding to fundamental changes in the demand level. Low values provide very "stable" forecasts that are not likely to be heavily influenced by randomness in the time series.

Compromise values for α typically range from 0.01 to 0.3, although higher values may be used for short time periods when anticipated changes will occur, such as a recession, an aggressive but temporary promotional campaign, the discontinuing of some products in the line, or the starting of the forecasting procedure when little or no historical sales results are available. A good rule to follow when searching for an α value is to choose one that will allow the forecast model to track major changes occurring in the time series and average the random fluctuations. This is an α to minimize forecast error.

Correcting for Trend

The basic exponential smoothing model gives good performance when applied to a time series pattern, as shown in Figure 8-1(a), or where the changes in trend and seasonal components are not great. However, when there is a substantial trend or a significant seasonal pattern in the data, the inherent forecast lag in this type of model may give unacceptable forecast error. Fortunately, the model can be expanded to provide better tracking when trend and seasonal elements are significant from the randomness in the data, as shown in Figure 8-1(b) and (c).

Correcting the basic model for forecast time lag due to trend is a simple embellishment to the "level only" model in Equation (8-2). The trend-corrected version of the model is a set of equations that can be stated as

$$S_{t+1} = \alpha A_t + (1 - \alpha)(S_t + T_t) \tag{8-3}$$

$$T_{t+1} = \beta(S_{t+1} - S_t) + (1 - \beta)T_t \tag{8-4}$$

$$F_{t+1} = S_{t+1} + T_{t+1} \tag{8-5}$$

where the additional symbols not previously defined are

F_{t+1} = trend-corrected forecast for period $t+1$
S_t = initial forecast for period t
T_t = trend for period t
β = trend smoothing constant

Example

Recall the previous example having the following data:

	QUARTER			
	1	2	3	4
Last year	1,200	700	900	1,100
This year	1,400	1,000	$F_3 = ?$	

We still want to make a forecast for the third period of this year, but with a correction for trend. We will use an arbitrary starting value of $S_t = 975$ (average of last year's demand) and $T_t = 0$ (no trend). The smoothing constant β is assumed 0.3 and α remains the previous value of 0.2. Now begin the forecasting procedure.

The forecast for the first quarter of this year is

$$S_1 = .2(1,100) + .8(975 + 0) = 1,000$$

$$T_1 = .3(1,000 - 975) + .7(0) = 7.5$$

$$F_1 = 1,000 + 7.5 = 1,007.5$$

Using the results from the first quarter, the forecast for the second quarter of this year is

$$S_2 = .2(1,400) + .8(1,000 + 7.5) = 1,086$$
$$T_2 = .3(1,086 - 1,000) + .7(7.5) = 31.05$$
$$F_2 = 1,086 + 31.05 = 1,117.05$$

Using the results from the second quarter, the forecast for the third quarter of this year is

$$S_3 = .2(1,000) + .8(1,086 + 31.05) = 1,093.64$$
$$T_3 = .3(1,093.64 - 1,086) + .7(31.05) = 24.03$$
$$F_3 = 1,093.64 + 24.03 = 1,117.67, \text{ or } 1,118$$

Summarizing,

	QUARTER			
	1	2	3	4
Last year	1,200	700	900	1,100
This year	1,400	1,000		
Forecast	1,008	1,117	**1,118**	

Correcting for Trend and Seasonality

In addition to trend, the effects of seasonal fluctuations in the time series may also be taken into account. Before applying this type of model, two conditions should be met.

1. There must be a known reason for the periodic peaks and valleys in the demand pattern, and these peaks and valleys should occur at the same time every year.
2. The seasonal variation should be greater than the random variations, or "noise."

If seasonal demand is not stable, significant, and discernible from random variations, then it becomes extremely difficult to develop a model that will accurately predict the direction of the next period's demand. If this is the case, a basic form of the exponential smoothing model, with a high value for the smoothing constant to reduce the effects of lag, may give a lower forecast error than the more complicated model. Caution is needed in model choice.

The level-trend-seasonal model is built around the concept of forecasting the index of actual demand to the trend, and then deseasonalizing it to produce the forecast. The equations for this model are

$$S_{t+1} = \alpha\,(A_t/I_{t-L}) + (1 - \alpha)(S_t + T_t) \tag{8-6}$$

$$T_{t+1} = \beta(S_{t+1} - S_t) + (1 - \beta)T_t \tag{8-7}$$

$$I_t = \gamma(A_t/S_t) + (1 - \gamma)I_{t-L} \tag{8-8}$$

$$F_{t+1} = (S_{t+1} + T_{t+1})I_{t-L+1} \tag{8-9}$$

where symbols not previously defined are

F_{t+1} = trend and seasonally corrected forecast for period $t + 1$
γ = smoothing constant on the seasonal index
I_t = seasonal index for period t
L = the time period for one full season

Solving this model involves the same procedures as the previous versions. The number of calculations makes it rather impractical to compute forecasts manually. Computer packages, such as the forecast module in LOGWARE,[2] have been written not only to make the forecast, but also to assist the user in setting the initial values to start the forecasting process and determine the best smoothing constants.

Forecast Error Defined

To the extent that the future is not perfectly mirrored by the past, the forecast of future demand will generally be in error to some degree. Since the exponential smoothing forecast is a prediction of the average demand, we seek to project a range within which the actual demand will fall. This requires a statistical forecast.

The error in the forecast refers to how close the forecast comes to the actual demand level. It is properly expressed statistically as a standard deviation, variance, or mean absolute deviation. Historically, the mean absolute deviation (MAD) has been used as the measure of forecast error with reference to exponential smoothing. Early proponents of exponential smoothing may have preferred standard deviation as the proper measure, but accepted the simpler MAD computation because of the limited memory of early computers. Since computers now have adequate memory for the forecasting task, the standard deviation is developed as the measure of forecast error.

---

[2]Software available with this text.

The forecast error is defined as

$$\text{Forecast error} = \text{actual demand} - \text{forecasted demand} \qquad \text{(8-10)}$$

Since the forecasted demand is an arithmetic mean value, the sum of the forecast errors over a number of periods should be zero. However, the magnitude of the forecast error can be found by squaring the errors, thus eliminating the canceling of positive and negative errors. The common form of the standard deviation is developed, and it is corrected for the one degree of freedom that is lost in producing the forecast; that is, the α in the "level only" forecast model. The expression for this standard deviation is[3]

$$S_F = \sqrt{\frac{\sum_t (A_t - F_t)^2}{N - 1}} \qquad \text{(8-11)}$$

where

S_F = standard error of the forecast
A_t = actual demand in period t
F_t = forecast for period t
N = number of forecast periods t

The form of the frequency distribution of forecast errors becomes important when making probability statements about the forecast. Two typical generalized forms of the forecast error distribution are shown in Figure 8-3. Assuming that the forecast model is tracking the average of actual demand levels quite well and the variation of actual demand about the forecast is small relative to the forecast level, the normal frequency distribution, or approximations to it, is a likely form to be found in practice. This will especially be the case for the distribution of average forecast errors. The central limit theorem[4] applies, and the normal frequency distribution is the proper distribution form. Where the forecast interval is short, a skewed distribution may result like that shown in Figure 8-3(b).

A way to determine the frequency distribution that applies in any particular situation is through using the chi-square goodness of fit test.[5] Alternately, the following test can be used to select between the normal (symmetrical) distribution and the exponential distribution form as a simple representation of a skewed distribution.

In a normal distribution, about 2% of the observations exceed a level two standard deviations above the mean. In an exponential distribution, the probability of exceeding the mean by more than 2.75 standard deviations is about

---

[3]Alternately, the mean squared error and the root mean squared error are popular formulations. They differ as to whether the square root is taken of the sum of the squared errors and whether a correction is made for the degrees of freedom lost. The degrees of freedom lost depends on the number of smoothing constants estimated in the model equations.
[4]For a definition, see any good book on applied statistics, or John Neter, William Wasserman, and G. A. Gilmore, *Applied Statistics* (Boston: Allyn and Bacon, 1988), pp. 262–263.
[5]Ibid.

Figure 8-3
Typical Forecast
Error Distributions

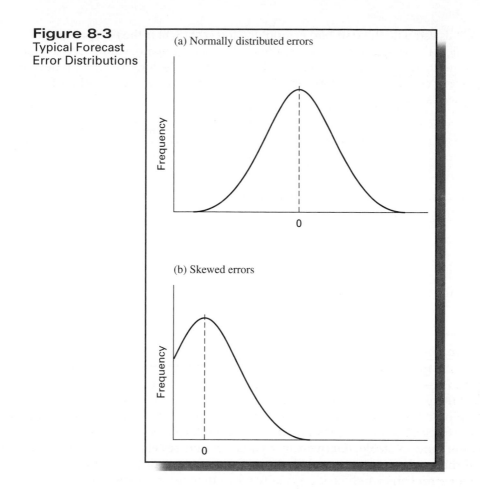

(a) Normally distributed errors

Frequency

0

(b) Skewed errors

Frequency

0

2%. Therefore, if the number of standard deviations it takes to account for all but about 2% of the observations is near 2, a normal distribution should be used. If it is above 2.7, the exponential distribution should be used.[6]

Example

Recall the "level only" forecast that had the following data and results:

	QUARTER			
	1	2	3	4
Last year	1,200	700	900	1,100
This year	1,400	1,000		
Forecast	1,000	1,080	**1,064**	

[6]Robert G. Brown, *Materials Management Systems* (New York: John Wiley & Sons, 1977), p. 146.

Now, let's estimate the standard error of the forecast (S_F) for the two periods (N = 2) for which the forecast has been made and actual demand values are available. Assuming that demand is normally distributed about the forecast, we can develop a 95 percent confidence band around the third quarter forecast. Based on Equation (8-11), we estimate S_F.

$$S_F = \sqrt{\frac{(1,400 - 1,000)^2 + (1,000 - 1,080)^2}{2 - 1}}$$
$$= 407.92$$

The best estimate for the actual demand level (Y) for the third quarter with $z_{@95\%} = 1.96$ from a normal distribution table (see Appendix A) is

$$Y = F_3 \pm z(S_F)$$
$$= 1,064 \pm 1.96(407.92)$$
$$= 1,064 \pm 800$$

Hence, the 95 percent confidence range for the forecast of actual demand (Y) is

$$264 < Y < 1,864$$

Monitoring Forecast Error

One of the notable advantages of using exponential smoothing for short-term forecasting is its ability to adapt to changing patterns in the time series. How well the model maintains its accuracy is directly related to the smoothing constant value at any point in time. Therefore, sophisticated forecasting procedures involve monitoring the forecast error and making adjustments in the smoothing constant values. If the time series is stable, relatively low values would be selected. During periods of rapid change, high values would be used. By not being limited to single values, the forecast error can be reduced, especially when demand patterns are dynamic.

A popular method for monitoring the forecast error is by means of a tracking signal. The tracking signal is a comparison, usually a ratio, of the current forecast error to an average of past forecast errors. This ratio may be continuously or periodically evaluated. As a result of this computation, the exponential smoothing constants may be recomputed or specified again if the ratio exceeds a specified control limit.

In general, the best smoothing constant values are the ones that minimize the forecast error over time for a stable time series. Adjusting the values as the characteristics of the time series change offers further opportunity to reduce forecast error. Adaptive models that allow the smoothing constants to be revised continuously perform well when the demand time series is changing rapidly, but they do not seem to perform as well during stable periods. Conversely, smoothing constants revised to specified limits offer good performance during stable demand periods and can give remarkably good performance during periods of sudden or rapid change in the series.[7] Flowers has suggested optimum values for these specified smoothing

---

[7]From computer simulation experiments as reported in D. Clay Whybark, "A Comparison of Adaptive Forecasting Techniques," *Logistics and Transportation Review*, Vol. 8, No. 3 (1972), pp. 13–25.

Figure 8-4
Example of the
Performance of a
Well-Specified
Exponential
Smoothing Model

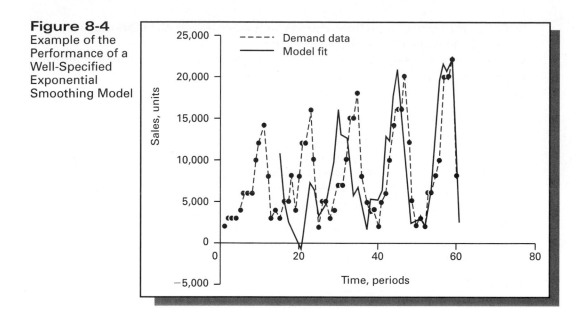

constants.[8] Performance of a well-specified exponential smoothing model should look like the latter periods of the time series shown in Figure 8-4.

Classic Time Series Decomposition

A class of forecasting models that has been useful over the years is that of time series decomposition. These methods include spectral analysis, classic time series analysis, and Fourier series analysis. Classic time series decomposition analysis is discussed here mainly because of its mathematical simplicity and its popularity, and because more elegant methods have not offered increased accuracy.

Classic time series decomposition forecasting is built on the philosophy that a historical sales pattern can be decomposed into four categories: trend, seasonal variation, cyclical variation, and residual, or random, variation. Trend represents the long-term movement in sales caused by factors such as changes in population, changes in marketing performance of the firm, and fundamental changes in market acceptance of the firm's products and services. Seasonal variation refers to the regular hills and valleys in the time series that usually repeat every 12 months. The forces causing this regular variation include climatic changes, buying patterns pegged to calendar dates, and the availability of goods. Cyclical variation is the long-term (more than one year) undulations in the demand pattern. Residual, or random, variation is that portion of total sales that is unaccounted for by trend, seasonal, or

[8]A. Dale Flowers, "A Simulation Study of Smoothing Constant Limits for an Adaptive Forecasting System," *Journal of Operations Management*, Vol. 1, No. 2 (November 1980), pp. 85–94.

cyclical components. If the time series is well described by the other three components, the residual variation should be random.

Classic time series analysis combines each type of sales variation in the following way:

$$F = T \times S \times C \times R \qquad\qquad (8\text{-}12)$$

where

F = demand forecast (units or $)
T = trend level (units or $)
S = seasonal index
C = cyclical index
R = residual index

In practice, the model is often reduced to only trend and seasonal components. This is done because a well-specified model has a residual index value (R) of 1.0 and thus does not affect the forecast, and because it is difficult in many cases to decompose cyclical variation from random variation. Treating the cyclical index (C) as equal to 1.0 is not as serious as it first seems because the model is usually updated when new data become available. The effect of cyclical variation tends to be compensated for in the updating process.[9]

The trend value (T) in the model may be determined by several methods, such as fitting a line "by eye," using some form of the moving average, or using the method of least squares.

The popular least squares method is a mathematical technique that minimizes the sum of the squared differences between the actual data and the proposed trend line. A least squares line can be found for any trend-line form, whether linear or nonlinear. The mathematical expression for a linear trend line is $T = a + bt$, where t is time, T is the average demand level, or trend, and a and b are coefficients to be determined for the particular time series. These coefficients are found by

$$b = \frac{\sum D_t(t) - N(\bar{D})(\bar{t})}{\sum t^2 - N\bar{t}^2} \qquad\qquad (8\text{-}13)$$

and

$$a = \bar{D} - b\bar{t} \qquad\qquad (8\text{-}14)$$

where

N = the number of observations used in the development of the trend line
D_t = the actual demand in time period t
$\bar{D}$ = average demand for N time periods
$\bar{t}$ = average of t over N time periods

---

[9]The model is sometimes expressed in an additive form of $F = T + S + C + R$.

Nonlinear trend lines are more complex mathematically and are not discussed here.[10]

The seasonality component of the model is represented by an index value that changes for each period being forecasted. This index is a ratio of the actual demand in a given time period to the average demand. The average demand may be represented by a single average of the actual demand over a specified period, usually one year; a moving average; or the trend line. Inasmuch as the trend line was previously discussed, it will be used as the seasonal index base. Therefore,

$$S_t = D_t / T_t \qquad \text{(8-15)}$$

where

S_t = seasonal index in time period t
T_t = trend value determined from $T = a + bt$

Finally, the forecast is made for time period t in the future as follows:

$$F_t = (T_t)(S_{t-L}) \qquad \text{(8-16)}$$

where

F_t = the forecasted demand in time period t
L = number of periods in the seasonal cycle

These ideas are best illustrated by an example.

Example

A manufacturer of young women's clothing had to make purchase quantity decisions and set production and logistics schedules based on forecasts of market bookings (sales). Five seasons of the year were specified for planning and promotional purposes—summer, trans-season, fall, holiday, and spring. Sales data for approximately two and one-half years were obtained (see Table 8-2). A forecast was needed for two seasons ahead of the current accounting period to ensure adequate purchasing and production lead time. In this case, the forecast period was the holiday season, even though the sales for the intervening fall period were not yet known.

The first task was to find the trend line using Equations (8-13) and (8-14). Assuming a straight-line trend, the b coefficient was

$$b = \frac{1,218,217 - (12)(14,726.92)(6.5)}{650 - (12)(6.5)^2} = 486.13$$

and the a coefficient follows as

$$a = 14,726.92 - 486.13(6.5)$$
$$= 11,567.08$$

---

[10]A discussion of nonlinear trend lines can be found in John Neter, William Wasserman, and Michael H. Kutner, *Applied Linear Regression Models* (Homewood, IL: Irwin, 1983), Chapter 14.

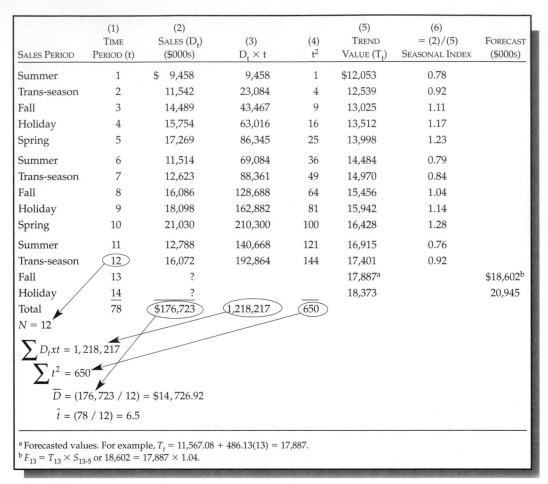

Sales Period	(1) Time Period (t)	(2) Sales (D_t) ($000s)	(3) $D_t \times t$	(4) t^2	(5) Trend Value (T_t)	(6) = (2)/(5) Seasonal Index	Forecast ($000s)
Summer	1	$ 9,458	9,458	1	$12,053	0.78	
Trans-season	2	11,542	23,084	4	12,539	0.92	
Fall	3	14,489	43,467	9	13,025	1.11	
Holiday	4	15,754	63,016	16	13,512	1.17	
Spring	5	17,269	86,345	25	13,998	1.23	
Summer	6	11,514	69,084	36	14,484	0.79	
Trans-season	7	12,623	88,361	49	14,970	0.84	
Fall	8	16,086	128,688	64	15,456	1.04	
Holiday	9	18,098	162,882	81	15,942	1.14	
Spring	10	21,030	210,300	100	16,428	1.28	
Summer	11	12,788	140,668	121	16,915	0.76	
Trans-season	12	16,072	192,864	144	17,401	0.92	
Fall	13	?			17,887[a]		$18,602[b]
Holiday	14	?			18,373		20,945
Total	78	$176,723	1,218,217	650			

$N = 12$

$$\sum D_t xt = 1,218,217$$

$$\sum t^2 = 650$$

$$\overline{D} = (176,723 / 12) = \$14,726.92$$

$$\overline{t} = (78 / 12) = 6.5$$

[a] Forecasted values. For example, $T_t = 11,567.08 + 486.13(13) = 17,887$.
[b] $F_{13} = T_{13} \times S_{13\text{-}5}$ or $18,602 = 17,887 \times 1.04$.

Table 8-2 Time Series Forecast from a Clothing Manufacturer's Sales Data

Therefore, the trend equation was

$$T_t = 11,567.08 + 486.13t$$

From this trend-line equation, the values were projected by substituting into the previous equation each value of t; see column 5 in Table 8-2.

The seasonal indices were computed according to Equation (8-15) and are displayed in column 6 of Table 8-2. For forecasting purposes, the most recently available season was used, mainly because the indices did not vary greatly from year to year. If this were not the case, the indices for several years might be averaged.

The forecast for the holiday season (period 14) was

$$Y_{14} = [11,567.08 + 486.13(14)] \times 1.14$$
$$= \$20,945 \text{ (in \$000s)}$$

The forecast for the fall period (period 13) was made in a similar manner.

Multiple Regression Analysis

In the forecasting models discussed thus far, time is the only variable that has been considered. To the extent that other variables show a relationship to demand, they may also be included in a model to forecast sales. Multiple regression analysis is a statistical technique that helps to determine the degree of association between a number of selected variables and demand. From this analysis, a model is developed that may use more than one variable to predict future demand. Information about the predictor (independent) variables is then converted by the regression equation to give a demand forecast.

Example

Reconsider the clothing manufacturer's problem discussed previously. An alternative approach to forecasting over the two-season interval was to use a regression model, preferably where the independent variables "lead" the demand variable in time. This permitted data to be obtained about independent variables in advance of the forecast period. One such forecasting equation was developed for the summer selling season:

$$F = -3{,}016 + 1{,}211X_1 + 5.75X_2 + 109X_3 \qquad \text{(8-17)}$$

where

F = estimated average summer season sales (in thousands of dollars)
X_1 = time in years (1991 = 1)
X_2 = number of accounts of purchasing during the season (from advanced bookings)
X_3 = monthly net change in consumer installment debt (percent)

The model explained 99 percent ($R^2 = 0.99$) of the total variation in demand and was statistically significant at the 5 percent level. The equation was deemed an accurate predictor of demand. For example, the actual sales for the summer season of 1996 were $20,750,000. The model inputs for 1996 were $X_1 = 6$, $X_2 = 2{,}732$, and $X_3 = 8.63$, and, when substituted in Equation (8-17), gave a sales forecast of $20.9 million, or $20,900,000.

Although a reasonable knowledge of statistical methodology is required to construct such a model, computer software, such as SPSS[11] and BMDP,[12] for performing a regression analysis is readily available for both microcomputer and mainframe computer installations. These programs perform the necessary computations for fitting an ordinary least squares line to the data and providing statistical information to evaluate the fit. However, care should be exercised in the use of these statistical packages since they alone cannot guarantee a valid model, that is, one that is free of specification and statistical problems.[13]

---

[11]A product of SPSS, Inc., 444 N. Michigan Ave., Chicago, IL.
[12]A product of BMDP Statistical Software, 1964 Westwood Blvd., Los Angeles, CA.
[13]For a discussion of these problems, see Marija J. Norusis, *SPSS/PC+* (Chicago: SPSS, Inc., 1986), Chapter 17; and Neter, Wasserman, and Kutner, *Applied Linear Regression Models*, op. cit.

SPECIAL PREDICTION PROBLEMS FOR LOGISTICIANS

Special problems are sometimes encountered when attempting to predict requirements. These problem areas are start-up, lumpy demand, regional forecasting, and forecast error. Although not all of these problems are necessarily unique to logistics, they are of great concern to the logistician in accurately determining requirements.

Start-Up

The logistician is often faced with the problem of predicting requirement levels for products or services for which there is not enough history to start the forecasting process. New product or service introductions and the need to provide logistical support for them create the common start-up conditions. Several approaches have been used during this early forecasting period.

First, put the initial estimation in the hands of the marketing personnel until a sales history begins to develop. They will know best the level of promotional effort, early customer response, and expected customer acceptance. Once a reasonable demand history has been generated, say, in six months, the established forecasting methods can be used with some confidence.

Second, an estimate may be made from the demand pattern of similar products in the line. Although many companies turn their product line on the average of once every five years, few products are radically new. They often represent changes in size, style, or revision of existing products. Therefore, demand patterns previously experienced may provide insight and a basis for estimating initial demand for new products.

Third, if the exponential smoothing model is used for forecasting, the exponential smoothing constant may be set at a high level (0.5 or higher) during the initial forecasting period. It will be reduced to a normal level once an adequate demand history has been generated.

Lumpy Demand

The problem of lumpy, or irregular, demand has been described previously and illustrated in Figure 8-2. It represents the condition where there is so much random variation in the demand pattern that trend and seasonal patterns can be obscured. The lumpy demand condition occurs when two or three times the standard deviation of the historical data exceed the forecast of the best model that can be fit to the time series. The lumpy demand pattern occurs frequently for a variety of reasons: The demand pattern is dominated by large, infrequent customer orders; demand may be derived from the demand of other products or services; seasonal peaking may not have been taken into account; and the demand pattern may be a result of exceptional data, outliers, or unusual conditions.

Lumpy demand patterns are, by nature, difficult to predict accurately by mathematical methods due to the wide variability in the time series; however, some suggestions on how to treat them can be offered. First, look for obvious reasons for the lumpiness and use them to produce the forecast. Separate the forecasting of lumpy demand products from those showing a regular pattern and use forecasting methods tailored to each.

Example

A chemical manufacturer had a product in its line used for cleaning apples at harvest time. Depending on the size of the apple crop, sales of the product could vary considerably from year to year. Exponential smoothing was used to forecast this as well as other products in the line. Inventory levels at warehouses that were set based on this forecast were typically either short or greatly in excess of reasonable needs. Grouping this lumpy demand product in with those having regular patterns did not permit the company to take advantage of the basic reasons why the demand level was changing throughout the year.

Second, do not react quickly to changes in the demand pattern for such products or services if no assignable causes can be found for the demand shifts. Rather, use a simple, stable forecasting method that does not react rapidly to change, such as a basic exponential smoothing model with a low smoothing constant value or a regression model that is refitted no more frequently than on an annual basis.

Third, because lumpy demand frequently occurs in low demand items, forecast accuracy may not be an overriding issue. If the forecast is used to establish inventory levels, carrying a little more inventory to compensate for forecast inaccuracy may be more economical than attempting to manage the forecast carefully.

Regional Forecasting

Although most of the discussion in this chapter has been directed toward forecasting time-related demand, geographic aggregation or disaggregation of the forecast is also of concern. That is, the logistician must decide whether to take a forecast of total demand and apportion it by regions, such as by plant or warehouse territories, or to forecast each region separately. Achieving the greatest accuracy in the forecast at the regional level is the concern. Forecasting all demands simultaneously very often will be more accurate than the sum of individual regional forecasts. If this is so, apportioning the aggregated forecast to the individual regions may preserve enough accuracy to give better results than individual forecasting. Research on the subject has not provided a definitive answer about which approach is better. Hence, the logistician should be aware of both possibilities and compare the methods in his or her particular situation.

Forecast Error

The final concern is to make the most of the available forecasting techniques. The discussion so far has centered on the use of individual models and methods. In practice, no single forecasting model may be best at all times. Rather, combining results of several models may give more stable and accurate forecasts.[14]

The following example shows combining multiple forecast methods according to their forecast error. This generally works well for long-term forecasts. For short-term forecasts, equally weighted forecasts have been shown to be particularly robust, and they give greater forecast accuracy than unequally weighted ones.[15]

Example

Reconsider the clothing manufacturer[15] forecasting problem. Because there were five selling seasons, there was no guarantee that one method of forecasting would consistently be superior throughout all seasons. In fact, four methods were used. There was a regression model (R) that predicted sales based on the two variables: (1) number of accounts; and (2) the change in consumer debt. Two versions (ES_1, ES_2) of an exponential smoothing model were used. The fourth model was the company's internal forecast based on managerial judgment and experience (MJ). The average forecast error realized by using each method during the different selling seasons is shown in Figure 8-5.

One way to combine the information from each forecast model is to weight the results according to the average historical error that they produced. In this way, no model results would be eliminated or would there be total reliance on the model result that happened to appear best historically.

To illustrate the weighting scheme, consider the fall selling season results shown in Figure 8-5. The average error for each model was MJ = 9.0 percent, R = 0.7 percent, ES_1 = 1.2 percent, and ES_2 = 8.4 percent. The weights should be inversely proportional to the forecast error and in the same ratio to their respective percentages. Table 8-3 shows the computation of the weighting factors.

Finally, given the forecast results of each model and the weighting factors, a weighted average forecast can be calculated, as shown in Table 8-4. The final forecast value for the fall selling season is $20,208,000 and represents inputs from a number of forecasting sources.

An expert system approach to combining forecast methods has shown encouraging results, especially for short-term forecast periods of less than one year. Known as rule-based forecasting, several time series methods are combined and rules derived from forecasting experts are applied to the input data and to the model application.

[14]M. J. Lawrence, R. H. Edmundson, and M. J. O'Connor, "The Accuracy of Combining Judgemental and Statistical Forecasts," *Management Science*, Vol. 32, No. 12 (December 1986), pp. 1521–1532, Essam Mahmoud, "Accuracy in Forecasting: A Survey," *Journal of Forecasting* (April–June 1984), p. 139; Spyros Makridakis and Robert L. Winkler, Average of Forecasts: Some Empirical Results," *Management Science*, (September 1983), p. 987; and Victor Zarnowitz, "The Accuracy of Individual and Group Forecasts from Business Outlook Surveys," *Journal of Forecasting* (January–March 1984), p. 10.
[15]Fred Collopy and J. Scott Armstrong, "Rule-Based Forecasting: Development and Validation of an Expert Systems Approach to Combining Time Series Extrapolations," *Management Science*, Vol. 38, No. 10 (1992), pp. 1394–1414.

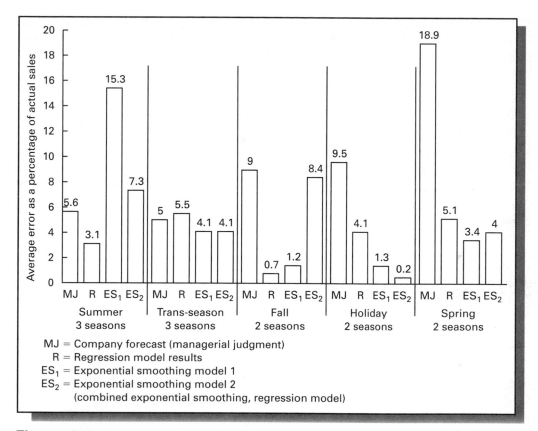

Figure 8-5 Forecast Error for Four Forecasting Techniques Applied to the Sales of a Clothing Manufacturer

Table 8-3 Calculation of Model Weights

Model Type	(1) Forecast Error	(2) = (1)/19.3 Proportion of Total Error	(3) = 1/(2) Inverse of Error Proportion	(4) = (3)/48.09 Model Weights
MJ	9.0	0.466	2.15	0.04
R	0.7	0.036	27.77	0.58
ES₁	1.2	0.063	15.87	0.33
ES₂	8.4	0.435	2.30	0.05
	19.3	1.000	48.09	1.00

Forecast Type	Model Forecast	Weighting Factor[a]	Weighted Proportion[b]
Regression model (R)	$20,367,000	0.58	$11,813,000
Exponential smoothing (ES_1)	20,400,000	0.33	6,732,000
Combined exponential smoothing–regression model (ES_2)	17,660,000	0.05	883,000
Managerial judgment (MJ)	19,500,000	0.04	780,000
Weighted average forecast			$20,208,000

[a]From Table 8-3
[b]Model forecast multiplied by the weighting factor

Table 8-4 Weighted Average Fall Selling Season Forecast Using Several Forecasting Techniques

The rules are various IF-THEN statements that guide actions to improve the forecast. Collopy and Armstrong develop 99 such rules, a few examples of which are

- IF an observation is an outlier, THEN set the observation equal to two standard deviations from the mean.
- For an exponential smoothing model, IF alpha (smoothing constant) is calculated to be greater than 0.7, THEN use 0.7. IF alpha is less than 0.2, THEN use 0.2.
- IF early data are irrelevant, THEN delete these data.
- IF observations are judged irregular based on knowledge of the application, THEN adjust the observations prior to analysis to remove their short-term effects.[16]

Applying these and additional rules to multiple forecasting methods such as random walk (using the most recent observation), exponential smoothing, and regression, significant reduction in forecast error can be achieved. This is especially true when the time series shows significant trends, low uncertainty, and stability, and the forecaster has good knowledge of the application. Each of the methods is weighted equally.

COLLABORATIVE FORECASTING

The forecasting methods that have been illustrated to this point in the chapter work best when demand does not show great variability. However, lumpy, highly uncertain, and dynamic demand brought about by such factors as promotions, few buyers purchasing in large qualities, seasonal/cyclical buying, and demand created by "acts of God" creates a special problem. Although some guidelines have already been offered to treat the lumpy demand case, collaborative forecasting is being suggested as an improved approach, especially for channel planning of the business

---

[16]Ibid.

processes. It is based on the premise that "two heads are better than one." That is, multiple parties have the likelihood of producing more accurate forecasts than a single party.

Collaborative forecasting refers to the development of forecasts using the inputs from multiple participants, whether they are from various functional areas within a single firm (marketing, operations, logistics, finance, purchasing, etc.) or from the various members in a supply channel such as vendors, carriers, and buyers. The goal is to reduce forecast error. This can best be accomplished when each party brings unique perspective to the forecasting process. Buyers or marketing personnel may be close to the final consumer and have the best "feel" of end demand. On the other hand, vendors or purchasing personnel may be attuned to supply shortages and capacity limitations that may place a cap on demand or that may ultimately affect product price that in turn affects price and product demand levels. Transportation personnel or carriers may be able to predict delivery times that affect customer service and sales.

Forecasting by means of collaboration requires administering a team of diverse parties with all the complications inherent in such a process. However, the key administrative steps can be identified, many of which are listed here:

- Someone should champion the process and provide the necessary communication and group meeting schedules.
- The kinds of information needed in the forecast and the processes for collecting them should be identified, including the timing, quantities, and person(s) responsible.
- Methods for processing the information from multiple sources, types, and formats should be established as well as the weights to be used for combining and reconciling forecasts from the multiple parties.
- Methods are needed for translating the final forecast into the form needed by each party, such as sales, shipments, and SKUs in total and by customer account, service territory, and so on.
- A process should be available for revising and updating the forecast on a real-time basis.
- Metrics should be established for appraising the forecast and determining whether collaborative forecasting is an improvement over traditional approaches.
- The benefits to each party of collaborative forecasting should be obvious and real.

Collaborative forecasting is a complex process that is inherently unstable, that is, forecasting will have the tendency to fall back to the individual members making their own predictions. Successful collaboration requiring sharing, coordination, compromise, consideration, commitment, and understanding is not easy to realize. However, the benefits of more accurate forecasting in the most difficult forecasting situations as well as the benefits of improved communication interfunctionally and interorganizationally may justify the extra effort required to operate in a coalition.

Applications

Although the supporting software for collaborative forecasting is new and under constant revision, several notable companies have reported early successes as they experiment with the collaborative forecasting approach. Heineken USA (the brewer) has close to 100 of its independent beer distributors submit forecasts electronically to Heineken USA's White Plains, New York, office using a third-party software product. Involving about 40 percent of Heineken's total volume, this setup has cut order-cycle times from 12 weeks to just four or five.[17]

Ace Hardware, a $2.8 billion hardware retailer, experimented with joint forecasting for stock replenishment with Manco, a supplier of tape, glues, and adhesives. Using Web-based software and the Internet, Manco can gain access to Ace's database. Ace presents Manco with its forecast for items through a Web browser screen, but Manco has the opportunity to change the forecast before it brings that forecast into its production planning system. Ace and Manco look at the same screens in real time and exchange messages before coming to a forecast consensus. Forecast accuracy is reviewed on a monthly basis. In the past, forecast accuracy was 20 percent over or under the actual demand. Now, it is less than 10 percent.[18]

FLEXIBILITY AND QUICK RESPONSE—AN ALTERNATIVE TO FORECASTING

The sales of some products or services are so unpredictable that using the types of forecasting methods already described results in such a high potential forecasting error that it makes them impractical. Lumpy demand patterns are an example, and so an alternative is needed. Recognizing that there can be no better forecast than to wait until customer demand materializes is a basis for responding accurately to demand. If the processes of the supply chain can be made to be flexible and to respond quickly to demand requirements, there is little need for forecasting. After all, statistical forecasting assumes the usual properties that the observations in the time series are random, independent, and each observation is a small portion of the total. When there is a time lag in matching supply to demand, forecasting serves to set the levels of production, purchasing, and inventories so that supply is available when demand occurs. Changing the nature of the supply chain so that the processes can respond flexibly and efficiently to the specific requirements of each customer request, and to do this almost instantaneously, makes forecasting unnecessary. Where demand is very unpredictable, this alternative approach should be explored.

---

[17]John Verity, "Collaborative Forecasting: Vision Quest" *Computerworld Commerce*, Vol. 31, No. 45 (November 1997), pp. 12–14.
[18]James A. Cooke, "Why ACE Is Becoming THE PLACE," *Logistics Management & Distribution Report*, Vol. 41, No. 3 (March 2002), pp. 32–36.

However, in many cases where demand is "regular," supplying to a forecasted demand remains the preferred choice.

Example

National Bicycle found that sports bikes—ten-speed and mountain bikes—had become fashion items, sold in part because of their bright, intricate color patterns that changed every year. National's inability to predict which color patterns would be hot each year was causing it to overproduce some colors and underproduce others, generating huge losses. To circumvent this forecasting problem, the company created a custom-ordering system by which customers were measured for their ideal frame dimensions and invited to choose their favorite color pattern from a wide selection. Their ideal bike was then created in the company's remarkably flexible plant in Kashiwara and delivered to their door two weeks later.[19]

CONCLUDING COMMENTS

The logistician frequently finds it necessary to provide his or her own forecasts of demand, lead times, prices, and costs for use in strategic and operational planning and control. Many times, the long-term forecasts needed are provided from outside the logistics function or are only partially the responsibility of the logistician. This is particularly true for strategic planning. Therefore, this chapter has focused on short to medium-term forecasting methods that the logistician is most likely to use. Within this period, those techniques that have proven to have the greatest utility are discussed—exponential smoothing, classic time series decomposition, and multiple regression.

Several special problems of producing a forecast are briefly discussed. These include starting the forecast with little or no previous information about the time series; dealing with lumpy or irregular time series patterns; forecasting demand within geographic segments; and using forecasting models in combination to reduce forecast error.

The logistics manager should also be aware of an alternative to forecasting that may be needed when demand is so unpredictable that forecasted results are unsatisfactory. By designing the supply chain for flexibility and quick response, supply can meet demand as it occurs and forecasting may not be needed at all.

QUESTIONS

A number of the problems in this chapter can be solved, or partially solved, with the aid of computer software. The software package that is most important in this

---

[19]Marshall L. Fisher, Janice H. Hammond, Walter R. Obermeyer, and Ananth Raman, "Making Supply Meet Demand in an Uncertain World," *Harvard Business Review*, Vol. 72 (May–June 1994), pp. 83–89+.

chapter is FORECAST (*F*) in LOGWARE. The CD icon **F** will appear where the FORECAST software is appropriate. A database has been prepared for the World Oil[20] case study. In general, the problems may be solved manually.

1. Why, and to what extent, is the logistician interested in demand forecasting? How do you suppose the interest might be different if the logistician were associated with
   a. a food manufacturer?
   b. an aircraft producer?
   c. a large retail chain?
   d. a hospital?
2. Give illustrations of
   a. spatial versus temporal demand
   b. lumpy versus regular demand
   c. derived versus independent demand
3. Contrast qualitative, historical projection, and causal models for forecasting. What strengths do you see in each type? How might the logistician use each? Categorize the models in Table 8-1 into these three basic types.
4. The Ace Trucking Company must determine the number of drivers and trucks to have available on a weekly basis. The standard schedule is to send drivers over the pickup and delivery route on Monday and return them to the originating point on Friday. The trucking requirements can be determined from the total volume to be moved for the week; however, they must be known a week in advance for planning purposes. The volume for the last ten weeks is given here:

Week	Volume	Week	Volume
10 weeks ago	2,056,000	5 weeks ago	2,268,000
9	2,349,000	4	2,653,000
8	1,895,000	3	2,039,000
7	1,514,000	2	2,399,000
6	1,194,000	1 (this week)	2,508,000

a. Using the simplest (level only) exponential smoothing model, predict the expected volume for the next week. [*Note*: You will need to estimate an exponential smoothing constant (α) that will minimize the forecast error. Use the four oldest weeks of data to start the forecast process, that is, find F_0, and search for α in increments of 0.1.]
b. Estimate the forecast error (S_F). Use the last six weekly periods.
c. Find the range over which the actual volume is likely to vary. (*Hint*: You must compute a statistical confidence band here. Assume a 95-percent confidence band and a normal distribution of requirements.)

---

[20]A database for this case study has been prepared in LOGWARE.

5. Suppose the data in problem 4 were given as follows:

Week	Volume	Week	Volume
10 weeks ago	1,567,000	5 weeks ago	2,056,000
9	1,709,000	4	2,088,000
8	1,651,000	3	1,970,000
7	1,778,000	2	1,925,000
6	1,897,000	1 (this week)	2,003,000

a. Using the trend-corrected version of the exponential smoothing model, with $\alpha = \beta = 0.2$, forecast next week's volume.
b. Estimate the error in the above forecast (S_F). Use the last six weekly periods.
c. Construct a 95-percent confidence band on the forecast assuming a normal distribution of requirements.

6. The High-Volt Electric Company has a difficult time predicting the quarterly sales for its room air conditioner line due to the substantial seasonality in product sales.

Quarterly sales data for the last three years are shown as follows:

LAST YEAR		TWO YEARS AGO		THREE YEARS AGO	
Quarter	Units	Quarter	Units	Quarter	Units
1	34,000	1	30,000	1	27,000
2	82,000	2	73,000	2	70,000
3	51,000	3	48,000	3	41,000
4	16,000	4	15,000	4	13,000

a. Determine the best straight-line trend using simple regression analysis.
b. Determine the seasonal indices for each quarter using the trend line values in your seasonal index computations.
c. By means of classic time series decomposition, forecast the sales for the next four quarters.

7. The materials manager at Metropolitan Hospitals must plan for inventories at three hospital locations within the region. His plan is to allocate stock to these locations. It is necessary to predict sales in order to have a basis for stock allocation. The manager wonders whether it would be more accurate to generate a forecast for each hospital or to generate one forecast from the aggregated data and apportion it to each region. (The more accurate the forecast for each region, the lower will be the inventories.)

To test the idea, the manager assembled the following monthly usage data for a particular syringe over the last year:

	Region 1	Region 2	Region 3	Combined
Jan.	236	421	319	976
Feb.	216	407	295	918
Mar.	197	394	305	896

Apr.	247	389	287	923
May	256	403	300	959
June	221	410	295	926
July	204	427	290	921
Aug.	200	386	285	871
Sept.	185	375	280	840
Oct.	199	389	293	881
Nov.	214	401	305	920
Dec.	257	446	337	1,040
Total	2,632	4,848	3,591	11,071

If the manager were to use simple (level only) exponential smoothing with $\alpha = 0.2$, which approach should he use? Why? [*Hint*: Find the initial forecast (F_0) by averaging the first four values in each series. Also, recall the law of variances where $S_T^2 = S_{E_1}^2 + S_{E_2}^2 + S_{E_3}^2$ and compare total errors of the forecast.]

8. A Texas manufacturer of concrete pipe and other precast concrete products for highway, farm, and commercial construction wished to project sales for improved planning of production and logistics operations. A number of variables were thought to affect sales—time, population, housing starts, construction employment, number of residential units, highway budget projections, number of farms, commercial structure construction permits, and number of competing firms in the state. A multiple regression analysis showed three variables to be key to projecting sales: population, construction employment, and construction permits of the previous year.
   a. Do you believe that there is a cause and effect relationship between these variables and company sales?
   b. Are there other important variables that should be considered that were not in the original list?

9. The purchasing agent for a hospital has collected data over the last five years on average monthly unit prices for a commonly used surgical item.

	Last Year	2 Years Ago	3 Years Ago	4 Years Ago	5 Years Ago
Jan.	210	215	211	187	201
Feb.	223	225	210	196	205
Mar.	204	230	214	195	235
Apr.	244	214	208	246	243
May	274	276	276	266	250
June	246	261	269	228	234
July	237	250	265	257	256
Aug.	267	248	253	233	231
Sept.	212	229	244	227	229
Oct.	211	221	202	188	185
Nov.	188	209	221	195	187
Dec.	188	214	210	191	189
Total	2,704	2,792	2,783	2,609	2,645

She believes that an accurate forecast of price would help improve the timing of her buying. Using the oldest four years of data as the base data and saving the most recent data (last year) for checking the forecast accuracy, do the following:

a. Plot the data on a graph. What important observations can you make about the data that would be useful to forecasting?

b. Construct a classic time series decomposition forecasting model based on two full years of data (years 2 and 3) and compute the error of the forecast (S_F) for the last full year. *Hint:* Use

$$S_F = \sqrt{\frac{\Sigma(A_t - F_t)^2}{N - 2}}$$

c. Construct an exponential smoothing model ($\alpha = 0.14$, $\beta = 0.01$, and $\gamma = 0.7$) with level, trend, and seasonal components, and compute S_F for the last year.

d. Create a weighted average model that combines both model types.

10. Hudson Paper Company is a small family-owned business that purchases paper in rolls from large mills. It then cuts and prints the paper into a variety of products, such as bags and wrapping paper, to customer order. The seasonality of sales has made forecasting a particularly difficult problem, especially because of the exact timing of seasonal surges. Management would like to develop an exponential smoothing forecasting model that will aid in forecasting sales. The model should be one that minimizes forecast error.

a. Based on the following aggregate product sales data that have been collected over the last five years, what forecasting model type and smoothing constant values would you suggest?

			SALES, ROLLS		
Month	2003	2002	2000	1999	1998
Jan.	7,000	8,000	7,000	10,000	10,000
Feb.	8,000	9,000	10,000	9,000	7,000
Mar.	8,000	8,000	10,000	9,000	8,000
Apr.	8,000	10,000	8,000	7,000	7,000
May	9,000	10,000	9,000	10,000	11,000
June	11,000	13,000	12,000	11,000	11,000
July	11,000	9,000	12,000	15,000	13,000
Aug.	11,000	13,000	15,000	19,000	15,000
Sept.	15,000	17,000	20,000	21,000	25,000
Oct.	17,000	17,000	20,000	21,000	25,000
Nov.	19,000	21,000	23,000	25,000	27,000
Dec.	13,000	15,000	13,000	17,000	13,000
Total	137,000	150,000	159,000	174,000	172,000

b. What is your forecast for January 2004?

c Construct a 95-percent confidence band on the forecast in part (b).

11. A steel distributor cuts sheets of steel from coils supplied by major mills. Accurate forecasting of coil usage can be very beneficial in controlling raw

material inventories. Eighty percent of the sales price is in the cost of purchased materials. Although determining purchase quantities involves many considerations, a three-month moving average is used to project the usage rate to the next month. Actual coil usage rates in lb for two products are given in the following table:

	COIL A569 CQ P&O			COIL A366 CQ CR		
	Two Years Ago	Last Year	This Year	Two Years Ago	Last Year	This Year
Jan.	206,807	304,580	341,786	794,004	735,663	633,160
Feb.	131,075	293,434	521,878	703,091	590,202	542,897
Mar.	124,357	273,725	179,878	757,610	601,401	692,376
Apr.	149,454	210,626	226,130	499,022	529,784	703,151
May	169,799	150,587	177,400	445,703	672,040	917,967
June	216,843	289,621	182,109	483,058	450,735	532,171
July	288,965	168,590	123,957	446,770	567,928	654,445
Aug.	219,018	171,470	54,074	806,204	549,355	546,480
Sept.	65,885	209,351	136,795	646,300	481,355	472,664
Oct.	179,739	203,466		470,551	419,846	
Nov.	251,969	145,866		682,611	612,346	
Dec.	205,806	203,742		606,968	447,021	

a. Will an exponential smoothing model provide improved forecasts compared with the three-month moving average? If so, what type of model and smoothing constants would you suggest?
b. What is your forecast of the usage for October of this year?
c. If the actual October usage for A569 is 369,828 lb and for A366 is 677,649 lb, how do you rationalize the difference from your forecasts of these items?

CASE STUDY

World Oil

World Oil is a worldwide refiner and distributor of fuel products for automobiles, aircraft, trucks, and marine operations, service stations, and bulk facilities as outlets. Keeping more than 1,000 such outlets supplied is a significant operating problem for the company. Maintaining adequate fuel levels at the auto service stations is its major concern, because fuel generates the most revenue for the firm and has the greatest demand for customer service (product availability). Being able to forecast usage rates by product at these service stations is one of the key elements of good distribution operations. In particular, the tanker truck dispatchers need an accurate forecast of fuel usage in order to schedule fuel deliveries at service stations to avoid stockouts.

SERVICE STATION OPERATION

Service stations may carry three or four different grades of fuel including 87-, 89-, and 92-octane gasoline and diesel fuels. These are stored in underground tanks. Due to the variations in the usage rates among the stations and the limited capacities of these tanks, the

frequency of replenishment may range from two or three times per day to only several times per week. Each tank is dedicated to one type of fuel. Fuel levels are measured periodically by placing a calibrated stick into a storage tank, although some of the more modern stations have electronic metering devices on their tanks. Tanker trucks, typically having four fuel compartments, are used for replenishment.

A FORECASTING SITUATION

Each service station's fuel grade represents a specific forecasting situation. A case in point is one of the lower-volume stations selling 87-octane fuel. With replenishment occurring only a few times per week, forecast of usage rates on a daily basis is adequate. Because usage does depend on the day of the week, forecasting for a particular day of the week may be quite different from any other day of the week. In Table 1, a history of Monday 87-octane fuel usage rates for the last 2-plus years is given for one low-volume station. A plot of this time series is shown in Figure 1. ∎

QUESTIONS

1. Develop a forecasting procedure for this service station. Why did you select your method?
2. How should promotions, holidays, or other such periods where fuel usage rates deviate from normal patterns be handled in the forecast?
3. Forecast next Monday's usage and indicate the probable accuracy of the forecast.

Table 1 Historical Daily (Monday) Usage Rates of 87-Octane Fuel for a Low-Volume Auto Service Station

Two Years Ago		Last Year		This Year	
Week	Usage, Gal.	Week	Usage, Gal.	Week	Usage, Gal.
1 (Jan.)	530	1 (Jan.)	660	1 (Jan.)	790
2	570	2	640	2	860
3	560	3	810[b]	3	890
4	530	4	790[b]	4	780
5	510	5	820[b]	5	810
6	560	6	650	6	?
7	610	7	710		
8	560	8	700		
9	580	9	670		
10	610	10	690		
11	650	11	730		
12	700	12	730		
13	670	13	760		
14	700	14	790		
15	760	15	810		
16	730	16	870		
17	760	17	890		
18	820	18	870		
19	780	19	890		
20	900	20	880		
21	840	21	930		
22	770	22	980		
23	820	23	900		
24	800	24	860		
25	760	25	890		
26	760	26	880		
27	770	27	870		
28	790	28	840		
29	760	29	860		
30	740	30	910		
31	720	31	870		
32	670	32	860		
33	690	33	840		
34	470[a]	34	540[a]		
35	670	35	780		
36	690	36	750		
37	620	37	780		
38	650	38	760		
39	610	39	710		

	Two Years Ago			Last Year			This Year	
Week	Usage, Gal.		Week	Usage, Gal.		Week	Usage, Gal.
40	620		40	730			
41	640		41	750			
42	590		42	750			
43	610		43	710			
44	600		44	750			
45	630		45	720			
46	600		46	770			
47	630		47	740			
48	640		48	750			
49	610		49	760			
50	590		50	780			
51	610		51	800			
52 (Dec.)	630		52 (Dec.)	850			
Totals	34,690			41,030			

[a]Holiday
[b]Promotional period

Figure 1 Fuel Usage on Mondays at a Low-Volume Service Station Over Approximately the Last Two Years

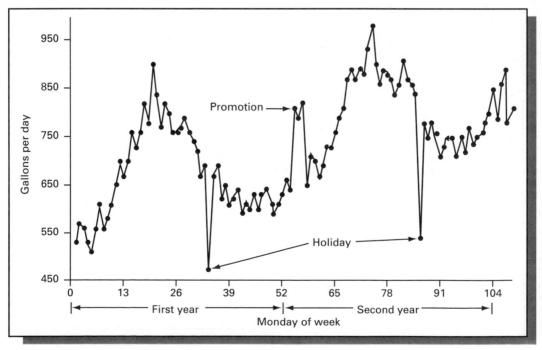

Chapter 9

Inventory Policy Decisions

> *Every management mistake ends up in inventory.*

—MICHAEL C. BERGERAC
FORMER CHIEF EXECUTIVE
REVLON, INC.

*I*nventories are stockpiles of raw materials, supplies, components, work in process, and finished goods that appear at numerous points throughout a firm's production and logistics channel, as shown in Figure 9-1. Inventories are frequently found in such places as warehouses, yards, shop floors, transportation equipment, and on retail

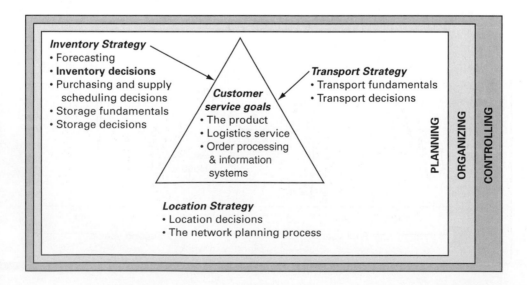

Inventory Strategy
• Forecasting
• **Inventory decisions**
• Purchasing and supply
  scheduling decisions
• Storage fundamentals
• Storage decisions

Transport Strategy
• Transport fundamentals
• Transport decisions

*Customer
service goals*
• The product
• Logistics service
• Order processing
  & information
  systems

PLANNING   ORGANIZING   CONTROLLING

Location Strategy
• Location decisions
• The network planning process

Figure 9-1 Inventories Are Located at Each Echelon of the Supply Channel

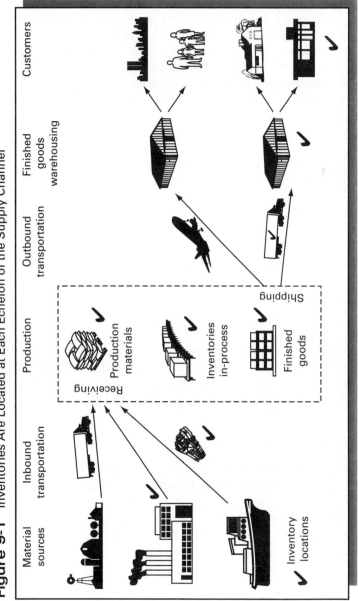

store shelves. Having these inventories on hand can cost between 20 and 40 percent of their value per year. Therefore, carefully managing inventory levels makes good economic sense. Even though many strides have been taken to reduce inventories through just-in-time, time compression, quick response, and collaborative practices applied throughout the supply channel, the annual investment in inventories by manufacturers, retailers, and merchant wholesalers, whose sales represent about 99 percent of GNP, is about 12 percent of the U.S. gross domestic product.[1] This chapter is directed toward managing the inventories that remain in the supply channel.

There is much to learn about inventory management and this chapter is rather lengthy because of it; however, the subject can be viewed in three major parts. First, inventories are most frequently managed as individual items located at single stocking points. This inventory control type has been researched extensively with methods for many specific applications. Second, inventory control will be viewed as management of inventory in the aggregate. Top managers are particularly interested in this perspective because of their need to control the overall inventory investment rather than individual stock-keeping units. Finally, managing inventories among multiple locations and multiple echelons within the supply channel will be examined.

APPRAISAL OF INVENTORIES

There are numerous reasons why inventories are present in a supply channel, yet in recent years inventory holding has been roundly criticized as unnecessary and wasteful. Consider why a firm might want inventories at some level in its operations, and why that firm would want to keep them to a minimum.

Arguments for Inventories

Reasons for holding inventories relate to customer service or to cost economies indirectly derived from them. Briefly consider some of these.

Improve Customer Service

Operating systems may not be designed to respond to customer requests for product or services in an instantaneous manner. Inventories provide a level of product or service availability, which, when located in the proximity of the customer, can meet high customer expectations for product availability. The availability of these inventories to customers can not only maintain sales, but they can also increase them.

---

[1]U.S. Bureau of the Census, *Statistical Abstract of the United States: 2001*, 121th ed. (Washington, DC: 2001), pp. 623, 644, and 657.

Application

Auto repair shops are faced with maintaining thousands of repair parts for a variety of automobiles from different model years. An automobile can contain 15,000 parts. To provide the fastest turnaround, repair shops carry a limited inventory of the more popular parts such as spark plugs, fan belts, and batteries. The auto manufacturer maintains a second inventory tier in regional warehouses from which parts can be transported using airfreight. The repair shops can, in some cases, receive these parts the same day they are requested. A high level of parts availability can be achieved with a minimum of on-site inventory.

Reduce Costs

Although holding inventories has an associated cost, their use can indirectly reduce operating costs in other supply channel activities that may more than offset the inventory carrying cost. First, holding inventories may encourage economies of production by allowing larger, longer, and more level production runs. Production output can be decoupled from the variation in demand requirements when inventories exist to act as buffers between the two.

Second, holding inventories fosters economies in purchasing and transportation. A purchasing department may buy in quantities beyond the firm's immediate needs in order to realize price-quantity discounts. The cost of holding the excess quantities until they are needed is balanced with the price reduction that can be achieved. In a similar manner, transportation costs can often be reduced through shipping in larger quantities that require less handling per unit. However, increasing the shipment size causes increased inventory levels that need to be maintained at *both* ends of the transportation channel. The reduction in transportation costs justifies the carrying of an inventory.

Third, forward buying involves purchasing additional product quantities at lower current prices rather than at higher anticipated future prices. Buying in quantities greater than immediate needs causes a larger inventory than does purchasing in quantities that more closely match immediate requirements. However, if prices are expected to rise in the future, some inventory resulting from forward buying can be justified.

Fourth, variability in the time that it takes to produce and transport goods throughout the supply channel can cause uncertainties that impact on operating costs as well as customer service levels. Inventories are frequently used at many points in the channel to buffer the effects of this variability and, thereby, help to smooth operations.

Fifth, unplanned and unanticipated shocks can befall the logistics system. Labor strikes, natural disasters, surges in demand, and delays in supplies are the types of contingencies against which inventories can afford some protection. Having some inventory at key points throughout the supply channel allows the system to operate for a period while the effect of the shock can be diminished.

Application

Papermaking requires expensive Fourdrinier machines and other pieces of equipment that have large capacities. The high fixed cost of this equipment dictates that it constantly be kept busy. Demand for industrial paper products (e.g., kraft wrapping papers, multiwall bags, and bulk products) is anything but stable and known for sure. Although large orders can be scheduled directly to the process, production of small orders would be too costly, considering that changeovers can take 30 minutes on machines costing $3,500 per hour to operate. Producing to an inventory and servicing the small-order demand for the more standardized products from that inventory reduces setup time, which more than compensates for the inventory-carrying cost.

Arguments Against Inventories

It has been claimed that management's job is much easier having the security of inventories. Being overstocked is much more defensible from criticism than being short of supplies. The major portion of inventory-carrying costs is of an opportunity cost nature and, therefore, goes unidentified in normal accounting reports. To the extent that inventory levels have been too high for the reasonable support of operations, the criticism is perhaps deserved.

Critics have challenged the holding of inventories along several lines. First, inventories are considered wasteful. They absorb capital that might otherwise be put to better use, such as to improve productivity or competitiveness. In addition, they do not contribute any direct value to the firm's products, although they do store value.

Second, they can mask quality problems. When quality problems occur, reducing existing inventories to protect the capital investment is often a first consideration. Correcting quality problems can be slow.

Finally, using inventories promotes an insular attitude about the management of the supply channel as a whole. With inventories, it is often possible to isolate one stage of the channel from another. The opportunities arising from integrated decision making that considers the entire channel are not encouraged. Without inventories, it is difficult to avoid planning and coordinating across several echelons of the channel at one time.

TYPES OF INVENTORIES

Inventories can be categorized in five distinct forms. First, inventories may be in the *pipeline*. These are inventories in transit between echelons of the supply channel. Where movement is slow and/or over long distances, or movement must take place between many echelons, the amount of inventory in the pipeline may well exceed that held at the stocking points. Similarly, work-in-process inventories between manufacturing operations can be considered as inventories in the pipeline.

Second, some stocks may be held for *speculation*, but they are still part of the total inventory base that must be managed. Raw materials such as copper, gold, and silver are purchased as much for price speculation as they are to meet operating requirements. Where price speculation takes place for periods beyond the foreseeable needs of operations, such resulting inventories are probably more the concern of financial management than logistics management. However, when inventories are built up in anticipation of seasonal selling or occur due to forward buying activities, these inventories are likely to be the responsibility of logistics.

Third, stocks may be *regular* or *cyclical* in nature. These are the inventories necessary to meet the average demand during the time between successive replenishments. The amount of cycle stock is highly dependent on production lot sizes, economical shipment quantities, storage space limitations, replenishment lead times, price-quantity discount schedules, and inventory carrying costs.

Fourth, inventory may be created as a hedge against the variability in demand for the inventory and in replenishment lead time. This extra measure of inventory, or *safety* stock, is in addition to the regular stock that is needed to meet average demand and average lead-time conditions. Safety stock is determined from statistical procedures that deal with the random nature of the variability involved. The amount of safety stock maintained depends on the extent of the variability involved and the level of stock availability that is provided. Accurate forecasting is essential to minimizing safety stock levels. In fact, if lead time and demand could be predicted with 100 percent accuracy, no safety stock would be needed.

Finally, some of the inventory deteriorates, becomes out of date, or is lost or stolen when held for a time. Such inventory is referred to as *obsolete*, *dead*, or *shrinkage* stock. Where the products are of high value, perishable, or easily stolen, special precautions must be taken to minimize the amount of such stock.

CLASSIFYING INVENTORY MANAGEMENT PROBLEMS

Managing inventories involves a variety of problem types. Since managing inventories cannot be handled using a single solution method, we need to categorize the methods into several major groups. Inventory management using just-in-time methods will not be included in this grouping, since the technique is discussed in Chapter 10. With the remaining inventory management methods, we assume that the conditions of demand level and its variability, lead time and its variability, and inventory-related costs are known, and that we must do the best job of inventory control, given these conditions. In contrast, the just-in-time philosophy (supply directly to demand as it occurs) is to eliminate inventories by reducing the variability in demand and replenishment cycle time, reducing lot sizes, and forging strong relationships with a limited number of suppliers to ensure quality products and accurate order filling.

Nature of Demand

The nature of demand over time plays a significant role in determining how we treat the control of inventory levels. Several common types of demand patterns are shown in Figure 9-2. Perhaps the most common demand characteristic is for it to continue into the indefinite future. The demand pattern is referred to as *perpetual*. Although demand for most products rises and falls through their life cycles, many products have a selling life that is sufficiently long to be considered infinite for planning purposes. Even though brands turn over at the rate of 20 percent per year, a life cycle of three to five years can be long enough to justify treating them as having a perpetual demand pattern.

On the other hand, some products are highly seasonal or have a one-time, or *spike*, demand pattern. Inventories that are held to meet such a demand pattern usually cannot be sold off without deep price discounting. A single inventory replenishment order must be placed with little or no opportunity to reorder or return goods if demand has been inaccurately projected. Fashion clothing, Christmas trees, and political campaign buttons are examples of this type of demand pattern.

Similarly, demand may display a lumpy, or erratic, pattern. The demand may be perpetual, but there are periods of little or no demand followed by periods of high demand. The timing of lumpy demand is not as predictable as for seasonal demand, which usually occurs at the same time every year. Items in inventory are typically a mixture of lumpy and perpetual demand items. A reasonable test to separate these is to recognize that lumpy items have a high variance around their mean demand level. If the standard deviation of the demand distribution, or the forecast error, is greater than

Figure 9-2
Examples of
Common
Product Demand
Patterns

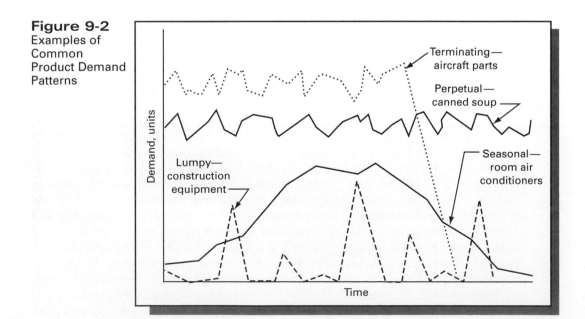

the average demand, or forecast, the item is probably lumpy. Inventory control of such items is best handled by intuitive procedures, or by a modification of the mathematical procedures discussed in this chapter, or through collaborative forecasting.

There are products whose demand terminates at some predictable time in the future, which is usually longer than one year. Inventory planning here involves maintaining inventories to just meet demand requirements, but some reordering within the limited time horizon is allowed. Textbooks with planned revisions, spare parts for military aircraft, and pharmaceuticals with a limited shelf life are examples of products with a defined life. Since the distinction between these products and those with a perpetual life is often blurred, they will not be treated differently from perpetual-life products for the purposes of developing a methodology to control them.

Finally, the demand pattern for an item may be derived from demand for some other item. The demand for packaging materials is derived from the demand for the primary product. The inventory control of such dependent demand items is best handled with some form of just-in-time planning such as MRP or DRP, which are discussed in Chapter 10.

Management Philosophy

Inventory management is developed around two basic philosophies. First, there is the *pull* approach. This philosophy views each stocking point, for example, a warehouse, as independent of all others in the channel. Forecasting demand and determining replenishment quantities are accomplished by taking into account only local conditions, as illustrated in Figure 9-3. No direct consideration is given to the effect

Figure 9-3
Pull Versus Push Inventory Management Philosophies

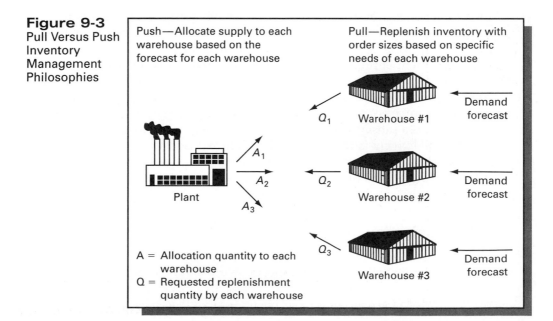

Push—Allocate supply to each warehouse based on the forecast for each warehouse

Pull—Replenish inventory with order sizes based on specific needs of each warehouse

Q_1 Warehouse #1   Demand forecast

A_1

A_2 Q_2 Warehouse #2   Demand forecast

Plant

A_3

Q_3 Warehouse #3   Demand forecast

A = Allocation quantity to each warehouse
Q = Requested replenishment quantity by each warehouse

that the replenishment quantities, each with their different levels and timing, will have on the economics of the sourcing plant. However, this approach does give precise control over inventory levels at each location. Pull methods are particularly popular at the retail level in the supply channel where over 60 percent of the hard goods and almost 40 percent of the soft goods are under replenishment programs.[2]

Alternatively, there is the *push* approach to inventory management (see Figure 9-3). When decisions about each inventory are made independently, the timing and replenishment order sizes are not necessarily well coordinated with production lot sizes, economical purchase quantities, or order size minimums. Therefore, many firms choose to allocate replenishment quantities to inventories based on projected needs for inventories at each location, available space, or some other criteria. Inventory levels are set collectively across the entire warehousing system. Typically, the push method is used when purchasing or production economies of scale outweigh the benefits of minimum collective inventory levels as achieved by the pull method. In addition, inventories can be managed centrally for better overall control, production and purchase economies can be used to dictate inventory levels for lower costs, and forecasting can be made on aggregate demand and then apportioned to each stocking point for improved accuracy.

Collaborative replenishment can be used as a hybrid of the pull and push methods. In this case, the channel members representing the source point and the stocking point jointly agree on the replenishment quantities and their timing. The result can be order replenishment that is more economical for the supply channel than if either party alone were to make the replenishment decision.

Degree of Product Aggregation

Much of inventory control is directed at controlling each item in inventory. Precise control of each item can lead to precise control of the sum of all item inventory levels. This is a bottoms-up approach to inventory management.

Management of product groups rather than individual items is an alternate, or top-down, approach—a common perspective of top management. Although daily operation of inventories may require item-level control, strategic planning of inventory levels can be accomplished by substantially aggregating products into broad groups. This is a satisfactory approach when managing the inventory investment of all items collectively is the issue, and the effort associated with an item-by-item analysis for thousands of items at many locations is not warranted. Methods of control tend to be less precise for aggregate inventory management than for item management.

Multi-Echelon Inventories

As supply chain management has encouraged managers to think about including increasingly more of the supply channel in their planning processes, inventories that

---

[2]Tom Andel, "Manage Inventory, Own Information," *Transportation & Distribution* (May 1996), p. 54ff.

span more than one channel echelon become a focus. Rather than planning inventories at each location separately, planning their levels in concert can lead to lower overall inventory quantities. Multi-echelon inventory planning has been a particularly difficult problem to solve, but some progress is being made in methods useful to managers.

Virtual Inventories

Historically, customers have been served from inventories to which they were assigned. If product was out of stock, either a sale was lost or the product was placed on back order. Improved information systems changed that. It became possible for firms to know product inventory levels at every stocking point in the logistics network, creating a virtual inventory of products. Because of this, out-of-stock items could be replaced by cross filling them from other locations. Satisfying demand when cross filling is an option can result in lower overall inventory levels and higher product fill rates.

INVENTORY OBJECTIVES

Inventory management involves balancing product availability, or customer service, on the one hand with the costs of providing a given level of product availability on the other. Since there may be more than one way of meeting the customer service target, we seek to minimize inventory-related costs for each level of customer service (see Figure 9-4). Let us begin the development of the methodology to control inventories with a way to define product availability and an identification of the costs relevant to managing inventory levels.

Figure 9-4
Design Curves for
Inventory Planning

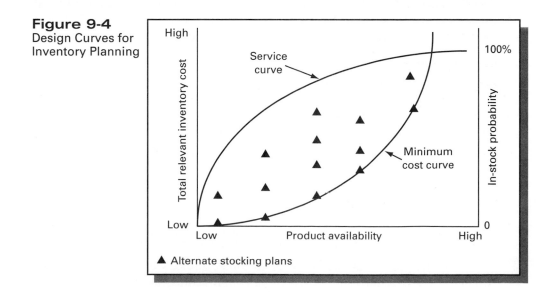

Product Availability

A primary objective of inventory management is to ensure that product is available at the time and in the quantities desired. This is commonly judged based on the probability of fulfillment capability from current stock. This probability, or item fill rate, is referred to as the service level, and, for a single item, can be defined as

$$\text{Service level } = 1 - \frac{\text{Expected number of units out of stock annually}}{\text{Total annual demand}} \qquad \textbf{(9-1)}$$

Service level is expressed as a value between 0 and 1. Since a target service level is typically specified, our task will be to control the expected number of stock out units.

We will see that controlling the service level for single items is computationally convenient. However, customers frequently request more than one item at a time. Therefore, the probability of filling the customer order completely can be of greater concern than single-item service levels. For example, suppose that five items are requested on an order where each item has a fill rate of 0.95, that is, only a 5 percent chance of not being in stock. Filling the entire order without any item being out of stock would be

$$0.95 \times 0.95 \times 0.95 \times 0.95 \times 0.95 = 0.77$$

The probability of filling the order completely is somewhat less than the individual item probabilities.

A number of orders from many customers will show that a mixture of items can appear on any one order. The service level is then more properly expressed as a *weighted average fill rate (WAFR)*. The WAFR is found by multiplying the frequency with which each combination of items appears on the order by the probability of filling the order completely, given the number of items on the order. If a target WAFR is specified, then the fill rates for each item must be adjusted to achieve this desired WAFR.

Example

A specialty chemical company receives orders for one of its paint products. The paint product line contains three separate items that customers order in various combinations. From a sampling of orders over time, the items appear on orders in seven different combinations with frequencies as noted in Table 9-1. Also from the company's historical records, the probability of having each item in stock is $SL_A = 0.95$; $SL_B = 0.90$; and $SL_C = 0.80$. As the calculations in Table 9-1 show, the WAFR is 0.801. There will be about one order in five where the company cannot supply all items at the time of the customer request.

Recall that additional measures for customer service were discussed in Chapter 4. Some of these measures encompass more than inventory and are not appropriate for

Item Combination on Order	(1) Frequency of Order	(2) Probability of Filling Order Complete	(3) = (1) × (2) Marginal Value
A	0.1	(.95) = 0.950	0.095
B	0.1	(.90) = 0.900	0.090
C	0.2	(.80) = 0.800	0.160
A, B	0.2	(.95)(.90) = 0.855	0.171
A, C	0.1	(.95)(.80) = 0.760	0.076
B, C	0.1	(.90)(.80) = 0.720	0.072
A, B, C	0.2	(.95)(.90)(.80) = 0.684	0.137
	1.0	WAFR =	0.801

Table 9-1   Computation of the Weighted Average Fill Rate

the discussion here. However, additional inventory performance measures might include percent of items on back order, percent of orders filled complete, percent of orders filled complete to a given percentage, and percent of items cross filled from secondary locations. These are not discussed further.

Relevant Costs

Three general classes of costs are important to determining inventory policy: procurement costs, carrying costs, and stockout costs. These costs are in conflict, or in trade-off, with each other. For determining the order quantity to replenish an item in inventory, these relevant costs trade-off are shown in Figure 9-5.

Figure 9-5
Trade-Off of the
Relevant Inventory
Costs with the Order
Quantity

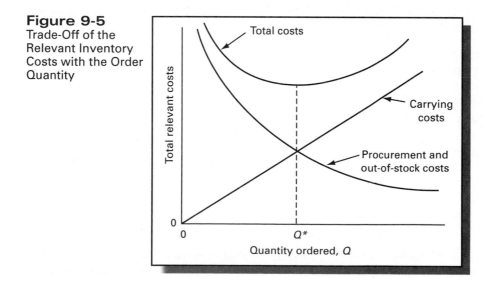

Procurement Costs

Costs associated with the acquisition of goods for the inventory replenishment are often a significant economic force that determines the reorder quantities. When a stock replenishment order is placed, a number of costs are incurred that are related to the processing, setup, transmitting, handling, and purchase of the order. More specifically, procurement costs may include the price, or manufacturing cost, of the product for various order sizes; the cost for setting up the production process; the cost of processing an order through the accounting and purchasing departments; the cost of transmitting the order to the supply point, usually using mail or electronic means; the cost of transporting the order when transportation charges are not included in the price of the purchased goods; and the cost of any materials handling or processing of the goods at the receiving point. When the firm is self-supplied, as in the case of a factory replenishing its own finished goods inventories, procurement costs are altered to reflect production setup costs. Transportation costs may not be relevant if a delivered pricing policy is in effect.

Some of these procurement costs are fixed per order and do not vary with the order size. Others, such as transportation, manufacturing, and materials-handling costs, vary to a degree with order size. Each requires slightly different analytical treatment.

Carrying Costs

Inventory carrying costs result from storing, or holding, goods for a period and are roughly proportional to the average quantity of goods on hand. These costs can be collected into four classes: space costs, capital costs, inventory service costs, and inventory risk costs.

Space Costs. Space costs are charges made for the use of the volume inside the storage building. When the space is rented, storage rates are typically charged by weight for a period of time, for example, $/cwt./month. If the space is privately owned or contracted, space costs are determined by allocating space-related operating costs, such as heat and light, as well as fixed costs, such as building and storage equipment costs, on a volume-stored basis. Space costs are irrelevant when calculating carrying costs for in-transit inventories.

Capital Costs. Capital costs refer to the cost of the money tied up in inventory. This cost may represent over 80 percent of total inventory cost (see Table 9-2), yet it is the most intangible and subjective of all the carrying cost elements. There are two reasons for this. First, inventory represents a mixture of short-term and long-term assets, as some stocks may serve seasonal needs and others are held to meet longer-term demand patterns. Second, the cost of capital may vary from the prime rate of interest to the opportunity cost of capital.

The exact cost of capital for inventory purposes has been debated for some time. Many firms use their average cost of capital, whereas others use the average rate of return required of company investments. The hurdle rate has been suggested as most accurately reflecting the true capital cost.[3] The hurdle rate is the rate of return on the most lucrative investments that the firm does not accept.

---

[3]Douglas M. Lambert and Bernard J. LaLonde, "Inventory Carrying Costs," *Management Accounting* (August 1976), pp. 31–35.

Table 9-2

Relative Percentages of Cost Elements in Inventory Carrying Costs

Interest and opportunity costs	82.00%
Obsolescence and physical depreciation	14.00
Storage and handling	3.25
Property taxes	0.50
Insurance	0.25
Total	100.00%

Source: Adapted from Robert Landeros and David M. Lyth, "Economic-Lot-Size Models for Cooperative Inter-Organizational Relationships," *Journal of Business Logistics*, Vol. 10, No. 2 (1989), p. 149.

Inventory Service Costs.   Insurance and taxes are also a part of inventory carrying costs because their level roughly depends on the amount of inventory on hand. Insurance coverage is carried as a protection against losses from fire, storm, or theft. Inventory taxes are levied on the inventory levels found on the day of assessment. Although the inventory at the point in time of the tax assessment only crudely reflects the average inventory level experienced throughout the year, taxes typically represent only a small portion of total carrying cost. Tax rates are readily available from accounting or public records.

Inventory Risk Costs.   Costs associated with deterioration, shrinkage (theft), damage, or obsolescence make up the final category of carrying costs. In the course of maintaining inventories, a certain portion of the stock will become contaminated, damaged, spoiled, pilfered, or otherwise unfit or unavailable for sale. The costs associated with such stock may be estimated as the direct loss of product value, as the cost of reworking the product, or as the cost of supplying it from a secondary location.

Out-of-Stock Costs

Out-of-stock costs are incurred when an order is placed but cannot be filled from the inventory to which the order is normally assigned. There are two kinds of out-of-stock costs: lost sales costs and back order costs. Each presupposes certain actions on the part of the customer, and, because of their intangible nature, they are difficult to measure accurately.

A *lost sales cost* occurs when the customer, faced with an out-of-stock situation, chooses to withdraw his or her request for the product. The cost is the profit that would have been made on this particular sale and may include an additional cost for the negative effect that the stockout may have on future sales. Products for which the customer is very willing to substitute competing brands, such as bread, gasoline, or soft drinks, are those that are most likely to incur lost sales.

A *back order cost* occurs when a customer will wait for his or her order to be filled so that the sale is not lost, only delayed. Back orders can create additional clerical and sales costs for order processing, and additional transportation and handling costs when such orders are not filled through the normal distribution channel. These costs are tangible, so measurement of them is not too difficult. There also may be the intangible cost of lost future sales. This cost is very difficult to measure. Products (automobiles and major appliances) that can be differentiated in the consumer's mind are more likely to be back ordered than substituted.

PUSH INVENTORY CONTROL

Let's begin to develop methods for controlling inventory levels with the *push* philosophy. Recall that this method is appropriate where production or purchase quantities exceed the short-term requirements of the inventories into which the quantities are to be shipped. If these quantities cannot be stored at the production site for lack of space or other reasons, then they must be allocated to the stocking points, hopefully in some way that makes good economic sense. Push is also a reasonable approach to inventory control where production or purchasing is the dominant force in determining the replenishment quantities in the channel. In either case, the following questions need to be addressed. How much inventory should be maintained at each stocking point? How much of a purchase order or production run should be allocated to each stocking point? How should the excess supply over requirements be apportioned among the stocking points?

A method for pushing quantities into stocking points involves the following steps:

1. Determine through forecasting or other means the requirements for the period between now and the next expected production run or vendor purchase.
2. Find the current on-hand quantities at each stocking point.
3. Establish the stock availability level at each stocking point.
4. Calculate total requirements from the forecast plus additional quantities needed to cover uncertainty in the demand forecast.
5. Determine net requirements as the difference between total requirements and the quantities on hand.
6. Apportion the excess over total net requirements to the stocking points on the basis of the average demand rate, that is, the forecasted demand.
7. Sum the net requirements and prorate the excess quantities to find the amount to be allocated to each stocking point.

Example

When the tuna boats are sent to the fishing grounds, a packer of tuna products must process all the tuna caught since storage is limited and, for competitive reasons, the company does not want to sell the excess of this valued product to other packers. Therefore, this packer processes all fish brought in by the fleet and then allocates the production to its three field warehouses on a monthly basis. There is only enough storage at the plant for one month's demand. The current production run is 125,000 lb.

For the upcoming month, the needs of each warehouse were forecasted, the current stock levels checked, and desired stock availability level noted for each warehouse. The findings are tabulated in Table 9-3.

WAREHOUSE	CURRENT STOCK LEVEL	FORECASTED DEMAND	FORECAST ERROR[a] (STD. DEV.)	STOCK AVAILABILITY LEVEL[b]
1	5,000 lb	10,000 lb	2,000 lb	90%
2	15,000	50,000	1,500	95%
3	30,000	70,000	20,000	90%
		130,000		

[a]Assumed to be normally distributed.
[b]Stock availability level is defined as the probability of stock being available during the forecast period.

Table 9-3 Basic Inventory Planning Data for a Tuna Packer

Now we need to compute the total requirements for each warehouse. Total requirements for warehouse 1 will be the forecast quantity and the added amount needed to ensure a 90 percent stock availability level. This is found from

$$\text{Total requirements} = \text{Forecast} + (z \times \text{Forecast error})$$

where z is the number of standard deviations on the normal distribution curve beyond the forecast (the distribution mean) to the point where 90 percent of the area under the curve is represented (see Figure 9-6). From the normal distribution curve in Appendix A, $z = 1.28$. Hence, the total requirement for warehouse 1 is 10,000 + (1.28 × 2,000) = 12,560. Other warehouse total requirements are computed similarly. The information is recorded in Table 9-4.

Net requirements are found as the difference between total requirements and the quantity on hand in the warehouse. Summing the net requirements (110,635) shows that 125,000 – 110,635 = 14,365, which is the excess production that needs to be prorated to the warehouses.

Figure 9-6
Area Under the
Forecast Distribution
for Warehouse 1

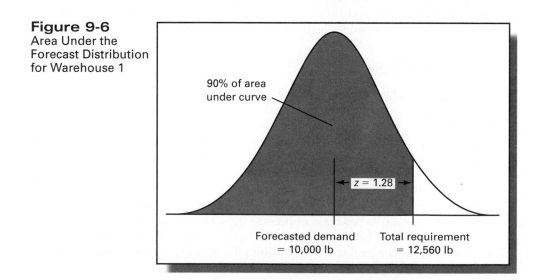

90% of area
under curve

$z = 1.28$

Forecasted demand
= 10,000 lb

Total requirement
= 12,560 lb

WAREHOUSE	(1) TOTAL REQUIREMENTS	(2) ON HAND	(3) = (1) – (2) NET REQUIREMENTS	(4) PRORATED EXCESS	(5) = (3) + (4) ALLOCATION
1	12,560 lb	5,000	7,560 lb	1,105 lb	8,665 lb
2	52,475	15,000	37,475	5,525	43,000
3	95,600	30,000	65,600	7,735	73,335
	160,635		110,635	14,365	125,000

Table 9-4 Allocation of Tuna Production to Three Warehouses

Prorating the excess production of 14,365 lb is made in proportion to the average demand rate for each warehouse. Average demand for warehouse 1 is 10,000 lb against a total demand rate for all warehouses of 130,000 lb. The proportion of the excess allocated to warehouse 1 should be $(10,000 \div 130,000)(14,365) = 1,105$. Prorate the excess for the remaining warehouses in a similar manner. The total allocation to a warehouse is the sum of its net requirement plus its portion of the production excess. The results are tabulated in Table 9-4.

BASIC PULL INVENTORY CONTROL

Recall that pull inventory control gives low inventory levels at stocking points because of its response to the demand and cost conditions particular to each stocking point. Although many specific methods have been developed to handle a variety of situations, the discussion here will attempt to highlight the fundamental ideas. Specifically, a contrast will be made between (1) demand that is one-time, highly seasonal, or perpetual; (2) ordering that is triggered from a particular inventory level or from a process of inventory level review; and (3) the degree of uncertainty in demand and replenishment lead time.

Single-Order Quantity

Many practical inventory problems exist where the products involved are perishable or the demand for them is a one-time event. Products such as fresh fruits and vegetables, cut flowers, newspapers, and some pharmaceuticals have a short and defined shelf life, and they are not available for subsequent selling periods. Others, such as toys and fashion clothes for the immediate selling season, hotdog buns for a baseball game, and posters for a political campaign, have a one-time demand level that usually cannot be estimated with certainty. Only one order can be placed for these products to meet such demand. We wish to determine how large the single order should be.

To find the most economic order size (Q^*), we can appeal to marginal economic analysis. That is, Q^* is found at the point where the marginal profit on the next unit sold equals the marginal loss of not selling the next unit. The marginal profit per unit obtained by selling a unit is

$$\text{Profit} = \text{Price per unit} - \text{Cost per unit} \qquad \textbf{(9-2)}$$

The per-unit loss incurred by not selling a unit is

$$\text{Loss} = \text{Cost per unit} - \text{Salvage value per unit} \qquad \textbf{(9-3)}$$

Considering the probability of a given number of units being sold, the expected profits and losses are balanced at this point. That is,

$$CP_n(\text{Loss}) = (1 - CP_n)(\text{Profit}) \qquad \textbf{(9-4)}$$

where CP_n represents the cumulative frequency of selling at least n units of the product. Solving the above expression for CP_n, we have

$$CP_n = \frac{\text{Profit}}{\text{Profit} + \text{Loss}} \qquad \textbf{(9-5)}$$

This says that we should continue to increase the order quantity until the cumulative probability of selling additional units just equals the ratio of Profit ÷ (Profit + Loss).

Example

A grocery store estimates that it will sell 100 pounds of its specially prepared potato salad in the next week. The demand distribution is normally distributed with a standard deviation of 20 pounds. The supermarket can sell the salad for $5.99 per pound. It pays $2.50 per pound for the ingredients. Since no preservatives are used, any unsold salad is given to charity at no cost.

Finding the quantity to prepare that will maximize profit requires that we first compute CP_n. That is,

$$CP_n = \frac{\text{Profit}}{\text{Profit} + \text{Loss}} = \frac{(5.99 - 2.50)}{(5.99 - 2.50) + 2.50} = 0.583$$

From the normal distribution curve (Appendix A), the optimum Q^* is at the point of 58.3 percent of the area under the curve (see Figure 9-7). This is a point where $z = 0.21$. The salad preparation quantity should be

$$Q^* = 100 \text{ lb} + 0.21(20 \text{ lb}) = 104.2 \text{ lb}$$

When demand is discrete, the order quantity may be between whole values. In such cases, we will round up Q to the next higher unit to ensure that at least CP_n is met.

Example

An equipment repair firm wishes to order enough spare parts to keep a machine tool running throughout a trade show. The repairperson prices the parts at $95 each if

Figure 9-7
Normally Distributed
Demand for Potato
Salad Problem

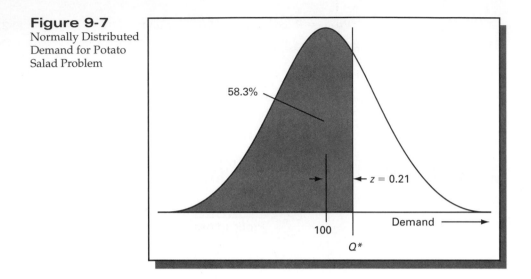

needed for a repair. He pays $70 for each part. If all the parts are not needed, they may be returned to the supplier for a credit of $50 each. The demand for the parts is estimated according to the following distribution:

Number of Parts	Frequency of Need	Cumulative Frequency
0	0.10	0.10
1	0.15	0.25
2	0.20	0.45
3	0.30	0.75 $\Leftarrow Q^*$
4	0.20	0.95
5	0.05	1.00
	1.00	

We should set the order quantity at

$$CP_n = \frac{\text{Profit}}{\text{Profit} + \text{Loss}} = \frac{(95 - 70)}{(95 - 70) + (70 - 50)} = 0.555$$

The CP_n value is between 2 and 3 units on the cumulative frequency column. Rounding up, we choose $Q^* = 3$.

Repetitive Order Quantities

In contrast to demand that occurs only periodically or possibly only once, demand may be perpetual. Inventory replenishment orders repeat over time and may be supplied instantaneously in their entirety, or the items in the orders may be supplied over time. Both cases are illustrated.

Instantaneous Resupply

When demand is continuous and the rate is essentially constant, controlling inventory levels is accomplished by specifying (1) the quantity that will be used to replenish the inventory on a periodic basis and (2) the inventory replenishment frequency. This is a problem of balancing conflicting cost patterns. In the simplest case, it requires balancing procurement costs against carrying costs, as was shown in Figure 9-5. Ford Harris recognized this problem as early as 1913 in his work at Westinghouse. The model that he developed for finding the optimum order quantity has become known as the basic *economic order quantity (EOQ)* formula,[4] and it serves as the basis for many of the pull inventory policies currently used in practice.

The basic *EOQ* formula is developed from a total cost equation involving procurement cost and inventory carrying cost. It is expressed as

$$\text{Total cost} = \text{Procurement cost} + \text{Carrying cost}$$

$$TC = \frac{D}{Q}S + \frac{ICQ}{2} \tag{9-6}$$

where

TC = total annual relevant inventory cost, dollars
Q = order size to replenish inventory, units
D = Item annual demand occurring at a certain and constant rate over time, units/year
S = Procurement cost, dollars/order
C = Item value carried in inventory, dollar/unit
I = carrying cost as a percent of item value, percent/year

The term D/Q represents the number of times per year a replenishment order is placed on its supply source. The term $Q/2$ is the average amount of inventory on hand.

As Q varies in size, one cost goes up as the other goes down. It can be shown mathematically that an optimal order quantity (Q^*) exists where the two costs are in balance and the minimal total cost results. The formula for this *EOQ* is

$$Q^* = \sqrt{\frac{2DS}{IC}} \tag{9-7}$$

The optimal time between orders is therefore

$$T^* = \frac{Q^*}{D} \tag{9-8}$$

and the optimal number of times per year to place an order is

$$N = \frac{D}{Q^*} \tag{9-9}$$

---

[4]F. W. Harris, "How Many Parts to Make at Once," *Factory, The Magazine of Management*, Vol. 10, No. 2 (February 1913), pp. 135–136, 152.

Example

An industrial machine tools manufacturer supplies replacement parts from its inventory. For a particular part, the annual demand is expected to be 750 units. Machine setup costs are $50, carrying costs are 25 percent per year, and the part is valued in inventory at $35 each. The economic order quantity placed on production is

$$Q^* = \sqrt{\frac{2DS}{IC}} = \sqrt{\frac{2(750)(50)}{(0.25)(35)}} = 92.58 \text{ or } 93 \text{ units}$$

This order size is expected to be placed in production every $T^* = Q^*/D = 92.58/750 = 0.12$ years, or 0.12 (years) $\times$ 52 (weeks per year) = 6.4 weeks. For practical reasons, we may wish to round this to 6 or 7 weeks with some slight increase in total costs.

A Lead Time for Resupply

Using this formula as part of a basic inventory control procedure, we see that a sawtooth pattern of inventory depletion and replenishment occurs, as illustrated in Figure 9-8. We can now introduce the idea of a *reorder point*, which is the quantity to which inventory is allowed to drop before a replacement order is placed. Since there is generally a time lapse between when the order is placed and when the items are

Figure 9-8 A Basic Pull Inventory Control Model for a Replenishment Part

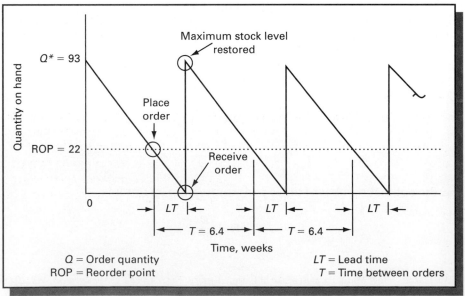

available in inventory, the demand that occurs over this lead time must be anticipated. The reorder point (ROP) is

$$ROP = d \times LT \qquad \text{(9-10)}$$

where

$ROP =$ reorder point quantity, units

$d =$ demand rate, in time units

$LT =$ average lead time, in time units

The demand rate (*d*) and the average lead time (*LT*) must be expressed in the same time dimension.

Example

Continuing the previous machine replacement part example, suppose that it takes 1.5 weeks to set up production and make the parts. The demand rate is $d = 750$ (units per year)/52 (weeks per year) = 14.42 units per week. Therefore, $ROP = 14.42 \times 1.5 = 21.6$, or 22 units. We can now state the inventory policy: When the inventory level drops to 22 units, place a replenishment order for 93 units.

Sensitivity to Data Inaccuracies

Demand and costs cannot always be known for sure. However, our computation of the economic order quantity is not very sensitive to incorrect data estimations. For example, if demand is in fact 10 percent higher than anticipated, Q^* should only be increased by $\sqrt{1.10} = 4.88$ percent. If the carrying cost is 20 percent lower than assumed, Q^* should be increased by only $\sqrt{1 / (1 - 0.20)} = 11.8$ percent. These percentage changes are inserted into the *EOQ* formula without changing the remaining cost and/or demand factors since they remain constant. Notice the stability of the Q^* values. If the incorrect order quantity were used in these two cases, total costs would have been in error by only 0.11 percent and 0.62 percent, respectively.

Noninstantaneous Resupply

A built-in assumption of Ford Harris's original *EOQ* formula was that resupply would be made instantaneously in a single batch of size Q^*. In some manufacturing and resupply processes, output is continuous for a time, and it may take place simultaneously with demand. The basic sawtooth pattern of on-hand inventory is modified, as shown in Figure 9-9. The order quantity now becomes the production run, or production lot size, quantity (POQ) labeled Q_p^*. To find Q_p^*, the basic order quantity formula is modified as follows:

$$Q_p^* = \sqrt{\frac{2DS}{IC}} \sqrt{\frac{p}{p - d}} \qquad \text{(9-11)}$$

where *p* is the output rate. Computing Q_p^* only makes sense when the output rate *p* exceeds the demand rate *d*.

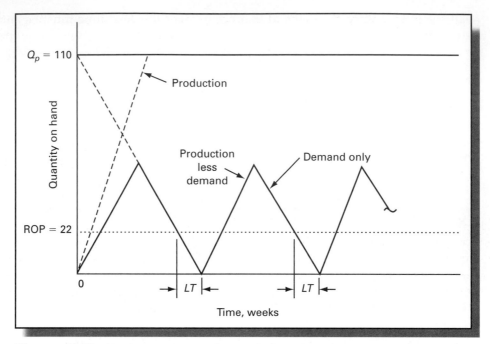

Figure 9-9 Noninstantaneous Resupply for a Parts Replacement Problem

Example

Again, for the previous parts replacement problem, suppose that the production rate for these parts is 50 units per week. The production run quantity is

$$Q_p^* = \sqrt{\frac{2(70)(50)}{(0.25)(35)}} \sqrt{\frac{50}{50 - 14.42}}$$

$$= 92.5 \times 1.185 = 109.74, \text{ or } 110 \text{ units}$$

The *ROP* quantity remains unchanged.

ADVANCED PULL INVENTORY CONTROL

Advanced pull control of inventories means that we recognize that demand and lead time cannot be known for sure. Therefore, we must plan for the situation where not enough stock may be on hand to fill customer requests. In addition to the regular stock that is maintained for meeting average demand and average lead time, an incremental quantity is added to inventory. The amount of this safety, or buffer, stock sets the level of stock availability provided to customers by controlling the probability of a stockout occurring.

Two inventory control methods form the foundation for most pull-type management philosophies with perpetual demand patterns. These are (1) the reorder point method and (2) the period review method. Practical control systems may be based on either of these methods or on a combination of them.

A Reorder Point Model with Uncertain Demand

Finding Q* and ROP

Reorder point inventory control assumes that demand is perpetual and continually acts on inventory to reduce its level. When inventory is depleted to the point where its level is equal to or less than a specified quantity called the reorder point, an economic order quantity of Q^* is placed on the supplying source to replenish the inventory. The effective inventory level at a particular point in time is the quantity on hand plus the quantity on order, less any commitments against the inventory, such as customer back orders or allocations to production or customers. The entire quantity Q^* arrives at a point in time offset by the lead time. Between the time when the replenishment order is placed at the reorder point and when it arrives in stock, there is a risk that demand will exceed the remaining amount of inventory. The probability of this occurring is controlled through raising or lowering the reorder point and by adjusting Q^*.

In Figure 9-10, the operation of the reorder point system is illustrated for a single item where the demand during the lead time is known only to the extent of a normal probability distribution. This demand during lead time (DDLT) distribution has a mean of X' and a standard deviation of s_d'. The values for X' and s_d' are usually not

Figure 9-10 Reorder Point Inventory Control Under Uncertainty for Item

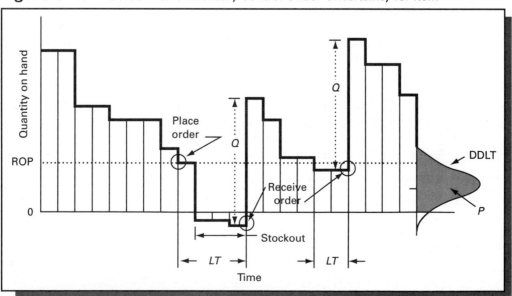

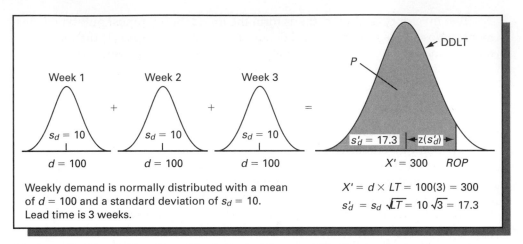

Figure 9-11   Rolling Up a Single Period Demand Distribution into a Demand During Lead Time (DDLT) Frequency Distribution

known directly, but they can be easily estimated by summing a single period demand distribution over the length of the lead time. For example, suppose weekly demand for an item is normally distributed with a mean $d = 100$ units and a standard deviation of $s'_d = 10$ units. Lead time is three weeks. We wish to roll up the weekly demand distribution into one 3-week DDLT demand distribution (see Figure 9-11). The mean of the DDLT distribution is simply the demand rate d times the lead time LT, or $X' = d \times LT = 100 \times 3 = 300$. The variance of DDLT distribution is found by adding the variances of the weekly demand distributions (see Figure 9-11). That is, $s'^2_d = LT(s_d^2)$. The standard deviation is the square root of s'^2_d, which is $s'^2_d = s_d\sqrt{LT} = 10\sqrt{3} = 17.3$.

Finding Q^* and the ROP is rather mathematically complex; however, a satisfactory approximation can be found if we first determine Q^* according to the basic EOQ formula (Equation 9-7).[5] Then, find

$$ROP = d \times LT + z(s'_d) \qquad \text{(9-12)}$$

The term z is the number of standard deviations from the mean of the DDLT distribution to give us the desired probability of being in stock during the lead time period (P). The value for z is found in a normal distribution table (Appendix A) for the area under the curve P.

Example

Buyers Products Company distributes an item known as a tie bar, which is a U-bolt used on truck equipment. The following data have been collected for this item held in inventory:

---

[5]Sven Axsäter, "Using the Deterministic EOQ Formula in Stochastic Inventory Control," *Management Science*, Vol. 42, No. 6 (June 1996), p. 830.

Monthly demand forecast, d	11,107 units
Std. error of forecast, s_d	3,099 units
Replenishment lead time, LT	1.5 months
Item value, C	$0.11/unit
Cost for processing vendor order, S	$10/order
Carrying cost, I	20%/year
In-stock probability during lead time, P	75%

The reorder quantity is

$$Q^* = \sqrt{\frac{2DS}{IC}} = \sqrt{\frac{2(11,107)(10)}{(0.20/12)(0.11)}} = 11,008 \text{ units}$$

The reorder point is

$$ROP = d \times LT + z(s_d')$$

where $s_d' = s_d\sqrt{LT} = 3,099\sqrt{1.5} = 3,795$ units . The value for z is 0.67 from Appendix A, where the fraction of the area under the normal distribution curve is 0.75. Thus,

$$ROP = (11,107 \times 1.5) + (0.67 \times 3,795) = 19,203 \text{ units}$$

So, when the effective inventory level drops to 19,203 units, place a replenishment order for 11,008 units.

It is common for the reorder point quantity to exceed the order quantity, as was the case in the previous example. This frequently happens when lead times are long or demand rates are high. For the reorder point control system to work properly, make sure that the timing of a replenishment order is based on the effective inventory level. Recall that the effective inventory level requires that all stock on order be added to the current quantity on hand when making a comparison to the reorder point. When $ROP > Q^*$, the result of this procedure is that a second order will be placed before the first arrives in stock.

Average Inventory Level
The average inventory level for this item is the total of the regular stock plus safety stock. That is,

$$\text{Average inventory} = \text{Regular stock} + \text{Safety stock}$$
$$AIL \qquad = \qquad Q/2 \qquad + \qquad z(s_d') \qquad \qquad \textbf{(9-13)}$$

Example

For the previous tie bar problem, the average inventory would be $AIL = (11,008/2) + (0.67 \times 3,795) = 8,047$ units

Total Relevant Cost

The total relevant cost is useful for comparing alternative inventory policies or determining the impact of deviations from optimum policies. We add two new terms to the total cost formula stated in Equation (9-6), which account for uncertainty. These are safety stock and out-of-stock terms. Total cost can now be expressed as

Total cost = Order cost + Carrying cost, regular stock
+ Carrying cost, safety stock + Stockout cost

$$TC = \frac{D}{Q}S + IC\frac{Q}{2} + ICzs'_d + \frac{D}{Q}ks'_dE_{(z)} \qquad \textbf{(9-14)}$$

where k is the stockout cost per unit. The stockout cost term requires some explanation. First, the combined term of $s'_d E_{(z)}$ represents the expected number of units out of stock during an order cycle. $E_{(z)}$ is called the unit normal loss integral whose values are tabled as a function of the normal deviate z (see Appendix B) Second, the term D/Q is the number of order cycles per period of time, usually a year. Hence, the number of order cycles times the expected number of units out of stock during each order cycle gives the total expected number of units out of stock for the entire period. Then, multiplying by the out-of-stock cost yields the total period cost.

Example

Continuing the tie bar example, suppose the stockout cost is estimated at $0.01 per unit. The total annual cost for the item would be

$$TC = \frac{11,107(12)10}{11,008} + 0.20(0.11)\left(\frac{11,008}{2}\right)$$
$$+0.20(0.11)(0.67)(3,795) + \frac{11,107(12)}{11,008}(0.01)(3,795)(0.150)$$
$$= 121.08 + 121.09 + 55.94 + 68.92 = \$367.03 \text{ per year}$$

Note: The value of 0.150 for $E_{(z)} = E_{(0.67)}$ is from the body of the table in Appendix B for $z = 0.67$.

Service Level

The customer service level, or item fill rate, achieved by a particular inventory policy was previously defined in Equation (9-1). Restating it in the symbols now being used, we have

$$SL = 1 - \frac{(D/Q)(s'_d \times E_{(z)})}{D} = 1 - \frac{s'_d(E_{(z)})}{Q} \qquad \textbf{(9-15)}$$

Example

The service level achieved for the tie bar problem is

$$SL = 1 - \frac{3,795(0.150)}{11,008} = 0.948$$

That is, the demand for tie bars can be met 94.8 percent of the time. Note that this is somewhat higher than the probability of a stockout during the lead time of $P = 0.75$.

Application

A manufacturer of quick-connect hose couplings uses an easy method for implementing a reorder point method of inventory control. A finished goods inventory is maintained at the factory from which customer orders are filled. The stock is divided into two sections. An amount of an item equal to the reorder point quantity is placed in a covered tray in the reserve section of the stocking area. A second tray contains the remainder of the stock. All orders are filled from the second tray first. When all stock is depleted from the second tray, the first tray is brought from reserve storage and inserted into its position. This action is the trigger to place a replenishment order on production. Little or no paperwork is needed to make a rather sophisticated inventory control system operate effectively.

The Reorder Point Method with Known Stockout Costs

When the stockout costs are known, it is not necessary to assign a customer service level. The optimum balance between service and cost can be calculated. An iterative computational procedure is outlined as follows:

1. Approximate the order quantity from the basic *EOQ* formula [Equation (9-7)] that is,

$$Q = \sqrt{\frac{2DS}{IC}}$$

2. Compute the probability of being in stock during the lead-time if back ordering is allowed

$$P = 1 - \frac{QIC}{Dk} \tag{9-16}$$

or if during a stockout the sales are lost

$$P = 1 - \frac{QIC}{Dk + QIC} \tag{9-17}$$

Find s_d'. Find the z value that corresponds to P in the normal distribution table (Appendix A). Find $E_{(z)}$ from the unit normal loss integral table (Appendix B).

3. Determine a revised Q from a modified EOQ formula, which is

$$Q = \sqrt{\frac{2D[S + ks_d'E_{(z)}]}{IC}} \tag{9-18}$$

4. Repeat steps 2 and 3 until there is no change in P or Q. Continue.
5. Compute ROP and other statistics as desired.

Example

Repeating the tie bar example, with the known stockout cost of $0.01 per unit and back orders are allowed.

Estimate Q

$$Q = \sqrt{\frac{2DS}{IC}} = \sqrt{\frac{2(11,107)(12)(10)}{0.20(0.11)}} = 11,008 \text{ units}$$

Estimate P

$$P = 1 - \frac{QIC}{Dk} = 1 - \frac{11,008(0.20)(0.11)}{11,107(12)(0.01)} = 0.82$$

From Appendix A, $z_{@0.82} = 0.92$. From Appendix B, $E_{(0.92)} = 0.0968$.

Revise Q The standard deviation of DDLT was calculated previously to be $s_d' = 3,795$ units. Now,

$$Q = \sqrt{\frac{2D[S + ks_d'E_{(z)}]}{IC}} = \sqrt{\frac{2(11,107)(12)[(10 + 0.01(3,795)(0.068)]}{0.20(0.11)}} = 12,872 \text{ units}$$

Revise P

$$P = 1 - \frac{12,872(0.20)/(0.11)}{11,107(12)(0.01)} = 0.79$$

Now, $z_{@0.79} = 0.81$ and $E_{(0.81)} = 0.1181$

Revise Q

$$Q = \sqrt{\frac{2(11,107)(12)[10 + 0.01(3,795)(0.1181)]}{0.20(0.11)}} = 13,246 \text{ units}$$

We continue this revision process until the changes in P and Q are so small that further calculation is impractical. The results are $P = 0.78$, $Q^* = 13,395$ units, and $ROP = 19,583$ units, with a total relevant cost of $TC = \$15,019$ and an actual service level (item fill rate) of $SL = 96$ percent.

The Reorder Point Method with Demand and Lead Time Uncertainty

Accounting for uncertainty in the lead time can extend the realism of the reorder point model. What we wish to do is find the standard deviation (s'_d) of the DDLT distribution based on uncertainty in both demand and lead time. Adding the demand variance to the lead time variance gives a revised formula for s'_d, which is

$$s'_d = \sqrt{LTs_d^{\,2} + d^2 s_{LT}^{\,2}} \qquad \text{(9-19)}$$

where s_{LT} is the lead time standard deviation.[6]

Example

In the tie bar problem, s_{LT} is 0.5 months. The value for s'_d would now be

$$s'_d = \sqrt{1.5(3,099)^2 + 11,107^2(0.5)^2} = 6,727 \text{ units}$$

Combining demand and lead time variability in this way can greatly increase $s_{d'}$ and the resulting safety stock. Brown warns that demand and lead time distributions may be dependent on each other.[7] Rather, when a replenishment order is placed, a fair idea is known as to the lead time for that order. Therefore, application of Equation (9-19) may lead to an overstatement of s'_d and the resulting amount of safety stock. If lead times do vary unpredictably, Brown suggests the following precise procedure for determining the standard deviation of demand during lead time:

> Forecast demand per lead time. A lead time starts when you trigger a replenishment order. Record the demand year-to-date at that time. Later, whenever material is received is, by definition, the end of the lead-time. Examine the demand year-to-date. The difference between the current demand year-to-date and the value when the order was released is precisely, by definition, the demand during the lead time. The values of this variable can be forecasted (usually with very simple forecast models) and the mean square error is the variance of demand during lead time, precisely the value being sought.[8]

Alternately and less precisely, the longest lead time may be used as the average lead time with s_{LT} set at zero (0). The standard deviation is then computed as $s'_d = s_d \sqrt{LT}$.

---

[6]Note that if demand is known for sure ($s_d = 0$) and lead time is uncertain, then $s'_d = d s_{LT}$.
[7]Robert G. Brown, *Materials Management Systems* (New York: John Wiley & Sons, 1977), pp. 150–151.
[8]Ibid.

Figure 9-12
Multiple Time
Elements
Throughout a
Supply Channel

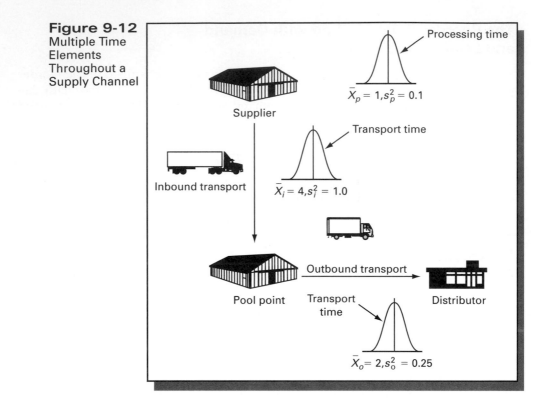

Processing time

$$\bar{X}_p = 1, s_p^2 = 0.1$$

Supplier

Transport time

$$\bar{X}_i = 4, s_i^2 = 1.0$$

Inbound transport

Outbound transport

Pool point   Transport
time

Distributor

$$\bar{X}_o = 2, s_o^2 = 0.25$$

Example

Suppose inventory is to be maintained on a distributor's shelf for an item whose demand is forecasted to be $d = 100$ units per day and $s_d = 10$ units per day. A reorder point is the method of inventory control. There are multiple points throughout the supply channel where time is incurred in the product flow between source point and customer. The distributions of these times that form the order replenishment lead time are shown in Figure 9-12. No significant amount of inventory is maintained at the pool point or in the trucks.

We also know that

$$I = 10\%/\text{year}$$
$$S = \$10/\text{order}$$
$$C = \$5/\text{unit}$$
$$P = 0.99$$

Determine the average inventory to be held at the distributor.

Solution   The reorder point inventory control method applies. However, determining the statistics of the demand-during-lead-time distribution requires taking the lead time for the *entire* channel into account.

Recall:

$$s_d' = \sqrt{LT s_d^2 + d^2 s_{LT}^2}$$

where from Figure 9-12

$$s_{LT}^2 = s_p^2 + s_i^2 + s_o^2 = 0.1 + 1.0 + 0.25 = 1.35 \text{ days}$$

and

$$LT = \overline{X}_p + \overline{X}_i + \overline{X}_o = 1 + 4 + 2 = 7 \text{ days}$$

Now,

$$s_d' = \sqrt{7 \times 10^2 + 100^2 \times 1.35} = \sqrt{14,200} = 119.16 \text{ units}$$

and

$$AIL = \frac{Q^*}{2} + z s_d'$$

where

$$Q^* = \sqrt{\frac{2(100)(10)}{0.1(5)}} = 63 \text{ units}$$

Finally, the average inventory level is

$$AIL = \frac{63}{2} + 2.33(119.16) = 309 \text{ units}$$

A Periodic Review Model with Uncertain Demand

An alternative to the reorder point method of control is the periodic review method. Although the reorder point method offers precise control over each item in inventory and, therefore, the lowest total relevant cost, it has some economic disadvantages. For example, each item is possibly ordered at a different time, thus missing joint production, transportation, or buying economies. Administratively, reorder point control requires constant monitoring of the inventory levels. Alternatively, under periodic review control, inventory levels for multiple items can be reviewed at the same time so that they may be ordered together, thus realizing production, transportation, or purchasing economies. Periodic review control results in slightly more inventory, but the added carrying costs may be more than offset by reduced administrative costs, lower prices, or lower procurement costs. Reasons for preferring a periodic review method can be summarized as follows:

1. A manual bookkeeping inventory system is used, and it is convenient to review inventory stocks on a definite schedule. This might be done on a *cycle count* basis, in which a portion of stock is reviewed each day or week, perhaps on an *ABC* basis (reordering *A* items more often than *B* items, etc). This also allows balancing of clerical workload.

2. A large number of items are to be jointly ordered from the same vendor sources.

3. Items ordered have a significant effect on the supplying plant's production output, and order predictability is desirable.

4. Significant transportation savings can sometimes result when several items are ordered at the same time.[9]

Single Item Control

The periodic review model is very similar to the reorder point model under uncertain demand conditions. However, one important difference in the periodic review model is that demand fluctuations during the order interval and the lead time must be protected against, whereas only demand fluctuations during the lead time are important in calculating safety stock using the reorder point method. This makes the periodic review model more complex to formulate precisely than the reorder point model, but an approximate solution will provide reasonable answers. Approximate solutions in inventory control are reasonable since the total cost curve usually has a flat bottom such that slight deviations from optimum values for the policy variables result in only small changes to the total cost.

Periodic review control operates as shown in Figure 9-13. That is, the inventory level for an item is audited at predetermined intervals (T). The quantity to be placed on order is the difference between a maximum quantity (M) and the amount on hand at the review time. Thus, inventory is controlled through the setting of T^* and M^*.

A good approximation for the optimum review interval begins with the basic inventory control model. That is,

$$Q^* = \sqrt{\frac{2DS}{IC}}$$

and the review interval is

$$T^* = \frac{\text{Order quantity}}{\text{Annual demand}} = \frac{Q^*}{D}$$

The order interval may also be assigned a particular value that best conforms to the practices of the firm. Of course, this does not necessarily assure an optimum policy.

Next, construct the distribution for demand over the order interval plus the lead time [$DD(T^* + LT)$], as shown in Figure 9-14. The point where the probability of a stockout during the protection period $(1 - P)$ equals the area under the normal distribution curve is the point of the maximum level (M^*). This point may be calculated as

$$M^* = d(T^* + LT) + z(s_d') \tag{9-20}$$

where $d(T^* + LT)$ is the mean of the $DD(T^* + LT)$ distribution, d is the average daily demand rate, and s_d' is the standard deviation of the $DD(T^* + LT)$ distribution. This standard deviation is now calculated as

---

[9]Lynn E. Gill, George Isoma, and Joel L. Sutherland, "Inventory and Physical Distribution Management," in James F. Robeson and Robert G. House (eds.), *The Distribution Handbook* (New York: The Free Press, 1985), p. 673.

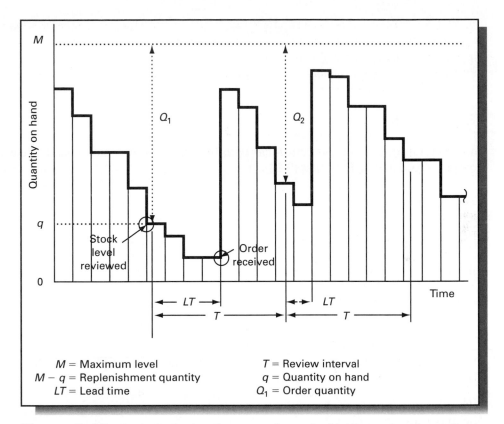

Figure 9-13 Periodic Review Inventory Control with Uncertainty for an Item

Where the labels within the figure read:

- M = Maximum level
- $M - q$ = Replenishment quantity
- LT = Lead time
- T = Review interval
- q = Quantity on hand
- Q_1 = Order quantity

Figure 9-14
A Distribution of Demand Over the Order Interval Plus Lead Time for the Periodic Review Inventory Control Method

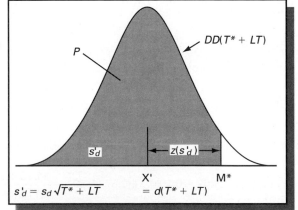

Labels within the figure:

P

$DD(T^* + LT)$

s'_d

$z(s'_d)$

X'
$= d(T^* + LT)$

M^*

$s'_d = s_d \sqrt{T^* + LT}$

$$s_d' = s_d\sqrt{T^* + LT} \tag{9-21}$$

where lead time is known for sure.

The average inventory level is found from

$$AIL = \frac{dT^*}{2} + z(s_d') \tag{9-22}$$

and the total relevant cost is computed with the same formula as under the reorder point method, that is, Equation (9-14).

Example

Let's use the tie bar problem data, but now develop a periodic review policy for it.

Find T^* and M^*   The optimal order quantity is the same as under the reorder point policy, or 11,008 units. The order interval is

$$T^* = \frac{Q^*}{d} = \frac{11,008}{11,107} = 0.991, \text{ or 1 month}$$

Then, the demand standard deviation during the review period plus lead time is

$$s_d' = s_d\sqrt{T^* + LT} = 3,099\sqrt{0.991 + 1.5} = 4,891 \text{ units}$$

The maximum level for a $P = 0.75$ is

$$\begin{aligned} M^* &= d(T^* + LT) + z(s_d') \\ &= 11,107(0.991 + 1.5) + 0.67(4,891) \\ &= 30,945 \text{ units} \end{aligned}$$

The inventory policy is to review the inventory level every month and to place a replenishment order for the difference between the quantity on hand and 30,945 units.

Average Inventory Level   This inventory policy can be expected to produce an average inventory level of

$$AIL = \frac{dT^*}{2} + z(s_d') = \frac{11,107(0.99)}{2} + 0.67(4,891) = 8,780 \text{ units}$$

Total Cost   The total relevant cost according to Equation (9-14) is

$$\begin{aligned} TC &= 121.08 + 121.09 + 0.20(0.11)(0.67)(4,891) + \frac{11,107(12)}{11,008}(0.01)(4,891)(0.150) \\ &= 121.08 + 121.09 + 72.09 + 88.83 = \$403.09 \end{aligned}$$

Note the slightly higher annual cost ($367.03 vs. $403.09) for the periodic review policy compared with the reorder point policy.

Service Level   The service level (item fill rate) achieved according to Equation (9-15) is

$$SL = 1 - \frac{4,891(0.150)}{11,008} = 0.933$$

Note: When using this method of determining service level (fill rate) in periodic inventory systems, researchers warn that accurate estimates are achieved when the fill rate is above 90 percent and demand variability is low.[10]

Joint Ordering

Both the reorder point and periodic review models discussed so far have been for single items. This assumes that each item in inventory is controlled independently of the others. In many cases, this is not the best practice since multiple items may be purchased from the same supplier or produced at the same time and location. Ordering multiple items at the same time and on the same order can result in economic benefits such as qualifying for price-quantity discounts or meeting vendor, carrier, or production minimum quantities, so inventory policy should reflect joint ordering. An inventory joint ordering policy involves determining a common inventory review time for all jointly ordered items, and then finding each item's maximum level (M^*) as dictated from its particular costs and service level.

The common review time for jointly ordered items is

$$T^* = \sqrt{\frac{2(O + \sum_i S_i)}{I \sum_i C_i D_i}} \tag{9-23}$$

where O is the common cost for procuring an order and the subscript i refers to a particular item. The maximum level for each item is

$$M_i^* = d_i(T^* + LT) + z_i (s_d')_i \tag{9-24}$$

The total relevant cost is

Total cost = Order cost + Regular stock carrying cost + Safety stock carrying cost
+ Stockout stock

$$TC = \frac{O + \sum_i S_i}{T} + \frac{TI \sum_i C_i D_i}{2} + I \sum_i C_i z_i (s_d')_i + \frac{1}{T} \sum_i k_i (s_d')_i (E_{(z)})_i \tag{9-25}$$

An example with only two jointly ordered items will be used. Using more items increases the computations needlessly.

---

[10]M. Eric Johnson, Hau L. Lee, Tom Davis, and Robert Hall, "Expressions for Item Fill Rates in Periodic Inventory Systems," *Naval Research Logistics*, Vol. 42 (1995), pp. 57–80.

Example

Two items are to be jointly ordered from the same vendor. The following data are available:

	Item	
	A	B
Demand forecast, units/day	25	50
Error of the forecast, units/day	7	11
Lead time, days	14	14
Inventory carrying cost, %/year	30	30
Procurement cost, dollars/order/item	10	10
with a common cost of, dollars/order	30	
In-stock probability during order cycle plus lead time	70%	75%
Product value, dollars/unit	150	75
Stockout cost, dollars/unit	10	15
Selling days per year	365	365

Review Time The common review time for these items according to Equation (9-23) is

$$T^* = \sqrt{\frac{2[30 + (10 + 10)]}{[0.30/365][150(25) + 75(50)]}} = 4.03, \text{ or 4 days}$$

Note that we have taken care to make demand and carrying cost conform to the same period.

Maximum Level From Equation (9-24), the maximal order quantity for item A can be found. First,

$$(s_d')_A = (s_d)_A \sqrt{T^* + LT} = 7\sqrt{4 + 14} = 29.70 \text{ units}$$

Then for $z_{P = 0.70} = 0.52$ (see Appendix A), M_A^* is

$$M_A^* = 25(4 + 14) + 0.52(29.70) = 465 \text{ units}$$

The maximum level for item B can be found similarly. First,

$$(s_d')_B = 11\sqrt{4 + 14} = 46.67 \text{ units}$$

Then for $z_{P = 0.75} = 0.67$, M_B^* is

$$M_B^* = 50(4 + 14) + 0.67(46.67) = 931 \text{ units}$$

Average Inventory Level The average inventory level for item A according to Equation (9-22) is

$$AIL_A = 25\frac{4}{2} + 0.52(29.70) = 65 \text{ units}$$

And for item B, it is

$$AIL_B = 50\frac{4}{2} + 0.67(46.67) = 131 \text{ units}$$

Total Relevant Cost Using Equation (9-25), the total annual cost for items A and B is

$$TC = \frac{30 + 2(10)}{4/365} + \frac{[4/365][0.30][150(25) + 75(50)][365]}{2}$$
$$+ 0.30[150(0.52)(29.70) + 75(0.67)(46.67)]$$
$$+ \frac{1}{4/365}[10(29.70)(0.1917) + 15(46.67)(0.1503)]$$
$$= 4{,}563 + 4{,}500 + 1{,}399 + 14{,}796$$
$$= \$25{,}258 \text{ per year}$$

Service Level The service level actually achieved for item A according to Equation (9-15) is

$$SL_A = 1 - \frac{29.70(0.1917)}{Q^*}$$

Applying a little algebra to Equation (9-8), $Q^* = T^* d = 4.03(25) = 101$. Thus,

$$SL_A = 1 - \frac{29.70(0.1917)}{101} = 0.944$$

For item B,

$$SL_B = 1 - \frac{46.67(0.1503)}{4.03(50)} = 0.9665$$

Practical Pull Inventory Control Methods

The models discussed so far in this chapter serve as a theoretical basis for the inventory control methods found in practice. Several realistic examples can be given.

A Min-Max System

The min-max system of inventory control is probably the most popular of all pull inventory control procedures. Historically, it has been implemented using manual

Figure 9-15 Min-Max Inventory Control Using a Kardex Record Card for an Office Supply Distributors' Standard Paper Item

Date	In/Customer	Sales	On hand
10/26	Bal Fwd		80,500
10/26	100M		180,500
10/30	Progression	20,000	160,500
10/30	Ogleby	25,000	135,500
11/2	Mid Ross	15,000	120,500
11/9	Unt Sply	50,000	70,500
11/29	Berea Lit	25,000	45,500
12/1	Dol Fed	10,000	35,500
12/13	Card Fed	20,000	15,500
12/14	Belmont	15,000	500
12/15	Shkr Sav	5,000	500*
1/8	BFK	500	0
1/8	100M		100,000
1/8	Card Fed	30,000	70,000
1/9	Pt of View	10,000	60,000
1/17	Am Safety	5,000	55,000
1/23	Foster	15,000	40,000
1/24	Gib Prtg	5,000	35,000
1/26	Bel-Gar	5,000	30,000
1/26	Copies	20,000	10,000
1/29	Slvr Lake	5,000	5,000
1/29	100 M		105,000
2/2	Sagamore	20,000	85,000
2/2	Copies	50,000	35,000
2/5	Bel-Gar	5,000	30,000
2/6	Bel-Gar	15,000	15,000
2/6	Superior	25,000	0*
2/6	Unt Sply	15,000	0*
2/6	Berea Prtg	15,000	0*
2/8	Sagamore	5,000	0*
2/14	100M		100,000
2/15	50M		150,000
2/16	Bel-Gar	5,000	145,000
2/21	Bel-Gar	15,000	130,000
2/26	Inkspot	5,000	125,000
2/27	Lcl 25UAW	50,000	75,000
2/28	Ptrs Dvl	2,500	72,500
2/28	Shkr Sav	25,000	47,500
3/1	Copies	35,000	12,500
3/2	Untd Tor	10,000	2,500
3/8	Sagamore	2,500	
3/8	Sagamore	12,500	0*
3/12	150M		150,000
3/12	Untd Tor	40,000	110,000
3/12	Preston	50,000	60,000
3/12	Midland	15,000	45,000
3/30	Sup Meats	25,000	20,000
3/30	Copies	50	19,950
3/30	Ptrs Dvl	5,000	14,950
3/30	Belmont	10,000	4,950
4/2	Berea Prtg	4,950	0*
4/2	Berea Prtg	15,050	0*
4/9	REM	500	0*
4/12	Mid Ross	5,000	0*
5/7	Ohio Ost	5,000	0*
5/8	Inkspots	5,000	0*
5/8	Prts Dvl	2,500	0*
5/11	100M		100,000
5/14	BVR	5,000	95,000
5/15	Guswold	10,000	85,000
5/16	ESB	15,000	70,000
5/16	Superior	50,000	20,000
5/16	J Stephen	5,000	15,000
5/16	Am Aster	15,000	0*
5/16	Am Aster	10,000	0*
5/22	Sagamore	15,000	0*

Size	M/Wgt	Basis	Grain	Color	Finish	Grade
8½ x 14	12.72	20	L	White	RmSeal	Advantage Bond

Coding	Location	Ctn. Skid Cont.	Att.
21200	F 14	5M	

M. Base Cost	Date	Min	Max
2.64	4/2	125M	250M

*No stock or insufficient stock to meet demand

control procedures and record keeping by ledger card (Kardex system), but it is also found in many computerized inventory control procedures. An example of such record keeping and control is shown in Figure 9-15.

The min-max inventory control procedure is a variant of the reorder point model; however, there are two differences. From Figure 9-16, we see that when an order is placed, it is for the amount determined by the difference between the target quantity, M (max level), and the quantity on hand, q, when the inventory level reaches the reorder point. Do not confuse this min-max control with the periodic review method. The max level M is simply the reorder point quantity (ROP) *plus* the economic order quantity (Q^*) found by the reorder point model. The reorder quantity is not always the same because the amount that the quantity on hand drops below the reorder point is added to Q^*. This extra amount is needed since the inventory level frequently drops in an amount greater than one unit, due to multiple units of the item being demanded from inventory between record updates. Q^* and ROP are approximated from the reorder point system as previously described. Although an exact computational procedure is available for min-max control,[11] this approximate approach results in a total cost of only 3.5 percent above optimum on the average.[12]

The Kardex card shown in Figure 9-15 is a record of the transactions for a particular grade of bond paper sold by an office supply distributor. Note the min and max values in the lower right-hand corner of the card. When the on-hand quantity drops to 125,000

Figure 9-16 A Min-Max System of Inventory Control, a Variant of the Reorder Point System

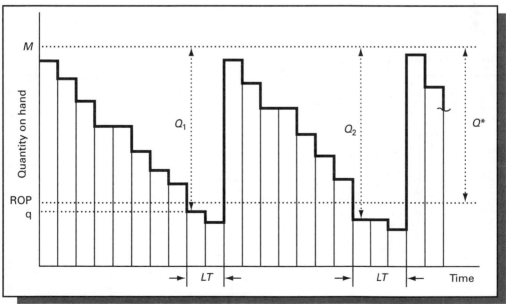

[11]Rein Peterson and Edward Silvers, *Decision Systems for Inventory Management and Production Planning* (New York: John Wiley & Sons, 1979), pp. 540–543.
[12]B. Archibald, "Continuous Review (s,S) Policies for Discrete Compound Poisson Demand Processes" (unpublished Ph.D. diss., University of Waterloo, 1976).

units, an order should be placed for 250,000 − 125,000 = 125,000 units. Note in the record that reorder quantity is not the 125,000 expected. Why? The company is ordering this item jointly with others from the same paper mill. Order minimum sizes are typically required such that when one item reaches its reorder point, the joint order may be "filled out" with other items that have not yet reached their *ROP*. In this way, the company forces single item, reorder point control to operate in a joint-ordered environment.

Although not necessarily better than just-in-time or quick response, the min-max approach to inventory control is an appropriate method to be used when demand is lumpy, or erratic. Lumpy demand is often associated with slow-moving items, but not necessarily limited to them. Actually, the lumpy demand characteristic may be seen in up to 50 percent of the product line items for many firms. Using what we have learned, the min-max approach can be slightly modified as follows to apply to items with lumpy demand:

1. Forecast demand by simply averaging the demand by period over at least 30 periods, if that much information is available. Compute the demand standard deviation over these same periods. If the standard deviation is greater than the average demand, declare demand to be lumpy and proceed to the next step.
2. Calculate the order quantity in any of the appropriate ways as previously discussed.
3. Because the on-hand quantity can drop significantly below the reorder point at the time that the order is placed, we adjust the *ROP* to compensate for it. That is, in addition to the demand during the lead time plus the safety stock that usually make up the *ROP*, we now add the *expected deficit* to *ROP*, which is the average amount that the quantity on hand is likely to fall before a replenishment order is placed. Refer to Figure 9-17.

Figure 9-17 Min-Max Inventory Control Under Lumpy Demand

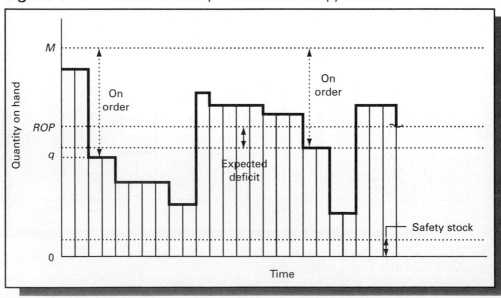

4. Approximate the expected deficit (average period sales) as one-half of the beginning and ending quantity on hand between quantity on hand record updates.
5. Set the max level as the *ROP* quantity *plus* the order quantity *less* the expected deficit.
6. Execute the min-max control system in the normal fashion as previously described. That is, when the effective inventory level falls to the *ROP* quantity, place an order for an amount equal to the difference between the max level (M^*) and the quantity on hand (q).

Example

The weekly requests for an item in inventory show a demand rate of $d = 100$ units and a standard deviation of $s_d = 100$ units. The item costs \$1.45, procurement costs are \$12 per order, annual carrying costs are 25 percent, and order lead time is 1 week. The in-stock probability during the lead time is to be at least 85 percent. The quantity on hand is updated daily, and the average daily sales quantity is 10 units, where an approximation for the expected deficit is $ED = 10$ units.

Since $s_d \geq d$, the item is believed to have a lumpy demand pattern. The order quantity can be found as

$$Q^* = \sqrt{\frac{2DS}{IC}} = \sqrt{\frac{2(100)(52)(12)}{0.25(1.45)}} = 587 \text{ units}$$

The ROP is

$$ROP = dLT + z(s'_d) + ED = 100(1) + 1.04(10) + 10 = 214 \text{ units}$$

where

$$z_{@0.85} = 1.04 \text{ from Appendix A}$$

$$s'_d = s_d\sqrt{LT} = 100\sqrt{1} = 100 \text{ units}$$

The maximum level is

$$M^* = ROP + Q^* - ED = 224 + 587 - 10 = 801 \text{ units}$$

Many times there are specific reasons why lumpiness occurs. Occasional spikes of high customer demand may be predicted with a high degree of accuracy. Hence, a great deal of inventory may be avoided. R. G. Brown provides an excellent illustration of this idea.

Example

In the U.S. Navy, there was an O-ring seal used in the boiler tubes on a particular class of carrier. The period demand history looked something like 0 0 1 3 2 0 0 1 307 0 1 0 0 4 3 5 307 0 3 1 0 0 3 307. . . . The demand certainly appeared to be lumpy.

However, most of the demand was in the single digits, with an occasional demand for 307 pieces. This large demand occurred when an overhaul was carried out in a shipyard, and overhauls were scheduled up to two years in advance.[13]

Stock-to-Demand

Sometimes companies prefer methods that are inherently simple to understand and easy to implement. Overall, such methods may provide better control if they are diligently followed, compared with the more elegant statistical methods of control. The stock-to-demand method is one such practical approach to pull inventory management.

The stock-to-demand method may be paraphrased as follows. At a specified time, a forecast is made for the item's demand rate. The forecast is multiplied by a factor that represents the review interval, the lead time for replenishment, and a time increment representing uncertainty in the demand forecast and lead time to obtain a target quantity. The on-hand quantity is noted at the time of the forecast and an order is placed for the difference between the target quantity and the on-hand quantity. Stock-to-demand inventory control is a periodic review system type.

Example

A materials manager for a large insurance company makes a forecast every month of the paper supplies needed by the office staff. For a particular month, copy machine paper usage is forecasted to be 2,000 reams. Inventory records show that 750 reams are currently on hand with none on order and none committed to users. It takes one week to receive an order placed with the paper distributor. The manager likes to have the equivalent of an extra week's demand on hand as safety stock.

The forecasted demand is multiplied by a factor of 6/4 that is calculated as follows:

Forecast/review interval	4 weeks
Lead time	1 week
Safety stock	1 week
Total	6 weeks

Since the forecast represents four weeks demand, total time is divided by the forecast interval. The order quantity is 2,000(6/4) − 750 = 2,250 reams.

Multiple Item, Multiple Location Control

The problem of inventory control in practice is truly large scale, often involving hundreds of products located at numerous stocking points that are served from multiple

---

[13]Brown, *Materials Management Systems*, p. 250.

plants. Different modes of transportation may be used to move product between plants and stocking points. Although inventory control may be handled as a number of single item, single location problems, an integrated approach may be used to focus on some important economic concerns, such as shipping in full truckload quantities or producing in economic lot sizes. Consider how a chemical company dealt with its inventory control problem.

Application

A manufacturer of industrial cleaning compounds used by restaurants, hospitals, car washes, manufacturers, and schools sold throughout the country over 200 products represented by more than 750 line items. The items were stocked in nearly 40 warehouses, but not all items were stocked in all warehouses. Of the $220 million annual soap products sales, 70 percent were handled through the warehousing system. A computerized inventory control system was developed that attempted to control the inventory levels in a manner as shown in Figure 9-18. Consider how it worked.

Each item in a warehouse was forecasted on a monthly basis using exponential smoothing. The forecasts were staggered throughout the month to balance the work-load on the computing system. The item amount on hand from warehouse computerized inventory records was checked daily.

Figure 9-18 Control of an Item in a Multiple-Item, Multiple-Location Inventory Control System for a Specialty Chemical Company

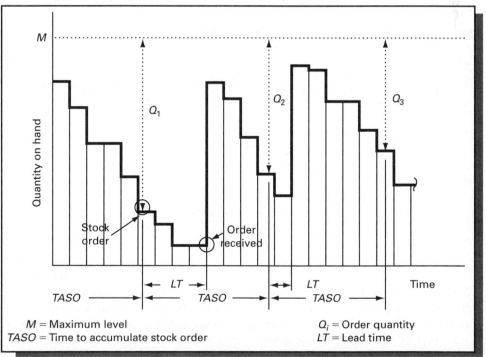

M = Maximum level
$TASO$ = Time to accumulate stock order

Q_i = Order quantity
LT = Lead time

Accumulating a truckload quantity was the main economic force in the design of the inventory control system. For all the items in the warehouse collectively, the *Time to Accumulate a Stock Order (TASO)* was computed as a truckload weight divided by the demand rate for the items stocked in the warehouse. Using this average review time, a maximum level was determined for each item.

Once a month, as the item forecast for a warehouse was made and the item stock level checked, a summation of the deficits between the item maximum level and its quantity on hand was determined. If the accumulated differences were greater than or equal to a truckload quantity, a replenishment order was placed on the serving plant. Although there was not precise control of each item, nevertheless major economies were achieved.

There were some side rules on the control process that helped it run smoothly. First, to prevent very small quantities of a particular item being included in an order, the deficit of an item had to be more than 10 percent of its max level. Second, to prevent an item from being out of stock in a warehouse when it alone might not have a deficit that would fill a truck, the inventory manager was issued a low-stock report, which showed that if the current demand rate continued, the item would be out of stock before the next expected warehouse replenishment shipment. The manager could then take action to replenish the item outside of normal ordering procedures, if it was desirable. Third, new items in the warehouse were not forecasted using exponential smoothing until they had accumulated at least a six-month sales history. Salespersons provided the interim forecasts. Stock-status reports, out-of-stock reports, forecasts, and shipping reports are examples of the report types that this system can produce.

Multi-Echelon Control

Recall in Figure 9-1 that inventories were located throughout the supply channel. These inventories are rarely independent of each other. That is, inventories at retail are backed up by inventories at their serving warehouses. In turn, warehouse inventories are backed up with inventories at the plants. If substantial amounts of inventory are maintained in field warehouses, then less may be needed at the next downstream echelon in the channel, namely, retail outlets, to maintain the same overall level of product availability. Managing the inventories throughout the *entire* channel becomes the important issue rather than the management at individual, independent stocking points.

Approximation to good multi-echelon inventory control is made using a base stock control system. The basis for this system is for any echelon in the supply channel to plan its stocking level on its inventory position *plus* the inventory from *all* downstream echelons. That is, planning the inventory level for a particular echelon is not determined from the demand information derived from just the next downstream echelon, but rather on the demand from the end customer. There is less demand variability for the particular echelon when end demand can be used in an upstream echelon inventory planning process. The demand characteristic throughout a supply channel: There is greater lumpiness at each echelon the further the echelon is upstream from the end customers. Inventory planning based only on orders

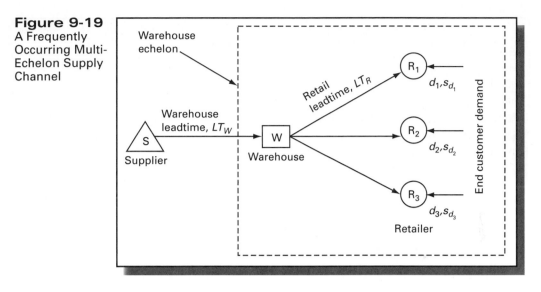

Figure 9-19
A Frequently
Occurring Multi-
Echelon Supply
Channel

from the next downstream echelon results in more safety stock than from planning using end customer demand.

A simple two-echelon supply channel might be like that shown for a warehouse-retailer channel as shown in Figure 9-19. Retailers serve the end customers from their inventories and the warehouse replenishes retailer stocks. In a base stock control system, retailer inventory levels are controlled using any appropriate method, such as reorder point control. Demand information for a retailer is derived from the end customers in the retailer's territory. The inventory position for a retailer is the quantity on hand plus the quantity on order from the warehouse.

For one echelon upstream from the retailers (the warehouse echelon), the demand for planning purposes is derived from the aggregation of the end customer demand on all retailers. The inventory position for the warehouse echelon, but not the warehouse itself, is the sum of the inventory at the retailers, the inventory in the warehouse, and the inventory in transit (on order) to and from the warehouse. The reorder point and reorder quantities are determined for the inventory position of the echelon and not for the warehouse itself. The average stocking level in the warehouse is found by subtracting the retailers' average inventory levels from the echelon inventory, assuming there is negligible inventory in transit.

The base stock system approach to inventory planning can be continued for additional echelons within the supply chain. Remember to plan inventory levels for any echelon based on end item demand and not on the orders from the next echelon downstream.

Example

Suppose a portion of a distribution network is illustrated in Figure 9-19. Retailers forecast their end customer demand for their particular territories. For a particular item, the retailers' monthly demand (normally distributed) is shown in Table 9-5.

	JAN.	FEB.	MAR.	APR.	MAY	JUNE	JULY	AUG.	SEPT.	OCT.	NOV.	DEC.	AVG.	STD. DEV.
Retailer 1	218	188	225	217	176	187	221	212	210	203	188	185	202.5	16.8
Retailer 2	101	87	123	101	95	97	93	131	76	101	87	114	100.5	15.6
Retailer 3	268	296	321	312	301	294	285	305	289	303	324	332	302.5	18.0
Combined	587	571	669	630	572	578	599	648	575	607	599	631	605.5	32.4

Table 9-5 Typical Retailer Monthly Demand and Combined Demand for Warehouse Echelon

The item has a value of C_R = \$10 per unit at the retail level and C_W = \$5 per unit at the warehouse level. Carrying costs are I = 20% per year. The cost to process a replenishment order for a retailer is S_R = \$40 per order and S_W = \$75 per order at the warehouse. The retailers' lead times are all one week (LT_R = 0.25 months) and the warehouse lead time is two weeks (LT_W = 0.5 months). An in-stock probability during the lead time of 90 percent is used for both warehouse and retailers. Using a reorder point inventory control method, find the reorder points and order quantities for both retail and warehouse echelons. How much inventory is needed at the warehouse?

First, compute the inventory policy for each retailer. For retailer 1, the order quantity (Q) is

$$Q_1 = \sqrt{\frac{2D_{R_1}S_R}{IC_R}} = \sqrt{\frac{2(202.5 \times 2)(40)}{0.20(10)}} = 311.8, \text{ or } 312 \text{ units}$$

The reorder point (ROP) is

$$ROP_1 = d_1 \times LT_R + zs_{d_1}\sqrt{LT_R} = 202.5 \times 0.25 + 1.28 \times 16.8\sqrt{0.25} = 61.38, \text{ or } 61 \text{ units}$$

The average inventory (AIL) is

$$AIL_1 = \frac{Q_1}{2} + zs_{d_1}\sqrt{LT_R} = \frac{311.8}{2} + 1.28 \times 16.8\sqrt{0.25} = 166.65, \text{ or } 167 \text{ units}$$

The inventory control rule: When the inventory level at retailer 1 falls to 61 units, place a replenishment order for 312 units.

Repeat the previous calculations for the remaining two retailers. The results are summarized in Table 9-6. The retailer echelon inventory is 167 + 120 + 202 = 489 units.

Next, compute the warehouse's inventory policy. Find the demand properties for the warehouse echelon by combining the retailers' demand, as shown in Table 9-5. The warehouse *echelon* order quantity is

$$Q_W = \sqrt{\frac{2D_W S_W}{IC_W}} = \sqrt{\frac{2(605.5 \times 12)(75)}{0.20(5)}} = 1,043.98, \text{ or } 1,044 \text{ units,}$$

Table 9-6
Inventory
Statistics for
Retailers

	RETAILER 1	RETAILER 2	RETAILER 3
Reorder quantity, Q	312	220	381
Reorder point, ROP	61	35	87
Average inventory, AIL	167	120	202

the ROP is

$$ROP_W = d_W \times LT_W + zs_W \sqrt{LT_W} = 605.5 \times 0.5 + 1.28 \times 32.4\sqrt{0.5} = 332.03, \text{ or } 332 \text{ units}$$

and AIL for the warehouse echelon is

$$AIL_W = \frac{Q_W}{2} + zs_W \sqrt{LT_W} = \frac{1,043.98}{2} + 1.28 \times 32.4\sqrt{0.5} = 551.32, \text{ or } 551 \text{ units}$$

However, the expected warehouse inventory is the warehouse echelon inventory less the retail echelon inventory, or 551 − 489 = 62 units. There is no inventory assumed to be in the pipeline.

The warehouse inventory control policy is to monitor the warehouse echelon inventory, which is the total of the inventory at each retailer, the inventory held in the warehouse, the inventory on order by the warehouse, and the inventory on order by the retail outlets less any inventory committed to end customers but not yet deducted from retail inventory. When this inventory echelon position falls to 332 units, place an order with the supplier for 1,044 units.

When the multi-echelon problems become too complex for the previous type of mathematical analysis, especially when more than two echelons are involved, computer simulation is an alternative. Simulations of this type are constructed from general simulation languages such a SLAM, DYNAMO, or SIMSCRIPT, or they may be conducted using custom packages such as *Long Range Environmental Planning Simulator* (LREPS)[14] or PIPELINE MANAGER.[15] The SCSIM module in LOGWARE software that accompanies this text illustrates this capability. The action of these simulators is to generate demand over time in a manner similar to that actually experienced by the operating channel. The product flows that take place to serve the demand are replicated. The product movement through the channel is observed, and statistics relating to product movement, inventory levels, stockouts, production rates, and transport shipments are reported. Alternative inventory policies can be tested through rerunning the simulation with different inventory stocking rules and service levels. Costs of alternatives can then be compared.

---

[14]Donald J. Bowersox, Omar K. Helferich, Edward J. Marien, Peter Gilmour, Michael L. Lawrence, Fred W. Morgan, Jr., and Richard T. Rogers, *Dynamic Simulation of Physical Distribution Systems* (East Lansing, MI: Division of Research, Graduate School of Business Administration, Michigan State University, 1972).
[15]Developed by Arthur Andersen & Company.

PIPELINE INVENTORIES

Pipeline inventories are in-transit stocks that reside in transportation equipment *moving* between inventory holding points. Management of these is a matter of controlling the time in transit, mainly through transport service selection. The inventories in transit can be surprisingly high, and good management can yield impressive cost reductions.

Example

A manufacturer of auto parts has assembly operations in the United States. It purchases components from companies located in the Pacific Rim and distributes them primarily in the United States. A diagram of the supply channel is shown in Figure 9-20. The average unit value of the product flowing in the channel is $50. Sales are 1,000 units per day. Carrying cost is 30 percent per year. The current in-transit inventories can be summarized as follows:

Pipeline	Days	Pipeline Inventory
Vendors to factory	21	21,000 units
In process at factory	14	—
Factory to warehouses	7	7,000
Warehouse storage	42	—
Warehouse to customers	3	3,000
Totals	87	31,000 units

Figure 9-20 A Typical Supply Channel Showing In-Transit Times

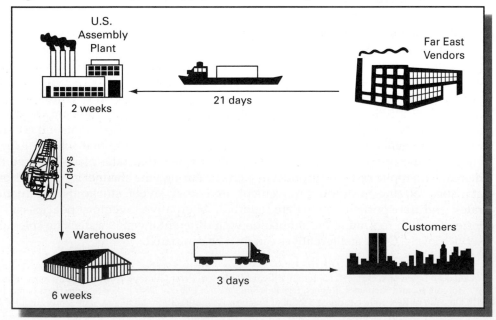

The total value of inventory in transit is $50 \times 31{,}000 = \$1{,}550{,}000$ and a carrying cost of $0.30 \times 1{,}550{,}000 = \$465{,}000$ per year.

If airfreight is used, the transit time between Far East vendors and the factory can be reduced to four days, most of which is ground handling. This would save $21 - 4 = 17$ days in the pipeline, $\$50 \times 17{,}000 = \$850{,}000$ in inventory value, and $0.30 \times 850{,}000 = \$255{,}000$ in annual carrying charges. This potential cost savings must be weighed against increased costs of using airfreight.

Reducing the average transit time in the pipeline usually has a coincident effect of reducing the transit time variability as well. Since transit time is a significant component of order lead time, the safety stocks in inventories will be lowered as an indirect benefit of reducing transit time uncertainty.

The annual in-transit inventory-carrying cost associated with a single link in the supply channel is calculated from

$$\text{In-transit inventory carrying cost } = \frac{ICDt}{365} \qquad \text{(9-26)}$$

where

I = annual carrying for product in transit, %/year
C = value of the product at the pipeline point in the supply channel, dollars/unit
D = annual demand, units
t = time in transit, days
365 = number of calendar days in a year

Note that I may be different from that for a stocking point since it does not need to include operating costs associated with storage. On the other hand, there may be operating costs for the transport of product in the pipeline, especially if private transportation is used. The costs in C should be those for holding the product and not for transporting it.

Example

Automobiles are imported to the United States through Boston, Massachusetts via Emden, Germany. The value of the automobile at the exit port in Germany is $9,000. Carrying cost is primarily the cost of the capital tied up in the vehicles, or 20 percent per year. The average sailing time to the United States is 10 days. The in-transit inventory cost per vehicle is found from $ICt/365 = (0.20)(9{,}000)(10)/365 = \$49.32$ per automobile.

Aggregate Control
of Inventories

Top management is frequently more interested in the total amount of money tied up in inventories and the service levels for broad item groups than in the control of individual items. Although carefully setting the policy for each item does provide precise control of individual item inventories as well as inventories taken together, management at this level of detail for general planning purposes becomes too cumbersome. Therefore, methods that collectively control items in groups have had a place among inventory control procedures. Turnover ratios, ABC product classification, and risk pooling are a few of the methods used to control aggregated inventories.

Turnover Ratios

Perhaps the most popular aggregate inventory control procedure is the turnover ratio. It is a ratio of the annual sales on inventory to the average investment in inventory for the same sales period, where sales and inventory investment are valued at the echelon in the logistics channel where the items are held. That is,

$$\text{Turnover ratio} = \frac{\text{Annual sales at inventory cost}}{\text{Average inventory investment}} \qquad \textbf{(9-27)}$$

The popularity of the measure undoubtedly stems from the ready availability of data (the company's financial statements) and the simplicity of the measure itself. Different turnover ratios may be specified for different product classes of, or for the entire, inventory. As a point of reference, the inventory turnover ratios for manufacturers, wholesalers, and retailers are 9:1, 9:1, and 8:1, respectively.[16]

By specifying the turnover ratio to be achieved, the overall inventory investment is controlled relative to the level of sales. It is appealing to have inventory investment change with the sales level; however, using the turnover ratio causes inventories to vary *directly* with sales. This is a disadvantage since we normally expect that inventories increase at a decreasing rate due to economies of scale. There is a price to be paid for simplicity!

ABC Product Classification

A common practice in aggregate inventory control is to differentiate products into a limited number of categories and then to apply a separate inventory control policy to each category. This makes sense since not all products are of equal importance to a firm in terms of sales, profit margin, market share, or competitiveness. By selectively applying inventory policy to these different groups, inventory service goals can be achieved with lower inventory levels than with a single policy applied collectively to all products.

It is well known that product sales display a life-cycle phenomenon where sales begin at product introduction with low levels, increase rapidly at some point, level off, and finally decline. A firm's products are usually in various stages of their life cycles and,

---

[16]*Statistical Abstract of the United States: 2001*, pp. 623, 644, and 657.

therefore, are contributing disproportionately to sales and profits. That is, a few items may be contributing a high proportion of the sales volume. This disproportionate relationship between the percent of items in inventory and the percent of sales has generally been referred to as the 80-20 principle, although rarely does exactly 20 percent of the items in a product line represent 80 percent of the sales. The 80-20 principle serves as a basis for the *ABC* classification of items. *A* items are typically the fast movers, *B* items the medium movers, and *C* items the slow movers. There is no precise way that the items are grouped into one category or another, or even of determining the number of categories to use. However, rank ordering the items by sales and then dividing them into a few categories is a start. Some of the items are reassigned to other categories as their importance dictates. Inventory service levels are then assigned to each category. The development of the *ABC* product classification scheme is more thoroughly discussed in Chapter 3.

Example

The Sorensen Research Company produces a limited line of high technology products for hospital use. The main products are arterial catheters (INTRASET); catheter-support devices (REGUFLO); and fluid-suction systems (VACUFLO, COLLECTAL). Annual sales data are summarized in Table 9-7.[17]

Table 9-7   Annual Sales Data for Sorensen Research Company

	NUMBER OF UNITS	VOLUME, DOLLARS	PRODUCT TYPE
INTRASET	1,000,000	$ 2,500,000	Catheter
SUBCLAVIAN II	250,000	137,000	Catheter
SUBVLAVIAN	150,000	975,000	Catheter
JUGULAR II	300,000	300,000	Catheter
CATHASPEC	100,000	150,000	Catheter
IV-SET	700,000	1,000,000	Catheter
CENTRI-CATH	500,000	3,500,000	Catheter
IV-12	15,000	74,700	Catheter
CSP	1,000,000	750,000	Catheter
Pressure Cuff	600,000	972,000	Catheter support
Pressure Tubing	25,000	825,000	Catheter support
EZE-FLO	4,200	65,100	Catheter support
REGUFLO	1,000,000	5,000,000	Catheter support
TRUSET	2,850,000	7,115,000	Catheter support
INTRAVAL	10,000	8,300	Catheter support
VACUFLO	355,000	350,000	Fluid suction
COLLECTAL Canisters	40,000	54,800	Fluid suction
COLLECTAL Liners	393,000	727,000	Fluid suction
	9,292,200	$24,503,900	

---

[17]Disguised data as reported in Sorensen Research Company, Harvard Business School Case 9-677-257 prepared under the direction of Steven C. Wheelwright.

	ITEM NUMBER	CUM. PERCENT OF ITEMS	VOLUME, DOLLARS	CUM. PERCENT OF SALES	ITEM CLASS
TRUSET	1	5.56%	$ 7,115,000	29.04%	A
REGUFLO	2	11.11	5,000,000	49.44	
CENTRI-CATH	3	16.67	3,500,000	63.72	
INTRASET	4	22.22	2,500,000	73.93	
IV-SET	5	27.78	1,000,000	78.01	B
SUBVLAVIAN	6	33.33	975,000	81.99	
Pressure Cuff	7	38.89	972,000	85.95	
Pressure Tubing	8	44.44	825,000	89.32	
CSP	9	50.00	750,000	92.38	
COLLECTAL Lin.	10	55.56	727,000	95.35	
VACUFLO	11	61.11	350,000	96.78	
JUGULAR II	12	66.67	300,000	98.00	
CATHASPEC	13	72.22	150,000	98.61	
SUBCLAVIAN II	14	77.78	137,000	99.17	C
IV-12	15	83.33	74,700	99.48	
EZE-FLO	16	88.89	65,100	99.74	
COLLECTAL Can.	17	94.44	54,800	99.97	
INTRAVAL	18	100.00	8,300	100.00	
			$24,503,900		

Table 9-8 Items Sorted in Descending Order Using Sales

For inventory control reasons, suppose these items are classified into three groups. The *A* items are to represent approximately the top 10 percent of items, *B* items are to be about the next 40 percent, and the *C* items are the remaining 50 percent. Table 9-7 is sorted in descending order according to item dollar sales. Computing the cumulative percent of items and the cumulative percent of sales on the sorted data yields Table 9-8:

Scanning down the cumulative percent of items column until approximately 10 percent of the items are accumulated will represent the *A* item category. Due to the small number of items, we cannot find exactly 10 percent. We may choose to round up. Next is the break point for *B* items, which is where the cumulative percent of items is 50 percent. We can now see that *A* items, or 11 percent of the items, account for 49 percent of the sales. *B* items, or 50% − 11% = 39%, of the items account for 92% − 49% = 43% of the sales. *C* items, representing 50 percent of the items, account for only 100% − 92% = 8% of the sales. Service levels can be set for these categories according to the importance of each to the company and to its customers.

Risk Pooling

Aggregate inventory level planning often involves projecting how stocking point inventory levels will change with changes in the number of stocking locations and their throughputs. In planning a logistical network, it is common to expand or contract the number of stocking points to meet customer service and cost objectives. As the number of locations is changed or even as the sales are reassigned among existing locations, the inventory in the system does not remain constant due to the risk pooling, or consolidation, effect. Risk pooling suggests that if inventories are consolidated into fewer locations, their levels will be reduced. Expanding the number of inventory locations has the opposite effect. System inventory levels are a result of balancing regular stock, which is affected by inventory policy, and safety stock, which is affected the degree of uncertainty in demand and lead time.

Illustration

Suppose that a product is stocked in two warehouses. Average territory monthly demand in warehouse 1 is $d_1 = 41$ units with a standard deviation $s_{d_1} = 11$ units/month. And for warehouse 2, $d_2 = 67$ and $s_{d_2} = 9$. Inventory replenishment quantities are determined using the economic order quantity formula. The replenishment lead time for both warehouses is 0.5 months, and the product value is $75 per unit. The replenishment order cost is $50 and the inventory-carrying cost is 2 percent per month. The probability of being in stock during the lead time is set at 95 percent. What inventory benefit would there be to consolidating the inventories into one warehouse?

First we estimate the regular and safety stock in the two warehouses.

Regular Stock. Compute the average amount of regular stock.

$$RS = \frac{Q}{2} = \frac{\sqrt{\frac{2dS}{IC}}}{2}$$

$$RS_1 = \frac{\sqrt{\frac{2(41)(50)}{0.02(75)}}}{2} = 26 \text{ units}$$

$$RS_2 = \frac{\sqrt{\frac{2(67)(50)}{0.02(75)}}}{2} = 33 \text{ units}$$

Regular system inventory for two warehouses is $RS_S = RS_1 + RS_2 = 26 + 33 = 59$ units.

Now compute the regular stock if held in one central warehouse. The average demand for the central warehouse is $d_C = d_1 + d_2 = 41 + 67 = 108$. Now,

$$RS_C = \frac{\sqrt{\frac{2(108)(50)}{0.02(75)}}}{2} = 42 \text{ units}$$

Safety Stock. Safety stock in two warehouses is found as follows.

$$SS = zs_d\sqrt{LT}$$
$$SS_A = 1.96(11)\sqrt{0.5} = 15.25 \text{ units}$$
$$SS_B = 1.96(9)\sqrt{0.5} = 12.47 \text{ units}$$

System safety stock in two warehouses is $SS_S = SS_A + SS_B = 15.25 + 12.47 = 27.72$, or 28 units.

For the safety stock in the central warehouse, estimate the demand standard deviation from

$$s_C = \sqrt{s_1^2 + s_2^2} = \sqrt{11^2 + 9^2} = 14.21.$$

Now, the safety stock is

$$SS_C = 1.96(14.21)\sqrt{0.5} = 19.69, \text{ or 20 units}$$

Total inventory is the sum of regular and safety stocks. For two warehouses $AIL_2 = 59 + 28 = 87$ units. In the central warehouse, $AIL_C = 42 + 20 = 62$ units. Note that regular and safety stock have decreased through consolidation.

Square Root Rule. The square-root rule is a well-known method for determining the consolidation effect on inventories. However, it measures only the regular stock reduction, not both regular and safety stock effects as described in the previous section. Assuming that an inventory control policy based on the *EOQ* formula is being followed and that all stocking points carry the same amount of inventory, the square-root rule can be stated as follows:

$$AIL_T = AIL_i\sqrt{n} \tag{9-28}$$

where

> $AIL_T =$ the optimal amount of inventory to stock, if consolidated into one location in dollars, pounds, cases, or other units
> $AIL_i =$ the amount of inventory in each of n locations in the same units as AIL_T
> $n =$ the number of stocking locations before consolidation

Note that inventory varies with the number of stocking points in the logistics network.

Example

Sorensen Research Company operated 16 regional public warehouses. Each warehouse carried $165,000 of inventory on the average. If all stocks are consolidated into one location at the plant, how much inventory can be expected?

Using Equation (9-28), we calculate

$$AIL_T = \$165,000\sqrt{16} = \$660,000$$

Note that the previous system of stocking points had a total of $16 \times 165,000 = \$2,630,000$ in inventory investment.

Example

Suppose that Sorensen wishes to consolidate inventories into two locations that equally divide the stock. How much inventory can be expected in each warehouse?

We already know that one location should have $660,000 in inventory investment. Now, we simply need to estimate from this value the amount to stock in two warehouses. By algebraically manipulating Equation (9-28), the inventory in a multiple warehouse system would be

$$AIL_i = \frac{AIL_T}{\sqrt{n}}$$

Hence, for two warehouses the inventory in each would be

$$AIL_i = \frac{\$660,000}{\sqrt{2}} = \$466,690$$

Systemwide inventory is $2 \times 466,690 = \$993,381$. Thus, reducing from 16 to two warehouse saves $\$2,630,000 - 933,381 = \$1,696,619$ in inventory investment.

Inventory Throughput Curve. Although the square-root rule of inventory consolidation is generally useful, the assumptions that there are equal amounts of inventory in all warehouses, inventories consolidate precisely as the square root of the number of warehouses, demand and lead time are known for sure, and order quantity is determined from the EOQ formula may be too limiting. Using a slightly different approach, these limitations can be dropped. First, from the company's stock status reports, construct a plot of average inventory (AIL_i) level against annual warehouse shipments (D_i), as shown in Figure 9-21. Each point on the plot represents a single warehouse. It is the turnover ratio for the warehouse. From a family of curves of the form $AIL = aD^b$, fit the best curve possible to the data. The data in Figure 9-21 are for a specialty chemical company, and give $a = 2.986$, $b = 0.635$. The taper in the curve indicates that the company is probably following a policy of inventory control based on the EOQ, but it is not necessary to know that. In practice, rarely do we see the square-root function due to the

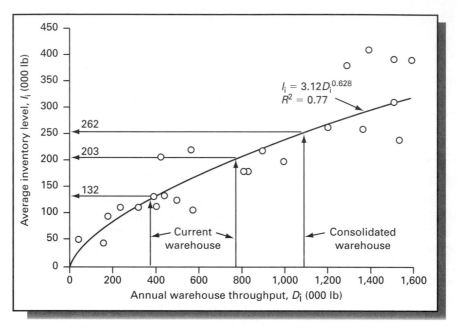

Figure 9-21 An Inventory Throughput Curve for a Producer of Industrial Cleaning Compounds

presence of some safety stocks.[18] Inventory levels for a warehouse with any projected demand throughput (shipments from the facility) can be computed from the mathematical formula for the curve or found directly from the plot of the inventory throughput curve.

Example

The specialty chemical company, whose data are represented in Figure 9-21, has 25 public warehouses and plants from which it distributes product. Suppose that two warehouses with 390,000 lb and 770,000 lb of throughput, respectively, are to be consolidated into a single warehouse with 390,000 + 770,000 = 1,160,000 lb of annual throughput. How much inventory should be stocked in the single warehouse?

From the plot in Figure 9-21, the inventory for the two current warehouses is 132,000 + 203,000 = 335,000 lb. Combining the throughput and reading the inventory from the plot gives 262,000 lb.

[18]Ronald H. Ballou, "Estimating and Auditing Aggregate Inventory Levels at Multiple Stocking Points," *Journal of Operations Management,* Vol. 1, No. 3 (February 1981), pp. 143–153; and Ronald H. Ballou, "Evaluating Inventory Management Performance Using a Turnover Curve" *International Journal of Physical Distribution and Logistics Management,* Vol. 30, No. 1 (2000), pp. 72–85.

Total Investment Limit

Inventories represent a substantial capital investment for many firms. Because of this, managers frequently will place a limit on the amount of inventory to be carried. The inventory control policy must then be adjusted to meet this goal, if total average inventory investment exceeds it. Suppose that inventory is controlled by a reorder point control policy under conditions of demand and lead time certainty. If a monetary limit is placed on all items carried at an inventory location, we can state that

$$\sum_i C_i \frac{Q_i}{2} \leq L \tag{9-29}$$

where

L = investment limit for i items in inventory, dollars
C_i = value of item i in inventory
Q_i = order quantity for item i in inventory

The order quantity can be determined from a modified Equation (9-7). When the average inventory value for all items exceeds the investment limit (L), the order quantities for the items need to be reduced to decrease the average item inventory levels and meet the investment limit. A reasonable way to do this is to artificially inflate the carrying cost I to a value $I + \alpha$; large enough to shrink the stock levels an appropriate amount. The basic economic order quantity formula is modified to be

$$Q_i = \sqrt{\frac{2D_i S_i}{C_i(I + \alpha)}} \tag{9-30}$$

where α is a constant to be determined. Equation (9-30) is substituted into Equation (9-29) and reworked to give a formula for α .

$$\alpha = \left(\frac{\sum_i \sqrt{2D_i S_i C_i}}{2L} \right)^2 - I \tag{9-31}$$

Once α is found, it is substituted into Equation (9-30) to find the revised Q_i.

Example

Suppose that an inventory contains three items. Management has placed a total dollar limit on the average inventory investment of $10,000 for these items. The annual carrying cost is 30 percent per year. Other relevant data are

Item i	Procurement Cost, S_i	Purchase Cost, C_i	Annual Demand, D_i
1	$50/order	$20/unit	12,000 units
2	50	10	25,000
3	50	15	8,000

We first compute each Q. That is,

$$Q_1 = \sqrt{\frac{2DS}{IC}} = \sqrt{\frac{2(12,000)(50)}{0.30(20)}} = 447.21 \text{ units}$$

Similarly,

$$Q_2 = \sqrt{\frac{2(25,000)(50)}{0.30(10)}} = 912.87 \text{ units}$$

$$Q_3 = \sqrt{\frac{2(8,000)(50)}{0.30(15)}} = 421.64 \text{ units}$$

Checking the total inventory investment by solving the left side of Equation (9-29) with the above computed values gives

$$\begin{aligned} \text{Inventory investment} &= C_1(Q_1/2) + C_2(Q_2/2) + C_3(Q_3/2) \\ &= 20(447.21/2) + 10(912.87/2) + 15(421.64/2) \\ &= \$12,199 \end{aligned}$$

Since the investment limit of $10,000 is exceeded, solve for α in Equation (9-31). That is,

$$\alpha = \left(\frac{\sqrt{2(12,000)(50)(20)} + \sqrt{2(25,000)(50)(10)} + \sqrt{2(8,000)(50)(15)}}{2(10,000)} \right)^2 - 0.30$$

$$= 0.146$$

We now can substitute $\alpha = 0.146$ into Equation (9-30) and solve for the revised order quantity for each item. That is,

$$Q_1 = \sqrt{\frac{2D_iS_i}{C_i(I + \alpha)}} = \sqrt{\frac{2(12,000)(50)}{20(0.30 + 0.146)}} = 366.78 \text{ units}$$

Similarly, the order quantities for the other items are computed to be $Q_2 = 748.69$ units and $Q_3 = 345.81$ units. The average investment now comes to $10,004. Close enough!

SUPPLY-DRIVEN INVENTORY CONTROL

There are situations where the previously discussed methodology does not seem appropriate. It assumes that supply and demand can be reasonably matched; however, there are situations where, in spite of management's best forecasting efforts, supply cannot be aligned well with demand. That is, supply may be so valuable that the producer will obtain all that is available. This can cause over- and understock in the supply channel. Little can be done when demand exceeds supply. On the other hand, when the producer pushes excess supply into the distribution channel, the producer has but one option to control excess inventory levels that can occur— increase demand to lower the inventory to more acceptable levels. Price discounting is commonly used as the variable to increase demand.

Applications

- StarKist operates a unique aggregate inventory-control system for its tuna products. Since the company is committed to purchase and pack all the tuna it can, the distribution system can become overloaded with finished product. To manage overstocking, the company will run sales on its products. Customers readily buy extra quantities of these highly prized products, thus reducing StarKist's inventory levels.
- The American Red Cross: Blood Services plans up to a year in advance for blood collections. Donors are highly valued and are not turned away, even if collections exceed anticipated levels or current blood needs. If inventory levels of specific blood types are high and outdating may occur, the Red Cross will either convert the whole blood to another blood product or reduce the price to their hospital customers. Price discounting is effective because hospitals obtain their blood supply from multiple sources, not just the Red Cross.

VIRTUAL INVENTORIES[19]

With improvements in corporate information systems, it has become an increasing practice to serve customer demand from more than one stocking location. Although customers may be assigned to a primary stocking site, it is rare that enough inventory will be maintained to meet all demand requests from the primary location all of the time. Such an inventory policy is reasonable since the inventory cost to ensure never being out of stock is exceedingly high. Alternatively, demand will be cross filled from other sites holding the same items, as illustrated in Figure 9-22 for an inventory system of two stocking points. The combination of inventory sites is referred to as a *virtual inventory*. Cross filling demand from the multiple stocking locations in the virtual inventory leads to the expectation that demand fill rates will be increased, systemwide inventory levels will be lower, or both, as compared with meeting demand from only the customer's primary stocking location and incurring some stockouts and order filling delays.

The logistician's problem is to decide the items to cross fill and those that should only be filled from the primary location. The solution requires a balance between the

[19]Ronald H. Ballou and Apostolos Burenetas, "Planning Multiple Location Inventories," *Journal of Business Logistics*, Forthcoming.

Figure 9-22
Illustration of
Inventory Cross
Filling

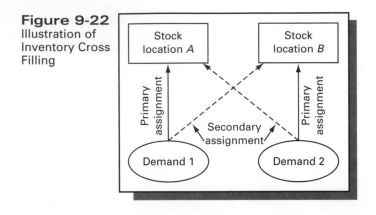

costs associated with regular stock versus safety stock. Recall that regular stock is the inventory to meet average demand and average lead time. Safety stock, on the other hand, is the extra inventory needed to meet uncertainty in demand and lead time. When it comes to cross filling, the economic forces associated with these two inventory types are opposed. That is, on a systemwide basis, regular stock increases with cross filling, whereas safety stock decreases. Consider how this happens.

Regular Stock

In a system of multiple stocking points, the maximum amount of inventory held system wide will occur when the demand on the stocking points is equally divided among them. On the other hand, when there is unequal demand dispersion, cross filling causes the effective demand throughout the system to be more balanced than was the primary demand. Effective demand refers to the demand actually realized on a stocking point through cross filling from other stocking points rather than the primary demand assigned to it.

To illustrate, suppose that there are two stocking points, as in Figure 9-22, with demand of 50 and 150 units per week, respectively, and an inventory fill rate of 90 percent. A 90 percent fill rate means that only 90 percent of each point's demand on the average can be filled from the primary location, with 10 percent being filled from the alternate location. Thus, the effective demand on location 1 is $50 \times 0.9 + 0.1 \times 150 = 60$ units per week. For location 2, the effective demand is $0.1 \times 50 + 0.9 \times 150 = 140$ units per week. Note that the effective demand has moved closer to the 100/100 demand split from the original 50/150 dispersion. If regular stock is determined from the EOQ formula in Equation (9-7), then the inventory at each stocking location is $AIL = K\sqrt{D}$ where K is a constant derived from the costs for a particular item. Therefore, the systemwide inventory (AIL_s) without cross filling is $AIL_s = \sqrt{50} + \sqrt{150} = 19.3$ units, where K is taken as one for illustration purposes. With cross filling, $AIL_s = \sqrt{60} + \sqrt{140} = 19.6$ units. Regular stock has increased.

Safety Stock

In a system of multiple stocking points, safety stock levels are affected by the fill rate and the dispersion of demand among the stocking locations. In contrast to regular

Table 9-9

Effective Demand Standard Deviation at Two Location, Units per Week

	STOCK, LOCATION A	STOCK, LOCATION B
Std. dev.	4.5[a]	0.5[b]
Std. dev.	1.5[c]	13.5
Combined std. dev.	4.7[d]	13.5

[a] $\sqrt{[FR(1 - FR)^{N-1}]^2 s^2} = \sqrt{[0.9(1 - 0.9)^{1-1}]^2 5^2} = 4.5$

[b] $\sqrt{[FR(1 - FR)^{N-1}]^2 s^2} = \sqrt{[0.9(1 - 0.9)^{2-1}]^2 5^2} = 0.45,\ \text{round to } 0.5$

[c] Round to 1.5

[d] $\sqrt{4.5^2 + 1.5^2} = 4.7$

stocks, minimum safety stocks occur when demand is balanced among the stocking locations.

To illustrate, suppose that the standard deviations (s) for regular stock demand given previously are 5 and 15 units per week, respectively, lead time (LT) is one week, and the fill rate is 90 percent. Recall that for a reorder point control system, safety stock (ss) can be estimated from $ss = zs\sqrt{LT}$, where $z = 1.28$ is from the normal distribution at 90 percent. (*Note:* It is assumed that the fill rate and the probability during the lead time or the probability during the lead time plus order review time depending on method of control are approximately the same.) With cross filling, the standard deviation for a particular location among multiple stocking points is $s_N = \sqrt{[FR(1 - FR)^{N-1}]^2 s^2}$, for the Nth stocking point. The effective standard deviations for the two stocking locations are shown in Table 9-9.

The safety stock at location A without cross filling is $ss = zs\sqrt{LT} = 1.28(5)\sqrt{1} = 6.4$ units, at B is 19.2 units, and for the entire system is 6.4 + 1.28 = 25.6 units. With cross filling, the safety stock at A is $1.28(4.7)\sqrt{1} = 6.0$ units, at B is 17.3 units, and for the system is 23.3 units. Cross filling gives a reduction of 25.6 − 23.3 = 2.3 units.

Now, the decision to cross fill or not cross fill an inventoried item is a result of balancing these opposing inventory-holding costs. In addition, transportation costs may be included for shipping to a customer from distant stocking points. This cost does not encourage cross filling. However, if the stockout costs incurred due to demand not being served on request from the primary stocking location are included, cross filling is encouraged. Computing these costs for each item maintained in inventory identifies those items whose demand should be filled only from the primary stocking location and those that should be filled from the virtual inventory.

Example

Suppose that a firm has two options to serve its customers in order to maintain a high level of product availability. First, the customers can be served from a designated warehouse in their vicinity. If there is a stockout, the sale may be lost or a back order will occur. Second, when a stockout occurs, the order may be filled from a secondary warehouse, with the company paying the extra transportation costs. For any given item in inventory, which of these designs should be selected?

A representative item is selected from inventory to be tested. The distribution system is similar to that illustrated in Figure 9-22. The item has a cost in inventory of $200 per unit, a carrying cost of 25 percent per year, a stock level of six weeks of demand, a replenishment lead time of eight weeks, and a target fill rate of 95 percent. The transport rate for cross hauling from a secondary warehouse outside of a customer's territory is $10 per unit. The item's weekly demand characteristics are as follows:

Location	Mean Demand	Standard Deviation
1	300	138
2	100	80
System	400	160

The inventory-control policy is not known for sure.

The cross filling decision curves of Figure 9-23 help with this type of decision making. It is necessary to make some preliminary estimates. Since there is no inventory throughput curve of the type described in a previous section, we will assume that the company is operating a well-run inventory control system with an $\alpha = 0.7$. We know that the average inventory level can be described as $AIL = KD^\alpha$ and K can be found from a manipulation of this formula. That is, $K = D^{1-\alpha}/TO$. AIL can be approximated as D/TO, where TO is the turnover ratio or 52 weeks per year/6 weeks of demand in inventory = 8.67. Hence, $K = (400 \times 52)^{1-0.7}/8.67 = 2.28$. Also, we assume that the fill rate and the in-stock probability during the lead time are approximately the same so that z can be found from the normal distribution (Appendix A) for the fill rate percentage, or $z_{@0.95} = 1.96$.

The X,Y parameters for Figure 9-23 can now be computed.

$$X = \frac{tD^{1-\alpha}}{ICK} = \frac{10([400 \times 52])^{1-0.7})}{0.25(200)(2.28)} = 1.73$$

and

$$Y = \frac{zs\sqrt{LT}}{KD^\alpha} = \frac{1.96(160)\sqrt{8}}{2.28([400 \times 52])^{0.7}} = 0.4$$

The demand ratio r is $100/400 = 0.25$.

In Figure 9-23, we now see that the intersection of X and r falls below the decision curve of $Y = 0.4$ (use $Y = 0.5$). Since the value falls below the curve Y, do not cross fill the item.

Additional curves of the type shown in Figure 9-23 are available for various FR and α values.[20] They permit virtual inventory planning problems to be handled for a variety of items.

---

[20]Ibid

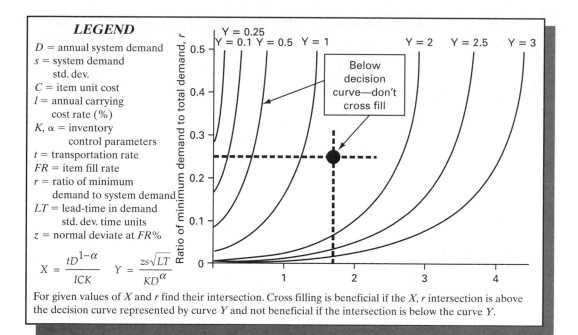

LEGEND

D = annual system demand
s = system demand std. dev.
C = item unit cost
l = annual carrying cost rate (%)
K, α = inventory control parameters
t = transportation rate
FR = item fill rate
r = ratio of minimum demand to system demand
LT = lead-time in demand std. dev. time units
z = normal deviate at $FR\%$

$$X = \frac{tD^{1-\alpha}}{lCK} \qquad Y = \frac{zs\sqrt{LT}}{KD^{\alpha}}$$

Below decision curve—don't cross fill

For given values of X and r find their intersection. Cross filling is beneficial if the X, r intersection is above the decision curve represented by curve Y and not beneficial if the intersection is below the curve Y.

Figure 9-23 Cross filling Decision Curves for FR = 0.95 and α = 0.7.

CONCLUDING COMMENTS

Inventories continue to represent a major use of capital in the supply channel. Good management of them means keeping them at the lowest possible level consistent with a balance of direct and indirect costs attributed to their level and with the need to maintain a desired level of product availability. Extensive research has been conducted on optimally managing inventories, and this chapter summarizes the key inventory control methods that have proven to be useful in practice. The differences between pull, push, supply driven, and aggregate approaches to inventory planning and control have been noted. Specific mathematical methods are illustrated for a variety of circumstances, such as certainty and uncertainty of demand and lead time, perpetual and seasonal demand patterns, single and multiple echelons, single and multiple stock locations, and inventories at rest and in transit. They are all useful in establishing sound policies for managing an expensive asset.

GLOSSARY OF TERMS

Q^* = optimal order quantity, units
Q = an order quantity, units
EOQ = economic order quantity, usually Q^*

CP_n = cumulative frequency of selling at least n units
D = average annual demand, units/year

S = item procurement cost, dollars/order

I = annual inventory carrying cost, percent of item value per year

C = item value in inventory, dollars/unit

T^* = optimal order interval expressed in units of time

T = a particular order interval expressed in units of time

N^* = optimal number of order intervals per year

ROP = reorder point quantity, units

d = average daily demand rate, units/day

LT = average lead time expressed in units of time

Q_p^* = optimum production run quantity, units

p = production output rate expressed in the same dimensions as d

s_d = standard deviation of demand, units

s_d' = standard demiation of the $DDLT$ or $DD[T + LT]$ demand distributions, units

X' = mean of the $DDLT$ or $DD[T + LT]$ demand distributions

s_{LT} = standard deviation of the lead time expressed in units of time

P = probability of being in stock during an order cycle (reorder point system) or during an order cycle plus lead time (periodic review system), expressed as a fraction or percent

z = normal deviate on the standardized normal distribution

SL = customer service level or item fill rate, expressed as a fraction or percent

AIL = average inventory level, units

$E_{(z)}$ = unit normal loss integral

TC = total relevant inventory cost, dollars/year

M^* = optimum max level for the periodic review system or min-max system

O = common order-processing cost for joint orders, $/order

k = stockout cost, dollars/unit

i = subscript to denote item number

Y = cumulative fraction of sales

X = cumulative fraction of items

A = a constant

n = number of stocking points in multiple stocking point system

L = inventory investment limit, dollars

K, α = inventory-throughput curve constants

ED = expected deficit, units

QUESTIONS

1. Why do inventories cost so much to maintain?
2. What are the reasons that inventories are held throughout a supply channel? Why should they be avoided?
3. Contrast a *push* inventory philosophy with a *pull* philosophy. When would each be most appropriately applied? Similarly, what is the difference between push and pull methods and aggregate control methods? When should each type be applied?
4. Identify the costs that are relevant to the control of inventories. Where do you think they might be obtained within a company?
5. Explain what safety stock is and why it is needed.
6. Explain the difference between the probability of a stockout during an order cycle and the service level, or item fill rate.
7. How might you decide which items in a company's product line are to be classified as A, B, and C items?
8. Explain what you think an executive meant by this statement: "Every management mistake ends up in inventory."

9. What is the square-root law in inventory planning, and to what problem types do you think it applies?
10. Why is the economic order quantity not very sensitive to inaccurate input data?
11. Where are pipeline inventories located in the supply channel, and how do we best control them?
12. How do you think one should go about setting the stock availability service level and determining stockout costs?
13. If the demand for an item in inventory showed the pattern of 0 1 2 5 150 0 1 0 3 4 150 1 0 0 5 1 150, what suggestions can you make on how the inventory level should be controlled?
14. Describe a supply-driven inventory system. How are inventory levels controlled compared with a pull system?
15. Contrast the stock to demand approach to inventory control with the *EOQ*-based period review method of control. Why is it simpler? Is there a price to be paid for this simplicity?
16. Explain the inventory pooling effect if the number of stocking points is varied.
17. What is the inventory throughput curve? How can it be determined? How is it useful?
18. What is a "virtual inventory"? What is the planning problem associated with such inventories?

PROBLEMS

A number of the following problems and case studies in this chapter can be solved or partially solved with the aid of computer software. The software packages in LOGWARE most important for this chapter are INPOL (*I*), and MULREG (*MR*). The CD icon (*I*) will appear with the software package designation where the problem analysis is assisted by one of these software programs. A database may be prepared for the problem if extensive data input is required. ( ) Where the problem can be solved without the aid of the computer (by hand), the hand icon is shown. If no icon appears, hand calculation is assumed.

1. A shopper goes to a drug store in search of six items. The store stocks these items with the following probabilities of their being in stock:

Item	In-stock Probability, %
Toothpaste	95
Mouthwash	93
Batteries	87
Shaving cream	85
Aspirin tablets	94
Deodorant	90

Assuming that only one item of each of these products is purchased, what is the probability that the shopper will fill his or her order completely?

2. Central Hospital Supply has a policy that a hospital can expect its orders to be filled directly from stock 92 percent of the time. If any one item on an order is out of stock, the entire order will be held as a back order to avoid additional shipping costs. Orders typically include up to ten items. A sampling of the orders over the last year shows that six combinations of products frequently appear on orders, as follows:

Order Item	Combination	Frequency of Order
1	A,C,F,G,I	0.20
2	B,D,E	0.15
3	E,F,I,J	0.05
4	A,B,C,D,F,H,J	0.15
5	D,F,G,H,I,J	0.30
6	A,C,D,E,F	0.15
		1.00

Inventory levels have been set so that products A, B, C, D, E, and F have a common service level of 0.95 each. The remaining products are set at 0.90 each.

a. Is the firm meeting its inventory service target?

b. If not, at what item service levels would these two groups of products have to be set to meet the 92 percent order fill rate?

3. An importer of television sets from the Far East distributes them throughout the European Union from four warehouses. Shipments are received monthly, and this month's shipment is 120,000 sets. Due to the long lead time, demand and supply for the sets are hard to match. Therefore, an allocation to the warehouses is based on a monthly demand forecast and the service level for each warehouse. The inventory records and forecast for the coming month show the following situation:

Warehouse	Quantity on hand, sets	Demand forecast, sets[a]	Forecast error, sets[b]	Service level[c]
1	700	10,000	1,000	90%
2	0	15,000	1,200	85
3	2,500	35,000	2,000	88
4	1,800	25,000	3,000	92

[a] Projected to the time of a stock replenishment based on the current sales rate.
[b] A standard deviation. Forecast errors are normally distributed.
[c] Probability of being in stock during the month.

If transportation to the warehouses takes one week and import handling requires one week after a shipment arrives, how should the allocation of the sets be made to the warehouses?

4. A computer-supply mail-order house has a memory chip in inventory that it sells to customers around the country. A Japanese manufacturer supplies the item using airfreight. It has the following characteristics:

Average annual demand	= 3,200 units
Replenishment lead time	= 1.5 weeks
Carrying cost	= 15% per year
Purchase price, delivered	= $55 per unit
Procurement ordering cost	= $35 per order

a. Design a reorder point method of control for this item.

b. What are the annual ordering and annual carrying costs if your design is used?

c. Suppose that the lead time stretches to three weeks, so that the $ROP > Q^*$. What adjustments would you suggest making in the control policy?

5. Helen's Secretarial School trains young people in word processing and other secretarial skills. Tuition for the course is $8,500, but she will rebate up to 10 percent of the fee annually until the graduate receives a job. Average annual demand for her graduates is 300 per year. (Note: Product value and setup costs are the same.)

a. How many potential secretaries should Helen admit per class?

b. How many times per year should she offer the course?

6. A retail store purchases computer software from a distributor for resale. For an upcoming promotion, the retailer needs to determine the best order size for a one-time purchase. One of the products is a word processing software program that will have a special sale price of $350. The retailer estimates the probabilities for selling various quantities as follows:

Quantity	Probability
50	0.10
55	0.20
60	0.20
65	0.30
70	0.15
75	0.05
	1.00

The program can be purchased from the distributor for $250 each, but there is a restocking charge of 20 percent of the purchase price for the return to the distributor of any unsold programs.

What size of a purchase order should the retailer commit to?

7. An automatic teller machine (ATM) is being installed at a branch of MetroBank. From the bank's research, it figures to indirectly benefit from offering this service. Estimates are that the bank will generate revenues at the rate of 1 percent of the money passed through the machine in the form of new customer accounts for checking services, loans, savings accounts, and the like. The average withdrawal from the teller machine is $75, and the bank figures its cost of money to be 10 percent per year.

Stocking the machine for the two-day weekend is its most difficult planning problem. From historical records for other ATMs, the bank estimates the average number of withdrawals to be 120 with a standard deviation of 20, with the distribution being normal.

How much money should the bank stock in the machine for the weekend? (*Hint*: Consider as a single order problem.)

8. Cabot Appliances, a retail chain, is trying to decide what size order it should place with its supplier of room air conditioners. Room air conditioner sales are highly seasonal, and the number of units sold is very dependent on summer weather patterns. Cabot places one order per year. Reorders are impractical after the selling season begins to develop. Although the actual sales level cannot be known for sure, Cabot analyzes past selling seasons, long-term weather reports, and the general state of the economy. The following probabilities of various sales levels are then estimated:

Sales, units	Probability
500	0.2
750	0.2
1,000	0.3
1,250	0.2
1,500	0.1
	1.0

A unit has a delivered price to Cabot of $320 and it is priced to customers at $400. Air conditioners unsold at the end of the season are discounted to $300, which clears them from inventory. Purchases can be made only in increments of 250 units, with a 500-unit minimum order.

a. Assuming no inventory is to be carried to the next year, what single order size should be placed?

b. Would you modify the order quantity in part a if Cabot can borrow money to support inventory at 20 percent per year? Excess units can be carried over to the next selling season.

9. Suppose that an auto part in a manufacturer's inventory has the following characteristics:

Forecast of demand	= 1,250 cases per week
Forecast error, std. dev.	= 475 cases per week
Lead time	= 2.5 weeks
Carrying cost	= 30% per year
Purchase price, delivered	= $56 per case
Replenishment order cost	= $40 per order
Stockout cost	= $10 per case
Probability of being in stock during the lead time, P	= 80%

a. Design a reorder point control system for this part, given the assigned P. How would you state the inventory control policy if the $ROP > Q^*$?

b. Design a periodic review system for this part. Now assume that the probability of being in stock extends to the order interval plus lead time.

c. Determine and compare the relevant costs of each approach.

d. What service level (fill rate) do you actually achieve with both designs?

e. Find the in-stock probability during the lead time that will optimize a reorder point system design. How does the total cost compare with that in part a?

10. Repeat Question 9, but include that the lead time is normally distributed with a standard deviation of 0.5 weeks.

11. A manufacturer of fractional horsepower motors for use in industrial sweepers and floor polishers produces its own wiring harnesses. These wiring harnesses are used in final assembly at the rate of 100 per day for 250 working days per year. It costs $250 to start up the wiring harness production. Production is at the rate of 300 per day when operating. The standard cost of a wiring harness is $75, and the company's inventory carrying cost is 25 percent per year.

a. What should the production run quantity be?

b. How long should each production run cycle be?

c. How many times per year should the part be produced?

12. A Japanese appliance manufacturer uses a valve in its refrigerator final-assembly operation. The valve is obtained from a local supplier in any quantity needed within one hour of an order request. The working day is eight hours. The production schedule calls for this part to be used at the constant rate of 2,000 per day, 250 working days a year. The company pays ¥35 for this valve delivered to the assembly line. Inventory-carrying costs are 30 percent per year. Due to contractual arrangements with the supplier, procurement costs amount to only ¥1.00 per order placed.

a. Design a reorder point method of inventory control for this item.

b. Suggest how a two-bin system could be used as a way of implementing this control method.

13. A large chemical company in Green River, Wyoming, mines soda ash used in glass manufacturing. Soda ash is sold to a number of manufacturers through annual contracts. The glass companies release their requests for soda ash against their contracts. The mining company sees demand in the form of rail-car quantities. A typical week shows demand to be normally distributed at 40 rail-car loads plus or minus 10 cars. They estimate the standard deviation at (max cars − min cars)/6 = (50 − 30)/6 = 3.33 cars.

Soda ash is valued at $30 per ton, and an average rail-car load is 90,000 lb of product. Annual carrying cost for the company is 25 percent per year. Setup costs at the mine are estimated to be $500 per order. It takes one week to produce the product and/or secure the rail-cars for shipment. A 90 percent in-stock probability during the lead time is desired.

a. The company must call for cars from the railroad to fill orders. How many cars should be requested at a time? (*Remember:* One ton is 2,000 lb.)

b. At what quantity of soda ash remaining in inventory should the request for cars be made?

14. A large hospital uses a certain intravenous solution that it maintains in inventory. Pertinent data about this item are as follows:

Forecasted daily usage[a]	= 50 units
Forecast error std. dev.[b]	= 15 units
Average lead time	= 7 days
Lead time std. dev.[b]	= 2 days
Annual carrying cost	= 30%
Procurement cost per order	= $50
Stockout cost	= $15 per unit
Product value	= $45 per unit
In-stock probability[c]	= 85%

[a]365 days per year
[b]Normally distributed
[c]During the lead time or during the order interval plus lead time, depending on the inventory control design

   a. Design a reorder point system of control for this item.
   b. Design a periodic review system of control for this item.
   c. Do you think the in-stock probability is correctly specified to minimize costs? Appraise with reference to the reorder point system design.

15. A periodic review method of inventory control is to be used for two products that are to be purchased from the same supplier at the same time. The following data have been collected for these items:

	PRODUCTS	
	A	B
Weekly demand forecast, units	2,000	500
Forecast error[a] (std. dev.), units	100	70
Lead time, weeks	1.5	1.5
Purchase price, dollar/unit	$2.25	$1.90
In-stock probability during lead time plus order cycle	90%	80%
Out-of-stock cost	Unknown	
Carrying cost, percent/year	30%	30%
Common purchase order cost, dollar/order	$100	

[a]Normally distributed

   a. Design the control system for these products. State how the control system will work.
   b. What is the average inventory level for each of these items?
   c. What is the customer service level that can be expected for these items?
   d. Suppose that the review time is set at four weeks. How will your answers to the previous questions change?

16. A company imports parts from Taiwan through the Port of Seattle on the West Coast. The parts are destined for its assembly operations on the East Coast. Shipments are by rail and require 21 days transit time. The parts are worth $250 each at the port, and 40,000 of them are used annually in assembly operations.

Inventory carrying costs are 25 percent per year. The rail rate to the East Coast is $6 per 100 lb, and crated parts weigh 125 lb each.

As an alternative, trucking can be used to cross the country in seven days. Truck rates are $11 per cwt. Do the savings from reduced in-transit inventories justify the higher cost of trucking?

17. At a point in Ohio, a manufacturer of hydraulic equipment (hoses, cylinders, and controls) consolidates the items on orders produced at various points in the United States. Consolidated orders are destined for Brazil and may be shipped via an ocean freight forwarder or using airfreight. The average order size is 292 lb. Ocean shipping ($4.94/lb) is less expensive than airfreight ($9.04/lb), but takes longer. Ocean movements from the consolidation center require transportation to the Port of Baltimore, vessel-waiting time for loading at the port, stop offs at Savannah and Miami for pickups, and sailing to São Paulo, Brazil. The total transit time averages 20 days. On the other hand, air shipments require only two days for handling and transit.

The manufacturer owns the goods in transit until they arrive at the destination port and is concerned with the cost of inventory while in transit. The product in transit is valued at $185/lb and 20,000 lb are shipped per year. The company's cost of capital is 17 percent per year.

From purely an inventory-transportation viewpoint, which transport mode should be used?

18. A distributor of truck and bus parts has a tie-down strap (B2162H) in inventory. The item has a monthly demand of 169 units with a standard deviation of 327 units per month, making the demand pattern quite lumpy. The lead time for the item is four months with a standard deviation of 0.8 months. The item costs $0.96 each at the factory with a $0.048 transportation charge from supplier to distributor. Carrying costs are 20 percent per year, and order-processing costs are $10 per order. The desired in-stock probability during the lead time is 85 percent. The inventory records are updated daily, and the average daily sales quantity is eight units.

Develop a min-max (reorder point system) inventory control policy for this lumpy-demand item.

19. Acme Computer maintains a stock of spare parts for the entire country at one warehouse in Austin, Texas. To provide improved customer service, the company will expand the number of warehouses to ten, and they will be of equal size. The total inventory investment in the current warehouse is $5,000,000.
   a. Using the square-root law, estimate the amount of inventory investment that the distribution system is likely to contain with ten warehouses.
   b. Suppose that nine warehouses are operating with $1,000,000 of inventory investment in each. If the company were to consolidate the inventory into three equal-size warehouses, how much inventory would be in each of them?

20. The California Fruit Growers' Association is a consortium of fruit farmers on the West Coast for product distribution. The association currently operates 24 warehouses throughout the country. For the most recent calendar year, the statistics on average inventory levels and warehouse throughputs were compiled as given in Table 9-10.

Warehouse	Annual Warehouse Throughput	Average Inventory Level
1	$ 21,136,032	$ 2,217,790
2	16,174,988	2,196,364
3	78,559,012	9,510,027
4	17,102,486	2,085,246
5	88,226,672	11,443,489
6	40,884,400	5,293,539
7	43,105,917	6,542,079
8	47,136,632	5,722,640
9	24,745,328	2,641,138
10	57,789,509	6,403,076
11	16,483,970	1,991,016
12	26,368,290	2,719,330
13	$ 6,812,207	$1,241,921
14	28,368,270	3,473,799
15	28,356,369	4,166,288
16	48,697,015	5,449,058
17	47,412,142	5,412,573
18	25,832,337	3,599,421
19	75,266,622	7,523,846
20	6,403,349	1,009,402
21	2,586,217	504,355
22	44,503,623	2,580,183
23	22,617,380	3,001,390
24	4,230,491	796,669
Totals	$818,799,258	97,524,639

Table 9-10 California Fruit Growers' Association's Inventory Versus Throughput Statistics

a. What overall turnover ratio is the association able to achieve? Compare the turnover ratio for the three smallest warehouses with the three largest ones in terms of throughput. Suggest why there is a difference.

b. Construct the inventory throughput curve by fitting a straight line to the data by hand or use a simple, linear regression model.

c. Warehouses 1, 12, and 23 are to be consolidated into one warehouse. How much inventory would you expect in the one warehouse using the curve from part b?

d. Warehouse 5 is to be expanded into two warehouses. Thirty percent of the throughput will be assigned to one warehouse, and the remainder to the other. How much inventory would you estimate to be in each warehouse using the curve from part b?

21. Three items in inventory have the following characteristics:

	A	B	C
Average demand per year	51,000	25,000	9,000
Lead time, weeks	0.5	0.5	0.5
Carrying cost per year	25%	25%	25%
Delivered purchase price per unit	$1.75	$3.25	$2.50
Procurement cost per order	$10	$10	$10

The average investment in these items is not to exceed $3,000. The items are purchased from different vendors and are not jointly ordered. Determine the order quantities for these items so that the investment limit is not exceeded.

22. A company has three items in its inventory that are purchased from the same vendor and are shipped together on the same delivery truck. The truck has a capacity of 30,000 lb. The items are under the periodic review method of inventory control and are purchased with a single purchase order that costs $60 to prepare. The annual carrying cost is 25 percent of each item's value. Other information about the items is as follows:

Item	Product Value, C_i	Product Weight, w_i	Weekly Demand Forecast, d_i
1	$50/case	70 lb/case	100 cases
2	30	60	300
3	25	100	200

Due to economic considerations, the shipment size is not to exceed the truck capacity for the combined order. What size should the order quantity be for each item? [*Hint:* Equation 9-29 becomes $\sum_i D_i T^* w_i \le$ Truck capacity, Equation (9-30) can be restated as

$$\alpha = \frac{2O}{\left(\dfrac{\text{Truck capacity}}{\sum_i D_i w_i}\right)^2 \sum_i C_i D_i} - I$$

and recall that $Q^* = D \times T^*$. Product weight is w_i and D_i is annual demand.]

23. Five items in a retail inventory make up the bulk of the items maintained. The inventory levels are controlled using the reorder point method. They have a fixed lead time of 15 days, a purchase order cost of $35 per order per item, and a daily inventory carrying cost of 0.08219 percent. Other information about the items is as follows:

	A	B	C	D	E
Daily demand forecast (d), cases	15	30	50	20	60
Forecast error (s_d), cases	2	4	5	3	7
Item value (C_i), dollar/case	36	45	24	13	16

An in-stock probability during lead time is targeted at 95 percent. The forecast errors are normally distributed.

What is the total average inventory, in cases, for these items?

24. A retail store controls its inventoried items using the reorder point method; however, the shelf space for these items is limited. (Retailers allocate a certain amount of shelf space to each item in the store.) Orders are placed on a central distribution center for replenishment. A typical item in the store might have the following data.

Demand forecast, boxes/week	123
Forecast error (s_d), boxes/week[a]	19
Lead time, weeks	1
Annual carrying cost, percent/yr.	17
Item value, dollar/box	1.29
Ordering cost, dollar/order[b]	1.25
Maximum shelf space for item, boxes	250
In-stock probability	93%

[a]Normally distributed.
[b]Prorated order cost for multiple items.

What order quantity should be used so that the shelf space restriction is not exceeded?

25. A Mexican firm, Recos Cementos, produces and distributes cement and concrete in bulk and bagged forms for the construction market. Inventory is maintained in nine terminals for serving customers (contractors) throughout the country. A graph of the average inventory level in a terminal vs. the annual shipments from the terminal for each of the nine terminals is shown in Figure 9-24.

What can you say to the company about its inventory management performance and opportunities?

26. A distributor of photographic equipment serves retailers in two cities from two warehouses. Retailers are normally supplied from the nearest warehouse to save on transportation expense. Two separate inventories of the same products are held. Although the distributor maintains an average fill rate of 95 percent, occasional stockouts can cause retailers' orders not to be filled or placed on back order. Since it is highly unlikely that an item will be out of stock at both warehouses at the same time, the distributor is contemplating filling out-of-stock orders in one region from the inventory of the other, that is, cross filling the orders. It is possible that system inventories will be less, but the extra transportation cost of shipping from a secondary location must be balanced against the inventory cost reduction.

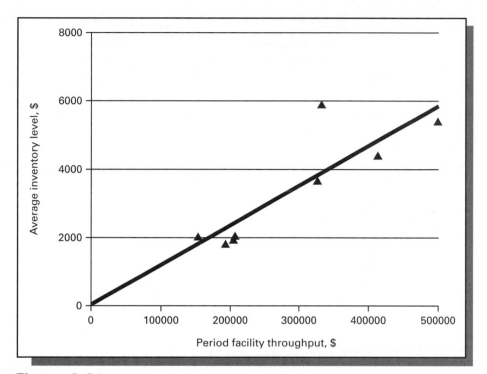

Figure 9-24   A Plot of Average Inventory Against Annual Terminal Shipments

To test the idea, a camera, worth $400 in inventory, is selected. The extra shipping and handling costs from a secondary warehouse are $12 per camera. Inventory-carrying cost is 20 percent per year. Replenishment lead time on this camera is two months.

The monthly forecast of demand in the first city is an average of 42 cameras with a standard deviation of seven cameras. In the second city, average demand is 75 cameras with a standard deviation of 13 cameras. The two cities combined have an estimated demand of 117 cameras and a standard deviation of $\sqrt{7^2 + 13^2} = 15$ cameras.

A reorder point method of inventory control is used to control the high-valued inventory and replenishment quantities are determined from the *EOQ* formula. An inventory turnover of six is currently achieved on a well-run inventory ($\alpha = 0.7$).

Should the item be cross filled or served only out of the assigned warehouse?

27. Suppose that a company has two of its warehouses that it would like to consolidate into a central warehouse. Three top-selling items stocked in both warehouses are selected for evaluation. From the monthly forecasts of the demand in the two warehouse territories, the following statistics are known:

Product	WAREHOUSE 1 Monthly Demand, Units	WAREHOUSE 1 Monthly Standard Deviation, Units	WAREHOUSE 2 Monthly Demand, Units	WAREHOUSE 2 Monthly Standard Deviation, Units	Product value, Units $/Unit
A	3,000	500	5,000	700	15
B	8,000	250	9,500	335	30
C	12,500	3,500	15,000	2,500	25

The product order quantities are determined locally at each warehouse using the *EOQ* formula and are ordered from separate vendors with an order-processing cost of $25 per order. Replenishment lead times average three weeks, or 0.75 months. Inventory carrying costs are 24 percent per year. The service level during the order cycle is set at 95 percent.

How much inventory can be saved through risk pooling if the inventory is consolidated into a central facility?

28. A distributor is positioned in the supply channel between his customers and suppliers. He knows that the customers maintain inventory that should be taken into account in planning his own inventory levels. In the spirit of cooperation, the customers share their end demand data with the distributor. For a particular item supplied by the distributor to three customers in his territory, the monthly demand for an item valued at the customer echelon at $35 per unit is as follows:

Customer	Avg. Demand, Units/Mo.	Demand Std. Dev., Units/Mo.
1	425	65
2	333	52
3	276	43
Combined	1,034	94[a]

[a]Estimated as $\sqrt{65^2 + 52^2 + 43^2} = 94$

The item is valued a little less at the distributor ($30 per unit) since some costs such as transportation to customers have not yet been added. Inventory-carrying cost is estimated at 20 percent per year at both echelons. Order-placement cost for the customers is $50 per order. The distributor can supply the customers within two weeks, but it takes vendors four weeks to fill the distributor's replenishment orders. Customers set their in-stock probability during the order cycle at 95 percent, whereas the distributor uses 90 percent. Both echelons use the reorder point method of inventory control. The distributor places orders on the vendor for 2,000 units to realize a purchase discount.

How much inventory of this item should the distributor stock if no inventory is assumed to be in transit to customers?

CASES

*Complete Hardware Supply, Inc.**

Tim O'Hare is the distribution manager for Complete Hardware Supply (CHS), with headquarters in Cleveland, Ohio. Consolidated, Inc., a holding company, recently acquired CHS. Consolidated's management has insisted that tighter control procedures be instituted to limit inventory investment at CHS.

CHS is a distributor of various hardware items to local hardware stores in the northeastern Ohio area. It purchases a wide variety of hardware items from a number of vendors located throughout the country. Hardware store orders are filled from the inventories held at CHS's Cleveland warehouse. Historically, Tim has used a reorder point method of inventory control to determine reorder quantities acquired from vendors and to control inventory levels.

To deal with the new investment limit placed on inventories, Tim selects for analysis 30 representative items from 500 in the product line. He collected the data on demand, product value, and lead times as shown in Fig. 1.

The cost for preparing and transmitting a purchase order is $15, and each item is purchased from a separate vendor on a separate order. The company's annual inventory-carrying cost is 25 percent, or 0.0048 per week. Tim currently uses a 98 percent in-stock probability during the lead time as a control on customer service, which was set in consultation with the company's salespersons.

The 30 products are sourced from various vendor-shipping points as follows:

Product Number	Vendor Shipping Area	Distance to CHS[a]
1, 2, 3, 5, 22, 23	New York, New York	471 mi
4, 6, 13	Cleveland, Ohio	25
7, 8, 9, 10, 11, 12, 20, 30	Chicago, Illinois	348
19, 24, 29	Atlanta, Georgia	728
14, 15, 16, 18, 25, 26, 27, 28	Los Angeles, California	2,382
17, 21	Dallas, Texas	1,189

[a]Approximate road distances.

The lead time to receive a replenishment order is composed of three elements: (1) the time to prepare and transmit an order, (2) the time to fill the order at the vendor location, and (3) the time to transport the order to Cleveland. Currently, orders are prepared by hand and mailed to vendors, a system where preparation takes two days and transmittal takes two days. Trucking is used to transport products to CHS. It takes approximately one day to transport product for every 300 miles of distance. Vendor order filling requires five working days.

Prorating the restrictions that Consolidated has placed on all items, the total investment for these 30 items should not exceed $18,000. However, to maintain revenues, Tim would like to have no more stockouts per year than he currently is experiencing.

---

*Paraphrased from a case study by Professor A. Dale Flowers, Case Western Reserve University.

Item Number	Weekly Demand Forcast	Weekly Forcast Error,[a] Std. Dev.	Unit Price,[b]	Lead Time,[c] Days
1	18	6	$37.93	10.6
2	9	2	85.06	10.6
3	113	30	1.32	10.6
4	20	5	2.41	9.5
5	7	2	5.19	10.6
6	490	101	0.51	9.5
7	44	11	2.36	10.2
8	68	23	1.30	10.2
9	48	15	7.38	10.2
10	7	1	9.69	10.2
11	6	2	1.38	10.2
12	4	1	3.25	10.2
13	90	22	7.79	9.5
14	5	1	5.48	16.9
15	3	1	19.04	16.9
16	7	2	2.03	16.9
17	6	2	68.97	13.0
18	3	1	21.65	16.9
19	14	4	56.28	11.4
20	5	1	19.85	10.2
21	104	35	35.51	13.0
22	30	9	2.19	10.6
23	8	2	14.24	10.6
24	15	6	12.16	11.4
25	6	2	4.04	16.9
26	4	1	66.13	16.9
27	7	2	68.10	16.9
28	5	1	11.18	16.9
29	20	5	26.41	11.4
30	14	4	40.86	10.2

[a]Forecast error is approximately normally distributed.
[b]Includes a transportation rate to Cleveland of 5% on the average.
[c]Lead times are expressed as the average number of working days. Assume 5 working days per week.

Figure 1 Sales, Price, and Lead Time Data at CHS

Reflecting on his dilemma, Tim has a number of action courses open to him to lower inventory levels:

- Transmit orders more rapidly

- Insist that vendors use a faster method of transportation
- Reduce the forecast error
- Compromise on customer service

Tim can buy electronic equipment (computer and software, facsimile machine, etc.) for approximately $1,500 (with a five-year life) and make order-transmittal time negligible. Of course, he figures that other related costs (EDI, Internet connection, telephone, etc.) will raise the purchase order cost from $15 to $17.

If special arrangements are made with United Parcel Service, a guaranteed delivery service of two days anywhere in the United States can be arranged. This would affect shipments over 600 miles and would add another 5 percent to the price of the items involved.

Finally, Tim has a line on a new forecasting software package that he can acquire for $50,000. If the software is implemented, he expects that the forecast error can be reduced by 30 percent. ∎

QUESTION

1. What course of action should Tim take, and how should he argue his case to Consolidated's management?

---

*American Lighting Products**

"I just love challenges like this—take out 20 percent of our finished-goods inventory without hurting customer service. I don't know how we are going to do it!" Sue Smith exclaimed to inventory analyst Bryan White. Sue had just returned from a meeting with the vice president of finance who had issued the directive, and she now had to come up with a plan.

BACKGROUND

Sue and Bryan work for American Lighting Products (ALP), a manufacturer of fluorescent lamps. ALP has two factories, both in Ohio. The Cleveland area plant produces the high-volume two-, three-, and four-foot lamps, with four-foot lamps accounting for 90 percent of the production. The Columbus area plant handles the low-volume types, ranging from six inches long to eight feet. Between both plants, ALP offers over 700 product line items, through three main sales channels: commercial and industrial (C&I), consumer, and original equipment manufacturers (OEM). The C&I market has long been the mainstay of the business, however with the emergence of home centers and deep discount merchants, the consumer channel is gaining in size and importance in the overall marketing strategy. The OEM market is small, but it is an important first step in the replacement market, since, as bulbs burn out, customers tend to purchase exactly what comes out of the fixture.

ALP is part of a larger corporation, American Electric Products (AEP), which manufactures a variety of other consumer and industrial products. Each division of AEP is run as a stand-alone business, and each fits into the overall strategy of AEP in its own way. ALP is a mature industry that provides AEP with a steady income from its operations. While the division's income earned is its primary measure of success, management also launches other major initiatives that focus on ways to increase the profitability of the corporation. The latest such initiative is a corporation-wide push to reduce inventories. The enhanced cash flow to be gained from reducing inventory is seen as a critical factor to the company's overall profitability.

To Sue Smith and her team at ALP, the inventory initiative is a new challenge. In the past, the focus has been on making sure that the

*Prepared by Cheryl Glanton under the supervision of Professor Ronald H. Ballou, Weatherhead School of Management, Case Western Reserve University, as a basis for class discussion rather than as an illustration of either effective or ineffective handling of an administrative situation. Data have been disguised.

inventory levels were sufficient to cover the seasonal peaks in demand and to cover the plant's three-week summer shutdown. Until this point, the costs of inventory have not been closely monitored, so reducing the overall inventory level is a completely new idea.

THE DISTRIBUTION SYSTEM

ALP warehouses its finished goods inventory in eight master distribution centers (MDCs) located throughout the United States, each servicing sales for its entire region. MDC and plant locations are shown in Figure 1. Each plant ships product to MDCs in full truckload quantities of 35,000 lamps. Shipping in large quantities allows the plants to manufacture product in economic lot sizes. Each plant schedules its production in weekly increments in order to minimize the impact of forecast errors that occur when production is based on monthly schedules.

Each MDC is set up as a hub to support its region, and the size of the center is based on the size of the region served. For instance, the

Hagerstown distribution center serves the northeastern United States as well as European and Middle Eastern exports. This large region results in Hagerstown being the largest inventory location for ALP. On the opposite end of the scale is the Seattle distribution center. It has the smallest region to serve and, therefore, the smallest inventory allotment. Table 1 shows the annual shipments and inventory by MDC.

For ease of control, inventory is primarily expressed in lamp quantities. The finance department assesses the average lamp value to be $0.88. The current carrying cost of an item held in inventory is 18 percent per year of lamp value before taxes.

As product is manufactured, the amount allocated to a certain distribution center is based on the following considerations:

1. The volume of current customer orders that exceeds available inventory
2. The volume that an MDC's inventory is below base stock levels
3. The volume of the sales forecast for an MDC service region

Figure 1 Production and Distribution Center Locations

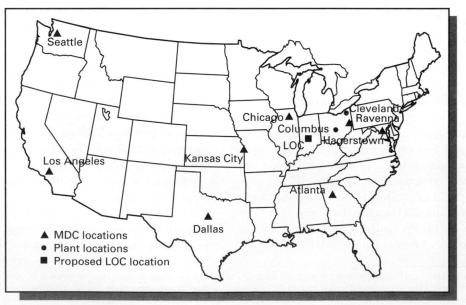

Table 1
Annual Units
Shipped and
Average Inventory
by MDC (in Lamps)

MASTER DISTRIBUTION CENTER	SHIPMENTS	INVENTORY
Atlanta	26,070,000	3,784,333
Chicago	23,321,000	2,188,417
Dallas	13,244,000	2,159,250
Hagerstown	38,193,000	5,824,583
Kansas City	15,950,000	1,592,333
Los Angeles	21,470,000	3,666,500
Ravenna	25,853,000	2,918,250
Seattle	4,922,000	959,833
Totals	169,023,000	23,093,499

The base stock level is set for each product item at each MDC based on historical sales levels. In the case of new products, stocking locations are based on the target customers and their estimated sales. The sum of the base stocks at all MDCs is the desired net system inventory objective (NSO) for a product. The NSO is the reorder point for the factory to produce another lot of product. Therefore, the average system inventory for a product is the NSO + 1/2 a lot size. The lot size was based on the plant's setup cost and manufacturing constraints.

ALP has a forecasting system that takes into account the past three years of sales history. Management adjusts the forecast when a known abnormality is expected, for instance, a special sales promotion. In general, the higher the level of the forecast, the more accurately sales can be predicted. For the total market, the forecast accuracy is in the 90 to 100 percent range. For product families, it is in the 70 to 90 percent range. For individual products, it is in the 50 to 70 percent range. For individual product items by MDC, the forecast accuracy is below 50 percent.

Customers place orders through regional salespeople, who send the orders to a central customer service center. The account specialists at the service center place the order in the order/ship/bill system. While inputting the order, they assign it to the MDC that serves the region for that customer. The system uses the customer zip code to determine the correct MDC. In the case of an order that consists of an entire truckload of one product, the order will be assigned to the plant producing the item instead of an MDC. The account specialist also enters the desired delivery date at the customer's site. If no future date is requested, the order is then scheduled for immediate delivery.

Inventory is allocated to each MDC based on the forecast for that region, as well as other considerations. Because of the high forecast error at the item level of detail, actual sales might be unexpectedly high in one region and low in another. When this happens, there may be a stockout at one warehouse while there is excessive stock at another, causing some orders to be back ordered at the primary location or filled from another location having the excess inventory.

CUSTOMER SERVICE

ALP measures its performance by first-time delivery rate, known at ALP simply as customer service. First-time delivery is defined as the proportion of line items delivered to the customer by the requested date. If an item is delivered from a source other than the assigned source, it does not count as a first-time delivery. Any back-ordered items are also not considered as first-time delivery. Figure 2 shows ALP's customer service level for the past two years.

The lighting business is extremely competitive and customers are becoming increasingly demanding of their suppliers. One of the demands is a high first-time delivery rate. The consumer channel expects 98 percent or better, while the C&I and OEM channels expect 95 percent first-time delivery. Over the past several years, ALP has struggled to meet these expectations. As customers become more sophisticated in their own ordering and inventory policies, they demand more of their suppliers. ALP is raising expectations. The current goal is to meet or exceed 95 percent service in all channels. The largest consumer accounts are being served at

the 98 to 100 percent rate, but it has taken extra inventory and resources to accomplish this result. Table 2 shows the items ordered and customer service level by channel for the past year.

INVENTORY POLICIES

Each channel of distribution has unique needs and inventory requirements. For instance, the consumer channel has a smaller variety of products, but the customer demands are the highest in the industry. Many consumer accounts have a ship-or-cancel policy. If an order is not delivered in the requested time window, it is canceled and the sale is lost. Many customers also release

Figure 2 First-Time Delivery Percentages by Month for the Last Two Years

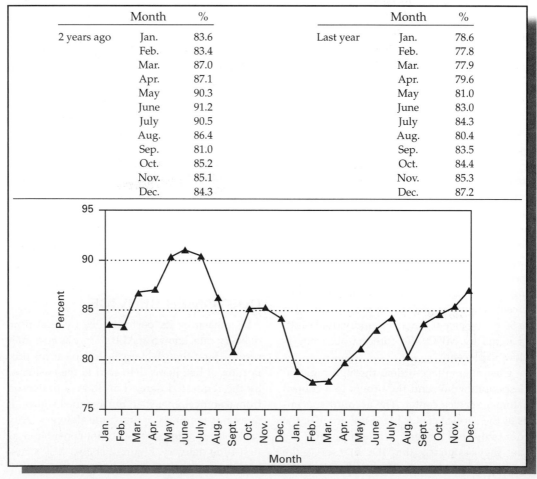

	Month	%		Month	%
2 years ago	Jan.	83.6	Last year	Jan.	78.6
	Feb.	83.4		Feb.	77.8
	Mar.	87.0		Mar.	77.9
	Apr.	87.1		Apr.	79.6
	May	90.3		May	81.0
	June	91.2		June	83.0
	July	90.5		July	84.3
	Aug.	86.4		Aug.	80.4
	Sep.	81.0		Sep.	83.5
	Oct.	85.2		Oct.	84.4
	Nov.	85.1		Nov.	85.3
	Dec.	84.3		Dec.	87.2

By Channel		Jan.	Feb.	Mar.	Apr.	May	June	July	Aug.	Sept.	Oct.	Nov.	Dec.
C&I	Items ordered	46307	55013	44683	54528	48492	42230	46709	50983	46792	65775	57932	47152
	B/O[a]	10795	13084	11083	11974	10173	7759	7979	11382	8719	10850	9571	6910
	%Service[b]	76.7%	76.2%	75.2%	78.0%	79.0%	81.6%	82.9%	77.7%	81.4%	83.5%	83.5%	85.3%
Consumer	Items ordered	24709	28023	21511	23487	29644	21204	24089	25958	26182	37272	33650	25482
	B/O	4214	5081	3331	3651	4373	2801	2925	3480	3196	4797	3652	2074
	%Service	82.9%	81.9%	84.5%	84.5%	85.2%	86.8%	87.9%	86.6%	87.8%	87.1%	89.1%	91.9%
OEM	Items ordered	1038	1396	1028	1260	1058	1019	1208	1215	1147	1526	1279	1122
	B/O	301	387	289	325	252	225	256	278	228	315	224	193
	%Service	71.0%	72.3%	71.9%	74.2%	76.2%	77.9%	78.8%	77.1%	80.1%	79.4%	82.5%	82.8%

[a] B/O = back orders.
[b] %Service = % first-time deliveries.

Table 2   Order Information by Channel

their orders weekly, based on point-of-sale information. Therefore, an order released on Friday has a shipping window of the following Monday through Wednesday. To meet these customer needs, ALP commits to having 4.5 weeks of inventory on hand of each consumer product.

On the other extreme is the OEM market. In this case, customer orders are typically of one product and shipped in a truckload quantity. However, OEM's want the product on the day they call. If the product is unavailable, they call a competing supplier.

The C&I market is not clear-cut. Some customers have sophisticated ordering schemes, but the majority use regular order procedures to replenish their shelves. Additional orders are placed because an end user is awarded a certain contract, for either a new building or a relamping project, and needs product. If the distributor does not carry the item, or is low on stock, it is ordered from ALP. Like the OEM customers, the contractor wants immediate delivery.

Historically, ALP's inventory management policy has been to maintain inventories to enable level production loading, while supporting heavy seasonal demand. Traditionally, the first and fourth quarters are the peak demand

seasons for ALP. Also factoring into the inventory profile is summer plant shutdowns. Each year in the summer, both ALP plants take from two to three weeks for equipment maintenance and vacations. An inventory buildup precedes this shutdown period to allow continuous product shipments. Figure 3 shows the system inventory levels by month for the past two years.

Reducing total inventories by 20 percent is going to be challenging. If the inventory levels are cut haphazardly, customer service will be at risk. Even though there is not a perfect correlation, inventory levels and service levels are somewhat related. So the question remains, How can ALP reduce inventory and increase service?

OPTIONS

Sue and Bryan both agree that in order to meet these new challenges, evaluating the distribution system is a good place to start looking for ways to make changes that will meet both goals. The first alternative Sue and Bryan developed is to create a large order center (LOC) for the national consumer accounts. The LOC would be a new MDC that serves only consumer accounts. The thought behind the LOC is to consolidate the consumer products in one warehouse and distribute from this central location.

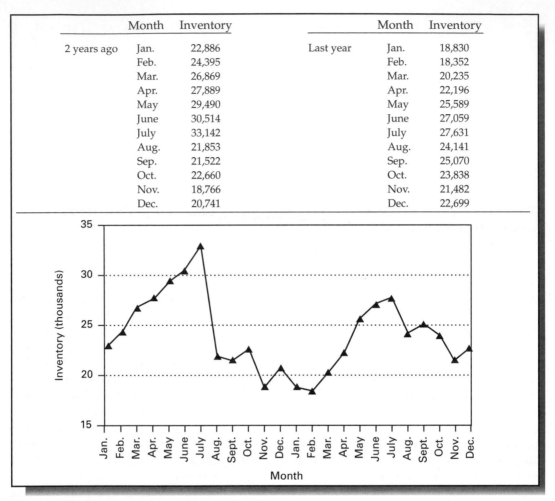

	Month	Inventory		Month	Inventory
2 years ago	Jan.	22,886	Last year	Jan.	18,830
	Feb.	24,395		Feb.	18,352
	Mar.	26,869		Mar.	20,235
	Apr.	27,889		Apr.	22,196
	May	29,490		May	25,589
	June	30,514		June	27,059
	July	33,142		July	27,631
	Aug.	21,853		Aug.	24,141
	Sep.	21,522		Sep.	25,070
	Oct.	22,660		Oct.	23,838
	Nov.	18,766		Nov.	21,482
	Dec.	20,741		Dec.	22,699

Figure 3 System Inventory for the Past Two Years

The advantage is that the consumer accounts typically had regular ordering patterns and the number of SKUs ordered by each account was defined at the beginning of the year. In the current distribution system, the inventory of the consumer items is kept at a higher level at each MDC. Sue and Bryan feel confident that the LOC will enable ALP to achieve 98 percent or greater customer service levels for the consumer channel, while reducing the total inventory, but it is unknown how much inventory can be taken out of the distribution system. Based on the warehouse locations of ALP's major consumer customers, Batesville, Indiana, was selected as the site for a future warehouse.

The risk of using a LOC is that it does not equally affect all product lines. In the case of C&I and OEM customers, another strategy is needed. The original theory in locating the MDCs was to have a distribution center at the hub of every major region in the country. The system worked well in shipping product to the customer, but the current inventory level is not sufficient to maintain a 95 percent service level. If the current distribution system is maintained, inventory needs to be added to reach the 95 percent goal.

MASTER DISTRIBUTION CENTER	TRANSPORT RATE, $/TRUCKLOAD	INBOUND LEAD TIME, DAYS	OUTBOUND LEAD TIME, DAYS
Atlanta	600	2	2
Chicago	350	1	2
Dallas	1200	3	2
Hagerstown	475	1	2
Kansas City	700	2	3
Los Angeles	1800	5	2
Ravenna	250	1	2
Seattle	1800	6	2
LOC	600	1	2

Table 3 Transportation Cost and Lead Times by MDC

Inventory reduction is the major concern of upper management, so this option is not feasible. An alternative is to reduce the number of MDCs and consolidate the inventory in such a way that each remaining MDC has a higher inventory level than before, but the total system inventory is lower.

MDC consolidation affects transportation costs and lead times as well as inventory levels. In order for MDC consolidation to be an economical alternative, the dollar value of the inventory reduction needs to be considered in light of any increase in transportation costs. Bryan and Sue investigated the current transportation costs and lead times, and the results are shown in Table 3. Inbound transportation is the in-transit time from the plant to an MDC, and outbound transportation is the in-transit time from the MDC to the customer. The outbound transportation costs are not shown since they represent thousands of rates to hundreds of customers from many existing and potential MDC locations.

The inbound lead-time varies from one day to four days around the average lead time, with the average variance being 2.5 days. On the outbound side, the majority of the territory is served within two days, with a variance of one day.

Sue and Bryan know that MDC consolidation might reduce total inventory, but they also know that the idea of building new MDCs around the country may not be easy to sell to upper management. At ALP, the investment constraint is that all projects must have at least a two-year payback.[1] Any plan to achieve MDC consolidation has to meet the investment criteria. Sue and Bryan feel that the best strategy is to consolidate MDCs at existing sites. For instance, the Chicago MDC could serve both its territory and Kansas City's from the current center. Consolidations like this minimize the investment needed.

What would happen to the warehousing cost is another concern with MDC consolidation. Currently, the finance department allocates a flat rate of $0.10 per lamp in inventory to warehousing cost. This rate covers the overhead of the distribution centers and the direct labor needed to handle product. If the number of MDCs were reduced, there would also be a reduction in the total warehousing costs for the entire system. However, the MDC selected as a consolidation site would have higher costs than before consolidation because of holding more lamps. The selected site is the one currently

---

[1] A two-year payback means that the cost savings associated with a project must equal or exceed the investment made in a project within two years.

having the greatest number of shipments among the consolidated group.

Options like the LOC and MDC consolidation have been brought up before, but they have always been discarded because of the additional costs involved. Upper management has had a feeling that transportation costs would increase. However, an in-depth analysis, considering inventory reduction, might yield a different answer. The new focus on inventory reduction provides an opportunity to question the status quo of the distribution system. At $0.88 per lamp inventory value, a 20 percent inventory reduction would yield a $4 million improvement in cash flow. However, any major construction projects required, as part of the MDC consolidation, would not be easily justified on a two-year payback basis. It would be acceptable to management to consolidate demand at the existing MDCs if the change can be economically supported and customer service maintained at least at current levels. Sue and Bryan know they need to find a solution that will meet both customer expectations and the business goals. ∎

QUESTIONS

1. Evaluate the company's current inventory management procedures.
2. Should establishing the LOC be pursued?
3. Does reducing the number of stocking locations have the potential for reducing system inventories by 20 percent? Is there enough information available to make a good inventory reduction decision?
4. How might customer service be affected by the proposed inventory reduction?

*American Red Cross: Blood Services**

Dr. Amy Croxton, the medical director of American Red Cross regional blood center for the northern Ohio region located in Cleveland, was in low spirits. In March, a severe outdating[1] of blood products had taken place; she now faced an extreme shortage of blood in April. The substantial outdating of blood products in March and their severe shortage in April had proved very costly. She reflected upon the stated mission of the American Red Cross (ARC) "to fulfill the needs of the American people for the safest, most reliable, most cost-effective blood, plasma, and tissue services through voluntary donations." She wondered if some changes in its blood inventory management program would reduce operating costs for the ARC and increase the availability of blood to the hospitals that it supplies.

INTRODUCTION

The American Red Cross is a nonprofit organization collecting 48 percent of the blood supply in the United States. The remainder is collected using independent members of America's Blood Centers (35%), by members of the Council of Community Blood Banks (15%), and by commercial blood banks (2%). Each year, over 2 million hospitalized Americans depend on the timely availability of the right type of blood products at over 6,000 hospital blood banks in the United States. If the right blood products are not available when required, then medical complications or postponements of surgical procedures can result. This translates to extra days of hospitalization and expense.

---

*This case was prepared with the assistance of Manish Batra and Benjamin Flossie.
[1]Outdating occurs when a blood product, due to age, is no longer usable for its intended purpose and is declared out of date.

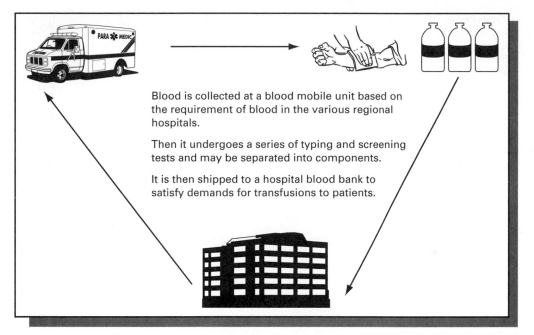

Figure 1 Collection, Testing, and Distribution of Blood

Human blood is a perishable product. It is collected in units of one pint per donor at collection sites such as churches, factories, schools, and regional blood centers; after undergoing a series of tests, it is ready to be processed and distributed to the various hospital blood banks in the region, as diagrammed in Figure 1.

There are eight major blood types, and their frequencies in the U.S. population vary from 38 percent for O+ to 0.5 percent for AB−, as shown in Table 1. Regional blood banks attempt to maintain inventories of some or all of the eight different types of blood in order to meet the variable daily demand for blood without incurring excessive outdating. The factors that affect the quantities to be maintained in inventory are as follows:

- *Demand.* The number of blood units (1 unit = 1 pint) of any one type that is required by the various hospital blood banks.
- *Shortage.* An occurrence when the demand exceeds the number of units of blood in inventory.
- *Shortage rate.* The long-term fraction (or percentage) of days on which a shortage occurs, that is, shortage rate = number of days a shortage occurs ÷ total number of days.
- *Outdate.* A blood unit discarded because of exceeding its shelf life (e.g., 35 days for whole blood).
- *Outdate Rate.* The ratio of mean number of blood units outdated to mean number of

Table 1 Relative Frequency of Blood Type in the U.S. Population

BLOOD TYPE	O+	A+	B+	AB+	O−	A−	B−	AB−	TOTAL
	38%	34%	9%	4%	7%	6%	1.5%	0.5%	100%

Figure 2
Generalized
Relationship
Between Outdating
and Shortage

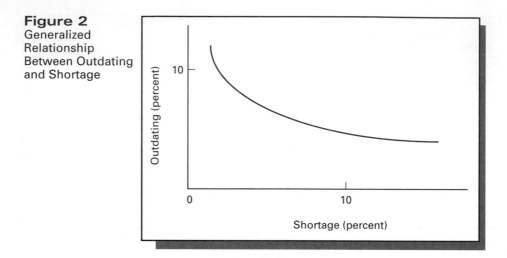

blood units collected, that is outdate rate =
mean number of units outdated ÷ mean
number of units collected.

When the shortage rate is decreased, the
outdate rate is increased, and vice versa. The
relationship between shortage and outdating is
shown in Figure 2. The optimal inventory level
for a specific blood product is found as a compromise between the shortage rate and the outdate rate. Shortage cost per unit equals the cost of
acquiring one unit (I) from another source, and
outdating cost per unit equals the cost of processing one unit (P). The number of units that can be
processed and outdated to cover the acquisition
cost of one unit is $I \div P$. For example, the cost of
acquiring one platelet unit from another source is
$30 and its processing cost is $3. Since the ratio of
I to P is 10 to 1, ten platelets could have been
processed and outdated for the cost of acquiring
just one unit from another source.

Once delivered to a hospital, a unit is
stored, under the appropriate conditions, in the
hospital's inventory. It is available to satisfy
physicians' requests for units to be put on
reserve for specific patients. These requests
arrive randomly during the course of each day,
each for a variable number of units. Upon
arrival of a request, the specified number of
units is selected from inventory according to a

first in, first out (FIFO) selection rule and put on
reserve. The units demanded but not used are
returned to inventory the next day.

A hospital is concerned with maintaining a
sufficient blood inventory to meet the variable
daily demand without outdating a large fraction
of the perishable blood. In trying to reach a
working compromise between the anticipated
outdate rate and shortage rate, most hospitals
exercise some judgment of their own in determining the quantities to order from the ARC. As
a result, the ideal blood distribution system is
one in which a hospital requests accuracy quantity of blood and the ARC tries to fulfill the
request as it occurs. This system results in a high
degree of uncertainty in the availability of blood,
and in inefficiencies in utilizing blood resources,
personnel, and facilities. To remedy this situation, alternative methods are employed, including the centralized management of blood, especially of the rare types, rather than management
by individual hospitals; prescheduled deliveries; and a distribution system in which blood is
"rotated" among the hospitals.

The timely availability and careful preser-
vation of blood are crucial to human life. Due to
blood's perishable nature, blood bank adminis-
trators find blood inventory management a
pressing problem. Shortages of blood often force
blood banks to adopt emergency procurement

procedures that result in high costs. Additional cost resulting from the adverse effects of shortages on patients is difficult to measure. Outdated blood causes blood centers to incur losses due to costs involved in procuring, processing, and storing blood.

BLOOD SOURCING: WHOLE BLOOD AND WHOLE BLOOD COMPONENTS

Whole blood is the blood drawn directly from a donor. This blood may be separated into various components: red blood cells, plasma, platelets, cryo, and so on. Unseparated whole blood is used directly for transfusion only in pediatric cases. In fact, less than 1 percent of total transfusions use whole blood.

Red blood cells are prepared by centrifugal or gravitational separation of the red cells from the plasma. Red blood cells are used for patients with a symptomatic deficit of oxygen-carrying capacity. They are also used for exchange transfusion and for helping to restore blood volume following significant hemorrhage.

Plasma is the liquid part of the blood. It consists of the anticoagulated, clear portion of blood that is separated by centrifugation or sedimentation no later than five days after the expiration date of the whole blood. It is used for patients with coagulation factors deficiency (deficiency in proteins that help in blood clotting). Plasma is stored frozen, while liquid plasma is refriger-

ated. *Fresh frozen plasma* is the plasma that is separated and frozen within eight hours after collection of whole blood. It contains plasma proteins including all coagulation factors.

Platelets occur on a concentrate separated from a single unit of whole blood and suspended in a small amount of the original plasma. These platelets are also known as *random platelets.* They are used for patients with bleeding problems and for patients requiring platelet transfusion, for example, certain cancer patients. Another type of platelets, called *pheresis platelets,* are also used.

Cryoprecipitate (or *cryo*) is prepared by thawing fresh frozen plasma between 1°C and 6°C and recovering the precipitate. The insoluble precipitate is refrozen. It is used for treatment of hemophilia and in the control of bleeding.

The above whole blood components are routinely extracted from the whole blood through appropriate procedures, which involve centrifuging, or spinning, the blood. The process used to extract various components/products from whole blood is shown in Figure 3.

The first spin should be completed within eight hours and the second within ten hours after drawing the blood. All of these components are perishable, with their lifetimes varying from five days (platelets) to one year (plasma and cryo). The lifetimes of the various components of blood are given in Table 2.

Figure 3 Extraction Process for Various Components/Products of Whole Blood

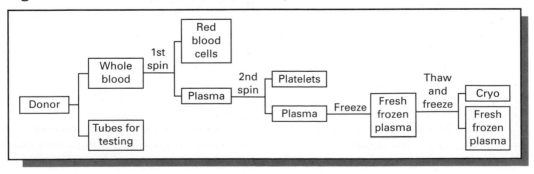

Product	Lifetime
Random platelets	5 days
Pheresis platelets	5 days
Whole blood	35 days
Red cells	42 days
Cryo	1 year
Fresh frozen plasma	1 year

Table 2 Lifetimes of Various Blood Products

Pheresis platelets have a lifetime of five days and serve the same purpose as random platelets. In fact, they are a better product than random platelets. Transfusion of one unit of pheresis platelets is equivalent to transfusing six units of random platelets. As a result, pheresis platelets required for a transfusion come from the same donor, and, thus, are safer to use. On the downside, pheresis platelets are more expensive to produce. From the prices of the various blood components in Table 3, one unit of pheresis platelets is priced at $408, while its equivalent of six units of random platelets is priced at $360. Because of this trade-off between cost of production and safety of use, pheresis platelets compete with random platelets. Deciding inventory levels for these two competing products, each with a short lifetime of five days, is a critical problem faced by the regional blood banks.

Product	Price
Random platelets	$60/unit
Pheresis platelets	408
Whole blood	169

Table 3 Prices of Various Blood Products

A SUPPLY-DRIVEN INVENTORY SYSTEM

Collecting blood for the region is one of the regional center's most important functions. It is done by (1) scheduled visits to organizations where donors have already signed up to give blood; (2) walk-in donors at the center's donor facilities; and (3) invited donors (or donor groups) who respond to emergency calls for blood. Out of these sources, the biggest portion of the center's supply comes from scheduled visits to schools, factories, churches, and the like. Collection sites are selected from a few months to up to a year in advance of a visit. Final scheduling must be done at least three to four weeks in advance. These long lead times and the resulting uncertainty make it difficult to collect the appropriate amount of blood needed at the time of collection. Since donors are volunteers and are not turned away, blood is collected from all qualified donors who arrive at a site. The number of collection sites is not easily changed with demand requirements since they too are volunteer in nature. In addition, the number of sites available and the quantities collected vary throughout the year. Often, demand for blood is at its highest, for example, in summer, a period with high accident rates, when the fewest sites are available (schools are in recess and factories are closed for vacation). The result can be substantial mismatches between supply and demand with little opportunity to adjust supply. Collection schedules are not easily adjusted to reduce supply; and when demand exceeds supply, emergency calls are made to donors to increase supply. Both are undesirable.

The various elements that affect the overall planning of this supply-driven inventory system are shown in Figure 4. All stages must be synchronized so that costs are controlled, and the need for blood is met.

An important aspect of uncertainty in the collection process comes from the fact that the center schedules collections from donors whose blood

Figure 4
Overview of the
Planning Process

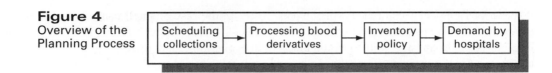

Scheduling collections → Processing blood derivatives → Inventory policy → Demand by hospitals

type is known only after the blood unit has been collected and typed. This means that the result of the blood drive, in terms of units collected for each blood type, can only be estimated, even if the exact number of donors is known beforehand. Even this knowledge is generally not possible, since the number of actual donors is usually less than the number of people who originally signed up. Approximately 14 percent of the people who signed up are not allowed to donate blood on that day and are deferred. This may happen because they are anemic, unhealthy, have engaged in risky behavior, have abnormal blood pressure, or have donated blood within the last 56 days.

DEMOGRAPHICS OF BLOOD DONORS

Only about 5 percent of the total U.S. population donates blood every year. Fifteen percent of these blood donors are first-time donors, while the rest are repeat donors. A person must be at least 17 years old to donate; there is no upper age limit.

Average age of a blood donor is 35. Fifty-two percent of the blood donors are male. Average number of donations per year per donor is 1.9. About 60 percent of the blood donors sign up to be V.I.P. donors (those who commit to donate blood at least four times a year). The average number of donations per year per V.I.P. donor is 2.9, a number less than four, since not all of the V.I.P. donors keep their commitment.

A majority of the donors belong to a community group. Donors also come from high schools; universities and colleges; and hospitals, industrial, business, and governmental organizations. Figure 5 gives a proportion of the various blood donor groups based on 203,018 units collected by the regional blood center over one year.

A COMPLEX DISTRIBUTION PROBLEM

The complexity of blood distribution is due to blood's perishable nature, the uncertainty in its availability to the regional blood center, and the

Figure 5
Blood Donor Groups

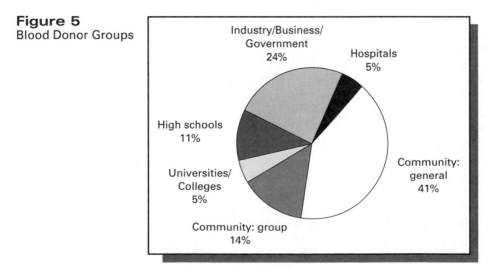

Industry/Business/Government 24%
Hospitals 5%
High schools 11%
Universities/Colleges 5%
Community: group 14%
Community: general 41%

demand variability at each of the hospital blood banks. The situation is further complicated by the large variation in the size of the hospital blood banks supplied, the incidence of the different blood groups, the requirements for whole blood and its various components at individual hospitals, and competition from other blood banks.

Since it is the ARC's policy for blood to be derived from volunteer donors, its availability is uncertain and donation is a function of a number of factors that cannot be controlled by the regional blood center, for example, public perception of the blood industry's quality control and fear of acquiring AIDS. The demand and usage of blood at hospital blood banks is also uncertain and varies from day to day and between hospital facilities. The hospital blood banks within a region may range from those transfusing a few hundred units per year to those transfusing tens of thousands of units per year.

A GENERAL APPROACH TO BLOOD INVENTORY MANAGEMENT

The transfusion services throughout the nation are characterized by diversity. Each regional blood center has independently evolved its own philosophies and techniques for blood distribution. Each region strives for self-sufficiency in supplying the blood needs of the hospitals in its region from regional donors. Because of these factors, it is essential that any strategy devised for inventory management be defensible from the point of view of both the regional blood center and each of the wide range of hospital blood banks that it serves. Furthermore, any strategy that involves interactions between regional blood centers must provide for clearly defined benefits for all participants. In addition, it is desirable that the implemented strategy be characterized by two management concepts: rotation of blood products between hospital blood banks and prescheduled deliveries to the hospital blood banks.

In the case of small usage hospital blood banks (these account for the largest part of the overall blood usage), any strategy that allocates blood products to be retained until transfused or outdated will result in low utilization. Consequently, some form of blood rotation is required, whereby freshly processed blood is sent to hospital blood banks, from which it may be returned some time later for redistribution according to the regional strategy. It is also desirable that a significant portion of the periodic deliveries to the hospital blood banks be prescheduled. This way, the uncertainty of supply faced by the hospital blood banks is reduced, with a resulting improvement in the planning of operations and the utilization of their resources.

Outdating of blood is undesirable and the ARC tries hard to avoid it. The uncertainties in supply and demand can result in too much blood that exceeds its acceptable use date. This usually occurs for specific blood types. That is, type O+ blood may be in short supply while type AB+ has excess inventory and is likely to be outdated. There is some opportunity at the time blood is collected to convert it into derivative products, considering different levels of anticipated product demand and the amount of product inventory on hand. However, outdating still can occur. When it does, there are several options available as the expiration date approaches. First, certain products can be converted into others with a longer shelf life, for example, whole blood may be converted into plasma. Second, the blood products may be sold to other regions of the American Red Cross, especially those having chronic blood supply deficits. Third, some, but not all, products may be sold to research laboratories. Fourth, they may be sold for a reduced price. Selling products outside of the local region generally results in less revenue for the products than if they were used to meet local demand.

Table 4 The ARC's Product Distribution to Its Largest Customers in Number of Units of Red Blood Cells Supplied to the Six Largest Customers Over One Year

HOSPITALS	RED BLOOD CELLS	TOTAL
A	30,000 units	15.00%
B	14,500	7.25
C	10,000	5.00
D	9,000	4.50
E	8,500	4.25
F	8,000	4.00
Others	120,000	60.00
Total	200,000 units	100.00%

AMERICAN RED CROSS REGIONAL BLOOD CENTER IN CLEVELAND, OHIO

The American Red Cross regional blood center in Cleveland supplies blood components to over 60 hospitals in the northern Ohio region. It supplies over 200,000 units of red blood cells per year, almost 40 percent of which is consumed by the six largest hospitals (see Table 4). The regional center decides on what the inventory levels at the hospitals should be, based on their past data of demand and usage. There are two options available for any hospital dealing with the ARC.

Option 1. The hospital decides its normal inventory levels based on past usage, and bears the risk of outdating. It is shipped blood daily to refill depleted quantities and rebuild inventories to their normal levels. This option is typically chosen by hospitals transfusing anywhere from a few hundred to a couple of thousand blood units per year.

Option 2. The hospital has a standing order, or a contract for a predetermined number of units of each blood component, to be delivered to it every day. This predetermined number of units is adjusted quarterly, based on the past usage. This option is the one chosen by hospitals transfusing anywhere from a couple of thousand to tens of thousands units of blood per year.

INVENTORY MANAGEMENT AT THE ARC'S REGIONAL BLOOD CENTER IN CLEVELAND, OHIO

Inventory management at the ARC's regional blood center uses a top-down planning approach (see Figure 6), which involves planning collections for the next year down to managing shortages and outdates that occur on a particular day.

Yearly Planning

An estimated usage for the next year is obtained from all the 60 hospitals that the ARC in Cleveland supplies. Then, using the historical data of demand and the estimated usage for the next year, collections are planned for the coming year. This takes into account the donors who

Figure 6 Top-Down Planning Approach to Inventory Management

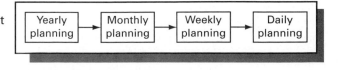

Figure 7
Recruitment and
Collections Analysis

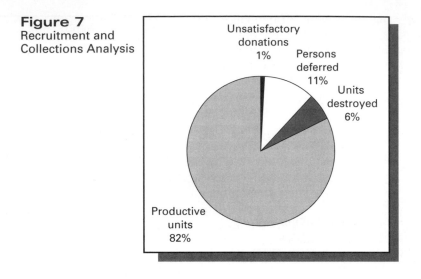

might be deferred due to illness or who have recently donated blood, the blood units that might be destroyed during testing, and the donations that might be unsatisfactory because less than one pint is collected. Figure 7, based on 233,352 yearly donors, shows that only 82 percent of the estimated collections result in productive units.

Monthly Planning

Monthly planning involves looking one month ahead and making sure that on every workday (Monday–Friday) in the next month, the estimated collections will exceed a predetermined number of units. This predetermined number of units is obtained by averaging the yearly requirements over the number of workdays in a year. If on a particular day in the coming month, the estimated collections are less than the predetermined number of units, ARC tries to recruit donors for that day. Collections are made on Saturdays and Sundays, but generally not as many units are collected on weekends as during the week.

Weekly Planning

Weekly planning involves looking at the inventory levels of various blood types, planning production of blood components, and planning distribution to the various hospitals for the whole

week. A projection of demand is made at the beginning of a week. Then, collections and production are planned based on projected demand in that week.

Daily Planning

Daily planning involves looking at the inventory and taking appropriate action in the case of shortages and products nearing their expiration date. A daily inventory report (see Table 5), which gives the inventory of each blood product by blood type, is generated during every shift. A product inventory report (see Table 6), which gives the inventory of a product by blood type and expiration date, is generated on every shift for platelets and at least once daily for all other products. A shipping report (see Table 7), which gives the number of units of each blood product shipped to the ARC's various customers on the previous day, is generated daily. A production report, which gives the number of units produced by blood type for a particular product, is generated daily.

A FIFO issuing policy is followed for all products, unless superseded by a standing order, which has to be fulfilled by relatively fresh units (with at least three days of remaining shelf life for platelets and 21 days for red cells).

PRODUCT	O+	A+	B+	AB+	O–	A–	B–	AB–	TOTAL
Red cells	472	1,349	99	539	142	91	83	105	2,880
Random platelets	77	67	16	17	13	14	2	9	215
Plasma	185	398	246	217	46	85	45	50	1,272
Pheresis platelets	4	7	5	0	1	3	0	0	20
Cryo	478	346	106	22	119	72	25	11	1,179

Table 5 Example of a Daily Inventory Report of Each Product by Blood Type (in Units)

An inventory, equal to at least three times the average daily demand, is maintained for each product and blood type. If the inventory falls below three times the average daily demand, a shortage is said to have occurred. Furthermore, if the inventory falls below the average daily demand, it is called an emergency, or a critical shortage. This may require emergency procedures for donor recruitment.

Products having excess inventory or nearing their expiration dates are sometimes reduced in price. This may be a $20 discount on red blood cells of blood type A+ to reduce excess inventory, or there may be a 50 percent

Table 6 Example of an Inventory Report of Products by Blood Type and Expiration Date (in Units)

PRODUCT	EXPIRATION DATE	O+	O–	A+	A–	B+	B–	AB+	AB–	TOTAL
Random platelets	02/15	—	—	4	—	2	—	—	—	6
Random platelets	02/16	48	7	5	3	35	11	4	2	115
Pheresis platelets	02/17	—	—	—	—	—	2	—	—	2
Random platelets	02/18	6	1	4	—	6	3	2	1	23
Random platelets	02/19	84	16	65	19	34	5	11	1	235
Pheresis platelets	02/19	3	1	3	3	2	—	—	—	12

Table 7 An Example Report on the Number of Daily Units of Each Blood Product Shipped to the ARC's Various Customers

TIME ORDERED	TIME SHIPPED	CUSTOMER NUMBER	RED CELLS/ WHOLE BLOOD	RANDOM PLATELETS	PHERESIS PLATELETS	FROZEN PLASMA	CRYO
12:28 A.M.	01:06 a.m.	19	0	12	0	0	0
01:33 A.M.	02:24 a.m.	31	57	0	0	0	0
02:16 A.M.	03:12 a.m.	31	1	0	0	0	0
01:38 A.M.	03:28 a.m.	5	94	0	0	0	0
02:19 A.M.	04:19 a.m.	5	1	0	0	0	0
01:32 A.M.	05:48 a.m.	20	25	0	0	0	0
07:06 A.M.	08:06 a.m.	6	12	0	0	0	0

	Red Blood Cells	Frozen Plasma	Cryo	Random Platelets	Pheresis Platelets
Total number of orders received	704	236	175	325	266
Number of orders filled at 100%	651	233	175	306	252
Percent filled at 100%	92.47	98.73	100.00	94.15	94.74

Table 8 Fill Rate As Determined by the Number of Orders Filled at 100% As Compared to the Total Number of Orders Received for Each Product Category in March

discount on platelets ready to expire. Shipping on consignment may also be initiated.

ASSESSING CUSTOMER SERVICE AT THE AMERICAN RED CROSS

The way customer service levels are assessed at the ARC's regional blood centers is by computation of a customer fill rate. This is done in two ways:

1. Fill rate is given by the ratio of the number of orders filled at 100 percent to the total number of orders received for each product category over a given month. It is computed for each of the five product categories (see Table 8).

2. Fill rate is given by the ratio of the number of units shipped to the number of units requested by the customer. Red blood cells constitute the only product for which the fill rate is computed by blood type, or ABO/Rh (i.e., for each of the eight blood types). For the other four product categories, the breakdown of the fill rate by the blood type, or ABO/Rh, is not done (see Table 9).

The regional blood center develops standards for fill rates by customer category, by product category, and by blood type (or ABO/Rh for red blood cells). This percentage may vary for different customers (depending on the negotiated standard for fill rates included in the customer's contract with the region), by

Table 9 Fill Rate As Determined by the Number of Units Shipped As Compared to the Number of Units Requested for Each Product Category in March

Red Blood Cells	O+	A+	B+	AB+	O–	A–	B–	AB–	Total
Units requested	2673	2988	2058	0	2425	270	247	56	10717
Units shipped	2461	2752	1864	0	1801	234	202	46	9360
Fill rate, %	92.07	92.10	90.57	—	74.27	86.67	81.78	82.14	87.34
Regional standard for fill rate, %	90	100	95	100	75	85	80	85	88.75
Percent difference	2.07	–7.90	–4.43	—	–0.73	1.67	1.78	–2.86	–1.41

	Frozen Plasma	Cryo	Random Platelets	Pheresis Platelets
Units requested	345	325	285	517
Units shipped	326	325	267	495
Fill rate, %	94.49	100.00	93.68	95.74
Regional standard for fill rate, %	100	100	95	98
Percent difference	–5.51	0.00	–1.32	–2.26

product, and by ABO/Rh. The difference between the negotiated or contract standard at the regional blood center and the regional blood center's actual performance is then computed. Monitoring fill rates provides valuable information to the regional blood center in its continuous effort to improve customer service.

COMPETITION

The American Red Cross guarantees an average fill rate of 97 percent to its customers, operating according to its stated mission. The smaller local blood banks are not capable of competing with the ARC on its high fill rate. However, since the local blood banks have lower fixed costs and provide no service level guarantee to their customers, they compete with the ARC on price. The ARC needs to collect the quantity and mix of blood products demanded by the hospitals (because of its high customer service level guarantee), while the local blood banks collect what they can. Very often, the hospitals shop arounded for the lowest price, and they might take their business, or

a part of it, to the local blood banks that offer prices lower than the ARC.

CONCLUSION

Dr. Croxton realized that she needed to do some major reflanking of her planning strategy. The amount of blood outdating that took place in March disturbed her. Volunteers donated blood with good intentions, but a good part of the blood became outdated. In April, when she tried to reduce outdating, extreme shortages occurred, resulting in lost revenue and lost goodwill. She could not forget that this was a business with a bottom line and that she must cover costs, or was it gradually becoming like any other business where the objective is making profits? More than ever before, competition existed in blood services. What was the best way to manage the blood supply? How should prices be set in the face of competition? She knew that the answers to some of the above questions were not easy and she had to do a lot of thinking. ■

QUESTIONS

1. Describe the inventory management problem facing blood services at the American Red Cross.
2. Evaluate the current inventory management practices in light of the ARC's mission.
3. Can you suggest any changes in ARC's inventory planning and control practices

that might lead to cost reduction or service improvement?
4. Is pricing policy an appropriate mechanism to control inventory levels? If so, how should price be determined?

Chapter 10

Purchasing and Supply Scheduling Decisions

*C*oordinating the flow of goods and services between physical facilities is a major issue in supply chain management. Deciding the product quantities to move, when to move them, how to move them, and from which locations to acquire them are frequent concerns. These scheduling decisions occur in the supply channel, and good management requires coordinating with other activities within the firm, especially production. In this chapter, we look at how such scheduling problems may be treated.

In addition, purchasing is considered an activity in the scheduling process. Although purchasing is primarily a buying activity, many of its

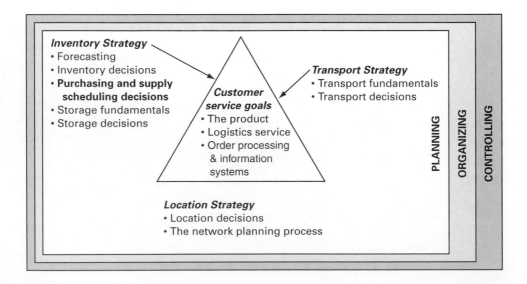

Inventory Strategy
• Forecasting
• Inventory decisions
• **Purchasing and supply scheduling decisions**
• Storage fundamentals
• Storage decisions

Customer service goals
• The product
• Logistics service
• Order processing & information systems

Transport Strategy
• Transport fundamentals
• Transport decisions

Location Strategy
• Location decisions
• The network planning process

PLANNING   ORGANIZING   CONTROLLING

decisions directly affect the flow of goods or services in a logistics channel. Therefore, only selected decisions are examined, and methods for solution are suggested. The entire purchasing function cannot be covered in this single chapter, so the reader is referred to one of the many good textbooks on purchasing for a more comprehensive discussion.[1]

COORDINATION IN THE SUPPLY CHANNEL

Good coordination among production, marketing, purchasing, and all other supply channel activities cannot be emphasized too strongly. Interrelationships between these activities frequently exist to the extent that optimizing one activity alone can be a detriment to one or more of the others. Failing to recognize this trade-off can negatively affect supply channel performance. For one company, purchasing policies and production scheduling rules interacted in such a way that the company's transportation manager thought inadequate transportation capacity alone was the reason for poor scheduling in the supply channel. Improved logistical supply was achieved when the elements of production scheduling, purchasing, and transportation were brought into proper balance. Consider in more detail from the following example the effect that poor coordination can have on channel activities.

Example

Anchor Hocking, a glass manufacturer, produced a line of dinnerware for the domestic consumer market. Demand for its products was reasonably constant throughout the year, with slight seasonality in demand at gift-giving times of the year.

The primary raw materials consisted of sand (75%); limestone (15%); and soda ash (10%). Sand was acquired locally, limestone was acquired regionally, and soda ash was acquired from mines in Wyoming. These materials were shipped using rail hopper cars as scheduled by production against an annual purchase contract. The suppliers knew how much was to be purchased from them annually, but the glass manufacturer decided when the suppliers should release (ship) the materials.

The supply cycle for soda ash is shown in Figure 10-1. After the production schedulers at the various plants released a shipping request to a vendor, the vendor would ship immediately, providing that covered hopper cars were available on the property. If not, a call for hopper cars would be placed to a local railroad. If no cars were available, premium transportation in the form of truck transportation was used. Preproduction materials were stored in silos with an average capacity of between three and six days of production output. Because of the relatively small storage capacity and the high cost to shut down a glass furnace when raw materials were not available, any potential delays in meeting the requirements of the production

---

[1]Michiel R. Leeders, Harold E. Fearon, and Anna Flynn, *Purchasing and Supply Management*, 12th ed. (Homewood, IL: Irwin, 2001); and Robert Monczka, Robert Trent, and Robert Handfield, *Purchasing and Supply Chain Management*, 2nd ed. (Mason, OH: South-Western, 2002).

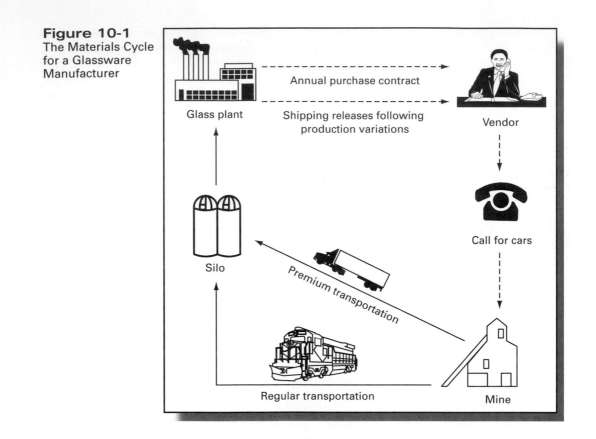

Figure 10-1
The Materials Cycle
for a Glassware
Manufacturer

Glass plant

Annual purchase contract

Shipping releases following
production variations

Vendor

Call for cars

Silo

Premium transportation

Regular transportation

Mine

schedule were avoided by using premium transportation with its associated higher-than-rail cost. Due to a perceived shortage of rail hopper cars in the country's rail system, management was willing to invest in its own railcars and place them in dedicated service.[2] The question that management posed was: How many rail cars are needed to minimize the cost of premium transportation?

The question presumes that railcar capacity was the answer to the marked increase in premium transportation costs. To a degree, it was. However, careful investigation showed that production schedulers at the plants were not allowing the 14 days between the time the material was to be shipped by a vendor and when it was needed in production. In fact, only about five days were being allowed, which was inadequate for shipping soda ash from Wyoming to plants in the East. Production schedulers appeared to be reacting to production requirements rather than adequately anticipating them. Adding to silo capacity so additional inventory could be stored was not practical because of the high investment cost. Therefore, with no change in scheduling procedures, an investment in 82 railcars could be justified. If good requirements planning techniques were used to guide shipment

---

[2]These cars were to be company owned, but the railroad would move them at a discount from its regular rate.

releases, only 40 railcars would be needed. Putting discipline in the shipment release methodology would reduce by 42 the number of railcars needed, thus reducing by one-half the potential investment.

The lesson of the Anchor Hocking case study is that poor production scheduling procedures can cause unnecessary transportation equipment investment. The transportation manager was trying to solve the problem entirely by acquiring more transportation capacity. Coordination among all the activities that affect physical supply was needed to realize a good solution to the problem.

SUPPLY SCHEDULING

The popularity of just-in-time, quick response, and time compression concepts highlights scheduling as an important activity in supply channels. Scheduling to requirements is an alternative to meeting requirements from inventories. Each represents the end points in a range of alternatives considered for meeting the demand, or requirements, of a supply channel. Chapter 9 was devoted to inventory management concepts, so we now turn our attention to the scheduling techniques referred to as requirements planning, which may minimize the inventory needed in a supply channel.

In the supply channel, it is the production requirements (or in the case of service firms, the operations requirements) that represent the demand to be met. A materials manager typically meets this demand in two ways. First, supplies are timed to be available just when they are needed for production. A popular technique for handling the mechanics of the scheduling process is materials-requirements planning. Second, requirements are met from supplies carried in inventory. The inventory replenishment rules maintain the stock levels. These rules specify when and in what quantities the materials will flow within the supply channel.

Many firms use both of these approaches simultaneously. To illustrate, consider how a manufacturer of industrial motors controlled its production output.

Example

The Power Equipment Division of the Lear Siegler Corporation produced a line of fractional horsepower motors for use in floor cleaners and polishers. These motors were sold as subcomponents to other manufacturers who produced the finished product. Because of this, the motors were custom-made to the buyers' specifications. Buyers typically placed firm orders several months in advance of their needs to ensure meeting their production schedules. Standard motors can be forecasted with reasonable accuracy and then produced to anticipated sales.

With this information, a build schedule (also called a master production schedule) was prepared for the coming three months. This build schedule, along with a materials list for each motor order, showed the production scheduler how much of each component was needed and when it was required. At this point, the production scheduler checked the available inventory for the necessary supplies. Normally, about 3,000 out of 3,300 parts, or about 90 percent, were made available through inventories. The remaining 300 parts were critical items of high value and were specific to each order, such as the motor shaft. These items were placed on a vendor shortage list until they were actually received and available to production. The same was true of any materials that were unavailable in inventory.

Offsetting by the length of the lead time, the production scheduler issued a purchase release order to the purchasing department so that the supplies were timed to arrive as needed for production. When all materials, parts, and supplies were on hand, the production scheduler released the customer orders to production for manufacture and assembly. As stocks were depleted from inventories, they were replenished according to a min-max inventory control policy.

The role of purchasing was to select the sources of supply, develop ordering procedures, negotiate price and terms of sale, specify the transportation services to be used, and estimate lead times. In this case, purchasing coordinates with production scheduling the flow of materials in the supply channel. The relationship of production scheduling to material supply is diagrammed in Figure 10-2.

Just-In-Time Supply Scheduling

Just-in-time (JIT) scheduling is an operating philosophy that is an alternative to the use of inventories for meeting the goal of having the right goods at the right place at the right time. It is a way of managing the materials supply channel that was first made popular by the Japanese, perhaps because of particular economic and logistical circumstances that have prevailed in that country in the last 40 years. Just-in-time scheduling may be defined as

> a *philosophy* of scheduling where the entire supply channel is synchronized to respond to the requirements of operations or customers.

It is characterized by

- Close relationships with a few suppliers and transport carriers
- Information that is shared between buyers and suppliers
- Frequent production/purchase and transport of goods in small quantities with resulting minimal inventory levels
- Elimination of uncertainties wherever possible throughout the supply channel
- High-quality goals

Economical replenishment quantities are driven toward single units as production setup and purchase-ordering costs are reduced to insignificant levels. Where there are economies of scale in purchasing or production, these economies are exploited to

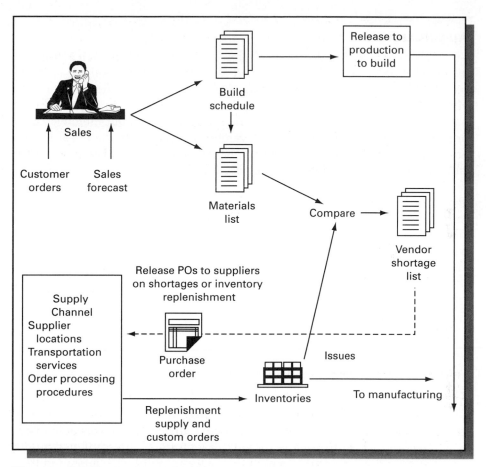

Figure 10-2   Relationship of Production Scheduling to Materials Supply

the maximum by using a few suppliers that are usually located in close proximity to the buyer's demand points. A close working relationship is developed with relatively few suppliers and carriers. Information from the buyer, mainly in the form of the production/operating schedule, is shared with the suppliers so that they might anticipate the buyer's needs, thereby reducing response time and its variability. The few selected suppliers are expected to perform with little variance in providing on-time deliveries. The overall effect of scheduling under a just-in-time philosophy is to create product flows that are carefully synchronized to their demands. Although more effort is likely to be expended in managing the supply channel under a JIT philosophy than with a supply-to-inventory philosophy, the benefit is to operate the channel with minimal inventory and with the attendant savings and/or service improvements. However, some of these benefits realized by the manufacturer may be a result of shifting costs and inventory onto the suppliers upstream in the supply channel.

Application

General Motors, a U.S. auto manufacturer, decided to implement a just-in-time supply scheduling system when it planned a major redesign of one of its best-selling cars. A previously used manufacturing plant, too small by today's standards, was reopened after installing doors along the long side of the building. This allowed materials to move a short distance to the production line, but there was little space for production inventories. A staging warehouse was constructed near the assembly building into which materials from suppliers would arrive and be unpacked prior to being moved, on demand, to the assembly line.

A significant reduction (to a few hundred from several thousand) in the number of suppliers and carriers was made, and suppliers could be no farther than 300 miles from the plant. For example, one supplier was selected as the sole provider of paint. However, this status came at a price. The paint supplier was required to maintain an inventory near the assembly plant. To assist in the supplier's planning, the automaker provided the supplier with the future auto production schedule. This established a level of trust between supplier and buyer not generally known in the industry.

Example

Hewlett-Packard applied just-in-time scheduling concepts to its distribution center operations. Over a one-and-a-half-year period, the company was able to achieve a 40 percent reduction in finished goods inventory, a 2 percent per month compounded growth in labor productivity, and a 44 percent improvement in the quality of customer shipments.[3]

Kanban

KANBAN is Toyota's production scheduling system and is perhaps the best-known example of just-in-time scheduling. KANBAN itself is a card-based production control system. A KAN card instructs a work center or supplier to produce a standard quantity of an item. The BAN card requests a predefined standard quantity of a component part or subassembly be brought to a work center. These cards are used as triggers for the production and movement of items.

The KANBAN/JIT scheduling system uses the reorder point method of inventory control to determine standard production-purchase quantities and involves very low setup costs and very short lead times. Several additional characteristics

---

[3]Patrick Guerra, "Just-In-Time Distribution," *Annual Proceedings*, Vol. 1 (St. Louis: Council of Logistics Management, October 27–30, 1985), p. 444.

make it effective as a just-in-time system. First, models in the master production schedule are repeated frequently and compared with a schedule built to take advantage of economies of scale. That is, a schedule of product models A and B that would exploit economies of scale and reduce setup costs might be

AAAAAAABBBBBBBAAAAAAABBBBBBBAAAAAAABBBBBBBB

However, the KANBAN schedule might look like this:

ABABABABABABABABABABABABABABABABABABABABABAB

Second, lead times are highly predictable because they are short. Suppliers are located near the site of operations and deliveries can be made frequently, often once an hour, without incurring great transportation expense.

Third, order quantities are small because setup and procurement costs are kept low. Since order quantities are related to setup or procurement costs, they become the target for cost reduction. Small order quantities mean low inventories. The classic reorder point method of inventory control is used to set the replenishment quantities.

Fourth, few vendors are used, with correspondingly high expectations of them. A high level of cooperation between the manufacturer and vendor is developed to assure that the desired level of product and logistical performance is achieved.

Just-in-time scheduling is in contrast with supply-to-inventory scheduling. Table 10-1 compares KANBAN/JIT to the supply-to-inventory approach for scheduling. Remember, they are alternatives, and one is not necessarily better than the other.

Observation

Since just-in-time systems operate with minimum inventory levels and few suppliers, the risk of immediate channel shutdown from interruptions in the supply chain is great. Toyota was at risk of shutting down 20 of its auto plants when a fire incinerated the main source of its supply of a crucial $5 brake valve. But five days after the fire, the factories started up again. The secret lay in Toyota's close-knit family of parts suppliers. In the corporate equivalent of an Amish barnraising, suppliers and local companies rushed to the rescue. Within hours, they had begun taking blueprints for the valve, improvising tooling systems, and setting up makeshift production lines. Thirty-six suppliers, aided by more than 150 other subcontractors, had nearly 50 separate lines producing small batches of the brake valve. The quick recovery is attributable to the power of the group, which handled the problem without thinking about money or business contracts.[4]

---

[4]Valerie Reitman, "Toyota's Fast Rebound After Fire at Supplier Shows Why It Is Tough," *Wall Street Journal*, May 8, 1997, A1.

Table 10-1 A Comparison of KANBAN/JIT Supply Scheduling and Supply-to-Inventory Scheduling Philosophies

Factors	Kanban/JIT Scheduling	Supply-to-Inventory Scheduling
Inventory	A liability. Every effort must be expended to do away with it.	An asset. It protects against forecast errors, equipment problems, and late vendor deliveries. More inventory is "safer."
Lot sizes, purchase quantities	Meet immediate needs only. A minimum replenishment quantity is desired for both manufactured and purchased goods, but it is determined from the EOQ formula.	Quantities determined by economies of scale or from the EOQ formula. No attempt is made to change setup costs to realize smaller production or purchase quantities.
Setups	Make them insignificant. This requires either extremely rapid changeover to minimize the impact on operations, or availability of extra machines already set up. Fast change over permits small lot sizes to be practical, and allows a wide variety of parts to be made.	A low priority. Maximize output is the usual goal, so setup costs may be a secondary consideration.
Work-in-process inventory	Eliminate them. When there is little inventory accumulation between processes, the need to identify and fix problems surfaces early.	A necessary investment. Inventory accumulation between processes permits succeeding operations to continue in the event of a problem with the feeding operation. Also, by providing a selection of jobs, the factory management has a greater opportunity to match varying operator skills and machine capabilities, and to combine setups so as to contribute to the operation's efficiency.
Vendors	Considered to be coworkers. The vendor takes care of the needs of the customer, and the customer treats the vendor as an extension of his factory. Few are used, but the risk of supply interruptions may increase.	A professional arm's-length relationship is maintained. Multiple sources are the rule, and it's typical to play them against each other to achieve the lowest prices.
Quality	Zero defects is the goal. If quality is not 100%, production and distribution are in jeopardy.	Tolerate some defects to keep products flowing and to avoid excessive costs to guarantee an exceedingly high level of quality.
Equipment maintenance	Preventive maintenance or excess capacity is essential. Process shutdown jeopardizes downstream operations when no inventory is available to act as a buffer.	As required. Not critical since inventories are maintained.
Lead times	Keep them short. This increases response times throughout the supply/distribution channel, and reduces uncertainties and the need for safety stocks.	Long lead times are not serious since they may be compensated for with additional inventories.

Requirements Planning

In the mid-1970s, requirements planning, which had been carried out for years, was formalized as materials requirements planning (MRP). Although MRP deals with supply scheduling, its logic base is different from that of KANBAN. It is a method primarily used for scheduling high-valued custom-made parts, materials, and supplies whose demand is reasonably well known. The purpose of MRP, from a logistics viewpoint, is to avoid, as much as possible, carrying these items in inventory. Theoretically, inventories do not need to be created when the amount and timing of the end-product requirements are known. Offsetting by the lead time the request for parts, materials, and supplies, the end-product requirements can be met at the time they develop. Precise timing of materials flows to meet production requirements is the principle behind materials requirements planning.

MRP is an important scheduling alternative to the supply-to-inventory scheduling philosophy. Except for the manner in which statistical inventory control procedures are used in KANBAN, they do not perform as well in the physical supply channel as they do in the physical distribution channel. The reason is that the assumptions on which statistical inventory control is based too often are not met. That is, demand is not regular, random, independent, and unbiased. Rather, demand patterns for parts, materials, and supplies that go into end products are derived from the end-product demand.

Derived demand patterns result from the knowledge that a predetermined number of parts, materials, and supplies, as specified on the bill of materials, goes into an end product. Therefore, the demand patterns for these materials of production are lumpy. If statistical inventory control procedures were used to set inventory levels, these levels would be unacceptably high due to the high variance of the lumpy demand patterns.

This demand lumpiness may also be caused from the application of standard inventory policies at multiple levels in the supply distribution channel. To illustrate, consider Figure 10-3. An end product is stocked in a field warehouse and is controlled using a reorder point inventory control procedure. The result of this policy is to send intermittent replenishment orders to the inventories at the plant. If only a few warehouses are being replenished from the plant stocks, or the orders from multiple warehouses occur simultaneously, a stair-step stock availability pattern results, as shown in Figure 10-3(b). Consequently, the supply inventory for a component that goes into the production of the end product must be even larger to meet the production requirements brought about through the replenishment of the plant end-product inventories [see Figure 10-3(c)]. Because of the intermittent depletions of the component inventory, high inventory levels must be maintained when they are not needed. If the depletion rate of the inventory level can even roughly be anticipated, components may be ordered just ahead of the depletion with a resulting substantial saving in inventory carrying costs.

MRP Mechanics

Only recently has the materials requirements planning methodology been formalized and computerized, although the requirements planning concept has been applied for many years. It can be described as

... a formal, mechanical method of supply scheduling whereby the timing of purchases or of production output is synchronized to meet period-by-period operating requirements by offsetting the request for supply from the requirements by the length of the lead time.

MRP has also been referred to as time-phased replenishment planning. Many computer software suppliers (e.g., SAP) now have programs that can readily be installed in a production environment to handle the MRP arithmetic required for thousands of items. To illustrate the basic concepts of the method, consider a simplified example.

Figure 10-3 Lumpy Demand for a Component When the End Product Is Under Reorder Point Control

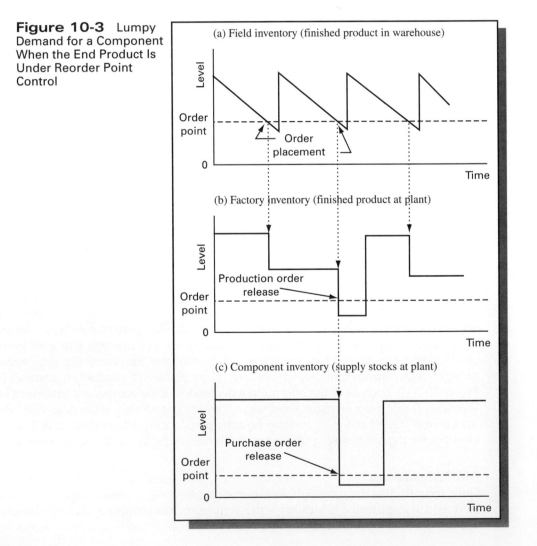

Example

Colonial Clocks produces and distributes, through catalogs, a line of authentic mechanical clock reproductions. Two clock styles, M21 and K36, use the same clock mechanism, R1063. Because these mechanisms wear out or are damaged in use, there is an independent replacement demand for the clock mechanism of 100 per week. Colonial assembles M21 and K36 in minimum production run quantities, but the clock mechanism is purchased from an outside supplier subject to a minimum purchase quantity. The estimated demand for M21 and K36 for the next eight weeks is itemized next.

Weeks from Now	M21	K36
1	200	100
2	200	150
3	200	120
4	200	150
5	200	100
6	200	90
7	200	110
8	200	120

Other vital information about each item follows:

Clock Style M21

Minimum production run quantity = 600 units
Production run time = 1 week
Inventory on hand = 500 units
Scheduled receipts = 600 units in period 2

Clock Style K36

Minimum production run quantity = 350 units
Production run time = 2 weeks
Inventory on hand = 400 units
Scheduled receipts = 0 units

Clock Mechanism R1063

Minimum purchase order quantity = 1,000 units
Purchase lead time = 2 weeks
Safety stock = 200 units to be maintained at all times
Inventory on hand = 900 units
Service parts demand = 100 units per week

The critical question for Colonial is, When and for what quantities should purchase orders be released to suppliers?

The MRP methodology begins with a product structure tree (bill of materials) that defines the quantity relationships between components and end product, as

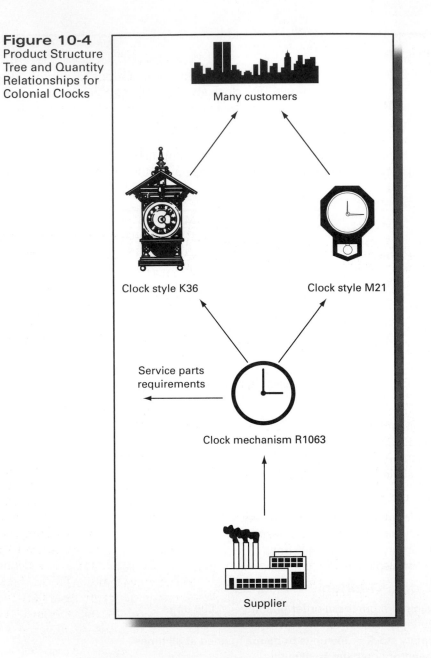

Figure 10-4
Product Structure
Tree and Quantity
Relationships for
Colonial Clocks

Many customers

Clock style K36

Clock style M21

Service parts
requirements

Clock mechanism R1063

Supplier

shown in Figure 10-4. Considering only one component (the clock mechanism), its derived demand comes from the production of the two clock models plus service parts requirements. Thus, if it is known when and in what quantities each model will be produced, a schedule for the purchase of the clock mechanisms can be developed. To organize these time-phased events and to keep track of incoming materials,

Figure 10-5
Computations for Determining the Planned Production Releases for Clock Style K36

(a) Initial MRP form

		Week							
		1	2	3	4	5	6	7	8
Projected gross clock requirements		100	150	120	150	100	90	110	120
Scheduled receipts									
Quantity on hand	400								
Planned production releases									

(b) Completed MRP form

		Week							
		1	2	3	4	5	6	7	8
Projected gross clock requirements		100	150	120	150	100	90	110	120
Scheduled receipts				350					
Quantity on hand	400	300	150	30	230	130	40	280	160
Planned production releases			350		350				

on-hand materials, and the requirements that must be met, a base chart is used, such as that in Figure 10-5(a). The projected requirements for the K36 clock are shown in their respective weekly "time buckets" (intervals of time, such as a week or month). The current on-hand inventory of these clocks is also noted.

To meet these end-product requirements, a product schedule needs to be developed showing when production should begin and when and in what quantities clock mechanisms should be available. To do this, begin with week 1 and deduct the requirements for week 1 from the available inventory on hand. Record the quantity on hand, as shown in Figure 10-5(b). This procedure is repeated for each subsequent week until the projected quantity on hand drops below zero. At this time, a scheduled receipt of finished K36 clocks is needed. Because a two-week lead time is required for production, the clock mechanisms must be available for production two weeks in advance of the scheduled receipt. Production determines the lot size quantity. The scheduled receipt adds to the quantity on hand so that enough stock is available to meet the requirements. Decreasing on-hand quantities continues until week 7, at which time another scheduled receipt must be planned. And so it goes to the end of the planning horizon.

Clock Style K36

Minimum production run quantity = 350 units
Production run time = 2 weeks
Inventory on hand = 400 units
Scheduled receipts = 0 units

Figure 10-6
Computations
for Determining
the Planned
Production
Releases for
Clock Style M21

		Week							
		1	2	3	4	5	6	7	8
Projected gross clock requirements		200	200	200	200	200	200	200	200
Scheduled receipts			600				600		
Quantity on hand	500	300	700	500	300	100	500	300	100
Planned production releases						600			

Next, the procedure is repeated for clock style M21, as shown in Figure 10-6. The major differences here are that a previously scheduled receipt is due in week 2, and the lead time offset is one week.

With the planned production releases now known for both clock styles, the gross requirements for the clock mechanism can be developed for each week. That is, the releases for K36 and M21 are summed into the corresponding week of the R1063 gross requirements time buckets. To these are added the demand for service parts. Once the projected gross requirements are established, the computations to determine when and how much should be purchased of the clock mechanisms proceed in the same manner as for K36 and M21. The result is to place a purchase order for 1,000 units in weeks 2 and 3 (Figure 10-7).

Clock Style M21

Minimum production run quantity = 600 units
Production run time = 1 week
Inventory on hand = 500 units
Scheduled receipts = 600 units in period 2

It should now be clear that the flow of materials is controlled through offsetting by the length of the lead time the call for materials from requirements. End-product requirements are assumed to be known for sure, as are lead times. Production-purchase lot sizes are given. Even though certainty is assumed, the effects of uncertainty in the requirements levels and in the lead times are always present. Transport rate breaks may alter the order release quantity. Consider how the MRP approach might be modified to handle these realities.

Demand Uncertainty in MRP

The MRP approach to purchase timing assumes that the requirements in the master schedule are known. To the extent that they may vary throughout the planning horizon, some safety stock protection is needed if the requirements are to be met. If the variability in requirements can be represented by a probability distribution, then the amount of safety stock needed in the schedule can be determined in a way that is

Figure 10-7 Determination of Gross Requirements and Purchase Order Releases for Clock Mechanisms R1063

CLOCK STYLE K36

		Week						
	1	2	3	4	5	6	7	8
Projected gross clock requirements	100	150	120	150	100	90	110	120
Scheduled receipts				350			350	
Quantity on hand 400	300	150	30	230	130	40	280	160
Planned production releases		350			350			

CLOCK STYLE M21

		Week						
	1	2	3	4	5	6	7	8
Projected gross clock requirements	200	200	200	200	200	200	200	200
Scheduled receipts		600				600		
Quantity on hand 500	300	700	500	300	100	500	300	100
Planned production releases					600			

CLOCK MECHANISM R1063

		Week						
	1	2	3	4	5	6	7	8
Projected gross clock requirements *(Service parts requirements)*	100	100	100	100	100	100	100	100
	0	350	0	0	350	0	0	0
	0	0	0	0	600	0	0	0
	100	450	100	100	1,050	100	100	100
Scheduled receipts								
Quantity on hand 900	800	350	250	1,150	1,100	1,000	900	800
Planned production releases		1,000	1,000					

Minimum purchase order quantity = 1,000 units

Purchase leadtime = 2 weeks

Safety stock = 200 units to be maintained at all times

Inventory on hand = 900 units

Service parts demand = 100 units per week

similar to inventory control. However, this may be impractical, because the require-ments for any product or component are likely to show wide variations due to changes in production schedules, canceled customer orders, and missed forecasts. This will lead to inaccurate estimates of the safety stock levels.

As an alternative, a fixed on-hand inventory level can be maintained that is determined from either practical experience or some other means. Once the minimal on-hand quantity is established, order releases are triggered in the normal MRP man-ner, except that the on-hand quantity drops to the minimum quantity rather than to zero. Although this method is approximate, it is probably the best that can be done considering the inherent lumpy nature of derived demand.

Lead Time Uncertainty in MRP

Lead times are not likely to be known for sure. When to release the request for mate-rials depends on the uncertainty in lead time as it affects over- and understocking. The optimal time T^* to release the request for materials ahead of requirements is a matter of balancing the expected cost associated with having the materials arrive before they are needed, thereby incurring a holding charge, with the expected cost of having the materials arrive after they are needed, thereby incurring a late-penalty charge. Assuming that requirements during a time bucket are filled at a constant rate and lead times are normally distributed, the expected number of units short of meet-ing production requirements is $s_{LT}E_{(z)}$, where s_{LT} is the standard deviation of the lead time distribution and $E_{(z)}$ is the normal unit loss integral. The expected number of units arriving too soon is $s_{LT}E_{(-z)}$. The total relevant cost then is

$$TC = P_c s_{LT} E_{(z)} + C_c s_{LT} E_{(-z)} \qquad \text{(10-1)}$$

where

P_c = cost per unit of having materials *after* they are needed ($ per unit per day)
C_c = cost per unit of having materials *before* they are needed ($ per unit per day)

Using calculus to find the minimum cost yields

$$P = \frac{P_c}{C_c + P_c} \qquad \text{(10-2)}$$

where P is the probability of having clock mechanisms available at the time needed for production. Given P, the number of standard deviations z is found from Appendix A such that the optimum release time T^* is

$$T^* = LT + z(s_{LT}) \qquad \text{(10-3)}$$

Example

Suppose that in the Colonial Clocks illustration the average purchase lead time for the clock mechanism is normally distributed with an average of 14 days and a stan-dard deviation of three days. There is a penalty cost for delaying or interrupting pro-duction: $500 per unit per day for each clock mechanism that is not available when

Figure 10-8
Lead Time
Distribution with
Order Release Point
T^*

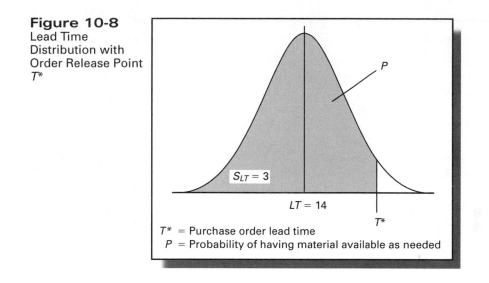

$S_{LT} = 3$

$LT = 14$

T^*

T^* = Purchase order lead time
P = Probability of having material available as needed

needed. If the clock mechanisms arrive ahead of schedule, a holding cost of $5 per unit per day is incurred.

The problem is one of determining how much time should be added to the average purchase lead time to protect against lead time variability. Specifically, we are looking for the optimum purchase order release time T^* on the lead-time distribution, as shown in Figure 10-8. This can be found after first determining P. That is,

$$P = \frac{P_c}{C_c + P_c} = \frac{500}{5 + 500} = 0.99$$

From the area under the normal distribution curve in Appendix A, $z_{@P = 0.99} = 2.33$. Therefore,

$$T^* = LT + z(s_{LT})$$
$$= 14 + 2.33(3)$$
$$= 21 \text{ days before production}$$

Over- and understocking costs will not always be known for sure. In such a case, P may be assigned a value and T^* computed according to Equation (10-3).

Order Release Quantity

Although production-purchase order quantities may be established through order quantity minimums or contractual amounts, they may also be established through balancing ordering costs against the inventory-carrying costs. This process has been referred to as part period cost balancing.

Example

Suppose that no minimum order release quantity has been specified for clock mechanisms, as previously shown in Figure 10-7. These clock mechanisms cost Colonial $15 each and the annual carrying charge is 25 percent, or $0.07 per unit per week. An order-processing cost of $150 is incurred every time an order is placed.

When an order is to be released in week 2 to meet the requirements for week 4, the question is whether the order quantity should be just large enough to meet the requirements for one week or whether the order quantity should be sufficient to cover the requirements for several weeks into the future. This can be determined by testing several obvious options, that is, testing order quantities equal to one week's requirements, two weeks' requirements, and so on. Assume the average inventory for the week is (beginning inventory + ending inventory)/2, where beginning inventory is scheduled receipts + quantity on hand. Ending inventory is beginning inventory – requirements. Starting with R1063 requirements for week 4, the strategies would be to order for week 4 only; weeks 4 and 5; weeks 4, 5, and 6; and so on. Given that a safety stock of 200 units is to be maintained, the order quantities to meet periods 4, 5, and 6 would be 50; 50 + 1050 = 1100; and 50 + 1050 + 100 = 1200, respectively.

When the carrying costs equal the ordering costs, the optimum order quantity is found. Find the inventory carrying cost for each strategy.

(Q = 50) Week 4	0.07(300 + 200)/2 = $17.50
(Q = 1,100) Weeks 4 & 5	0.07[(1,350 + 1,250)/2 + (1,250 + 200)/2] = **$141.75**
(Q = 1,200) Weeks 4, 5 & 6	0.07[1,450 + 1,350)/2 + (1,350 + 300)/2 + (300 + 200)/2] = $173.25

Because the carrying costs associated with an order release quantity of 1,100 is closest to the ordering cost of $150, this is the best strategy. If price discounts or transportation rate breaks were also present in this problem, even larger release quantities might be justified, as the additional carrying costs can be offset by these cost reductions.

Just-In-Time Distribution Scheduling

The concepts embodied in just-in-time supply scheduling can also be applied to the physical distribution channel. Compressing the time between when customer orders are placed and when they are received can be a competitive advantage. This quick response is based on many of the same ideas behind just-in-time scheduling. That is, use information to reduce uncertainties and substitute for assets, namely inventories. Use electronic information transmission to reduce the order-cycle time. Use computer technology to speed the production and/or filling of customer orders. Careful application of these concepts to the distribution channel can improve customer service and lower costs.

Integrated Supply Channel Management

From an operating viewpoint, the methods of MRP can be used in the distribution channel, called distribution-requirements planning (DRP), to allow integrated supply scheduling throughout a company's entire logistics channel, from suppliers to customers. Consider the supply channel as generalized in Figure 10-9. It is not rare to see physical distribution scheduling managed separately from production or supply scheduling. Pull methods of inventory management[5] in field warehouses are popularly taught as ways to manage inventory levels and to recommend to production when and in what quantities to produce. Applying the just-in-time concept expressed as DRP to the physical distribution channel offers an alternative with several benefits to the more traditional pull methods. These benefits are

- A similar information base is created for the entire production/logistics channel. This encourages integrated planning throughout the channel.
- The DRP concepts are compatible with those of MRP used at the plant.
- Since DRP shows planned future shipments, decision making is assisted in such areas as transport capacity planning, vehicle dispatching, and warehouse order filling. Increased flexibility and an improved ability to react to change are also noted.
- When developing a schedule, all demand sources can be incorporated, not just the forecast.
- Whereas ROP/EOQ systems generally manage individual items from independent multiple warehouses, DRP allows them to be managed collectively.

Companies are reporting that significant improvements have been realized when DRP is installed in their operations. Collins and Whybark offer several examples.[6]

Examples

- Abbott Laboratories, Canada, produced products in three plants and distributed them throughout Canada through distribution centers. Its DRP installation improved customer service levels from 85 to 97 percent while reducing inventories by 25 percent. The total distribution costs dropped by 15 percent. In addition, product obsolescence was reduced by 80 percent.
- A Midwest supplier of service parts for farm equipment, Hesston, served 1,200 dealers through eight distribution centers. The benefits of DRP were described both in qualitative and quantitative terms. In addition to a 20 percent cost reduction and an improvement of service levels to 97.5 percent, it noted an improvement in flexibility and ability to react to change. Planning for future requirements improved, and it reported improved productivity from its distribution analysis.

[5]See the discussion of the reorder point and periodic review methods of inventory control in Chapter 9.
[6]Robert S. Collins and D. Clay Whybark, "Realizing the Potential of Distribution Requirements Planning," *Journal of Business Logistics*, Vol. 6, No. 1 (1985), pp. 53–65.

Figure 10-9 A Generalized Supply Chain Order Information Flow from Suppliers to Customers

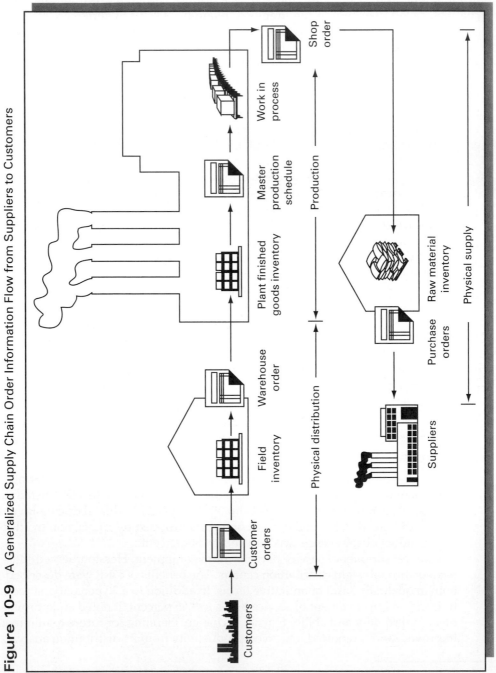

- Howard Johnson used DRP in distributing its ice cream on the East Coast. It reported a 12 percent improvement in service levels, and a reduction in inventories of 25 percent. The total distribution costs dropped by 10 percent. Improved control over inventories enabled it to realize an 80 percent reduction in obsolescence (freshness control) as well.

DRP Mechanics

DRP is an extension of the MRP logic that has already been described. Attention here will be drawn to the differences between the two. First, DRP begins with an item demand forecast as close to that of the customer as possible, which we will assume is the demand on a field warehouse. This demand is for a number of periods into the future and is developed from the item forecast, future customer orders, planned promotions, and any other information relevant to the demand pattern. This demand becomes the forecast requirements in the DRP—equivalent to the master production schedule in MRP. An example of the basic DRP record is shown in Figure 10-10. Note the similarity with the MRP record given in Figure 10-5(a).

The planned shipments for a single item from more than one warehouse are combined to generate the gross requirements on the central inventory, such as the plant finished-goods inventory. Suppose that plant inventories are used to meet field warehouse planned shipments and that production supplies plant finished-goods inventories. We then implode the planned shipments of an item for all warehouses to generate the gross requirements for the plant inventory. The imploding process is shown in Figure 10-11. Once the gross requirements are known for central inventory, a requirements planning record is developed to determine the planned order releases at the plant inventory level. These planned order releases are used to generate the master production schedule. The requirements planning process can continue upstream in the supply channel until the suppliers are reached, allowing full-channel scheduling.

Figure 10-10 Example of a Basic DRP Record for a Single Item in a Field Warehouse

		Period							
		1	2	3	4	5	6	7	8
Forecast requirements		100	200	100	150	100	100	200	200
In transit			300		300			300	300
Quantity on hand	250	150	250	150	300	200	100	200	300
Planned shipments		300		300			300	300	

Safety stock = 50 units   Shipping quantity = 300 units
Lead time = 1 period

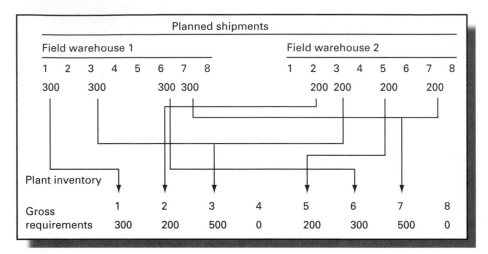

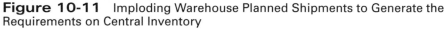

Figure 10-11 Imploding Warehouse Planned Shipments to Generate the Requirements on Central Inventory

PURCHASING

Purchasing involves buying the raw materials, supplies, and components for the organization. The activities associated with it include the following:

- Selecting and qualifying suppliers
- Rating supplier performance
- Negotiating contracts
- Comparing price, quality, and service
- Sourcing goods and services
- Timing purchases
- Setting terms of sale
- Evaluating the value received
- Measuring inbound quality, if this is not a responsibility of quality control
- Predicting price, service, and sometimes demand changes
- Specifying the form in which goods are to be received

Buying indirectly affects the flow of goods in the physical supply channel, although not all buying activities are of direct concern to the logistician. Decisions relating to the selection of vendor shipping points, the determination of purchasing quantities, the timing of supply flows, and the selection of the product form and transport methods are some of the important decisions affecting logistics costs. Conversely, activities relating to the negotiation of contracts, vendor performance evaluation, quantity assurance, and value analysis do not have a direct bearing on movement and storage of goods in the supply channel. Consequently, it is fair to say that purchasing should not be the entire responsibility of the logistician. However, the interrelationship between purchasing and move-store activities can be substantial. The discussion here is focused on those purchasing activities most directly related to product flows.

Importance of Purchasing

Purchasing commands an important position in most organizations since purchased parts, components, and supplies typically represent 40 to 60 percent of an end product's sales value. This means that relatively small cost reductions gained in the acquisition of materials can have a greater impact on profits than equal improvements in other cost-sales areas of the organization. This has been known as the *leverage principle*.

Example

The leverage principle can be illustrated using a simple profit-and-loss statement. The objective is to double profits. Currently, a firm with gross sales of $100 million and a profit of $5 million spends 60 percent of its sales for purchased goods and services. Remaining costs include labor, salaries, and overhead. The question is, How much of an increase or decrease in sales, price, labor and salaries, overhead, or purchases would be needed to increase profits from their current level of $5 million to $10 million?

Table 10-2 shows how much of a change in each category is required to double profits. In every column, except for Price and Purchases, the change must be dramatic in order to double profits. Even in the case of Price, competition in the marketplace may preclude an increase. Although a major portion of the cost of purchased goods cannot be managed, often such simple procedures as requiring two supplier quotes on each item purchased, working closely with suppliers to control costs, taking advantage of vendor quantity discounts, or paying careful attention to the sourcing, routing, and selection of transport modes can lead to substantial cost reductions. The percentage reduction need not be great in order to realize substantial absolute dollar cost reduction and profit improvement.

The return-on-assets effect also illustrates the importance of purchasing. In addition to increasing profits, reduced purchasing prices lower the asset base for the firm. This results in a return on assets that is disproportionately higher than the extent of the price reduction.

Table 10-2 Illustration of the Leverage Principle in Purchasing to Achieve a Doubling of Profits ($000,000)

	CURRENT	SALES +17%	PRICE +5%	LABOR AND SALARIES −50%	OVERHEAD −20%	PURCHASES −8%
Sales	$100	$117	$105	$100	$100	$100
Purchased goods and services	60	70	60	60	60	55
Labor and salaries	10	12	10	5	10	10
Overhead	25	25	25	25	20	25
Profit	$ 5	$ 10	$ 10	$ 10	$ 10	$10

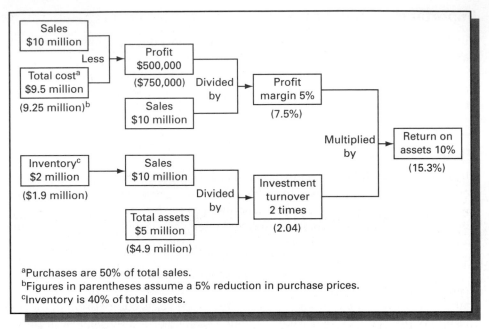

Figure 10-12 Return on Assets Before and After a 5 Percent Purchase Price Reduction

Source: Adapted from Michiel R. Leeders and Harold E. Fearon, *Purchasing and Supply Management*, 11th ed. (Burr Ridge, IL: Irwin, 1997), p. 17.

Example

Suppose a firm has $10 million in annual sales with total expenses of $9.5 million. Assets are $5 million, of which $2 million are for inventory. Cost of purchased materials is 50 percent of sales. Using the standard return-on-assets model, we can develop Figure 10-12. Purchasing can achieve an across-the-board price reduction of 5 percent. What increase in return on assets is likely to occur?

This modest price reduction can achieve a 50 percent increase in profits. This is due to the leverage effect. On the other hand, the price reduction lowers the asset base by valuing inventory at 95 percent of its previous value. This increases the velocity of asset turnover to 2.04 from the previous 2.00. The return on assets increases to 15.3 percent from its previous 10 percent, a 53 percent increase.

When companies such as GE, General Motors, and United Airlines undertake cost-saving initiatives, it is common for them to seek price cuts from their suppliers. Recognizing that purchased materials average more than 50 percent of their expenses, suppliers are the obvious focus of cost reductions. Some of the strategies used can be summarized in the following four points.

- *Renegotiate contracts.* Send suppliers letters demanding price cuts of 5 percent or more; rebid the contracts of those who refuse to cut costs.
- *Offer help.* Dispatch teams of experts to suppliers' plants to help reorganize and suggest other productivity-boosting changes; work with suppliers to make parts simpler and cheaper to produce.
- *Keep the pressure on.* To make sure improvements keep coming, set annual, across-the-board cost-reduction targets, often of 5 percent or more a year.
- *Pare down suppliers.* Slash the overall number of suppliers, sometimes by up to 80 percent, and boost purchases from those that remain to improve economies of scale.[7]

It is clear that these companies understand the leverage principle and the return-on-assets effect.

Internet auctioning is another way that firms seek to lower prices for their purchased goods and services. An inherent advantage of the Internet is that many suppliers can be brought together in the purchasing process conveniently and inexpensively. Lower prices are achieved because the marketplace is expanded with more potential sellers offering their services and products. In other words, a perfect marketplace is approached where prices are driven to their lowest levels.

Observation

United Technologies needed suppliers to make $24 million worth of circuit boards. FreeMarkets, an online B2B bidding service, evaluated 1,000 potential suppliers and invited 50 especially qualified to bid. FreeMarkets planned for three hours of on-line competitive bidding. FreeMarkets divided the job into 12 lots, each of which was put up for bid. At 8 A.M., the first lot valued at $2.25 million was put up. The first bid was $2.25 million, which was seen by all. Minutes later, another bidder placed a $2 million bid. Further bidders reduced the price again. Minutes before the bid closed on the first lot, at 8:45 A.M., the forty-second bidder placed a $1.1 million bid. When it all ended, the bids for all 12 lots totaled $18 million (about a 35 percent savings to United Technologies).[8]

Where the logistician sees opportunity in the purchasing activities to reduce costs substantially is in the timing of material flows, in determining the buying quantities, in the sourcing of materials, and in setting the terms of sale. That is, the key questions are how much to buy and when, where to buy (shipping point), and what should the weight, shape, and size of delivered material be. To some extent, these questions have been dealt with in previous chapters. The methods for answering these will be supplemented here.

---

[7]"Cut Costs or Else: Companies Lay Down the Law to Suppliers," *Business Week*, March 22, 1993, pp. 28–29.
[8]Jay Heizer and Barry Render, "How E-Commerce Saves Money," *IIE Solutions* (August 2000), pp. 22–27.

Order Quantities and Timing

The purchase quantities and their timing affect prices paid, transportation costs, and inventory-carrying costs. One strategy is to buy only to meet requirements as they occur. This is the just-in-time strategy, also referred to as hand-to-mouth buying. Alternately, some form of forward, or anticipatory, buying may be used. This can be advantageous when prices are expected to be higher in the future. In addition, speculative buying may be engaged in, where buyers attempt to hedge on future price increases. The materials, often commodities such as copper, silver, and gold, may be resold at a profit. Speculative buying differs from forward buying to the extent that purchase quantities may exceed any reasonable amount dictated by future requirements.

Purchase quantities may also be affected by the special price reductions that sellers offer from time to time. Buyers may wish to "stock up" at a good price. On the other hand, buyers may wish to negotiate for a good price, but not actually take delivery of the goods until they are needed, thus avoiding an inventory buildup.

A Mixed Buying Strategy

When a commodity has a reasonably predictable seasonable price pattern, engaging in a mixed strategy of hand-to-mouth and forward buying can result in a lower average price than hand-to-mouth buying alone. Forward buying is the act of buying in quantities exceeding current requirements, but not beyond foreseeable future requirements. It is an attractive strategy when prices are expected to rise so that additional quantities are purchased at low prices, but some inventory is created and must be balanced against the price advantages. On the other hand, hand-to-mouth buying is advantageous when prices are dropping, thus avoiding buying greater quantities now when delayed buying can yield lower prices. Effectively combining these two strategies when requirements are seasonal can yield substantial price advantages.

Example

Suppose that a commodity has a seasonal price pattern, as shown in Table 10-3. Projected requirements for the year are a constant 10,000 units per month. The

Table 10-3
A Seasonal Price Pattern for the Example Commodity

MONTH	PRICE ($/UNIT)	MONTH	PRICE ($/UNIT)
Jan.	3.00	July	1.00
Feb.	2.60	Aug.	1.40
Mar.	2.20	Sept.	1.80
Apr.	1.80	Oct.	2.20
May	1.40	Nov.	2.60
June	1.00	Dec.	3.00

	HAND-TO-MOUTH PURCHASES	2-MONTH FORWARD BUYING	3-MONTH FORWARD BUYING	6-MONTH FORWARD BUYING
MONTH	PURCHASE COST	PURCHASE COST	PURCHASE COST	PURCHASE COST
Jan.	$ 30,000	$ 30,000	$ 30,000	$ 30,000
Feb.	26,000	26,000	26,000	26,000
Mar.	22,000	22,000	22,000	22,000
Apr.	18,000	18,000	18,000	18,000
May	14,000	14,000	14,000	14,000
June	10,000	10,000	10,000	10,000
July	10,000	20,000[a]	30,000b	60,000[c]
Aug.	14,000	—	—	—
Sept.	18,000	36,000	—	—
Oct.	22,000	—	66,000	—
Nov.	26,000	52,000	—	—
Dec.	30,000	—	—	—
Subtotal	$240,000	$228,000	$216,000	$ 180,000
Inventory carrying cost	50,000	75,000	100,000	175,000
Total	$290,000	$303,000	$316,000	$ 355,000

[a] Purchase two months' requirements at the July price.
[b] Purchase three months' requirements at the July price.
[c] Purchase six months' requirements at the July price.

Table 10-4 Mixed Purchase Strategy Using Various Time Periods for Forward Buying When Prices Are Rising

objective is to choose the best combined strategy of hand-to-mouth and forward buying. Table 10-4 summarizes several forward buying periods: two-month, three-month, and six-month forward buys. Since prices are dropping from January through June, only a hand-to-mouth strategy need be considered for this time period. Selecting the best combined strategy requires balancing the purchase cost reductions achieved from forward buying against the increased inventory-carrying costs resulting from buying ahead of requirements. If the holding cost of a unit is $10 per year, the average inventory-carrying cost for the hand-to-mouth option is $(10,000/2)$ $10 = $50,000 per year. This assumes that a shipment of 10,000 units arrives at the beginning of the month and is depleted to 0 by the end of the month. For the two-month forward buying strategy, the inventory-carrying cost for the year would be

$$|\leftarrow \quad \text{First half} \quad \rightarrow|\leftarrow \text{Second half} \rightarrow|$$
$$[(10,000/2) \times 6/12 + (20,000/2) \times 6/12] \times \$10 = \$75,000/\text{year}$$

The inventory cost for the three-month and six-month forward buying strategies would be $100,000 and $175,000, respectively. The minimum total cost is for the hand-to-mouth buying strategy throughout the entire year. As longer forward buying periods are explored, the cost of carrying inventory increases more rapidly than the benefits of not paying for price increases. However, if there were price discounts or transportation rate breaks based on the size of the purchase, forward buying might be economical. This possibility should be considered.

Dollar Averaging

Forward buying, to be effective, requires that seasonal price patterns be reasonably stable and predictable. To accomplish the same lowest purchase price goal as forward buying, dollar averaging can be used. This method assumes that prices will generally rise over time, but otherwise they will fluctuate with uncertainty. Purchases are made at fixed intervals, but the quantity to buy depends on the price at the time of the buy. A budget is established based on the average price for a reasonable time into the future—at least a full seasonal cycle. The price is divided into the budget amount to determine the quantity to buy. The result is that more units are purchased when prices are low than are purchased when they are high, if prices are generally rising. The danger in this strategy is that quantities not large enough to meet requirements may occur when prices are high. Protection in the form of carrying some inventory may be necessary.

Example

An office supply product is expected to cost $2.50 for each unit throughout the next year. Usage is also expected to be at the rate of 20,000 units per month, with purchases made every three months. Inventory carrying costs are 25 percent per year.

The first step in dollar averaging is to develop the three-month purchasing budget. Simply put, this is 20,000 × 3 × 2.50 = $150,000. We spend this amount at each purchase. Suppose that the actual prices for the next year unfold as shown next.

Month	Price ($/unit)	Month	Price ($/unit)
Jan.	2.00	July	2.55
Feb.	2.05	Aug.	2.65
Mar.	2.15	Sept.	2.75
Apr.	2.25	Oct.	2.80
May	2.35	Nov.	2.83
June	2.45	Dec.	2.86

If we sum the prices and divide by 12, the actual average price is $2.47 per unit. The first three-month purchase quantity in January would be

$$\$150,000/\$2.00 \text{ per unit} = 75,000 \text{ units}$$

Continuing this type of calculation for each three-month period, we would have

Month	No. of Units	Price ($/unit)	Total Cost	Average Inventory
Jan.	75,000	2.00	$150,000	37,500[a] units
Apr.	66,667	2.25	150,000	33,334
July	58,824	2.55	150,000	29,412
Oct.	53,571	2.80	150,000	26,786
	254,062		$600,000	31,758[b] units

[a] 75,000/2 = 37,500 units.
[b] Annual average, or (37,500 + 33,334 + 29,412 + 26,786)/4 = 31,758 units.

The average unit cost is $600,000/254,062 = $2.36. Compared with monthly hand-to-mouth purchases, this gives a price reduction of $[(2.47 - 2.36)/2.47] \times 100 = 4.45\%$. The total hand-to-mouth purchase cost would be $254,062 \times \$2.47/\text{unit} = \$627,533$.

Now we account for inventory-carrying costs. The annual average carrying cost for monthly hand-to-mouth buying is $(20,000/2) \times 2.47 \times 0.25 = \$6,175$. And for dollar averaging, it is $31,758 \times 2.36 \times 0.25 = \$18,737$.

Summarizing the annual costs for the two strategies, we have

Strategy	Purchase Cost	Inventory Cost	Total Cost
Monthly hand-to-mouth	$627,533	+ 6,175	= $633,708
Dollar averaging	$600,000	+ 18,737	= **$618,737**

The most economical strategy in this rising price market is dollar averaging. (*Note:* Adequate inventory will need to be maintained so that demand can be met during periods of small purchase quantities.)

Quantity Discounts

The purchasing agent is frequently encouraged to buy in large quantities. Suppliers may offer lower prices if larger quantities are purchased, since suppliers benefit from economies of scale and pass along some of these benefits to the buyers through price incentives. Two forms of price incentives are popular: inclusive and noninclusive. An inclusive quantity discount-price-incentive plan is one where, for progressively larger purchase quantities, a lower price is offered that applies to all units purchased. It is commonly seen for many consumer items. In contrast, under the noninclusive quantity discount-price-incentive plan, the price reduction applies to only those units within the quantity discount-price interval. The in-excess rate in transportation is an example. If quantities purchased are already large—that is, larger than the last quantity price break—nothing further needs to be considered. However, when purchase quantities are small, the buyer faces the dilemma of whether to pay a high price for the small quantity or to increase the purchase quantity and incur additional inventory carrying costs. We will explore these two pricing policies.

Inclusive Quantity Discount-Price-Incentive Plan. A simple inclusive quantity discount-price schedule can be expressed as

Quantity, Q_i	Price, P_i
$0 < Q_i < Q_1$	P_1
$Q_i \geq Q_1$	P_2

where Q_i is the quantity purchased, and P_i is the price paid per unit for all of Q_i. P_1 ranges from 1 to less than Q_1, otherwise P_2 applies. P_2 is less than P_1.

Finding the optimal purchase quantity requires finding the lowest total cost comprising purchase cost, ordering cost, and inventory-carrying cost. Mathematically, this total cost is

$$TC_i = P_i D + \frac{DS}{Q_i} + \frac{IC_i Q_i}{2} \qquad \text{(10-4)}$$

where

TC_i = total relevant cost for the quantity Q_i
P_i = price per unit for quantity Q_i
D = average annual demand in units
S = procurement cost in dollar per order
Q_i = quantity to purchase in units
I = carrying cost in percent per year
C_i = cost of the item at the point inventoried in dollars per unit

The total cost curve for an inclusive quantity discount-price-incentive plan is shown in Figure 10-13. Finding the optimal purchase quantity is not as simple as under a

Figure 10-13
A Total Cost Curve for a Single Break, Inclusive Quantity Discount-Price Incentive Plan

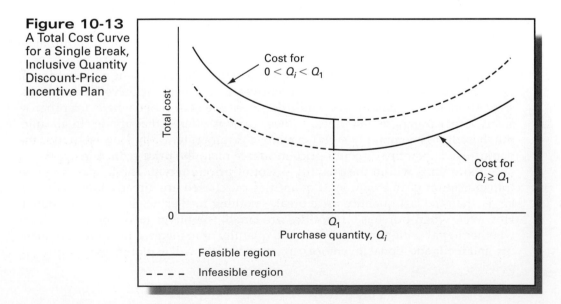

Cost for
$0 < Q_i < Q_1$

Cost for
$Q_i \geq Q_1$

Total cost

0

Q_1

Purchase quantity, Q_i

——— Feasible region

- - - - Infeasible region

single price plan because of the discontinuity point in the total cost curve. However, a computational procedure can be developed that requires a minimal number of calculations. It can be paraphrased as follows:

- Compute the economic order quantity (*EOQ*) for each price, P_i. Find the one *EOQ* that is within the feasible range of its total cost curve. If the feasible *EOQ* is on the lowest cost curve, the optimal Q has been found. If it is not, compute TC_{EOQ} and proceed with the next step.
- Set Q_i at the minimum quantity within the quantity price range i and compute TC_i. Compare all TC_i and TC_{EOQ}.
- Select the quantity Q_i representing the minimal total cost.

Example

An item is regularly purchased with an estimated demand of 2,600 units per year. Purchase order preparation costs are $10 per order, and the inventory-carrying cost is 20 percent per year. The supplier offers two prices—$5 per unit for a purchase quantity of less than 500 units, and a 5 percent discount that applies to all units when quantities of 500 or more units are purchased. The prices include delivery. What order size should the purchasing agent place?

We first compute the economic order quantities for the prices below and above 500 units. Hence, for P_1,

$$Q_{EOQ1} = \sqrt{\frac{2DS}{IC}} = \sqrt{\frac{2(2600)(10)}{0.20(5)}} = 228 \text{ units (feasible)}$$

And the total cost according to Equation (10-4) is

$$TC_{EOQ1} = 5(2600) + \frac{2600(10)}{228} + \frac{0.20(5)(228)}{2} = \$13,228.04$$

For P_2:

$$Q_{EOQ2} = \sqrt{\frac{2(2600)(10)}{0.20(4.75)}} = 234 \text{ units (infeasible)}$$

Notice that Q_{EOQ2} on the lower cost curve is infeasible considering the price used in the calculation. That is, the price of 4.75 is not consistent with the order quantity of less than 500 units. Q_{EOQ2} is eliminated from further consideration. Now test the quantity just at the break point, or $Q = 500$ units.

$$TC_{500} = (5 \times 0.95)(2600) + \frac{2600(10)}{500} + \frac{0.20(5 \times 0.95)(500)}{2} = \$12,639.50$$

Since TC_{500} is less than TC_{EOQ1}, a quantity of 500 units should be ordered to minimize costs.

Noninclusive Quantity Discount-Price-Incentive Plan.   When the quantity price incentive plan is of the noninclusive type, a slightly modified solution procedure is required. Beyond the price break quantities, the average unit price continues to drop, as shown in Figure 10-14. We can find the optimal purchase quantity by trial and error.[9] That is, the total cost for progressively larger order quantities is computed until the minimum cost is found.

Example

Using the previous example, the 5 percent price discount now applies only to purchases *greater* than 500 units, that is, to $Q_{i > 500}$. To find the optimal order quantity, we prudently select Q_s to be evaluated. Let's begin with a $Q = 300$ and incrementally add to this quantity until the total cost stops dropping and begins to increase. We use Equation (10-4) for our calculations, where average price Pi is found from one of two formulas. If Q_i is less than or equal to 500 units, $P_i = P_1$; otherwise, $P_i = [500 \times P_1 + (Q_i - 500) \times P_2] / Q_i$. The computations can now be summarized as follows:

Q_i	Average Unit Price, P_i	$P_i \times D$	$+D \times S/Q_i$	$+I \times C_i \times Q_i/2$	$=$ Cost
300	5	$13,000.00	$86.67	$150.00a	$13,237
400	5	13,000.00	65.00	200.00	13,265
500	5	13,000.00	52.00	250.00	13,302
600	$\dfrac{500(5) + 100(4.75)}{600} = 4.96$	12,896.00	43.33	297.60	13,237
800	$\dfrac{500(5) + 300(4.75)}{800} = 4.91$	12,766.00	32.50	392.80	13,191
900	$\dfrac{500(5) + 400(4.75)}{900} = 4.89$	12,714.00	28.89	440.10	**13,183 ←**
1000	$\dfrac{500(5) + 500(4.75)}{1000} = 4.88$	12,688.00	26.00	488.00	13,202
1100	$\dfrac{500(5) + 600(4.75)}{1100} = 4.86$	12,636.00	23.64	534.60	13,194

a $P_i = C_i$

Within the increments of 100 units that were tested, the optimum purchase order quantity with the lowest total annual cost is 900 units.

Deal buying.   It is quite common for vendors to offer occasional price discounts for the purpose of promoting their business or clearing excess inventory. The purchasing

---

[9]For an exact approach to the noninclusive discount-price problem, see Richard J. Tersine, *Principles of Inventory and Materials Management*, 4th edition (Upper Saddle River, NJ: Prentice Hall, 1994), pp.110–113.

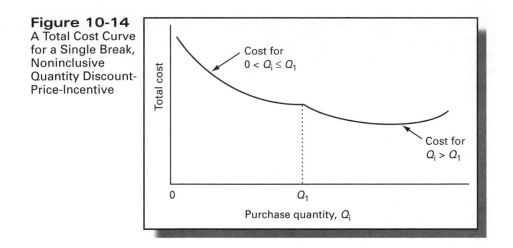

Figure 10-14
A Total Cost Curve for a Single Break, Noninclusive Quantity Discount-Price-Incentive

Total cost

Cost for
$0 < Q_i \leq Q_1$

Cost for
$Q_i > Q_1$

0

Q_1

Purchase quantity, Q_i

agent for the buyer is faced with the question of how much to buy if the discount appears to be attractive. The purchasing agent may already be buying from the vendor and has optimized the quantities to be purchased under the existing price. For a time, such purchases create higher-than-normal inventory levels. This may be acceptable if the price reduction more than compensates for the added carrying costs. The special order quantity can be found from

$$\hat{Q} = \frac{dD}{(p - d)I} + \frac{pQ^*}{p - d}$$
(10-5)

where

d = unit price decrease, dollars/unit
p = price per unit before the discount, dollars/unit
S = order cost, dollars/order
I = annual carrying cost, percent/year
D = annual demand, units
Q^* = optimal order quantity before the discount, units
$\hat{Q}$ = special order size, units

The offer is a one-time event, the demand for the product is expected to remain unchanged, and after the offer expires, the order pattern returns to its original buying quantity and timing.

Example

Jaymore Drugstores sells a line of coffeemakers in its drugstore chain. The vendor of the coffeemakers normally sells the product for a delivered price of $72 per unit. Jaymore's stores typically sell 4,000 units per year. The purchasing agent finds that carrying costs are 25 percent/year and the cost to prepare purchase orders is $50 per order.

The vendor is offering to give a one-time $5 discount off the regular price to reduce its factory inventory. Jaymore believes that the coffeemakers will continue to sell at the normal sales rate and any excess inventory created from a larger-than-normal purchase quantity will be depleted. How large an order should be placed with the vendor?

The typical order size can be determined by solving for the economic order quantity. That is,

$$Q^* = \sqrt{\frac{2DS}{IC}} = \sqrt{\frac{2(4,000)(50)}{0.25(72)}} = 149 \text{ units}$$

Now, the special order size is found from Equation (10-5), or

$$\hat{Q} = \frac{dD}{(p-d)I} + \frac{pQ^*}{p-d} = \frac{5(4000)}{(72-5)0.25} + \frac{72(149)}{(72-5)} = 1,354 \text{ units}$$

Instead of holding an order quantity for $Q^*/D = (149/4,000) = 0.037$ yr, or two weeks, the units from the special order will be in inventory for $\hat{Q} = (1,354/4,000) = 0.339$ yr, or 18 weeks.

Contract buying. A buyer may wish to negotiate the best possible price but not take delivery of the full purchase amount at one time. Therefore, the buyer offers to purchase a given unit quantity or a dollar amount over time. This contract may be for a specific item or it may be for a variety of items covered under a blanket dollar contract. For example, suppose that a buyer has agreed to purchase $500,000 worth of goods from a particular supplier for the coming year. The quantities of individual items are not known at contract time, only the monetary amount is "guaranteed."[10] As the need develops throughout the year, the buyer calls on the seller to deliver the items requested in the desired quantities. The dollar purchase amount of individual items within the contract may vary considerably. For the buyer, this is *stockless purchasing*, yet the buyer has the advantage of volume buying and its associated price benefits. It is attractive where the just-in-time supply philosophy guides operations and inventories are to be minimized. For the seller, more efficient operations can be expected from better planning due to the certainty of the purchases from its customers.

Sourcing

Fixed Sourcing

Another important decision is selecting the shipping points from which purchased materials should be supplied, when the price policy requires the buyer to do this.

---

[10]The guaranteed dollar amount often has some flexibility in it, such as ± 10 percent.

Determining these sourcing points may depend on the inventory availability, performance and cost of the transportation services used, and the price level and price policy used. For example, if the price policy is a delivered or prepaid one, transportation selection is not likely to be an issue. If there is only one possible shipping point to serve one destination point, the decision is straightforward. However, when there are multiple source and destination points with restrictions on the amount that can be shipped from each source, the decision problem is more complex. One way to approach such a problem is to use linear programming.

Example

The Regal Company has received vendor quotes for a component that is part of a larger assembly. The prices, quoted f.o.b. vendor shipping point, are as follows:

Supplier	Shipping Location	F.o.b. Price
Philadelphia Tool	Philadelphia	$100 each
Houston Tool & Die	Houston	101
Chicago-Argo	St. Louis	99
L.A. Tool Works	Los Angeles	96

Regal has three plants to be supplied—Cleveland, Atlanta, and Kansas City. The transportation rates (in $/cwt.) and the plant requirements for January are

Shipping Point	Cleveland	Atlanta	Kansas City
Philadelphia	$2/cwt.	$3/cwt.	$5/cwt.
Houston	6	4	3
St. Louis	3	3	1
Los Angeles	8	9	7
Requirements	**4000 units**	**2000 units**	**7000 units**

Los Angeles can supply an unlimited amount, as can Houston. However, Philadelphia can supply up to 5,000 units and St. Louis can supply up to 4,000 units. Each unit weighs 100 pounds.

The purchasing department's policy is to buy from the supplier offering the lowest price. What is the optimal sourcing plan, and how much would it save Regal?

This problem type may be dealt with using linear programming's transportation method. The solution matrix for this problem is shown in Figure 10-15. Notice that the cell cost value (the cost of shipping a single unit between two points) includes the f.o.b. price as well as per-unit shipping costs. The available supply from Houston and Los Angeles has been set at arbitrarily high values to represent unrestricted supply. A dummy column has been added as a destination point to absorb the excess supply over requirements. All cell costs of zero are used in the dummy column, although any values will do.

Figure 10-15
The Optimum
Sourcing Pattern
for the Regal
Company

Supply points	Cleveland	Atlanta	Kansas	Dummy	Supply
Philadelphia	102 **4,000**	103 **1,000**	105	0	5,000
Houston	107	105	104	0 **15,000**	15,000
St. Louis	102	102	100 **4,000**	0	4,000
Los Angeles	104	105 **1,000**	103 **3,000**	0 **11,000**	15,000
Requirements	4,000	2,000	7,000	26,000	39,000

For the company's policy of purchasing from the least expensive source, all purchases would be made from the Los Angeles source with a total landed cost of

From Los Angeles		
To Cleveland	$104/unit × 4,000 units =	$ 416,000
To Atlanta	105/unit × 2,000 units =	210,000
To Kansas City	103/unit × 7,000 units =	721,000
	Total landed cost	$ 1,347,000

One revised, optimal sourcing plan (there is another equally as good) is shown in Figure 10-15. This plan can be summarized as follows:

Philadelphia to Cleveland	$102/unit × 4,000 units =	$ 408,000
Philadelphia to Atlanta	103/unit × 1,000 units =	103,000
St. Louis to Kansas City	100/unit × 4,000 units =	400,000
Los Angeles to Atlanta	105/unit × 1,000 units =	105,000
Los Angeles to Kansas City	103/unit × 3,000 units =	309,000
	Total	$1,325,000

In this case, Regal could save $22,000 in the month of January by using multiple sources as indicated. It should also be recognized from Figure 10-15 that both Philadelphia and St. Louis are being sourced to the limit of their available supply. Regal should negotiate for increased supply from these sources to reduce costs further. Houston does not appear to be a particularly attractive source point since it is not used. Perhaps Regal could present this information to Houston Tool & Die and discuss a price reduction of about $1 or $2 per unit. This would allow Houston to compete for the Atlanta and Kansas City requirements, which would be desirable if Houston is a favored supplier for reasons other than price.

Flexible Sourcing

It may not always be practical to specifically assign destination requirements to particular sources. Changing requirements during long lead-time periods may lead to a flexible sourcing arrangement. One manufacturer of glass products used this method to keep glass furnaces operating when limited raw materials storage capacity was available at the plant sites. Against an annual purchase quantity, multiple suppliers were requested to ship materials as scheduled by production. Once en route, production schedules could be shifted either as to product mix, and therefore the raw materials needed, or by changes in the volume to be produced. Because of this, it was a common practice to divert in-transit railcar shipments to plants other than those originally scheduled. This method better matched supply to requirements while avoiding a buildup of material shortages at plants. The disadvantage was that higher overall transportation costs would be incurred because a plant was not always tied to a specific source.

Terms of Sale and Channel Management

When we think of terms of sale, it is often with price and financial considerations in mind. However, specifying in the terms of sale the form in which goods are to be supplied and the methods by which they will be handled can be very important to product movement and storage efficiency within the supply channel. Since suppliers have their own logistics systems, there is no guarantee that these systems will be compatible with those of the buying firm. It is possible that package sizes, transport methods, and handling procedures will not match, causing additional time and effort to force compatibility. Where possible, purchasing should specify how shipments must conform to a desired pattern. If such patterns cannot be forced through contractual arrangements, then cooperative efforts should be undertaken with suppliers to encourage the desired system compatibility.

Observation

Constellation Supers, Inc., was a supermarket chain in the Minneapolis area. National Home Food Products was its largest supplier, with a distribution center located just seven miles from Constellation's Edina facility. Yet, National would depalletize Constellation's order from 40 in. by 48 in. pallets and ship it to Constellation using rail. Constellation would repalletize the goods on 32 in. by 40 in. pallets in order to match its handling and storage system. Since Constellation's purchases amounted to less than 1 percent of National's total sales, National was reluctant to incur a charge for repalletizing to 32 in. by 40 in. pallets. Without incurring the cost of retrofitting the Edina warehouse to accommodate the 40 in. by 48 in. pallets, Constellation seemed powerless to overcome the inefficiencies of extra handling. What suggestions can you make to correct this supply channel incompatibility?

CONCLUDING COMMENTS

Purchasing and scheduling involve decisions that can substantially affect the efficient movement and storage of goods within the supply channel. Scheduling ensures that goods arrive at a designated point at the time and in the quantities needed. Using inventory-control methods is one approach to ensuring the availability of goods. Just-in-time scheduling procedures have become popular. Specifically, both Toyota's KANBAN system and the materials-requirements planning (MRP) system are frequently used in the United States. The basic procedures for developing an MRP schedule were presented in this chapter. As an extension of MRP, distribution-requirements planning was also discussed. Combining MRP and DRP allows integrated scheduling of the entire supply chain from suppliers to customers.

Purchasing is primarily a buying activity. This important activity accounts for 40 to 60 percent of the sales dollar. Many of the decisions involving purchasing have an impact on the efficiency with which logistical activities in the supply channel can be conducted. In this chapter, several key purchasing decisions were examined and methods suggested for treating them. Key purchasing decisions include determining purchase quantities, timing purchases, and sourcing shipments.

This chapter suggests a strong relationship between production scheduling, purchasing, and logistics. Integrating these is the essence of supply chain management. The goal is to achieve maximum efficiency effectiveness of product flows through the careful management of cross-functional activities.

QUESTIONS

1. How is just-in-time scheduling different from the supply-to-inventory philosophy of scheduling? How is it that JIT scheduling can eliminate the need for inventories in the supply channel?
2. Why is just-in-time a philosophy and not a technique?
3. How are the methods for determining the optimal purchase quantity different under inclusive and noninclusive quantity discount-price plans?
4. What are the similarities and differences between MRP and DRP?
5. How is KANBAN different from the MRP approach to JIT scheduling?
6. Considering the many parts, components, and supplies that a firm would need in order to supply a production or service operation, what characteristics would these items likely have to be scheduled by requirements planning versus being stocked in supply inventories?
7. What are the characteristics of JIT supply scheduling, and why are they important to the effectiveness of this scheduling approach?
8. What is the leverage principle in purchasing? The return-on-assets effect?
9. Under what circumstances is forward buying a good practice? When is dollar averaging a good buying practice?
10. How do compatibility in the form of goods and the movement methods between supplier and buyer affect logistics efficiency? How might purchasing contribute to improved efficiency in the channel?
11. What is the future of product and service auctioning on the Internet?

PROBLEMS

Some of the problems and the case study in this chapter can be solved or partially solved with the aid of computer software. The software packages in LOGWARE that are most important in this chapter are TRANLP (*T*), and INPOL (*I*). The CD icon ⓣ will appear with the software package designation where the problem analysis is assisted using one of these software programs. A database may be prepared for the problem if extensive data input is required. Where the problem can be solved without the aid of the computer (by hand), the hand icon 👆 is shown. If no icon appears, hand calculation is assumed.

1. A furniture manufacturer sells a line of desks with the same general design. The desks are made from veneered plywood sheets, and the purchase plan for the plywood is to be determined for the next seven weeks. The desks are offered in three styles, each with minor modifications in the drawer layout. Marketing forecasts for the three styles are given as follows:

Desk	WEEKLY DEMAND FORECAST (UNITS)							
	1	2	3	4	5	6	7	8
Style A	150	150	200	200	150	200	200	150
Style B	60	60	60	80	80	100	80	60
Style C	100	120	100	80	80	60	60	40

It takes one week to produce the desks, with a production run of 300 for style *A* and 100 each for styles *B* and *C*. Currently, 80 style *B* desks and 200 style *C* desks are on hand. Current production plans will make available 200 style *A* desks in week 1, with none currently on hand. No production is currently scheduled for styles *B* and *C* desks. All other parts for the desks are readily available and cause no delay in producing the finished desks.

For the plywood veneer sheets (three sheets = one desk), there are 2,400 sheets on hand and 600 more are to be received in week 2. Once an order is placed, it takes, on the average, two weeks to obtain a plywood order. Minimum orders are for 1,000 sheets with a safety stock of 200 sheets to be on hand at all times.

a. Develop a schedule for timing the release of plywood purchase orders over the next seven weeks.

b. Suppose the costs for delaying production are $5 per day for each plywood sheet that has not arrived in time to meet production needs.

Correspondingly, the cost for carrying plywood that arrives in advance of needs is $0.10 per sheet per day. The average order cycle time on purchase orders is two weeks (14 days) with a standard deviation of two days. These lead times are normally distributed. How should purchase order release time be adjusted to account for this uncertainty?

		WEEK							
		1	2	3	4	5	6	7	8
Projected gross requirements		100	450	100	300	850	100	100	100
Scheduled receipts					?				
Quantity on hand	900	800	350	250					
Planned purchase order releases									

Table 10-5 A Materials Requirements Planning Schedule in Units

2. A certain item is scheduled using production-requirements planning with the purchase order releases being time-phased. A schedule is shown in Table 10-5. The materials manager believes that this schedule may not be the most economical from a supply point of view. The following additional information has been obtained:

Carrying cost = 20% per year
Year = 365 days
Production downtime cost = $150 per day per unit
Item price = $35 per unit
Purchase order preparation cost = $50 per order

Lead time is normally distributed with an average of 14 days and a standard deviation of four days
a. How much time should be allowed in advance of scheduled receipts for the release of orders?
b. In period 4, a scheduled receipt is needed to maintain a minimal safety level of 200 units. If there are no minimums on the purchase (order release) quantity, what is the most economic order release size?

3. The physical distribution channel of a major food manufacturer consists of plant stocks from which regional warehouses are restocked. These regional warehouses in turn supply the field warehouses assigned to them. There is one plant serving two regional warehouses that, in turn, serve three field warehouses each. The field warehouses have the following weekly demand forecasts for a particular item and the following inventory on hand:

Regional Warehouse	Inventory on Hand (Cases)	Field Warehouse	Inventory on Hand (Cases)	Weekly Forecasted Demand (Cases)
1		1	1,700	1,200
1	52,300	2	3,300	2,300
1		3	3,400	2,700
2		4	5,700	4,100
2	31,700	5	2,300	1,700
2		6	1,200	900

The regional warehouse will supply its assigned warehouses only when the accumulated order quantity at each warehouse equals or exceeds 7,500 cases, and then in increments of 7,500 cases. The 7,500 cases are equal to a truckload shipment. In turn, the plant will supply regional warehouses in increments of 15,000 cases, which is a railcar shipment. The lead time for the supply of field warehouses is one week. Lead time is two weeks for supplying regional warehouses. Production has a lead time of three weeks for materials in lots of 20,000 cases. No shipments are in the pipeline to field warehouses; however, a previously scheduled shipment of 15,000 cases is due to arrive at regional warehouse 2 in the second week.

Over the next ten weeks, plan the materials flow through the network, estimate the average inventory in the system, and project what the production schedule should be.

4. A firm with annual sales of $55 million pays out 50 percent of its sales dollar as cost of goods sold. Overhead amounts to $8 million. Labor and salaries are $15 million. Thus, a profit of $4.5 million is realized. Assets are $20 million, of which 20 percent are in inventories.
   a. If the firm can (1) increase sales volume, (2) raise price, (3) reduce labor and salaries, (4) decrease overhead, or (5) reduce the cost of goods sold, how much change (in percent) in each category would be required to increase profits to $5 million?
   b. If prices of purchased materials (i.e., cost of goods sold) can be reduced by 7 percent, what return on assets can be realized? How does this compare with the current ROA?

5. A firm purchases a material that shows definite price seasonality throughout the year with relatively minor fluctuations within each month. Requirements for the material are constant throughout the year at 50,000 units per month. The prices throughout the year are projected as follows:

Month	Price ($/unit)	Month	Price ($/unit)
Jan.	4.00	July	6.00
Feb.	4.30	Aug.	5.60
Mar.	4.70	Sept.	5.40
Apr.	5.00	Oct.	5.00
May	5.25	Nov.	4.50
June	5.75	Dec.	4.25

Inventory-carrying cost is 30 percent per year. The current buying strategy is to purchase directly to requirements at the going price.
   a. Does a mixed strategy of forward and hand-to-mouth buying lower purchasing costs? Which is the best strategy mix?
   b. If a mixed strategy is better, what concerns might there be in using it?

6. A magnet manufacturer purchases copper on the open market at monthly intervals throughout the year. The best estimate of the average price for the next year is $1.10 per lb. A fixed quantity of 25,000 lb per month is needed to meet the expected requirements for a four-month planning horizon. Inventory carrying cost is 20 percent per year.

a. Develop a dollar-averaging budget for future purchases.

b. Suppose, at the time of the purchases, the actual prices per pound for the next four months turn out to be $1.32, $1.05, $1.10, and $0.95, respectively. If dollar averaging is used, what quantities should be purchased in each month? Is there any advantage over a hand-to-mouth strategy?

7. A large medical clinic uses 500 cases of floor polish per year. Purchases are made at an ordering cost of $15 per order. Inventory-carrying cost is 20 percent per year. The price schedule, which includes the transportation cost, shows that orders of less than 50 cases will cost $49.95 per case; between 50 and 79 cases will cost $44.95 per case; and 80 cases or more will cost $39.95 per case. Prices apply inclusively to all units bought. What is the optimum purchase order size that should be placed, and what is the total cost?

8. An East Coast electric company buys motors from a supplier on the West Coast for use in pumping equipment. Production needs 1,400 motors per year. Procurement costs, including clerical and expediting costs, are $75 per order. Inventory-carrying cost is 25 percent per year. The supplier has provided the following price schedule:

Units per Order	Unit Price[a]
First 200	$795
Next 200	750
Over 400	725

[a] Includes transportation

Given this noninclusive price schedule, what is the optimal purchase quantity (to the nearest 50 units), and what is the total annual cost?

9. The central purchasing group for Ortega Foods buys cornmeal for the company's four plants that produce taco shells. Three source points are available, but contractual agreements limit supply from some of the sources. The cornmeal is shipped in 100-lb bags. Data on plant requirements, supply availability, and f.o.b. prices for a typical week are shown in Table 10-6. The transportation rates (in $/cwt.) between the various sources and plants are as follows:

or

	PLANTS			
Sources	Cincinnati	Dallas	Los Angeles	Baltimore
Minneapolis	0.15	0.19	0.24	0.21
Kansas City	0.10	0.08	0.20	0.18
Dayton	0.05	0.12	0.27	0.15

The purchasing group currently supplies Cincinnati and Baltimore plants from Dayton. Dallas is served by Kansas City, and Los Angeles is served by Minneapolis.

a. What sourcing plan would be best for Ortega, and how much would it save?

b. Are there any actions that the purchasing group might pursue to reduce costs further?

Table 10-6
Supply and Demand
Data for Ortega Food
Problem

Source	Supply Availability (cwt.)	Price ($/cwt.)
Minneapolis	1,200	$3.25
Kansas City	4,800	3.45
Dayton	Unlimited	3.40

Plant	Requirements (cwt.)
Cincinnati	5,000
Dallas	2,500
Los Angeles	1,200
Baltimore	1,000

    c. Is Ortega contracting with too many suppliers? Why or why not? (*Hint*: Use the transportation method of linear programming to help solve this problem.)

10. A-Mart sells small-screen television sets in its many retail outlets. Typical total sales for all stores are projected to be 120,000 units. The vendor in South Korea normally sells the sets for $100US, however, the vendor will offer a $5 discount if a buyer will place a special order of at least 20,000 units. The buyer's carrying cost is 30 percent per year and the cost to prepare purchase orders is $40 per order. Transportation costs are included in the price.

    a. Should the buyer accept the discount? If so, what should the special order size be?

    b. If the special order is placed, how long will the order size need to be held in inventory?

CASE STUDY

Industrial Distributors, Inc.

As director of purchasing for Industrial Distributors, Walter Negley had to plan the purchasing quantities for the higher-valued products that Industrial Distributors inventoried and resold to its industrial customers on a short order cycle. One such product was a replacement motor used in conveyors. Replacement sales were received from customers located in North America and were approximately constant throughout the year. These motors were manufactured in West Germany and imported through the Port of Baltimore. They were transported by truck to Industrial's privately owned warehouse in the Chicago area. Although the West German manufacturer had a price policy that included transportation to Baltimore, Industrial incurred the transportation expense from Baltimore to Chicago. To help determine the purchase quantities, Walter gathered the following information:

Information Description	Quantities/Costs	Source of Information
Average annual sales	1,500 units	Sales
Replenishment lead time	1 month (0.083 yr.)	Purchasing
Clerical cost per requisition	$20	Accounting
Expediting cost per requisition	$5	Traffic
Inventory-carrying cost	30% per year	Finance
Packaged weight per unit	250 lb	Traffic
Unloading cost at warehouse	$0.25 per cwt.	Accounting
Storage capacity at warehouse[a]	$300 units	Warehouse manager
Public warehouse storage rates	$10 per unit per year	Public warehouse

[a] There is only enough space in the company's warehouse to store 300 units. If a replenishment order size greater than 300 units is received, the excess over 300 units must be stored in a public warehouse.

The manufacturer has just announced its new price schedule for motors at the Port of Baltimore. Checking with the trucking company to move the motors from Baltimore,

Units per Order	Unit Price
First 100	$700
Next 100	$680
All over 200	$670

Walter found it practical to contract for either full truckload shipments at $12 per cwt. (100 lb) for truckload (TL) quantities of 40,000 lb or more, or for less-than-truckload (LTL) quantities at $18 per cwt. ∎

QUESTIONS

1. What replenishment order size, to the nearest 50 units, should Walter place, given the manufacturer's noninclusive pricing policy?

2. Should Walter change his replenishment order size if the manufacturer's pricing policy were one where the price in each quantity break includes all units purchased?

Chapter 11

The Storage and Handling System

$\mathcal{I}$n contrast with transportation, product storage and handling take place primarily at the supply chain network nodal points. Storage has been referred to as "transportation at zero miles per hour." This chapter focuses on the characteristics and costs of warehousing and materials handling activities. It has been estimated that these activities can absorb 20 percent of a firm's physical distribution cost, and thus they are worthy of careful consideration.[1]

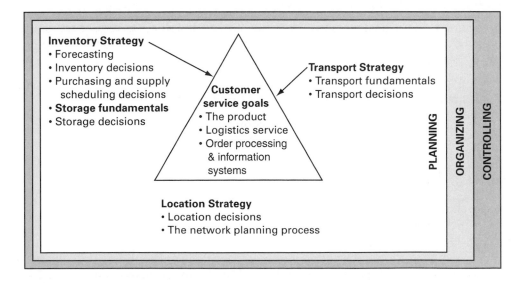

Inventory Strategy
• Forecasting
• Inventory decisions
• Purchasing and supply
  scheduling decisions
• **Storage fundamentals**
• Storage decisions

Customer service goals
• The product
• Logistics service
• Order processing
  & information
  systems

Transport Strategy
• Transport fundamentals
• Transport decisions

Location Strategy
• Location decisions
• The network planning process

PLANNING ORGANIZING CONTROLLING

---
[1]Recall Table 1-3.

Need for a Storage System

Do firms really need storage and materials handling as part of the logistics system? If demand for a firm's products were known for sure and products could be supplied instantaneously to meet the demand, theoretically storage would not be required since no inventories would be held. However, it is neither practical nor economical to operate a firm in this manner since demand usually cannot be predicted exactly. Even to approach perfect supply and demand coordination, production would have to be instantly responsive, and transportation would have to be perfectly reliable, with zero delivery time. This is just not available to a firm at any reasonable cost. Therefore, firms use inventories to improve supply and demand coordination and to lower overall costs. It follows that maintaining inventories produces the need for warehousing and the need for materials handling as well. Storage becomes an economic convenience rather than a necessity.

The warehousing and materials handling costs are justified because they can be traded off with transportation and production-purchasing costs. That is, by warehousing some inventory, a firm can often lower production costs through economical production lot sizing and sequencing. By this means, the firm avoids the wide fluctuations in output levels due to uncertainties and variations in demand patterns. In addition, warehousing inventories can lead to lower transportation costs through the shipment of larger, more economical quantities. The object is to use just enough warehousing so that a good, economical balance can be realized among warehousing, production, and transportation costs.

Reasons for Storage

There are four basic reasons for using storage space: (1) to reduce transportation-production costs; (2) to coordinate supply and demand; (3) to assist in the production process; and (4) to assist in the marketing process.

Transportation-Production Cost Reduction

Warehousing and the associated inventory are added expenses, but they may be traded off with the lower costs realized from the improved efficiency in transportation and production. To illustrate the trade-off idea, consider the distribution problem of Combined Charities, Inc.

Example

The national office of Combined Charities prepared literature for the fund-raising campaigns of a number of well-known charitable and political organizations. The company printed the literature and distributed it to campaign points at the local geographic level. When a job was contracted, the typical procedure was to dedicate the company's entire workforce and printing equipment to preparing the literature for a single campaign. Overtime was often used. After production was completed, the literature was sent directly from the printing site to local distribution points using UPS.

The company's president, who had a good feel for logistics/SC management, thought that overall costs might be lowered if warehouse space could be rented at various regional locations around the country. Although warehousing would be an added expense, he thought that he could ship truckload quantities to the warehouses and use UPS for shipping the short distance from the 35 warehouses he had chosen to the local areas. Production costs could also be reduced because the local areas could draw from warehouse stocks rather than placing orders directly on the printing operation, which often caused a change in the production schedule.

The president made the following rough cost calculations for a typical campaign in which 5 million pieces of literature would be produced:

	Ship Direct from Plant	Ship Through 35 Warehouses	Change in Costs
Production costs	$500,000	$425,000	$ −75,000
Transportation costs:			
To warehouse	0	50,000	+50,000
To local area	250,000	100,000	−150,000
Warehouse costs	0	75,000	+75,000
Total	$750,000	$650,000	$−100,000

The increased warehousing expense is more than offset with reduced production and transportation expenses. Using warehousing appears to be an attractive option.

Coordination of Supply and Demand

Firms with highly seasonal production, along with reasonably constant demand have a problem coordinating supply with demand. For example, food companies producing canned vegetables and fruits are forced to stockpile production output in order to supply the marketplace during the nongrowing season. Conversely, those firms that must supply a product or service to a seasonal and uncertain demand typically produce at a constant level throughout the year in order to minimize production costs and to build inventories needed to meet the demand during a relatively short selling season. Room air conditioners and snowblowers are examples. Whenever it becomes too expensive to precisely coordinate supply and demand, warehousing is needed.

Commodity price considerations may also produce a need for warehousing. Those materials and products that experience wide swings in price from one time to another (copper, steel, and oil) may encourage a firm to purchase these commodities in advance of their needs in order to obtain them at lower prices. Warehousing usually is needed, but its cost can be offset with the better price obtained for the commodities.

Production Needs

Warehousing may be part of the production process. The manufacturing of certain products such as cheeses, wines, and liquors requires time for aging. Warehouses serve not only to hold the product during this manufacturing phase, but in the case where products are taxed, to secure, or "bond," the product until the time of sale. In this way, companies can delay paying taxes on the product until the product is sold.

In certain cases, the warehouse may perform some "value-added" services in addition to holding inventory. Examples of such services for the customer are special packaging, private labeling, and custom product preparation. Value-added services are an extension of the production process that takes place at a forward point in the supply chain.

Marketing Considerations

Marketing is frequently concerned with how readily available the product is to the marketplace. Warehousing is used to put value into a product. That is, by warehousing a product close to customers, delivery time can often be reduced or supply made readily available. This improved customer service through faster delivery can increase sales.

STORAGE SYSTEM FUNCTIONS

The storage system can be separated into two important functions: inventory holding (storage), and materials handling. These functions can be seen when tracing product flow through a typical food distribution warehouse, as shown in Figure 11-1. Materials handling refers to those activities of loading and unloading, moving the product to and from various locations within the warehouse, and order picking. Storage is simply the accumulation of inventory over time. Different locations in the warehouse and different lengths of time are chosen, depending on the purpose for storage. Within the warehouse, these move-store activities are repetitive and are analogous to the move-store activities occurring between various levels of the supply channel (recall Figures 1-2 and 1-4). Thus, in many ways, the storage system is a microlevel distribution system. Specific identification of the major system activities promotes understanding of the system as a whole and helps to provide a basis for generating design alternatives.

Storage Functions

Storage facilities are designed around four primary functions: holding, consolidation, break-bulk, and mixing. Warehouse design and layout often reflect the particular emphasis on satisfying one or more of these needs.

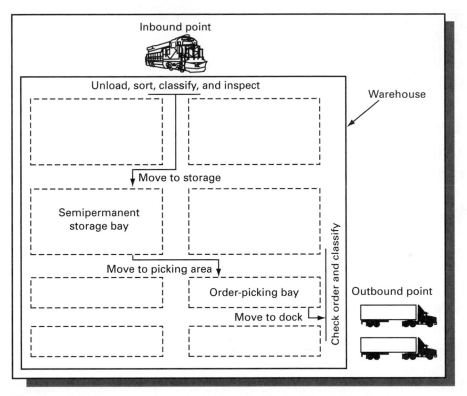

Inbound point

Unload, sort, classify, and inspect

Warehouse

Move to storage

Semipermanent
storage bay

Move to picking area

Check order and classify

Order-picking bay

Outbound point

Move to dock

Figure 11-1   Move-Store Activities of a Typical Food Distribution
Warehouse

Holding

The most obvious use of storage facilities is to provide protection and the orderly
holding of inventories. The length of time for holding goods and the requirements
for storage dictate the facility's configuration and layout. Facilities vary from long-
term, specialized storage (aging liquors, for example), to general-purpose merchandise storage (seasonal holding of goods), to temporary holding of goods (as in a
trucking terminal). In the last case, goods are held only long enough to build efficient
truckload quantities. Products stored in these various modes include finished goods
ready for the market, semimanufactured goods awaiting assembly or further processing, and raw materials.

Consolidation

Transportation rate structures, especially rate breaks, influence the use of storage facilities. If goods originate from a number of sources, it may be economical to establish a
collection point (a warehouse or a freight terminal) to consolidate the small shipments
into larger ones (Figure 11-2) and to reduce overall transportation costs. This assumes
that the buyer does not purchase enough to warrant volume shipments from each
source. The freight differential may more than offset the field warehousing charges.

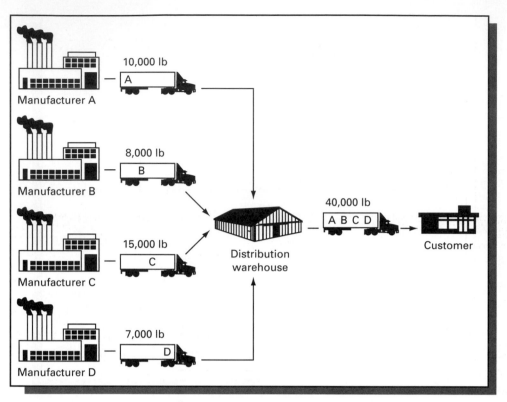

10,000 lb
A
Manufacturer A

8,000 lb
B
Manufacturer B

15,000 lb
C
Manufacturer C

7,000 lb
D
Manufacturer D

Distribution warehouse

40,000 lb
A B C D

Customer

Figure 11-2   Distribution Warehouse Used to Consolidate Small Inbound Shipments into Larger Outbound Shipments

Example

Suppose the customer in Figure 11-2 normally receives mixed-product shipments from the four manufacturers A, B, C, and D, in quantities of 10,000, 8,000, 15,000, and 7,000 lbs, respectively. If all shipments are made less-than-truckload to the customer, the total distribution cost would be $966 per shipment, as shown in Table 11-1(a). By consolidating shipments at a distribution warehouse, the total distribution cost is reduced to $778 per shipment, as shown in Table 11-1(b). In this case, a savings of $188 per shipment results, even after the warehousing cost is considered.

The term *distribution warehouse*[2] is used here primarily to make a contrast with a holding warehouse. The difference is a matter of how much emphasis is placed on holding activities and the time goods are stored. A holding warehouse implies that much of the warehouse space is devoted to semipermanent or long-term storage, as

---

[2]*Distribution warehouse* is used synonymously with *field warehouse* and *distribution center*.

(a) Without Consolidation

MANUFACTURER	SHIPPING WEIGHT (LB)	LTL RATE TO CUSTOMER	COST
A	10,000	$2.00/cwt.	$200
B	8,000	1.80	144
C	15,000	3.40	510
D	7,000	1.60	112
Total			$966

(b) With Consolidation

MANUFACTURER	SHIPPING WEIGHT (LB)	LTL RATE TO DISTRIBUTION CENTER	TOTAL LTL	DISTRIBUTION WAREHOUSE CHARGE	TL RATE FROM DISTRIBUTION WAREHOUSE TO CUSTOMER	TOTAL TL	COST
A	10,000	$0.75	$ 75	$10	$1.00/cwt.	$100	$185
B	8,000	0.60	48	8	1.00	80	136
C	15,000	1.20	180	15	1.00	150	345
D	7,000	0.50	35	7	1.00	70	112
Total	40,000						$778

Table 11-1 Example of the Potential Cost Savings Associated with Consolidating at a Distribution Warehouse

shown in Figure 11-3(a). In contrast, the distribution warehouse has most of its space allocated to temporary storage, and more attention is given to speed and ease of product flow in Figure 11-3(b). Obviously, many warehouses operate in both capacities, and the difference is a matter of degree.

At the limit, a warehouse may focus only on receiving and shipping activities, eliminating storage and order picking activities. Such warehouses are referred to as cross docks, or pool points. Goods are transferred directly from inbound to outbound docks with little or no storage. The transfer is typically completed in less than 24 hours. Compared with shipping goods directly from source points, cross docking is justified from the transportation economies that can be achieved.

Break-Bulk

Using storage facilities to break-bulk (or transload) is the opposite of using them to consolidate shipments. A generalized break-bulk situation is illustrated in Figure 11-4. Volume shipments having low transport rates are moved to the warehouse and then reshipped in smaller quantities. Break-bulk is common in distribution or terminal warehouses, especially when inbound transportation rates per unit is less than the outbound rates per unit, customers order in less-than-vehicle-load quantities, and the distance between manufacturer and customers is great. While transportation rate differentials tend to favor a distribution warehouse location near customers for break-bulk operations, the opposite is true for freight consolidation.

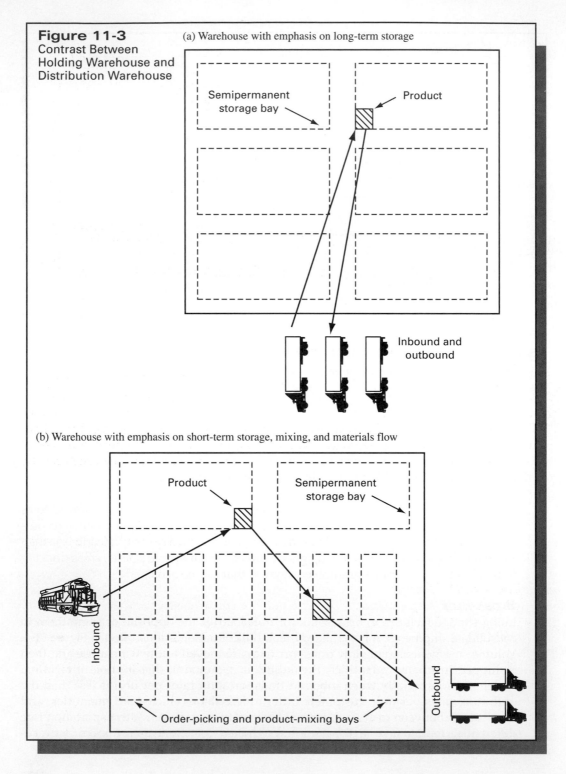

Figure 11-3
Contrast Between
Holding Warehouse and
Distribution Warehouse

(a) Warehouse with emphasis on long-term storage

Semipermanent
storage bay

Product

Inbound and
outbound

(b) Warehouse with emphasis on short-term storage, mixing, and materials flow

Product

Semipermanent
storage bay

Inbound

Outbound

Order-picking and product-mixing bays

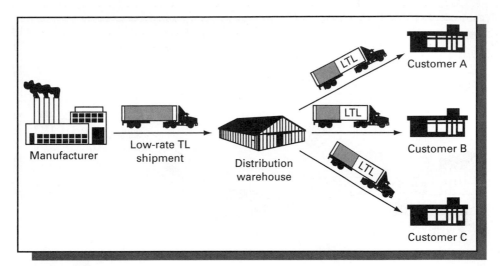

Figure 11-4 Distribution Warehouse (Pool Point, Cross Dock, or Terminal) Used to Break-Bulk

Mixing

The use of storage facilities for product mixing is shown in Figure 11-5. Firms that purchase from a number of manufacturers to fill a portion of their product line at each of a number of plants may find that establishing a warehouse as a product mixing point offers transportation economies. Without a mixing point, customer orders might be filled directly from producing points at high transportation rates on small-volume shipments. A mixing point permits volume shipments of portions of the product line to be collected at a single point and then assembled into orders and reshipped to customers.

Materials Handling Functions

Materials handling within a storage and handling system is represented by three primary activities: loading and unloading, movement to and from storage, and order filling.

Loading and Unloading

The first and last activities in the materials-handling events chain are loading and unloading (recall Figure 11-1). When the goods arrive at a warehouse, they must be offloaded from the transportation equipment. In many cases, unloading and movement to storage are handled as one operation. In others, they are separate processes, sometimes requiring special equipment. For example, ships are unloaded at dockside using cranes, and rail hopper cars are turned upside down with mechanical unloaders. Even when unloading equipment is not different from the equipment used to move goods to storage, unloading may be treated as a separate activity because goods may be offloaded and then sorted, inspected, and classified before moving on to a storage location in the warehouse.

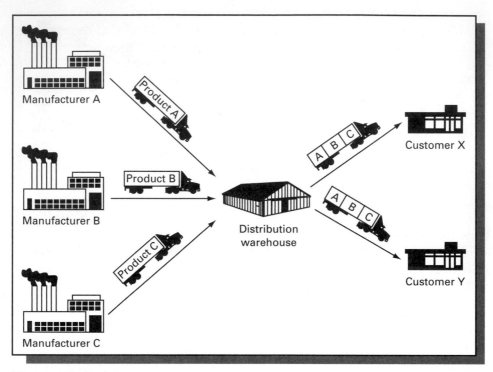

Figure 11-5   Generalized Example of a Distribution Warehouse Used for Product Mixing

Loading is similar to unloading; however, several additional activities may take place at the loading point. A final check concerning order content and order sequence may be carried out before the shipment is loaded onto the transportation equipment. In addition, loading may include an additional effort to prevent damage, such as bracing and packing the load.

Movement To and From Storage

Between the loading and unloading points in a storage facility, goods may be moved several times. Movement first is from the unloading point to a storage area. Next, movement proceeds from the shipping dock or from the order-picking area for stock replenishment. Using an order-picking area in the handling operation causes an additional movement link and nodal point in the storage system network, as was seen in Figure 11-1.

The actual movement activity can be accomplished using any number of the many materials handling equipment types available. These types vary from manual push trucks and carts to fully automated and computerized stacking and retrieval systems.

Order Filling

Order filling is the selection of stock from the storage areas according to the sales orders. Order selection may take place directly from semipermanent or bulk storage areas or from areas (called order-picking areas) that are especially laid out to enhance orderly materials flow in break-bulk quantities. Order filling is often the most critical materials handling activity because the handling of small-volume orders is labor intensive and relatively more expensive than the other materials handling activities.

STORAGE ALTERNATIVES

Storage may take place under a number of financial and legal arrangements. Each presents a different alternative to the logistician in evaluating his or her logistics system design. Four distinct alternatives are important, though various combinations of the four can create an almost infinite variety. The basic alternatives are ownership, rental, lease, and store in transit.

Space Ownership

Most manufacturing firms and service organizations own storage space in some form, ranging from a back room for office supplies to a finished goods warehouse with space in the hundreds of thousands of square feet. However, the common feature is that the firm or organization has a capital investment in the space and in the facility's materials handling equipment. For this investment, the company expects a number of advantages:

1. Less expensive warehousing than is possible with renting or leasing, especially if there is high utilization of the facility most of the time.
2. A higher degree of control over warehousing operations, which helps to ensure efficient warehousing and a high level of service.
3. Private ownership may be the only practical alternative when the product requires specialized personnel and equipment, such as with pharmaceuticals and certain chemicals.
4. The benefits that accrue from real estate ownership.
5. The space may be converted to other uses at a future time, such as to a manufacturing facility.
6. The space may serve as a base for a sales office, private truck fleet, traffic department, or purchasing department.

In summary, private warehousing has the potential of offering better control, lower costs, and greater flexibility as compared with rented warehouse space, especially under substantial and constant demand conditions or where special warehousing skills are needed.

Rented Space

Thousands of firms are in the business of providing warehousing services to other businesses. These firms may be public warehouses, but they also can be third-party logistics service providers or freight forwarders, both providing warehousing as part of their service offerings. They perform many of the same services that are carried out under a private warehousing arrangement, that is, receiving, storage, shipping, and related activities. These warehouse providers are similar to common carriers in transportation and hold essentially the same relationship to the private warehouse as the common carrier holds to private truck fleet ownership.

Types of Warehouses

Warehouse types for company-owned warehouses exist in an almost infinite variety because of customized designs that follow specialized needs. In contrast, a public warehouse holds itself out to serve a wide range of company needs. Thus, when compared to private warehouses, public warehouses are far more standardized in space configuration and use of multipurpose equipment. Many such warehouses are converted facilities—often buildings that were previously used as manufacturing facilities.

Public warehouses can be classified into a limited number of groups.

1. *Commodity warehouses.* These warehouses limit their services to storing and handling certain commodities, such as lumber, cotton, tobacco, grain, and other products that easily spoil.
2. *Bulk storage warehouses.* Some warehouses offer storage and handling of products in bulk, such as liquid chemicals, oil, highway salts, and syrups. They also mix products and break bulk as part of their service.
3. *Temperature-controlled warehouses.* These are warehouses that control the storage environment. Both temperature and humidity may be regulated. Perishables, such as fruits, vegetables, and frozen foods, as well as some chemicals and drugs, require this type of storage.
4. *Household goods warehouses.* Storage and handling of household items and furniture are the specialty of these warehouses. Although furniture manufacturers may use these warehouses, the major users are the household goods moving companies.
5. *General merchandise warehouses.* These warehouses, the most common type, handle a broad range of merchandise. The merchandise usually does not require the special facilities or the special handling as noted above.
6. *Miniwarehouses.* These are small warehouses, having unit space from 20 to 200 square feet and are often grouped together in clusters. They are intended as extra space, and few services are provided. Convenient location to renters is an attraction, but security may be a problem.

In practice, a public warehouse may not strictly be any one of these types. For example, a general merchandise warehouse handling food products may find the operation of a refrigerated section a necessity. In addition, in some cases it is good practice to combine bulk storage with general merchandise storage.

Inherent Advantages

Public warehousing, or rented warehouse space, offers many advantages, a number of which are the opposites of those for privately owned warehouses. Several of these are noted as follows:

1. *No fixed investment.* The use of public warehousing requires no investment for the firm renting space. All warehousing costs to the using firm are variable, that is, in direct proportion to the extent that warehouse services are used. Having no investment in storage facilities is beneficial when a firm has other preferred uses for the capital or simply does not have the capital to invest in this manner.

2. *Lower costs.* Public warehousing can offer lower costs than private or leased warehousing when the utilization of private space would be low, as when seasonal inventories must be stored. Inefficiencies may be encountered in private warehousing due to under- or overutilization of space. The public warehouseman attempts to counterbalance seasonal inventory patterns of a number of manufacturers and benefits from relatively constant and full utilization of capacity, as shown in Figure 11-6.

3. *Location flexibility.* Because arrangements with public warehouses are usually on a short-term basis, it is easy and inexpensive to change warehouse locations as markets shift. This lack of a long-term commitment offers important flexibility necessary to maintain an optimal logistics network.

Services

Public warehouses offer a wide variety of services to attract and retain customers. Most warehouses provide such basic services as receiving, storing, shipping, consolidating,

Figure 11-6 Balancing Seasonal Peaks and Valleys in Inventory Levels Among Several Manufacturers to Maintain Full Utilization of Usable Capacity in Public Warehouses

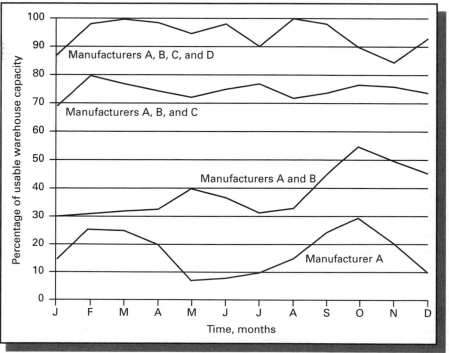

mixing, and break-bulk. Frequently, they offer much more. According to the American Warehousemen's Association, the following services can be expected from a public warehouse:

- Handling, storage, and distribution services, per package or per hundredweight
- In-transit storage
- U.S. Customs bonded storage
- U.S. Internal Revenue bonded storage
- Controlled temperature and humidity space
- Space rental on a square foot basis
- Office and display space; special clerical and telephone service
- Traffic information
- Handling and distribution of pool cars and consolidated shipments
- Physical inventories
- Modern data facilities
- Freight consolidation plan
- Packaging and assembly service
- Fumigation
- Marking, tagging, stenciling, wrapping
- Parcel post, UPS, and express shipments
- Dunnage and bracing
- Loading and unloading of cars and trucks
- Repairing, coopering, sampling, weighing, and inspection
- C.o.d. collections
- Compiling special stock statements
- Maintenance of and delivery to accredited customer lists
- Local and long-distance trucks
- Appliance delivery and installation
- Warehouse receipts forms, negotiable and nonnegotiable
- Overage, shortage, and damage reports prepared
- Prorating freight charges
- Prepaying of freight bills
- Credit information
- Loans on stored commodities
- Field warehousing services
- Waterborne freight terminal services
- Storage of machinery, steel, and other items requiring special handling equipment
- Yard storage
- Dry bulk commodity handling, storage, and bagging
- Liquid bulk handling, storage, drumming, and bottling
- Handling and storage of containerized materials[3]

Several of these services require special mention, either because they are unique to public warehousing or because they are important to potential users.

---

[3]American Warehousemen's Association, Chicago, IL.

Bonding arrangements are made with the government for certain goods, such as tobacco and liquor, on which taxes or duties are levied. The arrangement is between the merchandise owner and the government, whereby the goods cannot be removed from the warehouse (unless to another bonded warehouse) until the required taxes or duties are paid. The owner of the goods benefits by not having to pay the taxes or duties until the goods are sold, thus minimizing the capital tied up in inventoried goods. Public warehousemen acting as agents assure the government that goods claimed to be in the warehouse are actually there. The concept of bonding extends to goods stored in private warehouses as well.

The concept of bonding can be applied to goods entering the country that are destined for domestic or foreign markets. Free trade zones have been established around the country, usually in port areas. These fenced-in areas may contain manufacturing or warehousing facilities. A foreign company may land goods in the free trade zone, carry on light manufacturing, store the goods, and not pay import duties until the goods enter the country outside the zone. If the goods move on to foreign markets, no import duties are paid.

Field warehousing is a method by which the public warehouseman helps the owner of stored goods increase working capital. It is the conversion of private warehouse space to public warehouse space for securing credit. The public warehouse company usually leases from the owner of the goods a portion of the private warehouse in which goods are stored and issues a warehouse receipt. The owner then can use the receipt to obtain credit, using the goods as collateral for a loan. Because the goods are in legal custody of the public warehouseman, the public warehouse company acts as a third party to guarantee that the collateral for the loan exists. Establishing the warehouse on the owner's property saves the expense of moving the goods to a public warehouse and the storage expenses while in the warehouse. The arrangement is usually temporary, lasting the duration of the loan.

Stock spotting is a collective term for a number of activities related to order filling and is an extension of the break-bulk function. Public warehouses have responded to manufacturers' increasing need to provide a high level of customer service to wholesalers and retailers who maintain little inventory to meet their sales needs. Producers "spot" an assortment of their goods in public warehouses close to their markets. The public warehouse serves as a branch warehouse by performing all the functions normally handled by a producer's own warehouse. The order cycle time is considerably shortened compared with more centralized private warehousing that the producer may be using.

The public warehouseman may also assist in *inventory control*. With many stocks located around the country, keeping accurate records on inventory can be a problem, even if the company has its own record-keeping system. Public warehousemen help in this regard by keeping perpetual inventory balances, noting unsalable stock, noting stock damaged in transit, keeping records of stock arrival at the warehouse, and listing disbursements. Public warehouses use computers for much of the record keeping.

If the public warehouseman, or similar service provider, handles order processing and delivery for his customers, order tracking may also be a service. Such tracking information may interface with other information systems of the supply channel so that end customers can trace their order status from order entry to delivery.

We should not expect all public warehouses to provide the full range of services. Most are small, locally owned and operated enterprises. Only the largest of these have the resources for an extensive service offering. Therefore, it is important for the user of public warehousing services to be selective.

Documentation and Legal Considerations

Public warehouses are custodians of public property. With this responsibility, there are certain liabilities that the public warehouseman agrees to accept. From the standard contract terms and conditions approved by the American Warehousemen's Association, the following section on liability is highlighted:

> The warehouseman shall not be liable for any loss or injury to goods stored however caused unless such loss or injury resulted from failure by the warehouseman to exercise such care in regard to them as a reasonably careful man would exercise in like circumstances, and the warehouseman is not liable for damages which could not have been avoided by the exercise of such care.[4]

The essence of this statement is that the legal responsibility of public warehousemen is to exercise reasonable care in the handling and storage of the goods in their custody. If the damages or losses could not have been avoided through reasonable care, the warehouseman is not held liable unless specific contractual arrangements have been made to cover these. The merchandise owner may wish to extend his or her protection against liability and casualty through insurance protection or by writing into the contract with the public warehouse a provision for added liability, for which the warehouseman makes an additional charge.

Because public warehouses operate in the public interest, several states maintain regulatory control through a public utilities commission in the particular state. However, regulation is not as extensive as it once was and now involves warehouses only in California, Minnesota, and Washington. The Uniform Commercial Code, which covers public warehouses in all states except Louisiana, defines the responsibilities of the public warehouseman, and establishes uniformity in issuing warehouse receipts. In Louisiana, the Uniform Warehouse Receipts Act defines the responsibilities of warehousemen.

Several types of documentation become important to the smooth public warehouse operation. The principal documents are the warehouse receipt; the bill of lading; the over, short, and damage report; and the inventory status report.

The *warehouse receipt* is the primary document identifying what is being stored, where the goods are stored, who owns the goods, to whom they are to be delivered, and the terms and conditions of the storage contract. The contract terms and conditions, specified under the Uniform Commercial Code or the Uniform Warehouse Receipts Act, typically appear on the back of the warehouse receipt.

---

[4]Ibid.

Warehouse receipts may be negotiable or nonnegotiable. The difference lies in the ease of passing the goods from one person to another. A nonnegotiable receipt is issued to a designated person or company. The goods cannot be passed to another person without written instructions to the warehouse to release the goods. In contrast, the negotiable receipt may be issued to a person or company, or it may not be issued to any specific person. It may simply pass from one person to another by endorsement of the receipt. The warehouseman releases the goods to whoever holds the receipt. The negotiable feature of the warehouse receipt makes it easy to use the goods as collateral for a loan.

The *bill of lading* is the contract document used in the movement of goods. It spells out the terms and conditions under which a carrier moves goods. Because origin, public warehouse, and destination location of goods are usually separated, the public warehouseman often issues this document on behalf of the owner of the goods.

The *over, short, and damage (O.S.&D.) report* is issued upon receipt of the goods at the warehouse, and only if goods do not arrive in good condition or as stated on the bill of lading. The O.S.&D. report serves as a basis for filing a claim with a carrier.

The *inventory status report* shows the inventory position in the warehouse at the end of the month in terms of item, quantity, and weight. It also may be used as the basis for computing storage charges.

Leased Space

Leasing space for many firms represents an intermediate choice between short-term space rental in a public warehouse and the long-term commitment of a private warehouse. The advantage of leasing storage space is that a lower rate may be obtained from the space owner. However, because the space user must guarantee, through a lease contract, that space rental for a specified time will be paid, some location flexibility is lost. However, depending on the length of the lease, the user may also have control over the storage space and the associated operations, which is to the user's advantage.

Storage space for lease may be obtained in a variety of ways. Public warehousemen may offer extended time contracts on their space. Space may be available from manufacturers who cannot fully utilize their private warehouses. Third-party logistics providers offer warehouse space as well as other logistics services. Finally, owners of private warehouses may find it to their advantage to sell their warehouses and lease them back from the buyers.

Storage in Transit

Storage in transit refers to the time that goods remain in the transportation equipment during delivery. It is a special form of warehousing that requires coordination with the choice of a transportation mode or service. Because different transportation choices mean different transit times, it is possible for the logistician to select a transportation service that can substantially reduce or even eliminate the need for conventional warehousing. This alternative is particularly attractive to those companies dealing with seasonal inventories and shipments over long distances.

Example

The United Processors Company harvests and processes a variety of fruits and vegetables in southern and western farming regions of the country. For products such as strawberries and watermelon, there tends to be strong demand in the East and Midwest just ahead of the local growing season. Because United Processors must harvest earlier than in the northern climates, supply builds before demand peaks. Inventories normally build in the growing areas before truck shipments are made to the demand areas. By switching to rail service and the longer transit times associated with it, the company could, in many cases, ship immediately after harvesting and have the products arrive in the marketplace just as strong demand develops. The railroad serves the warehousing function. The result is a substantial reduction in warehousing costs and transportation costs as well.

MATERIALS HANDLING CONSIDERATIONS

Materials handling considerations are an integral part of the storage space decision. If the choice is public warehousing, compatibility of the company's materials handling system with that of the public warehouse is a prime consideration. If a company-controlled warehouse is selected, the efficiency of the entire materials-handling operation is of concern. Materials handling is largely a cost-absorbing activity, although it has some impact on the customer's order cycle time and, therefore, on customer service. Thus, the objectives for materials handling are cost centered, that is, to reduce handling cost and to increase space utilization. Improved materials-handling efficiency develops along four lines: loading unitization, space layout, storage equipment choice, and movement equipment choice.

Load Unitization

A fundamental principle in materials handling is that

> generally, materials handling economy is directly proportional to the size of load handled.[5]

That is, as the load size increases, the fewer the number of required trips to store a given quantity of goods and the greater the economy. The number of trips relates directly to the labor time necessary to move goods, as well as the time that the materials-handling equipment is in service. Efficiency often can be improved through consolidating a number of small packages into a single load and then handling the consolidated load. This is referred to as load unitization and is most commonly accomplished through palletization and containerization.

---

[5]Stanley M. Weir, *Order Selection* (New York: American Management Association, 1968), pp. 4–5.

Palletization

A pallet (or skid) is a portable platform, usually made of wood or corrugated cardboard, on which goods are stacked for transportation and storage. Goods are often placed on pallets at the time of manufacture and they remain palletized until order filling requires breaking the bulk quantities. Palletization aids movement by permitting the use of standardized mechanical materials handling equipment to handle a wide variety of goods. Further, it aids in load unitization with a resulting increase in weight and volume of materials handled per worker-hour. It also increases space utilization by providing more stable stacking and, hence, higher stacks in storage.

Pallets may be made in any desired size. The most popular size in the United States is 40 by 48 inches, which allows two pallets to be placed side by side in a standard container or truck trailer. Additional common sizes are 32 by 40 inches, 36 by 42 inches, and 48 by 48 inches. Other countries do not necessarily use these sizes. For example, Australia has a standard pallet size of 46 by 46 inches and Brazil favors 1200 mm by 1000 mm. Pallet size and configuration depend on the size, shape, weight, and crushability of the goods and materials handling equipment capacity. In addition, choosing a pallet size should take into account compatibility within one's own materials handling system and compatibility with materials handling systems outside the firm that must also handle the goods, such as those of public warehouses and the firm's customers. After accounting for these needs, the largest suitable pallet size should be selected to minimize the number of pallets required and to minimize handling. Loading the pallet should take into consideration the distribution and stability of the load.

The pallet is an added cost item to the materials handling system. It must be justified based on the savings realized from its use.

Containerization

The ideal in load unitization and materials handling system compatibility is the container. Containers are large boxes in which goods are stored and transported. They can be waterproofed and locked for security so that ordinary warehousing is not necessary. Storage can take place in an open yard. Standardized materials handling equipment can be used to move them, and they are interchangeable among different transportation modes.

Size standardization will be the key to widespread container use. Because of the many interest groups throughout the storage-transportation systems here and abroad, container sizes are still not standardized. Containers are expensive, and probably some cost-sharing plan and container-exchange program will need to emerge before containerization becomes a common materials handling method for other than international movements.

Space Layout

Location of stock in the warehouse directly affects the total materials-handling expense of all goods moving through the warehouse. A balance is sought between the materials handling costs and the warehouse space utilization. Specifically, there are storage space and order-picking considerations in internal warehouse design.

Layout for Storage

In warehouses where the turnover is low, the primary concern is to configure the warehouse for storage. Storage bays may be both wide and deep, and stacking may be as high as ceiling height or load stability permits. Aisles may be narrow. This layout assumes that the extra time required for moving stock in and out of storage areas is more than compensated for by the full space utilization.

As stock turnover increases, such a layout becomes progressively less satisfactory, and modification must be made to keep handling costs reasonable. Thus, aisles will tend to become wider and the stack height may be decreased. These reduce the time spent placing and retrieving the stock.

Layout for Order Picking

Because the usual flow pattern in a warehouse is for goods to come into the warehouse in larger unit quantities than they leave, order-picking considerations become prime warehouse layout determinants. A disproportionately greater amount of labor time can be spent on filling orders than on receiving and storing the stock. The simplest layout for order picking is to use existing storage areas (referred to as an *area system*), with any modification as to stacking height, location of goods relative to outbound docks, and bay size, as may be needed for efficiency [see Figure 11-7(a)]. If the turnover of goods is high and order filling requires breaking bulk, using storage bays to fulfill both storage and order-picking needs may result in higher than necessary materials handling costs and in poor warehouse space utilization. That is, the traveling time is great as long distances are encountered in routing through the warehouse to fill orders, unit loads are broken such that orderly stacking and placement of goods is diminished, and space utilization is reduced.

An alternate layout plan is to establish stock bays in the warehouse according to their primary function. This is called a *modified area system*. Certain warehouse areas would be designed around storage needs and full space utilization, while others would be designed around storage order-picking requirements and minimum travel time for order filling [Figure 11-7(b)]. The storage (reserve) bays are used for semipermanent storage. When stock is low in the order-picking bays, it is replenished with stock from the storage bays. With the exception of large, bulky items, which may still be picked from storage areas, all unit loads are broken in the order-picking area. Order-picking bays tend to be smaller than storage bays, often only two pallets deep or using storage racks half the size of those in the reserve section. The order-picking stack height is limited to a comfortable reach for the workers. Using order-picking areas separate from the reserve area will minimize the routing time and service time to fill orders.

Order-picking travel time may be further reduced through the choice of specialized order-picking equipment, such as flow racks, conveyors, towlines, scanners, and other materials handling equipment; and through operational design, such as sequencing, zoning, and batching. Because materials handling equipment will be discussed in a later section of this chapter, only operational considerations will be mentioned at this point.

Sequencing is the arrangement of items needed on an order in the sequence in which they appear on the order-picking route through the warehouse. Avoiding

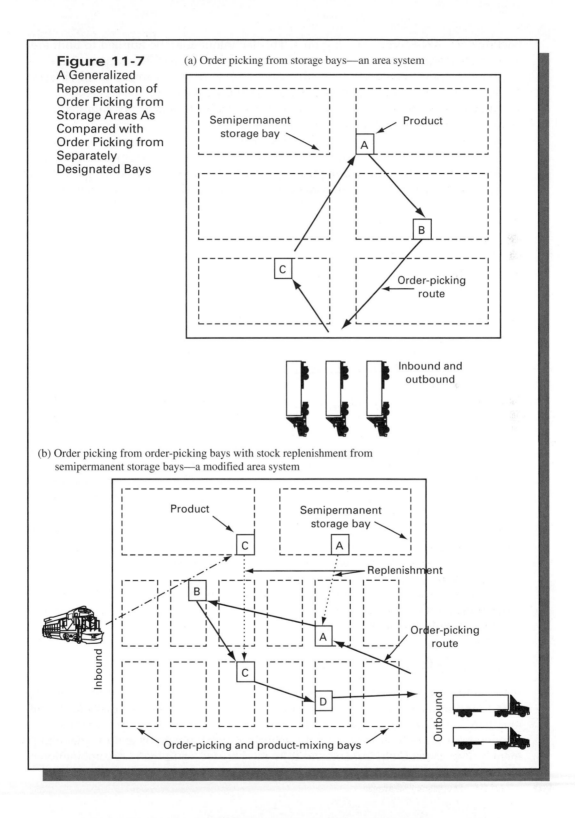

Figure 11-7
A Generalized Representation of Order Picking from Storage Areas As Compared with Order Picking from Separately Designated Bays

(a) Order picking from storage bays—an area system

Semipermanent storage bay

Product

A

B

C

Order-picking route

Inbound and outbound

(b) Order picking from order-picking bays with stock replenishment from semipermanent storage bays—a modified area system

Product

Semipermanent storage bay

C

A

Replenishment

B

A

Order-picking route

C

D

Inbound

Outbound

Order-picking and product-mixing bays

backtracking saves order-picking time. This technique may be applied to both area and modified-area systems, however, it does carry a penalty. The sequencing must occur on the sales order itself through cooperation with the customer or salesperson, or else the product item data must be sequenced after the order is received.

Zoning refers to assigning individual order pickers to serve only a limited number of the stock items instead of routing them through the entire stock. An order picker may select the stock in a single aisle or designated area, filling only a portion of the total customer order. Although zoning permits balanced labor utilization and minimum travel time in order picking, it also has some shortcomings. First, it requires that stock be located in zones according to ordering frequency, item weight, item similarity, and the like so that the order picker workload is balanced. Second, sales orders must be subdivided and a picking list for each zone developed. Third, the various portions of the orders must be reassembled into a complete order before leaving the warehouse. If the order filling proceeds from one zone to another to avoid the problem of reassembly, then the order-picking pace becomes dependent on the order-picking pace in other zones.

Batching refers to the selection of more than one order on a single pass through the stock. This practice obviously reduces travel time, but it also increases the complication of reassembling orders and partial orders for shipment. It also may increase order-filling time for any one order because its completion is dependent on the number and size of the other orders in the batch.

Storage Equipment Choice

Storage and materials handling must be considered in concert. In a way, storage is simply a temporary halt in the materials flowing through a warehouse. Storage aids promote the full space utilization and improve the materials handling efficiency.

Probably the most important storage aid is the rack. Racks are shelves, usually of metal or wood, on which goods are placed. When a wide variety of items in small quantities must be stored, stacking loads one on top of another is inefficient. Racks promote floor-to-ceiling stacking, and the items on the top and bottom shelves are equally accessible, though items with high turnover should be placed near the bottom to reduce total service time at the rack. Racks also aid in rotating stock, as in a first-in-first-out inventory control system.

Other available storage aids include shelf boxes, horizontal and vertical dunnage, bins, and U-frames. All such equipment assists the orderly storage and handling of irregularly shaped products.

Movement Equipment Choice

A tremendous variety of mechanical equipment for loading and unloading, picking orders, and moving goods in the warehouse is available. Movement equipment is differentiated by its degree of specialized use and the extent that manual power is required to operate it. Three broad equipment categories can be distinguished: manual equipment, power-assisted equipment, and fully mechanized equipment. A combination of these categories is generally found within a materials handling system rather than a single category used exclusively.

Manual Equipment

Hand-operated, materials handling equipment, such as two-wheeled hand trucks and four-wheeled platform trucks, provides some mechanical advantage in movement of goods and requires only a modest investment. While much of this equipment can be used for a great many goods and under a wide variety of circumstances, some of this equipment is designed for special use, for example, carpet handling, furniture handling, and pipe handling.

In general, manual equipment's flexibility and low cost make it a good choice when the product mix in a warehouse is dynamic, the volume flowing through the warehouse is not high, and the investment in more mechanized equipment is not desirable. However, the use of this equipment is somewhat limited to the operator's physical capabilities.

Power-Assisted Equipment

Materials handling can be speeded up and the output per worker-hour increased with the use of power-assisted materials handling equipment. Such equipment includes cranes, industrial trucks, elevators, and hoists; however, the industry workhorse is the forklift truck and its variations.

The forklift truck is usually only one part of a materials handling system. It is combined with palletized loading and sometimes with pallet racks. The power-assisted equipment permits high load stacking (over 12 feet) and load movements of substantial size. The most common forklift truck has a lifting capacity of about 3,000 pounds. The use of the forklift truck, pallet, and rack in a modified area warehouse layout is shown in Figure 11-8.

The pallet and forklift truck materials handling system has high flexibility. The pallet permits a variety of goods to be moved with standard handling equipment. The system as a whole is not likely to become obsolete or require expensive modification as storage requirements change. In addition, because only a modest investment is required, the system is a popular one.

Fully Mechanized Equipment

With computer-controlled handling equipment, bar coding, and scanning technology, some materials handling systems have been developed that come close to full automation. Such systems are referred to as *automated storage and retrieval systems*, or AS/RS, for short. They represent the most extensive application of technology of all the materials handling alternatives.

Applications

- At the peak of trading stamp popularity, the huge S&H Green Stamp Distribution Center in Hillsdale, Illinois, served more than 150 stamp redemption centers, stocked 2,000 items from 700 suppliers, and processed more than 16,000 cartons during a single 7 1/2-hour shift. A computerized conveyor system was used to move goods from order-picking areas, to police the flow of orders through the conveyor system, and to control the accumulation of orders at the dock.

- The handling system at Rohr Corporation, which handles 90,000 aircraft parts, represents a step closer to a fully automated storage and retrieval system. With the exception of the shipping and receiving area and the audit area for paperwork and load checking, incoming loads are moved via conveyor to storage racks, stored in racks by automated cranes, and retrieved by the reverse process. A schematic diagram of this system is shown in Figure 11-9.

Stories of high-tech materials handling can excite the imagination, but an AS/RS is not a good alternative for most warehouse operations. Unless a constant

Figure 11-8 Pallet, Rack, and Forklift Truck Materials Handling System in a Modified Area Warehouse Layout

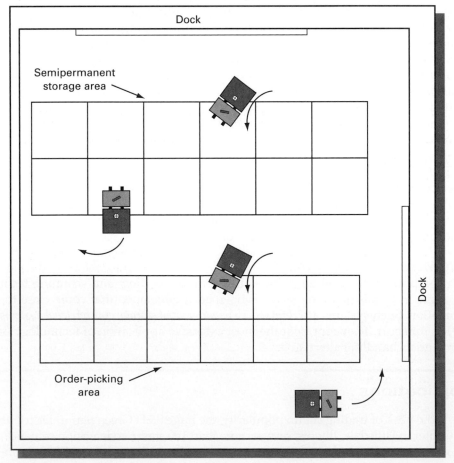

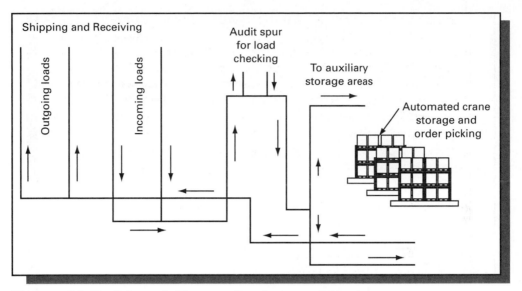

Figure 11-9 Schematic Diagram of an Automated Warehouse

and substantial volume flows through a warehouse, it is difficult to justify the large investment required for such systems. In addition, they have the following drawbacks: inflexibilities in terms of future product mix and volume and in terms of warehouse location, and mechanical failures that can shut down the entire system. However, given favorable circumstances for its development, the fully mechanized warehouse offers more potential for lower operating costs and for faster order picking than any other type of materials handling system.

STORAGE SYSTEM COSTS AND RATES

A company must pay storage system costs either through rates charged by an outside firm offering such services or through internal costs generated from the particular materials handling system in a company-controlled warehouse. To provide an overview of the various storage system costs, four different systems are noted: public warehousing; leased warehousing, manual handling; private warehousing, pallet and forklift truck handling; and private warehousing, automated handling. Each represents a different level of fixed and variable costs, as shown in Figure 11-10. Note that this is not an exhaustive list of all possible combinations of space alternatives and handling methods.

Public Warehousing

With the exception of a few states (for example, Washington and Minnesota) where public warehouse rates are disclosed to the public, warehouse rates are confidential

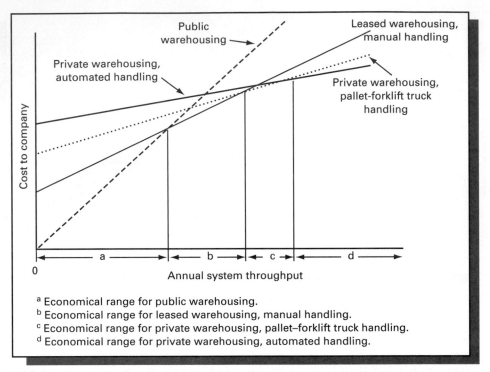

Figure 11-10 Generalized Total Cost Curves for Four Alternative Storage Systems

and a matter of negotiation between the warehouseman and the customer. The agreed-upon rate will be based on such factors as the volume of goods to be handled and stored; the time the warehouse space will be needed; the number of separate items in the product mix; any special requirements or restrictions for storage; the average outbound order size; and the amount of clerical work required.

These cost factors are generally grouped into three basic categories: storage, handling, and accessorial costs. Each exhibits different characteristics and usually separate rates are quoted in the three areas. Specifically, storage rates are often quoted on a per hundredweight, per month basis. The monthly rate reflects the time dimension of storage. In contrast, handling rates are typically quoted on a per hundredweight basis. The number of times that the goods must be handled is the important dimension in handling costs. Clerical costs are charged to the customer on a direct basis. For example, bill of lading preparation costs are charged on a per bill basis.

Public warehousemen may use several other methods of quoting rates:

1. On a per case basis with an in and out per case charge for handling
2. By the actual space merchandise occupies, usually computed on a square foot or cubic foot basis
3. By a lease agreement for space and a contract for the handling function by the warehouse personnel

In all cases except method 3, the customer is billed monthly unless other arrangements have been made.

Public warehousing to the customer is an all-variable-cost storage system. If a company generates a substantial and steady volume of business, public warehousing may become more expensive than private warehousing. Flexibility and improved customer service may be reasons for selecting public warehousing, even if an alternative's costs are higher.

Leased Warehousing, Manual Handling

Another storage system type is to combine leased warehousing space with manual materials handling. Though leasing is a long-term commitment compared with public warehousing, the charges for the space are incurred at regular intervals, so leased space can be treated as a variable cost for a given warehouse throughput. Handling equipment requires a modest investment, if the equipment is company owned, that must be amortized over time. Labor costs tend to be substantial for this system, which imparts a strong variable cost component into the total storage system cost curve (Figure 11-10).

Private Warehousing, Pallet and Forklift Truck Handling

This is a commonly chosen alternative to public warehousing. All costs within this system are internal company costs, provided that handling equipment is not leased or rented. Owning both warehouse and equipment introduces a substantial fixed-cost level in the total cost curve, as shown in Figure 11-10. High levels of mechanization in handling and low direct costs for operating a private warehouse mean low variable costs. However, substantial volume is needed before this alternative becomes economically viable, as compared with those alternatives noted previously.

The pattern of throughput for a private (or leased) warehouse is important in assessing the costs for the storage system. Seasonal variations in warehouse usage cause capacity under- and overutilization. During periods of low utilization, there is idle capacity and indivisibilities of some labor units that create high variable costs. Conversely, straining the warehouse capacity limits again causes high variable costs as materials handling inefficiency and damage to the stored goods increase. (The typical private warehouse per unit cost curve is shown in Figure 11-11.) Therefore, the cost level associated with this alternative depends on the extent of warehouse utilization and the diseconomies caused from fluctuating warehouse throughput.

Private Warehousing, Automated Handling

In terms of costs, the private warehouse, automated handling storage system is a limiting case of the other alternatives mentioned. It represents a high level of fixed investment in the warehouse and the automated handling equipment, such as computer-controlled conveyors and cranes, and a low level of variable costs, as the system requires little in the way of labor, light, heat, and the like. As Figure 11-10

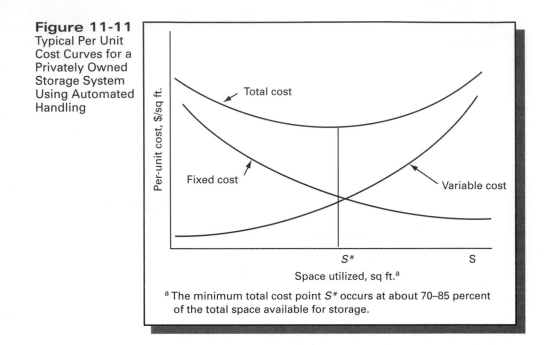

Figure 11-11
Typical Per Unit
Cost Curves for a
Privately Owned
Storage System
Using Automated
Handling

Per-unit cost, $/sq ft.

Total cost

Fixed cost

Variable cost

S^*

S

Space utilized, sq ft.[a]

[a] The minimum total cost point S^* occurs at about 70–85 percent
of the total space available for storage.

shows, at very high warehouse throughput levels, private warehousing with auto-mated handling has the potential for being the lowest-cost storage system per throughput unit.

Beyond simply comparing one storage system against another, it is useful for further analysis and control to break down total costs into the three basic cost components in a storage system: storage, handling, and clerical costs. For the public warehouse, these costs provide the basis for establishing rates and providing a ready comparison with the public warehousing alternative. In the private warehouse, they are valuable for controlling the various expenses. Allocation of the various costs incurred in warehouse operation requires a good deal of judgment. One such allocation is illustrated in Table 11-2. Once total storage, handling, and clerical costs are identified, they can be expressed on a per hundredweight basis, a square-foot basis, or any other useful dimension.

VIRTUAL WAREHOUSING

An extension of the concept of a virtual inventory is the virtual warehouse. Whereas virtual inventories satisfy customer requests from alternate inventories in a company's logistics system, a virtual warehouse is one where not all items for sale are stocked in a company's warehouse. Rather, selected items are shipped directly to customers from supplier inventories with no intention of a company stocking them. Some items that are stockout in the warehouse may be handled in a similar manner. Consider a company such as Amazon, which stocks high-volume book titles in its own warehouse but cannot practically stock low-volume and rare titles. Alternately,

Table 11-2 Allocation of a Set of Warehouse Expense Items Into Basic Storage System Cost Categories

Account Code	Account Name	Total	Storage	Handling	Clerical	G & A[b]
1	Rent	$16,281	$13,980	$1,345	$ 506	$ 450
2	Taxes—payroll[a]	2,390[a]	63[a]	1,187[a]	810[a]	330[a]
3	Taxes—highway	10		7	3	
4	Taxes—real estate	2,259	1,852	313	94	
5	Taxes—franchise	775	275			500[a]
6	Maintenance—building	225	25		200	
7	Maintenance—elevator	50	50			
8	Maintenance—tools and equipment	185	70	115		
9	Maintenance—furniture	60			50	10
10	Maintenance—air conditioning	1,500	1,400	50	50	
11	Utilities	950	380	190	380	
12	Insurance—liability[a]	222[a]	4[a]	75[a]	101[a]	42[a]
13	Insurance—worker's comp.[a]	691[a]	35[a]	652[a]	3[a]	1[a]
14	Insurance—other	80	25	26	29	
15	Insurance—group	847[a]	24[a]	434[a]	262[a]	127[a]
16	Labor[a]	34,170[a]	1,200[a]	23,550[a]	9,420[a]	
17	Salaries	6,500				6,500
18	Dues and subscriptions	150				150
19	Motor equipment	500				500
20	Demurrage	110	110			
21	Donations	25				25
22	Legal and accounting	100				100
23	Loss and damage	700	10	690		
24	Miscellaneous	573	33	4		536
25	Packing materials	295		295		
26	Postage	175		25		150
27	Bad accounts	210				210
28	Stationery—supplies	350			350	
29	Telephone	1,125				1,125
30	Subcontracts	500	500			
31	Equipment rental	175		175		
32	Travel	800				800
33	Equipment interchange		200	(200)		
34	Gasoline and oil	400		300	100	
35	Amortization—organization expense	500				500
36	Tires	30		30		
37	Depreciation expense	4,857	507	4,209	141	

Table 11-2 (*cont.*)

ACCOUNT CODE	ACCOUNT NAME	TOTAL	STORAGE	HANDLING	CLERICAL	G & A[b]
38	Garage	500		500		
39	Subtotals	79,270	20,743	33,972	12,499	12,056
40	Prorata G & A		3,721	6,093	2,242	(12,056)
41	Total expense	$79,270	$24,464	$40,065	$14,741	

[a]Denotes labor and labor-related expenses.
[b]General and administration expenses.
Source: Howard Way and Edward W. Smykay, "Warehouse Cost Analysis," *Transportation & Distribution Management*, Vol. 4 (July 1964), p. 32.

the handling is contracted to third parties or shipments are made directly from vendors. The result is that less investment is needed in the logistics infrastructure while high levels of customer service are maintained.

Since the intention is not to stock all products being sold, handling customer orders might proceed as follows: Say, an order contains seven items. The company's order management system (OMS) identifies that two of the items are in the warehouse and sends the requested items to the company's warehouse management system (WMS) for picking, packing, and shipping from a company owned and operated warehouse. Requests for the remaining items are sent to vendors who hold physical inventories of the items. Each vendor's OMS transfers the order request to its WMS for processing.

A key to using the virtual warehousing concept effectively is sharing critical information with vendors. The seller shares information with vendors on what is in transit, what is in the warehouse, what is on order. The vendor, in turn, shares production schedules and his own inventory status. This instant visibility of product availability, often with communication through a Web site, allows quick response to customer demand trends and minimizes capital investment in inventory and warehouses.

Example

Land's End maintains its own well-stocked warehouses, but the catalog retailer also depends on vendors who ship direct to customers. Also an Internet retailer, Land's End uses a demand management process to distribute forecasts to suppliers on a regular basis. Suppliers share their production process with Land's End, which, in turn, distills the information down to product availability dates for customers. Land's End refers to this process of inventory control as *net position management*.[6]

---

[6]Helen L. Richardson, "Virtually Connected," *Transportation & Distribution* (March 2000), pp. 39–44.

CONCLUDING COMMENTS

This chapter provides a brief overview of the storage and handling system in a supply chain network. The discussion is directed toward the types of systems available, the functions they serve, and their inherent advantages. Storage and handling alternatives are also discussed along with their associated costs. This is the storage and handling system environment. Logistics decision making draws upon this information in generating reasonable courses of action.

QUESTIONS

1. Why does the logistician consider the storage system an economic convenience rather than a necessity?
2. Why is the storage system a micrologistics system problem? Compare the storage system with the logistics system network in Figure 2-4.
3. Compare and contrast private ownership of storage space to rented storage space with reference to the following:
   a. Services that can be realized from each
   b. Cost for storage
   c. Degree of administrative control
   d. Flexibility in meeting future uncertainties
   Under what general circumstances is private warehousing a better choice than public warehousing?
4. How is storage in transit an alternative to conventional warehousing?
5. What benefits does containerization offer over conventional forms of load unitization? Why is it not more widely used?
6. For the following situations, indicate whether an area or modified-area layout of a warehouse would likely be used and why.
   a. A food distribution center
   b. A furniture warehouse
   c. Storage of major appliances
   d. Storage of a steel company's products
   e. A drug and sundries distribution center
7. Explain and define the following:
   a. Stock spotting
   b. Negotiable warehouse receipt
   c. O.S.&D. report
   d. Containerization
   e. Unitization
   f. Bonding
   g. Field warehousing
   h. Palletization
   i. Automated storage and retrieval systems
   j. Order picking
   k. Storage in transit
   l. Breaking bulk
   m. Zoning

8. How does storage contribute to the time value of goods? Explain.
9. How can a materials handling system overcome the disadvantages of size, configuration, and shape of storage space?
10. Explain what the logistician should generally know about the storage and materials handling system.
11. What is virtual warehousing? When is it likely to be used? What is required for it to work well?

Chapter 12

Storage and Handling Decisions

> *Perfection is not attainable, but if we chase perfection, we catch excellence.*
>
> —VINCE LOMBARDI

*T*he logistician often becomes involved with activities that supplement a firm's primary move-store activities. Storage and materials handling are such activities. They can be quite important since they affect the time that it takes to process customer orders in the distribution channel or to make supplies available in the supply channel. They are cost absorbing and worthy of careful management.

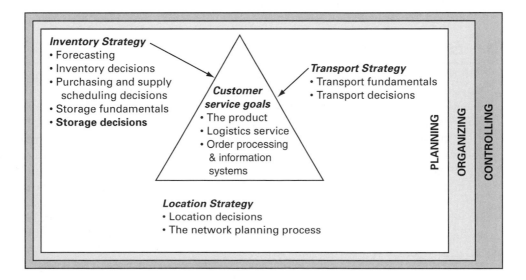

Inventory Strategy
- Forecasting
- Inventory decisions
- Purchasing and supply scheduling decisions
- Storage fundamentals
- **Storage decisions**

Transport Strategy
- Transport fundamentals
- Transport decisions

Customer service goals
- The product
- Logistics service
- Order processing & information systems

Location Strategy
- Location decisions
- The network planning process

PLANNING   ORGANIZING   CONTROLLING

Although storage and handling do not play the same role in all logistics systems, this chapter focuses on these activities as they take place in warehouses and other locations where inventories are held. Warehousing displays the full range of storage and handling decisions that are included in various logistics systems.

The importance of warehousing activities was previously documented. As shown in Table 1-3, storage and materials handling activities account for roughly one-fourth of logistics expenses, excluding the cost of carrying inventories. Of this expense, approximately one-half is for labor, one-fourth is for space, and the remaining is for energy, equipment, material, and other. Neglecting to manage these activities effectively can result in inefficiencies that outweigh gains in good management of such key activities as transportation, inventory maintenance, and information flow. Many storage and handling activities are repetitive, so careful management can produce substantial economies and customer service improvements over time.

We want to consider the planning problems for the design and operation of the nodal points in the logistics network. Nodal points usually are represented by warehouses. However, nodal points also may refer to inventory accumulations in whatever form they may take, whether held outdoors, underground, or within partially protecting shelters. Because warehousing is a complex and widely used storage form, the major emphasis will be on warehouse design and its operation, with implications for other methods of storage and handling. Specifically, this chapter deals with planning for facility design, which includes facility sizing, financial type, configuration, space layout, dock design, materials handling system selection, and stock layout. An overview of storage and handling activities was presented in Chapter 11, and this chapter continues by dealing with many of the associated decisions.

SITE SELECTION

Before a discussion of the detailed decisions about warehouse design and operation proceeds, the question of where the warehouse is to be located needs to be resolved. Chapter 13 presents a number of mathematical models that give a rough approximation to final location in terms of a region, metropolitan area, or city. Within the defined area, the specific site must be selected. Site selection refers to the specific piece of real estate on which the facility will be located, and its methodology is more of an art than a well-defined process. It frequently involves weighing a number of tangible and intangible factors. From a survey of the readers of *Transportation & Distribution* magazine, the most important site selection factors for a distribution center are identified by whether the responding member's firm was engaged in manufacturing, retailing, or distributing.[1] The factors and their ranking are shown in Table 12-1.

---

[1]Les B. Artman and David A. Clancy, *Transportation & Distribution*, Vol. 31, No. 6 (June 1990), pp. 17–20.

Factor	Overall	Manufacturer	Retailer	Distributor
Transportation access	1	1	2	1
Outbound transportation	2	2	3	5
Customer proximity	3	3	6	6
Labor availability	4	5	1	3
Labor costs	5	6	7	4
Inbound transportation	6	4	4	2
Union environment	7	7	5	9
Taxes	8	8	10	7
State incentive/laws	9	10	—	—
Land costs	10	—	8	8
Utilities	—	—	9	10
JIT requirements	—	9	—	—

Source: Les B. Artman and David A. Clancy, *Transportation & Distribution*, Vol. 31, No. 6 (June 1990), p. 19.

Table 12-1 Distribution Center Site Selection Factors by Industry Type

Of course, when the warehouse already exists, as in the case of a public warehouse or a facility to be leased, selection is usually restricted to the available facilities. When selection is among public warehouses, site selection is concerned with rates and services to be provided. On the other hand, selecting a facility to be leased involves many of the factors just noted, but the physical characteristics of the buildings to be leased also act as constraints on warehouse operations.

Planning the private warehouse offers the maximum design flexibility of all the warehousing alternatives. Thus, the following discussion of the planning for design and operation is directed primarily toward the privately operated warehouse.

PLANNING FOR DESIGN AND OPERATION

Planning for facility design is concerned with the long-range decision making needed to establish the facility for efficient temporary product storage and the flow of products through the facility. Such decisions often require a substantial capital investment that commits the company to a design for many years. However, careful design planning can mean years of efficient warehouse operation.

Sizing the Facility

Size is probably the most important factor in designing a storage facility. Once warehouse size is determined, it acts as a constraint on warehouse operations that may last 20 years or longer. Whereas internal facility layout may be changed with relative ease, altering overall size is much less likely to occur. Although the facility may be expanded later or unused space may be leased to other users, the resulting quality of the space may not be ideal. In general, the result of poor size planning is either to cause higher than necessary materials handling costs (in the case of underbuilding), or to force unnecessary space costs on the logistics system (in the case of constructing more space than needed).

Specifically, what is size? Size simply refers to the overall cubic content of the building—its length, width, and height. Determining the needed building volume is a task complicated by the many factors that affect the size decision. Such factors as the type of materials handling system to be used, aisle requirements, stock layout arrangements, dock requirements, local building codes, office area, and product throughput (both now and in the future) influence the final choice of building size. A starting point is the minimum space required for accommodating the inventory stored in the building over time. The remaining factors influence size by adding to the basic inventory-determined size.

Let us look at inventory-determined warehouse size under two different conditions. The first is when there will be no significant changes in the need for space in the reasonable future. No trend in space needs is expected. However, in the short term there will be seasonal changes in space needs as sales through the warehouse and warehouse stock replenishment vary throughout the year. The second is when average inventory levels are anticipated to change over a period of years. This dynamic sizing problem seeks the best size for the warehouse in each year of the planning horizon.

Before a detailed sizing analysis is carried out, a company typically has made its general location decision, although not necessarily its site selection decision. In the location analysis, it is necessary to assign sales territories to warehouses. This assignment is the basis for projecting the product throughput (demand) for the warehouse. With this throughput and the warehouse's inventory turnover ratio, the amount of inventory can be estimated. Rough warehouse size approximations can be made from these inventory needs, and further analysis begins with this preliminary information.

The No-Trend Sizing Problem

There are generally two basic choices for warehousing. The first is to rent space, such as from a public warehouse or subcontracted operation. The second is to operate owned or leased warehouse space. Depending on which is least expensive, a company may use only one type, assuming there is little fluctuation in the space needs over time. However, when space requirements fluctuate widely, there is the possibility that a mixed strategy would be better. If privately operated space is sized to peak space requirements, there can be substantial space underutilization during a portion of the year. A better strategy would be to skim the space requirements so that a high level of utilization is realized and to use rented space on a short-term basis to meet peak space requirements. This strategy is graphically illustrated in Figure 12-1.

Finding the best mixed strategy is a matter of trying different sizes of privately operated space and determining the associated total cost for meeting all space needs

Figure 12-1
A Mixed Strategy of
Rented and Privately
Operated
Warehouse Space
for Variable Space
Requirements

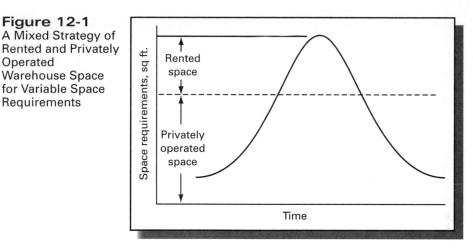

throughout the year. Privately operated space is characterized by a combination of fixed and variable costs, whereas rented space is essentially an all-variable cost to the user. Thus, as privately operated space is increased in size, the combined cost will initially drop until the point where fixed costs and space underutilization of progressively larger warehouses causes total costs to increase. We seek the minimal cost point.

Example

Douglas-Biehl, a small chemical company, is planning to build a warehouse on the West Coast. Projections of average monthly demand on the warehouse are as follows:

Month	Demand, lb	Month	Demand, lb
Jan.	66,500	July	1,303,000
Feb.	328,000	Aug.	460,900
Mar.	1,048,500	Sept.	99,900
Apr.	2,141,000	Oct.	15,300
May	2,820,000	Nov.	302,200
June	2,395,000	Dec.	556,700
		Total	11,537,000

A *monthly* inventory turnover ratio[2] of 3, or 36 turns per year, is to be maintained for the warehouse. Of the total warehouse space, 50 percent is used for aisles, and only 70 percent is to be utilized to anticipate variability in space requirements. An average

---

[2]Monthly sales divided by average inventory.

mix of chemical products occupies 0.5 cubic feet of space per lb and can be stacked 16 feet high on racks.

The warehouse, with equipment, can be constructed for $30 per square foot, amortized over 20 years, and operated at $0.05 per lb of throughput. Annual fixed costs are $3 per sq. ft. of total space. Space may be rented for a space charge of $0.10 per lb per month and an in-and-out handling charge of $0.07 per lb. What warehouse size should be constructed?

We first need to develop a space requirements table showing the space requirements throughout the year in square feet. We know from the turnover ratio that for every 3 lb of chemicals moving through the warehouse per month, 1 lb is maintained in inventory. For each pound stored, 0.5/16 sq. ft. of space is needed. Due to aisles, this space requirement needs to be doubled (1/0.50) and then increased for the rate of space utilization (1/0.70). Therefore, to convert demand to space requirements in square feet, we have

$$\text{Space (sq. ft.)} = \text{Monthly demand (lb)} \times (1/3)(0.5/16)(1/0.50)(1/0.70)$$
$$= \text{Monthly demand (lb)} \times 0.029762$$

The space requirements table is developed in Table 12-2.

Next, we select a warehouse size to be tested. Let us try 60,000 sq. ft. A warehouse of this size costs $30/sq. ft. × 60,000 sq. ft. = $1,800,000 to build. Amortizing the construction cost over 20 years would yield an annual fixed cost of $90,000. A working cost table (Table 12-3) for this warehouse size alternative is developed. Repeating the same calculations for various warehouse sizes provides us with the data to develop the total annual cost curve as shown in Figure 12-2. The most economical warehouse size is 60,000 sq. ft. It can be anticipated that rented space will be needed during the months of April through June, with May being the peak month, requiring enough rented space to handle $(2,820,000 \times 0.29)/3 = 272,600$ lb of chemicals.

Table 12-2   The Projected Space Requirements for Douglas-Biehl's West Coast Warehouse

MONTH	WAREHOUSE DEMAND, lb	SPACE REQUIREMENTS, sq. ft.	MONTH	WAREHOUSE DEMAND, lb	SPACE REQUIREMENTS, sq. ft.
Jan.	66,500	1,979[a]	July	1,303,000	38,780
Feb.	328,000	9,762	Aug.	460,900	13,717
Mar.	1,048,500	31,205	Sept.	99,900	2,973
Apr.	2,141,000	63,720	Oct.	15,300	455
May	2,820,000	83,929	Nov.	302,200	8,994
June	2,395,000	71,280	Dec.	556,700	16,568
			Totals	11,537,000	343,362

[a] $66,500 \times 0.029762 = 1,979$

Table 12-3 Costs for a Mixed Warehouse Size Strategy Using a 60,000 Square Foot, Privately Operated Warehouse

Month	Warehouse Throughput, LB	Space Requirements, Sq. Ft.	Privately Operated			Rented			Monthly Cost
			Private Allocation	Monthly Fixed Cost	Monthly Variable Cost	Rented Allocation	Monthly Storage Cost	Monthly Handling Cost	
Jan.	66,500	1,979	100%	$22,500[a]	$ 3,325[b]	0%	$ 0	$ 0	$ 25,825
Feb.	328,000	9,762	100	22,500	16,400	0	0	0	38,900
Mar.	1,048,500	31,205	100	22,500	52,425	0	0	0	74,925
Apr.	2,141,000	63,720	94[c]	22,500	100,627[d]	6	4,282[e]	8,992[f]	136,401
May	2,820,000	83,929	71	22,500	100,110	29	27,260	57,246	207,116
June	2,395,000	71,280	84	22,500	100,590	16	12,773	26,824	162,687
July	1,303,000	38,780	100	22,500	65,150	0	0	0	87,650
Aug.	460,900	13,717	100	22,500	23,045	0	0	0	45,545
Sept.	99,900	2,973	100	22,500	4,995	0	0	0	27,495
Oct.	15,300	455	100	22,500	765	0	0	0	23,265
Nov.	302,200	8,994	100	22,500	15,110	0	0	0	37,610
Dec.	556,700	16,568	100	22,500	27,835	0	0	0	50,335
Totals	11,537,000	343,362		$270,000	$510,377		$44,315	$93,062	$917,754

[a][$90,000 + (3 × $60,000)]/12 = $22,500
[b]66,500 × 0.05 = $3,325
[c]60,000/63,720 = $0.94
[d]2,141,000 × 0.94 × 0.05 = $100,627
[e]Given a monthly turnover ratio of 3 and 6% of the demand through the rented warehouse, then [(2,141,000 × 0.06)/3] × $0.10 = $4,282
[f]2,141,000 × 0.06 × 0.07 = $8,992

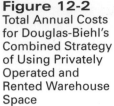

Figure 12-2
Total Annual Costs
for Douglas-Biehl's
Combined Strategy
of Using Privately
Operated and
Rented Warehouse
Space

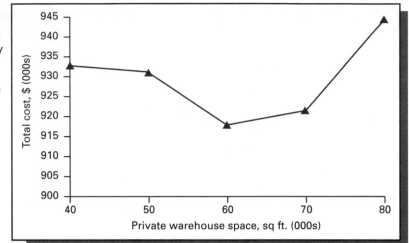

Sizing with Trend

Warehouse sizing is a strategic, or long-run, planning problem. When the trend in space requirements is not constant over time, as was assumed in the no-trend sizing analysis, we should be prepared to factor fundamental changes in space requirements into our analysis. The problem now becomes a dynamic one, so we must consider the additional questions of *when* the warehouse size should be changed, and *by how much*. Determining the best warehouse size at any point in time requires balancing the benefits of being in a particular size with the costs of moving to another size. A methodology for this sizing problem is very similar to that presented for the dynamic location problem in Chapter 13. No further discussion of the methodology will be presented here.

Appraisal of the Sizing Method

The method for sizing a warehouse, although largely of a trial-and-error nature, offers some major benefits.

1. The method specifically draws attention to the problem of seeking the best privately operated warehouse size, in terms of a combination of owning and renting alternatives, rather than providing space in the form of either all privately operated space or all rented space.
2. The variability of space requirements due to seasonal fluctuations in supply and demand and the uncertainties associated with forecasting are considered.
3. The timing and magnitude of public warehouse space needs are defined and can be planned.
4. The timing and magnitude of private space needs are defined at present to permit lead time for planning and/or construction of space changes.

The method is not without its limitations. Chief among these are the following:

1. Inventory levels are used as the primary determinant of space needs. The space requirements of aisles, docks, staging areas, and order-picking areas are approximated and incorporated into the cost for a given warehouse size. They are not specifically treated. Therefore, the suggested size can only be an estimate of the final size to be built.

2. As with any dynamic model, long-range forecasts are required. Any errors in the plan, due to inaccurate forecasts, must be weighed against the alternative approach of changing the warehouse size as changes in space requirements are observed.

3. The selection of the sizing alternatives to be examined is based on judgment. As such, some size combinations may not be explored by the analysis. However, the improvement to be gained from additional size alternatives in the analysis should be minor.

Selecting the Space Type—Financial Considerations

Although seasonal fluctuation in space requirements plays a role in determining the space type to use, it is equally important to recognize that even when there is little seasonality in space needs, there is a choice of renting, leasing, or owning the space. The selection among these options is usually based on a financial comparison. Since the time horizon of the decision can be long, perhaps 20 years, the time value of money can be important in the selection process. That is, we want to compare the net present value of money according to

$$PV = \text{Lease payment} \times \frac{(1 + i)^n - 1}{i(1 + i)^n}$$ (12-1)

where

NPV = net present value at time 0
I = initial investment, or cash outlay, at time 0
j = time period in the planning horizon between 0 and n
n = the time period at the end of the planning horizon
C_j = the cash flow difference (cash outflow) between alternatives in time period j
i = the discount rate, or hurdle rate, that such investments are expected to return annually
S_n = the cash return, or salvage value, of the asset at time period n

A positive NPV encourages investment, whereas a negative NPV discourages it. Alternately, NPV can be set to 0 and i found. This is the internal rate of return (IRR), which can then be compared to the company's hurdle rate. If IRR exceeds the hurdle rate, the investment is encouraged.

The present value formula [Equation (12-1)] is general and can be manipulated in many ways and applied to a broad range of financial problems. Only one example will be illustrated here.

Application[3]

A company's warehouse facilities have reached capacity in the mid-Atlantic region. Currently, the firm owns and operates two facilities in the area and utilizes approximately 150,000 sq. ft. of outside public warehouse space. The most pressing need is for overflow storage, which is now being handled by a public warehouse. Overflow requirements are expected to grow substantially in the next several years.

It is estimated that approximately 210,000 sq. ft. of space will be required. The alternatives have been reduced to the following: (1) Use public warehousing or (2) lease 210,000 sq. ft. for five years at $2.75 per sq. ft. per year with a five-year renewal option. Company federal taxes are at the rate of 39 percent per year.

For space of this size, the annual public warehousing charges are expected to be

Handling charges	$ 760,723
Storage charges	413,231
Total annual charges	$1,173,954

There are several categories of charges for the leased warehouse.

1. The estimated annual operating expenses are $309,914.
2. The annual lease payment is $577,500. According to one philosophy of financial analysts, the lease should be capitalized; that is, it should be treated as a debt or fixed asset. The company has an after-tax cost of capital of 10 percent. Discounting the ten equal lease payments to the present at a 10 percent discount rate gives $3,548,500. That is,

$$PV = \text{Lease payment} \times \frac{(1 + i)^n - 1}{i(1 + i)^n}$$

$$= 577{,}500 \times \frac{(1 + 0.10)^{10} - 1}{0.10(1 + 0.10)^{10}}$$

$$= 577{,}500 \times 6.1446$$

$$= \$3{,}548{,}500$$

3. Other fixed assets and one-time charges for the leased facility.

Handling equipment	$170,800
Computer systems	26,740
Racks	252,000
Subtotal	$449,540
Startup costs	10,500
Total initial cash outlay	$460,040

4. Since all equipment is used up in ten years, there is no salvage value in it. The lease has no salvage value.

---

[3]Based on an example given in Thomas W. Speh and James A. Blomquist, *The Financial Evaluation of Warehousing Options: An Examination and Appraisal of Contemporary Practices* (Oxford, OH: The Warehousing Research Center, an affiliate of the Warehousing Education and Research Council, 1988), pp. 26–28.

The yearly cash flow difference between a public warehouse and a leased warehouse is $1,173,954 − 309,914 = $864,040, which we will call a *savings* (i.e., −C_j) to maintain the convention of Equation (12-1). Because of taxes, we need to account for depreciation on the assets. The depreciation schedule on the $460,040 of initial outlay is

Year	Depreciation	Year	Depreciation
1	$136,000	6	$25,000
2	109,000	7	21,000
3	71,000	8	3,000
4	50,000	9	0
5	45,000	10	0

To determine the after-tax cash flow, consider the effect of taxes for the first year:

Savings	$ 864,040
Depreciation	−136,000
Net profit (before tax)	$ 728,040
Federal taxes (39%)	−283,936
Net profit (after tax)	$ 444,104
Depreciation	+136,000
After-tax cash flow	$ 580,104

Similar cash flow calculations can be made for each year (see Table 12-4).

We are now able to calculate the present value on the after-tax cash flow stream. Recalling that the after-tax hurdle rate is 10 percent and the discount formula is $1/(1 + i)^j$, we can calculate the following discounted cash flow stream:

Year	(1) After-Tax Net Cash Flow	(2) Discount Factor $1/(1 + 0.1)^j$	(3) = (1)(2) Discounted Net Cash Flow
0	($4009)		($4009)
1	580	0.9091	527
2	570	0.8264	471
3	555	0.7513	417
4	547	0.6830	374
5	545	0.6209	338
6	537	0.5645	303
7	535	0.5132	275
8	528	0.4665	246
9	527	0.4241	224
10	527	0.3855	203
		NPV =	($ 631)

The net present value is a *negative* $631,000, meaning that the hurdle rate of 10 percent after taxes cannot be realized with a leased warehouse. Public warehousing should be used.

Table 12-4 Ten-Year Cash Flow Stream for Public Versus Leased Warehouse Comparison

Year	Savings: Lease vs. Public	Pre-Tax Net Cash Flow	Depreciation Schedule	Savings Less Depreciation	Taxes (39%)	Savings Less Depreciation & Tax	Savings Less Tax	After-Tax Net Cash Flow
0	$ 0	($4,009)[a]	$ 0					($4,009)
1	864	864	136	$ 728	$ 284	$ 444	$ 580[b]	580
2	864	864	109	755	294	461	570	570
3	864	864	71	793	309	484	555	555
4	864	864	50	814	317	497	547	547
5	864	864	45	819	319	500	545	545
6	864	864	25	839	327	512	537	537
7	864	864	21	843	329	514	535	535
8	864	864	3	861	336	525	528	528
9	864	864	0	864	337	527	527	527
10	864	864	0	864	337	527	527	527
Total	$8,640	$4,631	$460	$8,180	$3,189	$4,991	$5,451	$1,442

[a] Capitalized lease plus initial cash outlay, i.e., $3,548,500 + 460,040 = $4,008,540

[b] Add back depreciation, i.e., 444 + 136 = $580

Facility Configuration

Warehouses come in various shapes as well as various sizes. Any given warehouse size may be constructed in many different length, width, and height combinations. It is now assumed that the basic warehouse size has been established, and the next question is, What is the best configuration for the warehouse? A distinction is made between warehouses that are for general storage and handling and those that are used as crossdock, or high throughput, facilities.

Ceiling Height

In the previous sizing analysis, a given usable ceiling height was assumed. Determining this height for a medium throughput facility depends on construction costs, materials handling costs, and product load-stacking characteristics. If we were to double the ceiling height, thereby doubling the cubic content, the construction costs would not necessarily double. The roof and floor remain the same in both cases. Balancing construction costs, however, are the added materials handling costs due to the greater service time required for stacking and picking loads at a greater average height. Finally, the stacking characteristics of the stored goods can influence the desired ceiling height. Stability of the goods stacked individually in columns or in pallet-load units may put an upper limit on the height. Of course, using storage racks increases cube utilization and overcomes product-stacking limitations. Height limitations may then shift from the product characteristics to the characteristics of storage and materials handling equipment. Local building codes regarding sprinkler clearance may also influence the final ceiling height.

Choosing a ceiling height is a matter of trading off construction and equipment costs with materials handling costs in light of product, equipment, and legal constraints. In addition, there should be a minimum of extra space between the goods and the effective warehouse ceiling. The needed additional height is determined from an analysis of uncertain future requirements. In a general merchandise warehouse, product is typically stacked on racks about 16 feet high with the ceiling height at about 20 feet. There is no particular ceiling height limitation to storage warehouses or to those with automatic storage and retrieval systems. High throughput facilities such as cross docks or order-picking areas of distribution warehouses may limit stacking to one or two tiers with enough additional height to accommodate a fire protection system.

Length Versus Width

The length and width or configuration, of the warehouse building should be decided in relation to the materials handling costs of moving products through the warehouse and to the warehouse construction costs. Francis explored the question of configuration design in a theoretical way.[4] He examined configuration with the inbound-outbound dock located at X and then at Y, as shown in Figure 12-3. The warehouse uses rectangular aisles, stores n different item types, and has a floor area

[4]Richard L. Francis, "On Some Problems of Rectangular Warehouse Design and Layout," *Journal of Industrial Engineering*, Vol. 18 (October 1967), pp. 595–604.

Figure 12-3
Outline of a
Warehouse with
Width *W* and Length
L and with Possible
Inbound-Outbound
Dock Locations at *X*
and *Y*

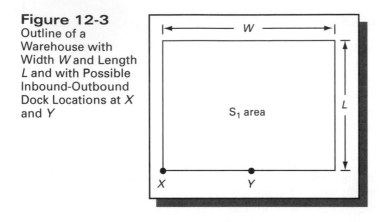

of S. The optimum width W^* and length L^* are found by balancing materials handling costs against warehouse perimeter costs. Perimeter costs are defined as the
annual construction and maintenance costs per foot of warehouse perimeter. For the
dock located at X, Francis concluded, assuming out-and-back selection in a medium
throughput facility, that the optimum width W^* is

$$W^* = \sqrt{\frac{C + 8k}{2C + 8k}}\sqrt{S} \qquad (12\text{-}2)$$

and the optimum length L^* is

$$L^* = \frac{S}{W^*} \qquad (12\text{-}3)$$

where

C = the sum of the total cost per foot to move an item of a given type in
      and out of storage multiplied by the expected number of items of a
      given type in and out of storage per year (dollar/ft.)
k = annual perimeter cost per foot (dollar/ft.)
S = required floor area of the warehouse (sq. ft.)

For the dock centered in the warehouse at location Y, the optimal width is

$$W^* = \sqrt{S} \qquad (12\text{-}4)$$

and the optimal length is

$$L^* = \sqrt{S} \qquad (12\text{-}5)$$

That is, the warehouse becomes square rather than rectangular. Of these two limiting
cases, locating the dock in the center of the warehouse is the least expensive.
Locating the dock at X has a total relevant cost $TC_{X \text{ of}}$

$$TC_X = 2\sqrt{[(1/2)C + 2k][(1/4)C + 2k]}\sqrt{S} \qquad (12\text{-}6)$$

The relevant cost TC_Y for locating the dock at Y is

$$TC_Y = [(1/2)C + 4k]\sqrt{S} \qquad\qquad (12\text{-}7)$$

The difference $TC_X - TC_Y$ is the premium that must be paid for locating the dock at X instead of at Y.

Example

A privately operated spare parts warehouse has a monthly throughput of 100,000 cases and an average in and out materials handling cost of $0.005 per foot per case moved. Order picking requires a trip to and from the outbound dock for each item requested. The total square footage needed for the operation is 300,000. Construction estimates show that a 500×600 sq. ft. warehouse can be built for $90 per sq. ft. The effective warehouse life is 20 years. The loading/unloading dock is to be located near to a corner of the proposed building. What are the best dimensions for the building and the total relevant cost?

The annual perimeter cost needs to be developed. There are $2(500) + 2(600) = 2,200$ ft. in the perimeter. The construction cost is $90 \times 300,000 = \$27,000,000$. Annualized, it is $\$27,000,000/20 = \$1,350,000$. On a perimeter-foot basis, it is $\$1,350,000/2,200 = \$613.64/\text{ft}$. This is k. C is $0.005 \times 100,000 \times 12 = \$6000/\text{ft}$.

To determine the warehouse width, Equation (12-2) applies. That is,

$$W^* = \sqrt{\frac{6,000 + 8(613.64)}{2(6,000) + 8(613.64)}}\sqrt{300,000}$$
$$= 440 \text{ ft.}$$

and the length according to Equation (12-3):

$$L^* = 300,000/440 = 682 \text{ ft.}$$

The relevant cost for this rectangular warehouse from Equation (12-6) is

$$TC = 2\sqrt{[(1/2)6,000 + 2(613.64)][(1/4)6,000 + 2(613.64)]}\sqrt{300,000}$$
$$= 6,790.87(547.72)$$
$$= \$3,719,495 \text{ per year}$$

It should be noted that these formulas might not be valid where a conveyorized materials handling system is used, since conveyors decouple dock location and warehouse configuration from variable materials handling costs. Thus, conveyor systems can neutralize the disadvantages of multistory, L-shaped, or other configurations that deviate from the theoretical design.

Jenkins expanded the previous analysis by noting that when rail and truck docks are centered but at opposite ends of the building, the least expensive configuration is the square.[5] On the other hand, movement costs may not be the primary determinant of the warehouse dimensions.[6] Rather, the length of the warehouse may be dictated by the dock requirements for rail or truck. The long and narrow building configuration of LTL truck terminals is an example. The number of truck stalls for inbound and outbound production movement and the length of the siding necessary for efficient product flow would need to be compared with the theoretical findings. How to determine these dock dimensions is discussed in the section on dock design.

Configuring high throughput facilities, known as cross dock warehouses and transfer terminals, requires a different cost balance than for the typical warehouse. Cross docking is limited to receiving and shipping, eliminating storage and order picking activities of the typical warehouse. The function is to unload goods and immediately transfer them to another truck, which is as close to the receiving point as possible to minimize handling expense. Ideally, this would be to assign a shipping dock directly across from the receiving dock. This suggests that the best building design is a long, narrow rectangle, or I-shape, assuming no conveyors are used to move goods about the building.

Not all goods received at a particular dock are transferred to the dock immediately across from it due to the allocation of dock spaces and the breakdown of inbound merchandise destined for multiple destinations. From a materials handling standpoint, a building configuration has a *centrality index*, which is the weighted average distance that all goods move in the building. As the number of doors increases, the centrality index also increases. To reduce the index, and therefore the handling cost, alternatives to the I-shape can be used, such as the T-shape, L-shape, and H-shape. Although T-, L-, and H-shapes reduce centrality, their configuration has the disadvantage of losing some door spaces for trailers at the inside corners. Therefore, the basic trade-off that determines building configuration is a balance of freight handling cost and the cost of constructing a building with the needed number of doors. Research suggests that building shape depends on the number of doors needed.[7] The best shape for small to midsize cross docks is a rectangle, or I-shape. As building size increases to 150 to 250 doors, a T-shape is best. For buildings in excess of 250 doors, the H-shape is best.

Space Layout

Once certain decisions have been made concerning the general configuration of the warehouse, the next decision is to lay out the storage bays, shelves, and aisles. The problem is one of determining the number of slots to place along a shelf, the number of shelves to use, and whether the shelves should be placed parallel or perpendicular to the longest wall. Several formulas and decision rules have been developed to help make this decision.[8] Two of several configurations are discussed.

---

[5]Creed H. Jenkins, *Complete Guide to Modern Warehouse Management* (Upper Saddle River, NJ: Prentice-Hall, 1990), pp. 104–107.
[6]C. E. Hancock and H. F. Kraemer, "The Economic Sizing of Warehouses—A Comparison of Evaluation Models," a paper presented at the TIMS-ORSA Joint National Meeting, Minneapolis, October 7–9, 1964.
[7]John J. Bartholdi III and Kevin R. Gue, "The Best Shape for a Crossdock," Working paper.
[8]Joseph Bassan, Yaakov Roll, and Meir J. Rosenblatt, "Internal Layout Design of a Warehouse," *AIIE Transactions*, Vol. 12, No. 4 (December 1980), pp. 317–322.

Two possible shelving layouts are shown in Figure 12-4. The product is received through a door on one side of the building and is shipped out a door on the opposite side. An item requires four movements between a door and a storage location. Dock doors are located in the center of the building, and all parts of the warehouse have an equal likelihood of being utilized. Shelving is double-sided except for shelves against a wall, which are single-sided. The layout objective is to minimize the sum of materials handling cost, annual warehouse area cost, and annual cost associated with the size (perimeter) of the building. The following notation is useful:

w = width of double shelf (ft.)
L = length of storage space; for example, width of a pallet (ft.)
m = number of storage spaces along a shelf
h = number of storage levels in the vertical direction
n = number of double shelves; two single ones are considered as one
  double shelf
K = total warehouse capacity in storage spaces
a = width of an aisle (ft.), where all aisles are assumed to be of the same width
u = length of the warehouse (ft.)
v = width of the warehouse (ft.)
d = yearly throughput (demand) of the warehouse, in storage units (for example,
  pallets). It is assumed that a storage item occupies one space unit (items/yr.)
C_h = materials handling cost of moving a storage item one length unit (dollars/ft.)
C_s = annual cost per unit of warehouse area (heat, light, maintenance) (dollars/sq. ft.)
C_p = annual cost per unit length of external walls (dollars/ft.)

For layout 1, shown in Figure 12-4(a), the optimal number of shelf spaces should be

$$m_1^* = \frac{1}{L} \sqrt{\left[\frac{dC_h + 2aC_s + 2C_p}{2(dC_h + C_p)} \right] \left[\frac{K(w + a)L}{2h} \right]}$$

(12-8)

and the optimal number of double shelves is

$$n_1^* = \frac{1}{w + a} \sqrt{\left[\frac{2(dC_h + C_p)}{dC_h + 2aC_s + 2C_p} \right] \left[\frac{K(w + a)L}{2h} \right]}$$

(12-9)

The best warehouse configuration will have a length of

$$u_1 = n_1^* (w + a)$$

(12-10)

and a width of

$$v_1 = 2a + m_1^* L$$

(12-11)

For alternative layout 2, shown in Figure 12-4(b), the optimal parameters are

$$m_2^* = \frac{1}{L} \sqrt{\left[\frac{2dC_h + 3aC_s + 2C_p}{dC_h + 2C_p} \right] \left[\frac{K(w + a)L}{2h} \right]}$$

(12-12)

Figure 12-4 Aerial View of Two Possible Layouts of Shelving in a Rectangular Warehouse Configuration

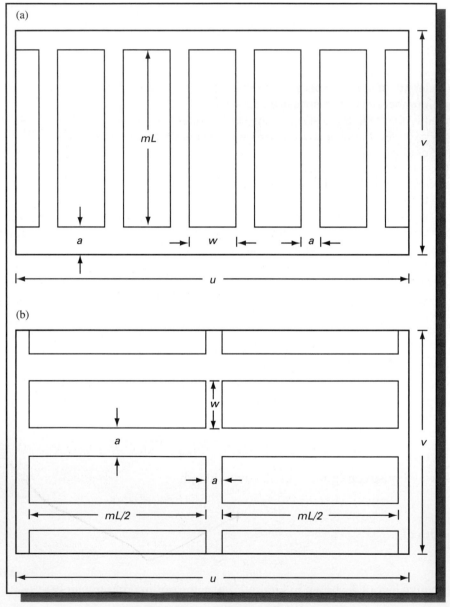

and

$$n_2^* = \frac{1}{w + a} \sqrt{\left[\frac{dC_h + 2C_p}{2dC_h + 3aC_s + 2C_p}\right]\left[\frac{K(w + a)L}{2h}\right]}$$

(12-13)

where

$$u_2 = 3a + m_2^* L$$

(12-14)

and

$$v_2 = n_2^* (w + a)$$

(12-15)

To minimize costs between these two layout choices, the following decision rule can be applied: If $d < C_p/C_h$, then layout 1 is preferred to layout 2. If $d > 2C_p/C_h$, then layout 2 is preferred. However, if $C_p/C_h < d < 2C_p/C_h$, no conclusion can be drawn.

Example

Suppose that a warehouse is to be configured according to the layout in Figure 12-4(b). The building is to handle a throughput of 400,000 pallets per year. These pallets require storage space of $4 \times 4 \times 4$ ft., and can be stacked four pallets high. Back-to-back pallet racks are 8 ft. wide. Aisles are 10 ft. wide. The materials handling cost is $0.001 per ft., annual space costs are $0.05 per sq. ft., and the annual cost per foot of perimeter wall is $3. The warehouse turnover is eight times per year with total warehouse capacity of 50,000 slots. What size building should be planned?

First, the number of storage spaces for the longitudinal bay, according to Equation (12-12), should be

$$m^* = \frac{1}{4} \sqrt{\left[\frac{2(400,000)(0.001) + 3(10)(0.05) + 2(3.00)}{400,000(0.001) + 2(3.00)}\right]\left[\frac{50,000(8 + 10)(4)}{2(4)}\right]}$$

$$= 237 \text{ spaces}$$

The number of double storage racks, according to Equation (12-13), should be

$$n^* = \frac{1}{8 + 10} \sqrt{\left[\frac{400,000(0.001) + 2(3.00)}{2(400,000)(0.001) + 3(10)(0.05) + 2(3.00)}\right]\left[\frac{50,000(8 + 10)(4)}{2(4)}\right]}$$

$$= 26 \text{ racks along one side of the warehouse.}$$

The length and width of the warehouse from Equation (12-14) and Equation (12-15) should be:

$$u = 3(10) + 237(4) = 978 \text{ ft. of length}$$

and

$$v = 26(8 + 10) = 468 \text{ ft. of width}$$

Dock Design

Dock design begins with the need for a rail or a truck dock at the warehouse. Nearly every warehouse requires at least one truck dock. The need for a rail dock is not as universal and depends on whether the product is to be received or shipped in large enough quantities to justify rail movement. Even if there is a need, a rail siding may not be possible if the warehouse is not located on a rail spur and the railroad is not willing to provide a spur. For purposes of discussion, let us assume that both dock types are needed.

Rail Dock

A primary consideration in dock design is the dock length that is needed to handle the product flow efficiently. Preliminary estimates can be made by multiplying the total average demand by the average length of rail cars used and dividing this quantity by the average quantity stored in the average rail car multiplied by the number of car changes per day. That is,

$$L = \frac{DS}{QN}$$

(12-16)

where:

L = length of rail dock needed (ft.)
D = daily demand from all orders (cwt./day)
S = length of the average rail car used (ft.)
Q = average product weight placed in each car (cwt./car)
N = number of car changes per day (number/day)

Example

A food warehouse receives by rail, on the average, 14,000 cwt. of merchandise per day. The railcars have a capacity of 570 cwt. for this type of merchandise and their effective length is 75 ft. Two car changes along the siding can be completed each day.

The length of rail siding needed can be estimated from Equation (12-16) as

$$L = \frac{14,000(75)}{570(2)} = 921 \text{ ft.}$$

In addition to dock length, there are several other dock design considerations. For example, should the extra expense of enclosing the dock be incurred? An enclosed dock provides weather protection, gives some protection against theft, and contributes to labor efficiency in loading and unloading. The required platform depth is another question. If forklift trucks are to be used for loading and unloading, a minimum of 12 feet is necessary for safe maneuvering. If the dock is also to serve as a staging area for temporary holding while checking the incoming order or palletizing the received goods, a much greater dock depth is required, perhaps 40 or 50 feet. Finally, the level of the dock in relation to the rail car bed is of concern. Either the dock level must be raised to meet the car bed, or the car bed must be lowered to the dock level. Because only slight inclines are possible with most materials handling equipment and because of the expense of raising the entire warehouse floor, it is usually more economical to recess the tracks below the dock level. A well of 45 inches puts the car bed at the dock level. The gap between the car bed and the dock is bridged using a steel dock plate.

Truck Dock

Most of the factors affecting truck dock design are the same as those affecting rail dock design. However, instead of computing a length of dock, truck docks are frequently referred to as the number of dock doors, or stalls, required. Of course, a truck door has a standard width that can be converted to the total required dock length. Very simply, the number of truck dock doors needed can be found by

$$N = \frac{DH}{CS} \qquad \text{(12-17)}$$

where

N = total number of truck dock doors
D = average dock throughput per day
H = time required to load or unload a truck
C = truck capacity
S = time per day available to load or unload trucks

This formula calculates the average number of truck doors. It does not account for the variation in trucks available for loading and unloading, dock throughput, or the truck loading and unloading rate. Some additional doors may be needed to meet these uncertainties.

Example

A warehouse for Rico Discount Drug Stores replenishes 250 drug retail stores in its region on a weekly basis. The average store order is 6,500 lb and 4 stores' orders can be placed on a single truck. It takes two workers a total of two hours to load a truck and they work an eight-hour shift. Rico assigns as many workers as may be needed to load the trucks in eight hours. How many truck doors are needed to meet this average level of activity?

We can estimate that 50 stores are served each day of a five-day workweek. Therefore, $50 \times 6{,}500 = 325{,}000$ lb of merchandise is picked and loaded for delivery to stores each day. If orders for four stores are placed on a truck, a truckload is $4 \times 6{,}500 = 26{,}000$ lb. Using Equation (12-17), we can estimate the number of doors as

$$N = \frac{325{,}000(2)}{26{,}000(8)} = 3.15, \text{ or 4 doors}$$

Four doors allow Rico extra capacity for contingencies. In fact, with the throughput of $26{,}000(8)(4) = 416{,}000$ for 4 doors in total, there is a $(416{,}000 - 325{,}000) \times$

$100/325{,}000 = 28\%$ increase in dock throughput. A $([26{,}000(8)(4)/325{,}000] - 2) \times 100/2 = 28\%$ slowdown in loading the trucks using four doors can occur while still meeting store requirements.

MATERIALS HANDLING SYSTEM DESIGN

Materials handling within a warehouse or storage area is typically a labor-intensive activity, since most materials handling throughout the world is conducted manually or at best semiautomatically. The merchandise layout, the extent to which equipment is used, and the degree of automation all affect materials handling costs. Finding the best combination of these is the task of materials handling design.

White has suggested that materials handling system design has evolved through five developmental stages.[9] To him, the basic dimensions of materials handling are the moving, storing, and controlling materials. These have evolved chronologically as

- Manual materials handling characterized by a high degree of human activity
- Materials handling aided by mechanical assists such as conveyors and industrial trucks to move materials; shelving, storage racks, and carousels for storage; and switches and solenoids for equipment control
- Automated handling characterized by the use of guided vehicles, automated palletizers, automated storage and retrieval equipment, and automated identification of material
- Integration of the "islands" of automation so as to create synergy among the various materials handling activities
- Intelligent materials handling through the use of artificial intelligence and associated expert systems

The first three of these have been well implemented. Even the oldest of these—manual handing—is being strongly advocated by the just-in-time proponents because of its flexibility. Integration has not been well achieved, and intelligent handling systems are the goal of the twenty-first century. This suggests that good practices around the basic system design remain the backbone of good materials handling.

According to White, good materials handling practice involves "moving less, storing less, and controlling less."[10] Ackerman and LaLonde are more specific and suggest the following ways in which materials handling costs can be reduced: Reduce the distances traveled, increase the size of the units handled, seek round-trip opportunities in the order picking or storage route, and improve cube utilization.[11] These suggestions guide the following discussion of key materials handling decisions.

---

[9]John A. White, "Materials Handling in Warehousing: Basics and Evolution," *Annual Proceedings*, Volume II (Boston: Council of Logistics Management, October 9–12, 1988).
[10]Ibid.
[11]Kenneth B. Ackerman and Bernard J. LaLonde, "Making Warehousing More Efficient," *Harvard Business Review* (March–April 1980), pp. 94–102. See also, David R. Olson, "Seven Trends of Highly Effective Warehouses," *IIE Solutions* (February 1996), pp. 12–15.

Materials Handling System Selection

The materials handling system should be selected to be an integral part of the entire storage system activity. It is not necessarily the beginning point of storage system design nor its ending point; however, management can make some rough, first approximations to the final design without attempting to balance all factors simultaneously. In this analysis, management should take into account several things. First, do materials handling systems of outsiders impose constraints on the choice? For example, if major suppliers to the warehouse make deliveries on 48 × 48 in. pallets, a materials handling system designed for 32 × 40 in. pallets may require repalletizing the incoming goods to avoid equipment incompatibilities or storage space inefficiencies.

Second, does the warehouse design impose constraints on equipment choice? Low ceilings, multistory buildings, narrow aisles, and long distances within the warehouse may make some equipment impractical. That is, where travel distances are long, moving goods manually in warehouses results in excessive labor costs. Similarly, using forklift trucks and elevators in multistory warehouses may be inefficient.

Third, the nature and level of the system load bear heavily on equipment selection. When throughput volume in the warehouse varies considerably or the product mix handling characteristics are not reasonably constant, a manual materials handling system, with its low investment cost and high degree of flexibility to changing conditions, often is the best choice. Conversely, when a substantial, steady volume is anticipated, more mechanized equipment is justified. Capital, in the form of equipment, is used to replace labor, but the greater investment levels may not be recovered if the system becomes obsolete too quickly. This is a particular danger with fully mechanized systems, such as automated storage and retrieval systems. Undoubtedly, the reason for the popularity of forklift truck and pallet systems is that they offer a good balance between mechanization and flexibility.

Fourth, product characteristics can be determining. Bulk products, such as powders and liquids, can be more efficiently handled in bulk by a system of tanks and pipes rather than in packaged form by pallets and forklift trucks. A mixture of product sizes, weights, and configurations may limit equipment to the more flexible types or require that a combination of equipment types be used to meet various product characteristics.

Finally, planning for contingencies can influence system design. As materials handling systems become more automated and integrated, they also become more subject to total shutdown when any individual segment fails. If system reliability greatly affects customer service, system-related costs (such as demurrage and detention charges), or system operating costs, then less mechanized systems or mechanized systems with built-in redundancy may be the best direction for the final system design.

Once the basic materials handling system has been roughed out, more detailed design questions must be answered. Selecting the system type and the equipment replacement policy are major considerations.

System Type

A decision that is coincident with sizing the warehouse is selecting the type of materials handling system to use. Common choices include a manual system, a forklift truck and pallet system, a conveyorized system, an automated storage and retrieval system, or some combination of these system. Choosing among these can begin with a financial analysis similar to that used for selecting a warehouse type. The final choice must be tempered with subjective considerations such as risk, flexibility, and obsolescence.

Example

A manufacturer of office copying equipment is to construct a warehouse for spare parts. The choices for the internal materials handling system design reduce to a fork-lift truck and pallet system with conveyorized order picking and an automated storage and retrieval system. The company projects 3,000,000 orders to be picked per year and expects a return on projects of 20 percent per year before taxes.

The conveyor and forklift truck system requires an investment in racks of $2,000,000 and trucks and conveyors of $1,500,000. Racks have a 20-year life and a salvage value of 30 percent of their initial value at the end of 20 years. The trucks and conveyors have a 10-year life with a 10 percent salvage value at the end of 10 years. The throughput cost is $0.50 per order.

The automatic storage and retrieval system requires an investment in racks of $3,000,000 and $2,000,000 in equipment and controls. The racks have a 20-year life with a 30 percent salvage value at the end of that life. The equipment and controls have a 10-year life with a 10 percent salvage value at the end of 10 years of use. The throughput cost is $0.10 per order.

A financial analysis is conducted to determine the preferred alternative. We wish to compare the net present value of each alternative according to Equation (12-1). However, Equation (12-1) is modified slightly to account for the different life spans of racks versus equipment, and the term C_j represents a cost (cash outflow) and not a savings (cash inflow). That is, the NPV for racks is

$$NPV = -I - \frac{C_j}{(1+i)^j} + \frac{S_{20}}{(1+i)^{20}}$$

whereas for the equipment, *NPV* is

$$NPV = -I - \frac{C_j}{(1+i)^j} + \frac{S_{10}}{(1+i)^{10}} - \frac{I}{(1+i)^{10}} - \frac{C_{j+10}}{(1+i)^{j+10}} + \frac{S_{20}}{(1+i)^{20}}$$

We judge the best alternative to be the one having the least negative *NPV*.

Two tables are now developed—one for the conveyor and forklift truck system (Table 12-5), and one for the AS/RS (Table 12-6). Since the *NPV* for the AS/RS is less negative than that for the conveyor and forklift truck system, the AS/RS offers the better return (costs less) and is the one that should be considered for implementation.

YEAR	INVESTMENT RACKS	INVESTMENT EQUIPMENT	ANNUAL OPERATING COST	CASH FLOW	DISCOUNTED CASH FLOW[d]
0	($2,000)	($1,500)		($ 3,500)	($ 3,500)
1			($1,500)	(1,500)	(1,250)
2			(1,500)	(1,500)	(1,042)
3			(1,500)	(1,500)	(868)
4			(1,500)	(1,500)	(723)
5			(1,500)	(1,500)	(603)
6			(1,500)	(1,500)	(502)
7			(1,500)	(1,500)	(419)
8			(1,500)	(1,500)	(349)
9			(1,500)	(1,500)	(291)
10		(1,350)[a]	(1,500)	(2,850)	(460)
11			(1,500)	(1,500)	(202)
12			(1,500)	(1,500)	(168)
13			(1,500)	(1,500)	(140)
14			(1,500)	(1,500)	(117)
15			(1,500)	(1,500)	(97)
16			(1,500)	(1,500)	(81)
17			(1,500)	(1,500)	(68)
18			(1,500)	(1,500)	(56)
19			(1,500)	(1,500)	(47)
20	600[b]	150[c]	(1,500)	(750)	(20)
				NPV =	($11,003)

[a]Equipment is replaced with a net investment equal to the cost of new equipment less the salvage value of the old; i.e., $1,500,000 - (1,500,000)(0.10) = $1,350,000.
[b]Salvage value of $2,000,000(0.30) = $600,000.
[c]Salvage value of $1,500,000(0.10) = $150,000.
[d]Cash stream discounted at 20% according to $1/(1 + 0.2)^j$.

Table 12-5 Cash Flow Analysis for the Conveyor and Forklift Truck Materials Handling Alternative

On a smaller scale than the entire materials handling system, individual pieces of equipment vary in their capacities and capabilities. Each has a different initial investment, annual operating expense, and salvage value. Again, selection is by comparing present values of the alternatives. When operating expenses are equal for all years over the useful life, and the useful life of the equipment is the same among alternatives, the net present value equation can be rewritten as follows:

$$NPV = I + C \frac{(1 + i)^n - 1}{i(1 + i)^n} - \frac{S_n}{(1 + i)^n} \qquad (12\text{-}18)$$

	INVESTMENT	ANNUAL			
YEAR	RACKS	EQUIPMENT	OPERATING COST	CASH FLOW	DISCOUNTED CASH FLOW[d]
0	($3,000)	($2,000)		($5,000)	($5,000)
1			($ 300)	(300)	(250)
2			(300)	(300)	(208)
3			(300)	(300)	(174)
4			(300)	(300)	(145)
5			(300)	(300)	(121)
6			(300)	(300)	(100)
7			(300)	(300)	(84)
8			(300)	(300)	(70)
9			(300)	(300)	(58)
10		(1,800)[a]	(300)	(2,100)	(339)
11			(300)	(300)	(40)
12			(300)	(300)	(34)
13			(300)	(300)	(28)
14			(300)	(300)	(23)
15			(300)	(300)	(19)
16			(300)	(300)	(16)
17			(300)	(300)	(14)
18			(300)	(300)	(11)
19			(300)	(300)	(9)
20	900[b]	200[c]	(300)	800	21
				NPV =	($6,722)

[a]Equipment is replaced with a net investment equal to the cost of new equipment less the salvage value of the old; i.e., $2,000,000 - (2,000,000)(0.10) = $1,800,000.
[b]Salvage value of $3,000,000(0.30) = $900,000.
[c]Salvage value of $2,000,000(0.10) = $200,000.
[d]Cash stream discounted at 20% according to $1/(1 + 0.2)^j$.

Table 12-6 Cash Flow Analysis for the AS/RS Materials Handling Alternative

where

NPV = net present value of equipment over its useful life
I = initial investment
C = annual operating cost
i = the discount, or hurdle, rate that such investments are expected to return
S_n = salvage value in year n
n = useful life of the equipment (years)

For convenience, the sign convention has been reversed from the previous example. The goal now is to select the alternative with the minimum net present value.

Example

Suppose that two type A forklift trucks can move the same amount of goods as three type B trucks. The following additional data are available:

	Two Type A Trucks	Three Type B Trucks
Total initial investment	$20,000	$15,000
Useful life (planned)	7	7
Salvage value (estimated)	$ 5,000	$ 2,000
Annual operating expenses	$ 4,000	$ 6,000
Hurdle rate	0.20	0.20

Applying Equation (12-18) to both truck types, we have

$$NPV_A = 20,000 + 4,000 \frac{(1 + 0.2)^7 - 1}{0.2(1 + 0.2)^7} - \frac{5,000}{(1 + 0.2)^7} = \$33,023 \quad \longleftarrow \boxed{\text{Best choice}}$$

and

$$NPV_B = 15,000 + 6,000 \frac{(1 + 0.2)^7 - 1}{0.2(1 + 0.2)^7} - \frac{2,000}{(1 + 0.2)^7} = \$36,040$$

Since $NPV_A < NPV_B$, selecting two trucks of type A seems to be the best financial choice.

Equipment Replacement

Materials handling equipment frequently has a shorter life than storage racks, bins, mezzanines, and other nonmechanical devices used in the handling process. Therefore, it is often necessary to develop a policy to replace equipment when it wears out or becomes obsolete. The need for a replacement policy is quite clear in the case of forklift trucks, where the economic life is not long and they must be replaced often. The need for a policy also occurs in various segments of bulk-handling systems or conveyor systems, where the useful life of the equipment may be much longer. It is common for management to have replacement rules of thumb, such as to replace forklift trucks every five years. Rules of thumb based on experience may be quite good. However, when such experience is not available to help develop policy guidelines, or when these rules of thumb have not been tested by "hard" economic analysis, it is useful to have an analytical means of developing replacement policies.

For developing replacement policies, special forms of present value analysis can be useful, although other methods such as payback and simple return on investment may be employed. There are several key features to note about such problems. First, the replacement cycle is expected to continue indefinitely into the future. Second, equipment-operating costs tend to increase over the years as equipment ages. Third, subsequent equipment is more efficient as technological improvements occur. To compare a stream of replacement cycles of different lengths, a form of present value analysis known as *equivalent annual cost (AC)* is used. That is,

$$AC_n = \left[I + \sum_{j=1}^{n} \frac{C_j}{(1+i)^j} - \frac{S_n}{(1+i)^n} \right] \left[\frac{i(1+i)^n}{(1+i)^n - 1} \right]$$

(12-19)

The period n for replacement that gives the minimum AC_n value is sought.

Example

Suppose a fleet of specialized materials handling trucks is used in a warehouse. Trucks are continually being replaced at an initial cost of $30,000 each. The salvage value declines proportionately with the age of a truck such that $S_n = I(1 - R \times n)$, where R is $1/N$, N is the normal life of a truck, and n is the replacement cycle time. N is 10 years for these trucks. Trucks can be sold at any time for the net undepreciated value. Operating cost for a truck, including maintenance, is $2,000 during the first year and tends to increase at the rate of $300 per year squared after the first year. However, because of technological improvement, it is expected that there will be a $200 per year reduction in operating expenses. A 20 percent return before taxes is the guideline on all company projects.

The operating cost for a truck, including the effect of technological improvements, can be approximated as $C_j = a + b(j - 1) + c(j - 1)^2$ where a = constant level of annual operating costs (dollars), b = rate of increase (or decrease) in annual operating costs due to technological improvements (dollars/year), c = rate of increase in annual operating costs (dollars/year/year), and j = the particular year of the cost estimate. Using this C_j cost function, as well as other data about the problem, we can compute the equivalent annual cost for a one-year ($n = 1$) replacement cycle. That is,

$$AC_1 = \left[30,000 + \sum_{j=1}^{1} \frac{2,000 - 200(0) + 300(0)^2}{(1 + 0.2)^1} - \frac{27,000}{(1 + 0.2)^1} \right] \left[\frac{0.2(1 + 0.2)^1}{(1 + 0.2)^1 - 1} \right] = \$11,000$$

Repeating this type of calculation for increasing values of n produces the series of annual cost values shown in Table 12-7. The lowest equivalent annual cost is for $n = 3$. Thus, this suggests that to minimize costs, the best policy is to replace the forklift trucks at the end of three years of service, but replacing trucks between two and five years of service results only in costs that are a maximum of 3 percent greater than optimum.

Product Layout Decisions

An important warehouse design decision concerns the internal layout of the items. After a building configuration is known; after receiving and shipping facilities are

Table 12-7 Example of Calculations for Determining Optimum Equipment Cycle Time[a]

	(1)	(2)	(3)	(4)	(5)	(6)	(7) = (1+3−5)(6)
Replacement Cycle Time, n	Initial Investment, I	Total Operating Costs, C_I	Discounted Operating Costs, $\sum_{j=1}^{n} \dfrac{C_j}{(1+i)^j}$	Salvage Value, S_n	Discounted Salvage Value, $\dfrac{S_n}{(1+i)^n}$	Discounted Factor, $\dfrac{i(1+i)^n}{(1+i)^n - 1}$	Equivalent Average Annual Cost, AC_n
1	$30,000	$2,000[b]	$1,667	$27,000[c]	$22,500	1.20	$11,000
2	30,000	4,100	3,125	24,000	16,667	0.65	10,698
3	30,000	6,900	4,745	21,000	12,153	0.47	10,618 ⟵
4	30,000	11,000	6,722	18,000	8,680	0.39	10,936
5	30,000	17,000	9,133	15,000	6,028	0.33	10,925
6	30,000	25,500	11,979	12,000	4,019	0.30	11,388
7	30,000	37,100	15,216	9,000	2,512	0.28	11,957
8	30,000	52,400	18,774	6,000	1,395	0.26	12,319
9	30,000	72,000	22,572	3,000	581	0.25	12,998
10	30,000	96,500	26,528	0	0	0.24	13,567

[a]All costs in thousands of dollars
[b]Computed as $C_j = 2000 − 200(j−1) + 300(j−1)^2$ and accumulated when there is more than one year in the replacement cycle
[c]Computed as $S_n' = I[1 - 0.1(n)]$

specified; after space blocks are defined for hazardous products, for products under theft protection, and for order picking; and after considering the materials handling system to be used, decisions need to be made as to where stock items are to be located, how they should be arranged, and what method should be used for finding stock in the warehouse. These questions have long concerned the industrial engineer in the layout of production facilities, and much of the decision methodology developed for production layout is transferable to the warehouse layout problem. Such methods supplement those dealing more directly with the layout problem in the warehouse, and these methods are blended into the following discussion.

Stock Location

Stock location is the problem of deciding the physical layout of merchandise in a warehouse to minimize materials handling expenses, to achieve maximum utilization of warehouse space, and to meet certain constraints on merchandise location such as for security, fire safety, product compatibility, and order-picking needs. Stock retrieval (or placement) generally occurs in three ways. First, there is out-and-back selection, where only one item or load is picked from a particular location. A typical trip would be to go out from the outbound dock, pick a product, and return to the outbound dock.

Second, there is picker routing, where several items on an order are picked before returning to the outbound point, or staging area. The volume picked on any one route may be limited by the truck capacity of the order picker.

Third, there is a designated order-picking area per worker. Order pickers retrieve items by out-and-back selection or picker routing within the limits of their specified work areas.

The objective of location planning in each of these problems is to minimize the total handling costs. This often translates into minimizing the total travel distance throughout the warehouse. In addition, order picking is typically of greater concern than item storage because the labor expense to pick merchandise from a warehouse is much greater than that required to store it. This is due to the smaller average load sizes moving from a storage location than moving to it. Therefore, our primary concern is with minimizing materials handling costs in the order picking activity of a warehouse.

Intuitive methods have appeal in that they provide some useful guidelines for layout without the need for higher-level mathematics. Layout is often intuitively based on four criteria: complementarity, compatibility, popularity, and size. *Complementarity* refers to the idea that items often ordered together should be located near each other. Examples of such items are paint and brushes, razor blades and shaving cream, and pens and pencils. This factor is particularly important when order picking is of the picker-routing type or when laying out storage, or flow, racks in designated order-picking area systems.

Compatibility includes the question as to whether items can be practically located next to each other. Auto tires are not compatible with foodstuffs, and gasoline is not compatible with cylinders of oxygen. Therefore, they should not be located near each other. Products are considered compatible if there is no restriction on their location proximity.

Compatibility and complementarity may be decided before order-picking costs are taken into consideration. In addition, there is concern with balancing workloads, minimizing fatigue, and equalizing travel distance when multiple workers are used to fill orders, as in a designated order-picking area design. Once these restrictions have been taken into account, layout by popularity or by size becomes appropriate.

Layout by *popularity* recognizes that products have different turnover rates in a warehouse, and materials handling cost is related to the distance traveled in the warehouse to locate and pick the stock. If stock is retrieved from a location in smaller volumes per trip than it is supplied, materials handling costs can be minimized by locating the fast-moving items close to the outbound point, or staging area, and the slower-moving items to the rear of these. This assumes that the items requiring a large number of trips for a given level of demand will have the shortest possible travel distance per order-picking trip.

Layout by popularity neglects the size of the item being stored and the possibility that a larger number of smaller items can be located near the outbound point, or staging area. This suggests that handling costs might be minimized if the *size* (cubic volume) of the item is used as the layout guide. By locating the smaller items near the outbound point in the warehouse, materials handling may be less than in the arrangement by popularity, as a greater density of items can be located close to the shipping dock.

However, layout by size does not guarantee lower costs than layout by popularity. The by-size method would be a good choice when high turnover is concentrated in the smaller items.

Layout by popularity or by size is not completely satisfactory because one neglects an important factor of the other. Heskett combined both features into a cube-per-order index.[12] *The index is the ratio of the average required cubic footage of the product for storage to the average number of daily orders on which the item is requested.* Products having *low* index values are located as near as possible to the outbound point. The cube-per-order index (COI) attempts to load the warehouse space so that the greatest volume of stock moves the shortest possible distance. When compared with a corresponding linear programming approach, it was found to be an optimizing method.[13] In addition, it has been used for more extended analyses of the layout problem.[14]

Davies, Gabbard, and Reinholdt compared four layout strategies including the COI method.[15]

---

[12]J. L. Heskett, "Cube-per-Order Index—A Key to Warehouse Stock Location," *Transportation and Distribution Management*, Vol. 3 (April 1963), pp. 27–31; and J. L. Heskett, "Putting the Cube-per-Order Index to Work in Warehouse Layout," *Transportation and Distribution Management*, Vol. 4 (August 1964), pp. 23–30.

[13]Carl Kallina and Jeffery Lynn, "Application of the Cube-per-Order Index Rule for Stock Location in a Distribution Warehouse," *Interfaces*, Vol. 7, No. 1 (November 1976), pp. 37–46. See also Hoyt G. Wilson, "Order Quantity, Product Popularity, and the Location of Stock in a Warehouse," *AIIE Transactions*, Vol. 9, no. 3 (September 1977), pp. 230–237.

[14]Charles J. Malmborg and Stuart J. Deutsch, "A Stock Location Model for Dual Address Order Picking Systems," *IIE Transactions*, Vol. 20, No. 1 (March 1988), pp. 44–52.

[15]Arthur L. Davies, Michael C. Gabbard, and Ernst F. Reinholdt, "Storage Method Saves Space and Labor in Open-Package-Area Picking Operations," *Industrial Engineering* (June 1983), pp. 68–74.

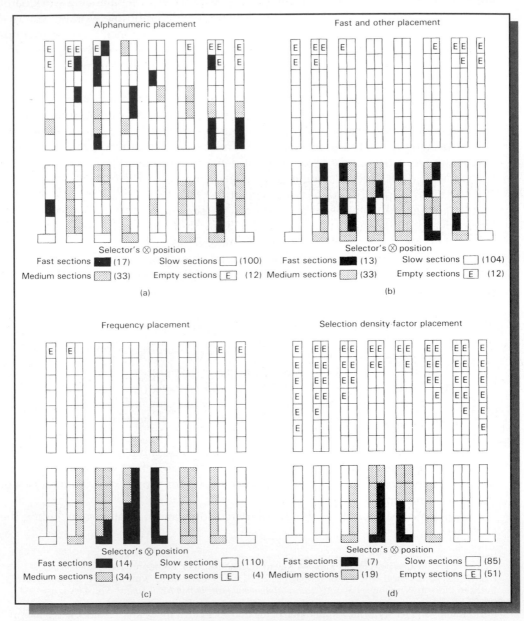

Figure 12-5 Comparison of Four Stock Location Strategies

Source: Arthur L. Davies, Michael C. Gabbard, and Ernst F. Reinholdt, "Storage Method Saves Space and Labor in Open-Package-Area Picking Operations," *Industrial Engineering* (June 1983), p. 70. Copyright Institute of Industrial Engineers, Norcross, GA.

1. *Alphanumeric placement*—all items are placed in strict alphanumeric sequence.
2. *Fast and other placement*—selected items are segregated from the remaining, or "other," items and stored in alphanumeric sequence as close as possible to the selector's work position.
3. *Frequency placement*—the fastest moving items are placed as close as possible to the selector's work position. (*Note:* This is the same as the layout-by-popularity method.)
4. *Selection density factor (SDF) placement*—the higher the ratio of number of selections per year to the required storage volume in cubic feet, the closer the item is placed to the selector's work position. (*Note:* This is the inverse of the cube-per-order index.)

A simulation study was conducted of 800 stock items that had an average of 800 selections per day. They found SDF, or COI, placement superior to the others, as shown graphically in Figure 12-5. It produced (1) the lowest average distance per selecting trip; (2) the lowest average time per selecting trip; (3) the lowest time per line items selected; and (4) the least total space. The SDF placement method has been widely implemented at Western Electric's material distribution warehouses.

Example

A warehouse has the internal configuration shown in Figure 12-6. Each storage bay can accommodate 40,000 cubic feet of product. Data have been collected on the cubic footage of storage required for the smallest shipping unit of the item for which an order can be placed, the expected number of orders on which the item appears over the planning horizon of one year, and the expected number of units to be shipped throughout the year. The basic data for seven items are shown in Table 12-8, as well as the computation of the COI for each item. Assigning the items with the lowest COI to storage bays nearest the outbound dock leads to the following acceptable product layout:

Bay No.	Product	Percentage of Bay Capacity Used
1Y	A—4,800 cu. ft.	
	E—35,200 cu. ft.	100%
1Z	E—2,400 cu. ft.	
	G—13,600 cu. ft.	
	C—24,000 cu. ft.	100
2Y	C—1,120 cu. ft.	
	B—38,880 cu. ft.	100
2Z	B—25,120 cu. ft.	
	F—14,880 cu. ft.	100
3Y	F—4,800 cu. ft.	
	D—35,200 cu. ft.	100
3Z	D—40,000 cu. ft.	100
4Y	D—40,000 cu. ft.	100
4Z	D—33,600 cu. ft.	84

Figure 12-6
Internal Warehouse Storage Bay Structure for Example Problem with a Cube-Per-Order Index Layout

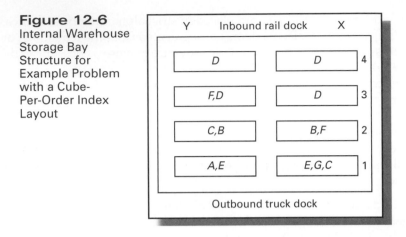

Intuitive layout methods are simple to use but do not guarantee that the lowest cost materials handling layout pattern will be found. For example, the methods just described best relate to order picking when it is of the out-and-back type. When a picker router is involved, methods for vehicle routing (see Chapter 7) are more appropriate.[16] Also, various methods that have been developed for plant layout are useful for warehouse layout as well. One such well-known model is computerized relative allocation of facilities technique (CRAFT)[17] and its various spin-off versions.[18] Computerized facilities design (COFAD) not only minimizes the move-

Table 12-8 Cube-Per-Order Index Computations for Example Problem

PRODUCT	(1) ITEM SIZE, cu. ft.	(2) EXPECTED NUMBER OF ORDERS/YEAR	(3) AVERAGE INVENTORY UNITS	(4) = (2)/250 AVERAGE NUMBER OF DAILY ORDERS[a]	(5) = (1) × (3) REQUIRED STORAGE SPACE, cu. ft.	(6) = (5)/(4) CUBE-PER-ORDER INDEX
A	6.0	6,750	800	27	4,800	177.8
B	4.0	15,750	16,000	63	64,000	1015.9
C	1.0	11,250	25,120	45	25,120	558.2
D	8.0	25,500	18,600	102	148,800	1458.8
E	3.0	17,750	12,533	71	37,599	529.6
F	5.0	3,500	3,936	14	19,680	1405.7
G	15.0	6,250	907	25	13,605	544.2
Totals		86,750	77,896		313,604	

[a]Based on 250 selling days per year

---

[16]See also James A. Chisman, "The Clustered Traveling Salesman Problem," *Computers and Operations Research*, Vol. 2, No. 2 (September 1975), pp. 115–119; and Marc Goetschalckx and H. Donald Ratliff, "Order Picking in an Aisle," *IIE Transactions*, Vol. 20, No. 1 (March 1988), pp. 53–62.
[17]Elwood S. Buffa, Gordon C. Armour, and Thomas E. Vollman, "Allocating Facilities with CRAFT," *Harvard Business Review*, Vol. 42 (March–April 1964), pp. 136–158.
[18]R. L. Francis and J. A. White, *Facility Layout and Location: An Analytical Approach* (Upper Saddle River, NJ: Prentice Hall, 1974).

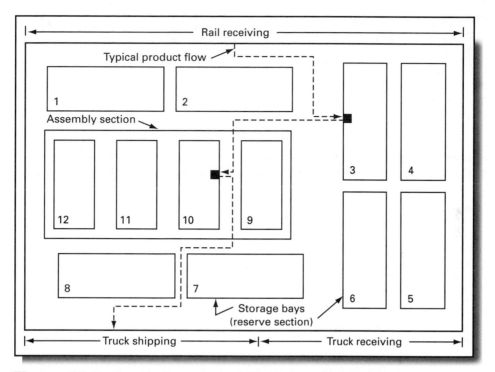

Figure 12-7 Sample Arrangement of Reserve and Assembly Areas in Grocery Warehouse

ment cost but also assigns materials handling equipment to given types of moves.[19] SPACECRAFT extends the CRAFT model to multistory facilities by appending additional floors to a first floor.[20] In an interesting comparative study, Trybus and Hopkins found that computer methods (specifically, CRAFT) gave better results than human subjects could find as problem size increased.[21] CRAFT always did as well, regardless of problem size. MULTIPLE extends CRAFT to multiple stories and realizes improved solutions from using space filling curve technology.[22] Now, even the expert systems approach is being applied to the layout problem.[23]

A more complex problem is two-stage layout, as shown in Figure 12-7. Product is received at rail or truck docks and is moved to semipermanent (reserve) storage. As

---

[19]"COFAD—A New Approach to Computerized Layout," *Modern Materials Handling* (April 1975), pp. 40–43.
[20]Roger V. Johnson, "Spacecraft for Multi-Floor Layout Planning," *Management Science*, Vol. 28, No. 4 (April 1982), pp. 407–417.
[21]Thomas W. Trybus and Lewis D. Hopkins, "Humans vs. Computer Algorithms for the Plant Layout Problem," *Management Science*, Vol. 26, No. 6 (June 1980), pp. 570–574.
[22]Yavuz A. Bozer, Russell D. Meller, and Steven J. Erlebacher, "An Improvement-type Layout Algorithm for Single and Multiple-floor Facilities," *Management Science*, Vol. 40, No. 7 (July 1994), pp. 918–932.
[23]John G. Carlson and Andrew C. Yao, "A Visually Interactive Expert System for a Distribution Center Environment," *International Journal of Production Economics*, Vol. 45, No. 1 (August 1, 1996), pp. 101–109.

			SPACE REQUIREMENTS		BAY CAPACITIES	
PRODUCT	MODE OF DELIVERY	TURNOVER RATIO	WAREHOUSE	ASSEMBLY[a]	RESERVE	ASSEMBLY
1	Rail	15	9,300	62	5,000	2,500
2	Truck	14	1,600	18	1,000	500
3	Truck	17	3,800	69	4,000	2,000
4	Rail	16	5,700	96	2,000	1,000
5	Rail	20	18,000	160	8,000	4,000

[a]These are minimum requirements for the assembly.

Table 12-9 Storage Bay Capacities and Space Requirements in Units for the Reserve and Assembly Areas for the Sample Grocery Warehouse

stock is depleted in the order-picking (assembly) area, replenishment stock is moved from the storage section to the order-picking section. As orders are filled, product is moved from the order-picking section to the outbound dock. The questions are where to place each product in the warehouse and how much space should be allocated for each product in the semipermanent and order picking sections. Table 12-9 illustrates a hypothetical example of this problem using only a few products and data to show contrasts.

A linear programming model can be formulated as an approach to this problem. It is shown in the Technical Supplement to this chapter. What we wish to do is minimize the total costs of moving the products through the warehouse, subject to limitations on minimum amounts of product to be stored in the assembly section, in a particular bay, and in the warehouse. Since products cannot occupy the same locations, this becomes an allocation problem to be solved. Once the per unit handling costs are estimated for the various product flow paths through the warehouse, the problem can be easily solved by most general-purpose linear programming computer programs. Although not all data for this problem are given here, the general nature of the solution would be as shown in Table 12-10.

Conceptually, linear programming is a good choice for solving the layout problem because, in effect, all possible arrangements are searched to find an optimum, and the assembly and reserve sections can be laid out simultaneously. However, practical problems involving thousands of products may be too large to be reasonably solved by linear programming. Therefore, application of methods discussed in this section, especially those developed for plant layout, may require creating zones of product in the warehouse or grouping of products into families to limit problem size. In addition, a method such as CRAFT achieves a higher computational speed than linear programming with little loss in solution accuracy. As Buffa, Armour, and Vollman point out: "The answers generated are not as surely the best ones as the answers to linear programming problems are, but they do represent solutions that cannot easily be improved on."[24]

---

[24]Buffa, Armour, and Vollman, "Allocating Facilities with CRAFT."

BAY	PRODUCT				
	1	2	3	4	5[a]
1	4,238			305	
2	5,000				
3		5		1,190	
4		510			
5		1,000			
6		67	3,371		
7				1,309	2,765
8				2,000	
9		18		96	3,472
10					4,000
11	62				4,000
12			69		3,763
Total requirements	9,300	1,600	3,800	5,700	18,000

[a]Much of product 5 is located in the assembly section, due to the high product turnover. If this creates too much of an imbalance with the other products, either the space requirements on products 1 to 4 can be increased, or a constraint can be added to the model that will limit the amount of a product that should be stored in the assembly section.

Table 12-10 Amount of Each Product Assigned to Respective Bays to Achieve Minimum Total Handling Cost for a Grocery Warehouse

Activity Profiling

A warehouse is not typically an area in which a singular layout occurs. Rather, the area is frequently divided into several subareas with specialized functions. Depending on the activity level and product mix, defined areas can be (1) full pallet/full case, (2) split case, (3) bulk, (4) bonded, (5) promotional, (6) returned merchandise, and (7) administrative. To determine the need for these areas and their size, Frazelle suggests a data mining process referred to as *activity profiling*.[25] Statistical distributions are obtained from actual sales data on order mix, lines per order, cube per order, and lines-and-cube per order. These data are also useful for applying the stock location methodology described in the previous section.

A first step in activity profiling is to generate an order mix distribution. We seek to find how much of the order volume is in pallet-load, full case, and broken-case quantities. Since stock retrieval is distinctly different for these three areas in both storage configuration and handling procedures, sampling warehouse throughput for a reasonable time, say, one year, provides the activity level needed to design these areas. Other merchandise classified as bulk, bonded, and promotional can be handled in a similar manner. Apportioning the warehouse space to the various uses might lead to the space allocation shown in Figure 12-8 for a high-volume warehouse.

---

[25]Edward Frazelle, *World-Class Warehousing and Material Handling* (New York: McGraw-Hill, 2002), Chapter 2.

Figure 12-8
Area Configuration
for a High
Throughput
Warehouse Based
on Activity Profiling

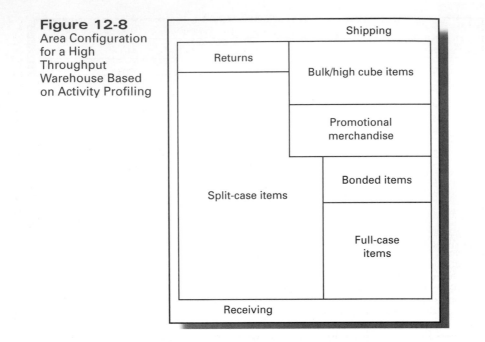

The same order data are subdivided along area lines. For example, merchandise assigned to a split-case picking area is separated from the remaining data. From these data, items can be ranked by number of orders on which the item appears (representing order-picking trips) and by item size. Inventory held for each item is also obtained, but not from the sales data. These data can then be used to calculate layout assignments by popularity, by cube, or by cube-per-order index.

Another distribution would be that of demand correlation. Here, the items most often ordered together are ranked from the highest frequency of occurrence to the lowest. This establishes item complementarity suggesting those items that should be located adjacent to each other. Similarly, the data may be analyzed for seasonal patterns with the purpose of locating items within the same zone that have opposing seasonal patterns. By colocating these items, storage space requirements are reduced.

Not all areas of the warehouse require activity profiling. Once the overall size of the area has been established from a first-level statistical analysis, layout may be a matter of convenience and good judgment. The area for promotional merchandise has goods purchased in quantities exceeding normal replenishment amounts that are temporarily stored until sales from aggressive pricing deplete them. The uncertain nature of the goods and their space requirements within the promotional area suggests that systematic layout planning is not required. Activity profiling is most beneficial where handling costs are high, many items are to be stored, and there are substantial differences in the physical characteristics of the items.

Figure 12-9
Pallet Positioning
Alternatives

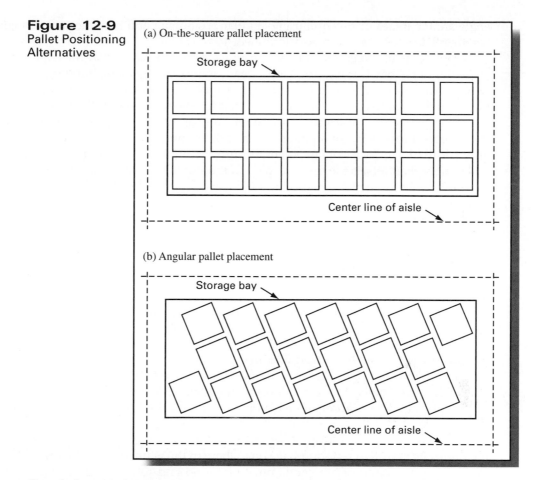

(a) On-the-square pallet placement

Storage bay

Center line of aisle

(b) Angular pallet placement

Storage bay

Center line of aisle

Stock Arrangement

Efficiency in warehousing can also be enhanced by stock positioning within storage bays. Positioning is a major consideration where palletized storage is used, and palletization of goods is a common practice in many warehouse operations.

Positioning specifically refers to the angle at which pallets are laid out relative to the service aisle. The most widely used positioning is the on-the-square, or 0 degrees, placement angle Figure 12-9(a). Most warehouse operators prefer the on-the-square pallet positioning. As an alternative, pallets may be positioned at some angle to the centerline of the service aisle Figure 12-9(b). "Angling" is not used a great deal by warehouses, probably because of the continuing controversy as to whether any efficiency results from angular positioning. The controversy can be seen in those studies that have suggested angles from 0 to 60 degrees as best.[26] More important than a generally suggested

[26]Joseph J. Moder and Herbert M. Thorton, "Quantitative Analysis of Factors Affecting Floor Space Utilization of Palletized Storage," *Journal of Industrial Engineering*, Vol. 16 (January-February 1965), pp. 8–18; Donald J. Bowersox "Resolving the Pallet Controversy," *Transportation and Distribution Management* (April 1963), pp. 27–31; and Ronald H. Ballou, "The Consideration of Angular Pallet Layout to Optimize Warehouse Space Utilization" (master's thesis, The Ohio State University, 1963).

angle are the issues involved in using angular positioning and how the correct angle, whether 0 degrees or not, can be determined.

Opponents to angling complain that unused space is created at the front, back, and sides of the bay [see Figure 12-9(b)]; that column arrangement, building configuration, and floor area place limitations on the implementation of an angular positioning plan; that angled pallets are more difficult to spot in the bay at the correct angle; and that the one-way aisles that naturally result contribute to higher materials handling costs. Proponents of angling, on the other hand, argue that the reduction in aisle width due to the less-than-90-degree turn required of a forklift truck servicing a pallet more than offsets the unused space in the storage bay. In addition, some operating efficiency is gained because the forklift truck makes less than a full 90-degree turn to place or retrieve a pallet.

Resolving this controversy is primarily a matter of balancing space utilization considerations against materials handling efficiencies. The effect of angling on total space requirements has been examined, and formulas or computation forms are available for determining the exact angle for any combination of pallet size, bay configuration, and forklift truck.[27] The effect of angling on operating efficiency can be determined from a time study of forklift truck operations under different pallet angles. Converting space and time measures to economic terms, we say that the angle yielding the lowest cost can be found.

Stock Locator-Identification Methods

An important design consideration that can substantially affect materials handling efficiency is the method used to identify merchandise location in the storage bays. Two opposing identification and location schemes are the fixed locator and the random locator methods.

Consider a common location problem. When goods arrive at the warehouse, they must be placed in a storage bay somewhere in the warehouse. When an order is to be filled, the appropriate goods must be found and retrieved from the storage location. How can this be accomplished with efficiency when the existing products show increasing and decreasing stock levels due to variations of supply and demand and when the product mix is changing because of additions and deletions from the product line?

The *fixed locator-identification method* assigns a given storage bay or storage rack number to each product. These locations can be determined from the stock location methods (by popularity, COI, and the like) already discussed. This locator-identification method is simple, and no formal code is needed to identify locations if only a few items are stored in the warehouse. Personnel who place and retrieve the stock can simply memorize the locations. If the product line is extensive, a formal code can be created to identify warehouse section, bay number, and slot.

The primary disadvantage of this method is that much underutilized space may be created. Space capacity should be established for the peak stocking requirements

---

[27]See Moder and Thorton, "Quantitative Analysis of Factors Affecting Space Utilization of Palletized Storage"; and Ronald H. Ballou, "Pallet Layout for Optimum Space Utilization," *Transportation and Distribution Management* (February 1964), pp. 24–33.

of each product. Because product peak stocking levels usually do not occur simulta- neously, poor utilization of the space can result.

The *random locator-identification method* is designed to overcome the disadvantage of the fixed locator-identification method. When goods arrive at the warehouse, they are routed to any open space that is available. There are no preassigned locations. This method offers better use of available storage space, but to keep track of many items, when each may be located in several places, requires an effective retricval code. Because of a continually shifting space availability pattern in the warehouse, an elaborate manual or computer-based stock-filing system is needed to support this manner of operation.

Although the random locator-identification method offers improved space uti- lization, longer travel times are usually encountered because a single item on an order may require picking from several locations. This method, and modified ver- sions of it, has been popular in automated storage and retrieval systems, where space costs are high relative to handling costs.

In high-volume and palletized handling systems, a blend of the two methods has proved practical. A popular modification is to confine items to designated zones in the warehouse, as suggested by stock location methods. Within these zones, prod- ucts can be stored on a space-available basis.

Example

A steel distributor put the designated-zones idea to good use to store its finished coils and sheet goods. The storage area was divided into a number of smaller areas that were given color designators—pink, violet, orange, and so on. The colors pro- vided easy identification of each area and of the product within. The product stored in a given area was allowed to "float" without a specifically assigned spot. Although the product could move randomly within its designated area, the area was not so large that product would be easily lost yet provided good utilization of the space.

ORDER-PICKING OPERATIONS

The labor-intensive nature of order picking makes it a target for productivity improve- ments. Several operational considerations can improve materials handling efficiency.

Order Handling

How the incoming order is managed affects handling costs. Generating picker lists from the sales order can lower costs.

Product Sequencing

Sequencing is the arrangement of items on picking route lists so that they are picked in an efficient route through the stock. Order-picking time is saved by avoiding backtracking through aisles and merchandise. Sequencing the items as they occur on the sales order may require the cooperation of sales personnel and customers to list items in the designated order. Alternately, a popular approach is the use of computers to sequence sales order items into efficient picker lists.

Picker Zoning

Zoning refers to assigning individual order pickers to serve only a limited number of the stock items instead of routing them through the entire stock layout. An order picker selects stock only within a designated area and usually fills only a portion of the total customer order. To achieve low materials handling cost (reduce picker fatigue and maximize throughput), careful attention needs to be paid to several factors. First, stock should be located between and within picker zones according to order frequency, complementarity, item weight, rack position, and item cube so that order picker workloads between zones are balanced. Second, the sales order must be broken down into picker lists for each zone. Third, the various portions of the order must be assembled into a complete order before leaving the warehouse. If the order filling proceeds sequentially from one zone to another to avoid the problem of reassembly when the zones are dispersed, then the order-picking pace becomes dependent upon the pace of order picking in other zones.

Although picker zoning has been the popular approach to dividing workload in high throughput warehouses, an alternative philosophy is emerging. It is derived from "swarm intelligence," the collective behavior of social insects such as ants, bees, and wasps.[28] Watching how ants move food from source to nest, the "bucket brigade" approach is observed. That is, ants pass food from one member to another along a food gathering chain. The ants are not stationary and the transfer points are not fixed. Starting with the food source, an ant carries the food down the chain until it reaches the next ant. After transferring the food, it returns upstream until it reaches the previous ant to receive the next load. This process continues along a chain of multiple ants where the only fixed locations are the food source and the nest.

Swarm intelligence has been applied to order picking in large distribution centers where a 31 percent improvement over the zone approach has been reported.[29] The zone approach does not recognize the wide variation in rate at which the pickers complete their tasks. The quickest person could be four times faster than the slowest. This tends to underutilize the fast people and aggravate the slower ones who are under pressure to keep up. Even if all worked at the same rate, the normal variation in completing the tasks in each zone would make it difficult to balance the workload. The better approach is for an upstream worker in an order-filling chain to continue picking items on the order until the person downstream takes over the work; then, head back upstream to take over the next person's work. The optimal way to arrange the workers is to begin upstream and sequence them from *slowest to fastest*.

---

[28]Eric Bonabeau and Christopher Meyer, "Swarm Intelligence: A Whole New Way to Think About Business," *Harvard Business Review*, Vol. 79, No. 5 (May 2001), pp. 106–114.
[29]Ibid.

Order Splitting

Order splitting is an extension of the ideas of picker zoning. When the stock does not reside at a single location, it is necessary to divide the sales order before routing it to a warehouse.

Application

Rico Drug Stores receives weekly replenishment orders from its retail stores. The orders are first split between over-the-counter (OTC) merchandise and pharmaceuticals. Pharmaceuticals are stocked at one location in the country. The remainder of the order is sent to the local distribution center where OTC merchandise is stocked. The order is further divided between bulk merchandise, which is stocked at a public warehouse, and the remainder, which is held in a leased facility. The flow of merchandise is coordinated from these separate locations so that the order arrives at the retail store at the promised time. Tagging and labeling the items and computer tracking of the split-order items become critical to achieving overall order coordination.

Item Batching

Batching is the selection of more than one order on a single pass through the stock. This practice obviously reduces travel time, but it also adds to the complication of reassembling orders and partial orders for shipment. It also may increase order-filling time for any order because its completion is dependent upon the number and size of the other orders in the batch.

Interleaving

A special problem in order-picking operations occurs when storage and order picking take place at the same time on the same route from the same origin-destination point. This has been referred to as *interleaving* and it is a common problem found in automatic storage and retrieval systems. For random storage assignment, where any open rack is selected for storage, a common rule is to select the open location nearest to the origin-destination point. However, a storage-retrieval rule based on turnover (popularity) has been shown to reduce substantially the average trip time for storage alone or for interleaving.[30]

Setting Standards

High levels of materials handling efficiency cannot be guaranteed by the application of rules, concepts, or optimization methods alone. The worker is an important ingredient

---

[30]Leroy B. Schwarz, Stephen C. Graves, and Warren H. Hausman, "Scheduling Policies for Automatic Warehousing Systems: Simulation Results," *AIIE Transactions*, Vol. 10, No. 3 (September 1978), pp. 260–270.

in the total cost equation. Performance standards are important to providing norms so that a reasonable number of workers can be assigned to the work of warehousing, to provide a benchmark against which superior or substandard performance can be judged, and to provide a base wage for incentive systems so that increased productivity can be rewarded.

CONCLUDING COMMENTS

This chapter deals with planning the design and operation of storage facilities with emphasis on the warehouse. Logisticians will have varying needs for this material, depending on how storage is provided in their firms. If public warehousing is used, the managers of the public warehouses plan the operation and the user firms evaluate the rates and services on a comparative basis with other public warehousing firms. On the other end of the scale, if the storage space is to be company owned, the logisticians will face the full range of warehouse design and operations decisions.

The discussion focuses on the various planning decisions relating to the major space and materials handling problems, once the general warehouse location is known. These major decisions include structure size and financial arrangement, facility configuration, space layout, dock design, materials handling systems selection, equipment replacement, stock arrangement, stock locator-identification methods, and order-picking operations. Concepts as well as mathematical models for decision making are illustrated. Although storage and materials handling decisions are presented here as seemingly independent of each other, and of the logistics system as a whole, the logistician is cautioned to watch for the economic impact that each of the noted warehouse decision problems has on other decisions outside their immediate scope. Activity profiling is suggested as a means for providing the initial information needed for warehouse design.

QUESTIONS

Some problems in this chapter can be solved or partially solved with the aid of computer software. The software packages in LOGWARE that are most important for this chapter are LNPROG (*LP*) and LAYOUT (*LO*). The CD icon

LP will appear with the software package designation where the problem analysis is assisted by one of these software programs. A database may be prepared for the problem if extensive data input is required. Where the problem can be solved without the aid of the computer (by hand), the hand icon is shown. If no icon appears, hand calculation is assumed.

1. A warehouse is to be located somewhere in your hometown. What factors do you think should be evaluated in making the selection of a particular site?

2. The Acme Manufacturing Company is concerned about its warehouse needs and how they can best be met. The company produces a line of spare parts for appliances. Due to the combination of production policies and demand patterns, warehousing space requirements vary considerably throughout the year. Space requirements are known with a great deal of certainty because the product line satisfies a replacement market. Growth, or decline, in production and sales is not anticipated in the near future. Monthly sales rates for a typical year are as follows:

Month	Sales, $
Jan.	5,000,000
Feb.	4,000,000
Mar.	3,000,000
Apr.	2,000,000
May	1,000,000
June	250,000
July	1,250,000
Aug.	2,250,000
Sept.	3,000,000
Oct.	3,500,000
Nov.	4,000,000
Dec.	4,500,000
Total	33,750,000

Warehouse inventory turns at the rate of two times per *month*. A dollar's worth of merchandise occupies 0.1 cubic feet of warehouse space and can be stacked 10 ft. high. The product density is $5 per lb. Given aisles, administrative space, and normal operating efficiency, only 40 percent of the total warehouse space is actually used for storage.

A private warehouse can be constructed and equipped for $35 per sq. ft. and can be amortized over 20 years. The cost of operation is $0.02 per dollar of throughput (lb). Annual fixed costs amount to $10 per sq. ft. of total space. Space may also be rented for a storage charge on inventory of $0.06 per lb per month and a handling charge of $0.05 per lb of throughput.

What size of private warehouse should be constructed, to the nearest 10,000 sq. ft., or what amount of public warehouse space should be rented? To what extent and when should each type of space be used?

3. O'Neal Consumer Products is in need of 150,000 sq. ft. of warehouse space for its East Coast market, where annual sales are $30,000,000. If a public warehouse is used, annual costs can be estimated as $600,000 for handling and $300,000 for storage. If leased space is used, the annual lease cost is $3 per sq. ft. for a ten-year lease. Leased-space operating cost is $250,000 per year. Equipment and start-up costs are $400,000, which can be depreciated over a seven-year period. A straight-line depreciation schedule is to be used.

The company's required return on projects is 11 percent after taxes, and its federal tax rate is 35 percent per year.

Which alternative makes the best economic sense?

4. A private warehouse has an annual throughput of 10,000 items and an average materials handling cost per item of $0.01/ft. The warehouse size is to be 100,000 sq. ft. Annual construction and maintenance costs are $210/ft. of perimeter. The loading and unloading dock is to be located at a warehouse corner. What is the best length and width of the warehouse? What is the total relevant cost for this design?

5. Using the data given in the space layout example from the chapter, design the layout and the length and width dimensions of a warehouse in the style of Figure 12-4(a).

6. A food distribution center makes deliveries to food stores on a weekly basis. On the average, 75 stores are served daily. A typical store places an order for 12,000 lb of various products. Three store orders can be placed on a delivery truck. Trucks are loaded in three hours. The distribution center operates an eight-hour shift.

   How many truck doors are needed on the average?

7. A firm uses a number of narrow-aisle forklift trucks and can purchase these in three types. Type 1 costs $20,000 each; type 2 costs $10,000 each; and type 3 costs $5,000 each. Such equipment can be sold at the end of its useful life (ten years) for 15 percent of its original cost. The annual operating costs for each type of equipment are $2,000, $2,500, and $3,000, respectively per truck. Three type-1 units can do the work of five type-2 units or of seven type-3 units. If investments are to return 20 percent before taxes per truck, which equipment would be the best buy?

8. A certain narrow-aisle forklift truck costs $4,000. When it is replaced, it will be replaced with a truck of the same kind. Operating costs for this truck are $500 for the first year and increase at the rate of $40 per year *squared* thereafter. Technological improvements reduce operating costs by an estimated $30 per year. The salvage value of the trucks declines linearly over their seven-year life. The desired rate of return is to be 20 percent before taxes.

   When should the equipment be replaced?

9. Suppose that a warehouse contains eight storage bays. Product enters the rear of the warehouse through a rail dock. Product is picked from the storage locations by an out-and-back selection method and shipped from a truck dock at the front of the building (see the design in Figure 12-6). Each bay can hold 2,500 sq. ft. with product stacked 10 ft. high. Ten products are maintained in the warehouse. The following data have been collected:

Product	Storage Space Required (sq. ft.)	Individual Product Size (cu. ft.)	Average Number of Daily Orders in Which Item Appears
A	500	1.5	56
B	3,000	10.6	103
C	1,500	4.3	27
D	1,700	5.5	15
E	5,500	2.7	84
F	1,100	15.0	55
G	700	9.0	26
H	2,800	6.7	45
I	1,300	3.3	94
J	900	4.7	35

a. Lay out the warehouse using the (1) by-popularity method, (2) the by-cube method, and (3) cube-per-order index method.

b. To what extent are these methods appropriate when more than one item is picked on a route, and when pickers are zoned to pick only a limited part of the product line on each order?

10. The Able Company is a local division of a large public warehousing firm. The management of this company has successfully applied the techniques of scientific management in the past and is currently looking at its layout problem to see if these techniques can indicate whether cost savings can be made in this area. The company has selected a particular warehouse for consideration. This warehouse has two receiving docks (R_1, R_2) and one shipping dock (S_1). The three major products handled by the warehouse are stored in six storage bays.

Management finds that because of order sizes, receiving locations, quantities received, and the like, different times are required to supply and distribute from a storage bay, and these service times depend on the particular product and location of the storage bay in the warehouse. There is a direct relationship between handling costs and handling times for each product and storage bay.

HANDLING TIMES (HR.)[a] PER 100 UNITS OF PRODUCT STORED IN VARIOUS BAYS

Storage Bay	1	2	3
1	0.90	0.75	0.90
2	0.80	0.65	0.95
3	0.60	0.70	0.65
4	0.70	0.55	0.45
5	0.50	0.50	0.45
6	0.40	0.45	0.35

[a]For a three-month period

Each storage bay has a certain capacity depending on the product. The following information on storage bay capacity is known:

Product	Storage Bay Capacity (units)
1	5,000
2	3,000
3	6,000

Management forecasts that it must plan storage space for at least 11,000 units of product 1, 4,000 units of product 2, and 12,000 units of product 3 over the next three months. The decision problem is how to allocate the products to the various storage bays (in the proper quantities) so as to minimize the total handling time (cost) required for all products. (*Hint*: Solve as a linear programming problem using the following model):

Objective function

$$z_{min} = \sum_i \sum_j C_{ij} X_{ij}$$

subject to

$$\sum_j \frac{1}{G_j} X_{ij} \leq 1.0 \quad \text{for} \quad i = 1, 2, \dots, M$$

and

$$\sum_i X_{ij} \geq R_j \quad \text{for} \quad j = 1, 2 \dots, N$$

where

G_j = capacity of bay for product j
R_j = number of units of product j required to be stored
M = number of storage locations
N = number of products

11. What space trade-offs are involved in angular pallet positioning? What additional considerations would enter into the decision to use angular pallet positioning?

12. What alternative methods of stock location and retrieval can you think of? Discuss the advantages and disadvantages of the methods that you propose.

13. A leading manufacturer of rubber and vinyl houseware products uses a random stock locator-retrieval system in its plant warehouse. All orders in the country are filled through this location. The internal warehouse design shows seven-tier racks laid out in rectangular patterns. The materials handling system involves narrow-aisle forklift trucks and palletized storage. Why would this company likely find such a storage materials handling system an advantage over other types?

14. A parts warehouse has two types of storage areas. The first type is carousels having many bins in which small and frequently requested items are placed. The remaining items are placed on storage racks (second type) from which items are retrieved using forklift trucks. What data distributions would you construct and how you would use them (activity profiling) to determine the size of the carousel/storage rack space? Next, how would the data distribution be used to lay out the items within theses areas?

15. For order picking in a warehouse, contrast the zone approach with the bucket brigade approach.

Appendix

Technical Supplement

The general linear programming formulation for the product layout problem involving both reserve storage and order picking areas is as follows:

The objective is to minimize the total materials handling cost, that is,

$$z_{min} = \sum_{i=1}^{M} \sum_{j=1}^{N} C_{ij} X_{ij}$$

subject to

1. a reserve section bay capacity constraint:

$$\sum_{j=1}^{N} \frac{1}{G_j^s} X_{ij} \leq 1.0 \quad \text{for } i = 1, 2, \dots, L$$

2. an assembly section bay capacity constraint:

$$\sum_{j=1}^{N} \frac{1}{G_j^a} X_{ij} \leq 1.0 \quad \text{for}$$
$$i = L + 1, L + 2, \dots, M$$

3. the minimum number of units of each product to be stored in the assembly section:

$$\sum_{i=L+1}^{M} X_{ij} \geq R_j^a \quad \text{for } j = 1, 2, \dots, N$$

4. the total number of units to be stored throughout the warehouse:

$$\sum_{i=1}^{M} X_{ij} \geq R_j \quad \text{for } j = 1, 2, \dots, N$$

5. a negative amount of product j cannot be stored:

$$\text{all } X_{ij} \geq 0$$

where

X_{ij} = amount of product j stored in bay i
C_{ij} = cost for handling product j when stored in bay i
M = number of storage bays in both reserve and assembly sections
N = number of different stock items handled by the warehouse
L = number of storage bays in the reserve section
G_j = amount of product j that can be stored in a bay
R_j = the required amount of product j to be stored in the warehouse
R_j^a = the minimum amount of product j to be stored in the assembly section

s and a = superscripts to denote the reserve and assembly sections, respectively

Chapter 13

Facility Location Decisions

> *Experience teaches that men are so much governed by what they are accustomed to see and practice, that the simplest and most obvious improvements in the most ordinary occupations are adopted with hesitation, reluctance, and by slow graduations.*
>
> —ALEXANDER HAMILTON, 1791

*L*ocating fixed facilities throughout the supply chain network is an important decision problem that gives form, structure, and shape to the entire supply chain system. This design defines the alternatives, along with their associated costs and investment levels, used to operate

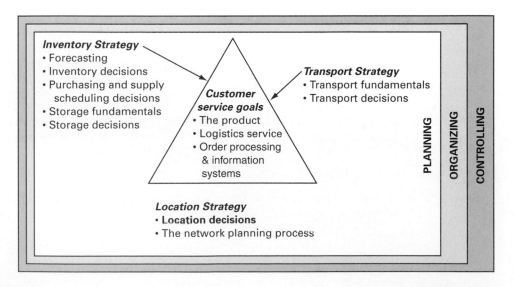

the system. Location decisions involve determining the number, location, and size of the facilities to be used. These facilities include such nodal points in the network as plants, ports, vendors, warehouses, retail outlets, and service centers—points in the supply chain network where goods temporarily stop on their way to final consumers.

Developing methods for locating facilities has been a popular area for research.[1] In this chapter, we will look at a selected number of the available methods for strategic network planning. The focus will be on those methods that (1) are representative of the types of solution methods available; (2) address a variety of common business location problems; and (3) illustrate the issues facing the decision maker in network planning.

CLASSIFICATION OF LOCATION PROBLEMS

When discussing location methods, it is useful to classify location problems into a limited number of categories, namely, by (1) driving force, (2) number of facilities, (3) discreteness of the choices, (4) degree of data aggregation, and (5) time horizon.

Driving Force

Facility location is often determined by one critical factor. In the case of plant and warehouse location, economic factors usually dominate. In retail location, revenue generated by a location is often the determining factor, with site costs subtracted from revenues to determine profitability. Where a service operation (hospital, automated bank teller, charity collection center, or maintenance facility) is to be located, accessibility to the site may be the primary location factor, especially when revenue and costs are not easily determined.

Number of Facilities

Locating one facility is a considerably different problem from locating many facilities at one time. Single facility location avoids the need to consider competitive forces, division of demand among facilities, inventory consolidation effects, and facility costs. Transportation costs are typically the primary consideration. Single facility location is the simpler of the two problem types.

Discreteness of the Choices

Some methods will explore every possible location along a space continuum and select the best one. These we refer to as *continuous* location methods. Alternatively,

[1]For a survey of many of these methods, see Margaret L. Brandeau and Samuel S. Chiu, "An Overview of Representative Problems in Location Research," *Management Science*, Vol. 35, No. 6 (June 1989), pp. 645–674; and Zvi Drezner, *Facility Location* (New York: Springer-Verlag, 1995).

location methods may select from a list of possible choices that have been identified for their reasonableness. These are *discrete* location methods. The latter are more commonly used in practice, mainly for multiple facility location.

Degree of Data Aggregation

Location problems typically involve the evaluation of an exceedingly large number of network design configurations. To manage problem size and obtain a solution, it is generally necessary to use aggregate data relationships when solving a practical location problem. This results in methods whose accuracy limits locations to wide geographic areas such as entire cities. On the other hand, methods using little data aggregation, especially those for site selection, can differentiate between locations separated only by a city street. The latter is particularly needed for retail location, intracity locations, and making final plant and warehouse site selections.

Time Horizon

The time nature of location methods is to be static or dynamic. That is, static methods find locations based on data for a single period, such as one year. Location plans may cover many years at once, however, especially if facilities represent a fixed investment and the costs of relocating from one location to another are high. Methods that handle multiperiod location planning are referred to as dynamic.

A HISTORICAL PERSPECTIVE ON LOCATION[2]

Much of the early theories about location were postulated by land economists and regional geographers such as Johann von Thünen,[3] Alfred Weber,[4] T. Palander,[5] August Lösch,[6] Edgar Hoover,[7] Melvin Greenhut,[8] and Walter Isard.[9] A common theme throughout all of these early works was the importance of transportation costs in determining location. Although much of the work was conducted in an agrarian and early industrial society, a number of the concepts that they suggested are still applicable today. Consider a brief outline of just a few of these.

---

[2]For a review of the history of location modeling, see T. Puu, *Mathematical Location and Land Use Theory* (New York: Springer-Verlag, 1997).

[3]Johann Heinrich von Thünen, *Der Isolierte Staat in Beziehung auf Landwirtschaft und Nationalökonomie*, 3rd ed. (Berlin: Schumacher-Zarchlin, 1875).

[4]Alfred Weber, *Uber den Standort der Industrien* (Mohr, Tubingen, 1909), translated by Carl J. Friedrich as *Alfred Weber's Theory of the Location of Industries* (Chicago: University of Chicago Press, 1929).

[5]T. Palander, *Beitrage zur Standortstheorie* (Uppsala, 1935).

[6]August Lösch, *Die Raumliche Ordnung der Wirtscaft* (Jena: Gustav Fischer Verlag, 1940).

[7]Edgar M. Hoover, *Location Theory and the Shoe and Leather Industries* (Cambridge, MA: Harvard University Press, 1957).

[8]Melvin L. Greenhut, *Plant Location in Theory and Practice* (Chapel Hill, NC: University of North Carolina Press, 1956).

[9]Walter Isard, et al., *Methods of Regional Analysis: An Introduction to Regional Science* (New York: John Wiley & Sons, 1960); and Walter Isard, *Location and Space Economy* (Cambridge, MA: MIT Press, 1968).

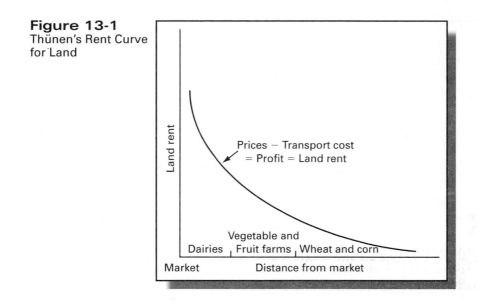

Figure 13-1
Thünen's Rent Curve
for Land

Land rent

Prices − Transport cost
= Profit = Land rent

Vegetable and
Dairies | Fruit farms | Wheat and corn
Market   Distance from market

Bid-Rent Curves

Thünen recognized that the maximum rent, or profit, that any economic development could pay for land was the difference between the price for the goods *in* the
marketplace and the cost of transporting the goods *to* the marketplace. He visualized
an isolated city-state (marketplace) situated on a plane of equal fertility. Economic
activity would locate itself around this city-state according to its ability to pay for the
land. In an agricultural economy, agricultural activity might locate out from the
marketplace, as shown in Figure 13-1. Today, this idea still seems to hold as we
observe the pattern of retail, residential, manufacturing, and agricultural locations
that ring the city center. Those activities that can pay the most for land will be located
nearest the city center and along major transportation links.

Weber's Classification of Industries

Alfred Weber recognized the role that raw materials play in the production process
and how they affect location. He observed that some processes are weight losing,
such as steelmaking. That is, the sum of the weight of raw materials is greater than
the weight of the finished product. Weight is lost in processing due to unusable by-
products. Therefore, to avoid shipping by-products to the marketplace, such
processes are drawn toward their raw material sources in order to minimize transportation costs (see Figure 13-2).

On the other hand, processes may be weight gaining. This commonly occurs
when ubiquities enter into the process. According to Weber, ubiquities include the
raw materials available everywhere, such as air and water. Therefore, to minimize
transportation costs by shipping ubiquities the shortest possible distance, such

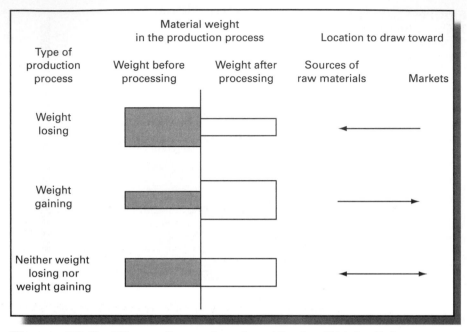

Type of production process	Material weight in the production process		Location to draw toward	
	Weight before processing	Weight after processing	Sources of raw materials	Markets
Weight losing			←	
Weight gaining			→	
Neither weight losing nor weight gaining			← →	

Figure 13-2   Effect on Process Location of Product Weights Before and After Processing

processes should be located as close to markets as possible (see Figure 13-2). An example of an industry that locates its plants in this manner is soft drink bottling. Syrups are shipped into the bottling plants and mixed with water. These plants are typically located in the general region of the markets for the products.

Finally, there are processes where there is no change in weight between raw materials and finished product. Assembly operations are representative of this category, where the finished product is a sum of the weight of the parts and components assembled into it. Such processes, according to Weber, are bound neither to the sources of the raw materials nor to the markets (see Figure 13-2). That is, the total of inbound and outbound transportation costs is the same at any location between source and market points.

Hoover's Tapered Transportation Rates

Hoover observed that transportation rates are tapered with distance. To minimize inbound plus outbound transportation costs where they are the dominant location force, a facility located between a raw material source and a market point will have a minimum transportation cost at one of these two points. As shown in Figure 13-3, location between these points is economically unstable. Since Y is lower than X on the cost curves, location should be at Y.

Figure 13-3
Tapered
Transportation Rates
Force Location to the
Source of Materials
or to the Market

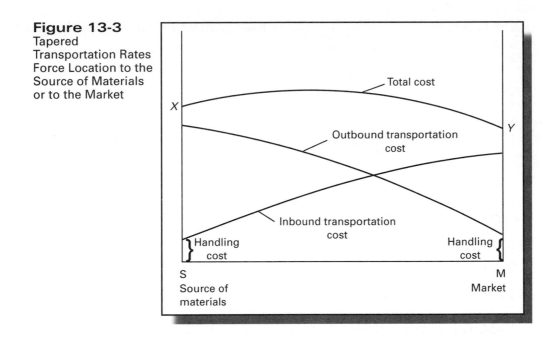

SINGLE FACILITY LOCATION

Let us now turn to contemporary ways of looking at facility location. With the popularity of applied mathematics and computers, these approaches are mathematical in nature rather than conceptual. We begin with a popular model that is used for locating a single plant, terminal, warehouse, or retail or service point. It has been variously known as the exact center-of-gravity approach, *p*-median, the grid method, and the centroid method. The approach is simple, since the transportation rate and the point volume are the only location factors. This model is classified mathematically as a static continuous location model.

Where should the facility be located given a set of points representing source points and demand points, their volumes that are to be moved to or from a single facility of unknown location, and their associated transportation rates? We seek to minimize the sum of the volume at a point multiplied by the transportation rate to ship to the point multiplied by the distance to the point, which is the total transportation cost. That is,

$$\text{Min } TC = \sum_i V_i R_i d_i \qquad \textbf{(13-1)}$$

where

TC = total transportation cost
V_i = volume at point i
R_i = transportation rate to point i
d_i = distance to point i from the facility to be located

The facility location is found by solving two equations for the coordinates of the location.[10] These exact center-of-gravity coordinates are

$$\overline{X} = \frac{\sum_i V_i R_i X_i / d_i}{\sum_i V_i R_i / d_i}$$

(13-2)

and

$$\overline{Y} = \frac{\sum_i V_i R_i Y_i / d_i}{\sum_i V_i R_i / d_i}$$

(13-3)

where

$$\overline{X}, \overline{Y} = \text{coordinate points of the located facility}$$
$$X_i, Y_i = \text{coordinate points of source and demand points}$$

The distance d_i is estimated by

$$d_i = K \sqrt{(X_i - \overline{X})^2 + (Y_i - \overline{Y})^2}$$

(13-4)

where K represents a scaling factor to convert one unit of a coordinate point to a more common distance measure, such as miles or kilometers.

The solution process involves several steps, which are outlined as follows:

1. Determine the X,Y coordinate points for each source and demand point, along with point volumes and linear transportation rates.
2. Approximate the initial location from the center-of-gravity formulas by omitting the distance term d_i as follows:

$$\overline{X} = \frac{\sum_i V_i R_i X_i}{\sum_i V_i R_i}$$

(13-5)

and

$$\overline{Y} = \frac{\sum_i V_i R_i Y_i}{\sum_i V_i R_i}$$

(13-6)

---

[10]These equations are derived from Equations (13-1) and (13-4) by taking the partial derivatives of TC with respect to X and Y, setting them equal to zero, and rearranging terms.

3. Using the solution for $\overline{X}, \overline{Y}$ from step 2, calculate d_i according to Equation (13-4). (The scaling factor K need not be used at this point.)
4. Substitute d_i into Equations (13-2) and (13-3), and solve for the revised $\overline{X}, \overline{Y}$ coordinates.
5. Recalculate d_i based on the revised $\overline{X}, \overline{Y}$ coordinates.
6. Repeat steps 4 and 5 until the $\overline{X}, \overline{Y}$ coordinates do not change for successive iterations, or they change so little that continuing the calculations is not fruitful.
7. Finally, calculate the total cost for the best location, if desired, by using Equation (13-1).

Example

Consider the problem of Limited Distributors, Inc., with two plants supplying the warehouse, which, in turn, supplies three demand centers. The spatial arrangement of the plants and market points is shown in Figure 13-4. We seek the location for the single warehouse that will minimize transportation costs. A grid overlay on a highway map is used as a convenience in establishing the relative point locations. Each plant and demand center location is expressed as a geometric coordinate point. Product A is supplied from P_1 and product B from P_2. These products are reshipped to the markets. Coordinate points, volumes, and transportation rates are summarized in Table 13-1.

Figure 13-4
Location Map of Plants P_1 and P_2 and Markets M_1, M_2, and M_3 and Suggested Warehouse Location

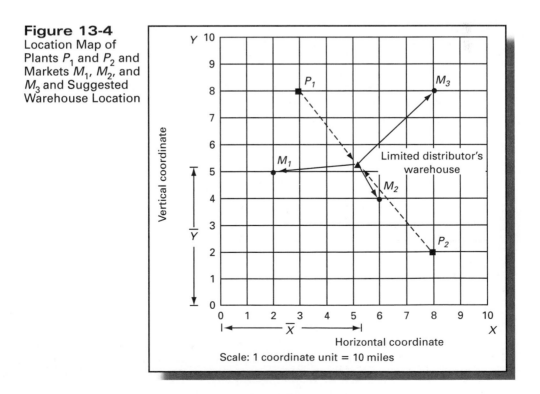

Point (I)	Product (s)	Total Volume Moving, V_I (cwt.)	Transportation Rate ($/cwt./mi.)[a]	Coordinates, X_I	Coordinates, Y_I
1-P_1	A	2,000	$0.050	3	8
2-P_2	B	3,000	0.050	8	2
3-M_1	A&B	2,500	0.075	2	5
4-M_2	A&B	1,000	0.075	6	4
5-M_3	A&B	1,500	0.075	8	8

[a]Determined by dividing a representative quoted rate ($/cwt.) by the distance (miles) over which the rate applies.

Table 13-1 Volume, Transportation Rates, and Coordinates for Market and Supply Points

Using Equations (13-5) and (13-6), we can find an initial, or approximate, location for the warehouse. Calculations are easy if we solve the equations in a tabular form. That is,

i	X_i	Y_i	V_i	R_i	V_iR_i	$V_iR_iX_i$	$V_iR_iY_i$
1	3	8	2,000	0.050	100.00	300.00	800.00
2	8	2	3,000	0.050	150.00	1200.00	300.00
3	2	5	2,500	0.075	187.50	375.00	937.50
4	6	4	1,000	0.075	75.00	450.00	300.00
5	8	8	1,500	0.075	112.50	900.00	900.00
					625.00	3,225.00	3,237.50

Now, we have

$$\overline{X} = 3{,}225.00/625.00 = 5.16$$

and

$$\overline{Y} = 3{,}237.50/625.00 = 5.18$$

These coordinates define the warehouse location, as shown in Figure 13-4. The total transportation cost associated with this location is determined in Table 13-2.

The previous example was terminated at step 2 of the solution process. This is an approximate solution. In many applications, it will provide a location that is reasonably close to the optimum. It will provide a first approximation to the least cost solution and will give an optimum when there is perfect symmetry in location, volume, and costs associated with the points. When these conditions are not fully met, research has shown that the potential error still can be quite small, if the volume associated with one or a few points is not substantially larger than the rest; there is a

Table 13-2
Calculation of Transportation Cost for Limited Distributors' Warehouse Location

i	X_i	Y_i	(4) V_i	(5) R_i	(6) d_i (MI.)[a]	(7) = (4) ×(5) ×(6) COST, $
1	3	8	2,000	0.050	35.52[b]	$ 3,552
2	8	2	3,000	0.050	42.64	6,395
3	2	5	2,500	0.075	31.65	5,935
4	6	4	1,000	0.075	14.48	1,086
5	8	8	1,500	0.075	40.02	4,503
			Total transportation cost			$21,471

[a] These distances have been rounded to the nearest 1/100 mile.

[b] From Equation (13-4), $d_i = 10\sqrt{(3 - 5.16)^2 + (8 - 5.18)^2} = 35.52$ mi.

large number of demand or supply points in the problem; and the transportation rates are linear, or nearly linear, with distance.[11] For example, a modest problem involving 50 demand points with randomly dispersed locations, volumes, and linear transportation rates had an average error of 1.6 percent from optimum when using this method. Of course, this error can increase substantially as the number of demand points is decreased.

Finding a more exact center-of-gravity solution requires completing the remaining steps in the solution process. We are not able to find the solution directly and must resort to an iterating procedure. A rather simple and straightforward method is that of successive approximations. Although there are others, this procedure serves us well in this application. It can be time-consuming for hand calculation, but lends itself nicely to computer solution.

Example

Continuing with the Limited Distributors' problem, we would now use the center-of-gravity solution as the starting solution in Equations (13-1) and (13-2) to find the exact location. The location coordinates for the first iteration can be found by solving the equations in the following tabular form, using results from the previous example.

i	(2) $V_i R_i$	(3) $V_i R_i X_i$	(4) $V_i R_i Y_i$	(5) d_i	(6) = (2)/(5) $V_i R_i / d_i$	(7) = (3)/(5) $V_i R_i X_i / d_i$	(8) = (4)/(5) $V_i R_i Y_i / d_i$
1	100.00	300.00	800.00	35.52	2.815	8.446	22.523
2	150.00	1,200.00	300.00	42.63	3.519	28.149	7.037
3	187.50	375.00	937.50	31.65	5.924	11.848	29.621
4	75.00	450.00	300.00	14.48	5.180	31.077	20.718
5	112.50	900.00	900.00	40.02	2.811	22.489	22.489
					20.249	102.009	102.388

[11]Ronald H. Ballou, "Potential Error in the Center of Gravity Approach to Facility Location," *Transportation Journal* (Winter 1973), pp. 44–49.

Table 13-3
One Hundred
Computational
Cycles of Location
Coordinates and
Total Transportation
Costs As Generated
from the COG
Software Module

ITERATION	$\overline{X}$ COORD.	$\overline{Y}$ COORD.	TOTAL COST, $	
0	5.160	5.180	21,471.00	⟸ Center of gravity
1	5.038	5.057	21,431.22	
2	4.990	5.031	21,427.11	
3	4.966	5.032	21,426.14	
4	4.951	5.037	21,425.69	
5	4.940	5.042	21,425.44	
6	4.932	5.046	21,425.30	
7	4.927	5.049	21,425.23	
8	4.922	5.051	21,425.19	
9	4.919	5.053	21,425.16	
10	4.917	5.054	21,425.15	
11	4.915	5.055	21,425.14	
.	.	.	.	
.	.	.	.	
.	.	.	.	
100	4.910	5.058	21,425.14	⟸ Exact solution

The revised location coordinate points can be calculated as

$$\overline{X} = 102.009/20.249 = 5.038$$

and

$$\overline{Y} = 102.388/20.249 = 5.057$$

with a total cost of $21,431.

Using the computer software module in LOGWARE known as COG, we can complete 100 iterations of this procedure. The results are given in Table 13-3. In this problem, note that the total cost does not decline further after the eleventh iteration, and there is little change in the location coordinates. This is the nature of this particular problem, but other problems may show dramatic differences.

Extensions to the Single Facility Location Model

The continuous location nature and simplicity of the exact center-of-gravity approach, given its appeal either as a location model unto itself or as a submodel in more elaborate methods, has encouraged researchers to extend its capability. Primary among these extensions are to include customer service and revenues,[12] to handle multiple locations,[13] and to represent nonlinear transportation costs.[14]

---

[12]See Donald J. Bowersox, "An Analytical Approach to Warehouse Location," *Handling & Shipping*, vol. 2 (February 1962), pp. 17–20; and Ronald H. Ballou, *Business Logistics Management*, 2nd ed. (Upper Saddle River, NJ: Prentice Hall, 1985), pp. 311–314.
[13]See Allan E. Hall, "Program Finds New Sites in Multi-Facility Location Problem," *Industrial Engineering* (May 1988), pp. 71–74; and Ballou, *Business Logistics Management*, pp. 316–323.
[14]Leon Cooper, "An Extension of the Generalized Weber Problem," *Journal of Regional Science*, Vol. 8, No. 2 (1968), pp. 181–197.

Appraisal of Single Facility Location

In addition to the center-of-gravity model, other single facility location approaches include graphical techniques[15] and approximating methods.[16] All vary in the degree of realism that they portray, in their speed and ease of computation, and in their ability to guarantee an optimum solution. Clearly, no single model is likely to have all of the features desired for a particular location problem so that the solution will lead directly to a final decision and management can merely delegate location decisions to an analyst. Therefore, these models can only provide solution guidelines and their effective use requires a good understanding of their strengths as well as their shortcomings.

The benefit of these single location models is quite clear—they aid the search for the best solution to a location problem, and they capture enough of the reality of the actual problem so that the solution is meaningful to management. The shortcomings may not be so obvious, and they need to be noted. Although any model will exhibit some shortcomings when applied to a real problem, this does not mean that the model is not useful. What is important is the sensitivity of the location model's results to a poor representation of reality. If a simplifying assumption, such as linearity in transportation rates, has little or no effect on a model's suggestion for a facility location, a simpler model may well prove to be more effective than elegant ones.

Some of the simplifying assumptions in single location models are listed next.

1. Demand volumes are frequently assumed concentrated at one point, when in fact they are generated from a number of customer points that are dispersed over a wide area. The market center of gravity is often used as the demand cluster, but this is subject to some error in calculating transportation costs to the demand cluster instead of to individual demand points.
2. Single facility location models typically find a location based on variable costs. They make no distinction between the differences in capital cost required for establishing a warehouse at various locations and other costs such as labor, inventory-carrying costs, and utilities associated with operating a facility at different locations.
3. Total transportation costs usually are assumed to increase proportionately with distance; however, most transport rates are composed of a fixed component and a variable component that varies with distance. Rate minimums and rate blanketing may further distort their linearity.
4. Straight-line routes are commonly assumed between the facility and other network points. This is rarely true, since travel is over a defined road network, established rail system, or through a rectilinear city street network. A proportionality factor can be included in the model to convert straight-line distances to approximate highway miles, rail miles, or whatever. This conversion factor, called a *circuity factor*, varies by location. For U.S. intercity transport, calculated straight-line miles should be increased by 20 percent to get highway direct-

---

[15]Alfred Weber, *Uber den Standort der Industrien*.
[16]G. O. Wesolowsky and R. F. Love, "A Nonlinear Approximation Method for Solving a Generalized Rectangular Distance Weber Problem," *Management Science*, Vol. 18(1972), pp. 656–663.

route miles and by 24 percent to get rail short-line miles. For city streets, a factor of 41 to 44 percent can be used. A table of circuity factors for truck travel in different countries is given in Chapter 14.

5. There is some concern that location models such as these are not dynamic. That is, they do not find a solution that reflects future changes in revenues and costs.

Applications

- Leaseway Transportation Corporation was able to make use of the exact center-of-gravity model to locate a truck maintenance facility in Boston. The company leased varying numbers of trucks to many accounts throughout the Boston metropolitan area. The truck maintenance facility was to be located for maximum convenience of all accounts. The location of each account and the number of trucks leased was known. The transportation rate was the same throughout the region. The center-of-gravity model gave the general location within which a specific site could be selected.

- An oil company used the center-of-gravity method to locate oil collection platforms in the Gulf of Mexico. Many wellheads were located throughout the floor of the Gulf. A group of these was connected using pipe that moved the oil to a collection platform on the surface. The center-of-gravity method was appropriate for finding the collection platform location that would minimize the total length of pipe needed.

MULTIPLE FACILITY LOCATION

The more complex, yet more realistic, location problem for most firms occurs when two or more facilities must be located simultaneously, or additional facilities are to be located when at least one already exists. This problem is common because all but the smallest companies have more than one facility in their logistics systems. It is complex because these facilities cannot reasonably be treated as economically independent, and the number of possible location configurations becomes enormous.

Observation

A few years ago, a company producing industrial cleaning compounds sold its products in approximately 2,000 U.S. counties, used 105 public warehouses, and manufactured its products in four plants. There were more than 800,000 possible plant-warehouse-customer combinations to be considered among only the existing locations. Finding an optimum warehouse configuration was further complicated by the several hundred product items sold and several modes of transportation used.

Let us direct our attention to the warehouse location problem as a general class, since it is a common problem experienced by many kinds of businesses. It can be characterized by several basic planning questions:

1. How many warehouses should there be in the supply chain network? How large should they be, and where should they be located?
2. Which demand points should be assigned to a warehouse? Which warehouses should be assigned to each plant, vendor, or port?
3. Which products should be stocked in each warehouse? Which products should be shipped directly from plants, vendors, or ports to customers?

A number of location methods have been developed that aid in answering some or all of these questions. Several of these, although by no means an exhaustive selection, are presented here to show the variety and power of the approaches. Mathematical location methods may be categorized as exact, simulation, and heuristic.

Exact Methods

Exact methods refer to those procedures with the capability to guarantee either a mathematically optimum solution to the location problem, or at least a solution of known accuracy. In many respects, this is an ideal approach to the problem of location; however, the approach can result in long computer running times, huge memory requirements, and a compromised problem definition when applied to practical problems. Calculus[17] and mathematical programming models are examples of this approach, and both will be illustrated.

Multiple Center-of-Gravity Approach

The nature of the multiple facility location problem is seen if we use the exact center-of-gravity approach in a multilocation format. Recall that this is a calculus-based model that finds the minimum transportation cost solution for an intermediate facility located among origin and destination points. If more than one facility is to be located, then it is necessary to *assign* the origin and destination points to arbitrary locations. This forms clusters of points equal to the number of facilities being located. Then, an exact center-of-gravity location is found for each of the clusters. These assignments to the facilities can be made in many ways, especially when considering multiple facilities and a large number of origin and destination points in the problem. One approach is to form the clusters by grouping the points that are the closest to each other. After the center-of-gravity locations are found, the points are reassigned to these locations. New center-of-gravity locations are found for the revised clusters. The process is continued until there is no further change. This completes the computations for a specified number of facilities to be located. It can be repeated for different numbers of facilities.

---

[17]For other calculus models, see Edward H. Bowman and John B. Stewart, "A Model for Scale of Operations," *Journal of Marketing*, Vol. 20 (January 1956), pp. 242–247; and Arthur M. Geoffrion, "Making Better Use of Optimization Capability in Distribution System Planning," *AIIE Transactions*, Vol. 11, No. 2 (June 1978), pp. 96–108.

As the number of facilities is increased, it is quite common for transportation costs to decline. In trade-off with these decreasing transportation costs are the increases in the total fixed costs and system inventory carrying costs. The best solution is the one that minimizes the sum of all of these costs.

Although this method is optimal if all the ways of assigning points to clusters are evaluated, it becomes computationally impractical for realistic-size problems. Assigning many customers to even a small number of facilities is an enormous combinatorial task. Another approach is needed.

Mixed Integer Linear Programming

Mathematicians have labored for many years to develop efficient solution procedures that have a broad enough problem description to be of practical value in dealing with the large, complex location problem frequently encountered in supply chain network design and yet provide a mathematically optimum solution. They have experimented with the use of sophisticated management science techniques, either to enrich the analysis or to provide improved methods for solving this difficult problem optimally. These methods are goal programming,[18] tree search methods,[19] and dynamic programming,[20] among others.[21] Perhaps the most promising of this class is the mixed integer linear programming approach.[22] It is the most popular methodology used in commercial location models.[23]

The primary benefit associated with the mixed integer linear programming approach—a benefit not always offered by other methods—is its ability to handle fixed costs in an optimal way. The advantages of linear programming in dealing with the allocations of demand throughout the network, which is at the heart of such an approach, are well known. Although optimization is quite appealing, it does exact its price. Unless special characteristics of a particular problem are exploited, computer-running times can be long and memory requirements substantial. There is no guarantee that the optimal solution will be found unless all possible alternatives are evaluated. Even if the optimal solution is found, slight changes in the data can cause subsequent runs to require substantial computational time.

---

[18]Sang M. Lee and Richard L. Luebbe, "The Multi-Criteria Warehouse Location Problem Revisited," *International Journal of Physical Distribution and Materials Management*, Vol. 17, No. 3 (1987), pp. 56–59.
[19]U. Akinc and B. M. Khumawala, "An Efficient Branch and Bound Algorithm for the Capacitated Warehouse Location Problem," *Management Science*, Vol. 23 (1977), pp. 585–594.
[20]Robert F. Love, "One-Dimensional Facility Location-Allocation Using Dynamic Programming" *Management Science*, Vol. 23, No. 6 (January 1976), pp. 614–617.
[21]Recall the survey of location methods by Brandeau and Chiu, "An Overview of Representative Problems in Location Research."
[22]A. M. Geoffrion and G. W. Graves, "Multicommodity Distribution System Design by Benders Decomposition," *Management Science*, Vol. 20, No. 5 (January 1974), pp. 822–844; P. Bender, W. Northrup, and J. Shapiro, "Practical Modeling for Resource Management," *Harvard Business Review*, Vol. 59, No. 2 (March-April 1981), pp. 163–173; and Jeffrey J. Karrenbauer and Glenn W. Graves, "Integrated Logistics Systems Design" in James M. Masters and Cynthia L. Coykendale, eds., "Logistics Education and Research: A Global Perspective," *Proceedings of the Eighteenth Annual Transportation and Logistics Educators Conference* (St. Louis, MO: October 22, 1989), pp. 142–171.
[23]Ronald H. Ballou and James M. Masters, "Commercial Software for Locating Warehouses and Other Facilities," *Journal of Business Logistics*, Vol. 14, No. 2 (1993), pp. 71–107.

Warehouse location problems are presented in many variations. Researchers who have applied the integer programming approach have described one such warehouse location problem as follows:

There are several commodities produced at several plants with known production capacities. There is a known demand for each commodity at each of the number of customer zones. This demand is satisfied by shipping via warehouses, with each customer zone being assigned exclusively to a single warehouse. There are lower as well as upper limits on the allowable total annual throughput on each warehouse. The possible locations for the warehouses are given, but the particular sites to be used are to be selected so as to result in the least total distribution cost. The warehouse costs are expressed as fixed charges (imposed for the sites actually used) plus a linear variable charge. Transportation costs are taken as linear.

Thus, the problem is to determine which warehouse locations to use, what size warehouse to have at each selected location, what customer zones should be served by each warehouse, and what the pattern of transportation flows there should be for all commodities. This is to be done so as to meet the given demands at minimum total distribution cost, subject to plant capacity and warehouse configuration of the distribution system.[24]

In descriptive language, this problem can be expressed in the following manner:

Find the number, size, and locations of warehouses in a supply chain network that will minimize the fixed and linear variable costs of moving all products through the selected network subject to the following:

1. The available supply of the plants cannot be exceeded for each product.
2. The demand for all products must be met.
3. The throughput of each warehouse cannot exceed its capacity.
4. A minimum throughput of a warehouse must be achieved before it can be opened.
5. All products from the same customer must be served from the same warehouse.

The problem can be solved using general integer linear programming computer software packages. Historically, such practical problems were not solved, even with the most powerful computers. Researchers now apply such techniques as decomposing a multiproduct problem into as many subproblems as there are products, eliminating parts of the problem irrelevant to the solution, and approximating data relationships in forms that complement the solution approach in order to achieve acceptable computer running times and memory requirements. Today, researchers are claiming to be able to extend substantially the number of echelons in the network that can be modeled, include multiple periods in the model, and cautiously handle nonlinear cost functions.[25]

---

[24]Geoffrion and Graves, "Multicommodity Distribution System Design," p. 822.
[25]Karrenbauer and Graves, "Integrated Logistics System Design."

Example

Considering a small multiproduct problem and a standard integer programming software code, solving a location problem by integer programming can be illustrated. Suppose we have the problem as shown in Figure 13-5. There are two products demanded by three customers, but a customer can be served out of only one warehouse. There is a choice between two warehouses. Warehouse 1 has a handling cost of $2/cwt. of throughput; a fixed cost of $100,000 per year if held open; and a capacity of 110,000 cwt. per year. Warehouse 2 has a handling cost of $1/cwt., a fixed cost of $500,000; and an unlimited capacity. There is no minimum volume to keep a warehouse open. Two plants can be used to serve the warehouses. The plants may produce either product, but the production costs per cwt. differ for each product. Plant 1 has a product capacity constraint (60,000 cwt. for product 1 and 50,000 cwt. for product 2). Plant 2 has no capacity constraint for either product. Our task is to find which warehouse(s) should be used, how customer demand should be assigned to them, and which warehouses and their throughput should be assigned to the plants.

The problem formulation is shown in the Technical Supplement to this chapter. The problem is solved using the MIPROG module in LOGWARE. The solution is to open only warehouse 2 and to serve it from plant 2. The cost summary is

Category	Cost
Production	$1,020,000
Transportation	1,220,000
Warehouse handling	310,000
Warehouse fixed cost	500,000
Total	$3,050,000

Application

Digital Equipment Corporation evaluates global supply chain alternatives and determines worldwide manufacturing and distribution strategy using the global supply chain model (GSCM), which recommends a production, distribution, and vendor network. GSCM minimizes cost or weighted cumulative production and distribution times or both, subject to meeting estimated demand and restrictions on local content, offset trade, and joint capacity for multiple products, echelons, and periods. Cost factors include fixed and variable production charges, inventory charges, distribution expenses via multiple modes, taxes, duties, and duty drawback. GSCM is a large mixed integer linear program that incorporates a global, multiproduct bill of materials for supply chains with arbitrary echelon structure and a comprehensive model of integrated global manufacturing and distribution decisions. The supply chain structuring has saved over $100 million.[26]

[26]Bruce C. Arntzen, Gerald G. Brown, Terry P. Harrison, and Linda L. Trafton, "Global Supply Management at Digital Equipment Corporation," *Interfaces*, 25, No. 1 (January–February 1995), pp. 69–93.

Figure 13-5 A Small Multiproduct Warehouse Location Problem for Mixed Integer Linear Programming

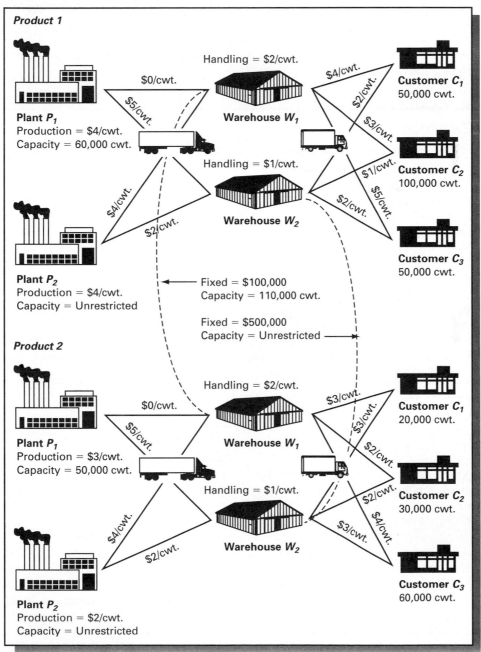

Another location method that utilizes mixed integer programming is a modified *p-median* approach. It is less complicated and less robust than the previous formulation. Demand and supply points are located by means of coordinate points. Facilities are restricted to be among the demand or supply points. The costs affecting location are variable transportation rates expressed in units as $/cwt./mi. and the annual fixed costs associated with the candidate facilities. The number of facilities to be located is specified before solution. The solution process finds this specified number among the candidate facilities.

Example

Environment Plus incinerates toxic chemicals used in various manufacturing processes. These chemicals are moved from 12 market areas around the country to its incinerators for disposal. The company provides the transportation due to the special equipment and handling procedures required. Transportation services are contracted at a cost of $1.30 per mile and the trucks are fully loaded at 300 cwt. Trips are out and back from an incinerator. Therefore, the effective transport rate is $1.30/mi. ×2 / 300 cwt. = $0.0087/cwt./mi. The market locations, annual processing volume, and annual fixed operating costs, regardless of throughput volume, are shown in Table 13-4.

The metropolitan areas of Baltimore, Memphis, and Minneapolis will not permit the incinerators, and therefore are not candidate locations. If five locations are to be used, which should they be?

The PMED software module in LOGWARE can help to solve this problem. A database for this problem is available as PMED02.DAT. The results show the preferred locations to minimize the cost.

Table 13-4
Market Location, Volume, and Cost Data for Environment Plus

No.	Market	Annual Latitude,°	Fixed Longitude,°	Volume, cwt.	Operating Cost, $
	Boston MA	42.36	71.06	30,000	3,100,000
	New York NY	40.72	74.00	50,000	3,700,000
2	Atlanta GA	33.81	84.63	170,000	1,400,000
	Baltimore MD	39.23	76.53	120,000	—
1	Cincinnati OH	39.14	84.51	100,000	1,700,000
	Memphis TN	35.11	89.96	90,000	—
	Chicago IL	41.84	87.64	240,000	2,900,000
	Minneapolis MN	44.93	93.20	140,000	—
3	Phoenix AZ	33.50	112.07	230,000	1,100,000
4	Denver CO	39.77	105.00	300,000	1,500,000
	Los Angeles CA	34.08	118.37	40,000	2,500,000
5	Seattle WA	47.53	122.32	20,000	1,250,000

No.	Facility Name	Volume	Assigned Node Numbers					
1	Cincinnati OH	680,000	1	2	4	5	7	8
2	Atlanta GA	260,000	3	6				
3	Phoenix AZ	270,000	9	11				
4	Denver CO	300,000	10					
5	Seattle WA	20,000	12					
	Total	1,530,000						

Total cost: $9,455,339

A map of the solution is shown in Figure 13-6.

Mixed integer linear programming has great appeal as a methodology, but the potentially long solution times of the method to handle large-scale location problems remains bothersome, although faster computers have helped. In addition, the difficulty of handling nonlinear functions as may occur in inventory policies, transportation rates, and sales and customer service relationships allows other approaches to remain competitive with mixed integer linear programming.

Simulation Methods

Although it may appear that location models providing mathematically optimum solutions are best, it should be remembered that the optimum solution to the

Figure 13-6 Plot of the Solution Results for the Environment Plus Location Problem

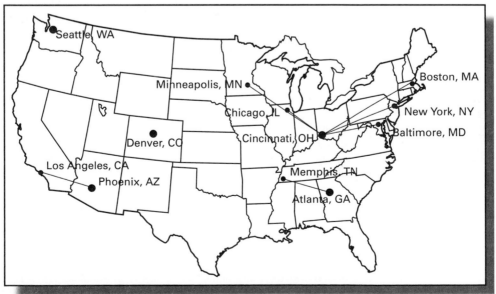

real-world location problem is no better than the model's description of the problem realities. In addition, such optimizing models are often difficult to understand and require technical skills that many managers do not possess. Therefore, proponents who demand that an accurate problem description be of the highest priority often rely on simulation as the planning method of choice. They prefer to risk finding an improved but suboptimum solution to an accurately described problem, rather than an optimum solution to an approximate problem description.

A simulation facility-location model refers to a mathematical representation of a logistics system by algebraic and logic statements that can be manipulated with the aid of a computer. Given a realistic representation of the economic and statistical relationships, the simulation model is used to evaluate the impact of various configurations. Simulation models are unlike algorithmic location models in that the analyst or manager must specify the particular facilities in the network to be evaluated. Whether optimal or nearly optimal location patterns are uncovered depends on the particular warehouses and the allocations to them that are selected for evaluation. Whereas algorithmic models search for the best number, location, and size of the facilities, a simulation model attempts to find the best network through repeated application of the model, given different warehouse and allocation pattern choices. The quality of the results and the efficiency with which they are obtained depend on the skill and insight of the user in selecting the locations to be analyzed.

Application

A now classic simulation model for warehouse location purposes was developed for the H. J. Heinz Company and later applied to the distribution problems of the Nestlé Company.[27] The simulation provided answers to the basic warehouse location questions (number, location, allocation of demand to warehouses, etc.) and could handle up to 4,000 customers, 40 warehouses, and 10 to 15 factories. Contrasted with many algorithmic models, this simulation has a broad problem scope. The major distribution cost elements in the Heinz Company simulation were

1. *Customers.* The characteristics of the customers that affect distribution costs are
   a. Customer location
   b. Annual volume of demand
   c. Types of products purchased. Different products fall into various commodity classifications and, therefore, will call for different freight rates. When there are regional variations in product mix, an average rate for all products will not do.
   d. The order size distribution. Different size shipments call for different freight rates.

---

[27]Harvey N. Shycon and Richard B. Maffei, "Simulation—Tool for Better Distribution," *Harvard Business Review*, Vol. 38, No. 6 (November–December 1960), pp. 65–75.

2. *Warehouses.* The characteristics of the warehouses that affect costs are

   a. Fixed investment in company-owned warehouses. Some companies prefer public warehousing, implying a relatively small fixed investment.
   b. Fixed annual operation and administrative costs.
   c. Variable costs of storing, handling, stock rotation, and data processing.

3. *Factories.* The location of the factories and the products available at each factory are the elements that most affect distribution costs. Certain warehousing and handling charges at the factory may be properly attributable to distribution costs, but insofar as these costs are largely independent of the warehouse configuration, they may be excluded from the analysis.

4. *Transportation costs.* The freight costs of moving product from factory to warehouse are termed transportation costs. These depend on the location of the factory and warehouse involved, the size of the shipment, and the commodity classification of the product.

5. *Delivery costs.* The costs of moving the product from warehouse to customer, termed delivery costs, depend upon the size of shipment, the location of the warehouse and customer, and the commodity classification of the product.[28]

Processing of the input data was handled in two parts. First, a preprocessing program separated customer orders that could be filled via a warehouse from those orders that were sufficiently large to be economically filled from a plant. Next, the test, or main, program computed distances from customers to warehouses and plants to warehouses from a longitude and latitude coordinate system.[29] Customers were assigned to warehouses by examining the five closest warehouses and then selecting the warehouse offering the least cost in terms of delivery costs from warehouse to customer, handling and storage costs at the warehouse, and transportation costs from plant to warehouse. The computer then performed the necessary computations to evaluate a particular warehouse configuration, given the assigned product flows through the warehouse system and geographic data read into the test program. A linear programming approach was used to resolve any capacity limitations at the factories. Many warehouse location configurations were evaluated. Figure 13-7 is a flow diagram of the model's operation.

Simulation models continue to play an important role in warehouse location. They are often written primarily as inventory simulators (LREPS[30] and PIPELINE MANAGER[31]), but others are developed more directly to be warehouse locators.[32] A

[28]Martin L. Gerson and Richard B. Maffei, "Technical Characteristics of Distribution Simulators," *Management Science*, Vol. 10 (October 1963), pp. 62–69.
[29]This coordinate system limits errors between actual and computed distances to about 2 percent.
[30]Donald J. Bowersox, "Planning Physical Distribution with Dynamic Simulation," *Journal of Marketing*, Vol. 36 (January 1972), pp. 17–25.
[31]Robert Sloan, "Integrated Tools for Managing the Total Pipeline," *Annual Conference Proceedings* (Chicago: Council of Logistics Management, 1989), pp. 93–108.
[32]Donald B. Rosenfield and William C. Copacino, "Logistics Planning and Evaluation Using 'What-If' Simulation," *Journal of Business Logistics*, Vol. 6, No. 2 (1985), pp. 89–109.

Figure 13-7
Flow Chart for a
Warehouse Location
Simulation
Developed for the
H. J. Heinz Company

Source: Harvey N.
Shycon and Richard B.
Maffei, "Simulation—
Tool for Better
Distribution," *Harvard
Business Review,* Vol. 38
(November–December
1960),
p. 73.

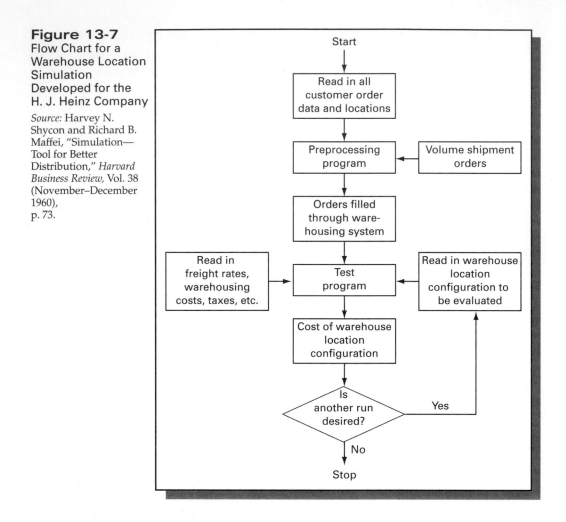

desirable feature inherent in them is their ability to handle time-related aspects of inventory along with the geographical aspects of location. On the other hand, massive data requirements and long computer-running times can be a problem for this methodology. Nevertheless, the precise descriptions of reality are the primary reasons for their appeal.

A major problem with location simulators is that the user may not know how close the chosen warehouse configurations are to the optimum. Of course, we do know that the total cost curve for the location problem usually has a "flat bottom." Therefore, costs between closely ranked alternatives change little in the region of the optimum. As long as a reasonable number of prudently selected configurations have been evaluated, we can have a high degree of confidence that at least a satisfactory solution has been found.

Heuristic Methods

Heuristics can be referred to as any principles or concepts that contribute to reducing the average time to search for a solution. They are sometimes referred to as *rules of thumb* that guide problem solving. When applied to problems of location, such rules of thumb, which are a consequence of insight into the solution process, allow good solutions to be obtained quickly from numerous alternatives. Although heuristic methods do not guarantee that an optimum solution has been found, the benefits of reasonable computer running times and memory requirements, a good representation of reality, and a satisfactory solution quality are reasons to consider the heuristic approach to warehouse location.

Heuristic methods have been popular as a methodology for warehouse location. A classic yet still useful heuristic approach to the warehouse location problem was developed by Kuehn and Hamburger.[33] Other examples abound.[34] To help understand a heuristic model type for realistic problems, consider the nature of the location problem typically encountered in practice.

The location problem is one of trading off the costs relevant to location, which include

- Production and purchase costs
- Warehouse storage and handling costs
- Warehouse fixed costs
- Cost for carrying inventory
- Stock order and customer order processing costs
- Warehouse inbound and outbound transportation costs

Each of these cost categories should reflect geographic differences, volume and shipping characteristics, policy variations, and economies of scale.

The nature of the cost trade-offs is graphically shown in Figure 13-8. Inventory, storage, and fixed costs are in direct trade-off with inbound and outbound transportation costs. Production and order processing costs also enter into the cost trade-off, but they cannot be adequately shown in this particular figure. The task of a location model is to seek out the warehouse/plant configuration that results in the minimum total relevant cost, subject to customer service and other practical restrictions placed on the problem.

Figure 13-8 shows that transportation costs decline with the number of warehouses in the distribution system. This is generally true because inbound shipments to a warehouse are made in larger quantities, and at lower rates, than outbound

---

[33]A. A. Kuehn and M. J. Hamburger, "A Heuristic Program for Locating Warehouses," *Management Science*, Vol. 10 (July 1963), pp. 643–666.
[34]Brandeau and Chiu, "An Overview of Representative Problems in Location Research," pp. 666–667; and Ronald H. Ballou and James M. Masters, "Commercial Software for Locating Warehouses and Other Facilities," *Journal of Business Logistics*, Vol. 14, No. 2 (1993).

Figure 13-8
Generalized Cost
Trade-Offs in the
Facility Location
Problem

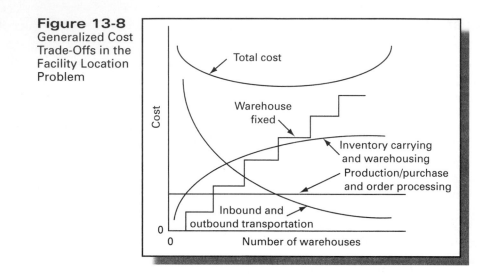

shipments. As more warehouses are put into the system, the warehouses are closer to customers, such that the inbound cost is increased but the outbound cost is disproportionately reduced. The transportation cost curve continues to decline in this manner until so many warehouses are used in the network that it is no longer practical to maintain full vehicle-load shipments to all warehouses. The transportation curve would turn up at this point.

The inventory-carrying and warehousing cost curve is shown to increase at a decreasing rate as the number of warehouses in the network increases. This is primarily a result of the inventory policy of a firm, as well as how that policy is executed, and the increasing amount of fixed cost in the network. With more warehouses, there is a proliferation of the amount of safety stock in the network. If the firm is controlling inventories by means of economical order quantity procedures, a tapered average inventory level and inventory-carrying cost curve results. Other policies may result in somewhat different inventory-carrying and warehousing cost curves, ranging from linear to tapered.[35] If the warehouses are privately owned or leased, there will be an annual fixed charge per warehouse. Total fixed costs in the network then will increase with the number of warehouses.

Selective Evaluation

A heuristic procedure can be developed from a method that has already been presented in this chapter, namely the multiple center-of-gravity method. The procedure is to solve for a specified number of facilities. Since the method only accounts for transportation costs, additional costs such as inventory and facility fixed costs may be added to create a more representative total cost. By repeating the procedure for various numbers of facilities, the best number of facilities, and their associated locations, can be found.

---

[35]Ronald H. Ballou, "Estimating and Auditing Aggregate Inventory Levels at Multiple Stocking Points," *Journal of Operations Management*, Vol. 1, No. 3 (February 1981), pp. 143–153.

Example

Suppose we have data for ten markets and their corresponding transportation rates, as given in file MCOG01.DAT of the LOGWARE software. The markets are shown in Figure 13-9. In addition, there is an annual fixed charge of $2,000,000 for each warehouse. All warehouses have enough capacity to handle the entire market demand. The amount of inventory in the logistics system is estimated from $I_T(\$) = \$6,000,000 \sqrt{N}$, where N is the number of warehouses in the network. Inventory-carrying costs are 25 percent per year. Handling rates at the warehouses are all the same; therefore, they do not affect the location outcome. How many warehouses should there be, where should they be located, and which markets should be assigned to each warehouse?

Using the MULTICOG software module in LOGWARE and repeatedly solving for various numbers of warehouse, a spreadsheet can be developed as shown in Table 13-5.

Four warehouses yield the best cost balance. As seen in Figure 13-9, warehouses should be located in markets 3, 7, 9, and 10. Markets 2, 3, 4, and 5 are assigned to the warehouse at 3; markets 1, 6, and 7 are assigned to the warehouse at 7; markets 8 and 9 are assigned to the warehouse at 9; and market 10 is assigned to the warehouse at 10.

Figure 13-9
Markets for Example Problem and a Solution with Four Warehouses

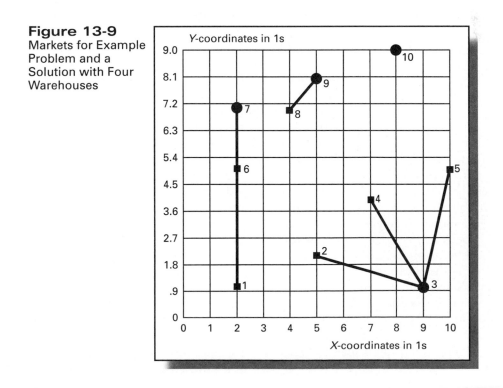

Table 13-5
Selection
Evaluation Location
Alternatives

NUMBER OF WAREHOUSES	TRANSPORTATION COST, $	FIXED COST, $	INVENTORY COST, $	TOTAL COST, $	
1	41,409,628	2,000,000	1,500,000	44,909,628	
2	25,989,764	4,000,000	2,121,320	32,111,084	
3	16,586,090	6,000,000	2,598,076	25,184,166	
4	11,368,330	8,000,000	3,000,000	**22,368,330**	←
5	9,418,329	10,000,000	3,354,102	22,772,431	
6	8,032,399	12,000,000	3,674,235	23,706,634	
7	7,478,425	14,000,000	3,968,627	25,447,052	
8	2,260,661	16,000,000	4,242,641	22,503,302	
9	948,686	18,000,000	4,500,000	23,448,686	
10	0	20,000,000	4,743,416	24,743,416	

The selection evaluation approach is heuristic for several reasons. First, the multiple center-of-gravity method includes some rules that are used to determine initial warehouse locations. This may cause sub-optimality in the results. Second, fixed costs and inventory costs are added to transportation costs *after* the warehouse locations are determined. It is preferred that these costs combine *during* the process that determines warehouse location for more optimal results. Regardless of its shortcomings, the approach has value when there is a minimum of information available to solve a location problem. It is useful in generating candidate locations that may be more thoroughly evaluated using procedures that are more robust.

Another form of selective evaluation specifies the number of warehouses to be evaluated and the particular warehouses in that number. Although the overall analysis is similar to that just presented using the center-of-gravity method, the analyst uses human judgment, logic, cognitive skills, and results from other model types to select the warehouses for evaluation. Since models seeking the optimum cannot hope to consider all the factors necessary for finding a satisfactory network design, this type of what-if analysis becomes very useful for practical network design. Linear programming is commonly used to allocate demand throughout the specified network. Choosing specific warehouses for evaluation is an effective way of dealing with practical issues in network design and making sure that desired warehouse combinations are considered. Most location analyses are dominated by selective evaluation of this type.

Selective evaluation may be used in solving location problems where the model used in the analysis is not primarily of a location nature. A common problem of this type is the location of a truck depot from which trucks are dispatched. Multiple trucks are routed to multiple stop-off points, and the route configuration is dependent on the location of the depot in proximity to the stop-off points. Depot location is dominated by transportation costs such that solving the truck routing problem is critical to depot location. A vehicle routing model such as ROUTER in LOGWARE can be used to form routes and minimize transportation cost. Then, selecting a particular depot location, solving the routing problem for the selected location, and

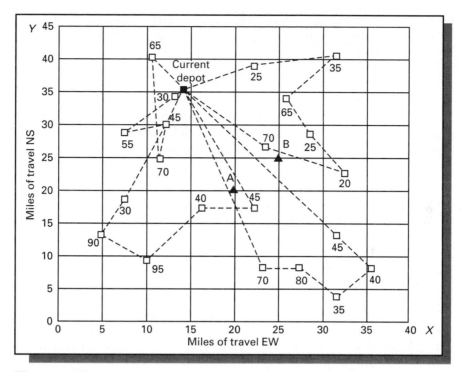

Figure 13-10 Current Depot Location with Stop Volumes in Cwt and Truck Routes

adding costs specific to the location allow each location to be evaluated. This is a trial-and-error procedure, and a satisfactory solution to the location problem depends on the quality of the locations selected for evaluation.

Example

A restaurant supply house makes deliveries to its customers (restaurants) on a daily basis. Currently, four trucks are dispatched on routes from a depot located in a city as shown in Figure 13-10 for a typical day's delivery volume. Considering that the trucks are amortized at a cost of $20 per day per truck, gas and maintenance costs to operate each truck are $0.40 per mile, and drivers are paid $11 per hour for wages and benefits, the current daily cost to serve the customers is $508. The company is considering a move to one of two central locations indicated in Figure 13-10 as A and B. The facility operating costs are expected to be about the same, but the amortized one-time moving cost is estimated as $40 per day. Using the ROUTER program in LOGWARE to generate routes from depots at A and B gives the revised transportation costs. Comparing the three alternatives on a daily cost basis, we have:

Location	Number of Trucks	Routing Cost	Truck Cost	Moving Cost	Total daily Cost
Current	4	$508	80	—	$588
A	5	497	100	40	637
B	4	484	80	40	604

Since the savings in routing costs cannot overcome the cost of moving to a new location, the economic decision is to keep the depot at the current location.

Guided Linear Programming

When serious heuristic procedures are developed for real-world location problems, they generally will include linear programming as part of the solution methodology. The appeal is that linear programming gives optimal results and can handle capacity restrictions that elude many other approaches. However, to be a truly robust procedure for location, fixed costs and nonlinear inventory costs need to be handled as well. Heuristic procedures need to be employed with linear programming to create an effective model.

Consider the small, single product problem shown in Figure 13-11. The first step is to construct a matrix that is formatted like the transportation problem of linear programming. By giving it a special structure, two logistics network echelons can be

Figure 13-11 A Single-Product Location Problem with Warehouse Fixed Costs and Inventory Costs

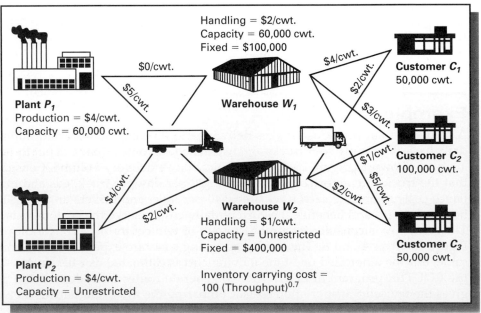

		Warehouses		Customers			Plant and warehouse capacities
		W_1	W_2	C_1	C_2	C_3	
Plants	P_1	4[a] 60,000	9	99[b]	99	99	60,000
	P_2	8	6 140,000	99	99	99	999,999[c]
Warehouses	W_1	0	99	9.7[d]	8.7 60,000	10.7	60,000
	W_2	99[b]	0	8.2[e] 50,000	7.2 40,000	8.2 50,000	999,999[c]
Warehouse capacity and customer demand		60,000	999,999[c]	50,000	100,000	50,000	

[a] Production plus inbound transport rates, that is, 4 + 0 = 4.
[b] Used to represent an infinitely high cost.
[c] Used to represent unlimited capacity.
[d] Inventory carrying, warehousing, outbound transportation, and fixed rates, that is, 3.2 + 2 + 4 + 0.5 = 9.7.
[e] 3.2 + 1 + 2 + 2.0 = 8.2.

Figure 13-12 Matrix of Cell Costs and Solution Values for the First Iteration in the Example Problem

represented in the matrix of Figure 13-12. The heuristic process is guided by the manner in which the cell costs are entered into the matrix. Since the production and transportation costs between plants and warehouses are linear, they enter the plant-warehouse cells directly. For example, the cell cost representing the flow between P_2 and W_1 is the production plus transportation costs, or $4/cwt. + $4/cwt. = $8/cwt.

The cellblock for warehouses and customers combines warehouse handling plus transportation plus inventory-carrying plus fixed costs. Handling and transportation rates can be read directly from Figure 13-11. However, there are no *rates* for inventory-carrying and fixed costs, and they must be developed, depending on each warehouse's throughput. Since this throughput is not known, we must assume starting throughputs. For fixed costs, each warehouse is initially given the most favorable status by assuming that all demand flows through it. Thus, the rate associated with fixed costs for warehouse 1 would be the annual warehouse fixed cost divided by the total customer demand, or $100,000/200,000 = $0.50/cwt. For warehouse 2, it is $400,000/200,000 = $2.00/cwt.

For inventory-carrying costs, the per cwt. rate depends on the number of warehouses and the demand assigned to them. Again, to give each warehouse the greatest opportunity to be selected, the assumed throughput for the warehouses is equal, or the throughput for each warehouse is the total customer demand divided by the number of warehouses being evaluated. The "per unit" inventory-carrying cost is defined as the average inventory value in a warehouse divided by the warehouse period throughput, or $IC_i = K(\text{Throughput}_i)^a/\text{Throughput}_i$. Initially for each warehouse, the per cwt. inventory carrying cost is

$$100[(200,000/2)^{0.7}]/(200,000/2) = \$3.2/\text{cwt.}$$

with "Total customer demand" labeling the numerator term and "Number of warehouses" labeling the denominator term.

The estimated per unit fixed and inventory-carrying costs are now entered into the warehouse-customer cells of the matrix of Figure 13-12. The problem is solved in a normal manner using the TRANLP module of LOGWARE. The computational results are shown as the bold values in Figure 13-12. This now completes round one of the computations.

Subsequent computational rounds utilize warehouse throughputs from its previous round to improve upon the estimate of the per unit inventory-carrying and fixed costs for a warehouse. To make these estimates, we note from the solution that the throughput for W_1 is 60,000 cwt. and for W_2 it is 140,000 cwt. (see Figure 13-12). The allocated costs for the warehouses are

Warehouse	Per Unit Fixed Cost, $/cwt.	Per Unit Inventory Carrying Cost, $/cwt.
W_1	$\$100,000/60,000$ cwt. $= 1.67$	$\$100(60,000 \text{ cwt.})^{0.7}/60,000$ cwt. $= 3.69$
W_2	$\$400,000/140,000$ cwt. $= 2.86$	$\$100(140,000 \text{ cwt.})^{0.7}/140,000$ cwt. $= 2.86$

The cell costs in the matrix for warehouses to customers (see Figure 13-12) are recalculated to be:

	C_1	C_2	C_3
W_1	11.36[a]	10.36	12.36
W_2	8.72[b]	7.72	8.72

[a] $2 + 4 + 1.67 + 3.69 = 11.36$
[b] $1 + 2 + 2.86 + 2.86 = 8.72$

The remaining cells are unaltered. Now, solve the problem again.

The second iteration solution shows that all production is at plant 2 and all demand is to be served from warehouse 2. That is,

	C_1	C_2	C_3	
W_1	0	0	0	
W_2	50,000	100,000	50,000	← Produced at plant 2

Subsequent iterations repeat the second iteration solution, since the allocation of inventory and fixed costs remain unchanged. A stopping point has been reached. To find the solution costs, recalculate them from the actual costs in the problem. Do not use the cell costs of Figure 13-12, since they contain the estimated values for warehouse fixed and inventory-carrying costs. Rather, compute costs as follows using the rates from Figure 13-11.

Cost Type	Warehouse 1 0 cwt.	Warehouse 2 200,000 cwt.	
Production	$0	$200,000 \times 4$	$= \$800,000$
Inbound transportation	0	$200,000 \times 2$	$= 400,000$
Outbound transportation	0	$50,000 \times 2$	$= 100,000$
		$100,000 \times 1$	$= 100,000$
		$50,000 \times 2$	$= 100,000$
Fixed	0		$400,000$
Inventory carrying	0	$100(200,000)^{0.7} =$	$513,714$
Handling	0	$200,000 \times 1$	$= 200,000$
Subtotal	$0	$2,613,714$	
Total		$2,613,714$	

The previous example illustrates a heuristic procedure for a single product. However, many practical location problems require that multiple products be included in the computational procedure. With slight modification where fixed costs for a warehouse are shared among the products according to their warehouse throughput, the guided linear programming procedure can be extended to handle multiple product case.[36]

Appraisal of Multiple Facility Location Methods

Large-scale, multiple facility location models are impressive in the decision-making assistance that they provide a manager. Applications have ranged from large supply and distribution networks involving more than 100 warehouses, 20 product groups, 15 plants, and 300 customer demand zones to supply networks where hundreds of vendors supply a master warehouse that in turn supplies customers. Defense, retail, consumer goods, and industrial goods industries operating in both domestic and international environments have applied models of this scale. The primary reasons for location modelings' popularity are (1) they offer decision support to solving a problem of great consequence to management; (2) they are sufficiently robust to replicate a wide variety of logistics networks in acceptable detail for planning purposes; (3) they are inexpensive to apply, such that the benefits derived from their use far exceed their application cost; and (4) the data required by them are readily obtainable in most firms. These models have come a long way in representing reality since the early models of the land economists.

---

[36]Ronald H. Ballou, "DISPLAN: A Multiproduct Plant/Warehouse Location Model with Nonlinear Inventory Costs," *Journal of Operations Management*, Vol. 5, No. 1 (November 1984), pp. 75–80.

However, these models are not yet all they can be.[37] First, nonlinear and discontinuous cost relationships observed in inventory policies, transportation rate structures, and production and purchasing economies of scale continue to present mathematical difficulties in dealing with them accurately or efficiently. Second, facility location models should be expanded to deal more effectively with inventory and transportation decisions[38] simultaneously; that is, they should be truly integrated network planning models rather than requiring each problem to be dealt with in a separate, approximate way. Third, more attention should be given to incorporating revenue effects into the network design process, since the result generally is to recommend more warehouses than when customer service is treated as a constraint and costs are minimized.[39] Fourth, the models should be made readily accessible to managers and planners so that they may be used frequently for tactical planning and budgeting rather than just for occasional strategic planning purposes. This will require closer ties to the firm's management information system so that the data to run them can be supplied immediately and in the form needed for model use.

Overall, each of these models, although they vary in terms of scope and solution procedures, can be used by the skilled analyst or manager to give valuable results. Making the existing technology easier to use and more accessible to the decision makers is a future direction in which development must move.

DYNAMIC WAREHOUSE LOCATION[40]

The location models discussed so far represent the type of sophisticated research that is being conducted to assist logisticians in solving practical warehouse location problems. Although many improvements have made the models more representative and computationally efficient, they remain essentially static in nature. That is, they do not provide optimal location patterns over time.

Demand and cost patterns shift over time, so implementing a location model's solution based on today's data may prove to be suboptimal under tomorrow's economic conditions. Optimal network configuration is a matter of changing from one configuration to another throughout a planning horizon to maintain an optimal

---

[37]Ronald H. Ballou, "Unresolved Issues in Supply Chain Network Design" *Information Systems Frontiers*, Vol. 3, No. 4 (December 2001), pp. 417–425.
[38]For an example of transportation planning integration into location models, see Jossef Perl and Mark S. Daskin, "A Unified Warehouse Location-Routing Methodology," *Journal of Business Logistics*, Vol. 5, No. 1 (1984), pp. 92–111; and for inventory-holding costs integrated into location decisions, see Steven J. Erlebacher and Russell D. Meller, "The Interaction of Location and Inventory in Designing Distribution Systems," *IIE Transactions*, Vol. 32 (2000), pp. 155–166.
[39]Peng-Kuan Ho and Jossef Perl, "Warehouse Location under Service-Sensitive Demand," *Journal of Business Logistics*, Vol. 16, No. 1 (1995), pp. 133–162.
[40]This section is based on Ronald H. Ballou, "Dynamic Warehouse Location," *Journal of Marketing Research*, Vol. 5 (August 1968), pp. 271–276. Extensions to this work appear in D. Sweeney and R. L. Tatham, "An Improved Long-Run Model for Multiple Warehouse Location," *Management Science*, Vol. 22, No. 7 (March 1976), pp. 748–758; G. O. Wesolowsky and W. G. Truscott, "The Multi-Period Location-Allocation Problem with Relocation of Facilities," *Management Science*, Vol. 22 (1975), pp. 57–65; Tony Van Roy and Donald Erlenkotter, "A Dual-Based Procedure for Dynamic Facility Location," *Management Science*, Vol. 28, No. 10 (October 1982), pp. 1091–1105.

configuration over time. This is not simply the problem of finding the best number, sizes, and locations of warehouses in each of the years throughout the planning horizon. There is a cost to change from one configuration to another. If the network uses public warehouses, it may be practical to change the configuration frequently, since there is little cost associated with closing out the stocks in one warehouse and starting them up in another. On the other hand, if there is a substantial cost of moving from one configuration to another, as might be the case if the warehouses are owned or leased, changing the network configuration should not occur often. Thus, it becomes important to implement the best design initially.

Finding the best configurations over time can be handled in several ways. First, the best warehouse locations can be found using the current conditions and those projected for some future year. The network configurations between the current year and the future year can then be averaged.

Second, the best current network configuration can be found and implemented. Then, in each year, as it arrives and data become available for the year, the best new configuration is found. If the location savings between the new configuration and the previous one are greater than the costs associated with moving to the new configuration, the change should be considered. This method has the benefit of always working with actual data—not those that need to be forecasted.

Third, an optimal configuration path can be found over time that will precisely show when a change to a new configuration is needed and the configuration to which the change should be made. The methodologies that have already been discussed for static warehouse location can be incorporated into a dynamic programming procedure to find the optimal configuration path. A simple, single location problem can be used to illustrate the methodology.

Example

Suppose we have the problem as shown in Figure 13-13. A plant at Granville ships through a single warehouse to a number of markets at Arlington, Concordia, Stanton, Morton, and Chardon. It is projected that over time demand will increase and shift westward. The center-of-gravity locations for each year in the next five years are shown as points A, B, C, D, and E. The profits, discounted to the present, associated with each of these best locations, are given in Table 13-6. In addition, the discounted profits associated with locating in each of the other locations throughout the five years are also given. We know that it requires $100,000 to move from one location to another in any year. The cost of capital is 20 percent per year.

Finding the best location-relocation plan requires searching the profit table (Table 13-6) for the maximum profit path, after accounting for the appropriate moving charges. This is not an easy task, since, even for this small problem, there are $5^5 = 3125$ possible location-relocation plans. However, the technique of dynamic programming[41] can be applied here, and it will reduce the number of required

---

[41]For an introduction to dynamic programming, see Frederick S. Hillier, *Introduction to Operations Research*, 7th ed. (New York: McGraw-Hill, 2000), Chapter 10.

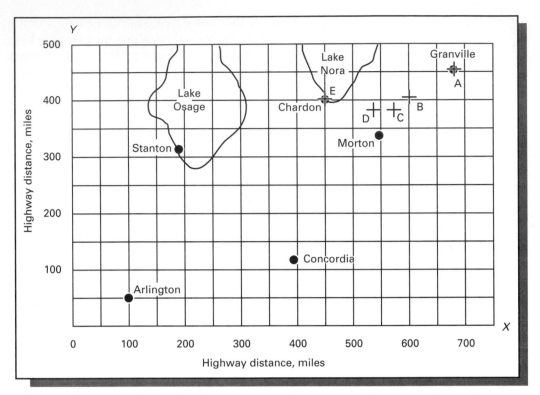

Figure 13-13 Plant-Market Location Map with Maximum-Profit Warehouse Location Points (+) for Each of Five Years

Table 13-6 Projected Discounted Profits for Each Location in Each Year of the Planning Horizon with Maximum Profits Along the Main Diagonal

WAREHOUSE LOCATION ALTERNATIVES	YEAR FROM PRESENT				
	1ST	2ND	3RD	4TH	5TH
A	$194,000[a]	$ 356,100	$ 623,200	$ 671,100	$1,336,000
B	176,500	372,000[a]	743,400	750,000	1,398,200
C	172,300	344,700	836,400[a]	862,200	1,457,600
D	166,700	337,600	756,100	973,300[a]	1,486,600
E	159,400	303,400	715,500	892,800	1,526,000[a]

[a]These alternatives are the maximum profit locations for each year of the planning horizon, as shown in Figure 13-13.

computations to find the optimum plan to $5 \times 5 = 25$. Dynamic programming permits us to recast this multi-period problem into a series of single-decision events.

Starting with the last year, we compute the profit associated with being in location A or of moving to one of the other locations. The discounted cost of moving in the beginning of year 5 would be $\$100,000/(1 + 0.20)^4 = \$48,225$. Given the location profits for the fifth year (see Table 13-6), we want to select the best strategy, assuming that we are in location A at the beginning of the fifth year. We evaluate the following choices:

	Alternative (x)	Location Profit	Moving Cost		Net Profit
	A	$1,336,000	–	0	= $ 1,336,000
	B	1,398,000	–	48,225	= 1,349,975
$P_5(A) =$	C	1,457,600	–	48,225	= 1,409,375
	D	1,486,600	–	48,225	= 1,438,375
	E	1,526,000	–	48,255	= 1,477,775 ←

If the warehouse is located in A, we should move it to E to maximize profit.

We proceed to make similar computations for each location in the fifth year. The strategy and the associated profits are recorded in Table 13-7.

When strategy calculations are made for years other than year 5, we must include the profits accumulated from subsequent years. Consider the calculations that would be made for location D in year 3. The discounted moving cost would be $\$100,000/(1 + 0.20)^2 = \$69,444$. The location profits are found in Table 13-6. The cumulative profits for the subsequent year (year 4) are found in Table 13-7. We now can find the best strategy.

	Alternative (x)	Location Profit	Moving Cost		Cumulative Profit for Subsequent Years $P_4(x)$		Cumulative Profit for Year 3 $P_3(D)$
	A	$623,200	–	69,444	+ $2,402,030	=	$2,955,786
	B	743,000	–	69,444	+ 2,402,030	=	3,075,986
$P_3(D) = $ max.	C	836,400	–	69,444	+ 2,402,030	=	3,168,986
	D	756,100	–	0	+ 2,459,900	=	3,216,000 ←
	E	715,500	–	69,444	+ 2,418,800	=	3,064,856

Similar computations are carried out until Table 13-7 is complete. The optimum dynamic location can be traced through the table. We search the first year for the maximum cumulative profit ($\$3,755,430$), which is location C. From this point, the strategy indicated is $S_C\ S_C\ S_C\ S_D\ S_D$. This means to initially locate in C, stay in C for the first three years, and then switch to location D at the beginning of the fourth year. Stay in location D the remainder of the planning horizon. Note also in Table 13-7 that should we wish initially to locate in any of the other locations, we may trace an optimum strategy given that starting location.

Table 13-7 Location-Relocation Strategies Over a Five-Year Planning Horizon with Cumulative Profits Shown from Year j to Year 5

					YEAR FROM PRESENT DATE j					
WAREHOUSE LOCATION ALTERNATIVES (x)	1ST		2ND		3RD		4TH		5TH	
	$P_1(x)$	STRATEGY[a]	$P_2(x)$	STRATEGY[a]	$P_3(x)$	STRATEGY[a]	$P_4(x)$	STRATEGY[a]	$P_5(x)$	STRATEGY[a]
A	$3,719,086	S_A	$3,525,086	S_A	$3,168,986	M_C	$2,402,030	M_D	$1,477,775	M_E
B	3,717,486	S_B	3,540,986	S_B	3,168,986	M_C	2,402,030	M_D	1,477,775	M_E
C	[b] → **3,755,430**	→ S_C	→ **3,583,130**	→ S_C	**3,238,430**	S_C	2,402,030	M_D	1,477,775	M_E
D	3,720,300	S_D	3,553,600	S_D	3,216,000	S_D	→ **2,459,900**	S_D	**1,486,600**	→ S_D
E	3,659,197	S_E	3,499,797	M_C	3,168,986	M_C	2,418,800	S_E	1,526,000	S_E

[a] Strategy symbol refers to "staying" (S) in the designated location or "moving" (M) to a new location as indicated.
[b] Arrows indicate maximum profit location plan when warehouse is initially located at C.

RETAIL/SERVICE LOCATION

Retail and service centers are often the final stocking points in a physical distribution network. These include such facilities as department stores, supermarkets, branch banks, emergency medical centers, churches, recycling centers, and fire and police stations. Location analysis for these points often must be highly sensitive to revenue and accessibility factors rather than the cost factors so important to plant and warehouse location. Factors such as proximity to competition, population makeup, customer traffic patterns, nearness to complementary outlets, parking availability, proximity to good transportation routes, and community attitudes are just a few of the many factors that can influence retail or service location. Therefore, the previous methodology does not directly apply to these problems. Since the logistician is less likely to be directly responsible for retail or service location, we will examine only a few of the more popular methodologies.

Weighted Checklist

Often, many of the factors important to retail or service location are not quantified easily or inexpensively. Judgment remains an integral part of the location decision, yet it is difficult to make comparisons among sites unless the analysis can be quantified to some degree, even if crudely. One possibility is to form a weighted matrix of location factors, like that shown in Table 13-8, and score each factor for potential sites. An index number, which is the sum of the factor weights multiplied by the factor scores, is the total score for the site. Sites with high index values are preferable to sites with low index values.

Table 13-8 An Example List of Factors Important to Retail or Service Site Selection

LOCAL DEMOGRAPHICS	SITE CHARACTERISTICS
Population base of the local area	Number of parking spots available
Income potential in local area	Distance of parking areas to site
	Visibility of site from street
	Size and shape of the lot
	Condition of existing building (if any)
	Ingress and egress quality
TRAFFIC FLOW AND ACCESSIBILITY	**LEGAL AND COST FACTORS**
Number of vehicles	Type of zoning
Type of vehicles	Length of lease
Number of pedestrians	Local taxes
Type of pedestrians	Operations and maintenance
Availability of mass transit	Restrictive clauses in lease
Access to major highway	Voluntary regulations by local merchants
Level of street congestion	
Quality of access streets	

RETAIL STRUCTURE

Number of competitors in area

Number and types of stores in area

Complementarity of neighboring stores

Proximity to commercial areas

Joint promotion by local merchants

Source: Avijit Ghosh and Sara L. McLafferty, *Location Strategies for Retail and Service Firms* (Lexington, MA: D. C. Heath and Company, 1987), p. 49.

Table 13-8 (*cont.*)

Example

Suppose that a major paint manufacturer wants to site a retail outlet for its products. Outside experts, as well as standard checklists, would be consulted to generate a list of factors relevant to the problem of where to put the retail store. An abbreviated list of factors is shown in Table 13-9. Factor weights are assigned a number from 1 to 10, according to the relative importance of each factor, with 10 being most important. A particular site is scored on a scale from 1 to 10, with 10 representing the most favorable status. This particular site has a total index of 391. Other sites can be scored and the total index values compared. Of course, special care must be taken to score different sites consistently so that the index values can be reasonably compared.

Table 13-9
A Hypothetical Weighted Factor Checklist for a Retail Location Example

(1) FACTOR WEIGHT (1 TO 10)[a]	LOCATION FACTORS	(2) FACTOR SCORE (1 TO 10)[b]	(3) = (1) ×(2) WEIGHTED SCORE
8	Proximity to competing stores	5	40
5	Space rental/lease considerations	3	15
8	Parking space	10	80
7	Proximity to complementary stores	8	56
6	Modernity of store space	9	54
9	Customer accessibility	8	72
3	Local taxes	2	6
3	Community service	4	12
8	Proximity to major transportation arteries	7	56
	Total index		391

[a]Weights approaching 10 indicate great importance.
[b]Scores approaching 10 refer to a favored location status.

Observations

- When Dave Thomas, founder of Wendy's, was asked how his firm decided on new locations for its restaurants, he replied, "We see where a McDonald's restaurant is and locate as near to it as possible."
- The Original Mattress Factory, which was founded by a former CEO of the Sealy Mattress Company (the largest mattress producer in the United States), established a factory and retail store and promoted its mattresses heavily through advertising on radio and television. It was not long before competing mattress retail stores were located immediately next door or directly across the street.

Spatial-Interaction Model

One of the most popular approaches to determining the drawing power, or overall desirability, of a site is the gravity model. An early version was known as Reilly's law of retail gravitation,[42] which is remarkably similar to Newton's law of gravity. The basic idea is that two competing cities attract trade from an intervening town in direct proportion to each city's population but in inverse proportion to the square of distances between the cities and town. Although this model is quite simplistic, it has been enriched through using the *mass* or *variety* offered by a retail outlet instead of *population*. Mass variables are square footage of the store, number of different items in stock, levels of inventory maintained, or other features that can attract customers. *Distance* in the original formula becomes customer driving distance or driving time to competing retail outlets and the proposed site. The power to which distance or driving time is raised can be empirically determined, usually by scaling from a map or driving the actual routes, to better reflect how distance or time repels trade.

The gravity concept has been modified into a more practical working model by Huff.[43] This spatial-interaction model developed an empirical basis for how consumers trade attractiveness of alternate retail sites with accessibility. This model is expressed as

$$E_{ij} = P_{ij}C_i = \frac{S_j/T_{ij}^a}{\sum\limits_i S_j/T_{ij}^a} C_i$$

(13-7)

where

E_{ij} = expected demand from population center i that will be attracted to retail location j

---

[42]William J. Reilly, *The Law of Retail Gravitation* (New York: Knickerbocker Press, 1931).
[43]David L. Huff, "A Computer Program for Location Analysis," in Raymond M. Hass (ed.), *Science, Technology, and Marketing*, (Chicago: American Marketing Association, 1966), pp. 371–379.

P_{ij} = probability of customers from population center i traveling to retail location j

C_i = customer demand at population center i

S_j = size of the retail location j

T_{ij} = travel time between population center i and retail location j

n = number of retail locations j

a = empirically estimated parameter[44]

Note that size S may include all variables that attract customers to a retail site (store attractiveness, inventory availability, price, parking space, etc.). The retail site may be a single outlet or a service center of a group of outlets such as a shopping center. Travel time T may include all variables that repel customers (distance, traffic congestion, limitations to access, detours, etc.). The purpose of the model is to estimate the share of the total market that will be captured by various retail and service center sites.

The Huff model is a basic model for spatial interaction. Over the years, researchers have improved its ability to represent real problems, have reformulated it as a multiplicative model, and have suggested different definitions of the variables to improve its predictive performance.[45]

Example

Suppose that there are two shopping centers (R_A and R_B) within a metropolitan region located in relation to one another as shown on the time map in Figure 13-14. R_B is a potential site and R_A is an existing site. Customers (C_1, C_2, and C_3) who are attracted to the shopping centers are concentrated at the centroids of their neighborhoods. The total sales potentials from the three neighborhoods are $10, $5, and $7 million, respectively. Shopping center A has 500,000 square feet of selling area and B has 1 million square feet. The parameter a is estimated to be 2.

The market share for each center can be approximated as shown in Table 13-10. First, the travel time is computed by using the coordinate point locations. For example, the travel time between C_1 and R_B is $D_{1B} = \sqrt{(X_1 - X_B)^2 + (Y_1 - Y_B)^2} = \sqrt{(10 - 50)^2 + (20 - 60)^2} = 56.6$. Second, the repelling time T^a is found—$T_{1B}^2 = 3,200$. Third, the probability P_{ij} of a dollar of revenue flowing to a center is computed. For example, the probability of customer 1 selecting center B is

$$P_{1B} = \frac{1,000,000/3,200}{(500,000/900) + (1,000,000/3,200)} = \frac{312.5}{868} = 0.36$$

[44]One way to determine this parameter is to compare actual sales for an existing retail configuration with the model-generated sales. The parameter is set so that the two are equal. For another way to calibrate the model, see Avijit Ghosh and Sara L. McLafferty, *Location Strategies for Retail and Service Firms* (Lexington, MA: Heath, 1987), pp. 95–100.

[45]For a review of these extensions, see Ghosh and McLafferty, Chapter 5.

Figure 13-14
A Time-Grid Map for
Shopping Center
Location Example

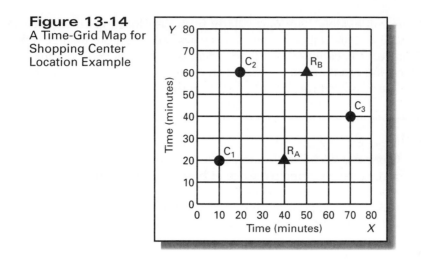

Fourth, the probability multiplied by the total sales potential of a customer neighborhood is the sales contribution that each neighborhood makes to the shopping center sales. The expected contribution of neighborhood C_1 to R_B would be $0.36 \times 10 = \$3.6$ million. Finally, the neighborhood contributions are summed to give total shopping center sales. In this case, the potential site R_B should be able to generate $13 million in sales. This expected revenue can now be compared to operating costs, rents, and construction costs to see if the investment should be made.

Other Methods

A variety of additional methods plays a role in solving retail or service location problems. Regression analysis is important to forecasting the revenues that a specific site

Table 13-10   Estimated Total Shopping Center Sales for Example Problem

Customer i	Time from Customer i to Location j A	Time from Customer i to Location j B	T_{ij}^2 A	T_{ij}^2 B	S_j/T_{ij}^2 A	S_j/T_{ij}^2 B	$P_{ij} = \dfrac{S_j / T_{ij}^2}{\sum_j S_j / T_{ij}^2}$ A	$P_{ij} = \dfrac{S_j / T_{ij}^2}{\sum_j S_j / T_{ij}^2}$ B	$E_{ij} = P_{ij}C_i$ A	$E_{ij} = P_{ij}C_i$ B
C_1	30.0	56.6	900	3200	555	313	0.64	0.36	$6.4	$3.6
C_2	44.7	30.0	2000	900	250	1111	0.18	0.82	0.9	4.1
C_3	36.1	28.3	1300	800	385	1250	0.24	0.76	1.7	5.3
					Total shopping center sales ($ million)				$9.0	$13.0

can expect. Covering models[46] are particularly useful for locating emergency services such as police and fire stations. Game theory has been suggested where competition is a key factor.[47] Location-allocation models such as goal programming and integer programming can be used. Consider an example of the use of integer programming to locate a bank's principal place of business.

Example[48]

The Ohio Trust Company wishes to locate within the 20 counties of northeast Ohio where it does not now have a principal place of business. According to the banking laws in Ohio, if a banking firm establishes a principal place of business (PPB) in any county, then branch banks can be established in that county and in any adjacent county. Ohio Trust would like to know in which counties to establish a minimum number of PPBs.

The 20 counties of northeastern Ohio are identified in Figure 13-15. In Table 13-11, those counties that are adjacent to each of the counties are listed.

To solve this problem as an integer-programming problem, we define

$$x_i = 1 \text{ if a PPB is to be located in county } i; 0 \text{ otherwise}$$

Based on the data in Table 13-11, we can formulate the problem as follows:

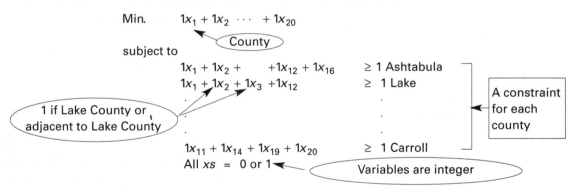

Min. $1x_1 + 1x_2 \cdots + 1x_{20}$ (County)

subject to

$1x_1 + 1x_2 + \quad + 1x_{12} + 1x_{16} \quad \geq 1 \text{ Ashtabula}$

$1x_1 + 1x_2 + 1x_3 + 1x_{12} \quad \geq 1 \text{ Lake}$

(1 if Lake County or adjacent to Lake County)

$1x_{11} + 1x_{14} + 1x_{19} + 1x_{20} \quad \geq 1 \text{ Carroll}$

All $xs = 0$ or 1 (Variables are integer)

(A constraint for each county)

Using any appropriate integer programming code to solve this problem (e.g., MIPROG in LOGWARE), we find that 3 PPBs are needed, and they should be located in Ashland, Stark, and Geauga counties.

Service facilities may also be located by the integer programming method.

---

[46]C. S. Craig and A. Ghosh, "Covering Approaches to Retail Facility Location" in *AMA Educators Proceedings* (Chicago: American Marketing Association, 1984).
[47]K. S. Moorthy, "Using Game Theory to Model Competition," *Journal of Marketing*, Vol. 22 (1985), pp. 262–282.
[48]Based on a problem shown in David R. Andersen, Dennis Sweeney, and Thomas A. Williams, *An Introduction to Management Science*, 5th ed. (St. Paul: West Publishing Co., 1988), pp. 335–339.

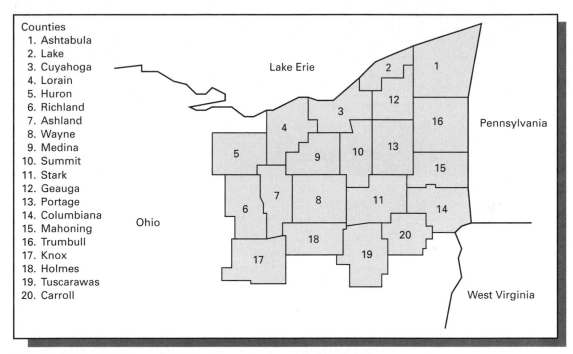

Figure 13-15 Northeastern Ohio Counties for Possible Principal Business Location by Ohio Trust Company

Source: Reprinted by permission from David R. Andersen, Dennis Sweeney, and Thomas A. Williams, *An Introduction to Management Science*, 5th ed. (St. Paul: West Po., 1988), p. 336. Copyright © 1988 by West Publishing Company. All rights reserved.

Table 13-11 Adjacent Counties to Each County Under Consideration for Ohio Trust Company

COUNTIES UNDER CONSIDERATION	ADJACENT COUNTIES BY NUMBER	COUNTIES UNDER CONSIDERATION	ADJACENT COUNTIES BY NUMBER
1. Ashtabula	2,12,16	11. Stark	8,10,13,14,15,18,19,20
2. Lake	1,3,12	12. Geauga	1,2,3,10,13,16
3. Cuyahoga	2,4,9,10,12,13	13. Portage	3,10,11,12,15,16
4. Lorain	3,5,7,9	14. Columbiana	11,15,20
5. Huron	4,6,7	15. Mahoning	11,13,14,16
6. Richland	5,7,17	16. Trumbell	1,12,13,15
7. Ashland	4,5,6,8,9,17,18	17. Knox	6,7,18
8. Wayne	7,9,10,11,18	18. Holmes	7,8,11,17,19
9. Medina	3,4,7,8,10	19. Tuscarawas	11,18,20
10. Summit	3,8,9,11,12,13	20. Carroll	11,14,19

Example

MetroHealth Hospital would like to position emergency services in the surrounding communities of the large metropolitan area in which it operates. The objective is to have no patient drive more than ten minutes to reach an emergency room. The estimated patient driving times in minutes to potential locations is given as follows:

	To Potential Emergency Room Site					
From Neighborhood	1	2	3	4	5	6
A	0	5	15	25	25	15
B	5	0	20	30	15	5
C	15	20	0	10	25	15
D	25	30	i10	0	10	20
E	25	15	25	10	0	9
F	15	5	15	20	9	0

What is the minimum number of emergency rooms and where should they be located?

To solve this problem, we first note which emergency room sites are within the required ten-minute drive. The list is

Potential Site	Neighborhood
1	A, B
2	A, B, F
3	C, D
4	C, D, E
5	D, E, F
6	B, E, F

We can now write

$$\text{Minimize } X_A + X_B + X_C + X_D + X_E + X_F$$

subject to

$$
\begin{array}{ll}
X_A + X_B & \geq 1 \text{ (Site 1 constraint)} \\
X_A + X_B \qquad\qquad + X_F & \geq 1 \text{ (Site 2 constraint)} \\
X_C + X_D & \geq 1 \text{ (Site 3 constraint)} \\
X_C + X_D + X_E & \geq 1 \text{ (Site 4 constraint)} \\
X_D + X_E + X_F & \geq 1 \text{ (Site 5 constraint)} \\
X_B \qquad\qquad + X_E + X_F & \geq 1 \text{ (Site 6 constraint)}
\end{array}
$$

All Xs = 0 or 1

Solving this problem using the MIPROG module in LOGWARE gives $X_B = 1$ and $X_D = 1$, meaning that emergency rooms should be placed in neighborhoods B and D.

OTHER LOCATION PROBLEMS

There are so many location problems occurring in supply chain planning that it is not practical to thoroughly discuss all of them. However, following are a few additional problem that may use the solution methodology already presented or that may require specialized solution procedures. They are selective illustrations of the variety of problem types faced by logisticians.

Hub and Spoke

A location problem solution made popular by the airlines, small package delivery services (FedEx and UPS), and communication systems is the hub-and-spoke concept. Rather than moving traffic directly from origin to destination, the traffic is directed through one or two hubs, or transfer facilities. Traffic moves from a hub to destination points or through a high-volume interconnection to another hub. The design problem is to minimize the transportation cost plus the cost of hub operation by (1) determining the number of hubs, (2) specifying their locations, and (3) routing traffic through the hubs. Since the origin and destination identities must be tied together, the problem is not solved in the same manner as a warehouse location problem. Rather, to solve the problem precisely requires a specialized algorithm.[49]

Obnoxious Facilities

It is common that location is judged on cost minimizing or profit maximizing criteria. This has the tendency to place locations close to the centers of demand, which is sometimes a disadvantage. Obnoxious facilities such as waste dumps, water treatment plants, chemical reclamation plants, and prisons are located on a criterion that attempts to maximize the minimum distance between them and the population. The problem can be solved in a manner similar to the MetroHealth Hospital emergency room problem discussed above. The difference is to develop a matrix of population centers that exceed the minimum required distance from a potential location. The problem constraints are then found from this matrix. Integer programming is used to solve the problem.

Microlocation

Practical location problems often involve significant-size geographical areas where distance approximations over road, rail, water, and air networks are reasonable. However, where location involves small demand areas such as locating newspaper distribution terminals, truck delivery and pickup terminals, workstation location in plants, and product location in warehouses, inaccuracies in estimating travel distances cannot be tolerated. Although the methodology for these microlocation problems is not necessarily different from those previously described, the requirement for precise data can be.

---

[49]Hasan Pirkul and David A. Schilling, "An Efficient Procedure for Designing Single Allocation Hub and Spoke Systems," *Management Science*, Vol. 44, No. 12 (December 1998), pp. S235–S242.

Concluding Comments

Locating facilities in the network can be considered the most important logistics/SC strategic planning problem for most firms. It sets the conditions for the proper selection and good management of transport services and inventory levels. In many ways, facility location is the "bones" of the supply chain. Because there are often many facilities to be considered at one time, along with multiple products placed in them, multiple sources to serve them, and multiple customers served by them, the problem is often quite complex. Decision aids are typically useful.

The purpose of this chapter was to survey some of the more practical methods for the location of plants, warehouses, and retail or service facilities in the logistics network. We began with classifying location problems into a limited number of categories so that the major characteristics of location methodology could be identified. Next, the history of location theory was highlighted.

Single facility location methodology was represented by the exact center-of-gravity approach. This continuous location method is useful where transportation costs are the dominant location factor and there is to be no selection of candidate locations for testing, as in the case with mathematical programming methods.

Multiple facility location is the more important problem to most businesses. Three location approaches are typically used: (1) optimization; (2) simulation; and (3) heuristic methods. Although there are many models of each class that have been formulated, only one or two in each class have been used to illustrate the nature of the methodology. The extensions of both the static single and multiple facility models to deal with the problem of location over time were shown.

Finally, the problem of retail and service location was discussed. Several models were shown (weighted checklist and gravity models). The retail or service location problem stands in sharp contrast with the warehouse location problem primarily because it is revenue-based rather than cost-based, as is most warehouse location.

Questions

1. Refer to Weber's classification of industries. Should the following processes be (1) located near their markets; (2) located near their raw material sources; or (3) not necessarily located at markets or raw material sources?
   a. Bottling windshield washer fluid
   b. Assembling VCRs
   c. Smelting aluminum
   d. Refining crude oil
   e. Making apple cider
   How do transportation costs influence your suggestion?
2. According to Hoover, what characteristic in transportation rates makes location inherently unstable between markets and raw material sources?
3. What is a ubiquity? What impact does it have on location?
4. Multiple facility location models can be classified as exact, simulation, or heuristic. Explain the differences between these and cite examples of each type. Be sure to indicate why your example illustrates the type.

5. Why are single location methods not very appropriate for the multiple location problem?
6. What are the relevant costs for a multiple warehouse location problem? Why are these important to a proper location analysis?
7. What benefit does a "flat bottom" total cost curve have in making simulation a usable methodology for multiple warehouse location?
8. What is a heuristic method? What is an exact method? How are they useful in solving warehouse location problems?
9. What is dynamic warehouse location? When is it most appropriate to use this approach?
10. When is a weighted checklist a useful methodology for location?
11. In the location of a McDonald's restaurant, what factors would attract customers to particular locations? What factors would repel them? How would you go about determining the relative importance of each factor?

PROBLEMS

Some problems in this chapter can be solved or partially solved with the aid of computer software. The software packages in LOGWARE that are most important for this chapter are COG (C), MULTICOG (M), TRANLP (T), ROUTER (R), PMED (P), and MIPROG (IP). The CD icon **C** will appear with the software package designation where the problem analysis is assisted by one of these software programs. A database may be prepared for the problem if extensive data input is required. Where the problem can be solved without the aid of the computer (by hand), the hand icon is shown. If no icon appears, hand calculation is assumed.

1. Two plants are to serve three market points through one or two warehouses, as shown in Figure 13-16. Volume flowing either to or from each point, and the associated transportation rates, are given as follows.

Point No.	Point, i	Volume, V_i(cwt.)	Transportation Rate, R_i($/cwt./mi.)
1	P_1	5,000	0.04
2	P_2	7,000	0.04
3	M_1	3,500	0.095
4	M_2	3,000	0.095
5	M_3	5,500	0.095

a. Using the center-of-gravity method, find the approximate location for a *single* warehouse.
b. Using the *exact* center-of-gravity method, find the optimum *single* warehouse location.

Figure 13-16
Location of Plants
and Markets with
Grid Overlay

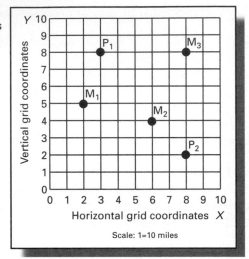

Scale: 1=10 miles

c. Evaluate the quality of the solutions obtained in terms of their optimality and usefulness. Evaluate the factors included or not included in the model. Explain how management might use the solution.
d. Find the optimum locations for *two* warehouses to serve these markets. Assume that each plant serves each warehouse in proportion to the market volume assigned to the warehouse.

2. The Care-A-Lot Hospital Group wishes to locate an outpatient clinic or clinics in a rural area of Africa. The construction costs and other considerations suggest that one or two centers would be about right. Since traveling is difficult for patients in this part of the world, proximity to such facilities often dictates their choice. Therefore, location is best determined based on weighted distance (number of patients times distance from the facility). Figure 13-17 shows the annual number of patients likely to visit the clinic(s) and their cluster locations. It is estimated that it costs an average of $0.75 per kilometer (prorated on the basis of a one-way trip) for a patient to travel or be transported to the clinic(s). This estimate is based on lost productivity, direct travel costs, and indirect travel expenses paid for by others.
   a. What is the best location for a single clinic?
   b. If two clinics are to be located, where is the best location for them?
   c. A clinic costs $500,000 (U.S. dollars) per year to equip and staff. This is paid through charitable contributions and government subsidies. On purely economic grounds, should the second clinic be built?

3. Bottoms-Up, Inc., is a small company that produces and distributes beer under the Old Wheez label. The company is examining the possibility of penetrating the North Shore City metropolitan area market. A plant location that would serve the area is sought. A grid overlay is placed over the selling area, as shown in Figure 13-18. North Shore City is area *E*. The suburbs surrounding *E* are designated as *A* to *I*. A market research study shows the following potential demand for Old Wheez.

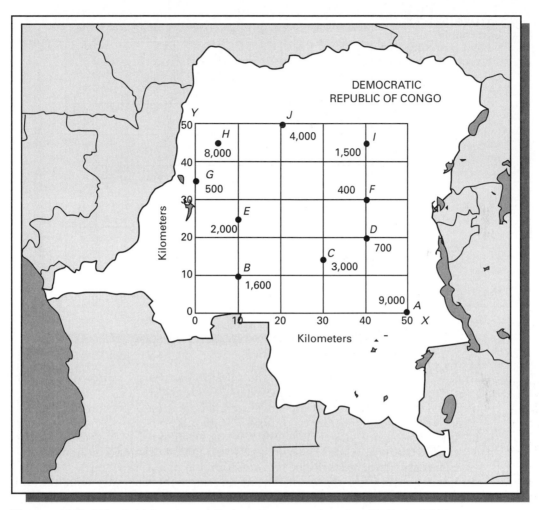

Figure 13-17 Grid Overlay on Patient Concentrations in a Region of Africa

Area	Annual Volume (cwt.)
A	10,000
B	5,000
C	70,000
D	30,000
E	40,000
F	12,000
G	90,000
H	7,000
I	10,000

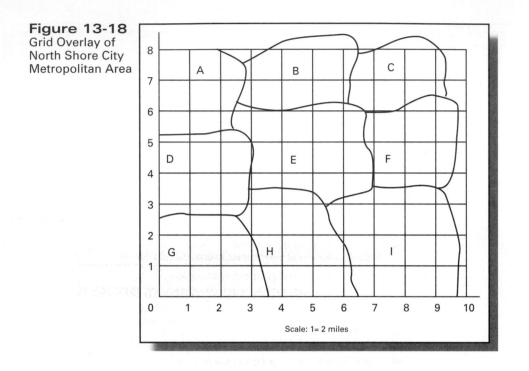

Figure 13-18
Grid Overlay of
North Shore City
Metropolitan Area

Scale: 1= 2 miles

Demand comes primarily from dealers that are scattered uniformly over the area. Transportation costs are estimated at $0.10/cwt./mi.

a. If the center-of-gravity approach is used, where should the bottling plant be located? Estimate the annual transportation bill.

b. If the *exact* center-of-gravity method is used to find the plant location, where should the location be? Does it make a substantial difference in transportation costs compared with the location found in part a?

c. If labor costs, property taxes, and site development costs vary with location, how would you propose accounting for these additional costs when deciding the location?

4. Recall the problem presented in Figure 13-10. Resolve it, assuming that both warehouses are public warehouses and, therefore, no fixed costs apply. Summarize your answer in terms of customer, warehouse, and plant assignments.

5. Recall the problem presented in Figure 13-10. Resolve it, assuming that warehouse 2 can handle only 100,000 cwt. Warehouse 1 is expanded to handle an unlimited throughput. The plant capacities remain unchanged. How much of a cost penalty can be expected from this change?

6. Recall the problem presented in Figure 13-10. Resolve the problem, assuming that the fixed cost on warehouse 2 (W_2) is $200,000 instead of $400,000 per year.

7. Develop a list of factors that you think would be important in deciding the location of
a. A Goodwill collection center
b. A Wendy's restaurant

c. An automobile assembly plant

d. A fire station

Also, indicate the weight that you would assign to each factor.

8. In the problem shown in Table 13-6 and Figure 13-13, suppose that the cost associated with moving from one location to another is $300,000 instead of $100,000. What location planning strategy would offer the maximum profits over the five-year planning horizon?

9. Recall the Environment Plus incinerator location problem and the data for the problem in the file PMED02.DAT of the PMED module in LOGWARE. Consider the following additional questions:

a. How many facilities will give the lowest operating cost plus transportation cost? Where should these incinerators be located? Show that the best number of incinerators has been found.

b. The company currently operates four incinerators at an annual operating and transportation cost of $35 million. Chicago, Atlanta, Phoenix, and Denver are the sites. The cost to establish a new incinerator site is a one-time cost of $6,000,000 per site. Is it economically reasonable for the company to establish the optimal number of sites found in part a?

c. If the West Coast market of Los Angeles and Seattle were to grow by 10 times, would your answer to part a be different?

10. Suppose that Farmers' Bank wishes to serve the nine customer clusters as shown in Figure 13-19. It has proposed locating a branch (A) at coordinates $X_1 = 20$, $Y_1 = 20$. A competing branch (B) is located at coordinates $X_2 = 40$, $Y_2 = 30$. Farmers' Bank is to be a full-service branch with a relative size (attractiveness) index of 1. The competing branch is a partial-line facility (no ATM, no drive-through capabilities) with a size index of 0.7. The travel time for customers to a bank is approximated as $T(\text{hours}) = D/50$, where $D = $ distance in miles. The average customer generates $100 in gross annual revenue for a bank. The

Figure 13-19
Number of Potential
Customers for
Branch Banks in a
Region

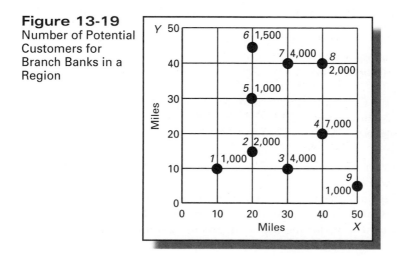

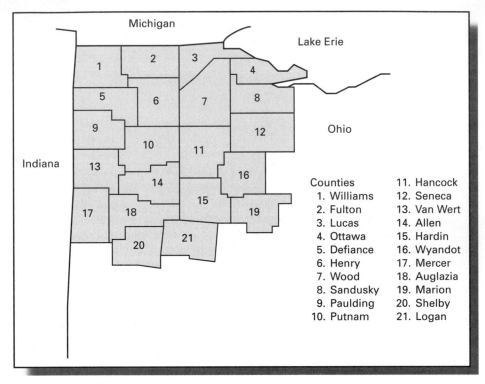

Figure 13-20 Northwest Ohio Counties for Ohio Trust Company Expansion

Counties	
1. Williams	11. Hancock
2. Fulton	12. Seneca
3. Lucas	13. Van Wert
4. Ottawa	14. Allen
5. Defiance	15. Hardin
6. Henry	16. Wyandot
7. Wood	17. Mercer
8. Sandusky	18. Auglazia
9. Paulding	19. Marion
10. Putnam	20. Shelby
	21. Logan

estimate of annual operating expense for Farmers' branch is $300,000, and the facility will cost $650,000 (20-year life) on land worth $100,000.

a. Apply Huff's retail gravity model to determine the branch's annual revenue. Assume $a = 2$.

b. Considering the level of investment required and the operating expenses, should the branch be constructed?

c. What additional information might you like to have before making a final decision?

11. The Ohio Trust Company wishes to expand its principal place of business locations to the northwestern counties of Ohio. The conditions for location were outlined in a previous example in Figure 13-15 on page 593. For the counties identified in Figure 13-20, find the minimum number of PPBs needed and the counties in which they should be located. (*Note:* A database is prepared for this problem in the module MIPROG.)

12. Biogenics is a start-up company that plans to produce biological materials used in medical research. Major customers for their products will be the large research hospitals located in major metropolitan areas. Customer location and projected annual sales are as follows.

No.	Customer	Latitude,°	Longitude,°	Sales, lb
1*	Boston	42.31	71.08	50,000
2*	New York	40.72	74.00	75,000
3	Washington	38.89	77.00	45,000
4*	Atlanta	33.75	84.38	65,000
5*	Miami	25.83	80.28	35,000
6*	Cleveland	41.48	81.66	25,000
7	Detroit	42.36	83.06	30,000
8*	Chicago	41.83	87.64	70,000
9	St. Louis	38.63	90.19	20,000
10*	Minneapolis	44.92	93.20	15,000
11	Kansas City	39.10	94.58	10,000
12*	Philadelphia	39.95	75.17	30,000
13*	Houston	29.78	95.38	25,000
14*	Dallas	32.98	96.78	20,000
15*	Phoenix	33.49	112.08	10,000
16*	Denver	39.73	104.98	15,000
17*	Seattle	47.63	122.33	10,000
18	Portland	45.46	122.67	10,000
19*	San Francisco	37.78	122.21	40,000
20*	Los Angeles	34.08	118.36	80,000

*Indicates a candidate site.

Products will be shipped UPS at a transport rate that averages $0.05/lb/mile. It is estimated that the annual operating costs (FOC) for a laboratory (plant) are given from $FOC(\$) = (\$5,000,000\sqrt{N})/N$, where N is the number of laboratories being operated. The vendors for the materials used in the production process are assumed concentrated at Chicago. The purchase weight is the same as the sales weight. The transport rate from Chicago to the laboratories is estimated at $0.02/lb/mile.

Determine the number and location of the laboratories to serve Biogenics' potential markets. Which customers should be served out of each site? Every customer location is a potential laboratory site, except St. Louis, Portland, Kansas City, Washington, Detroit, and Chicago vendors.

13. For the problem shown in Figure 13-5, suppose that the capacity restriction on warehouse 2 (W_2) for both products combined is 100,000 cwt. There is no capacity restriction on warehouse 1 (W_1). (*Note:* Data for the problem shown in Figure 13-5 are available in the MIPROG module of LOGWARE. Capacities are at the insertion point of Cap-W1/ZW1 and Cap-W2/ZW2 in the problem setup.)

14. Recalling the problem presented in Figure 13-5, how would the solution change if the following alterations were made to the problem setup?
   a. Demand for product 1 is doubled, but remains unchanged for product 2.
   b. The manufacturing cost for product 2 is raised to $5/cwt. at plant 2 only.
   c. The handling cost for warehouse 2 is increased to $4/cwt.

d. There is a limited capacity in plant 2 of 90,000 cwt. to produce product 1. Plant 1 capacity is increased from 60,000 cwt. to 150,000 cwt. There are no plant capacity changes for product 2.

e. Customer 2 for product 2 can no longer be served from warehouse 2.

Table 13-12
Times Between Zones for Globe Casualty Company, in Minutes

FROM ZONE	TO ZONE 1	2	3	4	5	6	7	8	9	10
1	5	23	34	15	45	55	25	10	9	19
2		5	18	12	53	37	27	33	26	16
3			5	6	14	41	31	28	24	17
4				5	15	29	45	60	31	23
5					5	25	27	14	39	43
6						5	7	13	42	53
7							5	33	14	8
8								5	26	10
9									5	19
10										5

Figure 13-21 Typical Daily Demand Pattern with Current and Potential Supply Yard Locations

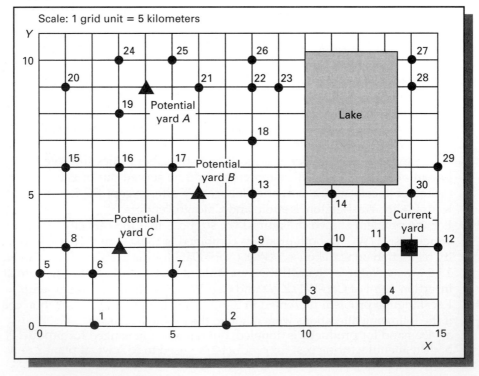

Resolve *separately* each of the above problem scenarios using the mixed integer linear programming approach. (*Note:* The problem setup for Figure 13-5 is available in the MIPROG module of LOGWARE.)

15. The Globe Casualty Company positions claims adjusters around a metropolitan area to respond quickly to insurance claims resulting from auto accidents, fires, crimes, and other such emergency situations. It is a competitive feature of the company's business for an adjuster to be on-site within 30 minutes of the time an accident is called in, so that customers feel they are being well served. The city has been divided into ten zones from which casualty calls originate and in which claims adjusters may be stationed. The response times in minutes between the ten zones are shown in Table 13-12. To meet the 30-minute response time, how many claims adjuster stations should be established, and in which zones should they be located?

16. A building supply firm supplies materials to construction sites throughout the metropolitan area of Mexico City, Mexico. Daily delivery trucks are dispatched from a materials yard. A typical daily demand pattern is shown in Figure 13-21, where a grid is overlaid on the metropolitan area. The map-scaling factor is 1 coordinate unit = 5 kilometers with a circuity factor of 1.44 to convert straight-line distance to approximate road distance. Demand is given in kilograms of merchandise in Table 13-13.

Table 13-13 Customer Demand Volume and Coordinate Locations with Yard Coordinates

STOP	X	Y	VOLUME, KG	STOP	X	Y	VOLUME, KG
1	2	0	300	16	3	6	300
2	7	0	250	17	5	6	150
3	10	1	600	18	8	7	275
4	13	1	175	19	3	8	375
5	0	2	100	20	1	9	475
6	2	2	375	21	7	9	150
7	5	2	400	22	8	9	475
8	1	3	50	23	9	9	325
9	8	3	100	24	3	10	350
10	11	3	200	25	5	10	225
11	13	3	350	26	8	10	250
12	15	3	100	27	14	10	300
13	8	5	200	28	14	9	200
14	11	5	450	29	15	6	150
15	1	6	225	30	14	5	50
Current Yard	14	3					
Yard A	4	9					
Yard B	6	5					
Yard C	3	3					

Trucks operate with a variable cost of 2.5 pesos per kilometer, driver's wages are 90 pesos per day, and a truck is amortized at 200 pesos per day. The materials are stored in open yards and in buildings at locations shown in Figure 13-21. The current materials yard from which trucks are dispatched operates at a cost of 350 pesos per day. The company is considering moving its operations. The potential materials yards have an estimated operating expense, including the moving expense from the current location, of 480 pesos per day for *A*, 450 pesos per day for *B*, and 420 pesos per day for *C*. There are ten trucks available, each with a hauling capacity of 1,000 kg, but not all may be needed for meeting average demand. Trucks travel over their routes at an average speed of 32 kph. After noon, drivers are permitted a one-hour lunch break and they usually return to the yard before needing additional breaks. Based on a company policy, routes should be no longer than ten hours in a day, and trucks are not to leave the yard before 8 A.M. If a truck has a short route and returns for reloading and rerouting, 1.5 hours for loading is required. Customers have a time window for delivery of between 8 A.M. and 5 P.M. Time for unloading at a customer location is estimated as 15 minutes plus 0.1 times the stop volume in kilograms.

Which yard location is most economically attractive?

CASE STUDIES

Superior Medical Equipment Company

Superior Medical Equipment Company supplies electrical equipment that is used as components in the assembly of MRI, CAT scanners, PET scanners, and other medical diagnostic equipment. Superior has production facilities in Phoenix, Arizona, and Monterrey, Mexico. Customers for the components are located in selected locations throughout the United States and Canada. Currently, a warehouse, that receives all components from the plants and redistributes them to customers, is located at Kansas City, Kansas. Figure 1 shows the geographical placement of these facilities.

Superior's management is concerned about the location of its warehouse since its sales have declined due to increasing competition and shifting sales levels among its customers. The lease is about to expire on the current warehouse, and management wishes to examine whether it should be renewed or warehouse space at some other location should be leased. The warehouse owner has offered to renew the lease at an attractive rate of $2.75 per sq. ft. per year for the 200,000 sq. ft. facility. It is estimated that any other location would cost $3.25 per sq. ft. for a similar-size warehouse. A new or renewed lease

Figure 1   Location of Superior's Plants, Warehouse, and Customers

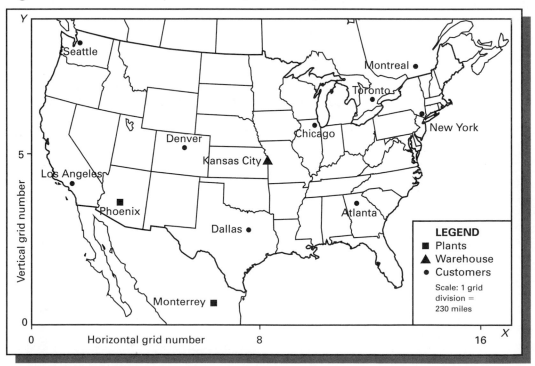

PLANT LOCATION	ANNUAL VOLUME, CWT.[b]	TRANSPORT RATE, $/CWT.	DISTANCE, MILES	GRID COORDINATES[a]	
				X	Y
Phoenix	61,500	16.73	1163	3.60	3.90
Monterrey	120,600	9.40	1188	6.90	1.00
Total	182,100				

[a]Miles = 230 × coordinate distance
[b]Cwt. = 100 lb.

Table 1 Volume, Rate, Distance, and Coordinate Data for Shipping from Plants to the Kansas City Warehouse in Truckload Quantities (Class 100) for the Most Recent Year

will be for five years. Moving the inventory, moving expenses for key personnel, and other location expenses would result in a one-time charge of $300,000. Warehouse operating costs are expected to be similar at any location.

In the most recent year, Superior was able to achieve sales of nearly $70 million. Transportation costs from the plants to the Kansas warehouse were $2,162,535, and from the warehouse to customers were $4,819,569. One million dollars was paid annually as warehouse lease expenses.

To study the warehouse location question, the data shown in Tables 1 and 2 were collected.

Although transport costs are not usually expressed on a $/cwt./mile basis, given that the outbound transportation costs for the most recent year were $4,819,569, the weighted average distance of the shipments was 1128 miles, and the annual volume shipped was 182,100 cwt., the estimated average outbound rate from a warehouse would be $0.0235/cwt./mile. ■

Table 2 Volume, Rate, Distance, and Coordinate Data for Shipping from the Kansas City Warehouse to Customers by Truck in 5,000 lb Quantities (Class 100) for the Most Recent Year

CUSTOMER LOCATION	ANNUAL VOLUME, CWT.	TRANSPORT RATE, $/CWT.	DISTANCE, MILES	GRID COORDINATES	
				X	Y
Seattle	17,000	33.69	1858	0.90	9.10
Los Angeles	32,000	30.43	1496	1.95	4.20
Denver	12,500	25.75	598	5.60	6.10
Dallas	9,500	18.32	560	7.80	3.60
Chicago	29,500	25.24	504	10.20	6.90
Atlanta	21,000	19.66	855	11.30	3.95
New York	41,300	26.52	1340	14.00	6.55
Toronto	8,600	26.17	1115	12.70	7.80
Montreal	10,700	27.98	1495	14.30	8.25
Total	182,100				
Kansas City				8.20	6.00

1. Based on information for the current year, is Kansas City the best location for a warehouse? If not, what are the coordinates for a better location? What cost improvement can be expected from the new location?
2. In five years, management expects the Seattle, Los Angeles, and Denver markets to grow by 5 percent, but the remaining markets to decline by 10 percent. Transport costs are expected to be unchanged. Phoenix output will increase by 5 percent, and Monterrey's output will decrease by 10 percent. Under these new conditions, would your decision about the warehouse location change? If so, how?
3. If by year 5 increases are expected of 25 percent in warehouse outbound transport rates and 15 percent in warehouse inbound rates, would your decision change about the warehouse location?
4. If the center-of-gravity method is used to analyze the data, what are its benefits and limitations for locating a warehouse?

Ohio Auto and Driver's License Bureaus

As a member of the planning commission for the state of Ohio, Dan Rogers was concerned about how the state could conserve tax dollars in providing services to its residents. Projected cutbacks in federal funds to the state, difficulties in increasing tax rates, and the general upward trend in operating costs encouraged a careful examination of how costs might be reduced throughout the state. Dan had a particular interest in how auto and driver's licensing bureaus might be operated more efficiently.

Dan thought that a study should be conducted to examine the locations, sizes, and number of license bureaus statewide. License bureaus issue motor vehicle license tags, driver's licenses, and motor vehicle registrations. The bureaus are located throughout the state for the convenience of the residents; however, the number of bureaus must be limited, due to the fixed costs associated with opening and maintaining a bureau location and the cost of operating it. Since population has shifted from central cities to the suburbs throughout the state and the network of license bureaus has not been evaluated in a number of years, Dan believed that there were too many bureau locations and

they were likely in the wrong locations. He thought that not only could costs be reduced, but service to the residents improved.

The Cleveland, Ohio, metropolitan area represents a typical service area that Dan believed would be a good test region to see if improvements might be made. A map of the region is shown in Figure 1. A linear grid was overlaid on the map, with grid divisions approximately 2.5-miles square. Population was used to represent the relative activity on a license bureau site. Approximate population levels for each grid block are given in Table 1, with clustering at the grid center. Locations of the existing bureaus are shown on the map.

Residents usually select a bureau location that is closest to their residence. Except for motor vehicle tags, which may be acquired through a mail-in program, there is no competition for a bureau's services. A major element of customer service is how far a resident must travel to a bureau.

Dan made some rough estimates of the costs involved. Operating costs for a site included rental charges on the space, salaries of personnel, and utilities. Space, staffing, and

Figure 1 Cleveland, Ohio, Area Auto and Driver's License Bureau Locations

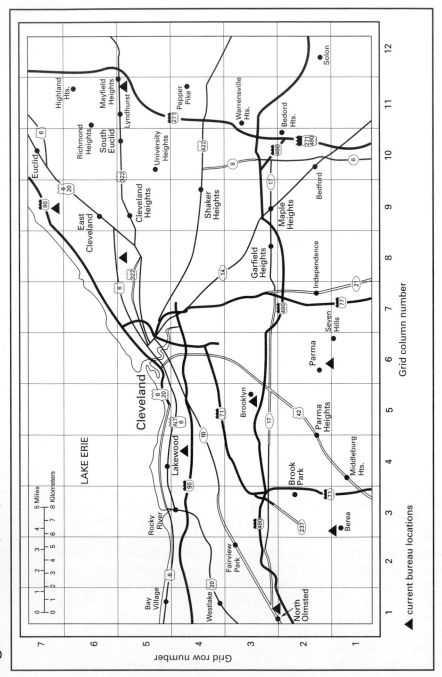

GRID COLUMN	GRID ROW (Y)						
NUMBER (X)	1	2	3	4	5	6	7
1	4,100	6,200	7,200	10,300	200	0	0
2	7,800	8,700	9,400	11,800	100	0	0
3	8,100	10,500	15,600	10,500	200	0	0
4	10,700	12,800	13,800	15,600	400	0	0
5	11,500	13,900	14,500	13,700	600	0	0
6	9,300	14,900	13,700	10,200	1,200	0	0
7	10,100	12,600	16,700	15,800	12,400	2,600	0
8	8,800	13,700	15,200	14,100	10,800	17,200	500
9	5,300	16,700	13,800	11,900	13,500	18,600	12,000
10	5,100	17,400	10,300	9,800	10,300	15,500	11,700
11	7,700	9,200	7,500	8,500	7,800	9,900	8,700
12	4,300	6,700	5,800	6,800	5,400	7,100	6,400
Totals	92,800	143,300	143,500	139,000	62,900	70,900	39,300

Table 1 Estimated Population by 2.5-mile Square Grids in the Cleveland Area

other costs for the existing locations are given in Table 2. For planning purposes, it was estimated that annual rental rates would be $22 per sq. ft., staff salaries would average $21,000 per year including benefits, and utilities would annually average $4 per sq. ft. The site space needed would be a minimum of 1,500 sq. ft. and additional space of 500 sq. ft. for each 100,000 of population served in excess of 100,000. A minimum of four staff persons would be needed, with an additional person for each 100,000 persons above the initial 100,000 served. Dan thought that a center-of-gravity type of location methodology might be used to deal with his planning questions.

Closing an existing site would involve moving equipment and paying separation expenses to any staff who could not be

Table 2 Current Bureau Locations and Associated Statistics

No.	BUREAU	GRID ROW NUMBER	GRID COLUMN NUMBER	SIZE, SQ. FT.	STAFF, PERSONS
1	Cleveland-Brooklyn	3.0	5.2	1,700	4
2	Cleveland-University Circle	5.5	7.8	1,200	4
3	North Olmsted	2.5	1.2	2,000	5
4	Berea	1.3	2.7	1,800	4
5	Parma	1.5	5.9	1,500	4
6	Lakewood	4.4	4.1	2,200	5
7	Euclid	6.9	9.0	2,700	5
8	Mayfield Heights	5.5	11.2	1,500	5
	Totals			14,600	36

transferred to other locations. Equipment moving would amount to $10,000 for each site, and separation expenses would be approximately $8,000 per staff member, if any existing positions were to be eliminated. These would be one-time expenses. For planning purposes, any unused equipment would be considered valueless and given to charity. To open a new site beyond the current eight bureaus would require the acquisition of new equipment ($60,000), if another site were not being closed so that equipment could be transferred. Initial hiring costs for staff not being transferred would be $3,000.

Dan was perplexed by the value that residents placed on bureau location. Since residents used their own means of transportation and rarely expressed their level of satisfaction with the effect of bureau location, there was no direct way to determine the benefits of location. However, he figured that the residents incurred a cost of travel and their proximity to bureaus was important. Based on the average number of trips residents made to the bureau, the cost of transportation, and the proportion of the population using the bureaus, an estimate of the annual travel cost between resident and a bureau location was 12¢ mile per resident. The territorial coverage of the current bureaus was not known. ■

QUESTIONS

1. Do you think there is any benefit to changing the network of license bureaus in the Cleveland area? If so, how should the network be configured?

2. Do you think that Dan Rogers's study approach is sound?

3. What concerns, besides economic ones, should Dan have before suggesting any network changes?

Southern Brewery

Southern Brewery is a regional brewer of a line of beer products. Markets for its products are limited to the southeastern portion of the United States, as shown in Figure 1. Southern's beers are local favorites and demand is growing rapidly among consumers over the age of 50. Its products are slightly lower in alcoholic content and are considerably lower in calories than the more popular brands. They are promoted as a healthy choice, and consumers are responding with increasing patronage.

To meet the growing demand for its products, Carolyn Carter, the director of logistics, has been asked to evaluate the effect on operating costs of constructing a brewery at Jacksonville, Florida. This proposal is brought about by the rapid growth in the southernmost markets of its region, and the projected strain on the Montgomery brewery's capacity. Carolyn begins her analysis by noting that the existing breweries at Richmond, Virginia, Columbia, South Carolina, and Montgomery, Alabama, vary in their costs and production capacities. The cost to produce a barrel of beer products is different among these locations, based on variations in equipment age; local labor rates; delivered costs of raw materials to breweries; and miscellaneous cost differences resulting from local property taxes, insurance rates, and utilities. These costs and capacities are summarized in Table 1. Each brewery produces a complete product line.

Southern maintains a uniform delivered price to distributors of $280 per barrel throughout its marketing region. Current average

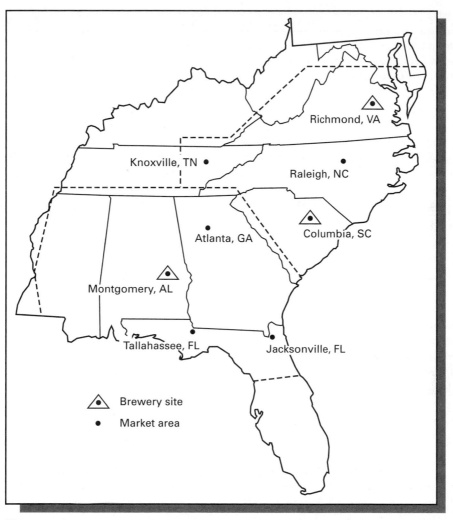

Figure 1 Map of Southern Brewery's Plants and Market Regions

Table 1
Production Costs and Capacities at Southern's Three Breweries

Brewery Location	Production Cost, $ per Barrel	Annual Production Capacity, Barrels[a]
Richmond, VA	$140	100,000
Columbia, SC	145	100,000
Montgomery, AL	137	300,000

[a] A unit of annual capacity is estimated to be currently worth (could be sold for) $50 per barrel.

Table 2
Current Average
Annual Sales by
Market Area and
Brewery of Origin

	MARKET AREA	BREWERY OF ORIGIN	ANNUAL SALES, BARRELS
1	Richmond, VA	Richmond, VA	56,000
2	Raleigh, NC	Richmond, VA	31,000
3	Knoxville, TN	Columbia, SC	22,000
4	Columbia, SC	Columbia, SC	44,000
5	Atlanta, GA	Montgomery, AL	94,000
6	Savannah, GA	Montgomery, AL	13,000
7	Montgomery, AL	Montgomery, AL	79,000
8	Tallahassee, FL	Montgomery, AL	26,000
9	Jacksonville, FL	Montgomery, AL	38,000
		Total	403,000

annual sales from each brewery for each market area are given in Table 2. A profit margin of 20 percent is earned on sales.

Transportation between the breweries is handled by a private trucking fleet owned by Southern. From the records of truck and driver expenses and the deliveries made, Carolyn constructed the average transport costs shown in Table 3. Based on her experience with the other breweries, Carolyn estimates the transport costs for the proposed breweries.

The primary reason for suggesting a new brewery at Jacksonville is the approximate dou-

bling of the Florida market, whereas the remaining markets are anticipated to grow between 15 and 50 percent. It is thought that the Jacksonville brewery would relieve the Montgomery brewery from serving the Florida market. The anticipated five-year demand pattern for each market area and the serving brewery is shown in Table 4.

A brewery at Jacksonville with a capacity of 100,000 barrels is planned. To construct a brewery of this size is expected to cost $10,000,000, with a useful life of 15 years. The company's expectation for such a project is a 20 percent

Table 3 Delivery Costs Between Breweries and Market Areas in Dollars per Barrel

		BREWERIES			
	MARKET AREA	RICHMOND	COLUMBIA	MONTGOMERY	JACKSONVILLE[a]
1	Richmond	$ 8.49	$12.54	$19.98	$17.13
2	Raleigh	10.70	9.78	16.35	14.25
3	Knoxville	16.38	12.81	13.80	15.48
4	Columbia	12.54	6.96	12.93	11.16
5	Atlanta	15.48	11.85	10.20	13.80
6	Savannah	14.64	9.54	13.80	9.54
7	Montgomery	19.98	12.93	6.96	13.80
8	Tallahassee	24.30	15.18	13.65	9.72
9	Jacksonville	18.84	12.27	15.18	7.68

[a]Proposed brewery

Table 4
Projected Fifth-Year Average Annual Sales by Market Area and Proposed Brewery of Origin

	MARKET AREA	BREWERY OF ORIGIN	ANNUAL SALES, BARRELS
1	Richmond, VA	Richmond, VA	64,000
2	Raleigh, NC	Richmond, VA	35,000
3	Knoxville, TN	Columbia, SC	33,000
4	Columbia, SC	Columbia, SC	55,000
5	Atlanta, GA	Montgomery, AL	141,000
6	Savannah, GA	Montgomery, AL	20,000
7	Montgomery, AL	Montgomery, AL	119,000
8	Tallahassee, FL	Jacksonville, FL; Montgomery, AL; and Columbia, SC	52,000
9	Jacksonville, FL	Jacksonville, FL	76,000
		Total	595,000

return before tax, and sales expenses and over-head are approximately 27 percent of sales. The new brewery is believed to be able to produce at a cost of $135 per barrel. ∎

QUESTIONS

1. If you were Carolyn Carter, would you agree with the proposal to build the new brewery? If you do, what plan for distribution would you suggest?
2. If the new brewery is not to be constructed, what distribution plan would you propose to top management?
3. What additional considerations should be taken into account before reaching a final decision?

Technical Supplement

This is the model formulation to the problem shown in Figure 13-5.[50]

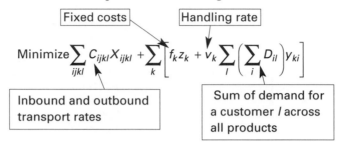

Minimize $\sum_{ijkl} C_{ijkl} X_{ijkl} + \sum_{k} \left[f_k z_k + v_k \sum_{l} \left(\sum_{i} D_{il} \right) y_{ki} \right]$

with annotations: **Fixed costs**, **Handling rate**, **Inbound and outbound transport rates**, **Sum of demand for a customer l across all products**

subject to:
Available production capacity cannot be exceeded

Plant capacity

$$\sum_{kl} X_{ijkl} \leq S_{ij} \quad \text{for all } ij$$

All customer demand must be met

Customer demand

$$\sum_{j} X_{ijkl} = D_{il} y_{kl} \quad \text{for all } ikl$$

Each customer must be served by a single warehouse

$$\sum_{k} y_{kl} = 1 \quad \text{for all } l$$

Keep warehouse throughput between minimum throughput $\underline{V}_k$ and capacity $\overline{V}_k$

Minimum warehouse throughput   **Warehouse capacity**

$$\underline{V}_k \leq \sum_{l} \left(\sum_{i} D_{il} \right) y_{kl} \leq \overline{V}_k$$

and

All $X \geq 0$
All $y = 0$ or 1
All $z = 0$ or 1

---

[50]Based on A. M. Geoffrion and G. W. Graves, "Multicommodity Distribution System Design by Benders Decomposition," *Management Science*, Vol. 20, No. 5 (January 1974), pp. 822–844.

where

i = index for commodities

j = index for plants

k = index for possible warehouses

l = index for customer zones

S_{ij} = supply (production capacity) for commodity i at plant j

D_{il} = demand for commodity i in demand zone l

$\underline{V}_k, \overline{V}_k$ = minimum, maximum allowed annual possession and operating cost for warehouse at site k

f_k = fixed portion of the annual possession and operating costs for a warehouse at site k

v_k = variable unit cost of throughput for a warehouse at site k

C_{ijkl} = average unit cost of producing, handling, and shipping commodity i from plant j through warehouse k to customer zone l

X_{ijkl} = variable denoting the amount of commodity i from plant j through warehouse k to customer zone l

y_{kl} = a 0–1 variable that will be 1 if warehouse k serves customer zone l, and 0 otherwise

z_k = a 0–1 variable that will be 1 if warehouse k is open, and 0 otherwise

Chapter 14

The Network Planning Process

*A*ny process that the logistician/supply chain manager uses to con-figure the network of facilities and define the product flow through it requires data, computational tools, and a process of analysis that leads to a good network design. In this chapter, the data requirements

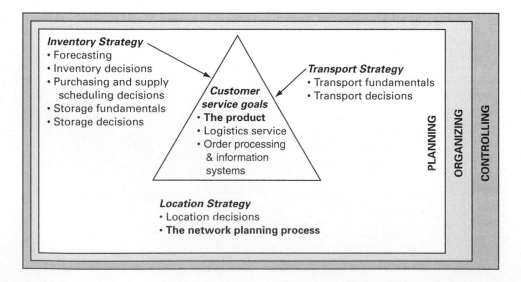

Inventory Strategy
- Forecasting
- Inventory decisions
- Purchasing and supply scheduling decisions
- Storage fundamentals
- Storage decisions

Customer service goals
- **The product**
- Logistics service
- Order processing & information systems

Transport Strategy
- Transport fundamentals
- Transport decisions

Location Strategy
- Location decisions
- **The network planning process**

PLANNING   ORGANIZING   CONTROLLING

for this type of planning and the information system that produces the needed data are examined. Next, the general methods by which alternative configurations can be evaluated efficiently are considered. Finally, an overall procedure is discussed for conducting the network design analysis. Among all supply chain planning problems, this is probably the most important since it provides the basic structure for building transportation, inventory, and information systems.

THE PROBLEM OF NETWORK CONFIGURATION

The problem of network configuration is one of specifying the structure through which products flow from their source points to demand points. This involves determining the facilities, if any, to be used; how many there should be; where they should be located; the products and customers assigned to them; the transport services used between them; the sourcing, interfacility, and distribution to customers product flows; and the inventory levels maintained in the facilities. A generalized product flow network is shown in Figure 14-1, where demand may be served from field warehouses or directly from source points such as plants, vendors, or ports. Field warehouses, in turn, are served by regional warehouses or directly from source points. This problem may be represented in a variety of forms where there may be more or fewer echelons than shown in Figure 14-1, and where there may be different configurations depending on the characteristics of the products flowing through the network. That is, there could be more than one network design for the products of one company.

This problem of network design has both spatial and temporal aspects. The *spatial*, or geographic, aspect refers to locating facilities on a geographic plane such as plants, warehouses, and retail outlets. Number, size, and locations of facilities are determined by balancing the following against the requirements for customer service as expressed geographically: production/purchase costs; inventory-carrying costs; facility costs (storage, handling, and fixed costs); and transportation costs.

The *temporal*, or time, problem in network planning is one of maintaining the product availability to meet customer service targets. Product availability may be realized through production/purchase order response time or through the maintenance of an inventory in the proximity of the customer. The customer's time to acquire the product is the major concern here. Balancing capital costs, order-processing costs, and transportation costs while meeting customer service targets dictates how the product flows through the network. Temporal-based decisions also affect the location of facilities.

Application

When the court ordered American Telephone & Telegraph (AT&T) to divest itself of local telephone operations, seven new regional telephone companies were formed to provide these services. Western Electric Company, a subsidiary of AT&T, maintained

Figure 14-1 Generalized Product Flow Network

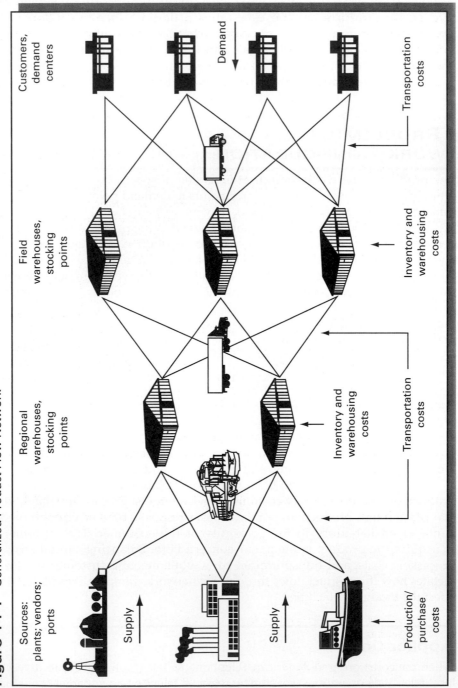

the warehousing for local telephone operations, but remained with AT&T after divestiture. The new telephone companies, each with revenues that ranged from $500 million to $700 million per year, were ordered out of the existing Western Electric warehouses, leaving the new companies without a logistics network to supply parts, components, and supplies to local installers. The first order of business was to configure logistics networks of warehouses, inventories, and trucking routes and schedules to meet the service requirements for each of the new, emerging telephone companies. Each telephone company conducted a network configuration study.

Network configuration cannot be limited to the forward movement of goods from suppliers to customers since, in some cases, firms must take back from downstream locations items such as packaging materials (e.g., pallets), leased products (e.g., copy machines), damaged goods (e.g., replaced auto engines), and products to be reworked and resold (e.g., disposable cameras). This reserve network often overlays the forward network and must be integrated into it. Network planning is complicated when the forward and reverse channels cannot be separated due to shared facilities.

The problem of network configuration is of great importance to top management. It is common that redesigning the logistics network can generate annual savings from 5 to 15 percent of total logistics costs. When we consider a company such as the Whirlpool Corporation that annually spends $1.5 billion on logistics, a 10 percent savings results in $150,000,000 per year. With cost reductions of this magnitude, it is not difficult to see why network reconfiguration tops the list of planning issues. This, of course, is in addition to the benefits that network design can have on customer service and the improved competitiveness of the firm.

DATA FOR NETWORK PLANNING

A Data Checklist

Network planning can require a substantial database that is derived from many sources. Although some data may be specific to a particular network configuration problem, much of the database can be generalized. It can include

- A listing of all products in the product line
- Locations of customers, stocking points, and source points
- Demand for each product by customer location
- Transportation rates or costs
- Transit times, order transmittal times, and order-fill rates
- Warehousing rates or costs
- Production/purchase costs
- Shipment sizes by product
- Inventory levels by location by product and the methods to control them
- Order patterns by frequency, size, season, and content

- Order-processing costs and where incurred
- Capital cost
- Customer service goals
- Available equipment and facilities with capacity limitations
- Distribution patterns of how sales are currently met

Data Sources

Most firms do not have formalized logistics information systems that specifically generate the data needed for logistics planning of the type just listed. This leaves the logistician to acquire the needed data from a variety of sources both internal and external to the firm. Primary sources for such data include business operating documents, accounting reports, logistics research, published information, and judgment.

Business Operating Documents

Every firm generates many documents to manage the various aspects of the business. Some of these may be related to logistics activities, but many are prepared for other purposes. They also may simply provide data, but not information, that is directly useful for planning. Let us examine some of these documents, beginning with the sales order.

The sales order, and its attendant documentation, is a primary data source from which a variety of essential logistics information can be derived. Customer locations, product sales levels over time by location, terms of sale, serving locations, shipment sizes, stock status and order-fill rates, and customer service levels are just a few of the kinds of information that can be derived from the sales order processing system. It is very common for companies to store such data in computers. This aids in their extraction and manipulation into information needed for planning.

Application

To complete a warehouse location study, a specialty chemical company was asked by its management consultant to provide data about sales throughout the country by chemical and paint products, and further to break out the sales data by large and small accounts. Since the company retained all of its sales transactions in a computer database, this database could be searched and sorted to provide the necessary sales data for an entire year. Further, the sales transactions could be cross-linked to a customer file that contained U.S. postal zip codes. Collecting contiguous zip codes into about 200 sales regions allowed sales to be aggregated into a manageable number of territories. This was all done without the need for any manual handling of the data.

Selling, manufacturing, purchasing, shipping, storing, and handling are all primary activities that firms conduct on a regular basis. Since they are to be measured and controlled, reports are frequently issued about their status. The logistician utilizes these reports to generate basic information about activity levels. For example, if we were interested in the percentage of shipments from a warehouse made in particular weight breaks, the freight bills or a report containing individual shipments, charges, and the carrier used might be appropriate sources for such data. These raw data can be transformed into a frequency distribution of shipment sizes.

Although it would be impractical here to examine all the activity reports and documents generated in the normal course of business operations, it is fair to say that business documents are a rich source for much of the data that the logistician needs for network planning. It is also worth noting that additional data are available from informal reports that individuals within the company generate for their own use.

Accounting Reports

Accounting data are also an important source of internal information available to the logistician. Accounting data focus on identifying the operating costs, including the costs for logistics activities.

Accounting practice, in general, does an excellent job of reporting on a majority of logistics costs. However, much of accounting practice is directed toward shareholder interests and not those of the manager. This is particularly true for logistics network planning. Within the guidelines of accepted accounting practice, some important costs go unreported, such as inventory-holding costs and the cost of inventory obsolescence. Others are reported in a manner that is confusing to the planning process. That is, should the line item cost for trash collection in a warehouse accounting report be categorized as a fixed, storage, or handling cost? Nevertheless, such accounting reports remain the primary source for cost data.

Logistics Research

Research provides information that neither an operating order-processing system nor an accounting system is likely to generate. Although there is little formal logistics research carried out by companies, such effort can be worthwhile in the defining of the basic relationships useful for network planning, such as sales-service relationships and transport rate-distance relationships. When such research is carried out, it is common for it to be conducted by internal or external consulting groups and by university professors.

Logistics research may also be conducted indirectly on behalf of the firm. Trade associations such as the Council of Logistics Management[1] and the Warehouse Education Research Council[2] regularly sponsor research efforts and report the results in publications distributed to members as well as nonmembers. It is a valuable source of logistical data about other firms in the same industry, and other industries. Such data enhance or supplement the data from the previously noted sources.

---

[1]www.CLM1.org.
[2]www.WERC.org.

Published Information

Much secondary, and sometimes primary, data are available to the logistician from outside the company. Trade magazines,[3] government-sponsored research reports,[4] and academic journals[5] are examples of sources of information on cost and industry trends, technological advances, activity levels, and forecasts.

Judgment

Executives within the firm, consultants to the firm, sales staff, operating personnel, and suppliers to the firm all represent data sources and are part of the logistics database. Little investment is typically needed to unlock this readily available data source.

Data Encoding

Data handling is facilitated by several techniques that have been used to code data. Chief among these are product coding and geographic coding.

Product Coding

Computer technology, the laser, and holography have brought about a way to enter data into computer memory banks without the necessity of manual entry. Bar codes, now popular for data entry, allow products, cartons, and shipments to be identified by the optical scanning of a numbering system. This facilitates the rapid and accurate transfer of data as well as its manipulation by sorting, selection, and rearrangement into information needed for planning. Particular attention should be paid to designing the code that potentially provides the data useful for planning as well as for operations.

Geocoding

Sales data are typically collected by a firm on a by-customer basis with reference to customers by name and address. Network planning is facilitated if sales data are referenced to a geographic base rather than an accounting base. Analysis for transportation decisions, facility location decisions, and inventory decisions are all enhanced by such a geographic database.[6] To the network planner, a customer account is a location, and a distance from other accounts. Preferably, logistics data should be referenced to a geographic customer code.

Geographic coding of data can be accomplished in several ways. A simple approach is to place a linear grid overlay on a map and use the horizontal and vertical grid numbers as the code. For example, a grid overlay is placed on a map of

---

[3]For example, *Transportation & Distribution, Distribution, American Shipper, Inbound Logistics, Warehousing Management, Modern Materials Handling, Traffic Management*, and *Transport Topics*.
[4]For example, RAND reports and the many reports available from the Superintendent of Documents, Washington, DC.
[5]For example, *Journal of Operations Management, Transportation Journal, Management Science, Logistics and Transportation Review, International Journal of Physical Distribution and Materials Management, IIE Transactions, Journal of Business Logistics*, and *International Journal of Logistics Management*.
[6]A time-related database is also an important basis on which to collect data. One can argue that customers are more interested in time dimensions of service rather than geographic dimensions and that network design should be based on time. However, networks are more practically designed around a geographic dimension.

Europe, as shown in Figure 14-2. Many maps give latitude and longitude coordinates that may be used as well, or these coordinates may be found by using a global positioning system locator device. Customers and sales data are then located within the various cells defined by the grid. That is, a customer account located within the cross-hatched cell would be aggregated along with other accounts falling within the cell. All are treated as if located at the midpoint or at the centroid of the cell. The location code for this point would be 008011, as shown in Fig. 14-2, which is a combination of horizontal and vertical coordinates. All data would be referenced to this and similar numbers, as shown in Table 14-1.

Figure 14-2 A Simple Linear Grid Placed Over a Map of Western Europe

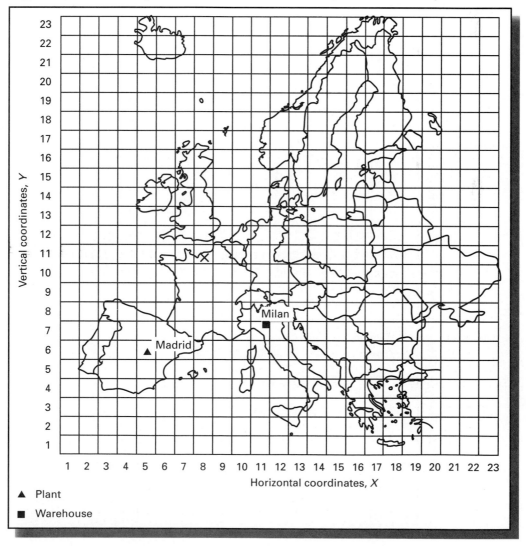

Table 14-1 An Example of Hypothetical Sales Order Data Summarized Around a Grid Location Code

Customer Grid Location Cell Code[a]	No. of Accounts in Cell	Total Annual Sales	Total Annual Shipping Weights	Average Order Size, Units	Average Customer Service Requirement[b]	Location Code of Serving Plant	Location Code of Serving Warehouse
001002	0	$0	0 lb	0	—	—	—
.	.	.	.	.	.	.	.
.	.	.	.	.	.	.	.
.	.	.	.	.	.	.	.
006009	123	890,000	600,000	153	1	005006	011007
007009	51	401,000	290,000	136	1	005006	011007
006008	37	295,000	175,000	127	2	005006	011007
.	.	.	.	.	.	.	.
006012	96	780,000	550,000	156	1	005006	011007
.	.	.	.	.	.	.	.
.	.	.	.	.	.	.	.
.	.	.	.	.	.	.	.

[a]Grid numbers are referenced to Figure 14-2.
[b]Requirements are expressed in the number of days for delivery acceptable to customers.

The grid size is a balance between overaggregation of data and the resulting loss of accuracy in representing the data, and the needless complexity and cost associated with grid cells so fine that they fail to group like customers and, therefore, fail to benefit from averaging.

In addition, numerous geopolitical, specialized areal, and grid location codes are available. A survey of such national geocoding systems identified 33 different coding systems, 8 of which were grid and coordinate codes.[7] In addition to the grid and longitude-latitude codes, several others have been popular for logistics planning purposes. In the United States, and in other countries as well, geographic codes developed for postal delivery are popular. They frequently serve as a basis for determining the distances between points on which transport rates are established, since they are typically tied to company sales data. In the United States, the Standard Point Location Code is often used in computerized transport rating and routing systems. Standard Metropolitan Statistical Areas are frequently used in marketing analysis, which may be a reason to tie logistics analysis to them. PICADAD, a computerized point reference system used by the U.S. Bureau of the Census, Transportation Division, assists in tabulating and analyzing traffic flows.

Application

Consolidated SMC[3], a company supplying technology, tools, and data to the transport community, offers transportation rates in electronic form, as do some trucking firms such as Yellow Freight Systems and Roadway. The database and computer program, called CzarLite™, allows the user to look up a rate between any two intercity points by their five-digit zip codes. The zip code serves as a convenient location code rather than city and state names, which might otherwise be used. The rates for other common carriers, UPS, and FedEx are similarly available and may be found on the Internet.[8]

Because the reference numbers in these codes refer to either an area or a point, mathematical manipulation of the code numbers is possible to determine distances and travel times, and to estimate transportation rates between pairs of areas or points. This ease of data manipulation is of great advantage in facility location analysis and for approximating transportation costs.

Coding generally requires only the simplest of arithmetic operations. As can be noted in Table 14-1, such a listing is produced by sorting the data according to geographic code and by summarizing and averaging data for each data category. This type of coded data is often stored as paper reports in the form of transportation

---

[7]Pamela A. Warner, *A Survey of National Geocoding Systems*, Technical Report no. DOT-TSC-74-26 (Washington, D.C. Superintendent of Documents, U.S. Government Printing Office, 1974).
[8]See www.UPS.com and www.FedEx.com.

rates, inventory costs, or inventory level records, to be retrieved when needed for planning.

Converting Data to Information

Data are facts without any particular purpose. Once gathered, they need to be organized, summarized, grouped, aggregated, or otherwise arranged in a manner that supports the network planning process. When this is done, data becomes information for decision making. For the network design problem, we want to look at the key information elements and their generation.

Units of Analysis

To begin network planning, the dimensions to be used in the analysis need to be decided. Common choices are some form of weight measure (lb, cwt., tons, or kg), a monetary measure (dollar, pound, or yen), a physical count (cases, units, or drums), or a volume measure (gallon, cube, or liter). A weight measure is the preferred choice by logisticians for most planning problems, since transportation rates, a dominant cost in network planning, are usually expressed in this dimension. What is commonly used by managers may be an overriding consideration, since the company's database and understanding of operations are in terms of this dimension. For example, firms primarily engaged in retail distribution view their businesses in monetary terms, whereas manufacturing firms commonly use a weight measure. Once the unit of analysis is decided, all the relevant costs for analysis need to conform to this dimension.

Product Grouping

Companies may have hundreds to thousands of individual items in their product line. This variety occurs not only because there are variations in product models and styles, but also because of the same product being packaged in many sizes (e.g., toothpaste may be offered in travel, regular, economy, and family sizes as well as in tube and pump packages). To collect all the necessary data and to conduct the analysis would be impractical for so many product items. Aggregating the items into a reasonable number of product groups is a practical approach to this problem. We seek to make this grouping so as not to substantially reduce solution accuracy.

Many of the items in any product line do not have different distribution patterns. That is, they may be warehoused at the same locations, bundled together on the same transport carrier, and be destined for the same customers. We want to exploit this by grouping those products sharing the same distribution channel, but create separate groupings for those that do not. Some common groupings would be those products that are shipped directly in bulk to customers because of their high order volume; and those that are shipped through a system of warehouses because of their low order volume requirements. Grouping products by the transport class of merchandise is another method. Of course, a company may wish to group products based on its sales groupings simply because management understands this breakdown. Whatever the method used to create product families, the aggregation of products is usually substantial. It is common to need no more than about 20 product groups for a network analysis.

Application

The Ford Motor Company purchased engines, transmissions, and wheel parts for its 13 eastern U.S. assembly plants from various vendors in Europe. The normal distribution pattern was to move these parts from vendor plants in the European hinterlands to European ports to U.S. ports to final assembly plants located in the U.S. interior. A staging warehouse was considered for location between the U.S. ports and the final assembly plants. Since the motivation for the warehouse was to save on inventories, a natural breakdown of the products was by shipment size. That is, demand was divided into less-than-container-load and full-container-load quantities, since the motivation for the warehouse was a trade-off between transportation costs and inventory-carrying costs. The favored container size was the variable used to decide product groups. A breakdown by product type was not meaningful.

Transport Rate Estimation

In network planning, transportation rates become a major problem because of the potential number of them. For a small network of only 2 product groups, 5 shipment weight breaks, 200 customers, 5 warehouses, and 2 plants, there are $2 \times 5 \times 200 \times 5 \times 2 = 20,000$ rates needed to represent all product flow combinations. Some form of rate estimation would speed computation and relieve the company personnel of the burden of looking up or acquiring so many rates. Such estimation must recognize the type of transportation used, whether privately owned or for hire.

Privately Owned Transport

Estimating an effective rate for privately owned transport, usually truck, requires knowledge of the operating costs and of how the vehicles are routed to their delivery or pickup points. Typically, good records are maintained of the operating costs that include driver wages and benefits, vehicle maintenance, insurance, taxes, depreciation, and overhead. Mileages are recorded from odometer readings. Therefore, a cost per mile is easily obtained.

Example

The Grand Island Biological Company produces and distributes culture media for growing and identifying certain bacteria useful in medical research. Customers primarily are the large medical research complexes located in such areas as New York and Washington, D.C. To evaluate private trucking (small refrigerated vans were used for delivery of these temperature-sensitive products), the company provided the following data about their trucking operations on a weekly basis in the Washington, D.C. area:

Data Category	Fact	Weekly Cost
Weekly mileage	2700 miles	
Weekly hours on duty	66 hrs./wk.	
Trips per week	3 trips/wk.	
Driver wages	$12.00/hr.	$ 792.00
Benefits	18.75% of wages	148.50
Fuel cost @ 10 mpg	$1.10/gal	297.00
Truck depreciation	$316.50/wk.	316.50
Maintenance	$45.00/wk.	45.00
Insurance	$51.00/wk.	51.00
Tolls, food, and lodging	$97.50/trip	292.50
Contingency	$30.00/trip	90.00
Total		$2,032.50

The trucking cost can then be calculated as $2,032.50/2700 mi. = $0.75 per mile.

It is more difficult to estimate the effective rate between origin and destination because the vehicle does not travel a direct route between the two. Rather, more than one stop is frequently made before returning to the depot. Suppose that there are five stops on a typical route and the average out-and-back driving distance is 300 miles, as might be determined by averaging a number of typical route patterns [see Figure 14-3a]. In this example, stem driving distance is a total of 200 miles and interstop driving distance is a total of 100 miles. If the average actual transport rate is taken as $1.30 per mile, the total actual transport cost for the five stops would be $1.30/mile × 300 miles = $390.00. Since, for planning purposes, we often estimate the distance to a customer in one direction only [see Figure 14-3b], the effective distance is 100 + 100 + 150 + 110 + 100 = 560 miles. The effective rate per direct mile would be $390.00/560 = $ 0.696 per mile. Hence, in planning, we calculate the straight-line distance to a customer and multiply it by the effective rate of $0.696/mile to find the transport cost to that customer.

For-Hire Transport
The process to estimate transport rates for for-hire transport is significantly different from the process just described for privately controlled transport. A characteristic of class rates for truck and rail, and rates for UPS and FedEx as well as other small-shipment carriers, is that the rates are reasonably linear with distance, a characteristic that we can use to advantage. This allows us to build a transport rate estimating curve that is based on distance traveled from a shipment origin point, like that shown in Figure 14-4. For a range of distances from a local delivery area of about 30 to 50 miles from the origin to the area of rate blanketing of about 1,000 to 1,500 miles from the origin, the rates are usually very linear with distance, typically having a coefficient of determination of 90 percent or higher. This has been observed for the United States as well as for other countries.

Figure 14-3
Actual Versus
Equivalent Driving
Patterns for Privately
Operated Vehicles

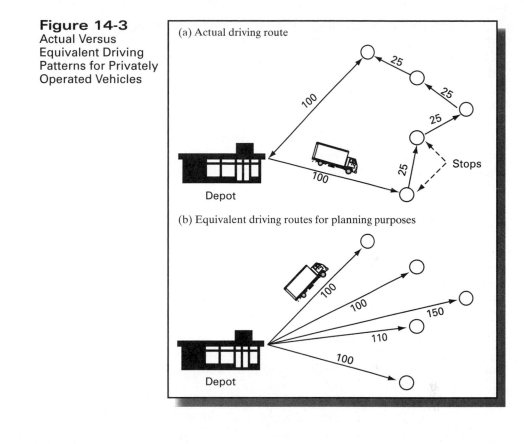

(a) Actual driving route

(b) Equivalent driving routes for planning purposes

Figure 14-4
Transport Rate
Estimating
Curve for
Selected
Distances from
Chicago

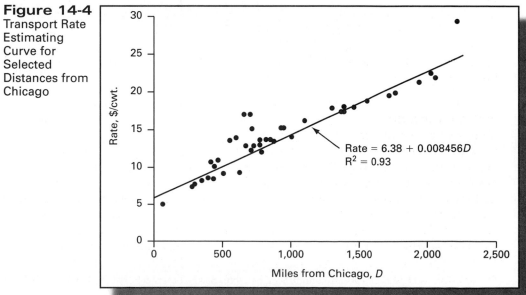

$$\text{Rate} = 6.38 + 0.008456D$$
$$R^2 = 0.93$$

The process for constructing a transport rate estimating curve involves sampling rates at varying distances radiating from an origin point, say, Chicago. A sample size of between 30 and 50 points is usually adequate. The rates may be found in tariffs or other rate quotations. In the case of Figure 14-4, the rates were taken from the Roadway Express rates without discounts or other service charges, as found on the Internet.[9] Since rates are quoted between postal codes, the distances may be found through map scaling or from tabulated distances in such publications as the Rand McNally Road Atlas,[10] Bartholomew Road Atlas Europe,[11] or from the mapping services on the Internet.[12] Commercial databases in electronic form are available. Distances also may be calculated from geographic coordinates, as discussed later in this chapter.

When a transport rate estimating curve does not produce a satisfactory degree of accuracy, specific rates may be used entirely or selectively in conjunction with a transport rate estimating curve. This may happen where rates are quoted on individual shipments such as for high-volume movements between specific points. Contract, commodity, and selectively discounted class rates may not show enough of a generalized relationship with distance to form a reasonable rate estimating curve.

Order and Shipment Profiles

Network design can be very sensitive to order size and the resulting shipment size. For example, if all customers had their orders shipped to them in full truckload quantities, there would be little economic incentive for warehousing, outside of having stock near customers for service reasons. On the other hand, very small customer orders frequently require extensive warehousing of stocks. However, a firm usually has many customers that it ships to in a variety of order weights. In Figure 14-5, the chemical company represented had divided its market into large and small accounts. Large accounts were generally managed by a direct sales force, whereas the small accounts were handled by telephone through a telemarketing program. This histogram shows the percentage of the shipments for each account type within a standard weight-break cell. Data for such distributions are generally available from shipping document samples or from the sales database.

The value of the shipment profile is to produce accurate estimates of transport rates. Between the same origin and destination points, there can be a substantially different rate, depending on the shipment weight. Therefore, transport rate estimating curves need to be developed for each standard weight break. Then, each rate curve can be weighted by the corresponding percentage of shipments in the weight break. One resulting transport rate curve can then represent a wide range of shipment sizes or a variety of transport modes, as the shipping profile may represent different modes as well as weight breaks.

---

[9]www.Roadway.com.
[10]*Rand McNally 2002 Road Atlas* (Skokie, IL: Rand McNally and Company, 2002).
[11]*Bartholomew Road Atlas Europe* (Edinburgh, Scotland: John Bartholomew & Son, Ltd., 1985).
[12]For example, see www.MapQuest.com or www.RandMcNally.com.

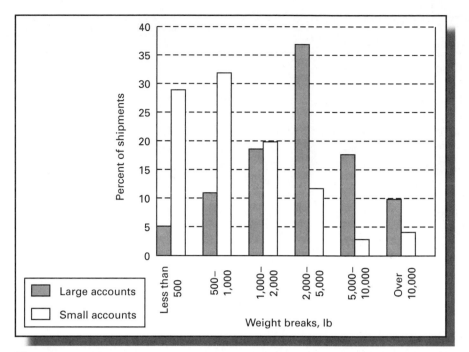

Figure 14-5 A Shipment Profile for Large and Small Accounts of a Chemical Company

Sales Aggregation

Customers for any firm's products or services are typically dispersed throughout a country, yet they are often concentrated in specific areas, usually population centers. From a network-planning viewpoint, it is not necessary to treat each customer separately. The product, or service, sales that thousands of customers generate can be geographically grouped into a limited number of geographic clusters without any significant loss in cost-estimating accuracy.

Sales clustering can affect the accuracy of estimating transportation costs to customers. With clustering, transport costs, rather than being computed to each customer location, are computed to the cluster center. Some error through using the average rather than actual distance will be introduced. This potential inaccuracy can be minimized if an adequate number of clusters are created, and these clusters are kept small around the greatest concentrations of sales. Based on research that determines the transportation cost error of assuming that shipments are made to the center of a customer cluster rather than to each customer, the appropriate number of clusters can be determined. Table 14-2 shows various cluster sizes depending on the number of facilities in a network and the allowable transport costing error.

Once the proper number of clusters is known, customer data can be aggregated into these clusters. Since sales are usually given by customer address, which includes zip code, it is common to group by zip code. Grouping zip codes by their proximity

Maximum Allowed Error	Largest Cluster Size[a]	Approximate Number of Source Points in Network					
		1	5	10	25	50	100
0.5%	0.5%	200[c]	325	350	500	650	750
	0.8%	150	150	175	375	450	650
	2.0%	75	100	300	450	600	650
	5.0%	75	150	250	500	600	750
	Unlimited[b]	50	350	400	500	700	750
1.0%	0.5%	200[c]	200[c]	200[c]	200[c]	250	500
	0.8%	200[c]	150	150	175	350	500
	2.0%	75	75	175	300	500	600
	5.0%	75	100	225	400	500	600
	Unlimited[b]	25	200	250	400	500	600
2.0%	0.5%	200[c]	200[c]	200[c]	200[c]	200[c]	350
	0.8%	150	150	150	150	250	450
	2.0%	75	75	100	250	350	500
	5.0%	75	75	175	300	450	500
	Unlimited[b]	25	75	175	300	450	500
5.0%	0.5%	200[c]	200[c]	200[c]	200[c]	200[c]	200[c]
	0.8%	150	150	150	150	150	300
	2.0%	75	75	75	100	225	300
	5.0%	75	75	75	175	275	350
	Unlimited[b]	25	50	75	200	275	350
10.0%	0.5%	200[c]	200[c]	200[c]	200[c]	200[c]	200[c]
	0.8%	150	150	150	150	150	150
	2.0%	75	75	75	75	125	175
	5.0%	75	75	75	75	150	200
	Unlimited[b]	25	50	75	100	175	225

[a] Largest cluster size among all clusters as a percentage of total demand.
[b] Cluster size is not specifically limited, but is approximately 7 percent of total demand.
[c] Mathematically the minimum number of clusters.
Source: Ronald H. Ballou, "Measuring Transport Costing Error in Customer Aggregation for Facility Location," *Transportation Journal*, Vol. 33, No. 3 (1994), pp. 49–59.

Table 14-2 Minimum Acceptable Number of Clusters for the Maximum Allowed Transport Costing Error and for Various Numbers of Network Source Points and Largest Customer Cluster Sizes

to each other gives a low transport costing error. Each cluster center can be identified using a geocode such as latitude and longitude. An example table of cluster centers, their geographical locations, and the zip sectional centers associated with each cluster can be formed, as shown in Table 14-3. Similar cluster tables can be generated for other parts of the world, using whatever postal code may be in effect in that particular region.

No.	Longitude[a]	Latitude[a]	Cluster Center City Name	Center Zip Code[b]	Zip Codes Represented[b]
1	73.25	42.45	Pittsfield, MA	012	012
2	71.81	42.27	Worcester, MA	016	015–016
3	71.08	42.31	Boston, MA	021	014, 017–024
4	71.43	41.82	Providence, RI	029	025–029
5	71.46	42.98	Manchester, NH	031	030–034
6	72.02	44.42	St. Johnsbury, VT	035	035, 058
7	70.97	43.31	Rochester, NH	038	038–039
8	70.28	43.67	Portland, ME	041	040–041, 045, 048
9	69.77	44.32	Augusta, ME	043	042–043, 049
10	68.75	44.82	Bangor, ME	044	044, 046
11	68.00	46.70	Presque Isle, ME	047	047
12	73.22	44.84	Burlington, VT	054	054, 056
.	.	.	.	.	.
.	.	.	.	.	.
.	.	.	.	.	.
180	117.05	32.62	San Diego, CA	921	920–921
181	119.00	35.56	Bakersfield, CA	933	932–934
182	119.78	36.76	Fresno, CA	937	936–937
183	122.21	37.78	Oakland, CA	946	939–954
184	124.07	40.87	Arcata, CA	955	955,960
185	121.46	38.55	Sacramento, CA	958	956–959
186	121.67	45.46	Portland, OR	972	970–974, 977, 986
187	121.75	42.22	Klamath Falls, OR	976	975–976
188	118.80	45.66	Pendleton, OR	978	978
189	122.33	47.63	Seattle, WA	981	980–985
190	120.47	46.60	Yakima, WA	989	988–989
191	117.41	47.67	Spokane, WA	992	835, 838, 990–992, 994
192	118.33	46.06	Walla Walla, WA	993	993

[a]Longitude and latitude coordinates in decimal degrees.
[b]Zip sectional center code.

Table 14-3 Partial Listing of a Geographic Clustering Scheme for the United States. Using 192 Clusters, Three-Digit Zip Sectional Centers, and Longitude-Latitude Coordinates

Mileage Estimates

The geographical nature of much of the network planning task requires logisticians to obtain distances. Distances are needed to estimate transport costs between origin and destination points, and they are frequently used as a substitute for time. For example, all customers may be required to be located within 300 miles of a warehouse, meaning that one-day delivery service can be achieved at that distance. As previously noted, distance data can be found in a number of commercial tables and road atlases in either printed or computerized form.[13] For other situations (e.g., planning truck routes through city streets), a handheld wheel-on-a-handle measuring device, available in many office supply stores, can be rolled over a map to obtain precise distances that a vehicle might actually travel. However, it is frequently more efficient, but not always as accurate, to simply compute distances from coordinate points.

When a simple, linear grid system is used, as previously shown in Figure 14-2, straight-line distances can be computed from the coordinates by means of the Pythagorean theorem. That is, if points A and B have given coordinate values, the straight-line distance between them can be determined by

$$D_{A-B} = K\sqrt{(X_B - X_A)^2 + (Y_B - Y_A)^2} \qquad (14\text{-}1)$$

where

D_{A-B} = distance between points A and B
X_A, Y_A = coordinates for point A
X_B, Y_B = coordinates for point B
K = scale factor to convert the coordinate measure to a distance measure

Example

Suppose that we want to estimate the distance between a plant at Madrid, Spain, and the warehouse at Milan, Italy, as shown in Figure 14-2. Madrid has coordinates $X_A = 5$, $Y_A = 6$ and Milan has coordinates $X_B = 11$, $Y_B = 7.5$. The map-scaling factor, or distance between successive coordinate numbers, is 194 kilometers. The computed straight-line distance is

$$D_{A-B} = 194\sqrt{(11 - 5)^2 + (7.5 - 6)^2}$$
$$= 1200\,\text{km}$$

The road distance from a road atlas is 1724 km. The road distance exceeds the computed distance because of the circuity with which a vehicle must normally travel.

If rectangular distances are desired to conform better to the rectangular layout of roads, especially in cities, a generalized distance formula can be used:

$$D_{A-B} = b_0 + b_1[|X_A - X_B| + |Y_A - Y_B|] + b_2\sqrt{(X_A - X_B)^2 + (Y_A - Y_B)^2} \qquad (14\text{-}2)$$

where $b_0, b_1,$ and b_2 are found by fitting the equation to active versus straight-line distances.[14]

---

[13]Many of the commercial computer products for mileage determination can be found in Accenture's annual guide to logistics software available through the Council of Logistics Management at www.CLM1.org.
[14]Jack Brimley and Robert Love, "A New Distance Function for Modeling Travel Distances in a Transportation Network," *Transportation Science*, Vol. 26, No. 2 (1992), pp. 129–137.

Due to distortions caused by various mapping techniques for projecting a globe onto a plane, the simple grid overlay technique may produce computational errors that vary, depending on the map projection method and where on the map the distances are computed. A more reliable technique is to use longitude-latitude coordinates and the great circle (spherical trigonometry) distance formula. Not only does the formula avoid mapping distortions, it also accounts for the curvature of the earth. The great circle formula is

$$D_{A-B} = 3959\{\arccos[\sin(LAT_A) \times \sin(LAT_B)$$
$$+ \cos(LAT_A) \times \cos(LAT_B) \times \cos|LONG_B - LONG_A|]\} \qquad \textbf{(14-3)}$$

where

D_{A-B} = great circle distance between points A and B (statute miles)
LAT_A = latitude of point A (radians)[15]
$LONG_A$ = longitude of point A (radians)
LAT_B = latitude of point B (radians)
$LONG_B$ = longitude of point B (radians)

Although this formula appears to be rather intimidating, it can be easily computer programmed,[16] and its advantages can outweigh this disadvantage. Some of these advantages are

- Latitude and longitude coordinates can be used around the world.
- The coordinates are available from a wide variety of sources, including road maps, navigational maps, encyclopedias, government publications, and commercial services.
- The coordinate system is generally understood.
- Good accuracy is achieved.

Therefore, the great circle method of distance computation is frequently the method of choice in computer programs for logistics planning. However, to preserve computational accuracy, the two points in the formula should be within the same hemisphere.

---

[15]Radians are computed from degrees by dividing them by 57.3, i.e., $180/\pi$.
[16]A small program in the BASIC programming language to compute the great circle distance from coordinates in degrees would be

```
100   C = 57.3
110   A = SIN(LATA/C) * SIN(LATB/C) + COS(LATA/C) * COS(LATB/C)
          * COS(ABS(LONGB - LONGA)/C)
120   D = 3959 * ATN(SQR(1 - A^2)/A)
```

where

D = distance in statue miles from the first to the second point
C = a constant to convert degrees to radians
$LATA$ = latitude of the first point in degrees
$LONGA$ = longitude of the first point in degrees
$LATB$ = latitude of the second point in degrees
$LONGB$ = longitude of the second point in degrees

Example

Continue the previous example by computing the straight-line distance from Madrid to Milan, but use the great circle distance formula. The coordinates for Madrid are $LONG_A = 3.41°W$, $LAT_A = 40.24°N$ and for Milan the coordinates are $LONG_B = 9.12°E$, $LAT_B = 45.28°N$. Dividing each of these coordinates by 57.3 converts them to radians. Hence, $LONG_A = 0.0595$, $LAT_A = 0.7023$, $LONG_B = -0.1592$, $LAT_B = 0.7902$. Note that $LONG_B$ is negative since it is east of the Greenwich line and $LONG_A$ is positive being west of that line. Putting this information in Equation (14-3), we have

$$D_{A-B} = 3959\{arccos[sin\ (0.7023) \times sin\ (0.7902)$$
$$+ cos\ (0.7023) \times cos\ (0.7902) \times cos|-0.1592 - 0.0595|]\}$$
$$= 724\ miles$$

Since there are 1.61 kilometers per mile, $D_{A-B} = 724 \times 1.61 = 1166$ kilometers. (*Note*: Arccos, sin, and cos values are found from trigonometric tables.)

Computed distances will always understate the actual distance between two points. Vehicles do not travel in a straight line. Rather, they move through a network of road, rail, or navigational routes, balancing distance and time to traverse the network. Because of this, computed distances are adjusted using a circuity factor, or multiplier. When the grid is a simple, linear type and Equation (14-1) is used, the circuity factor is approximately 1.21 for roads and 1.24 for railroads in well-developed networks. When using latitude-longitude coordinates in the great circle formula to compute distance [Equation (14-3)], circuity factors for various regions of the world, as given in Table 14-4, are good starting values. A precise circuity factor for any particular region can be determined simply by taking a sample of distances between selected points and averaging the ratio of actual-to-computed distances.

In addition to mileage estimates, time estimates are sometimes needed to reflect customer service in the network. A common practice is first to estimate distances and then to convert them to time estimates by dividing distance by travel speed. However, some research has been done to estimate transit times for intercity and intracity networks. Camp and DeHayes developed regression equations for estimating intercity transit times using a grid system.[17] Ratliff and Zhang estimate speed and time for regions the size of cities.[18]

Facility Costs

Costs related to a facility such as a warehouse can be represented in terms of (1) fixed costs; (2) storage costs; and (3) handling costs. Fixed costs are those that do not change with the activity level of the facility. Real estate taxes, rent, supervision, and

---

[17]Robert Camp and Daniel DeHayes, "A Computer-based Method for Predicting Transit Time Parameters Using Grid Systems," *Decision Sciences*, Vol. 5 (1974), pp. 339–346.
[18]H. Donald Ratliff and Xinglong Zhang, "Estimating Traveling Time/Speed," *Journal of Business Logistics*, Vol. 20, No. 2 (1999), pp. 121–139.

Country	Number of Points	Average Circuity Factor	Standard Deviation
Argentina	66	1.22	0.15
Australia	77	1.28	0.17
Byelorussia	21	1.12	0.05
Brazil	120	1.23	0.11
Canada	49	1.30	0.10
China	66	1.33	0.34
Egypt	21	2.10	1.96
Europe	199	1.46	0.58
England	37	1.40	0.66
France	9	1.65	0.46
Germany	31	1.32	0.95
Italy	11	1.18	0.10
Spain	61	1.58	0.80
Hungary	36	1.35	0.25
India	105	1.31	0.21
Indonesia	16	1.43	0.34
Japan	36	1.41	0.15
Mexico	49	1.46	0.43
New Zealand	4	2.05	1.63
Poland	45	1.21	0.09
Russia	78	1.37	0.26
Saudi Arabia	21	1.34	0.19
South Africa	91	1.23	0.12
Thailand	28	1.42	0.44
Turkey	28	1.36	0.34
Ukraine	36	1.29	0.12
United States[a]	299	1.20	0.17
Alaska	55	1.79	0.87
US East[b]	143	1.20	0.16
US West[c]	156	1.21	0.17

[a]Excluding Alaska and Hawaii
[b]East of the Mississippi River
[c]West of the Mississippi River
Source: Ronald H. Ballou, Handoko Rahardja, and Noriaki Sakai "Selected Country Circuity Factors for Road Travel Distance Estimation," *Transportation Research*, Part A, Vol. 36 (2002), pp. 843–848.

Table 14-4 Circuity Factors for Selected Countries (and Areas of the United States)

depreciation are examples of fixed costs. However, we should recognize that all costs are variable at some activity level. Careful consideration must be given as to whether cost is likely to change over a reasonable activity range that may be applied to a facility when classifying a cost as fixed.

Storage costs are those that vary with the amount of stock stored in the facility. That is, if a particular cost will increase or decrease with the level of inventory maintained in the facility, then the cost will be classified as a storage cost. Typical costs here might be some utilities, personal property taxes, capital tied up in inventory, and insurance on inventory value.

Handling costs vary with the facility throughput. Typical examples are labor costs to store and retrieve items, some utility costs, and variable handling equipment costs.

Private or leased warehousing costs are tracked through a firm's accounting system. Reports are periodically issued as a list of accounts, giving costs and their associated descriptions. Judgment must be used to classify these data as annualized fixed, storage, and handling costs useful for network planning.

Example

A major oil company's warehouse stocks tires, batteries, and accessories that are sold through gasoline retail outlets. An accounting report of expenses associated with the operation of the warehouse for one year is shown in Table 14-5. This author has made judgments as to how the expenses might be allocated to fixed, storage, and handling cost categories as would be needed for network planning. See if you would allocate them any differently.

When public warehouses are involved, storage and handling rates are easily obtained. The service is for hire and can be purchased generally in direct proportion to the amount needed. Rates for storage ($/cwt./month) and handling ($/cwt.) appear on the public warehouse contract. No fixed costs apply since this is a for-hire service. However, there may be vendor discounts offered based on the length of contract and the projected volume.

Costs for plants and vendors are also easily found. The variable costs for the plant output by product are usually obtained from the accounting standard costs for production. For purchased goods, vendor costs are the prices quoted to the buyer.

Facility Capacities

Strict capacity limitations on plants, warehouses, and vendors can have a substantial impact on network configuration. Yet capacities, in practice, are not absolute, rigid values. While there may be a most efficient throughput at which a facility operates, working overtime, working additional shifts, storing product in the aisles, and securing additional equipment or space on a temporary basis are just a few of the ways that capacity may be expanded. Although these come at an increased cost, care should always be taken to not view capacities as too rigid a constraint.

ACCOUNT DESCRIPTION	TOTAL EXPENSE	ANNUAL FIXED COST	STORAGE COST	HANDLING COST
Salaries and wages[a]	$347,440	$36,500	$	$310,940
Overtime pay	40,351			40,351
Part-time temporary workers	23,551			23,551
FICA	27,747	2,915		24,832
Unemployment pay	4,437	466		3,971
Travel expense	5,716	5,716		
Meals for overtime	844			844
Benefit plan expense	19,619	2,061		17,558
Group insurance	14,860	1,561		13,299
Janitor expense—material	5,481	5,481		
Snow and rubbish removal	2,521	2,521		
Building and grounds maintenance	19,780	19,780		
Fire protection	2,032	2,032		
Landscaping	3,855	3,855		
Blacktop[b]	15,621	15,621		
Unsalable merchandise	4,995		4,995	
Security	583	583		
Office supplies and forms	38,697			38,697
Postage	518			518
General warehouse supplies	64,338			64,338
Electric	39,332	39,332		
Heat	28,974	28,974		
Telephone	8,750	8,750		
Books, subscriptions	1,017	1,017		
Membership dues and expense	3,993	3,993		
Taxes—real estate	43,570	43,570		
Taxes—personal property	35,354		35,354	
Truck expense	12,961			12,961
Materials handling equipment expense	29,042			29,042
Totals		$224,728	$40,349	$580,902

[a]Includes warehouse manager.
[b]Amortized over 10 years.

Table 14-5 Annual Warehouse Expenses Allocated to Fixed, Storage, and Handling Cost Categories

Inventory-Throughput Relationships

When planning involves the location of warehouses, it is usually necessary to esti-mate how inventory levels throughout the network will be affected as warehouse number, location, and size change. Recall from Chapter 9 on inventory, there are two forces acting on inventory levels—regular stock and safety stock. As the number of facilities is reduced in a network, the inventory levels will generally decline. Recall that the square-root law predicts the reduction in regular stock; it fails to estimate safety stock effects. Using the inventory throughput will help to estimate both effects.

Because the location problem is one of allocating demand among warehouses, we would like to be able to project the amount of inventory in a warehouse from the demand, or throughput, assigned to it. One way to find the inventory-throughput relationship is to generate it from the company's own inventory policy. That is, an inventory turnover ratio of eight turns per year may be the goal. Since the turnover ratio is annual sales to average inventory, the relationship is defined. However, this is an expression of what management intends and not what actually occurs. It simply may be the best relationship that we have if no other information is available.

Perhaps a better way to find the inventory-throughput relationship is to observe how management controls inventories. A common report for most firms is the stock status report that gives monthly inventory levels and shipments for each warehouse in the network. By averaging the inventory levels for each warehouse and summing the shipments, a data point on a graph can be found, as shown in Figure 14-6. Plotting similar data for all warehouses and plant locations that act as warehouses serving their local territories completes the data profile. We then fit the best mathematical equation to the data that can be found. From this equation, knowing the annual demand assigned to an existing or new warehouse, we can estimate, on the average, the amount of inventory that should be in a particular warehouse.

When (1) there are few warehouses in the existing network from which to generate a reasonable data profile; (2) the execution of the inventory policy is so varied between warehouses that an aggregate relationship cannot be accurately established;

Figure 14-6 An Inventory-Throughput Curve for a Producer of Industrial Cleaning Compounds

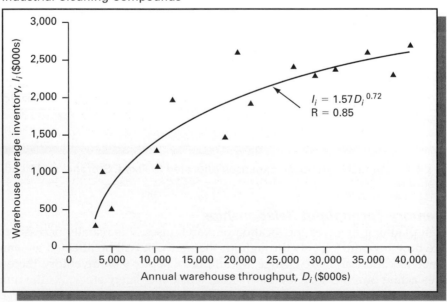

$$I_i = 1.57 D_i^{0.72}$$
$$R = 0.85$$

or (3) the inventory policy is to be changed, it then may be necessary to estimate the average inventory level from the inventory policies for individual product items. This can be accomplished by simulating the action of demand on individual items in a warehouse and summing the results to an aggregate inventory level for all items. How a company controls each of the items is reflected in the total inventory levels. By dividing demand among varying numbers of possible warehouses, simulated data can be generated as shown in Figure 14-6.[19]

Future Demand Estimation

It makes little sense to plan the network based on past or current demand data when the results of the planning are not likely to be implemented immediately. Therefore, we seek some future year for design purposes. Medium- to long-range forecasting methods may be useful here. As an alternative, many firms produce a five-year forecast for general planning purposes. This can be useful information for network planning as well.

Other Factors and Strictures

After the basic economic data has been gathered, information will still be needed on various restrictions that may affect network design. Bender outlines these as follows:

- Financial limitations, such as maximum allowable investment in new facilities
- Legal and political constraints determining, for example, the need to avoid certain areas in evaluating potential sites
- Manpower limitations, such as the number and quality of personnel available to support new strategies
- Deadlines to be met
- Facilities that must be kept operating
- Contractual conditions, both existing and anticipated[20]

Missing Information

One of the more perplexing problems in network planning is not having all the necessary data needed to carry out the analysis. This frequently occurs when the analysis involves facilities not currently operated by the company. For these facilities, no definitive costs are available concerning their operation. They must be either estimated or acquired externally. An estimating approach is to borrow from existing data, either from currently operated facilities in the same proximity of the potential facility, or from facilities having the same general characteristics. Transport rate curves may be duplicated at new locations or new samples of rates may be drawn from around these new origin points. Estimates of average inventory levels are taken from the average inventory-throughput curve.

---

[19]For an in-depth discussion of aggregate inventory-throughput relationship development, see Ronald H. Ballou, "Estimating and Auditing Aggregate Inventory Levels at Multiple Stocking Points," *Journal of Operations Management*, Vol. 1, No. 3 (1981), pp. 143–153; and Ronald H. Ballou, "Evaluating Inventory Management Performance Using a Turnover Curve," *International Journal of Physical Distribution and Logistics Management*, Vol. 30, No. 1 (2000), pp. 72–85.

[20]Paul S. Bender, "Logistic System Design," in James F. Robeson and Robert G. House (eds.), *The Distribution Handbook* (New York: Free Press, 1985), p. 173.

Information not available within the company may sometimes be found outside it. Economic data such as labor rates, leasing rates, taxes, and construction costs may be found from regional labor surveys periodically conducted by the Department of Labor. The various chambers of commerce conduct local economic surveys that provide data useful for developing warehouse costs. Roadway Pilot, Yellow Freight, and other trucking companies offer free disks, or Internet access to them, of their transportation rates between hundreds of intercity origin and destination points around the United States. Several vendors offer transport rates for sale, such as the SMC[3] Corporation.[21] Public warehousemen will quote rates. Although data from these sources do not represent "hard negotiation" on the part of the firm, they do provide ways of filling in some missing data.

THE TOOLS FOR ANALYSIS

When the appropriate information has been developed for network planning, analysis to find the best design can begin. For this problem type, the process of searching for the best designs is complex and is usually assisted through the use of mathematical and computer modeling. Consider some of the choices.

Choices for Modeling

Although there are numerous individual models that can be used for analysis, models may be classified in just a few categories, namely, (1) chart, compass, and ruler techniques; (2) simulation models; (3) heuristic models; (4) optimization models; and (5) expert system models. Some of these models were discussed in Chapter 13.

Chart, Compass, and Ruler Techniques

This is a general label referring to a wide variety of intuitive techniques aided by a relatively low level of mathematical analysis. However, the results need not be of low quality. Insight, experience, and a good understanding of network design allow an individual to generate satisfactory designs. Subjective factors, exceptions, costs, and constraints, many of which cannot be represented by the most elaborate mathematical model, can be taken into account. This enriches the analysis and is likely to lead to designs that can be directly implemented.

Methods used to support this type of analysis are likely to seem rudimentary in today's computerized world. Statistical charting, mapping techniques, and spreadsheet comparisons are just a few of the techniques that might be employed.

Application

When labor threatened to unionize at a brake manufacturing plant, its owner sought to move operations to another location. The plant was located in a Midwestern state where labor unions were traditionally strong. The plant's owner

---

[21]See www.SMC3.com.

wanted the new location to be in a right-to-work state. Given the limited number of locations that this stricture implied for a single new facility, each location was easily cost-analyzed with the use of a handheld calculator. Once the general region of the country for location was identified, the final site was selected by comparing many subjective factors, such as quality of local education, community attitudes about the operation, and the availability of transportation and utilities. Specific costs associated with the site were also considered, such as real estate and local taxes, utility rates, and rents.

Simulation Models

Simulation models are represented by two types: (1) deterministic simulation and (2) stochastic, or Monte Carlo, simulation. Deterministic simulators are essentially cost calculators, where the values of structural variables (e.g., product flows in a network) are given to the model and it in turn calculates the costs, services statistics, and other relevant information. On the other hand, stochastic simulators attempt to mimic actual events (e.g., order patterns, transport delivery times, and inventory levels over time in a supply channel) using probability distributions to represent the uncertainty in the time of events and the level of the event variables. Deterministic simulations are typically used to evaluate a company's current network design so that a "base case" can be established against which optimized network designs may be compared. Stochastic simulations are used to show the performance results of inventory control methods, transport service selection, customer service policies, and so on. Stochastic simulations deal effectively with the *time* dimension of supply chain planning whereas deterministic simulators are used in conjunction with spatial network design.

Simulating the network ordinarily involves replicating the cost structures, constraints, and other factors that represent the network in a reasonable manner. This replication is usually done by means of mathematical relationships, which are often stochastic in nature. Then, the simulation procedure typically is

> . . . nothing more or less than the technique of performing sampling experiments on the model of the system.[22]

That is, a particular network configuration is presented to the simulation model that then provides the costs and other data relevant to the operation of the system design. Repeating the experiment many times over with the same design and with different designs generates statistics that are useful in making comparisons among the design choices. Due to the complexity of the model relationships and the amount of information handled in simulations, they are ordinarily conducted on a computer. Manipulating the simulation model rather than the real system is done as a matter of convenience.

---

[22]Frederick S. Hiller and Gerald J. Lieberman, *Introduction to Operations Research*, 3rd ed. (San Francisco: Holden-Day, 1980), p. 643.

Simulations have been used to deal with about every planning problem in logistics. Some years ago, Shycon used a (deterministic) simulation to help locate warehouses.[23] Andersen Consulting (now Accenture) has used the technique (stochastic simulation) to analyze the flow of product through multiple echelons of facility locations with the purpose of answering questions relating to inventory levels, production output, and timing of flows in the supply-distribution channel.[24] Powers and Closs investigated the effects of trade incentives on logistical performance using simulation.[25] Many more examples exist.

Simulations are, for the most part, tailor-made to the particular problem being analyzed. Although a few simulators exist that specifically handle logistical problems, such as LREPS,[26] PIPELINEMANAGER,[27] LSD,[28] and LOCATE,[29] many other simulators may be created with the aid of general simulation languages. These include SIMSCRIPT, GPSS, SIMULA, DYNAMO, SIMFACTORY, and SLAM. A number of these languages now include a graphics feature whereby the action of product flows and stocking levels can be animated in simulated time on a video screen for easier interpretation of the results.

Stochastic simulation is the method of choice when substantial detail in a complex problem description is essential, when there are stochastic elements in the problem, and when finding the mathematically optimum solution is not critical. Practitioners rank simulation as the second most frequently used quantitative technique for analysis, ranking it only behind statistics.[30]

A stochastic simulator called SCSIM is available as part of the LOGWARE package. It replicates a multi-echelon supply channel and allows the testing of various forecasting methods, inventory policies, prices, transportation delivery times, production lot sizes and processing times, order processing times, and item fill rates. Results include projected revenue, various logistics and production costs by echelon, customer service statistics, inventory levels, back orders, and fill rates. More will be said about this simulator later in this chapter.

Heuristic Models

Heuristic models are something of a blend of the realism in model definition that can be realized by simulation models and the search for optimum solutions achieved by

---

[23]H. N. Shycon and R. B. Maffei, "Simulation-Tool for Better Distribution," *Harvard Business Review*, Vol. 38 (November–December 1960), pp. 65–75.

[24]PIPELINEMANAGER™, a proprietary computer simulation software package of Accenture, Chicago, Illinois.

[25]Thomas L. Powers and David J. Closs, "An Examination of the Effects of Trade Incentives on Logistical Performance in a Consumer Products Distribution Channel," *Journal of Business Logistics*, Vol. 8, No. 2 (1987), pp. 1–28.

[26]Donald J. Bowersox, O. K. Helferich, P. Gilmour, F. W. Morgan, Jr., E. J. Marien, G. L. Lawrence, and R. T. Rogers, *Dynamic Simulation of Physical Distribution Systems* (East Lansing, MI: Division of Research, Graduate School of Business Administration, Michigan State University, 1972).

[27]A simulator of logistics channel product flows developed by Andersen Consulting, a division of Arthur Andersen and Company.

[28]David Ronen, "LSD—Logistic System Design Simulation Model," *Proceedings of the Eighteenth Annual Transportation and Logistics Educators Conference* (Boston: October 9, 1988), pp. 35–47.

[29]A simulator for facility location developed by CSC Consulting.

[30]John L. Harpell, Michael S. Lane, and Ali H. Mansour, "Operations Research in Practice: A Longitudinal Study," *Interfaces*, Vol.19, No. 3 (May–June 1989), 65–74.

optimization models. They generally achieve a broad problem definition, but do not guarantee optimum problem solutions. The models are built around the concept of the heuristic, which Hinkle and Kuehn define as

> A short cut process of reasoning . . . that searches for a satisfactory, rather than an optimal, solution. The heuristic, which reduces the time spent in the search for the solution of a problem, comprises a rule or a computational procedure, which restricts the number of alternative solutions to a problem, based upon the analogous human trial-and-error process of reaching acceptable solutions to problems for which optimizing algorithms are not available.[31]

Heuristic modeling is a practical approach to some of logistics' most difficult problems. Heuristics are useful where the desire is for the model to search for a best solution, but too much might need to be compromised to solve the problem by optimizing methods. We often use heuristics in planning, where they may appear as principles or concepts. Examples of heuristic rules might be

- The most likely sites for warehouses are those that are in or around the centers of greatest demand.
- Customers that should be supplied directly from source points and not through a warehousing system are those that can purchase in full-vehicle-load quantities.
- A product should be warehoused if the differential in transportation costs between inbound and outbound movement justifies the cost of warehousing.
- Items in a product line that are best managed by just-in-time procedures, rather than statistical inventory control, are those that show the least variability in their demand and lead time patterns.
- The next warehouse to add to a distribution system is the one that shows the greatest cost savings.
- The most expensive customers from a distribution standpoint are those that purchase in small quantities and are located at the end of the transportation lanes.
- Economical transportation loads are built by consolidating small-volume loads into full-vehicle loads beginning from the most remote customers on the distribution network and combining loads along a line to the transportation origin point.[32]

Such rules as those in the preceding list can be programmed into a model, often a computer software program, to allow the search for a solution to follow the logic of these rules.

Optimization Models

Optimization models are based on precise mathematical procedures for evaluating alternatives and they guarantee that the optimum solution (best alternative) has been

[31]Charles L. Hinkle and Alfred A, Kuehn, "Heuristic Models: Mapping the Maze for Management," *California Management Review*, Vol. 10 (Fall 1967), p. 61.
[32]Ronald H. Ballou, "Heuristics: Rules of Thumb for Logistics Decision Making," *Journal of Business Logistics*, Vol. 10, No. 1 (1989), pp. 122–132.

found to the problem as proposed mathematically. That is, it can be proved mathematically that the solution produced is the best. Many of the deterministic operations research, or management science, models are of this type. These include mathematical programming (linear, nonlinear, dynamic, and integer programming); enumeration; sequencing models; various calculus-dominated models; and equipment replacement models. Many optimization models have been generalized and are available as computer packages.

When do you use optimization models? According to Powers, ". . . wherever and whenever possible."[33] He goes on to note several advantages of the optimization approach:

- The user is guaranteed to have the best solution possible for a given set of assumptions and data.
- Many complex model structures can now be handled correctly.
- A more efficient analysis is conducted since all alternatives are generated and evaluated.
- Reliable run-to-run comparisons can be made, since the very best solution is guaranteed for each run.
- The cost or profit savings between optimum and heuristic-generated solution can be significant.[34]

Although these are impressive advantages, the optimization models are not without their disadvantages. The primary disadvantage is that, as the complexity of the problem increases, an optimum solution cannot be achieved within a reasonable computational time and with the memory capabilities of even the largest computers. Often, the realism of the problem description must be considered in trade-off with solution time. Even so, a limited optimization model might be used in a heuristic model, where optimization solves part of the problem. On the other hand, optimization models involving mathematical programming (a major type for network planning) frequently include heuristics to guide the solution process and limit solution time since they cannot guarantee that the solution will be found without enumerating all possible alternatives with resulting unacceptable running time.

Example

A basic economic order quantity (EOQ) model that is used for inventory control is a good illustration of an optimization model. It is a calculus-based model that is very popular in practical application. Although of limited scope, it captures the essence of many inventory-control problems and is useful as a submodel within such planning models as a supply channel simulator. The EOQ model gives the optimum quantity of goods to reorder when the item inventory level drops to a predetermined amount. The model, which is a balance between the costs of ordering and the costs of carrying inventory, gives the optimum reorder quantity and has the following formulation:

[33]Richard F. Powers, "Optimization Models for Logistics Decisions," *Journal of Business Logistics*, Vol. 10, No. 1 (1989), p. 106.
[34]Ibid., pp. 111–115.

$$Q^* = \sqrt{2DS/IC}$$

where

Q^* = optimum reorder quantity (units)
D = annual demand (units)
S = cost to procure order (dollars/order)
I = annual inventory-carrying cost (annual % of unit value)
C = value of a unit held in inventory (dollars/unit)

This model was discussed in Chapter 9.

Expert Systems Models

When a planning problem, such as network design, is solved many times in a variety of situations, the planner is likely to develop insight into how the problem is solved. Such insight often transcends the most complex mathematical formulation possible. This knowledge and expertise, if they can be captured in a model setting or expert system, can be used to produce solutions of higher overall quality than previously obtained with the use of simulation, heuristic, or optimization methods alone. Cook defines an expert system as

> an artificially intelligent computer program that solves problems at an expert level by utilizing the knowledge and problem solving logic of human experts.[35]

Although expert systems are in their early stages of development, some applications have been reported, such as aids to medical diagnosis, mineral exploration, designing custom computer configurations, and stacking boxes on pallets. A few applications in logistics are beginning to be reported in the areas of inventory, transportation, and customer service.[36] According to Cook, expert systems have several distinct advantages over conventional planning systems:

---

[35]Robert L. Cook, "Expert System Use in Logistics Education: An Example and Guidelines for Logistics Educators," *Journal of Business Logistics*, Vol. 10, No. 1 (1989), p. 68.

[36]For example, see Mary K. Allen, *The Development of an Artificial Intelligence System for Inventory Management* (Oak Brook, IL: Council of Logistics Management, 1986); Robert L. Cook, Omar K. Helferich, and Stephen Schon, "Using an AI-Expert System to Assess and Train Logistics Managers: A Parts Inventory Manager Application," *Proceedings of the Sixteenth Annual Logistics Conference* (Anaheim, CA, October 5, 1986), pp. 1–24; Aysegul Ozsomer, Michel Mitri, and S. Tamer Cavusgil, "Selecting International Freight Forwarders: An Expert Systems Application, " *International Journal of Physical Distribution & Logistics Management*, Vol. 23, No. 3 (1993), pp. 11–21; James Bookbinder and Dominque Gervais, "Material-Handling Equipment Selection Via an Expert System," *Journal of Business Logistics,* Vol. 13, No. 1 (1992), pp. 149–172; Prabir K. Bagchi and Barin N. Nag, "Dynamic Vehicle Scheduling: An Expert Systems Approach," *International Journal of Physical Distribution & Logistics Management,* Vol. 21, No. 2 (1991); Lori S. Franz and Jay Woodmansee, "Computer-Aided Truck Dispatching Under Conditions of Product Price Variance with Limited Supply," *Journal of Business Logistics,* Vol. 11, No. 1 (1990), pp. 127–139; Peter Duchessi, Salvatore Belardo, and John P. Seagle, "Artificial Intelligence and the Management Science Practitioner: Knowledge Enhancements to a Decision Support System for Vehicle Routing," *Interfaces,* Vol. 18, No. 2 (March–April 1988), pp. 85–93; and Mary K. Allen and Omar K. Helferich, *Putting Expert Systems to Work in Logistics* (Oak Brook, IL: Council of Logistics Management, 1990), Chapter 3.

- They can process both qualitative and quantitative information, allowing critical subjective factors such as managerial judgment to more easily be part of the decision process.
- They can process uncertain information and provide solutions with only partial information, allowing more complex, unstructured problems to be solved.
- They provide solutions faster and at lower cost by using only the minimum information needed to solve a problem.
- They display the expert's problem solving logic, which allows the logistics manager to quickly improve decision-making capabilities.
- They provide portable, duplicatable, and documentable knowledge.[37]

Identifying experts, specifying the knowledge base (much of which may be qualitative), and acquiring their relevant knowledge are the greatest hurdles to be overcome in developing expert system models. Yet, the concept of capturing the techniques and knowledge associated with the artistry of planning in order to complement the scientific methods already used in planning has so much appeal that expert systems undoubtedly will increase in popularity.

Decision Support Systems

The database and the tools for analysis have been combined, with the aid of the computer, into what is now called a decision support system (DSS). A DSS aids the decision-making process by allowing the user to interact directly with the database, to direct data to decision models, and to portray results in a convenient form. According to Andersen, Sweeney, and Williams, a DSS has four basic subsystems:

- Interactive capability that enables the user to communicate directly with the system.
- A data manager that makes it possible to extract necessary information from both internal and external databases.
- A modeling subsystem that permits the user to interact with management science models by inputting parameters and tailoring situations to specific decision-making needs.
- An output generator with a graphics capability that enables the user to ask what-if questions and obtain output in easily interpretable form.[38]

Such systems may simply provide an environment in which the decision maker may interact, but he or she is given substantial latitude in making a final choice. On the other hand, the DSS may give the solution that the decision maker is to implement. The former may be more typical when strategic planning is involved, whereas the latter may be more characteristic of operational planning. In either case, the computer-based DSS gives an extended dimension to the planning process.

---

[37]Cook, "Expert System . . .," pp. 68–70.
[38]David R. Andersen, Dennis J. Sweeney, and Thomas A. Williams, *An Introduction to Management Science*, 4th ed. (St. Paul, MN: West, 1985), p. 722.

Application

The Batesville Casket Company produces and distributes a line of premium caskets to funeral homes throughout the United States. Distribution takes place regionally from about 50 warehouses that domicile the trucks making daily deliveries to meet funeral home orders. Batesville developed a decision support system for its truck dispatchers. Orders from all over the country are entered into the company's mainframe computer at Batesville, Indiana. Overnight, the order quantities, along with customer location information, are transmitted to a microcomputer at the appropriate warehouse. Combined with information stored locally in the computer, the database manager within the system prepares the data in the form needed by a truck-routing and scheduling model. The local dispatcher calls upon this model to find good routes and schedules for the day's deliveries. He uses the model results as a first solution to his problem, modifying them according to late-arriving orders, changes in equipment availability, and modified customer requirements. He can test his revised plan against the optimized design before deciding his final delivery schedule.

CONDUCTING THE ANALYSIS

We now turn our attention to the logic used to strategically plan the logistics network. The network design problem is positioned at the very top of the planning hierarchy, as illustrated in Figure 14-7. It differs from other logistics planning problems in both the frequency with which the planning is repeated and the degree of aggregation in the information used in the planning process. To contrast network design from the other planning problems, consider how Stenger classifies the problems at each level in the hierarchy.

- *Network design.* Designing the network to accomplish the firm's strategic objectives. The number, location, product assignments, and capacities/capabilities of distribution centers, plants, and consolidation points are specified. Targets are set for inventory levels throughout the network. The level of customer service to be provided will be determined. Aggregate data and long-term forecasts are used and the planning process is not likely to be repeated in less than one year.

- *Aggregate planning and allocation.* Planning at this hierarchical level determines loads, or allocates demand to distribution centers, plants, and material sources on an aggregate basis. The aggregate volumes for purchasing, production, warehousing, and traffic are specified. Planning here is repeated quarterly or monthly.

- *Flow planning and master production scheduling.* Planning at this level is similar to the previous one, except that allocation is for the individual stock-keeping unit. The objective is to ensure that forecasts and inventory targets are being met. The planning horizon is monthly or weekly.

Figure 14-7
A Hierarchy of
Logistics Decision
Making

Source: Adapted from
Alan J. Stenger,
"Electronic Information
Systems—Key to
Achieving Integrated
Logistics Management,"
*Proceedings of the
Seventeenth Annual
Transportation and
Logistics Educator's
Conference* (Atlanta, GA,
September 27, 1987),
p. 16.

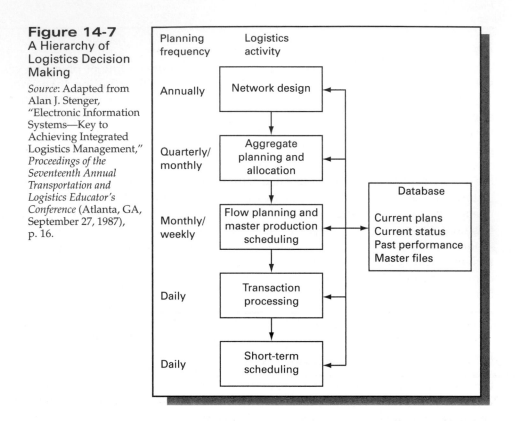

- *Transaction processing.* This is a short-term allocation planning problem whereby customer orders arriving in a random manner are assigned to be filled by location and carrier. Planning is daily.

- *Short-term scheduling.* A short-term planning problem that seeks to optimize the use of resources, such as transportation, to deal with specific open orders, while meeting explicit order processing deadlines. Planning is daily.[39]

The procedures used for strategic planning do vary from planner to planner and from project to project. However, good practice can be generalized into at least several basic elements. Consider the general steps in this procedure.

Auditing Customer Service Levels

A logical, but optional, first step in designing a network is to conduct a customer service audit. This involves asking customers about the level of logistics service they are currently receiving and the level that they would like to receive. Personal interviews with customers or mail questionnaires are typically used to answer such questions as

---

[39]Alan J. Stenger, "Electronic Information Systems—Key to Achieving Integrated Logistics Management," *Proceedings of the Seventeenth Annual Transportation and Logistics Educators Conference* (Atlanta, GA, September 27, 1987), pp. 12–26.

- What levels of service do customers expect?
- What levels of service do competitors provide?
- How do competitors achieve their service levels?
- To what extent has the firm assured itself that its strategy meets desired levels of costs and services to end users?
- To what extent has the firm employed "channel vision" in determining who should do what, when, where, and how in its channels of distribution?
- Does the firm's logistics strategy support its corporate strategy?[40]

This type of audit can help to establish the target logistics customer service level for the network design; however, it is quite common for service levels to be specified by management or to be set at the existing levels.

The external audit may be followed by an internal one. The purpose is to establish the level of service that the firm is actually providing and to define a benchmark for service. Sterling and Lambert suggest that the internal audit should answer the following questions:

- How is customer service currently measured within the firm?
- What are the units of measurement?
- What are the performance standards or objectives?
- What is the current level of attainment—results versus objectives?
- How are these measures derived internally?
- What is the internal customer service reporting system?
- How does each of the firm's business functions perceive customer service?
- How do these functions interface in a communications and control context?
- What is the variance in order cycle time, and how does this variability impact on the customer's business?[41]

Although it would be beneficial to conduct such an internal audit, most planners do not do it. Rather, they are more likely to rely on replicating the current network design as the best indication of the current customer service levels that the firm is providing.

It would be ideal if these audits could generate a reliable relationship between the customer service levels and the resulting revenues that would be realized from a particular network design. Since they rarely do, it is common to treat customer service as a *constraint* on the network design. The constraint can be changed to see the effect on total costs and, thereby, indirectly impute the worth of service.

Organizing the Study

The first phase of network design typically involves defining the scope and objectives of the project, organizing the study team, determining the availability of needed data, and establishing the collection procedures. The purpose is to determine

---

[40]Jay U. Sterling and Douglas M. Lambert, "Customer Service Research: Past, Present and Future," *International Journal of Physical Distribution & Materials Management*, Vol. 19, No. 2 (1989), pp. 1–23.
[41]Ibid.

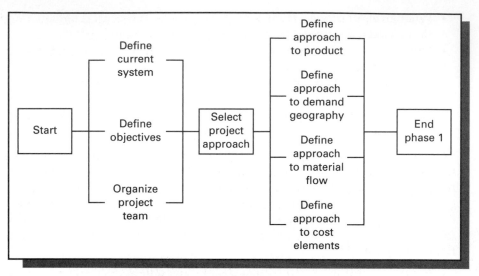

Figure 14-8 Logistics Network Design, Organization Phase

Source: Frank H. Mossman, Paul Bankit, and Omar K. Helferich, *Logistics Systems Analysis,* rev. ed. (Washington, D.C.: University Press of America, 1979), p. 307.

the feasibility of conducting a strategic planning study within a particular situation, the appropriate members to be included on the study task force, and the likelihood of the study having useful results. Mossman, Bankit, and Helferich have summarized this initial study phase (see Figure 14-8) and have given a description of the tasks involved:

- Review the present logistics situation to define costs, customer service levels, and logistics operations to provide a basis for evaluating logistics system alternatives (the logistics audit).
- Interview key management personnel and each member of the project team to ensure understanding of management objectives and to gain background for defining the specific questions and logistics systems alternatives to be evaluated in the study.
- Develop a preliminary list of critical management study assumptions, logistics operating and marketing policies, and guidelines that are critical to the evaluation of logistics alternatives and to the data collection effort.
- Specify the required evaluation criteria and study the output in terms of cost and customer service variables.
- Select the solution technique (model) based on the appropriateness for the alternatives to be evaluated, ease of preparing input data, cost and time estimates, and projected future utilization.
- Define the specific data requirements and provide the data collection procedures.
- Outline any major manual analyses required to supplement the computer model results to further evaluate the impact on cost and customer service.

- Conduct a working meeting with the project team to review findings, conclusions, model selection criteria, and preliminary project work plan.
- Estimate the benefits in terms of cost reduction (profit improvements) or customer service improvements expected from the study.
- Recommend, as appropriate, any suggestions for immediate cost or customer service improvements.
- Define project management procedures and estimate the personnel, computer, and other support requirements of the study.[42]

The task force should be organized with an eye toward strategy implementation. Careful attention should be given to including those people whose areas may be affected by the study and who may provide valuable insights and judgments as needed. It is particularly important to include persons from the production and marketing areas.

Benchmarking

Benchmarking, or validation of the modeling or other analytical processes used in planning, is the second phase of strategic planning. The philosophy here is to create a reference point, or base case, using a firm's current distribution patterns and policies. The methods used for analysis should be reasonably close to what standard accounting and reporting procedures produce. In addition to establishing the cost of the current distribution system so that changes may be made against it, the benchmarking process builds confidence that the methods used will accurately portray the firm's distribution costs and customer service performance.

Modeling is a popular approach to the network design problem, and benchmarking serves an important role in the analytical process. Analysis is directed at making comparisons between the network in its current configuration and a new, improved network configuration. Of course, management would like the comparisons to reflect actual conditions under which they must operate. However, models are much easier to manipulate than an actual network, so we use modeling as a way of making comparisons. The comparison of model results is a surrogate for what would be expected in actual practice. Therefore, benchmarking is the process whereby we validate that the modeling process faithfully replicates the cost and service levels of the current network. This builds confidence that when the model represents network configurations not now experienced by management, it will match to a reasonable degree the cost and service levels in practice.

Benchmarking typically proceeds in the following manner: Representative product groups are established. The number is determined as a balance between retaining the distinctive characteristics of the products with regard to service and costs, and the benefits of reduced data collection resulting from product aggregation.

Next, sales are aggregated geographically into a manageable number of demand centers. Customer service policies are defined for each product group. Data are collected for relevant cost categories, such as transportation, warehousing, inventories,

---

[42]Frank H. Mossman, Paul Bankit, and Omar K. Helferich, *Logistics Systems Analysis*, rev. ed. (Washington, D.C.: University Press of America, 1979), Chapter 8.

and production/purchase. Current product-flow paths are described for both movements through the warehouse as well as movements from plants/vendors/ports directly to customers. Inventory policies are also defined at this time.

Finally, various relationships between cost, demand, and service are established from the collected data. The information is organized in cost-service categories to be compared to actual expenditures made. The task force reviews the reasonableness of these results attempts to explain any deviations. Once this validation process is complete, selection of the best system design can begin.

Network Configuration

The modern approach to network configuration planning is to use the computer to manipulate the substantial amounts of data involved in the analysis. Computer models that deal with the problem of location in network planning have been particularly popular. They have been useful in answering questions that relate to the number, size, and location of plants, warehouses, and terminals; the way demand is assigned to them; and the products that should be stored at each facility. The objectives for network configuration are to

- Minimize all relevant logistics costs while meeting the constraints on logistics customer service.
- Maximize the logistics customer service level while holding the line on total logistics costs.
- Maximize the profit contribution made by logistics by maximizing the spread between the revenues generated by a logistics customer service level and the costs for providing that level of service.

The third objective is more in keeping with a firm's economic goals, but, due to the frequent lack of a sales and service relationship for the firm's products, most models are built around the first objective.

Models that help the planner search for the best configuration of facilities will do so by attempting to balance conflicting cost patterns that occur among production/purchasing, warehousing, and transportation, subject to practical limitations such as plant capacity, warehouse capacity, and customer service restrictions. The costs are associated with product movements as they take place from plants and vendors through intermediate stocking points and on to customer locations. An example of the type of output report that can be obtained from a commercial-grade model for location analysis is shown in Figure 14-9. This summary report is a result of one computer run where the user specifies the facilities and the manner in which the product flows through them or the model makes the facility selections and allocates to them. The network is potentially like that represented in Figure 14-1. Note that no regional warehouses are specified in this solution, only field, or level 1, warehouses.

Establishing Benchmark Costs and Service Levels
The first step in strategic network planning is to establish a benchmark of existing logistics costs and service levels. Surprisingly, few firms have carefully described

Figure 14-9 Sample Output for One Product Group from a Commercial-Grade Facility Location Model

```
ANALYSIS OF PRODUCT -- Canned goods-EU

                      -SUMMARIZED NETWORK SOLUTION RESULTS-
Revenue                                    E$                              0
Production/purchase cost                                    13,425,407
Level 3 facility operating cost                                      0
Level 3 facility fixed cost                                          0
Level 3 facility inventory carrying cost                             0
Level 2 facility operations cost                                     0
Level 2 facility fixed cost                                          0
Level 2 facility inventory carrying cost                             0
Level 1 facility operations cost                               243,478
Level 1 facility fixed cost                                    160,000
Level 1 facility inventory carrying cost                       283,761
  Transportation cost:
Plants/vendors to level 3 facilities                                 0
Plants/vendors to level 2 facilities                                 0
Plants/vendors to level 1 facilities                           584,014
Plants/vendors to customers                                          0
Level 3 to level 2 facilities                                        0
Level 3 to level 1 facilities                                        0
Level 3 facilities to customers                                      0
Level 2 to level 1 facilities                                        0
Level 2 facilities to customers                                      0
Level 1 facilities to customers                             11,533,930
  Total cost                                                26,230,590

    Profit contribution                   E$                  -26,230,590
```

```
                          -CUSTOMER SERVICE PROFILE-
Dist. from                               Dist. from
facility to      Percent of   Cum. % of  facility to      Percent of   Cum. % of
customer, (Km)   demand       demand      customer, (Km)   demand       demand
  0.0 to  100.0    .0           .0         800.0 to   900.0   42.6         73.8
100.0 to  200.0    .0           .0         900.0 to 1,000.0    .0          73.8
200.0 to  300.0   12.1         12.1      1,000.0 to 1,500.0    2.2         76.0
300.0 to  400.0    3.3         15.4      1,500.0 to 2,000.0   24.0        100.0
400.0 to  500.0    4.1         19.5      2,000.0 to 2,500.0    .0         100.0
500.0 to  600.0   11.7         31.2      2,500.0 to 3,000.0    .0         100.0
600.0 to  700.0    .0          31.2             > 3,000.0      .0         100.0
700.0 to  800.0    .0          31.2             Total        100.0
```

```
                   -PLANT/VENDOR THRUPUT AND ASSOCIATED COSTS-
Plant/        Plant/                                        Plant/
vendor        vendor        Maximum          Assigned       vendor
number        location      thruput, Kgr     thruput, Kgr   cost, E$
  1           PARIS         200,000          69,712         2,180,591
  2           ROME          400,000          354,950        11,244,816
              Totals        600,000          424,662        13,425,407
```

Figure 14-9 (cont.)

Plant/ vendor number	Plant/ vendor location	--------Transport Costs from Plants/Vendors--------			
		To level 3, E$	To level 2, E$	To level 1, E$	To customers, E$
1	PARIS	0	0	131,630	0
2	ROME	0	0	452,384	0
	Totals	0	0	584,014	0

-LEVEL 1 FACILITY THRUPUT AND ASSOCIATED COSTS-

Level 1 facility number	Level 1 facility location	Maximum thruput, Kgr	Assigned thruput, Kgr	Storage costs, E$	Handling costs, E$
1	MILAN	900,000	354,950	57,080	141,980
2	LIVERPOOL	900,000	29,411	7,010	16,176
3	HANNOVER	900,000	40,301	5,918	15,314
	Totals	2,700,000	424,662	70,008	173,470

Level 1 facility number	Level 1 facility location	Facility fixed costs, E$	Estimated inventory level, E$	Inventory carrying costs, E$	Transport— Level 1 to customers, E$
1	MILAN	50,000	1,364,567	231,976	11,418,378
2	LIVERPOOL	80,000	131,685	22,387	52,648
3	HANNOVER	30,000	172,928	29,398	62,904
	Totals	160,000	1,669,180	283,761	11,533,930

-CUSTOMER ASSIGNMENTS TO FACILITIES-

Volume, Kgr	Seq no.	Customer location	Seq no.	Serving point location	Serv. point type	Serv. dist., Km	Serv. time, Days	Landed cost, E$/Kgr
38,955	1	LISBON	1	MILAN	LVL 1	1,930	.00	133.31
148,384	2	BARCELONA	1	MILAN	LVL 1	837	.00	36.09
14,035	3	LONDON	2	LIVERPOOL	LVL 1	316	.00	39.24
22,966	4	BERLIN	3	HANNOVER	LVL 1	295	.00	36.61
19,794	5	BRUSSELS	1	MILAN	LVL 1	842	.00	36.10
49,891	6	ROME	1	MILAN	LVL 1	535	.00	35.66
15,376	7	DUBLIN	2	LIVERPOOL	LVL 1	277	.00	39.13
17,335	8	COPENHAGEN	3	HANNOVER	LVL 1	461	.00	36.97
12,537	9	BORDEAUX	1	MILAN	LVL 1	868	.00	36.14
9,327	10	PALERMO	1	MILAN	LVL 1	1,004	.00	133.31
62,993	11	ATHENS	1	MILAN	LVL 1	1,694	.00	133.31
13,069	12	LUCERNE	1	MILAN	LVL 1	239	.00	35.23

-LEVEL 1 FACILITY ASSIGNMENTS TO SERVING POINTS-

Volume, Kgr	Seq no.	Level 1 facility location	Seq no.	Serving point location	Serv. point type	Serv. dist., Km	Serv. time, Days	Thruput cost, E$/Kgr
354,950	1	MILAN	2	ROME	PLANT	563	.00	34.31
29,411	2	LIVERPOOL	1	PARIS	PLANT	719	.00	37.39
40,301	3	HANNOVER	1	PARIS	PLANT	762	.00	35.20

their distribution flow patterns, customer service performance, or the total costs of distribution. This process sets the base level of costs, service, and configuration against which improvements may be compared, as shown in Table 14-6. The results may be used to validate the modeling process as well as to increase confidence that the projected cost improvements will be accurate.

	MODEL RUN TYPE[a]			
COST TYPE	BENCHMARK	IMPROVED BENCHMARK[b]	MAX. SAVINGS NETWORK[c]	IMPLEMENTABLE NETWORK[d]
Inventory and warehousing				
Capital	$ 103,110	$ 87,008	$ 87,626	$ 100,737
Tax and insurance	38,756	47,957	19,037	34,022
Order processing	284,366	223,820	198,210	262,413
Storage	165,788	138,412	119,749	119,293
Handling	299,863	265,252	329,385	253,479
Subtotal	$ 891,883	$ 762,449	$ 754,007	$ 769,944
Transportation				
Plant to warehouse	$ 261,853	$ 213,567	$0	$ 206,542
Warehouse to customer	1,041,661	1,113,978	1,453,812	925,043
Subtotal	$1,303,514	$1,327,545	$1,453,812	$1,131,585
Production	_At current capacities_		_No capacity restrictions_	
@Atlanta	$3,861,765	$3,906,037	$ 832,112	$3,404,138
@Indianapolis	667,057	593,876	770,427	906,619
@Houston	587,140	498,835	2,408,764	692,441
Subtotal	$5,115,962	$4,998,748	4,011,303	$5,003,198
Total	$7,311,359	$7,088,742	$6,219,122	$6,904,727
Customer Service	_Closely matched_		_No restriction_	
Percentage of demand				
< 300 miles	65%	63%	30%	68%
< 500 miles	85%	82%	45%	98%
No. of warehouses	9	9	3	10
Savings vs. benchmark	0	$ 222,617	$1,092,237	$ 406,632[e]

[a]Costs are totals for three product groups.
[b]Plant capacity restrictions are at current levels but with no service restrictions. The result is direct shipments from plants.
[c]No plant capacity or customer service restrictions. The result is direct shipments from plants.
[d]Current plant capacities are in effect and the desired service level is set at 500 miles.
[e]Essentially no investment in plant or warehousing is required to realize these savings.

Table 14-6 Summary of Selected Results from a Network Analysis for a Specialty Chemical Company

Improved Benchmark

Over time, such occurrences as demand shifts, transport rate adjustments, and warehouse storage and handling rate changes may cause an otherwise well-planned network design to perform at a suboptimal cost-service level. Therefore, the next task in strategic network planning is to optimize the logistics patterns subject to the existing number and location of facilities, capacities of those facilities, current service levels, and the like. This is a no-investment strategy, where cost savings may be realized without an outlay of capital. As Table 14-6 shows, a specialty chemical company could realize more than $400,000 per year in cost savings (implementable network) from a total benchmark cost of $7.3 million, a reduction of 6 percent, by increasing the number of stocking points used and allowing customer service to be brought in line with stated service policy. This is an important result because further alterations to the network are properly compared with the improved benchmark rather than the benchmark cost level.

Maximum Opportunity

In strategic network planning, it is informative to determine the network with the lowest possible variable costs. This is accomplished by finding the optimum network without plant or warehouse capacity constraints, without customer service restrictions, and considering a large number of plant and warehouse locations. As Table 14-6 indicates, this result, although attractive from a cost savings standpoint, is usually achieved through reduced service and a shifting of demand to facilities beyond their capacity to handle it. Obviously, if these savings were not great enough to support a change beyond the improved benchmark, further exploration of alternatives would likely be fruitless because they would only have higher costs.

Practical Designs

Between the improved benchmark and the maximum savings design, there may be a number of acceptable network strategies. These may be found through repeated model runs that represent various network configurations and assumptions about demand, costs, and service. These configurations can produce a combination of cost and service levels, as shown in Figure 14-10. That is, for any given service level, there may be many different numbers of warehouses and their locations (configurations) that can realize a particular service level, but with different cost levels. Drawing a smooth line through the lowest cost points generates a network design curve that identifies the lowest cost alternative for each service level (see Figure 14-10). It is along this design curve that we seek an improved network configuration. If a current design is not optimal and, therefore, it lies above the design curve, then moving the design to the left increases customer service without increasing costs. Moving the design point down lowers costs while maintaining the same customer service level. Moving the design point to the design curve affords the maximum opportunity for cost or service improvement.

The costs and service results for one such practical design are shown in Table 14-6. Note that in this case the company chose a conservative design where the number of stocking points and the customer service level were higher than that of the benchmark

Figure 14-10
A Design Curve for Network Configuration Generated from the Lowest Cost Alternatives for a Particular Customer Service Level

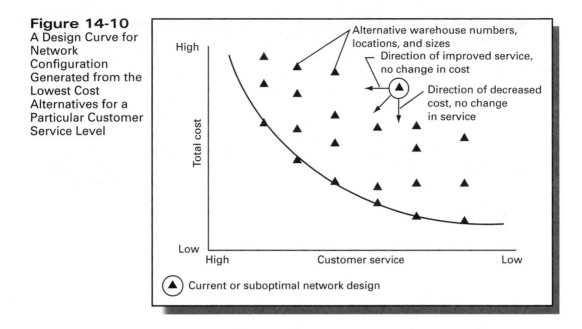

and the improved benchmark. The savings were still substantial at over $400,000 per year—more than 5 percent of total production and distribution costs. There was also some improvement in the logistics customer service level.

What-If Analysis

There will always be errors in estimating cost and capacity input information for network planning. There may be attractive designs that are suboptimal from a modeling standpoint, but better reflect practical considerations beyond the modeling process. Repeating the analysis using selected network scenarios and/or revised cost and capacity figures is referred to as *what-if analysis*. It is a way of using the analytical process to assist in bringing more reality into the search for a practical network design. What-if analysis is often considered more valuable to management than the modeling process's ability to find an optimal solution to a given set of data. This is because there is often little cost difference between closely configured networks, and because an improved network design around which the organization can rally is usually more valuable than a mathematically optimum solution.

Comparable Data[43]

It seems appealing to use actual company data to design a network, but this may lead to a biased design. Suppose that a warehouse in a company's distribution network

---

[43]This section based on Ballou, "Information Considerations," p. 12.

that may be poorly located has low per unit costs owing to its current high through-put volume and the related spreading of its fixed costs. On the other hand, another warehouse has a good location, but has been assigned high per unit costs due to its underutilization. If these costs are used in revising the network, the poorly located warehouse may survive and the other may be closed or continue to be underutilized. A similar situation may occur between rates assigned to existing warehouses and potential ones that would be new and have the most modern equipment.

A remedy for this kind of data incomparability is to assign a standard rate to each warehouse that neutralizes the effects of age and size, but preserves the cost differentials that are due to location. Of course, standardizing the rates in this manner may drive demand away from existing warehouses where there is a high sunk cost and an emotional investment by management. A choice must be made here.

Design Year Analysis

Ideally, designing or redesigning a network is based on some period in the future, since a new design cannot be implemented instantly. Of course, a forecast of demand can be made to the design year. A major question is whether costs should also be projected to the design year. Except for demand forecasting, projecting costs into the future results in losing touch with the benchmark and its associated comparability. It is usually a better practice to hold costs constant unless they are changed in the benchmark as well.

Channel Design

Configuration of the network mainly concerns location questions, where issues relating to inventory and transportation are dealt with on an aggregate level. There are several additional considerations regarding how the products should be directed through the configured network. Products flowing through a typical logistics/supply channel, like that shown in Figure 14-11, raise some of the following questions:

- How much of each product item should be stocked at each echelon and at each stocking point?
- What is the best transport service to use between each echelon?
- Should a make-to-order or make-to-stock strategy be followed?
- Should a push or pull inventory strategy or requirements planning be used?
- What methods of information transmittal between stocking echelons are best?
- Which forecasting methods perform best?

Therefore, channel planning is concerned with planning the configured network operation. The best design approach is to consider network configuration and channel design simultaneously. This is a very difficult problem, because the fundamental dimensions on which each is based are quite different. Network configuration is primarily based on a *spatial*, or geographic, dimension whereas channel design is based on a *temporal*, or time, dimension. Although combining spatial and temporal issues into a singular analysis is ideal, practical considerations require that they be treated separately and then worked iteratively to achieve a satisfactory overall design.[44]

---

[44]Waiman Cheung, Lawrence C. Leung, and Y. M. Wong, "Strategic Service Network Design for DHL Hong Kong," *Interfaces*, Vol. 31, No. 4 (2001), pp. 1–14.

Figure 14-11
A Multi-Echelon
Logistics/Supply
Channel

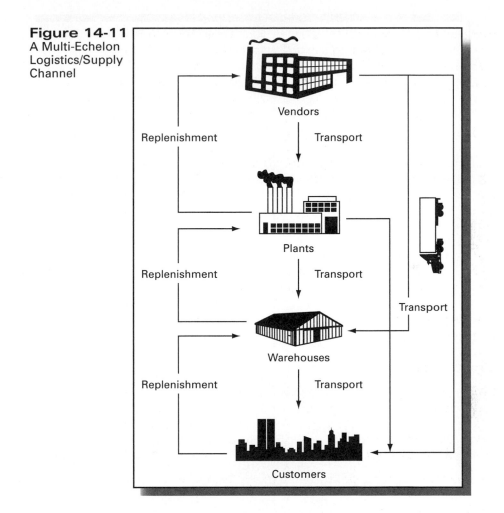

Because there are no effective, integrated models that deal with the entire strategic supply chain planning problem, it is usually necessary to break down the complex problem into manageable portions. This has meant solving facility location, inventory policy, and transport planning problems separately but recursively, where the results of one analysis are used as inputs to another. The process quickly converges on a satisfactory answer to the comprehensive problem.

A primary method for channel planning involves the use of computer simulation of the supply chain channel. The action of such simulators is to closely mimic the flow of orders and product through a configured network. Orders are generated in patterns similar to those a company actually experiences. Given a specific network configuration, its operating procedures, and policies, its transport services, and its customer service policies, product is tracked through the channel to meet the simulated order patterns. Sales, costs, and lead time statistics are typically captured by the simulation. Representative summary information generated by such a simulator is shown in Figure 14-12. By changing such elements as the method of forecasting sales,

Figure 14-12 An Illustrative Summary Report from PIPELINE MANAGER, a Supply Channel Simulator

```
PIPRPT01
                              ABC Manufacturing Co.
                              Pipeline Manager
                              Run Summary Report

Run Number: 001    Total Model Run Days: 364    #Items: 17                  #Finished Goods Warehouses: 03
Random Seed: 002       Total Periods: 13        #Vendors: 05                      #Central Warehouses: 01
                    Steady-State Days: 028       #Raw Material Warehouses: 03   #Customer Facing Warehouses: 05
                                                 #Plants: 03                             #Customers: 20
```

Statistic	Customers	Customer Facing Warehouses	Central Warehouses	Finished Goods Warehouses	Plants	Raw Material Warehouses	Vendors	Totals
Sales	105,300,000							105,300,000
Costs:								
Purchase							40,000,000	40,000,000
Production					15,000,000			15,000,000
Shipping		4,000,000	3,500,000	2,500,000	750,000	800,000		11,550,000
Warehousing		3,500,000	2,800,000	3,000,000	1,500,000	2,500,000		13,300,000
Inv. Carrying		1,250,000	750,000	800,000		600,000		3,400,000
Order Processing		900,000	550,000	400,000		450,000		2,300,000
Total Costs								85,550,000
Margin								19,750,000
Cust. Service Level	87%							87%
Fill Rate	90%	85%	93%		84%	86%		89%
Avg. Lead Time (Days)	4.8	4.5	6.8	6.3	8.4	2.4	22.0	55.2
Inventory Turnover		8.4	20.2	35.0		18.5		4.3

Avg. Inv. Units		150,200	62,600	44,700	81,000		298,000
Avg. Inv. $ Value		12,500,000	5,200,000	3,700,000	2,400,000		23,800,000
#Orders Placed	12,200	960	200		180		13,540
#Order Units Placed	1,300,000	1,285,000	1,310,000		1,296,000		5,191,000
Avg. Size (Units)	106	1,340	6,500		6,700		380
Avg. Size ($)	8,840	110,000	540,000		230,000		31,800
#Shipments Received	12,500	965	195	2,200	690	2,210	18,760
#Units Received	1,281,250	1,230,000	1,275,000	1,280,000	1,250,000	1,285,000	7,601,250
Avg. Size (Units)	103	1,275	6,540	580	1,800	581	405
Avg. Size ($)	8,510	100,000	545,000	48,300	58,000	18,350	32,400
#Backorders	845	850	55	45	350	450	1,750
#BO Units	71,500	85,000	48,400	171,000	206,500	270,000	782,650
Avg. Size (Units)	85	100	880	3,800	590	600	447
Avg. Size	7,565	8,100	73,000	317,000	19,000	49,800	35,780
#Splits & Partials	370	550	480	190			1,220
#Split/Part Units	38,850	35,000	28,000	15,200			78,200
Avg. Size (Units)	105	63	58	80			64
Avg. Size ($)	7,350	5,280	4,100	6,640			5,320
#Cancellations	150						150
#Cancelled Units	18,750						18,750
Avg. Size (Units)	125						125
Avg. Size ($)	10,750						10,750

Figure 14-13 Simulated Channel for SCSIM

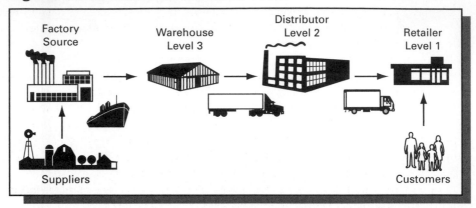

the modes of transportation, the inventory-control policies, and the methods for filling orders, the status of the channel design to meet customer service requirements in an efficient manner can be evaluated.

Channel Simulation in LOGWARE

A stochastic simulator called SCSIM is available in the LOGWARE software that accompanies this textbook. It has the capability of replicating the operating characteristics of a supply channel having the multiple echelons shown in Figure 14-13. Because the simulation is multi-echelon, the effect of the channel policies of one or more channel members can be tested for the effect on other members. Operating costs and performance factors describe the modes of transportation, order processing, and manufacturing. Different methods of forecasting and inventory control can be used with manual inventory control and user forecasting, if desired. Demand patterns can be specified, or they can be generated using statistical patterns. Product fill rates can be specified, or are the result of product flowing through the channel.

To run a simulation, prepare the database as instructed in the user's manual. There are at least two concerns to be aware of when running a stochastic simulator. First, recall that simulations should be treated as experiments. That is, conclusions result from a number of runs, or trials, that are analyzed statistically using hypothesis testing. Randomly selecting a seed number gives the result for one experiment, or trial. Using the same seed number produces the same result if no changes have been made in the database. Choosing a different seed number gives a different event sequence with different experimental results. A reasonable sample size (number of runs) should be obtained with the appropriate averaging of the results and statistical testing to compare one supply channel design to another.

The second concern is the length of simulated time. Simulations are subject to start-up conditions such that taking the results from early periods can give erroneous impressions. The simulation needs to be run for a sufficient time until steady-state conditions are reached. Plotting run results can show the initial unrepresentative periods, which can be eliminated. For example, if the simulation length is set to be five years, it may be reasonable to accept results from years 2 through 5. Year 1 results are sacrificed. For additional considerations in using simulators as analytical tools, refer to a good book on simulation modeling.[45]

To illustrate the use of the simulator, consider the "bull whip" effect that occurs in supply channels. In a multi-echelon supply channel where each member derives its demand pattern from the orders of the immediate downstream member, it is said that the demand patterns show increasing variability with each successive upstream member.[46] The uncertainty of increasing demand variability can cause poor planning and high operating costs. The "bull whip" phenomenon can be illustrated using the SCSIM simulator. Tracking sales through a supply channel consisting of a production point serving a warehouse serving a distributor serving a retailer, who finally serves the end customer (see Figure 14-13) gives the sales plot shown in Figure 14-14. A representative sales pattern for a simulated year is shown

Figure 14-14 Illustration of Increasing Demand Variability ("Bull Whip" Effect) in a Multi-Echelon Supply Channel

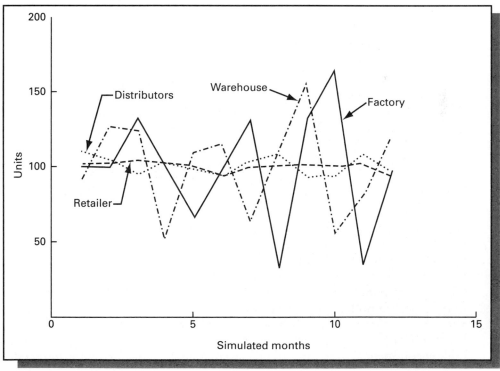

---

[45]For example, see Averill M. Law and W. David Kelton, *Simulation Modeling and Analysis*, 3rd ed. (New York: McGraw-Hill, 2000), especially Chapters 5 and 10.

[46]Frank Chen, Zvi Drezner, Jennifer K. Ryan, and David Simchi-Levi, "Quantifying the Bullwhip Effect in a Simple Supply Chain: The Impact of Forecasting, Lead Times, and Information, *Management Science*, Vol. 46, No. 3 (March 2000), pp. 436–443.

for each channel member. Notice the increasing oscillations for the upstream members. Some of the ways that the sales patterns can be smoothed and channel planning improved include:

- Reduce uncertainty throughout the channel by centralizing information, thereby making critical planning information, especially customer demand data, available to all members
- Plan echelon inventory levels on end-channel (customer) demand
- Improve forecasting
- Reduce lead times
- Improve inventory decision rules
- Form partnerships and collaborate on order sizes, deliveries, and order timing

The simulator is useful to test the effect of changing inventory decision rules, transportation modes, order-processing procedures, and forecasting methods without disturbing actual operations. The cost-service implications can be seen for the entire channel as well as for individual channel members.

Integrated Supply Chain Planning

Comprehensive supply chain planning is a process involving several elements, a number of which have previously been discussed in this chapter. Unless the relationship between customer service and logistics design is known, planning starts with determining a target customer service level. A survey of customer desires or a specified customer service level is needed. After assembling the appropriate data, analysis can begin.

Good planning involves both network configuration and channel design. Integration of these two is not generally achieved using a single model.[47] However, a network model can be used in concert with a channel simulator. Preliminary results for the number of facilities, their locations, and allocated volume to them are found from applying a location model. Then, these results are provided to the channel simulator so that inventory effects, transport mode analysis, and fill rate levels can be evaluated. Revised inventory-throughput relationships, transport modes with associated rates, and facility costs are inputted into the location model for reevaluation. Solving the two models recursively continues until there are no longer changes in the model inputs and outputs. This process allows converging on an optimal, or nearly optimal, solution to the integrated location-channel planning problem. However, in practice, most supply chain planning is conducted using only the location analysis while estimating the effects on operation issues.

---

[47]For an early attempt at creating a single planning model, see Donald J. Bowersox et al., *Dynamic Simulation of Physical Distribution Systems* (East Lansing, MI: Division of Research, Graduate School of Business Administration, Michigan State University, 1972).

A LOCATION CASE STUDY

To illuminate some of the major ideas presented in this chapter, consider the process of evaluating and making recommendations for the production and warehousing system of a specialty chemical company. Special attention is given to how various data elements were obtained and treated, the methods used to converge upon a final recommendation, the practical restrictions that had to be considered for a satisfactory solution, and the reporting of the results to management.

Problem Description

Aqua-Chem Company produced a line of water treatment chemicals that were used to control mineral deposits in boilers, algae formation in commercial air-conditioning systems, and bacteria growth in swimming pools. Customers were located throughout the United States; sales approximated $15 million per year for about 21 million pounds of chemicals. The company grew dramatically through the acquisition of similar small, regional firms, which eventually gave it market coverage of the entire country. Product distribution was continued from the acquired plants as it had been before acquisition. Six such companies and plants were merged under this program, but no systematic review of the entire logistics system had ever been made. Therefore, a supply chain network study was proposed to suggest improvements in the flow of product to customers.

The first order of business was to form a task force of company and consulting personnel who would guide the study. This group consisted of the director of purchasing, the vice president of marketing, the controller, the traffic manager, an analyst from the planning department, and a professor of logistics from a local university who would act as a consultant to the group. Priority was given to defining the scope of the study. Because purchasing costs play an important role in determining the final distribution network, all costs from the major vendors, through production of the products and on to the customer, were considered. Depending on whether the products were ordered by customers in full-truckload quantities or in less-than-truckload quantities, separate supply chain networks would have to be considered. Volume purchases would be shipped directly from one of the six plants located at Portland, Oregon; Phoenix, Arizona; Minneapolis, Minnesota; Dallas, Texas; Asheville, North Carolina; or Akron, Ohio. Smaller orders would be served from warehouses or from plants acting as warehouses for their local territories. The costs associated with each of these distribution channels are summarized in Figure 14-15.

Managing the Problem Size

The company distributed hundreds of individual product items to thousands of customers. Due to the enormous amount of data required, it was necessary in this study, as well as in most distribution studies, to make selective simplifications that reduce computational effort while retaining accuracy in representing the problem. First, rarely does all product volume need to be included in the study. Many products

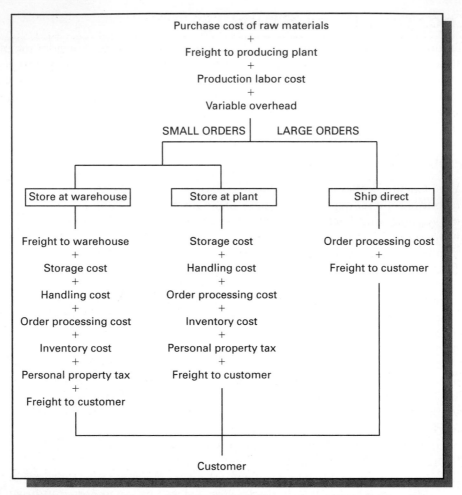

Figure 14-15 Alternative Distribution Channels and Distribution Costs for the Aqua-Chem Company

account for less than five percent of sales and can reasonably be eliminated. This is an application of the 80-20 principle.

Second, those products having similar distribution characteristics may be grouped together and treated as one. For this study, the products were separated into those rated as class 55 and those rated as class 60 by the motor vehicle products classification scheme. These product groups were further separated into those moving through the warehouse network and those moving in volume directly to customers from the plants without the need for storage.

Third, there is little advantage gained by accounting for each customer on an individual basis. Aggregating them by geographic region substantially reduces the computational effort as well as the data collection effort. In this study, 323 demand clusters were chosen, following three-digit zip codes

Finally, mathematical curves were used to estimate the transportation rates between selected points in the network. Little loss in transport rate estimation accuracy was expected because regression curves were fitted to class rates over various distances with coefficients of determination (R^2) of more than 90 percent. Alternatively, the number of individual rates to be obtained for 4 product groups, 6 plants, 22 current and potential warehouses, and 323 demand clusters would have been 170,544. For practical reasons, the latter was rejected.

The Analysis

The major questions for Aqua-Chem were, which plants should be used, and which warehouses should they serve? How many stocking points should be used, and where should they be located? These questions were to be answered in the context of no specific customer service restrictions and the customers paying the warehouse outbound freight costs. A computer model was used to evaluate alternative network configurations. The results of several of the more interesting runs are shown in Table 14-7.

Note first in Table 14-7 that the current production-distribution network has a total cost of $6,348,179, with 63 percent of the demand within 300 miles of a stocking point. Twelve stocking points were being used. Next, an improved benchmark was found. Recall that this is the case where no investment is to be made in the network. Only adjustments to plant and warehouse territories were allowed, closing of facilities was permitted, and service was to remain approximately the same as the benchmark level. The result was an annual savings of $109,669, or 2 percent from the benchmark cost level. Note that warehouse-to-customer transport costs were held constant.

The results from multiple computer runs revealed that the distribution network design was being dictated by production costs at the plant sites. That is, the raw material costs, which were about 80 percent of production costs, were subject to volume discounts due to purchase quantity and shipment size. This resulted in three plants being the optimum number, and they were located at Akron, Asheville, and Dallas (see Table 14-7). A further reduction in the number of plants decreased total production costs, but the savings were more than offset by increased distribution costs. The optimum network design appeared to be three plants with between 12 and 14 stocking points. The three plants were balanced in terms of their capacities to take maximum advantage of purchasing economies. The resulting savings were approximately $188,000, or 3 percent from the benchmark costs. These savings could be achieved with an investment of $11,000 to move some production equipment to the Dallas plant.

Reporting the Financial Results to Management

Addressing the financial concerns of top management involves three key measures: Cash flow, profit, and return on investment. Ideally, the network design changes being proposed increase each of these measures.

Cost Type	Benchmark	Improved Benchmark	3 Plants 9,000 mi.[a]	3 Plants 900 mi.[b]	3 Plants 700 mi.[c]	2 Plants 900 mi.[d]
Inventory						
Carrying cost	$ 77,974	$ 121,196	$ 95,549	NC[e]	$ 120,406	NC[e]
Order processing	188,863	137,050	168,990	NC	165,770	NC
Storage	6,294	6,176	4,240	NC	6,574	NC
Handling	17,241	25,319	20,450	NC	29,534	NC
Tax	12,545	40,532	24,066	NC	24,934	NC
Subtotal	$ 302,917	$ 330,273	$ 313,295	$ 341,830	$ 347,218	$ 355,331
Transportation						
Plant to warehouse	$ 40,212	$ 123,517	$ 212,014	$ 297,457	$ 331,658	$ 386,587
Warehouse to customer	1,109,026	1,101,988	1,137,232	1,059,713	1,041,467	1,064,781
Subtotal	$1,149,238	$1,225,505	$1,349,246	$1,357,170	$1,373,125	$1,451,368
Production:						
@Akron	$1,965,740	$2,969,211	$1,470,728	$1,470,728	$1,470,728	$2,232,639
@Asheville	898,941	302,464	1,460,730	1,460,730	1,460,730	0
@Dallas	534,117	693,787	1,529,343	1,529,343	1,529,343	2,220,233
@Phoenix	714,377	277,043	0	0	0	0
@Portland	335,989	376,769	0	0	0	0
@Minneapolis	446,860	63,458	0	0	0	0
Subtotal	$4,896,024	$4,682,732	$4,460,801	$4,460,801	$4,460,801	$4,452,872
Total	$6,348,179	$6,238,510	$6,123,342	$6,159,801	$6,181,144	$6,259,571
CUSTOMER SERVICE						
Percent of demand						
< 300 miles	63%	67%	61%	63%	65%	71%
< 500 miles	88	82	79	85	88	83
Savings vs. benchmark	0	$109,669	$224,837	$188,378	$167,035	$ 88,608

[a]No customer service constraint.
[b]900 mile customer service constraint.
[c]700 mile customer service constraint.
[d]900 mile customer service constraint.
[e]Not specifically computed.

Table 14-7 Alternative Distribution Network Design for the Aqua-Chem Company

Cash Flow

Does the changed network release any cash that might be used to pay salaries or other bills? Reduction in inventory value is an obvious place where an asset can be turned into cash. Although inventory value is not reported directly in Table 14-7, the change can be estimated. Inventory-carrying cost is approximately 30 percent of the subtotal in Table 14-7. Therefore, for the three-plant, 900-mile alternative, the inventory-carrying cost is estimated to be $0.30 \times 341{,}830 = \$102{,}549$. The carrying-cost change from benchmark is $\$121{,}196 - 102{,}549 = \$18{,}647$. If the carrying cost is 25 percent, the change in inventory value is $\$18{,}647/0.25 = \$74{,}588$. If the cost of capital is 80 percent of the carrying cost (i.e., 20 percentage points of 25%), the cash flow is *positive* at $0.80 \times 74{,}588 = \$59{,}670$ per year.

Profit

Profit is the saving in overall costs that can contribute to the profit of the company. It is the balance of all relevant costs. This is the difference between the costs of the improved benchmark and preferred network design. The profit contribution, or savings, is $\$188{,}378 - 109{,}669 = \$78{,}709$ per year. In addition, some part of the $\$109{,}669$ difference between the benchmark and the improved benchmark can be saved as well, but it is not clear how much will materialize. Both are *positive* savings.

Return on Investment

The return on investment measure reflects the expenditure that needs to be made to achieve the cost savings. Compared with the improved benchmark, this yields a $[(188{,}378 - 109{,}669)/11{,}000] \times 100 = 716$ percent simple return on investment. Again, the value is *positive* and, in this case, quite significant.

Conclusion

This case study briefly illustrates some of the procedures and logic used in the strategic planning of supply chain networks. In this particular case, physical supply considerations were a dominant influence on structuring the distribution network. In addition, pricing policy neutralized the impact of the warehouse outbound transportation costs that further caused production costs to be a dominant design factor. Finally, controlling or restricting customer service increased costs, as did proliferating the number of stocking points. The final design is a balance of all relevant costs, customer service considerations, and the traditions and risk concerns of management. Realizing acceptance of the design requires addressing the financial concerns so important to top management.

CONCLUDING COMMENTS

Supply channel performance cannot be any better than the configuration of the network will allow. Poor facility locations, misallocations to them, improper stocking levels, ill-suited transportation methods, and undesirable customer service levels can result from an out-of-date or inappropriately designed supply chain network. The result is a supply chain profit contribution that is lower than it should be. Periodic planning of the network configuration ensures a good base for an efficient and effective supply channel.

This chapter outlined a three-part process for planning the supply chain network. First, data requirements, sources, and conversion to relevant information needed for planning were discussed. Second, quantitative methods useful in the planning process were outlined. Finally, a logical process was presented using location and simulation methods leading to good network design. This general planning process is used by many management consultants and corporate planners.

QUESTIONS

Some problems in this chapter can be solved or partially solved with the aid of computer software. The software packages in LOGWARE most important for this chapter are MULREG (*MR*), MILES (*D*), SCSIM (*S*), and WARELOCA (*W*). The CD icon

MR will appear with the software package designation where the problem analysis is assisted by one of these software programs. A database may be prepared for the problem if extensive data input is required. Where the problem can be solved without

the aid of the computer (by hand), the hand icon is shown. If no icon appears, hand calculation is assumed.

1. Explain what strategic network planning is for a supply chain. Select several companies, manufacturing as well as service oriented, profit versus nonprofit, and outline how you would proceed to design the supply chain network. Discuss the data needed, sources where they might be found, and how you would convert the data to the information needed for analysis. Propose a methodology that you think would be appropriate to the network design problem.

2. Develop a workable list of those members that should be included in a strategic network planning study team to ensure the study's successful completion and implementation.

3. Compute the expected road distance between the following pairs of points using longitude and latitude as the coordinate points.

		Location		Longitude	Latitude
a.	From	Lansing, MI	USA	84.55°W	44.73°N
	To	Lubbock, TX	USA	101.84°W	33.58°N
b.	From	Toronto	CAN	79.23°W	43.39°N
	To	Atlanta, GA	USA	84.39°W	33.75°N
c.	From	São Paulo	BR	46.37°W	23.32°S
	To	Rio de Janeiro	BR	43.15°W	22.54°S
d.	From	London	UK	0.10°W	51.30°N
	To	Paris	FR	2.20°E	48.52°N

Use a road circuity factor of 1.15.

4. Suppose that a certain linear grid coordinate system has been overlaid on a map of the United States. The grid numbers are calibrated in miles, and there is a road circuity factor of 1.21. Find the expected road distances between the following pairs of points:

	Location	X-Coordinate	Y-Coordinate
a. From	Lansing, MI	924.3	1675.2
To	Lubbock, TX	1488.6	2579.4
b. From	El Paso, TX	1696.3	2769.3
To	Atlanta, GA	624.9	2318.7
c. From	Boston, MA	374.7	1326.6
To	Los Angeles, CA	2365.4	2763.9
d. From	Seattle, WA	2668.8	1900.8
To	Portland, OR	2674.2	2039.7

5. The following table presents a sample of common carrier truck rates in $/cwt. for shipments in the range of 2000 to 5000 lb, originating at Chicago, with destinations to various cities surrounding Chicago. The rates are taken from the *Rocky Mountain Motor Tariff* and the mileages are from the *Rand McNally Mileage Guide*.

No.	Rate	Miles	No.	Rate	Miles	No.	Rate	Miles
1	4.15	169	21	11.44	1438	41	16.60	2384
2	16.20	2220	22	16.35	3017	42	12.64	1653
3	9.11	1108	23	9.32	962	43	13.85	2272
4	6.81	427	24	10.48	1341	44	3.80	107
5	13.53	2197	25	12.36	1520	45	13.84	1830
6	9.84	1226	26	9.54	1091	46	9.01	929
7	15.28	2685	27	10.94	1390	47	10.94	1455
8	6.92	465	28	9.63	1092	48	10.85	1162
9	9.51	936	29	11.99	1507	49	11.05	1435
10	8.03	751	30	5.95	208	50	15.61	2752
11	7.80	848	31	7.27	581	51	15.93	2866
12	12.77	1923	32	12.79	1694	52	14.18	2376
13	11.28	1004	33	11.30	1469	53	14.88	2018
14	7.80	657	34	11.47	1301	54	16.35	2984
15	8.24	955	35	6.37	315	55	17.81	3128
16	8.40	801	36	17.60	2670	56	16.35	3016
17	13.38	1753	37	8.23	574	57	10.02	1207
18	12.77	1998	38	3.70	109	58	8.00	448
19	10.69	1337	39	16.69	3144	59	12.07	1634
20	8.50	799	40	16.00	1907			

From these data, construct a transport rate estimating curve of the form $R = A + B \times$ distance. Using this curve, what rate would you estimate for a shipment moving 500 miles? How well do you feel that the line accurately represents the rates?

6. The California Fruit Growers Association distributes various dried fruit products throughout the country using 24 public warehouses. Estimate the amount of inventory that a new warehouse would have if the annual sales through the warehouse were known. The company has collected the following data from their 24 warehouses:

No.	Annual Warehouse Throughput, $	Average Inventory Level, $	No.	Annual Warehouse Throughput, $	Average Inventory Level, $
1	21,136,032	2,217,790	13	6,812,207	1,241,921
2	16,174,988	2,196,364	14	28,368,270	3,473,799
3	78,559,012	9,510,027	15	28,356,369	4,166,288
4	17,102,486	2,085,246	16	48,697,015	5,449,058
5	88,228,672	11,443,489	17	47,412,142	5,412,573
6	40,884,400	5,293,539	18	25,832,337	3,599,421
7	43,105,917	6,542,079	19	75,266,622	7,523,846
8	47,136,632	5,722,640	20	6,403,349	1,009,402
9	24,745,328	2,641,138	21	2,586,217	504,355
10	57,789,509	6,403,076	22	44,503,623	2,580,183
11	16,483,970	1,991,016	23	22,617,380	3,001,390
12	26,368,290	2,719,330	24	4,230,491	796,669

Construct an inventory-throughput curve for these warehouses. If a warehouse has an annual throughput of $50,000,000, how much inventory would you estimate for this warehouse? What comments can you make about warehouse 22? Explain how this relationship might be used in network planning. Recall that you may have already constructed this curve in a problem in Chapter 9.

7. Several broad classes of model types are available to assist in network analysis. Identify and contrast them. Suggest the circumstances under which each might be an appropriate choice.

8. The expert system is a new approach to solving complex problems. The expert system is based on the way that humans solve problems as expressed by a set of IF-THEN statements. As if you were to explain to someone how to locate a warehouse, develop at least 10 IF-THEN statements that would guide him or her to good locational choices. For example, a statement might be "If one warehouse is to be located, then a good location is likely to be in the center of the demand being served by the warehouse."

9. What is the usefulness of each of the following in the methodology for finding the best network design?
   a. Benchmarking
   b. Improved benchmark
   c. Maximum opportunity design
   d. What-if analysis

10. Explain how the strategic design of the network may favorably or unfavorably affect the efficiency and effectiveness of the supply channel to operate on a routine basis.

11. Sealy is the largest manufacturer of mattresses in the United States, having the largest market share. The company focuses on the higher-quality, higher-priced market segment. Sealy manufactures to order and, therefore, it carries no finished goods inventory. Shipment to retailers takes a day or two. The vice president of manufacturing services is concerned that Sealy's raw materials inventories are too high. These raw materials consist of (1) wire for springs, (2)

foam rubber for padding, (3) wood for framing, and (4) ticking, or covering material. There are currently 20 plants located throughout the United States. How would you propose to approach her problem?

CASE STUDIES

Usemore Soap Company:
A Warehouse Location Case Study

The Usemore Soap Company produces a line of cleaning compounds, used mainly for industrial and institutional purposes. Typical products include general cleaning compounds, dishwasher powders, rinse agents, hand soaps, motor vehicle washing compounds, and cleaning products for the food industry. The product line is composed of more than 200 products and nearly 800 individual product items. Package sizes range from 18-pound cases to large metal drums weighing 550 pounds.

Sales are generated throughout the 48 contiguous United States, with additional sales in Hawaii, Alaska, and Puerto Rico. Customers typically purchase in quantities less than 10,000 pounds, that is, less-than-truckload (LTL) quantities. A few customers purchase in truckload and bulk quantities. Annual LTL sales, which pass through the warehouses, are running at the 150 million pound level. Volume sales, which are served directly from plants, add another 75 million pounds. These sales represent approximately $160 million in revenue.

The primary marketing effort comes from a direct selling force operating under the incentive of a liberal sales commission structure. Salespeople look upon themselves as individual entrepreneurs and have a great deal of autonomy within the company. This marketing strategy has generally proved successful for the company, as the company has often been referred to as one of

the most profitable divisions within its widely diversified parent organization.

In spite of the high profitability, company management is concerned about the costs of producing and distributing the product line to maintain its competitive edge. Growth and shifting demand patterns are straining the production capacity of the four existing plants. In addition, changing costs of distribution, as well as the fact that the distribution network has not been studied in 12 years, raise questions about the proper placement of the warehouses. What follows is a summary of the problem conditions being faced by management. You are to suggest an improved distribution network that meets the stated customer service policy and minimizes total network production-distribution costs.

BACKGROUND

The current distribution network consists of four full product line plants located at Covington, Kentucky, New York, New York, Arlington, Texas, and Long Beach, California. The plants are currently producing product for their low-volume customers at the level of 595,102 cwt.,[1] 390,876 cwt., 249,662 cwt., and 241,386 cwt., respectively. This output is shipped from plants either to field warehouses in the distribution network or to customers within the local areas of the plants. In the latter

---
[1]cwt. = 100 pounds

No.	Location	No.	Location	No.	Location
1	Covington, KY[a]	9	Cleveland, OH	17	Milwaukee, WI
2	New York, NY[a]	10	Davenport, IA	18	Orlando, FL
3	Arlington, TX[a]	11	Detroit, MI	19	Pittsburgh, PA
4	Long Beach, CA[a]	12	Grand Rapids, MI	20	Portland, OR
5	Atlanta, GA	13	Greensboro, NC	21	W Sacramento, CA
6	Boston, MA	14	Kansas City, KS	22	W Chester, PA
7	Buffalo, NY	15	Baltimore, MD		
8	Chicago, IL	16	Memphis, TN		

[a]Field warehousing as part of plant operations.

Table 1 Current Plant and Public Warehouse Locations

case, plants serve as field warehouses as well as producing centers.

Warehousing takes place at 18 public warehouses and at the four plant locations, as shown in Table 1. These warehouses are dispersed in such a fashion that the majority of the customers are within a one-day delivery time frame of a stocking point; that is, approximately 300 miles. Except for the plants serving as warehouses, the warehouses are supplied in full truckload quantities. Less-than-truckload shipments serve customers. Customer order processing takes place at each warehouse location.

In addition, two potential plant sites are being considered at Chicago, Illinois, and Memphis, Tennessee. Additional warehouse sites are considered at the locations shown in Table 2.

Potential warehouse sites are made based on sales personnel's suggestions, favorable warehousing rates, good warehousing service availability, proximity to demand concentrations, and filling out of the distribution network. Of the existing and potential warehouse sites, it is hoped that an improved mix of warehouses can be found. In addition, plant expansion, either at existing sites or at new sites, will be needed to meet future demand projections. Specifically, answers to the following questions are sought:

1. How many warehouses should be operated now and in the future?

Table 2
Possible Public
Warehouse
Locations

No.	Location	No.	Location	No.	Location
23	Albuquerque, NM	32	Phoenix, AZ	41	Louisville, KY
24	Billings, MT	33	Richmond, VA	42	Columbus, OH
25	Denver, CO	34	St Louis, MO	43	New York, NY
26	El Paso, TX	35	Salt Lake City, UT	44	Hartford, CT
27	Camp Hill PA	36	San Antonio, TX	45	Miami, FL
28	Houston TX	37	Seattle, WA	46	Mobile, AL
29	Las Vegas NV	38	Spokane, WA	47	Memphis, TN P[a]
30	Minneapolis MN	39	San Francisco, CA	48	Chicago, IL P[a]
31	New Orleans LA	40	Indianapolis, IN		

[a]Prefers to warehouses at additional plant sites.

2. Where should they be located?
3. Which customers and associated demand should be assigned to each warehouse and plant?
4. Which warehouses should be supplied from each plant?
5. Should production capacity be expanded? When, where, and by how much?
6. What level of customer service should be provided?

SALES DATA

Manufacturing of soap liquids and powders is an uncomplicated and easily duplicated process, which contributes to substantial competition in the marketplace. The undifferentiated nature of soap products results in keen competition in both price and service. Customer service is of particular concern because it is directly affected by the choice of warehouses. No specific dollar figure can be placed on the total value of good distribution service, as it depends on customer attitudes about service and resulting patronage. The general feeling in the company is that service should be maintained at a high level so as not to jeopardize sales. A "high" level of service is taken to mean delivery time of 24 to 48 hours or less. This generally places customers somewhere between 300 and 600 miles of warehouses.

Annual sales for the products that move through the warehousing network are 147 million pounds for annual revenue of slightly more than $100 million. Sales are distributed similarly to population centers with an average profit margin of 20 percent. Figure 1 shows the six major sales territories, with sales volume in pounds by state. The company has more than 70,000 individual customer accounts, and these are aggregated into 191 active demand centers. A demand center is a grouping of zip code areas into a zip sectional center as the focus of the collected demand. These demand centers, along with how they are currently being served, are given in Table 3. In addition, the sales territory

in which the demand center is grouped is shown.

The five-year plan shows volume growth throughout the United States. This growth will not be uniform due to population and business migration patterns, competition, and varying promotional efforts. The changes in volume compared with current volume levels are projected by sales territory as follows:

Region No.	Sales Territory	Five-Year Growth Factor[a]
1	Northeast	1.30
2	Southeast	1.45
3	Midwest	1.25
4	Northwest	1.20
5	Southwest	1.15
6	West	1.35

[a]Multipliers to the current sales volume.

PRODUCTION COSTS AND CAPACITIES

The production variable costs at existing plants vary by location. This variance results from labor rate differences, volume purchases of raw materials, and inbound transport cost differences due to the proximity of the plants to major raw materials sources. These costs are listed next.

Plant	Variable Production Cost
Covington, KY	$21.0
New York, NY	19.9
Arlington, TX	21.6
Long Beach, CA	21.1

The potential plant at Chicago has an estimated cost of $21.0 per cwt.; and the Memphis plant has a cost of $20.6 per cwt. Expansion at any existing plant site would have the current variable cost. Fixed costs are not included for existing plants because these are sunk costs. However, to construct a new plant or expand an existing one would cost a minimum of

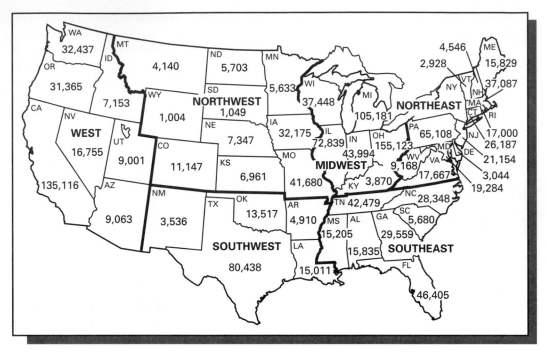

Figure 1 Usemore Soap Company Annual Sales in Cwt. by State, with Major Sales Districts Defined

$4 million. This cost would result in an output for the plant (or an output increase in the case of a plant addition) of up to 1 million cwt. per year for the near future.

According to current distribution patterns, the existing plants are producing, relative to throughput capacity (in cwt.), at the following rates:

Plant	Current Capacity	Current Production	Percent of Capacity
Covington, KY	620,000 cwt.	595,102 cwt.	96%
New York, NY	430,000	390,876	91
Arlington, TX	300,000	249,662	83
Long Beach, CA	280,000	241,386	86%
Total	1,630,000	1,477,026	91

WAREHOUSING RATES AND CAPACITIES

Company contracts with public warehousemen show that rates are categorized as storage, handling, and accessorial. Storage rates are quoted on a $/cwt./month basis of average inventory held. Handling charges are incurred whenever in or out movement of the product occurs and are assessed on a $/cwt. basis. Accessorial

charges are for a number of services, such as bill of lading preparation, local delivery, and stock status reporting. Similar charges are estimated for the four plant warehouses as a fair share of production operations.

Also associated with warehousing are the stock replenishment costs. These are costs for preparing the paperwork for normal replenishment and the expediting of stock into the warehouse. Stock order costs as well as customer order costs are computed by multiplying the average cost per order by the average number of orders for the warehouse.

The warehouse-related costs and other associated information are given in Table 3. Costs for existing points are taken from company records. Those for potential warehouses are determined from quotas by warehousemen in the appropriate cities. Estimates are made of costs where such information is not otherwise available.

There are no effective capacity limits on public warehousing. Usemore's space need is a small fraction of a public warehouseman's total capacity. On the other hand, a throughput of at least 10,400 cwt. per year, or a replenishment truckload every two weeks, is the desired minimum throughput needed to open a warehouse. Available space is limited at the four current plant sites. The stocking limits in terms of throughput at Covington = 450,000 cwt., New York = 380,000 cwt., Arlington = 140,000 cwt., and Long Beach = 180,000 cwt.

TRANSPORTATION COSTS

Three general transportation cost types are important to Usemore: inbound, outbound, and local delivery transport charges. Inbound transportation costs to a warehouse depend on the volume shipped and the distance between plant and warehouse. A sampling of truck common carrier rates at various distances from the plants for full truckload shipments shows that the transport rate between a plant and warehouse (P-W) can be reasonably approximated by a linear function. That is, the truckload rate is

P-W rate ($/cwt.) = 0.92 + 0.0034$d$ (miles)

where d is the distance between the two points.[2] Total inbound transport costs are determined by multiplying the P-W rate by the volume assigned to flow between the plant and warehouse.

Warehouse outbound transport costs depend on the distance that a customer is from the warehouse. If the customer is roughly within 30 miles of the warehouse, local cartage rates generally apply. These local delivery rates are shown by warehouse in Table 3. For distances greater than 30 miles, a linear function similar to that for the inbound rates can be developed. Given the average shipment size from the warehouses of approximately 1,000 pounds, the warehouse to customer (W-C) rate function is

W-C rate ($/cwt.) = 5.45 + 0.0037$d$

Computation of total warehouse outbound transport costs is carried out in the same manner as for inbound transport costs.

INVENTORY COSTS

Inventory costs depend on the average inventory maintained at a warehouse and the inventory rate factors that apply to the inventory level. These rate factors include the cost of capital, personal property taxes, and insurance costs. The average inventory at a warehouse will vary by the demand on the warehouse and by the method used to control the inventory. A mathematical function to express inventory based on annual warehouse throughput is found by plotting the annual average inventory against annual throughput at each active stocking point. The resulting curve is shown in Figure 2. Knowing that the annual cost-to-carry-inventory rate is approximately 12 percent of the average product value of $26 per cwt., the total cost to carry inventory at each warehouse is given by

$$IC_i = (0.12)(26)(11.3D_i^{0.58}) = 35.3D_i^{0.58}$$

where

IC_i = annual inventory carrying cost at warehouse i ($)

D_i = annual demand throughput at warehouse i (cwt.)

---

[2]For simplicity, one aggregated relationship is shown. In practice, several such relationships would be used to reflect the rate difference caused by geographic locations of the shipment origin points.

Table 3 Stocking Point Rate and Order Size Information

WHSE NO.	STORAGE ($/$)[a]	HANDLING ($/CWT.)[b]	STOCK ORDER PROCESSING ($/ORDER)	STOCK ORDER SIZE (CWT./ORDER)	CUSTOMER ORDER PROCESSING ($/ORDER)	CUSTOMER ORDER SIZE (CWT./ORDER)	LOCAL DELIVERY RATE[c] ($/CWT.)
1	0.0672	0.46	18	400	1.79	9.05	1.90
2	0.0567	0.54	18	400	1.74	10.92	3.89
3	0.0755	0.38	18	400	2.71	11.59	2.02
4	0.0735	0.59	18	400	1.74	11.30	4.31
5	0.0946	0.50	18	401	0.83	9.31	1.89
6	0.1802	0.75	18	405	3.21	9.00	4.70
7	0.0946	0.74	18	405	1.23	8.37	1.55
8	0.2072	1.14	18	405	1.83	13.46	1.79
9	0.1802	1.62	18	409	4.83	9.69	4.92
10	0.1442	1.14	18	410	2.74	8.28	2.23
11	0.0946	1.04	18	409	3.93	10.20	1.81
12	0.1982	1.06	18	410	3.18	15.00	1.00
13	0.0766	1.06	18	400	1.08	9.07	1.63
14	0.1262	1.22	18	423	1.56	11.72	1.17
15	0.1126	0.82	18	426	1.20	9.35	1.73
16	0.0991	0.64	18	433	1.78	8.70	0.50
17	0.1577	0.71	18	394	5.33	8.07	1.46
18	0.1307	0.79	18	398	0.91	7.66	2.29
19	0.1487	1.15	18	399	2.08	9.39	2.20
20	0.2253	0.80	18	490	1.10	7.31	1.49
21	0.1370	1.39	18	655	1.70	9.31	2.72
22	0.0991	0.83	18	400	2.46	10.14	4.17
23	0.1260	0.59	18	110	2.33	5.07	2.37
24	0.0631	0.45	18	134	1.88	6.80	1.36
25	0.0946	1.68	18	341	2.58	6.83	2.21
26	0.1216	0.88	18	149	1.83	14.32	0.80
27	0.0721	0.55	18	198	1.83	7.38	3.88
28	0.1532	0.80	18	420	1.58	9.70	2.14
29	0.1172	1.04	18	287	0.78	7.52	1.51
30	0.1080	1.46	18	408	5.33	11.46	1.70
31	0.1487	0.95	18	340	1.36	10.48	1.63
32	0.1396	0.69	18	333	1.50	6.67	1.66
33	0.1126	0.64	18	277	2.33	11.98	1.54
34	0.1712	1.35	18	398	0.93	10.13	1.84
35	0.1261	0.79	18	434	2.08	6.81	1.58
36	0.1352	0.80	18	323	0.88	7.67	1.93
37	0.2704	0.96	18	423	0.89	8.57	3.08
38	0.2250	0.80	18	425	2.88	7.61	1.43
39	0.1487	1.49	18	400	1.46	7.55	6.44
40	0.2073	1.14	18	400	2.75	10.13	2.83

WHSE NO.	STORAGE ($/$)[a]	HANDLING ($/CWT.)[b]	STOCK ORDER PROCESSING ($/ORDER)	STOCK ORDER SIZE (CWT./ORDER)	CUSTOMER ORDER PROCESSING ($/ORDER)	CUSTOMER ORDER SIZE (CWT./ORDER)	LOCAL DELIVERY RATE[c] ($/CWT.)
41	0.2073	1.14	18	400	2.75	10.13	2.83
42	0.1802	1.62	18	400	2.75	10.13	4.81
43	0.2613	1.39	18	400	2.71	11.59	3.89
44	0.1396	0.71	18	400	2.04	9.37	3.89
45	0.1036	0.55	18	400	2.75	10.13	1.74
46	0.0946	0.55	18	400	1.74	9.31	1.89
47	0.0682	0.64	18	400	1.78	8.70	0.50
48	0.0682	1.22	18	400	1.79	9.05	1.55

[a]Annual rate in $ per $ of average inventory in the warehouse.
[b]Annualized rate for moving 1 cwt. in and out of the warehouse.
[c]A transport rate that applies to customer shipments within 30 miles of a stocking point.

WAREHOUSE OPERATING COSTS

Warehouse operating costs refer to the combination of storage and handling costs incurred resulting from assigning demand to warehouses. Storage costs are computed by taking the storage rate and multiplying it by an estimate of the average inventory in the warehouse. Mathematically, this can be expressed as

$$SC_i = SR_i(26)(11.3D_i^{0.58})$$

where

SC_i = annual cost of stock storage at warehouse i ($)

SR_i = storage rate from warehouse i from Table 4

D_i = annual demand throughput at warehouse i (cwt.)

Figure 2 The Inventory-to-Warehouse Throughput Relationship for the Usemore Soap Company

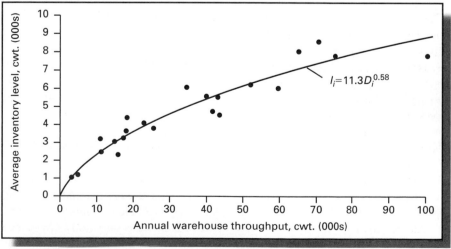

$I_i = 11.3D_i^{0.58}$

WAREHOUSE TO CUSTOMER DISTANCE	PERCENT OF DEMAND	CUMULATIVE PERCENT OF DEMAND	TOTAL DEMAND (CWT.)
0–100 mi.	56.4%	56.4%	833,043
101–200	21.3	77.7	314,607
201–300	15.7	93.4	231,893
301–400	2.1	95.5	31,018
401–500	1.5	97.0	22,155
501–600	0.5	97.5	7,385
601–700	2.0	99.5	29,541
701–800	0.5	100.0	7,384
801–900	0.0	100.0	0
901–1000	0.0	100.0	0
> 1000	0.0	100.0	0
	100.0%		1,477,026

Table 4 Benchmark Customer Service Profile

Handling costs are strictly a function of the warehouse throughput. They are determined by the handling rate multiplied by the throughput, or

$$HC_i = (HR_i)D_i$$

where

HC_i = annual handling cost at warehouse i ($)

HR_i = handling rate at warehouse i from Table 4

ORDER-PROCESSING COSTS

Order-processing costs refer to the charges incurred in handling the paperwork associated with stock replenishment and customer orders. Both types of costs are computed for each warehouse in essentially the same way. That is, the order-processing rate is multiplied by the annual demand on the warehouse and the result divided by the order size.

TOTAL COSTS

The total costs for various production distribution configurations can be determined by summing all the relevant costs. For the Usemore Soap Company, these are production costs; warehouse operating costs (storage, handling, stock order processing, and customer order processing); transportation costs (warehouse inbound, outbound, and local delivery); and inventory-carrying costs. Changing the number and location of plants and warehouses will cause a change in the balance of these cost factors. For example, adding warehouses will typically reduce transportation costs but increase inventory costs, as well as affect customer service. Assessing the trade-offs between costs and customer service is at the heart of this problem type.

The cost and customer service summaries for the current network design are shown in Tables 4 and 5. At present, Usemore Soap is able to place 93 percent of its demand within 300 miles of warehouses for a total annual cost of $42,112,463.

A COMPUTER-ASSISTED ANALYSIS

Although enough data have been provided to carry out an analysis manually, a computer program (WARELOCA, a module in LOGWARE) accompanies this case study. Given a particular combination of plants, plant capacities,

Table 5
Cost Profile for the
Current Distribution
Network

Cost Category	Cost
Production	$30,761,520
Warehouse operations	1,578,379
Order processing	369,027
Inventory carrying	457,290
Transportation:	
Inbound to warehouse	2,050,367
Outbound from warehouse	6,895,880
Total cost	$42,112,463

customer service constraints, and warehouses, the program optimally assigns demand centers to warehouses and warehouses to plants by means of linear programming. From the selected list of warehouses, the least expensive will be chosen if more than one choice is available within the prescribed service distance from a demand center. If a warehouse cannot be found within the service distance, the warehouse closest to the demand center will be selected.

Only linear variable costs are used in the allocation of demand centers to warehouses. Storage and capital costs, which are nonlinear, are not used in the allocation process. They are included in the system costs for a particular configuration. Fixed costs are neither included in the allocation, nor are they shown in the total system costs. They must be externally added to system costs.

WARELOCA is a program in which you provide the plant locations and capacities, warehouse locations, customer service distance, and demand and cost levels. Each run of the program represents an evaluation of a particular network configuration. The results of a sample WARELOCA run in which the current network is *approximated*[3] (not the true benchmark) where the existing 4 plants and 22 warehouses are evaluated are given in Figure 3. ∎

Figure 3 WARELOCA Results for an Approximated Benchmark Run

```
                          WARELOCA RESULTS

           SUMMARY OF ANALYSIS FOR
      22 POTENTIAL WAREHOUSE LOCATIONS


              -SYSTEM COSTS-
Production costs              $30,761,518
Warehouse operations           1,515,395
Order processing                 357,343
Inventory carrying               447,282
Transportation costs
  Inbound to whse              2,354,017
  Outbound from whse           6,657,464
                              _____

         Total costs         $42,093,020
```

[3]Plant capacities are set at current production levels, customer service set at 300 miles, and the current 22 warehouses are selected for evaluation.

Figure 3 (*cont.*)

CUSTOMER SERVICE PROFILE FOR A DESIRED
SERVICE DISTANCE OF 300 MILES

Distance from whse to customer (miles)			Percent of demand	Distance from whse to customer (miles)			Percent of demand
0	to	100	55.9	800	to	900	.0
100	to	200	18.2	900	to	1,000	.0
200	to	300	19.5	1,000	to	1,500	.0
300	to	400	1.8	1,500	to	2,000	.0
400	to	500	2.0	2,000	to	2,500	.0
500	to	600	.3	2,500	to	3,000	.0
600	to	700	2.0	>		3,000	.0
700	to	800	.4				
						Total	100.0

-PLANT THRUPUT AND COSTS-

Location	Thruput (cwt)	Production costs
COVINGTON KY	595,102	12,497,142
NEW YORK NY	390,876	7,778,432
ARLINGTON TX	249,662	5,392,699
LONG BEACH CA	241,386	5,093,244
MEMPHIS TN	0	0
CHICAGO IL	0	0
Totals	1,477,026	30,761,518

-WAREHOUSE THRUPUT AND COSTS-

Whse no.	Location	Thruput (cwt)	Whse Total, $	Storage	Handling	Capital
1	COVINGTON KY P	236,640	180,853	25,845	108,854	46,153
2	NEW YORK NY P	228,067	189,677	21,345	123,156	45,176
3	ARLINGTON TX P	104,081	86,246	18,033	39,550	28,662
4	LONG BEACH CA P	106,047	109,288	17,747	62,567	28,974
5	ATLANTA GA	46,949	55,775	14,239	23,474	18,062
6	BOSTON MA	49,350	83,524	27,919	37,012	18,592
7	BUFFALO NY	28,342	45,076	10,625	20,973	13,478
8	CHICAGO IL	87,860	170,997	44,858	100,160	25,979
9	CLEVELAND OH	0	0	0	0	0
10	DAVENPORT IA	13,068	33,837	10,337	14,897	8,602
11	DETROIT MI	82,999	131,269	19,815	86,318	25,135
12	GRD RAPIDS MI	17,330	45,238	16,736	18,369	10,132
13	GREENSBORO NC	31,832	57,362	9,203	33,741	14,417
14	KANSAS CITY KS	73,416	137,595	24,618	89,567	23,409
15	BALTIMORE MD	38,128	62,294	15,021	31,264	16,008
16	MEMPHIS TN	67,480	83,888	18,409	43,187	22,292
17	MILWAUKEE WI	28,121	51,015	17,632	19,965	13,417
18	ORLANDO FL	44,523	71,765	19,076	35,173	17,515
19	PITTSBURGH PA	21,553	50,534	14,249	24,785	11,499
20	PORTLAND OR	74,280	127,242	44,250	59,424	23,568
21	W SACRAMENTO CA	65,744	137,256	23,915	91,384	21,957
22	W CHESTER PA	31,216	51,936	11,772	25,909	14,255
	Totals	1,477,026	1,962,667	425,655	1,089,739	447,282

Whse no	Location	Order processing	Transport costs Inbound	Outbound
1	COVINGTON KY P	57,453	0	1,166,502
2	NEW YORK NY P	46,603	210,610	1,135,465
3	ARLINGTON TX P	29,020	96,128	511,022
4	LONG BEACH CA P	21,101	97,942	528,650
5	ATLANTA GA	6,293	112,810	212,015
6	BOSTON MA	19,794	82,324	261,289
7	BUFFALO NY	5,424	59,064	72,647
8	CHICAGO IL	15,850	168,091	276,774
9	CLEVELAND OH	0	0	0
10	DAVENPORT IA	4,898	30,896	74,424
11	DETROIT MI	35,631	154,332	173,983
12	GRD RAPIDS MI	4,434	34,705	46,545
13	GREENSBORO NC	5,222	71,933	129,723
14	KANSAS CITY KS	12,896	196,711	381,234
15	BALTIMORE MD	6,504	60,638	152,684
16	MEMPHIS TN	16,611	174,640	344,308
17	MILWAUKEE WI	19,857	62,954	42,548
18	ORLANDO FL	7,302	174,726	236,580
19	PITTSBURGH PA	5,746	45,302	47,416
20	PORTLAND OR	13,906	325,989	343,276
21	W SACRAMENTO CA	13,811	153,326	379,100
22	W CHESTER PA	8,977	40,887	141,269
	Totals	357,343	2,354,017	6,657,465

Essen USA

Essen is a German candy company that produces and distributes chocolate and other types of candies throughout Europe and the United States. For the U.S. market, the candies are manufactured in Essen, Germany, and shipped through the port at Amsterdam in the Netherlands. The product enters the United States through a port in New Jersey and is stored in a warehouse in Edison, New Jersey. From this central warehouse, the product is redistributed to the warehouses (there are many of these) of the purchasing companies that in turn ship it to their retail outlets (there are many of these). These buyers typically are large retailers such as Wal-Mart, Walgreens, and Giant Eagle, as well as many small retailers that purchase through distributors. Essen's supply channel is shown in Figure 1. Essen's distribution cost and customer service are affected by the product flow throughout the entire supply chain. Although Essen directly controls only a portion of the supply chain, good planning of the entire supply chain may benefit Essen, its buyers, and, ultimately, the customers. Essen may be able to influence its customers through price-quantity discounts and other incentives, if it can estimate the effect that these might have on its downstream channel members.

SALES

Essen had annual sales to its customers (level 2) of about $80 million in the United States on 36 million pounds of candies. Sales at retail (level 1)

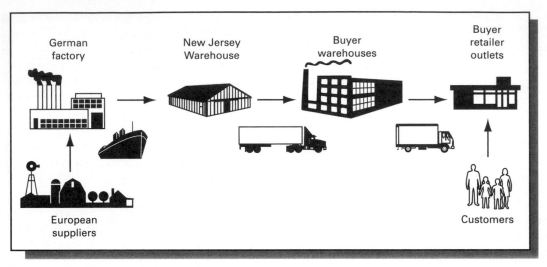

Figure 1   The Supply Channel for Essen

were about $104 million. This is an average price of $2.22 per lb to Essen's customers, who then add a 30 percent markup for an average price to end customers of $2.89 per lb. Sampling of sales data shows that daily sales average 100 thousand lb with a standard deviation of 15 thousand lb. Sales vary according to a normal distribution pattern. There is some increase in customer demand around holiday periods (Valentine's Day, Easter, Thanksgiving, and Christmas) with less-than-average sales in the fall and winter months. Summer months have slightly below average sales. Typical seasonal indices are as follows:

Month	Index	Month	Index	Month	Index	Month	Index
Jan	0.25	Apr	0.75	Jly	0.75	Oct	0.75
Feb	1.25	May	0.75	Aug	0.75	Nov	1.50
Mar	1.25	Jun	0.75	Sep	0.75	Dec	2.50

Sales growth has been modest at about 1 percent per year.

RETAILER OUTLETS/LEVEL 1

The retailers (level 1) in the channel restock their shelves on a weekly basis. Demand is forecasted from sales by averaging the last seven days of sales (seven-day moving average). The inventory-control policy is to stock to demand. That is, the amount of stock on the shelves is reviewed every seven days and a target inventory level of ten days sales is used for control

purposes. Ten days of demand is determined from the frequency for reviewing stock levels, the risk of running out, and the experience in providing adequate stock levels.

The approximate worth of 1,000 lb of product in inventory is $2,220. Inventory-carrying cost is nominally set at 25 percent of item value per year. The cost for filling customer orders is the result of dividing store overhead and labor by the units sold. For a single product line such as candy, it is no more than $1 per 1,000 lb. On the other hand, the retailer purchase order preparation cost includes form completion, order transmission, and miscellaneous checking. A cost of $35 per order is reasonable.

Time to fill a customer request for candy is nominally set at the minimum time of one day with no variation. This accounts for the time that the customer drives to the store, selects the product, checks out, and drives home.

A product such as this is generally not back ordered when an out-of-stock situation occurs. Sales are lost instead. Therefore, product is stocked at a high fill rate (98%). Back order costs are set at 0.67 per thousand lb to represent the lost sales effect.[1]

WAREHOUSES/LEVEL 2

Essen supplies to a number of its customers' warehouses. It is typical for these warehouses to forecast the volume of activity on them based on a 30-day moving average. Inventory levels are usually reviewed every 30 days and a target level of 45-days sales is used to replenish inventories. A fill rate of 95 percent is desired.

The cost to fill a retailer's order from warehouse stocks is estimated to be $20 per 1,000 lb, which includes some stock checking, credit checking, information transmission, and some overhead charges. Retailer store orders can be processed in two days with a standard deviation of 0.2 days. The cost to prepare and transmit the purchase orders for warehouse stock replenishment is $75 per order.

Inventory carrying cost is 25 percent of inventory value, which is estimated to be $2,220 per 1,000 lb. Orders that cannot be filled from available stock are back ordered at a cost of $100 per 1,000 lb.

ESSEN'S NEW JERSEY WAREHOUSE/LEVEL 3

The warehouse at New Jersey is the importation and redistribution point for Essen's products in the United States. It ships the full line of candy products to all its customers' warehouses from here. Overall requirements are forecasted using a 360-day moving average, even though there is a significant seasonal pattern in sales around the end of the calendar year. Inventory is planned on an aggregate basis (all products combined) with a stock-to-demand type of policy. Inventory review and forecasting take place every 30 days and a target quantity is 90-days sales. Rather high inventory levels are held because of the need for good stock availability to customers and the long lead times resulting from the distant supply source. One thousand pounds of product held in inventory is valued at $1,710 at cost. The company uses a 20 percent annual inventory-carrying charge. An in-stock probability (fill rate) of 95 percent is desired. Essen's customer order size averages 5,000 lb.

Preparing a purchase order on the factory is estimated to average $75 per order. The cost to process a buyer's order is $15 per 1,000 lb. The time to fill a distributor's order is three days, with a standard deviation of 0.3 days. All unfilled customer orders are back ordered at an estimated cost for the extra handling of $25 per 1,000 lb.

FACTORY/SOURCE

The factory purchases in Europe the materials for candy products at an average cost of U.S. $1,000 per 1,000 lb. The average lot size across all product line items is 10,000 lb. Production cost including overhead is about $850 per 1,000 lb. The time for production from when an order is received, reviewed, held for best time in the production schedule, and processed is eight days, with a standard deviation of two days. However, if larger batch sizes of 20,000 lb are produced, production cost can be reduced to $825 per 1,000 lb. Then production time is lengthened to 10 days, with a standard deviation of 2.1 days.

The cost for filling a warehouse order, mainly preparing the order for shipment, is $10 per 1,000 lb.

---

[1]This is the estimated profit earned on a lb of product, or $2.89 − 2.22 = $0.67 per lb.

TRANSPORTATION

Transport Between Factory and New Jersey Warehouse. Candy is shipped in containers by ocean freight from the Essen factory to the New Jersey warehouse. Sometimes refrigerated transport is needed for summer months, when the expected high temperatures would melt the chocolate candies. Transport costs are approximately $78 per 1,000 lb and transit time averages nine days, with a standard deviation of three days.

Alternately, warehouse orders can be airfreighted to the United States for $1,833 per 1,000 lb, with an average transit time of one day and a standard deviation of 0.2 days.

Transport from New Jersey Warehouse to Retailer Warehouses. Shipments are made from the New Jersey warehouse by LTL trucking, although the carriers frequently use pool points to build full truckload movements over the longer distances. Transport averages 1,000 miles for a cost of $70 per 1,000 lb. Transit time for these 1,000-mile deliveries averages five days, with a standard deviation of one day.

Transport from Retailer Warehouses to Retail Outlets. Shipments from retailer warehouses to multiple retail outlets typically combine numerous products destined for more than one store on a single truck route. The proportion of the delivery associated with just the candy products is estimated to cost $25 per 1,000 lb. Transit time is about one day with no appreciable variability. ■

QUESTIONS

1. What can you say about the logistics performance throughout the supply channel for Essen and its customers?
2. What steps would you suggest taking to improve logistics performance throughout the channel? Do any of the changes involve Essen? If so, does the company directly realize any cost or operating performance improvements?
3. Would shipping by airfreight from Germany be a benefit to channel performance? To Essen?
4. Is there a benefit to producing in the larger 20,000 lb batch size?
5. If non-Essen channel members hold the key to good channelwide performance and improved performance for Essen, how does Essen encourage them to cooperate?

Logistics/Supply Chain Organization

> *A good organization structure does not by itself produce good performance—just as a good constitution does not guarantee great presidents, or good laws, or a moral society. But a poor organization structure makes good performance impossible, no matter how good the individual managers may be. To improve organization structure . . . will therefore always improve performance.*[1]

—PETER F. DRUCKER

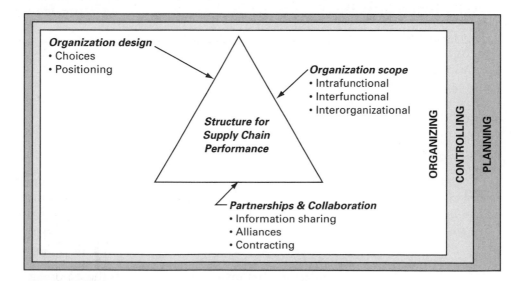

[1]Peter F. Drucker, *The Practice of Management* (New York: Harper & Row, 1954), p. 225.

*A*dministrative organization is the structure that facilitates the creation, the implementation, and the evaluation of plans. It is the formal or informal mechanism for allocating the firm's human resources to achieve its goals. The organization may appear as a formalized chart of functional relationships, an invisible set of relationships understood by the firm's members but not stated in any formal way, or a combination of these. Whichever is the case, attempting to establish human relationships in an optimal way is probably the firm's most difficult task. No precise algorithms exist for doing this. The best we can hope for are some guidelines that may be useful in establishing acceptable organizational structures.

The focus of this chapter is specifically on the organizational structure required for the management of the business logistics function. The discussion is separated into four parts. First is organizing the logistics effort. Concern here is with *why* a logistics/SC organization is needed. Second are the choices that management has available. These range from formal to informal organization forms, as well as the placement of the organizational form within the company's organization structure. The third concerns the management of logistics across different organizations. Finally, we will look at the alternatives to the organizational structure that have the purpose of operating a supply channel, namely, outsourcing some or all of the logistics effort through strategic logistics/SC alliances, logistics/SC partnerships, logistics/SC third-party providers, and collaborative arrangements.

ORGANIZING THE LOGISTICS/SC EFFORT

Positioning those persons in the firm who are responsible for logistics activities in a way that encourages coordination among them is the major problem of logistics/SC organization. Such organizational arrangements promote efficiency in the supply and distribution of goods and services by encouraging the cost trade-offs that are frequently encountered in planning and operating the logistics system.

Need for Organization Structure

Logistics/SC is a vital activity that must be carried out by virtually every type of firm or institution. This means that some organizational arrangement, whether formal or informal, will have been made to handle product and service movement. What then is the need for any specific consideration of organization structure?

Organizational Fragmentation

A traditional form of organization that many have adopted is the grouping of their activities around the three primary functions of finance, operations, and marketing, as

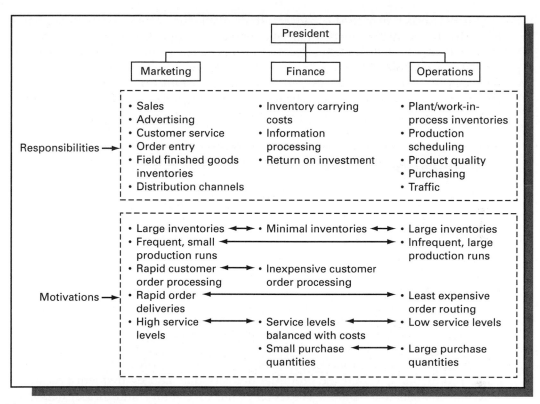

Figure 15-1 Organization of a Typical Manufacturing Firm with Reference to Logistics/SC Activities

shown in Figure 15-1. From a logistics point of view, this arrangement has resulted in a fragmentation of the logistics activities among these three functions whose primary purposes are somewhat different from those of logistics. That is, responsibility for transportation might be placed under operations, inventory divided among the three functions, and order processing placed under either marketing or finance. Yet marketing's primary responsibility may be to maximize revenue, operations' responsibility may be to produce at the lowest per-unit cost, and finance's responsibility may be to minimize the capital costs or maximize return on investment for the firm. These motivational cross-purposes led one executive some years ago to wisely observe:

> If permitted to run free, a salesman and his manager would promise his customer impossible delivery service from a plant or distribution center. On the other hand, the production manager, if permitted, would request that all orders be accumulated for long periods to reduce the cost of setups, and allow more time to plan economic materials procurement quantities.[2]

---

[2]Kenneth Marshall, "Bruning: Another Way to Organize Physical Distribution Management," *Handling & Shipping* (November 1966), pp. 61–66.

Such conflict of purpose can result in a logistics operating system that is suboptimal—so much so, that the efficiency of the firm as a whole may suffer. For example, marketing may desire fast delivery to support sales, whereas manufacturing, if it has the responsibility for traffic, may desire the lowest cost routing. Unless steps are taken to achieve compromise across the functional lines, the most advantageous logistics cost-service balance is not likely to be realized. Some organizational structure for the coordination of decision making of separate logistics activities is needed.

Observation

A paper products manufacturer was caught in the classic conflict between sales and production around logistics matters. This company produced and sold a variety of kraft paper products for such uses as grocery bags, commercial packaging and wrapping, and toilet tissue and napkins. Sales were often generated in large order quantities involving as much as 30 carloads for one customer. Organizationally, the company was oriented around the tasks of marketing and production.

Due to a lack of coordination between marketing and production, salespeople typically promised customers delivery when they wanted it, with little regard for production schedules. When important delivery dates were not being met, sales pressed production for the order. The philosophy was simple: "Squeeze the grape hard enough, and the seed will pop out."

On the other hand, production was often pressured by orders that were received at the production site after the promised delivery date and by frequent production schedule changes that resulted in expensive machine setups and further delays for some of the less pressing orders.

The poor coordination between demand and supply was causing an increasing number of customer complaints and threats by customers to seek other sources of supply.

Management

Providing some organizational structure to logistics/SC activities also defines the necessary lines of authority and responsibility to ensure that goods are moved according to plan and that replanning is carried out when needed. If the balance between customer service and the costs to produce the service are critical to the operation of a particular firm, someone should be placed in charge of overseeing product movement. In effect, someone has to manage logistics. Whereas such areas as order processing, traffic, and warehousing may be individually supervised for good control, a manager is often required to coordinate their combined operations. Only a manager has the scope to balance these operations to achieve the highest level of efficiency.

Importance of Organization to Logistics/SC

The attention that can be given to logistics organization and to the organizational arrangement depends on the nature of logistics/SC in a particular firm. Although every firm or institution conducts logistics/SC operations to some degree, logistics matters are not equally important to all. A firm spending a small fraction of its total operating costs on logistics or where logistics customer service levels are not of great importance to customers is not likely to give logistics any special organizational attention. However, for many consumer-product firms, food firms, and chemical firms in which logistics costs may average 25 percent or more of the sales dollar, the opposite is true.

In addition, the need for a given type of organization depends on *how* logistics costs are incurred and *where* service needs are the greatest. The organizational form may center on materials management, physical distribution, or the supply chain. Consider how the need for organization varies among various industry types.

Extractive industries are characterized as firms that produce basic raw materials, mainly for use by other industries. Examples of such firms are those engaged in lumbering, mining, and agriculture. Logistics operations involve securing a variety of goods needed in the extractive operations. Capital equipment and supplies for operations are typical of such purchases. Purchasing and transportation are the primary supply-side logistical activities. Outbound products typically are of limited diversity, are of relatively low value, and are shipped in bulk. Controlling shipping in terms of mode selection, routing, and equipment utilization is a major concern. Therefore, the firms in these industries are likely to have very visible materials management departments.

Service industries mainly concern themselves with supply-side logistics activities. Firms in this industry convert tangible supplies into service offerings. Hospitals, insurance companies, and transportation companies are good examples of service firms. A variety of product items are purchased, many of which are critical, from suppliers that are geographically dispersed. These items are entirely consumed in producing the service. Purchasing and inventory management are primary logistics activities to be managed, with slightly less concern about transportation since many of the supplies are received under a delivered pricing arrangement. Logistics costs can be significant to such firms, but the associated activities take place on the supply side of the firm. Organization for logistics centers on materials management, with typically little recognition given to any physical distribution activities.

Marketing industries are characterized as firms that purchase goods mainly for resale. Typical members of this industry are distributors and retailers. Firms in this industry do little to change the form of the product. Major concerns are with selling and logistics activities. Typically, such firms purchase many items from many suppliers that are geographically dispersed. These items are resold in diverse combinations and in small quantities, usually within a limited geographical area. Operations are characterized as purchasing, inbound traffic, inventory control, warehousing, order picking, and shipping. Organization for the management of logistics is significant and usually will involve both materials management and physical distribution activities, however greater emphasis is likely to be given to a strong physical distribution organization since many of the inbound supplies are priced by suppliers on a delivered basis.

Manufacturing industries are characterized by firms that purchase a wide variety of items from many suppliers for transforming them into items of relatively high value. There is substantial logistics activity, both on the supply side and the distribution side of these firms. Organization design includes both materials management and physical distribution.

Organizational Development

The philosophy about what is good logistics/SC management and the resulting organizational design has been evolving over the years. Bowersox and Daugherty have noted three distinct stages of development.[3] Stage I, which could be observed in the early 1970s, represented a clustering of activities that were important to realizing the cost trade-offs inherent to logistics management. Transportation activities were managed in concert with inventory and order-processing activities to achieve physical distribution cost and service goals. Purchasing, inbound transportation, and raw materials inventories were collected together under a single organizational banner for coordination. The recognition of the activities relevant to physical distribution and physical supply and the need for their careful coordination were there in the early 1970s, but organizational structures were rather weak. Many firms would rely on informal arrangements such as persuasion and staff coordinators to balance the interests among the activity areas. Since organizational design change seems to be more of an evolutionary process than a revolutionary one, early attempts at logistics organization were carried out without radical change to the "in-place" organizational structure.

The Stage II organization was directed at formal structures, where a top-level executive was placed in charge of the relevant logistics activities, usually those of physical supply or physical distribution, but not both. This gave direct control over the coordination of the logistics activities. This was an evolutionary step, as the benefits of good logistics management became better understood and appreciated among firms. Companies such as Kodak and Whirlpool were early leaders in this type of formalized structure. However, in 1985 larger firms (42%) remained in Stage I[4] or had moved on to Stage III (20%).

Stage III organization structure referred to the full integration of logistics activities, spanning both physical supply and physical distribution. Total integration of logistics activities, and the organizational structure of a scope to coordinate them, increased in popularity. Total integration was driven by the just-in-time, quick response, and time compression philosophies that required precise coordination among all activities throughout the entire firm. In addition, shared assets such as a truck fleet or warehouses that were used in both physical supply and physical distribution activities also required careful coordination to achieve their maximum utilization.

---

[3]Donald J. Bowersox and Patricia J. Daugherty, "Emerging Patterns of Logistical Organization," *Journal of Business Logistics*, Vol. 8, No. 1 (1987), pp. 46–60.
[4]A. T. Kearney, *Emerging Top Management Focus for the 1980s* (Chicago: Kearney Management Consultants, 1985).

Example

Micro-Kits sold one of its products—a toolkit for field repair of PC hardware—through three market channels: (1) retail stores; (2) catalog customers; and (3) wholesale customers. It purchased components from vendors and shipped them to a plant for assembly. Finished goods were shipped to a distribution center from which sales orders were filled. A JIT system was proposed that would mainly improve operating performance in the physical supply channel and in production.

The entire logistics and production channel was modeled using computer simulation. The results showed that JIT would make a substantial improvement compared with current operations. That is, the profit margin would increase by 106 percent, inventory turnover would increase from 7.2 to 7.8:1, and the channel lead time would be reduced from 24.2 to 13.7 days.

However, this view was shortsighted. By planning the entire channel in an integrated fashion where physical distribution and physical supply are planned collectively, further improvement was possible. Profit margins could be increased by an additional 6 percent, inventory turnover could be increased from 7.8 to 16.3:1, and the channel lead time reduced from 13.7 to 8.9 days.

It is this type of benefit from integrated planning that is also driving organization structure to span both physical supply and physical distribution activities.[5]

Now a Stage IV is being referred to as supply chain, or integrated logistics, management. This involves the full integration of the logistics activities of Stage III, but includes the logistics activities within the product transformation processes (production). That is, companies in Stage IV of their organizational development will view logistics as encompassing all those activities that take place between their sources of raw materials, through production, and on to the final consumer. The significant difference between Stage III and Stage IV is that the activities of the product transformation process such as product scheduling, work-in-process inventory management, and coordination of just-in-time scheduling both inbound and outbound are now included in the scope of integrated logistics.

A Stage V can be envisioned where logistics activities will be managed *between* firms in the supply channel that are separate legal entities. To this point, managerial attention has primarily focused on those logistics activities that are within the immediate control and responsibility of the firm. Managing this superorganization will bring new challenges, but it will also bring opportunities for efficiencies not yet tapped by current organizational thinking and structures.

ORGANIZATIONAL CHOICES

When the need for some form of organizational structure has been established, there are basic choices from which a firm may select. These can be categorized as informal,

---

[5]Robert Sloan, "Integrated Tools for Managing the Total Pipeline," *Annual Conference Proceedings*, Volume II (St. Louis: Council of Logistics Management, 1989), pp. 93–108.

semiformal, and formal types. No type is dominant. Organizational choice for any particular firm is frequently a result of evolutionary forces operating within the firm. That is, the logistics organizational form is often sensitive to the particular personalities within the firm, to the traditions regarding organization, and to the importance of logistics activities.

The Informal Organization

The major objective for logistics/SC organization is to achieve coordination among logistics activities for their planning and control. Given a supporting climate within a firm, this coordination may be achieved in a number of informal ways. These typically do not require any change in the existing organizational structure, but rely on coercion or persuasion to accomplish coordination among activities and cooperation among those who are responsible for them.

For firms that have designated separate areas of responsibility for such key activities as transportation, inventory control, and order processing, an incentive system can sometimes be created to coordinate them. Whereas the budget, which is a major control device for many firms, is often a disincentive to coordination, it can sometimes be turned into a mechanism for effective coordination. The budget may be a disincentive because a manager of transportation, for example, would find it unreasonable to incur higher than necessary transportation costs in order to achieve lower inventory costs. Inventory costs do not fall within the transportation manager's budget responsibility. The transportation manager's performance is measured by how transportation costs compare with the budget.

One possible incentive system to encourage cross-activity cooperation is to establish a number of cross charges or transfer costs among the various logistics activities. Consider how a transportation selection decision might be made when it indirectly affects inventory levels, but the transportation decision maker is unmotivated other than to seek the lowest possible transportation costs.

Example

Suppose that the inventory manager in a firm is to permit higher-than-desired levels of inventory in order to accommodate a less expensive but slower means of transportation, resulting from shipping in larger quantities. To the extent that the inventory costs are increased above the desired inventory levels, as determined strictly by inventory objectives, the incremental costs incurred above this level are charged to the transportation manager's account. The transportation manager can realistically appraise the impact of his or her transport selection decision on inventory costs and make a choice that balances costs across the firm by simply following his or her own budget objectives.

Another incentive is to establish some form of a cost saving and sharing arrangement. All managers of the separate logistics activities that show conflicting cost patterns could pool their cost savings. A predetermined schedule could be established to divide the savings for redistribution to salaries. There is incentive for cooperation because the greatest potential savings come about when cooperation leads to a balancing of activities having conflicting cost patterns. These so-called profit-sharing plans have had limited success among firms, but a few firms have used them effectively (e.g., Lincoln Electric).

The use of coordinating committees is another informal approach to logistics organization. These committees are made up of members from each of the important logistics areas. By providing a means through which communication can take place, then coordination may result. For companies in which there is a history of coordinating committees, the committee form can be quite satisfactory. Dupont is one example of a company famous for its effective management by committee. Although committees seem to be a simple, straightforward solution to the coordination problem, their shortcoming is that they generally have little power to implement their own recommendations.

A chief executive's review of logistics decisions and operations is a particularly effective way of encouraging coordination. Top management has the necessary position in the organizational structure to easily observe suboptimal decision making within the organization. Because subordinate managers in the logistics activity areas are responsible to top management, top management's encouragement and support of coordination and cooperation among these interfunctional activities goes a long way toward achieving the organizational goals without a formal organizational structure.

The Semiformal Organization

The semiformal organization form recognizes that logistics planning and operation usually cut across the various functions within a firm's organizational structure. The logistician, or supply chain coordinator, is then assigned to coordinate projects that involve the supply chain and that cover several functional areas. This type of structure is often called a *matrix* organization, and it has been especially popular in the aerospace industry. The concept has been adapted to logistics system management, as shown in Figure 15-2.

In a matrix organization, the logistics/SC manager has responsibility for the entire logistics system, but he or she does not have direct authority over the component activities. The traditional organizational structure for the firm remains intact, yet the logistics/SC manager shares the decision authority and accountability with the activity area manager. Expenses for the activities must be justified by each functional department as well as by the logistics program, which is the basis for cooperation and coordination. The logistics/SC coordinator may even assist in coordinating logistics activities among member firms of the supply channel beyond the boundaries of his firm.

Although the matrix organization can be a useful organizational form, we should recognize that the lines of authority and responsibility become blurred. Conflicts may arise that cannot be easily resolved. However, for some firms this choice is a good compromise between an informal form and a highly structured one.

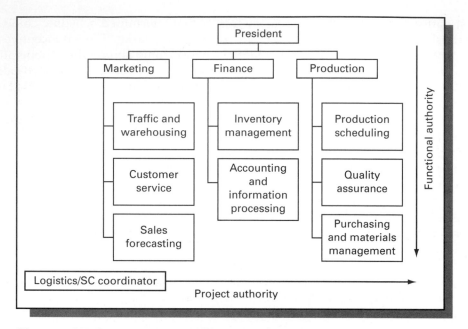

Figure 15-2 A Logistics/SC Matrix Organization

Example

United Fixtures manufactures plumbing hardware, with sales in the $80 million range. This firm recently created a distribution department to solve logistics problems. The new manager reported to the vice president of sales and marketing. The department was given the objective of defining customer service standards and then coordinating those standards with delivery schedules and production plans.

The sales department had previously been routing production orders from the plant to please large customers, and production control personnel could not keep up. The new department was quickly able to identify the bottleneck and institute a system that better coordinated order entry, production schedules, field warehousing, and transportation to meet customer demands.

At the same time, sales personnel devised new methods of circumventing the schedules, once again accommodating favored customers. Purchasing personnel further confounded the situation by complaining at length about the widely different materials requirements because of new production schedules.

Despite the favorable impact on transport costs and better on-time delivery, a number of problems remained. Most functions in the firm that interfaced or participated in the materials movement system felt that the distribution department was interested only in bettering a system that helped finished goods distribution. Furthermore, the distribution manager was upset because he had not been able to gain control over the inventory of finished goods. The vice president of manufacturing was "responsible for stock control for the company" and was not about to release control over finished goods.

The company was persuaded to implement a form of matrix organization. Substantial success has been achieved, but some difficulties have been experienced with the shared authority obstacle. An executive vice president in charge of materials was appointed. In this job, he had no responsibility for a large staff nor did he have any departments reporting to him. Owing in part to his prestigious title and his tactful approach, he and two assistants were nevertheless able to achieve the kind of overall coordination that had eluded other functional organizations.[6]

The Formal Organization

The formal organization is one that establishes clear lines of authority and responsibility for logistics/SC. This typically involves (1) placing a manager in a superior position relative to logistics activities; and (2) placing the manager's authority on a level in the organization's structure that allows effective compromise with the other major functional areas of the firm (finance, operations, and marketing). This elevates and structures logistics personnel in a form that promotes activity coordination. Firms seek the formal organizational form when less formal arrangements prove ineffective or when greater attention is to be given to logistics activities.

Practitioners frequently remind us that there is no such thing as a typical organization for logistics. Organizational structure is customized to individual circumstances within a firm. However, we can develop a generalized formal organization that makes good sense in terms of logistics management principles and appears, in at least partial form, in enough firms to use it as a model. This organizational structure is shown in Figure 15-3. It serves as a valuable guideline.

This formal design accomplishes several important ends. First, logistics/SC is elevated to a position in the organization where it is managed with the same authority as the other major functions. This helps to ensure that logistics activities receive the same attention as marketing, operations, and finance. It also sets the stage for the logistics manager to have an equal voice in resolving economic conflicts. Having logistics on a par with the other functional areas creates a balance of power for the economic good of the firm as a whole.

Second, a limited number of subareas are created under the chief logistics/SC officer. The five categories shown in Figure 15-3 are established with a separate manager for each and are managed as a distinctive entity. Collectively, they represent the major activities for which managers are typically responsible.[7] Why are there exactly five areas? Only as many areas are created as technical competencies

[6]Daniel W. DeHayes Jr. and Robert L. Taylor, "Making 'Logistics' Work in a Firm," *Business Horizons* (June 1972), pp. 38 and 45. Copyright © 1972 by the Foundation for the School of Business at Indiana University. Used with permission.

[7]Bernard J. LaLonde and Larry W. Emmelhainz, "Where Do You Fit In?" *Distribution*, Vol. 8, No. 11 (November 1985), p. 34.

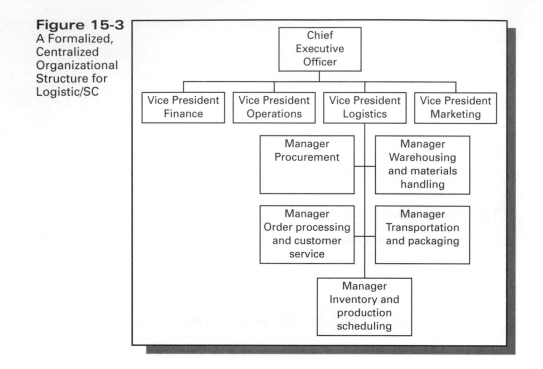

Figure 15-3
A Formalized,
Centralized
Organizational
Structure for
Logistic/SC

require. It might seem desirable to combine, say, transportation and inventory activities into a single area because their costs are naturally in conflict and better coordination could be achieved. However, the technical skills required in each area are substantially different, so finding management for the combined areas having both types of skills is difficult. It is often more workable to keep such activities under a separate manager and rely on the logistics manager to establish coordination through the informal or semiformal organizational types previously discussed. Similar arguments can be offered for the other activity areas. Therefore, the formal organization structure is a balance between minimizing the number of activity groups to encourage coordination while separating them to gain effectiveness in the management of their technical aspects.

The organizational form in Figure 15-3 is the most formalized and centralized that is generally found in industry today. It is a structure integrating both materials management and physical distribution under a single banner. Relatively few firms have, in fact, achieved this degree of integration (20% in 1985),[8] but cost and customer service trends are likely to increase its popularity. However, the basic model is useful, whether a firm organizes its logistics operations around supply-side activities, as in the case of many service firms, or around physical distribution activities, as in the case of many manufacturing firms.

---

[8]A. T. Kearney, *Emerging Top Management Focus for the 1980s*.

Example

Several years ago, a producer of corn and soybean products reorganized its distribution activities. Because of high shipping volumes, a great deal of attention was paid to traffic activities, with a vice president of traffic as a member of the board of directors. Performance of the traffic division was measured by the dollar size of the freight bill. Partly because of this, the distribution system grew to contain over 350 inventory-stocking points.

Because of an outside consultant's study and top management's support, the finished product service functions were grouped under one director. This integrated function is shown in Figure 15-4 and was created from the organizational fragments found throughout the company. A member of the marketing group was selected as the new head of physical distribution. Not only did the new organization result in greater control over the finished product, but also the number of late shipments was reduced by 88 percent, and greater stock availability was provided in the marketplace. This was all achieved at a lower total cost.

Figure 15-4 Distribution Division Organizational Design for a Producer of Corn and Soybean Products

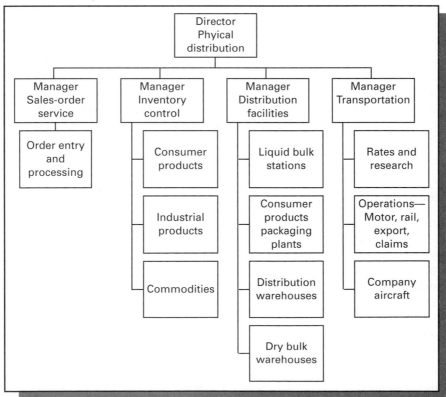

The results of distribution organization were so impressive that supply-side activities have been grouped under one executive and called materials management. Note how this organizational design was evolving toward that shown in Figure 15-3.

ORGANIZATIONAL ORIENTATION

According to a Michigan State University study of Fortune 500 firms, the type of organizational structure to be selected was found to depend on the particular strategy that the firm was pursuing.[9] Organizational design seems to follow three corporate strategies: process, market, and information.

Process Strategy

A process strategy is one where the objective is to achieve the maximum efficiency in moving goods from a raw materials state through work in process and on to a finished-goods state. Organization design is likely to focus on the activities that give rise to cost. That is, activities such as purchasing, production scheduling, inventory, transportation, and order processing will be collected together and managed collectively. The actual form of the organization will most probably be of the types previously discussed.

Market Strategy

Firms pursuing a market strategy have a strong customer service orientation. Both sales and logistics coordination are sought. The organizational structure is not likely to integrate the logistics activities that are inherent under the process strategy. Rather, those activities directly relating to customer service for both sales and logistics are collected together and often report to the same executive. The organizational structure is likely to span across business units to a high level of customer service. Of course, logistics costs may not be held at their lowest level.

Information Strategy

Firms that pursue an information strategy are likely to be those that have a significant downstream network of dealers and distribution organizations with substantial inventories. Coordination of logistics activities throughout this dispersed network is a primary objective, and information is the key ingredient for good management. In order to secure this information, the organizational structure is apt to span functions, divisions, and business units. When logistics activities span the legal boundaries of channel members, such as when goods are placed on consignment in retail outlets or returned goods are handled by the buying firms, information must be obtained across these organizational boundaries. Thus, the organizational structure must span the traditional legal boundaries of the firm itself.

---

[9]Bowersox and Daugherty, "Emerging Patterns of Logistical Organization."

We should recognize that no firm is likely to display a single organization design. Because mixed strategies often exist within the same firm, a variety of designs will appear for essentially similar firms. In addition, similar firms may be in different stages of organizational development. This can make it difficult to explain the rationale for any particular structure just from its design.

ORGANIZATIONAL POSITIONING

Organizational choice and orientation are the first considerations in organizational structure. Next comes the positioning of logistics activities for their most effective management. Positioning concerns *where* to place these activities in the organizational structure. This is determined by such issues as (1) decentralization versus centralization; (2) staff versus line; and (3) large company size versus small.

Decentralization Versus Centralization

One of the continuing controversies in organization is whether activities should be grouped close to top management or dispersed throughout the divisions of the larger firms. For example, a major electric company had a number of product divisions, such as industrial electrical equipment, nuclear power, small appliances, major appliances, and lamps. A centralized organization groups logistics activities at the corporate level for serving all product groups, as shown in Figure 15-5. On the other hand, the decentralized logistics organization puts the responsibility for logistics at the product group or division level, as shown in Figure 15-6. A separate decentralized logistics organization is established to serve each division.

There are some obvious advantages to each type, and a number of firms create organizational forms that blend both types to seek their combined advantages. The principal reason for the centralized form is to maintain close control over logistics activities and to benefit from the efficiencies associated with the scale of activities that can occur by concentrating all logistics activities for the entire corporation under a single director. Consider the traffic activity as an example. Many firms own private truck fleets. Utilization of the equipment is the key to efficiency. By having centralized control of all traffic activities, a firm might find that the forward haul of one division's products might be the back haul for another. These movements can then be balanced, whereas under a decentralized organization they might be overlooked. Similar efficiencies can be gained through shared warehousing, shared purchasing, and shared data processing.

Decentralization of organization often allows quicker and more customized logistics response to customer needs than the more removed, centralized organization. Decentralization makes a great deal of sense when product lines are distinctly different in their marketing, logistics, and manufacturing characteristics, and when few economies of scale can be found.

Rarely can we expect to find either a purely centralized or a purely decentralized design. For example, although there is managerial interest in divisional and even regional autonomy among the operating units of a firm, technical advances such as

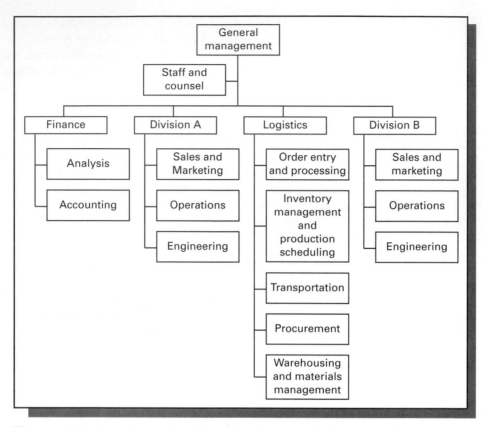

Figure 15-5 A Generalized Example of a Centralized Logistics/SC Organizational Structure

computerized data processing have made it more efficient to have centralized order processing and inventory control. Such conflicting trends help to explain the diversity of organizational forms in practice.

Staff Versus Line

A number of firms do not create organizations that have direct or line responsibility over goods movement and storage. They find it more satisfactory in their circumstances to establish an advisory, or staff, organization for logistics. The logistician in this case is placed in a consulting role to the other line functions such as marketing and operations. An advisory organization is a good alternative when (1) a line organization would cause unnecessary conflicts among the existing personnel; (2) logistics activities are less critical than selling, producing, and other activities; (3) planning is relatively more important than administration; and (4) logistics is treated as a shared service among the product divisions.

The staff type of organization may be attached to any of the functional areas at a centralized or decentralized level. Frequently, however, the logistics staff is located

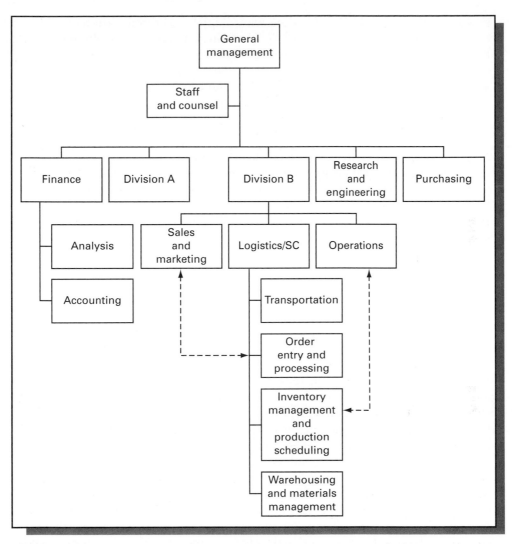

Figure 15-6 A Generalized Example of a Decentralized Logistics/SC Organizational Structure

near top management in geographical location and on the organization chart. Because the logistics staff is in an advisory role, authority that is more indirect can be given to logistics through this type of organizational positioning. In fact, some corporate level logistics staffs wield more authority than many division-level line organizations.

Large Versus Small

Most of the attention given here has been to the large, multidivisional firm. What about the small firm? We should recognize that the small firm has just as many logistics problems as the large firm. In some ways, logistics activities are more important because the small firm does not benefit from volume purchases and shipments, as does the larger firm. Organizationally, the small firm has some form of a centralized organization because, for practical purposes, no product divisions exist. In addition, logistics activities are not as likely to be clearly defined and structured as in the larger firm.

INTERFUNCTIONAL MANAGEMENT

Much of the previous discussion has dealt with organizing logistics as a separate, integrated function to reduce conflicts among logistics activities. While conflict is generally reduced among these activities, an additional functional area increases the level of conflict between logistics and the other functional areas within the organization. Since all activities of a firm are economically interrelated, to departmentalize them along functional lines to create a reasonable span of control for management promotes conflicts. Autonomy of responsibility, authority, accountability, and reward do not encourage interfunctional activity trade-offs and can lead to suboptimal performance by the firm as a whole. Thus, the logistician, as well as his or her superiors, must be prepared to deal with the problem of interfunctional management.

Several activities are at the interface of logistics and other areas of the firm, thus creating a shared responsibility. These can include customer service, order entry and processing, packaging, and retail location for the logistics-marketing interface; and plant location, purchasing, and production scheduling for the logistics-operations interface. Recall that interface activities are those that require some form of collective management among the functional areas involved to prevent suboptimal decisions from being made.

The benefits of interfunctional management between logistics and marketing can be seen if we consider packaging. Packaging is of concern to marketing because of its impact on sales. Protection, storage, and handling features of packaging are generally of little concern to marketing unless in some way marketing rewards are partially determined by package design. The logistics activity of the firm most often must suffer the consequences of poor package design through handling and storage inefficiencies. On the other hand, logistics performance is not typically measured by the promotional qualities of a package. Yet, the package is a single entity. Protective features cannot be divorced from promotional features. Some form of cooperation is needed to achieve a package design that will yield the best balance between marketing revenues and logistics costs. Operating alone, neither function is likely to come up with a package design that is as economically beneficial as the one created by working together.

Cooperation between operations and logistics on the setting of production schedules is a second example. Inventory is the common element between the two functions. The operations function seeks product schedules to balance inventory costs against manufacturing costs. On the other hand, logistics balances inventory costs against transportation costs in deciding production schedules. Without cooperation, there is no guarantee that an optimum balance will be achieved between transportation, inventory, and manufacturing costs.

Similar overlap between functional areas exists for the remaining interface activities.

Example

A steel processor cuts and shapes raw steel rolls, sheets, and plates obtained from major steel producers for customers who need the raw steel prepared for their own stamping and forming. Most business is made to order, with raw materials inventories and machine processing being the major cost components of price. Typically, customers place orders without advanced notification, which can cause imperfect planning by the steel distributor. There is little opportunity to realize economies by scheduling processing with other orders or economizing on raw material purchase and inventories. If customers can be encouraged to inform the steel processor of when their orders will be placed and what their requirements will be, operating efficiencies can be realized. Working with sales, operations can estimate the benefit of the advanced purchase commitments while sales uses the information to determine a price discount for customers pegged to the extent of advanced notification. By aligning the price discounts with operating benefits, overall channel profits can improve as well as there being profit improvement benefits for individual customers and for the steel processor. Sales and operations have cooperated interfunctionally for the company's greater good.[10]

INTERORGANIZATIONAL MANAGEMENT

So far, we have noted the organizational problems associated with realigning a firm's activities to achieve meaningful economic trade-offs and the problems associated with managing activities at functional area interfaces. Both of these managerial problems are internal to the firm. Since the supply and distribution policies of any one firm in the distribution channel can affect the performance of other firms in the channel, the question is raised about whether there might be some advantage to viewing the channel as a single entity, or "superorganization," and managing it to the benefit of all members involved. This proposition is probably not new, but the processes involved are little understood. As Stern and Heskett noted a while ago:

> The management of complex organizations has undergone considerable scrutiny by students of administrative processes. But only a small body of literature has been devoted to the management of interorganization systems, entities whose objectives transcend those of single organizations defined by legal boundaries.[11]

If effective organizational processes can be developed to deal with logistics matters external to the firm, the firm stands to gain in a way not otherwise possible. This is a

---

[10]Stephen M. Gilbert and Ronald H. Ballou, "Supply Chain Benefits from Advanced Customer Commitments," *Journal of Operations Management*, Vol. 18 (1999), pp. 61–73.

[11]Louis W. Stern and J. L. Heskett, "Conflict Management in Interorganization Relations: A Conceptual Framework," in Louis W. Stern, *Distribution Channels: Behavioral Dimensions* (Boston: Houghton Mifflin, 1969), p. 288.

key idea in supply chain management and is only now being actively pursued by researchers and practitioners.

The Superorganization

The superorganization is a group of firms related through their business processes and mutual objectives (satisfying customers and maximizing profits), but who are legally separate. They share a common interest in the individual decisions made by each, since the decisions of the other firms can affect their performance, and vice versa. For example, a carrier's pricing decision will influence the decision of the carrier's customer on how much service to purchase. The customer's purchase decision, in turn, influences the carrier's pricing decision. Normally, each firm makes its decision while pursuing individual goals. If profit maximization is the goal, making the purchase and price decisions individually not only leads to suboptimal profits for the firms taken collectively, but they also can result in suboptimal profits for the firms individually. Management of the superorganization is a relatively easy task if the cooperative efforts yield proportionately greater returns to each member and they are distributed fairly. The situation is self-motivating for the members, and the only need is to become aware of the possibility and benefits of cooperation. However, if the benefits of cooperation "pool" (disproportionately favor) with one or a few of the channel members, equitably distributing the benefits and dispersing information among the members about the effects of cooperation is needed.

Example[12]

Conflicts and opportunities within the superorganization can be illustrated through a simple, hypothetical example. Suppose that a supply channel consists of a buyer and a seller. The seller prices an item to the buyer and the buyer decides on the quantity to purchase. Demand on the buyer is relatively predictable and stable; the buyer determines the purchase quantity from the economic order quantity formula to minimize procurement and inventory-holding costs. The potential conflict in the channel arises when the order quantity for the buyer is not the preferred order quantity for the seller.

The buyer is an original equipment manufacturer producing $D = 10,000$ units of a certain model at a constant rate. This firm purchases a component for this model from an upstream supplier. Each time the buyer places an order, an ordering cost associated with administrative details, transportation, and so on is incurred. This ordering cost is $S_b = \$100$. The buyer also incurs an inventory-carrying cost of $I = 20\%$ per year for the component valued at $C = \$50$ per unit. Obviously, the buyer will attempt to determine an order quantity (Q_b) that balances ordering costs against

---

[12]Paraphrased from Ronald H. Ballou, Stephen M. Gilbert, and Ashok Mukherjee, "New Managerial Challenges form Supply Chain Opportunities," *Industrial Marketing Management*, Vol. 29, No. 1 (2000), pp. 7–18, with permission from Elsevier Science.

inventory-holding costs. From the *EOQ* formula (recall Equation 9-7), the optimal order quantity for the buyer is

$$Q_b^* = \sqrt{\frac{2DS_b}{IC}} = \sqrt{\frac{2(10,000)(100)}{(0.2)(50)}} = 447 \text{ units}$$

The supplier produces to order whenever one is received from the buyer. Each time the seller sets up to produce a batch of components, a production setup cost of $S_s = \$300$ is incurred, and the total annual setup cost (C_s) depends on the *buyer's* order quantity: $C_s = \$300D/Q_b$. The more frequently the buyer places orders, the more setup costs are imposed on the seller.

The optimal order quantity from the buyer (Q_b) is not the same as the optimal order quantity for the entire supply chain (Q_c). These two order quantities are labeled Q_b and Q_c, respectively, in Figure 15-7. If the supply chain were owned and operated by a single firm, the total cost of ordering and setting up for a batch of components would be $S_c = S_b + S_c$. The total inventory-carrying cost would be the carrying cost incurred by the buyer, *IC*. The optimal order quantity for the channel would be

$$Q_c^* = \sqrt{\frac{2D(S_b + S_s)}{IC}} = \sqrt{\frac{2(10,000)(100 + 300)}{(0.2)(50)}} = 894 \text{ units}$$

Unfortunately, when the buyer and the seller are legally separate entities, the buyer lacks motivation to deviate from his optimal order quantity of 447 units, even though the total costs to the supply chain would be lower if he did. In fact, the total setup and inventory carrying costs incurred by the supply chain are 25 percent higher, because the self-interested decision of the buyer causes him to order in quantities that are

Figure 15-7
Cost Curves for
the Buyer, Seller,
and Supply Chain

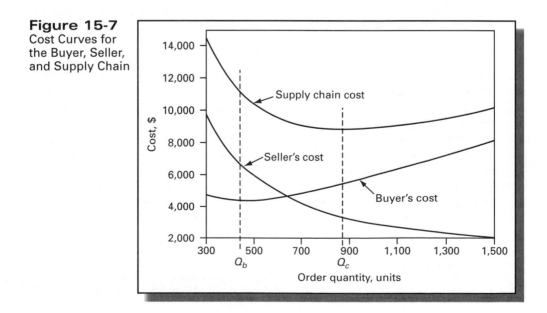

	Buyer Optimal, Q_b = 447 Units	Supply Chain's Optimal, Q_c = 894 Units	Cost Change from Buyer's Optimal, Q
Seller[a]	$ 6,711	$3,356	−50%
Buyer[b]	4,472	5,589	+25%
Supply chain[c]	11,183	8,945	−20%

[a]$TC_s = S_s D/Q_s$
[b]$TC_b = S_b D/Q_b + ICQ_b/2$
[c]$TC_c = (S_s + S_b)D/Q_c + ICQ_c/2$

Table 15-1 Annual Costs for Buyer, Seller, and Supply Chain under Various Order Quantities in Units

about half as large as what is optimal for the supply chain. The economic situation is summarized in Table 15-1 and is shown graphically in Figure 15-7.

It is clear that supply chain costs can be reduced by switching to order quantities based on the costs for the entire supply chain, rather than letting the buyer dictate the order size. If it were true that switching to the optimal order quantity for the supply chain resulted in *both* the seller and the buyer realizing lower costs, the channel would be economically stable, that is, no member wishes to alter the order quantity since his costs would be higher. As seen in Table 15-1, if a switch were made to the supply chain optimal quantity, the seller could benefit at the expense of the buyer, whose costs would increase by 25 percent. Since the buyer controls the quantity, he will not order the supply chain optimal quantity unless the benefits are redistributed to reward him for doing so. The benefits are accumulating with a channel member who is not responsible for creating them. Ways need to be found for resolving this conflict.

Managing the Conflict

The object of managing the superorganization is to establish the conditions so that each member of the coalition may benefit from his or her cooperation for the greater good. Managing the superorganization is not the same as managing within the confines of the firm. The reliance is more on bargaining and tacit arrangements than on formalized structural relationships. This type of management is generally little understood and is a subject for further research. However, the direction for successful superorganization management seems clear. First, metrics need to be established for identifying boundary-spanning opportunities and measuring performance due to cooperation. Second, there need to be ways of sharing relevant information among the superorganization members. Third, there needs to be the application of a strategy for conflict resolution. Fourth, there needs to be some method for distributing the gains achieved from cooperation and maintain the coalition.

Need for Metrics
Uncovering cost-saving/service-improvement opportunities in the supply chain from managing across company boundaries and quantifying them requires an

accounting system that few possess. Multienterprise accounting would need to report such costs as inventory holding, transportation, order or production setup, product storage and handling—all the costs, demand, and service information associated with product flows between the firms. Channel members must be able to evaluate the effect of their decision making on their performance as well as that of other members. They need to know where the benefits "pool" in the channel and to quantify the changes in logistics performance. Measures that specifically address boundary-spanning issues such as total channel cost/profit, total order cycle time, and channel productivity should be a part of channelwide reporting. Many of the metrics that firms use internally for their own managerial purposes need to be extended to their supply chain partners. Whatever form the metrics take, they should *encourage* the identification and measurement of superorganization opportunities.

Information Sharing

An adequate information base in the superorganization is needed for at least two reasons. First, in order for each firm to adjust its controllable variables so that optimum channel profits are achieved, knowledge is required of the economic factor inputs to the decision problems facing the other members, as well as accounting information on the level of profits accruing to each member. Second, an adequate information system also reduces the uncertainties among the autonomous members and contributes to their continued voluntary cooperation. An intermember information system could be established, but assuring adequate and accurate information among the membership is difficult because of the weak lines of accountability. However, sharing information related to the cooperative effort is essential since it helps to build trust among the members, a key ingredient for encouraging and maintaining cooperation.

Distribution of Benefits

Equitable redistribution of the benefits achieved through cooperation by the coalition is important. Recall Table 15-1, especially column 3. Under the revised order quantity, channel costs are at their lowest level, but the change in costs (see column 4) is not distributed equitably among the members. That is, both seller and the channel stand to gain from the buyer's change in order quantity. However, the buyer stands to lose as costs increase. The buyer lacks the incentive to cooperate since he can profit more by acting alone, as can be noted from his cost figures for Q_b in Table 15-1. The buyer might drop from the coalition. If a method for the redistribution of costs, possibly in proportion to the cost levels that are likely to exist under the situation where both members act alone, were established, each member could be satisfied. The buyer recovers the cost level he would have gained from acting alone, in addition to sharing in the additional cost benefits achieved through cooperation. Both members are likely to remain in the coalition, since both derive benefits from it. However, establishing a method for passing the benefits between channel members that will keep them acting in concert may be elusive.

Strategies for Conflict Resolution[13]

When cooperation produces an equitable distribution of benefits among channel members, no formal action is needed to redistribute the benefits. All members are better off and may be satisfied with the outcome. However, if the members believe that they gain, but inequitably or the benefits "pool" with some members at the expense of others, then there is a choice of using a formal or informal transfer mechanism.

A *formal* transfer mechanism is one where a product-flow variable under the control of one channel member can be altered in such a way to influence the action of another member to cause the systemwide optimum to be achieved. An example in the previous illustration would be to adjust price in the channel that is under the seller's control. In Table 15-1, the buyer's costs are shown to increase by $1,117 per year if he agrees to an order quantity of 894 units, whereas the seller's costs are reduced by $3,355 for this quantity. If the seller transfers some of his benefits in the form of a price discount that reduces the buyer's annual costs by a least $1,117, an economically rational buyer will take the incentive and order the supply chain optimal quantity. Although price is one variable that can be manipulated to achieve the redistribution of benefits, other formal transfer mechanisms might include order minimums, reapportionment of orders among channel members to reward cooperation, and incentives on future orders, depending on the configuration of the channel and where in the channel the benefits tend to collect.

Ensuring cooperation in a supply chain when a formal transfer mechanism is not present or is not to be used requires other mechanisms that are less direct and obvious, that is, *informal*. Informal cooperative mechanisms arise outside the scope of traditional economic understanding of exchange since, unlike the economic theory of pure and perfect competition, there is no development of a theory of pure and perfect cooperation.

At least two major and distinct informal mechanisms, *power* and *trust*, can be used to generate cooperation in a supply chain. These mechanisms are usually regarded as alternatives to each other. Power is a central concept because its mere existence is thought to condition others. Power is also seen as a central tenet in achieving cooperation. In contrast, it is theorized that central to relationship marketing is the presence of trust, not power, and its ability to condition others.

Consider the role of power as a mechanism to achieve cooperation. The exercise of power by a channel member might be used especially against the one worse off because of cooperation. A member might be so dominant that other members may be coerced into acting to achieve the systemwide benefits. In the example, if the seller has the status of being the only supplier, he might coerce the buyer to accept purchasing in the larger quantity. The buyer may have to accept the additional costs as a pseudo price increase, yet the seller has not changed his pricing policy with the attendant legal problems that might be involved.

Additional forms of power include reward power, expert power, and referent power. An example of *reward power* is to establish the buyer as a preferred customer, which might include for him faster and easier transactions or guaranteed service

---

[13]Ibid.

regarding quantity availability and delivery time. The benefit to the buyer is the reduction of uncertainty. Similarly, a member might use *expert power*. In this case, the seller might provide training, information, or problem-solving assistance as an incentive for cooperation. Another might be the use of *referent power*. Here, the seller's brand name or image may be so strong that the buyer may be permitted to use it in his advertising and to his benefit (e.g., Intel Inside). This is an indirect benefit to the buyer, who then may agree to supply chain cooperation. If the value of these incentives exceeds the $1,117 cost increase experienced by the buyer, then a rational buyer is likely to accept ordering in the larger order quantities.

Another informal mechanism, *trust*, is defined as a general expectancy held by a channel member that the word of the other can be relied on. That is, one party has confidence in an exchange partner's reliability and integrity. Once trust is established, parties learn that coordinated, joint efforts lead to outcomes that exceed what the firm can achieve acting solely in its own interest, which is exactly the phenomenon illustrated in the example. In buyer-supplier bargaining situations, trust is found to be central to the process of achieving cooperative problem solving and constructive dialogue.

Trust may lead directly to cooperation, or indirectly through development of commitment, which then leads to cooperation. A partner committed to the relationship will cooperate with another because of a desire to make the relationship work. In interfirm relationships, commitment and trust are seen to have strong positive relationships with cooperation. The concepts of trust and commitment are used as mechanisms to enhance relationship marketing, which refers to unique value-added partnerships for which the buyer may be willing to pay a price.

Given that trust and commitment lead to the desired outcome of supply chain cooperation, what are the precursors of trust and commitment in a supply chain? A major precursor of trust is *communication*, which can be defined broadly as the formal as well as informal sharing of meaningful and timely information between channel members. Information sharing is one of five building blocks that characterize solid supply chain relationships, according to LaLonde.[14] Timely communication fosters trust by assisting in resolving disputes and aligning perceptions and expectations about the benefits of cooperation. This accumulation of trust, in turn, leads to better communication. Thus, relevant, timely, and reliable information will result in greater trust. New ways of information sharing, as well as sharing of information between parties usually held in private, can be vital in attaining supply chain cooperation.

Another precursor of trust is *shared values*. Shared values are the beliefs in common that partners have about what behaviors, goals, and policies are important or unimportant, appropriate or inappropriate, and right or wrong. Behavior results from (1) sharing, identifying with, or internalizing the values of an organization or (2) cognitive evaluation of the instrumental worth of continued relationship with an organization. Thus, shared values lead to trust and commitment, and, in turn, cooperation. In a supply channel, channel members are likely to share common economic goals.

---

[14]Bernard J. LaLonde, "Building a Supply Chain Relationship," *Supply Chain Management Review*, Vol. 2, No. 2 (Fall 1998), pp. 7–8.

None of these methods can guarantee conflict resolution or force a particular channel member to perform in a manner that will benefit the channel as a whole. However, they should provide some guidelines for realizing the opportunities that lay dormant in managing the logistics channel among firms.

ALLIANCES AND PARTNERSHIPS

As an alternative to total ownership of the logistics capability and the need for an extensive logistics organizational structure or to loosely held together cooperative arrangements, some firms choose to *share* their logistics capability with other firms or to *contract* for the logistics activities to be performed by firms specializing in providing such services, called third-party providers (3PLs). Many firms are recognizing that there are strategic and operating advantages to be gained from logistics partnering. Some of the general benefits are

- reduced cost and lower capital requirements
- access to technology and management skills
- improved customer service
- competitive advantage such as through increased market penetration
- increased access to information for planning
- reduced risk and uncertainty

Of these, a potential reduction in transportation/distribution costs and freed up capital in noncore areas rank at the top of the benefits, with reduced personnel also being a noted advantage. The primary risk to the firm is the loss of control over critical logistics activities that may result in the potential advantages never being realized.

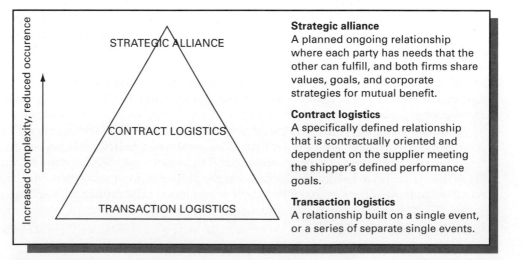

Figure 15-8 The Outsourcing Relationship Continuum

Source: "Strike Up Logistics Alliances," *Transportation & Distribution* (November 1988), pp. 38–42.

To some extent, firms have been outsourcing a portion of their logistics activities for many years. Every time a firm calls up UPS or a common carrier, or uses a public warehouse to store its goods, it is partnering with an outside firm to handle part of the supply chain activities. How extensive the relationship is between the firm and its outside partners is a matter of degree. The relationship may be based on single events to long-term contractual arrangements to shared systems of a strategic alliance. This outsourcing relationship continuum is illustrated in Figure 15-8.

Examples

Outsourcing logistics activities and partnering with others concerning logistical matters are quite common. Consider some of the opportunities for logistics cost reduction in several settings:

- MetroHealth, 1,000-bed community hospital, maintains a fleet of vans and drivers for transporting patients to and from its hospital complex to meet appointment times for examination and treatment. Vehicle and driver utilization is low, rarely exceeding 50 percent of the time available throughout the workday. Considering the cost pressures on the healthcare system, partnering with other area hospitals for this transport capability, while maintaining a desirable transport service level within the region, makes good economic sense, since hospital service territories typically overlap. Duplicate transportation systems could be avoided.
- A pharmaceutical manufacturer was constructing a new warehouse to meet its space needs for a considerable time into the future. The warehouse was sized to its future peak needs, and the fear of losing control over the inventory prohibited the company from seeking alternative space during the intervening years. Seeking partners to share the space for the time until the company needed to recapture the space due to inventory growth would save the expense of excess capacity. On the other hand, partners could acquire the space at rental rates, which were less than public warehousing or alternative contractual arrangements
- Abbott Laboratories and 3M consolidated their order entry and distribution functions for improved purchasing, materials handling, and inventory control. The two companies formed an alliance to allow hospitals to receive supplies from both firms through a single delivery. The alliance works well because the companies do not substantially compete with each other. The relationship has provided mutual marketing and distribution cost savings. IBM Information Network has joined the alliance to capitalize on increasing demand for on-line distribution service. Improved supply chain management and improved services for smaller suppliers are benefits of the alliance.[15]

---

[15]E. J. Muller, "The Coming of the Corporate Alliance," *Distribution*, Vol. 87, No. 8 (August 1988), pp. 82–84.

Figure 15-9
Selection Diagram
of Where to Perform
Logistics Activities

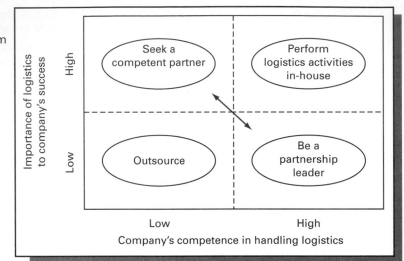

Deciding whether to perform the logistics function in-house or to seek other arrangements is a balance of two factors: how critical logistics is to the firm's success and how competent the firm is in managing the logistics function. As shown in Figure 15-9, the strategy to follow depends on the position in which the company finds itself.

A company that has high customer service requirements, significant logistics costs as a proportion of total costs, and an efficient logistics operation administered by competent personnel will likely find little benefit to partnering or outsourcing logistics activities. Logistics activities are best performed in-house. Wal-Mart is a company that, because of its superior supply channel, has these characteristics. On the other hand, for those companies where logistics is not central to strategy and a high level of logistics competency is not supported within the firm, outsourcing the logistics activities to third-party providers may well lead to significant cost reductions and customer service improvements. Dell Computer considers its core competencies to be marketing and manufacturing high-technology PC hardware rather than logistics. This direct-marketing firm contracts with several third-party logistics providers to coordinate distribution in geographical areas.

Where logistics is critical to strategy but logistics management competency is low, finding a firm with which to partner may provide significant benefits. A strong partner may provide facilities located in new and existing markets, a transportation capability, and administrative expertise not available within the company. Conversely, where logistics is not especially critical to strategy but managed by capable personnel, managers may want to be aggressive by taking the lead in seeking partners to share the logistics system, thus reducing the company's costs through increased volume and the economies of scale that result. Target partners would be those companies that fall into the northwest quadrant of Figure 15-9.

Alliances

It is quite natural for a firm that is heavily invested in transportation equipment, warehouses, inventories, order processing systems, logistics technology, and administrative personnel to question whether this investment might be shared with other firms to reduce its own costs. Conversely, being conscious of the high costs of logistics, a firm may seek to partner with another firm that has excess logistics capacity, strategic facility locations to markets, desirable technology, and outstanding administrative capabilities that the firm seeks to share. Of course, the firm may have certain skills and capabilities that are desirable to other firms. Forming a logistics alliance, or partnership, may benefit both parties. The firm that does not desire to build a high degree of management competency in logistics may also seek an alliance with a stronger logistics partner to strengthen its own competitive position.

A logistics alliance is built on *trust*, a *sharing of information* that aids logistics performance, *specific goals* to achieve a higher level of logistics performance than can be achieved alone, operating *ground rules* for each partner, and *exit provisions* for alliance termination. The benefits to be derived from a logistics alliance have already been noted. If these benefits are so obvious, why is it that there are so few alliances that actually have been created? The answer may lie in the concerns that a potential partner has about the alliance when supply channels are to be merged. Chief among these concerns may include

- Loss of control over the logistics channel
- Fear of being "written out of the logistics picture"
- Increased concern about logistics failures and no direct way to handle them for their customers
- Adequate checks and balances may not be able to be identified to the satisfaction of the partner
- Difficulty of identifying the economies to be achieved as compared with the partner's current logistics costs
- A reporting system that does not match that of the partner's or one that is inadequate to reduce uncertainty
- Difficulty of identifying the benefits to be shared, especially when the partner has some ownership in the logistics system
- There may simply not be enough trust to try such an arrangement
- Partners may not be viewed as equals where one partner's requirements may take precedence over another's
- Difficulty in seeing how trust, good faith, and cooperation can be achieved in such an arrangement
- Too few examples to show how such alliances work well in other companies

Logistics alliances are fragile. They can be difficult to form and they may fracture easily; however, their potential benefits encourage management to continue to explore ways of making them work.

Example

A domestic manufacturer of electrical and power transmission equipment with annual sales of about $1.5 billion was quite proud of the logistics system it had created, especially the information system used to operate the system. Product was made to stock at nine plants and distributed nationally through eight warehouses and distributors. Pressures to reduce logistics costs led the company to consider a partner that would share the company's distribution system. Economies resulting from the additional volume flowing through the distribution channel would improve customer service and lower costs.

The company created an alliance with a European partner, who also manufactured industrial products and had annual U.S. sales of about $250 million. The product line was manufactured at two domestic plants with supplemental imports. Products were produced to stock, and national sales were served from three warehouses. The service levels to customers were similar for both partners.

The partnership primarily involved sharing the domestic firm's warehouse space in the California area. The domestic manufacturer was able to recover some of the fixed warehousing cost and better utilize the transportation equipment in the California marketplace. The European partner gained easy access to the California market, which it had not penetrated particularly well, and warehousing and delivery expenses were modest when compared with other alternatives.

Contract Logistics

For years, companies have been using the services of other companies to support their own logistics activities. Common carriers provide trucking and rail services, public warehouses provide storage services, and specialty firms provide freight bill auditing and accounting services. In recent years, mainly since the deregulation of transportation, logistics companies have emerged that provide a full-service logistics capability. That is, they can handle the entire logistics operation for a client company for a contract price. They have variously been referred to as third-party providers, integrated logistics companies, and contract logistics specialists. Although there has been significant growth for these logistics service providers, the companies using them do so sparingly. Eighty-five percent of the companies using outside services spend less than 20 percent of their logistics budgets on them.[16]

Compared with alliances, contract logistics companies (3PLs) are often viewed as selling services rather than forming partnerships that benefit from the synergism between the members of the alliance. However, because there can be information sharing and close working relationships, the relationship between a company and its outside logistics provider is frequently referred to as a partnership. The contract logistics companies hold themselves out to provide high-level solutions to logistics problems and excellent performance in the execution of logistics operations. A primary

---

[16]Robert Lieb, "The Use of Third-Party Logistics Services by Large American Manufacturers," *Journal of Business Logistics*, Vol. 13, No. 2 (1992), pp. 29–42.

motivation for a company to outsource some or all of its logistics activities is that the third-party provider is more efficient because logistics is its primary business, while logistics is not the core competency of the buying firm.

The potential benefits of partnering were previously noted. On the other hand, there are some possible disadvantages, as well. From a survey by J. P. Morgan Securities, Inc., the most noted negatives to using a 3PL were the lack of understanding the client's business and overpromising service capabilities.[17] Barriers to maintaining a successful long-term relationship include (1) misalignment of company cultures; (2) change in leadership at either the 3PL or the user; (3) unreasonable expectations of the outsourced relationship; and (4) lack of good information.[18]

Failures in 3PL relationships have sometimes been spectacular. They have resulted in lawsuits and negative press, perhaps because expectations for the benefits were so high. Now that several years have passed since 3PLs became an option for logistics managers, practitioners having experience with outsourcing have the following 12 suggestions that can lead to a company's successful long-term relationship with a 3PL:[19]

1. Determine your current supply chain costs and service levels as a baseline for comparing performance with that of the 3PL.
2. Develop the necessary metrics and invest in the proper technology to accept and evaluate the information received from the 3PL.
3. Invest the time to make sure that you and the 3PL are in strategic alignment.
4. Establish trust by meeting promises, owning up to and working through mistakes, and accepting responsibility as appropriate.
5. Develop relationship management capabilities, especially strategic and organizational change management skills, necessary to manage relationships with 3PLs.
6. Measure performance of the 3PL in terms of costs, but also attempt to measure the 3PL's contribution to increased sales.
7. Be a good customer by treating the 3PL as a partner rather than a vendor.
8. Communicate openly and honestly.
9. Share both risk and reward.
10. Recognize the 3PL's team who is working on your behalf.
11. Work through the difficult situations rather than quickly changing providers.
12. Explore the frontiers for performance improvement as the relationship matures.

Example

With nearly 400 suppliers in 14 states shipping materials to 30 assembly plants on a call-and-demand basis, General Motors found its inventory and distribution costs rising and its facilities congested with less-than-truckload (LTL) truck traffic. GM turned to Penske Logistics, a third-party provider, for a customized solution. GM

---

[17]"Shippers Slam Ignorance of Many 3PLs," *American Shipper* (December, 2001), pp. 30–31.
[18]"Making a Long Term Commitment," *Inbound Logistics* (July 2002), pp. 98–104.
[19]Ibid.

had three objectives: reduce costs, improve inbound material management and information processing, and reduce its carrier base.

Penske evaluated the automotive manufacturer's distribution processes and recommended the use of a cross-dock distribution center strategically located in Cleveland. Staffed and managed by Penske Logistics personnel, this facility receives, processes, and consolidates inbound materials. Penske Logistics also implemented a dedicated fleet of 60 tractors and 72 trailers and handled route development and scheduled supplier pickups and JIT deliveries.

Penske schedules supplier pickups based on parts usage levels communicated via EDI from GM. Once received, a shipment crosses the dock for immediate staging and is labeled with in-plant routing instructions designed to expedite delivery at the proper location within the facility. The freight is then loaded on outbound trailers. The process involves 5 million pounds of freight each week.

Penske Logistics uses dynamic routing to increase the frequency of supplier pickups, thus reducing inventory levels and improving outbound material flow. On-board computers using satellite technology allow continuous two-way communication between drivers and dispatchers.

By consolidating inbound shipments at the distribution center and shipping full truckloads to the plants, Penske was able to lower LTL trucking costs and reduce GM's carrier base. Penske Logistics selects and manages those carriers necessary to supplement the dedicated fleet. This has reduced GM's administrative costs by processing "one bill" for LTL services and has cut transit times by 18 percent.[20]

Partnering Through Collaboration

The benefits of organization need not result from formal or informal designs where relationships are defined between people within an organization. As information technology has evolved, a new dimension to organization has emerged—partnering through collaboration. Partnerships among the supply channel members occur as information is shared among them for their mutual benefit. These partners collaborate to achieve their own organizational objectives, usually lowered cost from reduced inventories and improved customer service from higher fill rates.

Partnering with members across echelons in the supply channel has seen success when retail point-of-sale information was shared with suppliers who were better able to plan inventory levels at the retail level (vendor managed inventory control or VMIC) and with requirements plans shared with suppliers in just-in-time systems. There were early successes with collaborative planning and an organization called the voluntary inter-industry commerce standards (VICS) created collaborative planning, forecasting, and replenishment (CPFR).[21] CPFR is a program of information sharing that involves forecasts, production schedules, order replenishment quantities and their timing, and lead times. VICS established guidelines for explaining underlying business processes, supporting technology, and change-management issues.

---

[20]"Logistics' New Customer Focus," *Business Week*, March 10, 1997.
[21]www.cpfr.org

Collaboration among channel members has the potential for improving supply chain performance by reducing the uncertainty associated with demand and lead times. Recall the "bull whip" effect on demand forecasting that arises when each channel member forecasts demand based on information derived from the order patterns of an immediate downstream member. Sharing information about end customer demand is known to improve forecasting accuracy for all members. Improved forecasting reduces inventory levels in the supply channel.

However, a program such as CPFR encourages collaboration beyond forecasting. Although sharing information among partners reduces demand-estimating variability, decisions also need to be made about order quantities, shipment sizes, delivery methods, and production or supplier response times. In a partnering environment, information about these issues will be shared and the outcomes negotiated. Compared with traditional approaches in which each member makes his or her own decisions, early results from pilot tests have been impressive. From a VICS survey, retail participants have reported

- An 80 percent increase in business with a CPFR partner
- A $9 million increase in sales
- Simultaneous sales growth and inventory reductions of at least 10 percent
- Improved fill rates with less inventory
- Service level of 100 percent, with almost 40 turns per year[22]

However, collaborative partnerships are being adopted slowly. The greatest impediment to mass adoption appears to be *trust*. Companies remain reluctant to share vital data with firms outside their control and who may have business relationships with competitors. Formal agreements between partners may reduce distrust, but it is likely to remain a hurdle to overcome for some time. Yet, the potential for collaborative partnerships remains high.

Observations

The concepts of collaborative planning, forecasting, and replenishment have been pilot tested in a number of cases with the following results:

- Wal-Mart collaborated with Warner Lambert on the mouthwash Listerine and found that in-stock levels increased to 98 percent from 87 percent, lead times were reduced from 21 days to 11 days, on-hand inventory was cut by two weeks, orders were more consistent, and production cycles were smoothed. Listerine's sales increased by $8.5 million. Similarly, sales for Sara Lee items in Wal-Mart's CPFR pilot increased 32 percent, while inventories fell 14 percent. In-stock performance improved by 2 percent and gross margin return on investment was up 6 percent.
- For two unnamed chains and their trading partners, post-collaboration results showed for one retail participant an average sales gain of 12 percent, and a

---

[22]Walter McKaige, "Collaborating on the Supply Chain," *IIE Solutions*, Vol. 33, No. 11 (March 2001), pp. 34–37.

distribution center inventory reduction averaging 33 percent for the other retail participant.

- One of Kmart's pilots with Kimberly Clark resulted in a 14 percent increase in sales as well as in-stock improvements that went from 86 to 94 percent without increasing inventory.
- Walgreen's CPFR with Schering-Plough for a laxative product showed a forecasting accuracy improvement of 25 percent.
- In Ace Hardware's CPFR pilot with Manic, a tape supplier, sales were up 20 percent, freight costs were down 14 percent, and Manic's distribution costs were down 28 percent.

CONCLUDING COMMENTS

This chapter has shown the basic issues in logistics/SC organization and how to achieve coordination and cooperation among activities, functions, and firms so that logistics plans can be implemented effectively. Guided by the total cost concept, organization facilitates optimum logistics performance, except when customer service or information strategies are dominant. The organization should be considered on three levels. Grouping relevant activities together and managing them collectively as a logistics function has received the greatest attention. In certain cases, the payoffs have been great because of this activity realignment. Much less consideration has been given to the problems of interfunctional and interorganizational cooperation, coordination, and collaboration. The potential benefits may far exceed those from direct activity management. However, achieving cooperation among functions within the firm and among firms beyond their legal boundaries, when cooperation is likely to be largely voluntary, is a highly complex organizational problem. Undoubtedly in the future, logistics/SC organization at all levels will choose cooperation as a general theme for organizational effectiveness rather than simply selecting formalized organizational structures that create as many coordination problems as they resolve.

As an alternative to performing all logistics tasks in-house and, therefore, needing extensive logistics/SC organizations, many firms have sought to outsource logistics activities or to form logistics partnerships and share their logistics systems with other firms. Advocates have argued that such a strategy can lead to reduced costs and improved customer service, while allowing the firm to focus in its core competencies. Those opposing the strategy cite loss of control of the logistics activities and a resulting deterioration in customer service.

QUESTIONS

1. Explain why a firm would want to develop an organization chart for a logistics/SC.
2. If a firm does not wish to establish a separate, identifiable logistics function, how might the coordination, which is necessary for effective management of logistics activities, be achieved?

3. Explain the difference between a line and a staff organization structure for logistics.
4. What criteria would you use to determine whether a logistics/SC organizational structure should be centralized or decentralized?
5. What responsibilities, skills, and experiences would you want to include in a job description for the position of vice president of logistics/SC for a consumer products manufacturer (say, of housewares)? How would your description change, if at all, if the position were for a large medical clinic?
6. Indicate the firm's activities, such as purchasing, transportation, and inventory control, that should be included in a logistics/SC organization, if the company is one of the following:
    a. Miller Coal Mining Company (extractive firm)
    b. Titusville Community Hospital (service firm)
    c. March Department Stores (retailing firm)
    d. Romac Appliance Company (manufacturing firm)
7. If a firm is in Stage II of its logistics/SC organizational development, what would be required for it to move to Stage III? To Stage IV? To Stage V?
8. Why are customer service, packaging, and production scheduling considered interfunctional management activities? How can they be managed effectively within a functionally organized firm? What organizational structure would you propose for managing the superorganization? Contrast the structure with that for managing logistics activities that are strictly within the legal boundaries of the firm.
9. What is a superorganization? How does managing the superorganization compare with managing the logistics function within the firm?
10. Table 15-1 indicates that distribution channel profits can be higher if individual channel members cooperate in deciding purchase order quantities and pricing policies than if they act alone. Because the benefits of cooperation may tend to "pool" with one of the members, how might the members enjoy the increased benefits and be encouraged to continue to cooperate?
11. Describe the situation within a company where it is suggested that
    a. Some or all of the logistics activities be outsourced.
    b. The company seeks a partner to share its logistics system.
    c. The company actively takes the lead in forming a logistics alliance.
    d. All logistics activities be managed in-house.
12. Suggest the type of information that should be shared among supply channel partners to encourage cooperation and to maintain trust.
13. What methods are available for distributing the benefits of channel member collaboration?
14. Briefly describe CPFR.

Chapter 16

Logistics/Supply Chain Control

The logistician is now a process manager and no longer just an activities administrator.

*L*ogistics/SC plans may be made and implemented, but that alone does not ensure accomplishment of intended goals. It is necessary to think about another primary management function. This function is control—the process where planned performance is brought into line, or kept in line, with desired objectives. The control process is one of comparing actual performance to planned performance and initiating

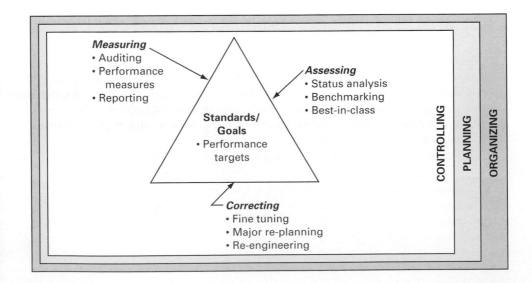

corrective action to bring the two more closely together, if required. Auditing provides the information necessary for control.

This chapter presents an overview of the audit and control processes, and discusses the control of the logistics/SC function and of logistics/SC activities. The major elements of control information, measurement, and corrective action are explored. Benchmarking and a supply chain operations reference (SCOR) model useful for identifying improvement opportunities are discussed. Finally, the role that artificial intelligence can play in the control process is examined.

A Control Process Framework

The basic need for a control activity in the management process centers on the future uncertainties that alter a plan's performance. Variation from design parameters will occur, as the many forces that act on the conditions of any plan cannot be predicted with certainty. In addition to what might be considered normal variations in conditions are the contingencies. These are the one-time, extraordinary occurrences, usually of major proportions (e.g., strikes, fires, floods), that drastically affect a plan's performance. Besides future uncertainties, there also may be fundamental changes occurring in the logistics/SC environment that will alter planned performance. For example, changes in economic conditions, technological changes, and shifts in customer attitudes may not have been foreseen at the time of planning but may affect the plan.

The control process is, in part, one of monitoring changing conditions with the anticipation that corrective action may be needed to realign actual performance with planned performance. Perfect planning and execution of plans would require no control. Because this is seldom possible, the logistician should provide a control mechanism to ensure the accomplishment of desired goals.

A Logistics/SC Control Model

The management control process is analogous to the many mechanical control systems encountered nearly every day. Perhaps most familiar is the heating system in the home or office building. The control mechanism is the thermostat, which senses the temperature of the air, compares it to the desired temperature setting, and initiates corrective action, if necessary, by calling for heat from the furnace or cool air from the air conditioner. In the logistics system, the manager seeks to control planned logistics activities (transportation, warehousing, inventories, materials handling, and order processing) in terms of customer service and activity costs. The control mechanism includes the audits and reports about system performance, the goals established for performance, and some means for initiating corrective action, which is often provided by the logistics/SC manager. This control mechanism, in relation to the associated factors in the process, is shown in Figure 16-1. The additional factors include plans, logistics activities, environmental influences, and performance.

Figure 16-1
A Schematic
Representation of
the Logistics/SC
Control Process

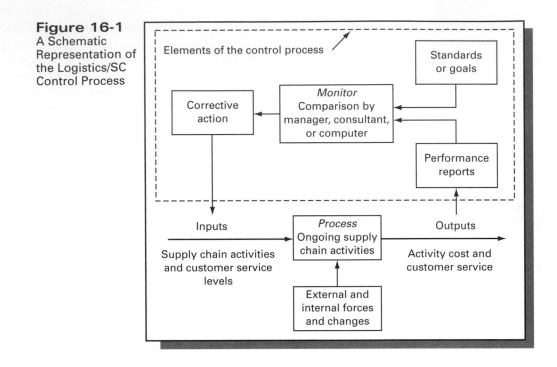

Inputs, the Process, and Output

The focus of the control system is on the process to be regulated. This process may be a single activity, such as filling orders and supplying inventories, or it may be a combination of all activities in the logistics function, both internal and external. There are inputs into the process in the form of plans. Plans indicate how the process should be designed. Examples are plans for transportation modes to use, for the safety stock to maintain, for the order processing system design, or a combination of all of these, depending on the goals for the control system.

Environmental influences are a second type of process input. The environment broadly includes all factors potentially affecting the process and that are not accounted for in the plans. These represent the uncertainties that alter the process output from the planned activity levels. Examples of some of the important environmental influences would be uncertainties in the actions of customers, competitors, suppliers, and government.

The process output is what we may, in general, call performance. Performance is the state of the process at any particular time. For example, if the process is the transportation activity, then the performance might be measured in terms of direct costs, such as transportation rates, indirect costs, such as loss and damage, or delivery performance.

The process, with its input plans and resulting performance, is the object of the control process. These factors result from the planning and implementation processes, and they are shown in relation to the control function in Figure 16-1.

Standards and Goals

The control function requires a reference standard against which logistics activity performance can be compared. The manager, consultant, or a computer program strives to match process performance with this standard. Typically, this standard is a cost budget, a customer service target level, or a contribution to profit.

In addition to standards set by company plans and policies, some firms have chosen to conform to external standards. The heightened interest in quality has led to firms setting their performance standards high enough to compete for quality awards, such as the Malcolm Baldridge National Quality Award, the Deming Prize, or the J. D. Powers & Associates Quality Award. Perhaps the most popular standards for quality assurance are those of the International Organization for Standardization,[1] referred to as ISO 9000.[2] For the logistician, quality may mean filling orders accurately, having few stockouts, or delivering product on time. Companies around the world seek to become certified and promote that they meet the certification criteria. Customers expect it from their suppliers, since this gives assurances that the products or services they receive will be as they expect. For the provider of products or services, the criteria for these quality awards or ISO 9000 certification may become the logistics process goal.

The Monitor

The monitor is the nerve center of the control system. It receives information about process performance, compares it with the reference goal, and initiates corrective action (see Figure 16-1). Compared with the thermostat in a heating and air-conditioning system, the information inputs to the logistics control system monitor are often not as electronically sophisticated. Information received by the monitor is primarily in the form of periodic reports and audits. Such information typically includes reports concerning inventory status, resource utilization, activity cost, and customer service level.

The monitor in the system is the manager, consultant, or a computer program. The monitor interprets and compares the performance reports with the activity goals. It decides whether performance is out of control and, if it is, chooses the corrective steps that must be taken to bring performance in line with objectives. For example, if customer service is too low compared with the desired service level, the manager might call for additional safety stock to be maintained in the warehouses. The exact nature of the corrective action depends on the degree of control process error and how permanent the manager hopes the correction to be. If the "error" between actual and desired performance is within acceptable limits, no corrective action is likely to be taken. On the other hand, if the error exceeds acceptable limits, the manager may choose immediate and possibly temporary tactical solutions to reduce the error, or he or she may initiate strategic planning that will alter the system design. It is a matter of judgment whether the manager seeks a tactical or strategic solution. That individual's understanding of the error's cause influences judgment,

---

[1] A worldwide federation of national standards bodies from some 100 countries, one from each country.
[2] A set of five universal standards for a quality assurance system accepted around the world.

for example, whether there is random variation or fundamental change in performance, whether the benefits to be gained from major replanning outweigh the costs involved, or whether there is a need for quick error correction.

Types of Control Systems

Control systems vary in design. They are generally categorized as open loop, closed loop, or modified feedback types.

Open-Loop Systems

The most common system for controlling logistics activities is the open-loop system as illustrated in Figure 16-2(a). The important feature of the open-loop system is the human intervention between the action of comparing actual and desired performance and the action to reduce the process error. The manager must intervene in a positive way before any corrective action can occur. Thus, the control process is said to be open.

Major advantages of the open-loop control system are its flexibility and low initial cost. The manager, at his or her discretion, can prescribe the type of information needed for control, the error tolerance that is acceptable at any particular time, and the form of the corrective action. This flexibility is particularly beneficial when goals, plans, and environmental influences are subject to frequent changes and when automated control procedures are expensive and constraining. To date, most individual logistics activities, plus the function as a whole, are under open-loop control systems.

Closed-Loop Systems

Much work has been done in recent years to find ways of reducing the need for the human element in control processes. A good deal of this work has centered on physical processes, such as controlling temperatures, voltages, pressures, speed, and position. Such control devices are broadly referred to as servomechanisms, regulators, and controllers. However, only recently has attention been given to similar control of logistics activities. The automatic control of inventories is the outstanding success to date.

In controlling logistics activities, the decision rule is used as a manager surrogate in closed-loop systems. The decision rule acts as the manager would if he or she had observed the performance error. Because the manager can be removed from the control process and control will be maintained by the decision rules, the control system is said to be closed.

Currently, the best example of a closed-loop control system in logistics management is the inventory-control system. As early as 1952, Simon suggested that servomechanism theory could be taken from its electrical and mechanical context and applied to the problems of business concerns, especially inventory-control problems.[3] It was not until the computer became useful as a business tool that inventory systems could be successfully controlled automatically. The importance of good inventory

---

[3]Herbert A. Simon, "On the Application of Servomechanism Theory in the Study of Production Control," *Econometrica*, Vol. 20 (April 1952), pp. 247–268.

Figure 16-2
Examples of
Various Control
Systems for
Inventory Control

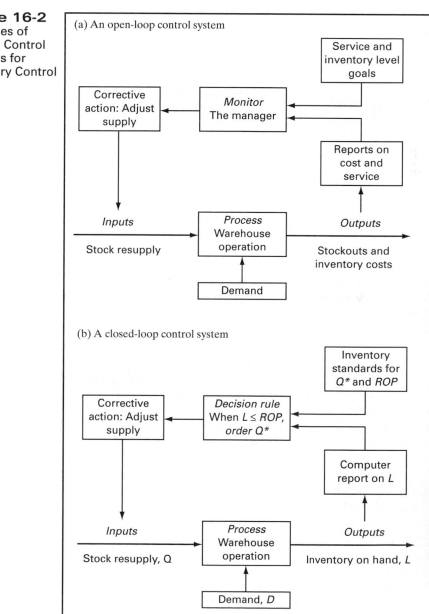

(a) An open-loop control system

Service and inventory level goals

Monitor The manager

Corrective action: Adjust supply

Reports on cost and service

Inputs

Stock resupply

Process Warehouse operation

Demand

Outputs

Stockouts and inventory costs

(b) A closed-loop control system

Inventory standards for $Q*$ and ROP

Decision rule When $L \leq ROP$, order $Q*$

Corrective action: Adjust supply

Computer report on L

Inputs

Stock resupply, Q

Process Warehouse operation

Demand, D

Outputs

Inventory on hand, L

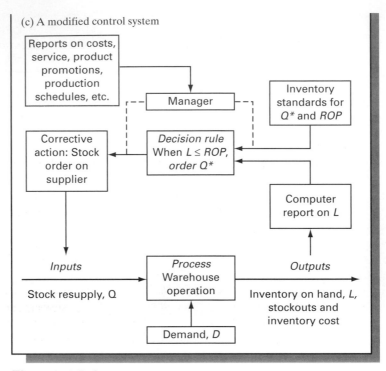

(c) A modified control system

Figure 16-2   *(cont.)*

management to many firms and the quantifiable nature of inventory problems have made it one of the first activities of the firm to be controlled by closed-loop methods.

Figure 16-2(b) shows a closed-loop control system for inventory control based on the fixed order quantity–variable order interval inventory control model with constant demand and lead time. It is contrasted with an open-loop control system for the same problem in Figure 16-2(a). The process is one of maintaining an inventory in a warehouse from which demand is served. Demand continually depletes the stock, and positive action must be taken to replenish it. In the simple system that we are examining, process output is the inventory on hand. Recalling the reorder point inventory model from Chapter 9, we can develop the performance standard and the decision rule for corrective action. That is, the decision rule would be, when the inventory on hand drops below the reorder point quantity *(ROP)*, place a stock order for Q^* units. If conditions remain the same as those assumed when the decision rule was developed, the control system will ensure optimum performance. Implementing the decision rule, reporting on inventory on hand at all times, and issuing the stock order can all be handled by a computer.

In contrast with the open-loop control system of Figure 16-2(a), closed-loop control systems have a great capacity for controlling numerous product inventories with speed and accuracy. However, the closed-loop system tends to be rigid in terms of meeting changing conditions outside its design parameters. It also may provide control over a portion of the total process and, therefore, may lack some of the scope of the open-loop system. Thus, automation may have reduced flexibility, more limited scope of control, and higher initial cost, but it offers increased speed and accuracy of control.

Modified Control Systems

In real-world applications, few things are implemented in their purest form, including control systems. Managers are reluctant to transfer extensive control of an activity or a group of activities to a set of decision rules. Environmental influences are too unpredictable to expect that an automatic control system will remain relevant for all time. Managers may even have a degree of distrust for computers and mathematical models. A combination open-loop, closed-loop (modified) control system is, in fact, what is most frequently used for logistics activity control. The modified system will generally appear as shown in Figure 16-2(c).

In a modified control system, the manager may at times substitute for the decision rules. In the case of the inventory-control problem of Figure 16-2(c), the logistics/SC manager is in a position to *override* the automatic decisions of when and how much to order. He or she generally has access to a much broader information base than the automatic control system and is in a position to judge the performance of the control system. Such information might include customer service complaints, inventory cost reports, marketing promotional announcements, transportation service changes, and production schedule changes. Because the automatic control system usually does not respond to this type of information, it may no longer ensure optimal inventory performance. Thus, the logistician may intervene in the control process either to make minor adjustments in the decision rule, the reference standard, or the information base, or he or she may make major changes in the control system and process design. If the control system is well designed, only infrequent minor adjustments will be necessary. For example, a higher-than-ordinary level of inventory may be needed for temporary item promotion, and the logistician would override the automatic control system by calling for a higher order quantity for the item than the automatic system would suggest.

The manager in a modified control system not only adds flexibility and scope to the system but also acts as a safety valve when the automatic system breaks down. In effect, the modified control system offers advantage in controlling complex activities without requiring the manager to relinquish managerial command over the system. This undoubtedly is the reason for its use over purely open loop or closed loop control systems.

CONTROL SYSTEM DETAILS

Once the type of control system for controlling single activities in the entire logistics function has been broadly defined, several system details need to be considered. These include the tolerance of the system for "error," the nature of system response, the setting of goals, and the nature of control information.

Error Tolerance

How great must the performance error be before corrective action is initiated? Just because the logistics activity costs are too high and the customer service level is too low may not mean that corrective action should be initiated. Corrective action does consume managerial time, especially if the control system is of the open-loop type, so that to take corrective steps to reduce the error when it is unnecessary leads to unneeded expense. Corrective action is unnecessary when the error is due to ordinary random events, and no fundamental changes in average process performance have occurred. In effect, a control system that tends to follow every slight performance error can have the characteristic of being "nervous." In general, a control system should not be designed to respond to random errors.

In contrast to too little tolerance for error is the control system that has too much tolerance for error. If the control monitor, say, the logistics/SC manager, is quite insensitive to performance errors, it is possible for him or her to miss fundamental changes in customer service and activity costs until some time after they have occurred. To bring the process back under control may require drastic alterations in activity levels, even in cases where minor adjustments may have proved satisfactory if the fundamental changes had been detected earlier. Thus, excess control expense can result from the control system designed to be too insensitive to error.

The best control system design is obviously the one that lies between these two extremes. That is, the best system is one that will detect fundamental errors but will not respond to random errors.

Response

When the error in a control system is no longer tolerable, corrective action must be taken. How the system responds to corrective action affects control costs. Response is a function of the characteristics of the system and the form in which corrective action is taken.

Logistics control systems are much like mechanical control systems in that they have varying degrees of mass. System mass governs how quickly actual error correction will occur and the pattern of process response. In a logistics system, mass determines the rate at which the needed change can be made. For example, if inventory levels are to be raised, the time required for realizing the desired levels will be a function of the rate at which production levels can be changed or the necessary quantities obtained from suppliers. The more mass there is in the system, the longer it will be before desired levels are reached, and the longer the out-of-control situation will prevail. Figure 16-3 illustrates the effect of mass on system response.

Information time lags are a second important factor in the pattern of response. In general, when there is a time lag between when a change in process occurs and when that change is detected in the control monitor, the system will tend to "hunt," as shown in Figure 16-4. That is, the control system can never stabilize at the desired level. If information lags, as well as system mass, are not too great, the variation around the desired level will remain within acceptable limits. If not, a more

Figure 16-3
Speed of Response
in an Inventory-
Control System,
Depending on the
Mass of the System

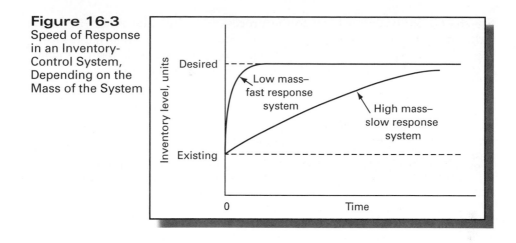

responsive information system, or possibly a more responsive production and delivery system, will need to be designed.

Process response is also influenced by the form in which corrective action is taken. Two modes of control are common. The most popular is the on-off, or two-position, mode. When an error is detected, full and constant corrective action is taken until it is observed by the monitor that the desired level has been reached. If the mass of the system and information lags are great, the on-off control mode promotes "overshooting" of the desired process performance level.

The *proportional* control system is the second familiar control mode. Corrective action here is in direct proportion to the observed error. When the error is great, so is

Figure 16-4 Control System Hunting Caused by Informational Time Lags

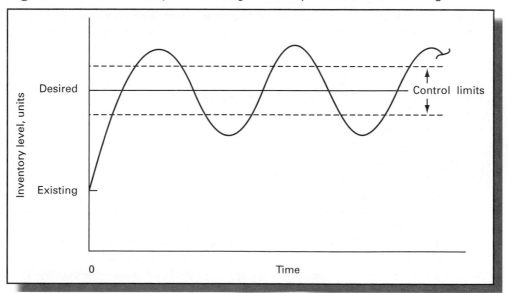

the change in the input level to the process to reduce the error. As the error is reduced, so is the change in process inputs. Such a system is more sophisticated and more expensive than an on-off system, but it may be justified in terms of more rapid system response without a loss in process performance stability.

CONTROL IN PRACTICE

Logistics control systems have been aided by the use of budgets, service targets, and even the profit center concept. There is increasing use made of the computer to aid in the control process through what is known as decision support systems.

Budgets

The most widely used aid for controlling logistics activities is the budget. Budgets are cost goals set by top management in concert with the logistics/SC manager to guide the cost performance of activities. Budgets serve as the reference standard in the control process and, it is hoped, ensure the profitability of the company through cost control. They also serve as a device for measuring the performance of the logistics/SC manager.

Budgets must be realistically set if the profit objectives of the firm are to be met. Nearly any budget can be met if customer service is reduced to low enough levels. However, if it is assumed that the firm desires long-run survival, the logistics service level should be set high enough to at least ensure a competitive service level.

Service Targets

Opposite to the budget is the customer service target. The customer service target focuses on the revenue side of the profit equation. The philosophy of control by setting the control reference standard equal to the service target is that costs will tend to follow revenues. This approach would be reasonable in cases where product sales are highly service-sensitive (e.g., low-valued, highly substitutable products). However, there is an important deficiency in using service targets as a control device. Often, too little is known about the effect of physical distribution service changes on revenues.

Profit Center Concept

An appealing approach for controlling logistics is to treat the logistics function as a separate business entity within the firm, that is, as a profit center. This makes sense because the logistics function employs capital, incurs cost, and adds value by distribution. It even contributes to sales through the customer service level provided. All the prerequisite elements exist for establishing a profit center. Control of the logistics function is in terms of the broader concept of profit and avoids the narrow control features of either budgets or service targets.

Making the profit-center concept work is more difficult than the use of budgets or service targets. The major problem centers on pricing the services provided by the logistics function. Pricing would not be a problem if there were some way of relating the customer service level provided and the contribution made to logistics function profits. If such a relationship were known, the logistics/SC manager would balance revenue against costs incurred in providing the service. Such a relationship generally does not exist. Even if it did, another problem would remain before the profit center concept could be effectively applied. That is, prices for incoming products to the logistics function have to be determined.

Pricing of logistics services and the prices paid for products to be handled by the logistics function are generally not serious problems. Transfer prices can be established in much the same way as goods are priced that move from one division to another in a multidivisional company. Production would price goods to logistics and logistics, after adding value, would price goods to marketing. The price to marketing might be the price paid to production plus logistics costs incurred in supply and distribution plus a markup equivalent to the company's overall return on investment. Once prices are fixed, the logistics/SC manager is free to improve profits in any way he or she wishes. Top management measures the logistics/SC manager through profit performance and periodically reviews the setting of transfer prices.

Decision Support Systems

Decision support systems (DSSs) involve the use of a computer, database systems, and decision, or control, models. An on-line database is maintained of the important data elements needed for control purposes. These might include transportation rates, demand forecasts, lead times, inventory levels, warehousing costs, and service targets. The computer is used to interrogate this database on command of the user. Integrated into the DSS are a number of models and report-generating programs useful for monitoring ongoing activities. These programs interrogate the database for information when activity levels are to be reviewed. In addition to generating activity reports, the DSS has the capability of determining the best level of performance, which serves as a standard against which current performance can be compared. This latter capability distinguishes the DSS from a manual system.

Application

When Xerox found it necessary to cut costs in order to compete in markets with rapidly falling prices, the company needed to know how to motivate personnel in the lower administrative levels to seek the desired cost goals. Logistics and Distribution (L&D) was a cost center of Xerox's Business Systems Group. Steps were taken to get this group to emulate the behavior of a profit center by providing services for a fee and incurring the costs associated with the services provided. L&D was permitted to offer its services to other units of Xerox on a competitive basis. In effect, L&D's 1,200 employees were to act as "intrapreneurs."

Four steps were necessary to realize the profit center status for the L&D group.

1. Establish Benchmarks   Since the L&D profit center must furnish services at competitive prices, it was necessary to know established norms for expenses and service levels relative to its competition. Data were gathered from vendors and companies with both similar and dissimilar operations. The data were represented in the form of indexes in order to neutralize the differences among the data sources.

2. Negotiate Service Levels   L&D contracted with the captive customers within its own group to establish level-of-service targets. L&D set up a fee schedule of expenses for various service levels that aided the selection process.

3. Bid for Business   L&D was permitted to bid for business in other business groups. Since each group had its own distribution organization, any business won was a clear savings to Xerox.

4. Vend to Outsiders   L&D could also sell its services to outside customers. The services offered were a complete network of services or elements of distribution such as transportation or warehousing.

Enhancement of employee morale, initiative, and professionalism were clear benefits of a profit center. In addition, Xerox was able to average a 12 percent productivity improvement over the three-year period following the introduction of the profit center concept to L&D.[4]

CONTROL INFORMATION, MEASUREMENT, AND INTERPRETATION

An effective logistics control system requires accurate, relevant, and timely information about activity or function performance. The major sources of this information are audits and various reports of logistics activities.

Audits

The logistics audit is a periodic examination of the status of logistics activities. Because of potential errors in reporting systems and the lack of reports about certain activities, it becomes necessary to periodically take stock of the situation. A control system may lose its effectiveness if the information available to it is inaccurate. Audit information is used to establish new reference points against which reports are generated and to correct errors resulting from the performance of certain logistics activities due to misinformation.

---

[4]Paraphrased from Frances G. Tucker and Seymour M. Zivan, "A Xerox Cost Center Imitates a Profit Center," *Harvard Business Review* (May–June 1985), pp. 168ff.

Total Function Audit

From time to time, management will find it necessary to take stock of how well the logistics function as a whole is being managed. Management needs to convince itself that the logistics activities are being performed effectively and efficiently. Such an audit might include an evaluation of all personnel, of the organizational structure, and of the overall network design. Network design can be effectively audited by analyzing the general determinants of logistics system design. Substantial changes in demand, customer service, product characteristics, logistics costs, and pricing policies can indicate the need for strategy revision.

Demand.   Geographic dispersion and level of demand greatly determine the configuration of distribution networks. Firms may project disproportionate growth or decline in one region of the country compared to a general growth or decline overall. The latter may require only expansion or recession at current facilities. However, shifting demand patterns may require that new warehouses be located in rapidly growing markets while facilities in slow-growth areas experience little or no expansion. Disproportionate growth of only a few percentage points a year indicates that replanning may be economically beneficial.

Customer service.   This usually includes inventory availability, speed of delivery, and order-filling speed and accuracy. The costs of transportation, warehousing, inventory carrying, and order processing rise disproportionately as service levels are increased. Therefore, logistics costs will be sensitive to the level of customer service provided, especially if the service level is already high.

Replanning is usually needed when service levels are changed due to competitive forces, policy revisions, or arbitrary service goals different from those on which the logistics strategy was originally based. Conversely, minor changes in service levels, when levels are already low, probably will not trigger the need for replanning.

Product characteristics.   Logistics costs are sensitive to product weight, volume, value, and risk. In the channel, these characteristics can be altered through package design or finished state of the product during shipment and storage. For example, shipping a product in a knocked-down form can considerably affect the weight-bulk ratio of the product and the associated transportation and storage rates. However, altering a product characteristic can substantially change one cost element of logistics without affecting others. This will create a new cost balance point for the distribution system. If so, replanning would be indicated.

Logistics costs.   The amount of money a firm spends on logistics often determines how often its strategy should be replanned. All other factors being equal, a firm producing highly engineered goods (such as machine tools and computers), with total distribution costs of 1 percent of sales or less, may give little attention to a logistics strategy. On the other hand, companies producing packaged industrial chemicals or food products may have physical distribution costs as high as 20 to 30 percent of sales. When costs are as high as this, even small changes in inventory-carrying costs and transportation rates can make reformulation of logistics strategy worthwhile.

Pricing Policy

Some suppliers transfer the responsibility and cost of transportation to the buyers, thus taking decisions on important logistics cost elements out of their own hands. Many firms do this through pricing policies such as f.o.b. factory, prepaid transportation charges, and invoice add-ons. Because these firms do not pay for transportation, there is little incentive to include it as an economic force in setting logistics strategy. If the price policy is changed to a delivered arrangement (transportation cost included in the price), the supplying firm directly incurs the transportation charges. This can add warehouses and inventory to the logistics system. Shifting the terms of the price policy, especially shipment routing and quantities, and shifting the responsibility for the transportation decision can signal a need for strategy reformulation.

Inventory Audits

Inventory audits are essential in inventory systems. A typical inventory-control system makes adjustments to inventory records due to demand depletions, replenishments, returns to plant, and product obsolescence. However, the occurrence of other events may cause disparities between inventory records and the actual inventories maintained in the warehouses. Theft, customer returns, damaged goods, and errors in various inventory reports can lead to substantial errors in the level of inventories believed to be on hand. A physical count of the inventories, from time to time, determines the true level of all product items. Adjustments are then made to inventory records so that once again the control system will provide more accurate tracking of inventory levels.

Taking a physical count of every item in an inventory can be quite time-consuming and disruptive to operations. Some firms may shut down operations annually while the item count is taken. As an alternative to the once-a-year count of all items, only a fraction of the items will be counted at a particular time, with the times for a count being staggered throughout the year. The frequency with which an item is counted can be set according to its criticality. This *cycle counting* process spreads the auditing workload throughout the year and causes fewer disruptions in operations.

Freight Bill Audits

Human mistakes commonly cause the extra expense of performing audits. In the control of transportation costs, many firms have found it worthwhile to audit their freight bills. Errors in rates, product description, weights, and routing are just a few of the ways that errors can creep into billing. It is common for a large company to have up to 750,000 freight bills a year, and even infrequent errors can result in sizable overcharges. There is a 3 to 5 percent overcharge to freight bills on an annual basis.

Checking freight bills can be handled by a company's traffic department; however, many firms prefer to have this audit performed outside the firm by freight bill auditing firms. These firms offer this service on a commission basis. That is, the audit firm receives a percentage of the claims that are recovered. Contracting with an outside agency is particularly beneficial to the small firm that cannot efficiently provide a staff for this activity. So common are errors that freight bill auditing is often carried out on a regular basis. The cost to have freight bills audited is typically about 50 percent of the amount recovered.

Benchmarking to Other Firms

When audits are conducted, it is common to wonder how well a firm's logistics/SC is performing compared with its competition. Costs and customer service performance data are sought for firms in similar businesses. Such data are made available through surveys. Typically, universities, trade associations, or consulting firms become repositories for such data submitted by many firms. The anonymity of the data from an individual firm is protected when the results are presented as averages and ranges. For example, Figure 16-5 shows total supply chain costs as a percent of revenue for a variety of industries. Since the best-in-class is given, this performance level may be used as a reference against which to compare. Other data besides costs may also be available, such as inventory turnover ratios, on-time delivery statistics, and logistics activity costs.

While appealing, benchmarking in this manner must be used with caution. A firm that is not performing as well as the best in class, or even as well as the average firm in its industry, must recognize that it may have chosen to balance its trade-offs differently. For example, a firm with low inventory turnover may be saving on transportation by shipping in large quantities. Transportation cost performance may be quite good, but inventory-carrying costs may be high. Similarly, logistics costs may be high, but exceptional customer service is given. Unless customer service is

Figure 16-5
Total Supply Chain
Costs As a Percent
of Revenue for
Selected Industries

Source: Pittiglio, Rabin,
Todd, & McGrath,
"The Keys to Unlocking
Your Supply Chain's
Competitive Advantage:
Integrated Supply-Chain
Benchmarking Study"
(1997), p. 4.

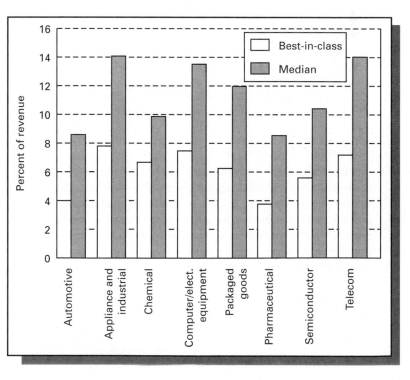

compared with costs, the firm with the high logistics costs may appear to be under-performing.

Example

Premier Industrial distributes lubricants to construction sites that may be up to 600 miles from a warehouse. Premier has found a profitable niche in the market-place by supplying its customers lubricants in small quantities and with quick response. Compared with the major oil companies used as a benchmark, Premier's logistics costs appear quite high. When customer service is brought into the comparison, logistics has been used as a key to its marketing strategy. Premier has been one of the most consistently profitable Fortune 500 companies for many decades.

Benchmarking has been referred to as a process with definable steps. It is a con-tinuous process of measuring and evaluating supply chain performance and prac-tices against others in the industry. The purpose is to identify differences that can lead to improvement. Benchmarking is conducted at the performance metrics, processes, or strategies level. Although the type of performance measurement using metrics has been previously discussed, benchmarking processes and strategies involves comparing such elements as information technologies used, methods for filling customer orders, transportation and inventory-management policies, make-to-stock or make-to-order strategies, and network configuration. Five steps for con-ducting a benchmark analysis have been suggested:

1. Collect and analyze baseline data
2. Identify and gather data on best practice companies
3. Identify and analyze performance gaps
4. Develop a plan to close process performance gaps
5. Implement the plan[5]

Collecting and analyzing baseline data involve mapping (describing) and reviewing the current supply chain. Data are assembled on key performance mea-sures, and processes are described using maps, flow diagrams, figures, and tables. Data gathering should focus on identifying symptoms of underperformance and causes for the performance problems. Preparing a data collection form that lists key questions and data items can be useful.[6]

Gathering data about best practice may be the most challenging part of the bench-marking process. Competitors are unlikely to share their data, and survey data may not separate best practice information from the generalized results. Nevertheless, the

---

[5]Sandor Boyson, Thomas M. Corsi, Martin E. Dresner, and Lisa H. Harrington, *Logistics and the Extended Enterprise* (New York: John Wiley & Sons, 1999), pp. 168–170.
[6]For an example, see Boyson et al., op. cit., pp. 201–219.

data sought should parallel that of the baseline information and problem causes noted in step 1. High-performing companies need to be identified that reflect characteristics similar to those of the baseline.

The third step is to compare the baseline data with that of the benchmark and best practice firms to note differences and measure the extent of the gap. Gaps may appear in performance measures such as transportation costs or item fill rates. In addition, the base company may be outsourcing logistics activities to a 3PL, whereas the best practice firm is managing its own transportation, which shows a difference in strategy.

Next, a plan is needed to close the gaps observed in step 3. Not all of the observed gaps will be of equal importance, so prioritize them. Many criteria can be used, such as greatest impact on revenue, greatest cost reduction, greatest customer service improvement, and ease of implementation for quick return. Top management approval of the initiatives may be needed whereby criteria important to these managers should be presented. Evaluating the plans on (1) the amount of cash flow generated, (2) the cost reduction, and (3) the return on investment will interest this level of management.

The final step is to implement the plans. A champion of the plan or an organizational structure to oversee implementation should be considered. A schedule for timing the various phases is needed to coordinate training, time resource availability, and so forth. Measuring performance change against the baseline is also useful.

Other Audits

Any number of other audits might also be carried out on an irregular basis. Warehouse space utilization, customer service levels, transportation fleet utilization, and inventory policy performance represent specific areas that might be audited. All provide basic information necessary for effective logistics control.

Observation

Technology is playing a major role in providing data for measurement and controlling operations. Take the control of trucking costs and on-time delivery. Just-in-time practices require that progress of truck deliveries be known precisely, since delayed shipments to customers can shut down their operations that have little or no backup inventory. With the high cost of trucking, it is imperative to carefully control costs. On many rigs, there now is a tiny data-beaming antenna that monitors the truck's location at all times—good for projecting arrival times. In addition, other electronic equipment helps with cost control. A special credit card helps the company check that the driver gets fuel only from approved stops. Electronic engine monitoring controls top speed, gear shifting, and maximum idling times. If the driver steps out of the truck, the engine shuts off. Cellular phones are common in many trucks so that the driver can be in constant contact with headquarters and can avoid long waits for phones at truck stops. Report preparation time is significantly reduced.[7]

---

[7]"New Gadgets Trace Truckers' Every Move," *Wall Street Journal*, July 14, 1997, B1.

Regular Reports

Many reports are generated in the normal course of business operations. A number of these are routinely available to the logistician. These include stock status reports, warehouse and truck fleet utilization reports, and warehouse and transportation cost reports. To achieve overall logistics function control, three key measurement reports are suggested: the cost-service statement, the productivity report, and the performance chart.

Cost-Service Report

Cost-service reports are similar to the profit-and-loss reports that are popular for financial accounting in most firms. They are intended to show total physical supply and physical distribution costs as well as the corresponding customer service levels achieved over time. The most important physical supply and distribution activities are presented, namely, transportation, handling, storage, inventory-carrying, and order processing costs. Total annual costs levels are given in this report, as shown in Table 16-1.

Costs for the various elements of the report can be determined from traditional accounting procedures. However, contemporary thinking is that *activity-based costing* gives a more accurate representation of logistics costs than traditional accounting practices.[8] The reason is that historically, process overhead costs were allocated to the process based on direct labor hours or machine hours. This was appropriate when operations were more focused, less automated, and more labor intensive, but as process improvements reduced volume-related costs in logistics activities, the traditional methodology has been questioned. Alternately, activity-based costing traces resource consumption to the consuming process and then to specific products, customers, and activities. Ultimately, cost drivers that influence costs are identified so that costs can be better managed.

It should be noted that the cost-service report includes opportunity costs, notably for inventories. This permits the proper comparison of these activities with those such as transportation and materials handling for which direct expenditures are made.

Ideally, the revenues associated with the physical distribution activity levels represented by the costs should be presented as well. Because it is impractical to determine accurately the relationship between sales and logistics service levels, revenues are not included in the report. Rather, measures of the customer service level itself are reported. No single customer service measure typically prevails. Therefore, many measures may be presented to provide a complete view of logistical performance (see Table 16-1).

The cost-service report may also give comparisons against previous periods or against budget. This can indicate trends in absolute cost-service levels. It is particularly good at showing the relative importance of each activity.

The report might logically be organized according to physical distribution costs, supply costs, and customer service. Distribution costs can be separated from supply

---

[8]Binshan Lin, James Collins, and Robert K. Su, "Supply Chain Costing: An Activity-Based Perspective," *International Journal of Physical Distribution & Logistics Management*, Vol. 31, No. 10 (2001), pp. 702–713.

Table 16-1 An Example of a Logistics Cost-Service Report

	THIS YEAR	LAST YEAR	BUDGET/TARGET
Physical Distribution			
Transportation of finished goods			
Freight charges inbound to warehouses	$ 2,700,000	$ 2,500,000	$ 2,800,000
Delivery charges outbound from warehouses	3,150,000	2,950,000	3,000,000
Freight charges on stock returns to plant	300,000	250,000	275,000
Extra delivery charges on back orders	450,000	400,000	400,000
Subtotal	$ 6,600,000	$ 6,100,000	$ 6,475,000
Finished goods inventories			
Inventories in transit	$ 280,000	$ 260,000	$ 250,000
Storage costs at warehouses[a]	1,200,000	600,000	1,000,000
Materials handling costs at warehouses	1,800,000	1,600,000	1,700,000
Costs of obsolete stock	310,000	290,000	300,000
Storage costs at plants[a]	470,000	460,000	460,000
Materials handling costs at plants	520,000	510,000	510,000
Subtotal	$ 4,580,000	$ 3,720,000	$ 4,220,000
Order-processing costs			
Processing of customer orders	$ 830,000	$ 840,000	$ 820,000
Processing stock replenishment orders	170,000	165,000	160,000
Processing of back orders	440,000	300,000	300,000
Subtotal	$ 1,440,000	$ 1,305,000	$ 1,280,000
Administration and overhead			
Proration of unallocated managerial expenses	$ 240,000	$ 220,000	$ 230,000
Depreciation of owned storage space	180,000	180,000	180,000
Depreciation of materials handling equipment	100,000	100,000	100,000
Depreciation of transportation equipment	50,000	70,000	50,000
Subtotal	$ 570,000	$ 570,000	$ 560,000
Total distribution costs	$13,190,000	$11,695,000	$12,535,000
Physical Supply			
Transportation of supply goods			
Freight charges inbound to plant	$ 1,200,000	$ 1,400,000	$ 1,115,000
Expedited freight charges	300,000	250,000	350,000
Subtotal	$ 1,500,000	$ 1,650,000	$ 1,465,000
Supply goods inventories			
Storage costs on raw materials	$ 300,000	$ 375,000	$ 275,000
Materials handling cost on raw materials	270,000	245,000	260,000
Subtotal	$ 570,000	$ 620,000	$ 535,000
Order processing			
Processing of supply orders	$ 55,000	$ 50,000	$ 50,000
Costs of expedited orders	10,000	10,000	10,000
Subtotal	$ 65,000	$ 60,000	$ 60,000

Table 16-1 *(cont.)*

	THIS YEAR	LAST YEAR	BUDGET/TARGET
Administration and overhead—supply goods			
Proration of unallocated managerial expenses	$ 50,000	$ 60,000	$ 40,000
Depreciation of owned storage space	30,000	30,000	30,000
Depreciation of materials handling equipment	40,000	40,000	40,000
Depreciation of transportation equipment	25,000	25,000	25,000
Subtotal	$ 145,000	$ 155,000	$ 135,000
Total supply costs	$ 2,280,000	$ 2,485,000	$ 2,195,000
Total distribution costs	$13,190,000	$11,695,000	$12,535,000
Total logistics costs	**$15,470,000**	**$14,180,000**	**$14,730,000**
Customer Service			
Percentage of warehouse deliveries within one day	92%	90%	90%
Average in-stock percentage[b]	87%	85%	85%
Total order-cycle time[c]			
(a) Normal processing	7 ± 2	6 ± 2	6 ± 2
(b) Back order–split delivery processing	10 ± 3	10 ± 3	10 ± 3
Back orders and split deliveries			
(a) Total number	503	490	490
(b) Percentage of total orders	2.5%	2.7%	2.5%
Orders filled complete	90%	86%	87%
Line item fill rate	95%	91%	95%
Customer returns due to damage, dead stock, order processing errors, and late deliveries[d]	1.2%	2.6%	1.0%
Percentage of available production time shutdown due to supply out-of-stocks	2.3%	2.4%	2.0%

[a]Includes space, insurance, taxes, and capital costs
[b]Percentage of individual product items filled directly from warehouse stocks
[c]Based on the distribution of order-cycle times at the 95th percentile
[d]Percentage of gross sales

costs because of the degree of independence in the systems that generate the costs. Supply warehouses may be different from finished goods warehouses, different transportation services may be used on the supply versus the distribution side of the firm, and the order processing networks may be different as well. Because of the degree of independence, separate management of these systems is sometimes possible. Thus, it is useful to separate the costs into two categories.

Distribution costs might include transportation costs from plant to customer, finished goods inventory costs, order processing costs, and administrative and overhead expenses associated with the distribution system. In the example in Table 16-1, transportation costs include inbound costs to and outbound costs from a finished goods warehouse, expenses from stock returns to plant, and charges associated with back orders. Finished goods inventory costs include those costs for maintaining inventories in field warehouses and at the plant, as well as the cost of goods in transit from plant to warehouse and warehouse to customer. In addition, materials handling costs at the warehouse and at the plant are listed because they are often computed separately from storage costs, and the separate classifications are useful in evaluating the efficiency and effectiveness of each of these subsystems. Obsolete stock costs are listed because, in this case, they are significant relative to the other costs in the category. Order processing costs are the third major item in distribution costs. These costs would include customer and stock order processing as well as the costs for processing the back orders. Finally, distribution costs would include prorating various administration and overhead expenses.

Physical supply costs are divided into the same general categories as physical distribution costs (see Table 16-1). Because the supply system often is simpler than the distribution system for many companies, fewer cost categories are needed for effective management.

Customer service is the final category in the cost-service statement. Logistics costs mean little unless there is some measure of logistics service against which to compare them. Knowing how any particular logistics system would affect revenues would be ideal. This is rarely available, so some physical rather than economic measure is used as a substitute. For example, distribution service might be measured in terms of percentage of warehouse deliveries within one day, average in-stock percentage, total order cycle time for normal processing and for back orders, the number and percentage of back orders, and percentage of sales returned due to distribution problems. On the supply side, customer service might be measured as a percentage of the available production time that operations were shut down due to raw material stockouts.

In general, the cost-service statement provides the kind of aggregate data necessary for broad control of the logistics function. When further information is required for detailed control of a single cost or service category, the logistician should be able to "explode" the category to obtain the information that produced the aggregate figure. This helps to trace the reason for being out of control to fundamental causes.

Productivity Report

The cost-service statement may be the proper report for budgeting purposes, but it does little to indicate efficiency in logistics activities. Examples of some of the top logistics management evaluation ratios that could be used for control to improve productivity include the following:

- Logistics cost to sales
- Activity cost to total logistics cost
- Logistics cost to industry standard and/or average
- Logistics cost to budget
- Logistics resources budget to actual (dollars, labor, hours, and the like) adjusted for actual throughput versus forecast activity

A productivity report of the type illustrated in Table 16-2 attempts to put activity performance in a relative perspective. That is, a ratio is formed of output performance to the input resources that gives rise to the output performance level. For example, ratios are created of freight costs to sales, sales to the average inventory level needed

PRODUCTIVITY MEASURE	THIS QUARTER	LAST QUARTER	THIS QUARTER LAST YEAR	COMPANY STANDARD	INDUSTRY AVERAGE[a]
Transportation					
Freight costs as a percentage of distribution costs	31%	30%	32%	29%	31%
Damage and loss claims as a percentage of freight costs	0.5%	0.5%	0.6%	0.5%	0.5%
Freight costs as a percentage of sales	9.6%	9.2%	10.2%	9.0%	8.8%
Inventories					
Inventory turnover	4.5	4.4	5.0	4.7	6.0
Obsolete stock to sales	0.1	0.1	0.3	0.1	0.2
Order Processing					
Orders processed per labor hour	50	45	55	50	50
Percentage of orders processed within 24 hours of receipt	96%	92%	85%	95%	93%
Order processing costs to the total number of orders processed	$5.50	$4.95	$5.65	$5.00	—
Warehousing					
Percentage of cube utilized	75%	70%	70%	70%	70%
Units handled per labor hour	200	250	225	200	200
Customer Service					
Stock availability (percentage of orders filled from primary stock)	98%	92%	90%	90%	85%
Percentage of orders delivered within 24 hours of receipt	72%	70%	61%	85%	90%

[a]For comparable firms

Table 16-2 An Example of a Logistics Productivity Report

to support them, and the number of items picked in a warehouse to labor hours. As sales of the company change, the ratio should either remain constant or change in a predictable way. Deviation may indicate any activity that is out of control.

Productivity reports of the type shown in Table 16-2 are particularly meaningful when one firm's logistics performance is compared with that of another or with that of the industry as a whole. Differences in the size of firms are neutralized, which enhances comparability. In addition, comparisons made between different periods are facilitated, as the sales level variations between periods are again neutralized in most ratios.

Graphic Performance Chart

Control charts of the type that have been so popular in manufacturing quality control can be used in logistics performance control to provide better tracking of costs, customer service, or productivity ratios over time and to pinpoint when adverse trends are occurring. When sufficient data are available, statistical procedures may be used to give signals as to when corrective action should be taken. Performance

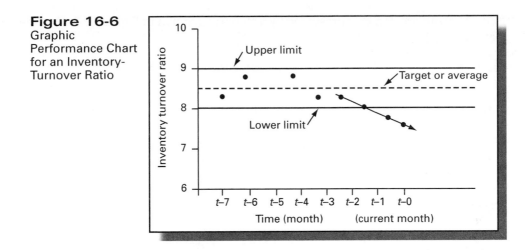

Figure 16-6
Graphic Performance Chart for an Inventory-Turnover Ratio

charts provide a graphic picture of performance as well as comparing performance measures over multiple, consecutive periods.

Figure 16-6 illustrates the use of the graphic performance chart for an inventory-turnover ratio. Normal variation for the ratio is between eight and nine turns per year. Actual turnover ratios can be plotted for the current period, including a representative number of the most recent periods. The actual performance, or turnover ratios, is observed for their trend, and whether they have penetrated the control limit. In either case, actual performance is no longer tracking within the norms set for the ratio. Management review of the reasons for the change would be in order.

Example

An express package service promises that packages will be delivered within 24 hours of pickup. Practically, the company wants at least 90 percent of the deliveries to be within this time period. Samples of 100 deliveries have been collected for each of ten representative operating days. The results were as follows:

Sample	Deliveries Made Within 24 hr.
1	94
2	93
3	94
4	95
5	94
6	93
7	92
8	93
9	96
10	95
Total	939

This process can be represented by a *p*-chart as shown in Figure 16-7. The process average $(\bar{p})$ is found by

$$\bar{p} = \frac{\text{Total number of on-time deliveries}}{\text{Total number of deliveries}} = \frac{939}{10(100)} = 0.94$$

The standard deviation of the sampling distribution for a sample size of $n = 100$ is

$$\hat{\sigma}_p = \sqrt{\frac{\bar{p}(1-\bar{p})}{n}} = \sqrt{\frac{0.94(1-0.94)}{100}} = 0.02$$

The upper and lower control limits on this process for a $z = 1.96$ at 95 percent confidence (Appendix A) are

$$UCL_p = \bar{p} + z(\hat{\sigma}_p) = 0.94 + 1.96(0.02) = 0.98$$
$$LCL_p = \bar{p} - z(\hat{\sigma}_p) = 0.94 - 1.96(0.02) = 0.90$$

The next three samples of 100 each show 92, 89, and 88 deliveries were made on time. The average number of late deliveries appears to be increasing, and corrective action would seem to be indicated in order to preserve the promised customer service level. An unfavorable trend is seen in Figure 16-7.

Figure 16-7
Graphic
Performance Chart
for On-Time
Deliveries

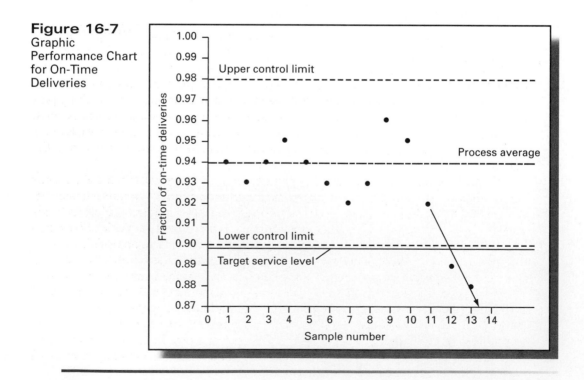

CORRECTIVE ACTION

The final element in the control function is the corrective action that must be taken when the difference between the system goals and actual performance is no longer tolerable. Action to reduce the difference depends on the nature and extent of the out-of-control condition. In this section, three types of action are delineated: minor adjustments, major replanning, and contingency action.

Minor Adjustments

Some variation of actual performance from desired performance will occur and can be anticipated, whether the control problem is one of managing the overall logistics function or a subactivity of the function. Just as the direction of an automobile must constantly be adjusted as it moves along a highway, so must the performance of a logistics activity. Activity performance is under constant change due to a dynamic and uncertain business environment that acts upon it. For example, the transportation activity of service selection, routing, and scheduling will vary over time in terms of its costs, due to changes in rates, available routes, equipment availability, loss and damage, and the like. Such dynamics usually do not require major changes in the way that the activity is performed. Minor adjustments to activity level mix, decision rules, and even system goals often suffice to maintain adequate control over the system. Most corrective action is of this type.

Major Replanning

Sweeping reevaluation of the logistics system, significant changes in logistics function goals, major changes in the logistics environment, and introduction of new products and dropping of existing ones, may necessitate major replanning for activity performance. Major replanning involves a recycling through the management planning process that generates new courses of action and, hence, a new activity performance level, control system reference standards, and error tolerance limits. Such replanning might result in a new warehouse configuration, alterations in order processing procedures, revision of inventory control procedures, and alterations to the product flow system within warehouses and plants.

The difference between corrective actions taken in the form of minor adjustments versus major replanning is that minor adjustments do not require any substantial changes to the control mechanisms. In fact, corrective action is often routine, as in the case of inventory control where action is initiated in the form of a stock order when stock is depleted to a predetermined level. Control adjustments are automatic through the application of a decision rule. In contrast, major replanning involves substantial changes to the process inputs in the form of new plans or major revision to old ones. There is no clear delineation as to when adjustments to maintain activity control should give way to major system revision. In theory, the optimal changeover point is when the incremental costs associated with continuing to use minor adjustments within the control system to maintain control over the process just equal the incremental benefits to be derived from major replanning. Finding this point is more a matter of managerial judgment than of precise mathematical calculation.

Contingency Plans

The third form of corrective action is that taken when there are possibilities of dramatic changes in the activity performance level. Such dramatic changes can occur when a warehouse is shut down due to fire, when computer failure renders the computerized inventory-control system inoperative, when labor strikes change the availability of transportation services, or when sources of raw materials suddenly become unavailable. The company's customer service may be severely jeopardized and/or the level of logistics costs to produce a given level of customer service may suddenly rise because of swift and dramatic changes in the conditions under which the process was operating. Minor adjustments to the process inputs often prove to be too little to restore control to a system that has suffered the shock of such an event. The pressures for continuing logistics operations put major replanning as a course for corrective action at a disadvantage, as good planning requires time.

Many companies have found that contingency plans developed in advance of their need are a good way of meeting the problem of shock changes to the system process.[9] Contingency plans represent predetermined courses of action to be implemented when a defined event occurs.

Application

Recall the previous illustration where the privately owned warehouse of a large and well-known manufacturer of office copier products was struck by fire on a Friday afternoon. The fire destroyed the warehouse and its contents. The warehouse served the entire West Coast area, and sales and customer service were jeopardized in this region. Because the company had the foresight to develop a contingency plan for just such an event, inventories were immediately shipped by airfreight to a public warehouse in the area to be ready for sales by Monday morning. Customers experienced no change in service

A SUPPLY CHAIN OPERATIONS REFERENCE (SCOR) MODEL[10]

To better measure supply chain performance and identify improvement opportunities, the Supply-Chain Council[11] in 1997 developed its first version of a business

---

[9]In a survey of the participants at an annual meeting of the Council of Logistics Management, 60 percent of the respondents claimed that their companies had contingency plans for logistics operations.
[10]Based on a SCOR model description in Scott Stephens, "Supply Chain Operations Reference Model Version 5.0: A New Tool to Improve Supply Chain Efficiency and Achieve Best Practice," *Proceedings of a Workshop on Supply Chain Management Practice and Research: Status and Future Directions* (University of Maryland, Rockville, MD, April 18–19, 2001), pp. 7-1–7-11.
[11]The Supply-Chain Council is a nonprofit organization composed primarily of practitioners dedicated to advancing supply chain management systems and practices. More information about the council and the SCOR model can be found at www.supply-chain.org.

process reference model. The model attempts to link supply chain process, or activity, description, and definition to performance measures, best practices, and software requirements. The objectives of model design were to provide a *structure* for linking business objectives to supply chain operations (e.g., interpreting the effect of order fulfillment statistics on revenue and costs) and to develop a *systematic approach* for identifying, evaluating, and monitoring supply chain performance. In a word, the supply chain operations reference (SCOR) model provides a way of defining supply chain activities in a standardized format, analyzing the supply chain interorganizationally at the product level, and comparing performance with statistics derived from the council's membership companies.

The model achieves its objectives first by having a broad scope that includes all elements of demand, beginning with customer demand forecast or order placement and ending with the final invoice and payment, which can include the supply chain elements from multiple enterprises. Second, process descriptions can be product specific, although a general company infrastructure description is possible as well. Third, a framework is established for process description based on five components of plan, source, make, deliver, and return. Finally, five performance dimensions are used: reliability, responsiveness, flexibility, cost, and efficiency in asset utilization.

At the highest level in the model (Level 1), the five business processes of plan, source, make, deliver, and return are described for each echelon in the supply channel, as shown in Figure 16-8. *Plan* activities balance demand and resources, and provide integration between activities and organizations. *Source* activities are those that are associated with acquiring raw materials and they connect organizations with their suppliers. *Make* activities transform raw materials into finished goods; however, some companies, such as distributors or retailers, do not perform make activities. *Deliver* activities are those associated with order management and delivery of finished goods. *Return* activities refer to those related to returning raw materials to suppliers or returning finished goods from customers. Whereas Level 1 is tied to the business objectives, the five processes may be decomposed in Levels 2 and 3 for further detail and greater insight

Figure 16-8 The Five Business Processes of the SCOR Model

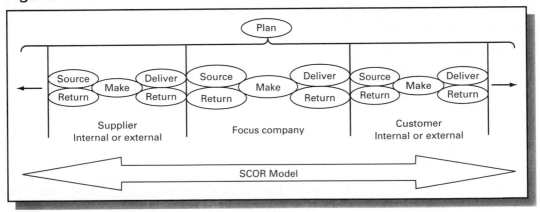

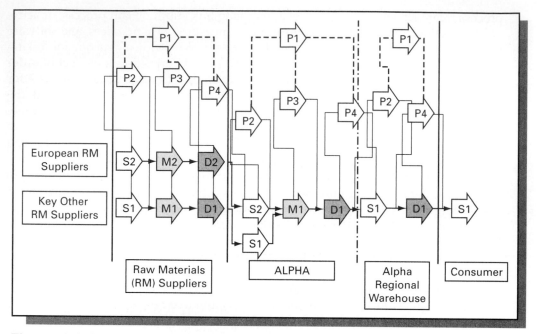

Figure 16-9 Process "Thread" Diagram for a Hypothetical Supply Chain, Where P = Plan, S = Source, M = Make, and D = Deliver

into supply channel operation. Standard references are used. Decomposing to Level 4 allows specific management practices to be modeled.

To further describe the supply chain, a process map is created. Often starting with a network diagram, a product "thread" diagram is prepared, as shown in Figure 16-9. This type of mapping helps to visualize the supply chain, but it still has insufficient information for knowing whether the supply chain is performing in accordance with business objectives. To do this, the model provides a number of measurements grouped into five performance dimensions. An example of the metrics for Level 1 is given in Table 16-3. For each of the process elements, the SCOR model identifies best practice and technology. Figure 16-10 shows a first step in linking processes and metrics within the SCOR model.

Finally, a table showing the best practice and technology is presented by the model. From these representative lists, options can be derived for improvement and implementation. The SCOR model is primarily a tool for communicating among practitioners, which leads to improved control over the supply channel.

CONTROL LINKS TO ARTIFICIAL INTELLIGENCE

It has been common practice for the logistics/SC manager to judge performance from the regular reports and audits that he or she receives and to take corrective action as appropriate. Computer technology that makes computer-based planning

Supply Chain Performance Attribute	Performance Attribute Level Definition	Level 1 Metric
Delivery reliability	The supply chain's performance in delivering the correct product, to the correct place, at the correct time, in the correct condition and packaging, in the correct quantity, with the correct documentation, and to the correct customer	• Delivery performance • Fill rates • Perfect order fulfillment
Responsiveness	The velocity at which a supply chain provides products to the customer	• Order fulfillment lead times
Flexibility	The supply chain's agility in responding to marketplace changes to gain or maintain competitive advantage	• Supply chain response time • Production flexibility
Costs	The costs associated with supply chain operations	• Cost of goods sold • Total supply chain management costs • Value-added productivity • Warranty/returns processing costs
Asset management efficiency	Organizational effectiveness in managing all assets to support demand fulfillment, including fixed and working capital	• Cash-to-cash cycle time • Inventory days of supply • Asset turns

Table 16-3 Level 1 Metrics for Supply Chain Performance Attributes

and control practical is moving a step ahead by permitting the application of the emerging concepts of artificial intelligence (coincidentally referred to as expert systems) to the logistics control process. There are many interpretations of artificial intelligence. For purposes here, it refers to computer recognition of adverse patterns in the performance reports and the resulting suggestions about the courses of action that might be taken to correct the adverse performance patterns. In a sense, the artificially intelligent computer acts as a consultant or assistant to the manager.

Pattern Recognition

The key to taking performance measurement to its next level of sophistication is pattern recognition. Businesses frequently hire consultants to audit logistics operations. These consultants use experience, concepts and principles, and philosophy to judge performance (as do analysts and managers). Judgment is then applied to decide which courses of action might relieve actual or potential out-of-control situations. Capturing this process within a computerized management information or decision support system brings a new level of sophistication to the control process.

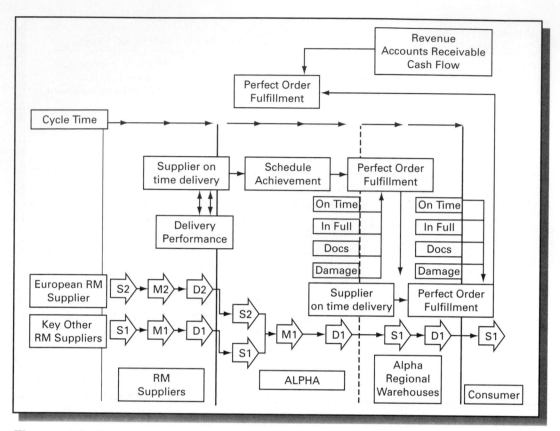

Figure 16-10 Linking Processes and Metrics Within the Model

Artificial intelligence is not new. Significant research in the area dates back over 20 years, and a Nobel prize was given for research in the field; however, the technology is beginning to be applied to control problems in logistics, although not extensively at this time. Out of 105 applications of artificial intelligence to logistical problems, Allen and Helferich classified only five as related to control.[12]

Applications

- Santa Fe Railway uses an artificially intelligent system, called TRACKS, to handle basic supply and demand aspects of operations. It predicts railcar demand, anticipates customer preferences, and controls cars to meet shipper orders.
- Digital Equipment Corportation's MOVER program coordinates and drives two robots that deliver work-in-process inventories from storage areas to production. The transport system consists of a robot that picks bar code labeled totes

[12]Mary K. Allen and Omar K. Helferich, *Putting Expert Systems to Work in Logistics* (Oak Brook, IL: Council of Logistics Management, 1990), p. 97.

from two carousels and moves them via one to three transporters to any of 75 production workstations. The robots deliver parts as needed by the plant six days per week, three shifts per day. MOVER has reduced materials handling labor costs $300,000 per year, decreased work in process (WIP) inventories 50 percent, and increased inventory account accuracy to 99 percent.[13]

Performance Patterns

Having the computer recognize performance trends or variations from standards is the first step toward an artificially intelligent control process. The basic concepts of logistics/SC management are the best guides to which performance information should be compared. Activities in significant cost conflict with each other (transportation with inventories and customer service levels with total distribution activity levels) are prime candidates to be monitored. Like the human as a monitor, we want the computer to recognize and interpret adverse logistics performance patterns.

The time when transportation and inventory costs are both rising yet customer service levels remain constant is an example of an adverse performance pattern. Because transportation and inventory costs typically show opposite, or conflicting, cost patterns, this trend is an indication that these two important performance factors are not moving in an expected manner and that inquiry and possible corrective action are needed.

Similarly, suppose that customer service levels are decreasing, yet total physical distribution costs are increasing. Alternatively, there is a decreasing item-fill rate on orders, but the inventory-turnover ratio is increasing. These comparisons reveal disturbing patterns that the artificially intelligent computer system should highlight.

Courses of Action

After recognizing performance patterns, the artificially intelligent control system will spell out appropriate courses of action that a manager should take to bring adverse performance patterns back in line with acceptable tolerance limits. This assumes that a computer can be instructed to discern performance patterns with accuracy and match them with appropriate corrective responses. Knowledgeable observers can do this now, and perhaps computers can emulate the process. In the short term, computers can track the performance information as generated by such reports as previously presented in this chapter. With specified performance pattern norms, the computer can assess actual performance against these norms and offer a range of possible courses of action.

Consider how this might work. Suppose a logistics/SC manager identifies the fact that the inventory-turnover ratios have been decreasing over the past several periods and are now outside the acceptable tolerance limits. The next step is to check the factors that could be causing the inventory levels to increase. The following questions that relate to inventories might be asked by the computer:

---

[13]Ibid., Chapter 3.

- Has there been a sudden or seasonal drop in sales?
- Have production or purchase quantities increased from previous levels?
- Are inbound shipments being received in larger quantities than they had been previously?
- Has the sales forecast error increased significantly?
- Have supply lead times increased or become more uncertain?
- Have outbound shipments been delayed?

There may be inadequate or unavailable data to answer some of these questions. As an example, suppose the answer to the third question is found to be yes because the computer interrogated the appropriate database. The answers to the remaining questions are no. Once the out-of-control condition has been isolated, appropriate courses of action may be suggested. For example, based on current cost relationships, the computer might indicate that inbound transport shipments need to be reduced to a specific level if an average inventory-turnover ratio of a given level is to be achieved. The manager may follow this advice, or reset the inventory-turnover control limits to reflect a new level of cost-service trade-offs. The manager might also decide to utilize various computer-based models of the decision support system to evaluate different logistics options, thus changing the relationship of transportation costs and the inventory-turnover ratio.

All other performance factors would be treated similarly. The intelligent, or "expertlike," interpretation by a computer of cost-service relationships is artificial intelligence.

CONCLUDING COMMENTS

Logistics control helps to ensure that the goals around which logistics plans were developed are achieved after the plan is put into action. The dynamics and uncertainties of the logistics environment over time can cause deviations from planned process performance. To keep process performance in line with desired performance objectives, some form of managerial control is required. Control usually takes the form of an open-loop system, closed-loop system, or a system that combines both of these. All are used in practice.

The logistician is involved in the control activity on a daily basis. He or she often serves as the monitor of logistics activities by measuring the activity level through the various audits and reports that are received and comparing these with targets for performance, such as budgets, profit standards, and customer service goals. Based on this comparison, the decision is made to take corrective steps to bring the activity back under control. In many ways, control is just short-term or tactical decision making.

As there is greater concern with control of logistics activities across company boundaries, traditional control systems are lagging. Not only is sharing information among supply chain partners a problem of trust, but companies may have not developed the metrics and report structures needed to operate in the multienterprise environment. The SCOR model is a first attempt to evaluate and modify logistics activities of the entire supply chain using a standardized structure.

Finally, we have artificially intelligent computer programs and expert systems to aid in interpreting performance patterns and in selecting the correct courses of action. How rapidly they come into widespread use depends more on our ability to articulate the nature of the control process, so that it can be programmed into a knowledge base, than on the state of computer technology. This depends on our clear understanding of the principles and concepts on which logistics/SC management is based. It is hoped that some of these principles and concepts have been communicated throughout this text.

QUESTIONS

1. What role does control play in the management of logistics activities?
2. A common carrier trucking firm controls its delivery performance in terms of average delivery time, delivery-time variability, and loss and damage claims. Sketch a generalized open-loop feedback control model for this process to maintain a desired level of delivery performance.
3. What advantages does the modified control system have over either the open loop or the closed loop control system?
4. Which logistics activities might successfully be controlled by a closed-loop control system? Explain.
5. What effect do you think that a mail order transmittal (slow) mode compared with an electronic order transmittal (fast) mode would have on the performance of an inventory control system?
6. Of what value is the audit in the logistics control process? Which audits would be of particular value to the control of logistics activities?
7. Logistics/SC managers can suffer from too many reports and from reports of the wrong kind. Select a typical activity, such as transportation or inventory control, and suggest the type and frequency of reports needed to control the activity.
8. Suppose you are in charge of managing a common carrier trucking operation. How would you establish the tolerance for substandard performance (average delivery time, reliability, loss and damage) before initiating minor corrective action such as tighter standards on performance, personnel changes, and the like? When should major replanning take place?
9. An appliance manufacturer has a large regional warehouse in Utah to store and distribute major appliances to West Coast markets. If you were a logistics/SC manager in charge of the distribution operation, what contingency plans would you make to ensure continued good logistics performance in case disaster strikes?
10. If you were developing an artificially intelligent computer system to control overall logistics costs and service, suggest the questions that the computer might raise if it detected the following patterns:
    a. Inventory-carrying costs and inventory stock availability are dropping.
    b. Transportation costs and inventory-carrying costs are increasing and customer service levels are constant.
    c. Transportation costs are increasing while inventory-carrying costs and customer service levels have not changed.

11. As a logistics/SC manager, you would like to compare your company's logistics performance with that of similar companies. Where would you find such benchmarking information? How would you use it in the logistics control process?

12. Sketch a framework for controlling the inventory levels and deliveries of purchased product between a supplier and a buyer. Suggest the information to be shared and the measurement system that would need to be developed.

Appendix A

Areas Under the Standardized Normal Distribution

A table entry is the proportion of the area under the curve from a z of 0 to a positive value of z. To find the area from a z of 0 to a negative z, subtract the tabled value from 1.

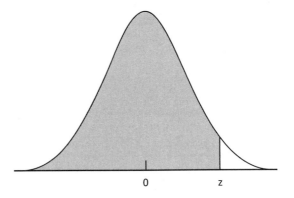

z	.00	.01	.02	.03	.04	.05	.06	.07	.08	.09
0.0	0.5000	0.5040	0.5080	0.5120	0.5160	0.5199	0.5239	0.5279	0.5319	0.5359
0.1	0.5398	0.5438	0.5478	0.5517	0.5557	0.5596	0.5636	0.5675	0.5714	0.5753
0.2	0.5793	0.5832	0.5871	0.5910	0.5948	0.5987	0.6026	0.6064	0.6103	0.6141
0.3	0.6179	0.6217	0.6255	0.6293	0.6331	0.6368	0.6406	0.6443	0.6480	0.6517
0.4	0.6554	0.6591	0.6628	0.6664	0.6700	0.6736	0.6772	0.6808	0.6844	0.6879
0.5	0.6915	0.6950	0.6985	0.7019	0.7054	0.7088	0.7123	0.7157	0.7190	0.7224
0.6	0.7257	0.7291	0.7324	0.7357	0.7389	0.7422	0.7454	0.7486	0.7517	0.7549
0.7	0.7580	0.7611	0.7642	0.7673	0.7704	0.7734	0.7764	0.7794	0.7823	0.7852
0.8	0.7881	0.7910	0.7939	0.7967	0.7995	0.8023	0.8051	0.8078	0.8106	0.8133
0.9	0.8159	0.8186	0.8212	0.8238	0.8264	0.8289	0.8315	0.8340	0.8365	0.8389
1.0	0.8413	0.8438	0.8461	0.8485	0.8508	0.8531	0.8554	0.8577	0.8599	0.8621
1.1	0.8643	0.8665	0.8686	0.8708	0.8729	0.8749	0.8770	0.8790	0.8810	0.8830
1.2	0.8849	0.8869	0.8888	0.8907	0.8925	0.8944	0.8962	0.8980	0.8997	0.9015
1.3	0.9032	0.9049	0.9066	0.9082	0.9099	0.9115	0.9131	0.9147	0.9162	0.9177
1.4	0.9192	0.9207	0.9222	0.9236	0.9251	0.9265	0.9279	0.9292	0.9306	0.9319

z	.00	.01	.02	.03	.04	.05	.06	.07	.08	.09
1.5	0.9332	0.9345	0.9357	0.9370	0.9382	0.9394	0.9406	0.9418	0.9429	0.9441
1.6	0.9452	0.9463	0.9474	0.9484	0.9495	0.9505	0.9515	0.9525	0.9535	0.9545
1.7	0.9554	0.9564	0.9573	0.9582	0.9591	0.9599	0.9608	0.9616	0.9625	0.9633
1.8	0.9641	0.9649	0.9656	0.9664	0.9671	0.9678	0.9686	0.9693	0.9699	0.9706
1.9	0.9713	0.9719	0.9726	0.9732	0.9738	0.9744	0.9750	0.9756	0.9761	0.9767
2.0	0.9772	0.9778	0.9783	0.9788	0.9793	0.9798	0.9803	0.9808	0.9812	0.9817
2.1	0.9821	0.9826	0.9830	0.9834	0.9838	0.9842	0.9846	0.9850	0.9854	0.9857
2.2	0.9861	0.9864	0.9868	0.9871	0.9875	0.9878	0.9881	0.9884	0.9887	0.9890
2.3	0.9893	0.9896	0.9898	0.9901	0.9904	0.9906	0.9909	0.9911	0.9913	0.9916
2.4	0.9918	0.9920	0.9922	0.9925	0.9927	0.9929	0.9931	0.9932	0.9934	0.9936
2.5	0.9938	0.9940	0.9941	0.9943	0.9945	0.9946	0.9948	0.9949	0.9951	0.9952
2.6	0.9953	0.9955	0.9956	0.9957	0.9959	0.9960	0.9961	0.9962	0.9963	0.9964
2.7	0.9965	0.9966	0.9967	0.9968	0.9969	0.9970	0.9971	0.9972	0.9973	0.9974
2.8	0.9974	0.9975	0.9976	0.9977	0.9977	0.9978	0.9979	0.9979	0.9980	0.9981
2.9	0.9981	0.9982	0.9982	0.9983	0.9984	0.9984	0.9985	0.9985	0.9986	0.9986
3.0	0.9987	0.9987	0.9987	0.9988	0.9988	0.9989	0.9989	0.9989	0.9990	0.9990
3.1	0.9990	0.9991	0.9991	0.9991	0.9992	0.9992	0.9992	0.9992	0.9993	0.9993
3.2	0.9993	0.9993	0.9994	0.9994	0.9994	0.9994	0.9994	0.9995	0.9995	0.9995
3.3	0.9995	0.9995	0.9995	0.9996	0.9996	0.9996	0.9996	0.9996	0.9996	0.9997
3.4	0.9997	0.9997	0.9997	0.9997	0.9997	0.9997	0.9997	0.9997	0.9997	0.9998

Unit Normal Loss Integrals[1]

Examples:

$E_{(z)} = E_{(0.85)} = 0.1100$
$E_{(-z)} = E_{(-1.79)} = 1.8046$

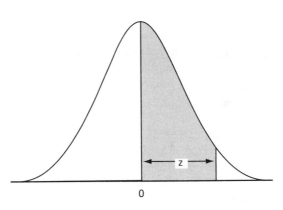

z	.00	.01	.02	.03	.04	.05	.06	.07	.08	.09
−3.4	3.4001	3.4101	3.4201	3.4301	3.4401	3.4501	3.4601	3.4701	3.4801	3.4901
−3.3	3.3000	3.3101	3.3201	3.3301	3.3401	3.3501	3.3601	3.3701	3.3801	3.3901
−3.2	3.2001	3.2102	2.2202	3.2302	3.2402	3.2502	3.2602	3.2701	3.2801	3.2901
−3.1	3.1003	3.1103	3.1202	3.1302	3.1402	3.1502	3.1602	3.1702	3.1802	3.1902
−3.0	3.0040	3.0104	3.0204	3.0303	3.0403	3.0503	3.0603	3.0703	3.0803	3.0903
−2.9	2.9005	2.9105	2.9205	2.9305	2.9405	2.9505	2.9604	2.9704	2.9804	2.9904
−2.8	2.8008	2.8107	2.8207	2.8307	2.8407	2.8506	2.8606	2.8706	2.8806	2.8906
−2.7	2.7011	2.7110	2.7210	2.7310	2.7410	2.7509	2.7609	2.7708	2.7808	2.7908
−2.6	2.6015	2.6114	2.6214	2.6313	2.6413	2.6512	2.6612	2.6712	2.6811	2.6911
−2.5	2.5010	2.5119	2.5219	2.5318	2.5418	2.5517	2.5617	2.5716	2.5816	2.5915
−2.4	2.4027	2.4126	2.4226	2.4325	2.4424	2.4523	2.4623	2.4722	2.4821	2.4921
−2.3	2.3037	2.3136	2.3235	2.3334	2.3433	2.3532	2.3631	2.3730	2.3829	2.3928
−2.2	2.2049	2.2148	2.2246	2.2345	2.2444	2.2542	2.2641	2.2740	2.2839	2.2938
−2.1	2.1065	2.1163	2.1261	2.1360	2.1458	2.1556	2.1655	2.1753	2.1852	2.1950
−2.0	2.0085	2.0183	2.0280	2.0378	2.0476	2.0574	2.0672	2.0770	2.0868	2.0966
−1.9	1.9111	1.9208	1.9305	1.9402	1.9500	1.9597	1.9694	1.9792	1.9890	1.9987
−1.8	1.8143	1.8239	1.8336	1.8432	1.8529	1.8626	1.8723	1.8819	1.8916	1.9013
−1.7	1.7183	1.7278	1.7374	1.7470	1.7566	1.7662	1.7758	1.7854	1.7950	1.8046
−1.6	1.6232	1.6327	1.6422	1.6516	1.6611	1.6706	1.6801	1.6897	1.6992	1.7087
−1.5	1.5293	1.5386	1.5480	1.5574	1.5667	1.5761	1.5855	1.5949	1.6044	1.6138

z	.00	.01	.02	.03	.04	.05	.06	.07	.08	.09
−1.4	1.4367	1.4459	1.4551	1.4643	1.4736	1.4828	1.4921	1.5014	1.5107	1.5200
−1.3	1.3455	1.3546	1.3636	1.3727	1.3818	1.3909	1.4000	1.4092	1.4118	1.4275
−1.2	1.2561	1.2650	1.2738	1.2827	1.2917	1.3006	1.3095	1.3185	1.3275	1.3365
−1.1	1.1686	1.1773	1.1859	1.1946	1.2034	1.2121	1.2209	1.2296	1.2384	1.2473
−1.0	1.0883	1.0917	1.1002	1.1087	1.1172	1.1257	1.1342	1.1428	1.1514	1.1600
−0.9	1.0004	1.0086	1.0168	1.0250	1.0333	1.0416	1.0499	1.0582	1.0665	1.0749
−0.8	0.9202	0.9281	0.9361	0.9440	0.9520	0.9600	0.9680	0.9761	0.9842	0.9923
−0.7	0.8429	0.8505	0.8581	0.8658	0.8734	0.8812	0.8889	0.8967	0.9045	0.9123
−0.6	0.7687	0.7759	0.7833	0.7906	0.7980	0.8054	0.8128	0.8203	0.8278	0.8353
−0.5	0.6978	0.7047	0.7117	0.7187	0.7257	0.7328	0.7399	0.7471	0.7542	0.7614
−0.4	0.6304	0.6370	0.6436	0.6503	0.6569	0.6637	0.6704	0.6772	0.6840	0.6909
−0.3	0.5668	0.5730	0.5792	0.5855	0.5918	0.5981	0.6045	0.6109	0.6174	0.6239
−0.2	0.5069	0.5127	0.5186	0.5244	0.5304	0.5363	0.5424	0.5484	0.5545	0.5606
−0.1	0.4509	0.4564	0.4618	0.4673	0.4728	0.4784	0.4840	0.4897	0.4954	0.5011
−0.0	0.3989	0.4040	0.4090	0.4141	0.4193	0.4244	0.4297	0.4349	0.4402	0.4456
0.0	0.3989	0.3940	0.3890	0.3841	0.3793	0.3744	0.3697	0.3649	0.3602	0.3556
0.1	0.3509	0.3464	0.3418	0.3373	0.3328	0.3284	0.3240	0.3197	0.3154	0.3111
0.2	0.3069	0.3027	0.2986	0.2944	0.2904	0.2863	0.2824	0.2784	0.2745	0.2706
0.3	0.2668	0.2630	0.2592	0.2555	0.2518	0.2481	0.2445	0.2409	0.2374	0.2339
0.4	0.2304	0.2270	0.2236	0.2203	0.2169	0.2137	0.2104	0.2072	0.2040	0.2009
0.5	0.1978	0.1947	0.1917	0.1887	0.1857	0.1828	0.1799	0.1771	0.1742	0.1714
0.6	0.1687	0.1659	0.1633	0.1606	0.1580	0.1554	0.1528	0.1503	0.1478	0.1453
0.7	0.1429	0.1405	0.1381	0.1358	0.1334	0.1312	0.1289	0.1267	0.1245	0.1223
0.8	0.1202	0.1181	0.1160	0.1140	0.1120	0.1100	0.1080	0.1061	0.1042	0.1023
0.9	0.1004	0.0986	0.0968	0.0950	0.0933	0.0916	0.0899	0.0882	0.0865	0.0849
1.0	0.0833	0.0817	0.0802	0.0787	0.0772	0.0757	0.0742	0.0728	0.0714	0.0700
1.1	0.0686	0.0673	0.0660	0.0647	0.0634	0.0621	0.0609	0.0596	0.0584	0.0573
1.2	0.0561	0.0550	0.0538	0.0527	0.0517	0.0506	0.0495	0.0485	0.0475	0.0465
1.3	0.0455	0.0446	0.0436	0.0427	0.0418	0.0409	0.0400	0.0392	0.0383	0.0375
1.4	0.0367	0.0359	0.0351	0.0343	0.0336	0.0328	0.0321	0.0314	0.0307	0.0300
1.5	0.0293	0.0287	0.0280	0.0274	0.0267	0.0261	0.0255	0.0249	0.0244	0.0238
1.6	0.0232	0.0227	0.0222	0.0217	0.0211	0.0206	0.0202	0.0197	0.0192	0.0187
1.7	0.0183	0.0179	0.0174	0.0170	0.0166	0.0162	0.0158	0.0154	0.0150	0.0146
1.8	0.0143	0.0139	0.0136	0.0132	0.0129	0.0126	0.0123	0.0120	0.0116	0.0113
1.9	0.0111	0.0108	0.0105	0.0102	0.0100	0.0097	0.0094	0.0092	0.0090	0.0087

z	.00	.01	.02	.03	.04	.05	.06	.07	.08	.09
2.0	0.0085	0.0083	0.0081	0.0078	0.0076	0.0074	0.0072	0.0070	0.0068	0.0067
2.1	0.0065	0.0063	0.0061	0.0060	0.0058	0.0056	0.0055	0.0053	0.0052	0.0050
2.2	0.0049	0.0048	0.0046	0.0045	0.0044	0.0042	0.0041	0.0040	0.0039	0.0038
2.3	0.0037	0.0036	0.0035	0.0034	0.0033	0.0032	0.0031	0.0030	0.0029	0.0028
2.4	0.0027	0.0026	0.0026	0.0025	0.0023	0.0024	0.0023	0.0022	0.0021	0.0021
2.5	0.0020	0.0019	0.0019	0.0018	0.0018	0.0017	0.0017	0.0016	0.0016	0.0015
2.6	0.0015	0.0014	0.0014	0.0013	0.0013	0.0012	0.0012	0.0012	0.0011	0.0011
2.7	0.0011	0.0010	0.0010	0.0010	0.0009	0.0009	0.0009	0.0008	0.0008	0.0008
2.8	0.0008	0.0007	0.0007	0.0007	0.0007	0.0006	0.0006	0.0006	0.0006	0.0006
2.9	0.0005	0.0005	0.0005	0.0005	0.0005	0.0005	0.0004	0.0004	0.0004	0.0004
3.0	0.0004	0.0004	0.0004	0.0003	0.0003	0.0003	0.0003	0.0003	0.0003	0.0003
3.1	0.0003	0.0003	0.0002	0.0002	0.0002	0.0002	0.0002	0.0002	0.0002	0.0002
3.2	0.0002	0.0002	0.0002	0.0002	0.0002	0.0002	0.0001	0.0001	0.0001	0.0001
3.3	0.0001	0.0001	0.0001	0.0001	0.0001	0.0001	0.0001	0.0001	0.0001	0.0001
3.4	0.0001	0.0001	0.0001	0.0001	0.0001	0.0001	0.0001	0.0001	0.0001	0.0001
3.5	0.0001	0.0001	0.0001	0.0001	0.0000	0.0000	0.0000	0.0000	0.0000	0.0000

[1]The values in this table can be approximated from $E_{(z)} = e^{[-0.92-1.19(z)-0.37z^2]}$ when z is positive.

SELECTED BIBLIOGRAPHY

Ackerman, Kenneth B. *Practical Handbook of Warehousing*, 4th ed. New York: Kluwer Academic Publishers, 1997.

Allen, Mary K., and Omar K. Helferich. *Putting Expert Systems to Work in Logistics*. Oak Brook, IL: Council of Logistics Management, 1990.

Arnold, J. R. Tony, and Stephen N. Chapman. *Introduction to Materials Management*, 4th ed. Upper Saddle River, NJ: Prentice Hall, 2001.

Ballou, Ronald H. *Basic Business Logistics: Transportation, Materials Management and Physical Distribution*, 2nd ed. Upper Saddle River, NJ: Prentice Hall, 1987.

Bauer, Michael J., Charles C. Poirer, Lawrence Lapide, and John Bermudez. *E-Business: The Strategic Impact on Supply Chain and Logistics*. Chicago: Council of Logistics Management, 2001.

Bell, Michael G. H., and Yasunori Iida. *Transportation Network Analysis*. New York: John Wiley & Sons, 1997.

Bender, Paul S. *Design and Operation of Customer Service Systems*. New York: American Management Association, 1976.

Berry, Brian J. L. *Geography of Market Centers and Retail Distribution*. Upper Saddle River, NJ: Prentice Hall, 1967.

Blanchard, Benjamin S. Logistics *Engineering and Management*, 5th ed. Upper Saddle River, NJ: Prentice Hall, 1998.

Blanding, Warren. *Blanding's Practical Physical Distribution/Customer Service*. Silver Spring, MD: Marketing Publications 1985.

Bloomberg, David J., Stephen Lemay, and Joe B. Hanna. *Logistics*. Upper Saddle River, NJ: Prentice Hall, 2002.

Bowersox, Donald J. et al. *Dynamic Simulation of Physical Distribution Systems*. East Lansing, MI: Division of Research, Michigan State University, 1972.

Bowersox, Donald J., and David Closs. *Logistical Management: The Integrated Supply Chain Process*. New York: McGraw-Hill, 1996.

Bowersox, Donald J., Pat J. Calabro, and George Wagenheim. *Introduction to Transportation*. New York: Macmillan, 1982.

Bowersox, Donald J., David J. Closs, and M. Bixby Cooper. *Supply Chain Logistics Management*. New York: McGraw-Hill, 2002.

Bowersox, Donald, Patricia J. Daugherty, Cornelia L. Dröge, Richard N. Germain, and Dale Rogers. *Logistical Excellence*. Burlington, MA: Digital Press, 1992.

Briggs, Andrew J. *Warehouse Operations Planning and Management*. New York: John Wiley & Sons, 1960.

Brown, Richard A. *Applying Physical Distribution Management Concepts: A NAWGA Introductory Manual*. Falls Church, VA: National-American Wholesale Grocers Association, 1984.

Brown, Robert G. *Materials Management Systems: A Modular Library*. New York: John Wiley, 1977.

Brown, Robert G. *Rules for Inventory Management*. New York: Holt, Rinehart & Winston, 1967.

Brown, Robert G. *Smoothing, Forecasting and Prediction of Discrete Time Series*. Upper Saddle River, NJ: Prentice Hall, 1963.

Bruce, Harry J. *Distribution and Transportation Handbook*. Boston: Cahners, 1971.

Cavinato, Joseph L. *Purchasing and Materials Management*. St. Paul, MN: West, 1984.

Cavinato, Joseph L. *Finance for Transportation and Logistics Managers*. Washington, DC: Traffic Service Corporation, 1977.

Chase, Richard B., and Nicholas J. Aquilano. *Production & Operations Management*, 6th ed. Homewood, IL: Irwin, 1992.

Chopra, Sunil, and Peter Meindl. *Supply Chain Management: Strategy, Planning, and Operation*, 2nd ed. Upper Saddle River, NJ: Prentice Hall, 2004.

Christopher, Martin. *Logistics and Supply Chain Management: Strategies for Reducing Cost and Improving Service*, 2nd ed. Upper Saddle River, NJ: Financial Times—Prentice Hall, 1998.

Christopher, Martin. *Logistics and Supply Chain Management*. New York: Irwin, 1994.

Christopher, Martin. *The Strategy of Distribution Management*. London: Gower Publishing, 1985.

Constantin, James A. *Principles of Logistics Management*. New York: Appleton-Century-Crofts, 1966.

Copacino, William C. *Supply Chain Management*. Boca Raton, FL: CRC Press, 1997.

Coughlan, Anne, Erin Andersen, Louis W. Stern, and Adel I. El-Ansary. *Marketing Channels*, 6th ed. Upper Saddle River, NJ: Prentice Hall, 2001.

Coyle, John J., Edward J. Bardi, and Joseph L. Cavinato. *Transportation*, 3rd ed. St. Paul, MN: West, 1990.

Coyle, John J., Edward J. Bardi, and C. John Langley, Jr. *The Management of Business Logistics: A Supply Chain Perspective*, 7th ed. Mason, OH: South-Western College Publishing, 2003.

Dobler, Donald W., and David N. Burt. *Purchasing and Supply Management: Text and Cases*, 6th ed. New York: McGraw-Hill, 1995.

Ellram, Lisa M., and Thomas Y. Chol. *Supply Management for Value Enhancement*. Tempe, AZ: Institute for Supply Management, 2000.

Ernst and Whinney. *Warehouse Accounting and Control: Guidelines for Distribution and Financial Managers*. Chicago: National Council of Physical Distribution Management, 1985.

Ernst and Whinney. *Transportation Accounting and Control: Guidelines for Distribution and Financial Management*. Oak Brook, IL: National Council of Physical Distribution Management, 1983.

Fair, Marvin L., and Ernest W. Williams, Jr. *Transportation and Logistics*. Plano, TX: Business Publications, 1981.

Fawcett, Stanley. *The Supply Management Environment*. Tempe, AZ: Institute for Supply Management, 2000.

Fearon, Harold E., Donald W. Dobler, and Kenneth H. Killen. *The Purchasing Handbook*, 5th ed. New York: McGraw-Hill, 1993.

Firth, Donald, Jim Apple, Ron Denham, Jeff Hall, Paul Inglis, and Al Saipe. *Profitable Logistics Management*, 2nd ed. New York: McGraw-Hill, 1988.

Forrester, Jay W. *Industrial Dynamics*. Cambridge, MA: MIT Press, 1961.

Francis, R. L., Leon F. McGinnis, and J. A. White. *Facility Layout and Location: An Analytical Approach*, 2nd ed. Upper Saddle River, NJ: Prentice Hall, 1992.

Frazelle, Edward. *World-Class Warehousing and Materials Handling*. New York: McGraw-Hill, 2002.

Ghosh, Avijit, and Sara L. McLafferty. *Location Strategies for Retail and Service Firms*. Lexington, MA: D. C. Heath, 1987.

Gilmour, Peter, ed. *Logistics Management in Australia*. Melbourne, Australia: Longman Cheshire, 1987.

Gilmour, Peter. *The Management of Distribution: An Australian Framework*, 2nd ed. Melbourne, Australia: Longman Cheshire, 1987.

Glaskowsky, Nicholas A., Jr., Donald R. Hudson, and Robert M. Ivie. *Business Logistics*, 3rd ed. New York: Dryden Press, 1992.

Greene, James H. *Production and Inventory Control Handbook*, 3rd ed. New York: McGraw-Hill, 1997.

Greene, James H., ed., *Production and Inventory Control Handbook*. New York: McGraw-Hill, 1997.

Greenhut, Melvin L. *Plant Location in Theory and Practice*. Chapel Hill, NC: University of North Carolina, 1956.

Guelzo, Carl M. *Introduction to Logistics Management*. Upper Saddle River NJ: Prentice Hall, 1986.

Handfield, Robert B., and Ernest L. Nichols, Jr. *Introduction to Supply Chain Management.* Upper Saddle River, NJ: Prentice Hall, 1999.

Harmon, Roy L. *Reinventing the Warehouse: World Class Distribution Logistics.* New York: The Free Press, 1993.

Hax, Arnold C., and Dan Chadea. *Production and Inventory Control.* Upper Saddle River, NJ: Prentice Hall, 1984.

Heinritz, Stuart F., Paul V. Farrell, Larry Giunipero, and Michael Kolchin. *Purchasing: Principles and Applications,* 8th ed. Upper Saddle River, NJ: Prentice Hall, 1991.

Helferich, Keith, and Robert L. Cook. *Securing the Supply Chain.* Oak Brook, IL: Council of Logistics Management, 2002.

Hillier, Frederich S., and Gerald J. Lieberman *Introduction to Operations Research,* 6th ed. New York: McGraw-Hill, 1995.

Hoover, Edgar M. *Location Theory and the Shoe and Leather Industries.* Cambridge, MA: Harvard University Press, 1957.

Hutchinson, Norman E. *An Integrated Approach to Logistics Management.* Upper Saddle River, NJ: Prentice Hall, 1987.

Isard, Walter. *Location and Space-Economy.* New York: John Wiley & Sons; Cambridge, MA: Technology Press of the Massachusetts Institute of Technology, 1956.

Jenkins, Creed H. *Complete Guide to Modern Warehouse Management.* Upper Saddle River, NJ: Prentice Hall, 1990.

Jetter, Otto. *Global Purchasing Management.* Upper Saddle River, NJ: Prentice Hall, 1996.

Johnson, James C., Donald F. Wood, Daniel Wardlow, and Paul Murphy. *Contemporary Logistics,* 7th ed. Upper Saddle River, NJ: Prentice Hall, 1999.

Kearney, A. T., INC. *Measuring Productivity in Physical Distribution.* Chicago: National Council of Physical Distribution Management, 1978.

Kotler, Philip. *Marketing Management: Analysis, Planning, Implementation, and Control,* 9th ed. Upper Saddle River, NJ: Prentice Hall, 1997.

Lalonde, Bernard J., and Paul H. Zinzer. *Customer Service: Meaning and Measurement.* Chicago: National Council of Physical Distribution Management, 1976.

Lambert, Douglas M. *The Development of an Inventory Costing Methodology.* Chicago: National Council of Physical Distribution Management, 1976.

Lambert, Douglas M., James R. Stock, and Lisa M. Ellram. *Fundamentals of Logistics Management.* New York: McGraw-Hill, 1998.

Leenders, Michiel R., Harold E. Fearon, Anna Flynn, and P. Fraser Johnson. *Purchasing and Supply Chain Management,* 12th ed. Chicago, IL: Irwin, 2001.

Lewis, Howard T., James W. Culliton, and Jack D. Steele. *The Role of Air Freight in Physical Distribution.* Boston: Division of Research, Graduate School of Business Administration, Harvard University, 1956.

Lieb, Robert C. *Transportation: The Domestic System,* 2nd ed. Reston, VA: Reston Publishing, 1981.

Losch, August. *The Economics of Location.* New Haven, CT: Yale University Press, 1954.

Magee, John F. *Industrial Logistics.* New York: McGraw-Hill, 1968.

Magee, John F., William F. Copacino, and Donald B. Rosenfield. *Modern Logistics Management: Integrating Marketing, Manufacturing, and Physical Distribution.* New York: John Wiley & Sons, 1985.

Martin, Andre J. *DRP: Distribution Resource Planning: The Gateway to True Quick Response and Continuous Replenishment,* rev. ed. New York: John Wiley & Sons, 1995.

McKeon, Joseph E., ed. *Managing Logistics Change Through Innovative Information Technology.* Cleveland, OH: Leaseway Transportation Corporation, 1987.

Mirchandani, Pitu B., and Richard L. Francis. *Discrete Location Theory.* New York: John Wiley & Sons, 1990.

Monczka, Robert, Robert Trent, and Robert Handfield. *Purchasing and Supply Chain Management,* 2nd ed. Mason, OH: South-Western College Publishing, 2002.

Morreale, Dick, and Bob Elliott. *Logistics Rules of Thumb, Facts & Definitions V*. Unpublished, 2001.

Morris, William T. *Analysis for Materials Handling Management*. Homewood, IL: Irwin, 1962.

Mossman, Frank H., Paul Bankit, and Omar K. Helferich. *Logistics System Analysis*. Washington, DC: University Press of America, 1977.

Mulcahy, David E. *Warehouse Distribution and Operations Handbook*. New York: McGraw-Hill, 1993.

Narasimhan, Seethrarama, Dennis W. McLeavy, and Peter J. Billington. *Production Planning and Inventory Control*, 2nd ed. Upper Saddle River, NJ: Prentice Hall, 1995.

Novack, Robert A. "Quality and Control in Logistics: A Process Model," *International Journal of Physical Distribution & Materials Management*, Vol. 19, No. 11 (1989).

Orlicky, Joseph. *Materials Requirements Planning*. New York: McGraw-Hill, 1975.

Plowman, E. Grosvenor. *Elements of Business Logistics*. Stanford, CA: Stanford University Press, 1964.

Raedels, Alan R. *Value-Focused Supply Management: Getting the Most Out of the Supply Function*. New York: McGraw-Hill, 1994.

Robeson, James, F., and William C. Capacino, eds. *The Logistics Handbook*. New York: The Free Press, 1994.

Rogers, Dale, and Ronald S. Tibben-Lembke. *Going Backwards: Reverse Logistics Trends and Practices*. Reno, NV: Reverse Logistics Executive Council, 1999.

Rose, Warren. *Logistics Management: Systems and Components*. Dubuque, IA: William C. Brown, 1979.

Sampson, Roy J., Martin T. Farris, and David L. Schrock. *Domestic Transportation: Practice, Theory, and Policy*, 6th ed. Boston: Houghton Mifflin, 1990.

Schary, Philip B. *Logistics Decisions*. New York: Dryden Press, 1984.

Schary, Philip, and Tage Skjott-Larsen. *Managing the Global Supply Chain*, 2nd ed. Copenhagen: Copenhagen Business School Press, 2001.

Shapiro, Jeremy F. *Modeling the Supply Chain*. Pacific Grove, CA: Duxbury, 2001.

Shapiro, Roy D., and James L. Heskett. *Logistics Strategy: Cases and Concepts*. St. Paul, MN: West, 1985.

Sherbrooke, Craig C. *Optimal Inventory Modeling of Systems: Multi-Echelon Techniques*. New York: John Wiley & Sons, 1992.

Silver, Edward A., and Rein Peterson. *Decision Systems for Inventory Management and Production Planning*, 2nd ed. New York: John Wiley & Sons 1985.

Simchi-Levy, Philip Kaminsky, and Edith Simchi-Levy *Designing and Managing the Supply Chain: Concepts, Strategies, and Case Studies*. New York: McGraw-Hill.

Smykay, Edward W., Donald J. Bowersox, and Frank H. Mossman. *Physical Distribution Management*. New York: Macmillan, 1961.

Stephenson, Frederick J. *Transportation USA*. Reading, MA: Addison-Wesley, 1987.

Stock, James R., and Douglas M. Lambert. *Strategic Logistics Management*, 4th ed. New York: McGraw-Hill Irwin, 2001.

Sussans, J. E. *Industrial Logistics*. London: Gower Press, 1969.

Taaffe, Edward J., Howard L. Gauther, Jr., and Morton E. O'Kelly. *Geography of Transportation*, 2nd ed. Upper Saddle River, NJ: Prentice Hall, 1996.

Taff, Charles A. *Management of Physical Distribution & Transportation*, 6th ed. Homewood, IL: Irwin, 1978.

Taylor, David H., ed. *Global Cases in Logistics and Supply Chain Management*. London: International Thomson Business Press, 1997.

Tersine, Richard J. *Principles of Inventory and Materials Management*, 4th ed. Upper Saddle River, NJ: Prentice Hall, 1994.

Tompkins, James A., and Dale Harmelink, eds. *The Distribution Management Handbook*. New York: McGraw-Hill, 1993.

Tompkins, James A., and John A. White. *Facilities Planning*. New York: John Wiley & Sons, 1984.

Tyworth, John E., Joseph L. Cavinato, and John C. Langley. *Traffic Management: Planning, Operations, and Control*. Reading, MA: Addison-Wesley, 1987.

Vanbuijtenen, Pieter, Martin Christopher, and Gordon Wills, eds. *Business Logistics*. The Hague: Martinus Nijhoff, 1976.

Vollmann, Thomas E., William L. Berry, and D. Clay Whybark. *Manufacturing, Planning, and Control Systems*, 4th ed. New York: McGraw-Hill Irwin, 1997.

Waters, C. D. J. *Inventory Control and Management*. New York: John Wiley & Sons, 1992.

Weir, Stanley. *Order Selection*. New York: American Management Association, 1968.

Wentworth, Felix, Martin Christopher, Gordon Wills, and Bernard Lalonde. *Managing International Distribution*. Hampshire England: Gower Press, 1979.

Wentworth, F. R. L. *Physical Distribution Management*. London: Gower Press, 1970.

Werner, Pamela A. *A Survey of National Geocoding Systems*, Report no. DOT-TSC-OST-74-26. Washington, DC: U.S. Department of Transportation, 1974.

Wight, Oliver W. *MRPII: Unlocking America's Productivity Potential*. Boston: CBI Publishing, 1981.

Wood, Donald F., Anthony P. Barone, Paul R. Murphy, and Daniel Wardlow. *International Logistics*. New York: AMACOM, 2002.

Wood, Donald F., and James C. Johnson *Contemporary Transportation*, 5th ed. Upper Saddle River, NJ: Prentice Hall, 1996.

Wood, Donald F., Daniel L. Wardlow, Paul R. Murphy, and James C. Johnson. *Contemporary Logistics*, 7th ed. Upper Saddle River, NJ: Prentice Hall, 1999.

Yaseen, Leonard C. *Plant Location*. Larchmont, NY: American Research Council, 1960.

Zenz, Gary J. *Purchasing and the Management of Materials*, 7th ed. New York: John Wiley & Sons, 1994.

Zipkin, Paul H. *Foundations of Inventory Management*. New York: McGraw-Hill, 2000.

AUTHOR INDEX

SUBJECT INDEX

A

ABC product classification, 69
 in aggregate control of
   inventories, 376–78
Accounting reports, in network planning
   process, 623
Agents, transportation,
   178–79
 international, 183–84
Aggregate control of inventories, 376–84
 ABC product classification
   in, 376–78
 risk pooling in, 378–82
 total investment limit in,
   383–84
 turnover ratios in, 376
Air transportation, 173–74,
   176
 cost characteristics of,
   188–89
Alliances, 716–24
 benefits of, 716
 decision making on, 718–19
 logistics, 719–20
Area system
 modified, as order-picking
   layout, 488, 489
 as order-picking layout, 488,
   489
Artificial intelligence, control
   links to, 754–58
Assembly postponement, 51
Audit(s)
 benchmarking of, to other
   firms, 741–43
 freight bill, 740
 inventory, 740
 in logistics/supply chain
   control, 738–43
 total function, 739

B

Auditing
 of customer service levels in
   network planning,
   652–53
 freight bill, in transportation
   management system,
   152–53

Back-haul costs, 186–87
Back order cost, 339
Basing point pricing, 81
Batching
 item, 543
 order, 146
 in order-picking layout, 490
Before-after experiments, in
   sales-service relationship modeling, 108
Benchmarking
 in network planning,
   655–56
 to other firms in audits,
   741–43
Bid-rent curves, 553
Bill of lading, 212–13, 485
Blanket transportation rates,
   191, 192
Bonding, as public warehouse
   service, 483
Break-bulk, as storage system
   function, 475, 477
Budget, in logistics/supply
   chain control, 736
Bulk storage warehouses,
   480
Business logistics, 1–32
 definition of, 3–7
Business logistics management, 3–7
 See also Logistics/supply
   chain management

C

Business logistics/supply
   chain management
 in firm, 24–27
 objectives of, 27–28
Business operating docu-
   ments, in network
   planning process,
   622–23
Buyer surveys, in sales-service
   relationship model-
   ing, 109
Buying
 contract, 458
 deal, 456–58

Capital costs, 338
Capital reduction, as strategic
   objective, 36
Carload quantity, in rail transportation, 172
Carrying costs, in inventory
   management, 338–39
Cash flow, in measuring supply chain strategy
   performance, 57
Centralization, of organization, 705–6
Channel management, 461
Channel simulation in
   LOGWARE, 666–68
Chart, compass, and ruler
   techniques, in net-
   work planning
   process, 644–45
Claims
 freight, 213–14
 processing of, in transportation management sys-
   tem, 151

checklist of, 621–22

converting of, to information, 628–43

  facility capacities in, 641

  facility costs in, 638, 640, 641

  for-hire transport in, 630–32

  future demand estimation in, 643

  inventory-throughput relationships in, 641–43

  mileage estimates in, 635–38, 639

  order and shipment profiles in, 632–33

  privately owned transport in, 629–30, 631

  product grouping in, 628–29

  sales aggregation in, 633–35

  transport rate estimation in, 629

  units of analysis in, 628

encoding of, 624–28

geographic coding of, 624–28

sources of, 622–24

Data inaccuracies, sensitivity of inventory control to, 347

Deal buying, 456–58

Decentralization, of organization, 705–6, 707

Decision support systems, 160–61

in logistics/supply chain strategy, 737–38

Decline, in sales-service relationship, 106–7

Deferred transportation rates, 205

Delay, claims for, 213–14

Delivery services, charges for, 210

Delivery time, 100

Demand

  coordination of supply with, storage in, 471

  forecasting, 287–91

  in inventory management, 332–33

  planning and, 43

  in total function audit, 739

  uncertain

    in materials requirements planning, 438–40

    periodic review inventory control with, 357–63

    reorder point inventory control with, 349–53, 355–57

Demand-related transportation rates, 192–93

Demurrage charges, 210–11

Derived demand, forecasting, 288, 290

Detention charges, 210–11

Differentiated distribution, 47–48

Diminishing returns, in sales-service relationship, 106

Discounts, quantity, 84–86

Distance-related transportation rates, 190–92

Distribution

  differentiated, 47–48

  normal, standardized, areas under, 761–65

Distribution channel, physical, 7

Distribution lines, lengthening and increased complexity of, 15–17

Distribution-requirements planning (DRP), 443

  mechanics of, 445–46

Distribution warehouse, 474–75, 476, 477

Diversion, of shipment, charges for, 205–6

Documentation

  for freight transportation, 212–15

  by public warehouses, 484–85

Dollar averaging, in purchasing, 452–53

DRP. *See* Distribution-requirements planning (DRP)

Dynamic warehouse location, 582–86

E

E-commerce, logistics information system and, 159–60

Economies of scale, transportation and, 166

80-20 curve, 68–71

Environment management, logistics/supply chain management in, 23–24

Equipment

  materials handling, replacement of, 527–28, 529

  movement, in materials handling, 490–93

  storage, in materials handling, 490

Error, forecast, prediction problems involving, 311–14

Error tolerance, in logistics/supply chain control system, 734

Expert systems models, in network planning process, 649–50

Exponential smoothing, in forecasting, 297–305

  correcting for trend and seasonality in, 300–301

  correcting for trend in, 299–300

Freight
  bill payment and auditing
      for, in transportation
      management system,
      152–53
  consolidation of
      decisions on, 252–54
      in transportation manage-
      ment system, 151
  containerized, 177–78
  equalization pricing of, 79,
      81
Freight-all-kinds (FAK)
      transportation rate,
      201
Freight bill, 213
Freight bill audits, 740
Freight claims, 213–14
Fulfillment process, 92–93

G

Game playing, in sales-service
      relationship model-
      ing, 108–9
General merchandise ware-
      houses, 480
Geocoding, of data in network
      planning process,
      624–28
Geographic pricing methods,
      77–83
Globalization, supply and dis-
      tribution lines and,
      15–17
Global positioning systems, in
      tracking shipments,
      152
Graphic performance chart,
      748–50
Guided linear programming,
      in facility location
      selection, 578–81

H

Heuristic models
  of facility location selection,
      573–81

guided linear program-
      ming as, 578–81
  selective evaluation as,
      574–78
  in network planning
      process, 646–47
Highway transportation,
      172–73, 176
  cost characteristics of,
      188
Holding, as storage system
      function, 473
Household goods warehouses,
      480
Hub and spoke location con-
      cept, 595

I

Importing, documentation for,
      215
Import rates, for transporta-
      tion, 204
Incentive pricing arrange-
      ments, 84–86
Independent demand, fore-
      casting, 288, 290
Industrial order processing,
      137–38
Industrial products, 65
Industries, classification of,
      facility location and,
      553–54
Information maintenance
      13
Information network, 42
Information substitution,
      116–17
Information system, 146–61
      See also Logistics informa-
      tion system (LIS)
Instantaneous resupply,
      345–46
Integrated supply channel
      management,
      443–45
Intelligence, artificial, control
      links to, 754–58

Interfunctional management,
      in logistics/supply
      chain organization,
      708–9
Interlining, charges for, 209
Intermodal transportation
      services, 176–78
Internationalization, supply
      and distribution lines
      and, 15–17
International transportation,
      180–84
  agencies for, 183–84
  documentation for, 214–15
  physical plant for, 181–83
  services in, 183–84
Internet, Web-based channel
      order planning and,
      141–45
Interorganizational manage-
      ment, 709–16
Inventory(ies)
  appraisal of, 328–30
  arguments against, 330
  arguments for, 328–30
  case studies on, 403–23
  consolidation of, 252
  control of, 340–85
      aggregate, 376–84
      (See also Aggregate
          control of
          inventories)
      pipeline, 374–75
      as public warehouse ser-
          vice, 483
      pull, 342–73 (See also Pull
          inventory control)
      push, 340–42
      supply-driven, 384–85
  decisions on, in system
      design, 40–41
  maintenance of, 12
  management of
      costs relevant to, 337–40
      demand and, 332–33
      objectives of, 335–40
          product availability as,
              336–37
      philosophy of, 333–34

minor adjustments in, 751
model of, 727–30
  inputs, process, and output of, 728
  monitor of, 729–30
  standards and goals of, 729
in practice, 736–38
pricing policy and, 740
profit center concept in, 736–37
reports in, 744–50 (*See also* Reports)
service targets in, 736
systems for, 730–33
  closed-loop, 730–33
  details of, 733–36
  error tolerance in, 734
  modified, 733
  open-loop, 730, 731
  response in, 734–36
Logistics/supply chain customer service, 91–129
See also Customer service
Logistics/supply chain management
  activity mix in, 9–13
  costs in, 13–14
  customer value and, 18–19
  in environment management, 23–24
  in firm, 24–27
  importance of, 13–24
  key activities in, 10–11, 12
  in military, 22–23
  in nonmanufacturing areas, 20–24
  objectives of, 27–28
  planning in, 28–30, 33–61
  quick response in, 19–20
  in service industry, 21–22
  strategic importance of, 17–18
  study of, approach to, 28–30
  supply chain in, 7–9
  support activities in, 11, 12–13
Logistics/supply chain organization, 691–725

alliances in, 716–24
choices in, 697–704
conflict management in, 712–16
decentralization versus centralization in, 705–6
development of, 696–97
formal, 701–4
importance of, 694–96
informal, 698–99
information strategy and, 704
interfunctional management in, 708–9
interorganizational management in, 709–16
large versus small, 707–8
market strategy and, 704
need for, 692–96
orientation of, 704–5
partnerships in, 716–24
positioning in, 705–8
process strategy and, 704
semiformal, 699–701
staff versus line in, 706–7
Logistics/supply chain planning, 38–53
  conceptualizing, 41–42
  levels of, 38–39
  major areas of, 39–41
  timing of, 42–44
Logistics/supply chain product, 62–90
See also Product(s)
Logistics/supply chain strategy, 35–37
  audits in, 738–43
  formulation of
    consolidation in, 52–53
    differentiated distribution in, 47–48
    guidelines for, 44–53
    mixed strategy in, 48–49
    postponement in, 50–52
    standardization in, 53
    total cost concept in, 44–47
  performance of, measuring, 57–58

selecting, 53–57
supply-to-order, 53–57
supply-to-stock, 53–55
Loss
  claims for, 213–14
  transportation service choice and, 169, 171
Loss function, 114–16
Lost sale cost, 339
Lot sizing, 146
Lumpy demand
  forecasting, 288, 290
  prediction problems involving, 310–11

M

Manufacturing postponement, 51
Marketing
  logistics and, 25, 26–27
  storage system and, 472
Materials handling
  considerations on, 486–93
  equipment for, replacement of, 527–28, 529
  as function of storage system, 477–79
  load unitization in, 486–87
  movement equipment choice in, 490–93
  order-picking operations in, 541–44
  space layout in, 487–90
  storage equipment choice in, 490
  system for
    design of, 522–41
    type of, 523–27
Materials requirements planning (MRP), 433–41
  demand uncertainty in, 438–40
  lead time uncertainty in, 440–41
  order release quantity in, 441–42
Microlocation problems, 595

Mileage, estimates of, in network planning, 635–38, 639
Military, logistics/supply chain management in, 22–23
Miniwarehouses, 480
Min-max system, of inventory control, 363–68
Mixed buying strategy, in purchasing, 450–52
Mixed integer linear programming, in multiple facility location selection, 564–69
Mixing, as storage system function, 477, 478
Movement, to and from storage, as materials handling function, 478
Movement equipment choice, in materials handling, 490–93
MRP. *See* Materials requirements planning (MRP)
Multi-echelon inventories, 334–35
  in pull inventory control, 370–73
Multiple center-of-gravity approach, to facility location, 563–64
Multiple item, multiple location method, of inventory control, 368–70
Multiple regression analysis, in forecasting, 309

N

Network configuration
  comparable data in, 661–62
  design year analysis in, 662
  establishing benchmark costs in, 656–59
  establishing service levels in, 656–59

improved benchmark in, 660
maximizing opportunity in, 660
in network planning, 656–62
practical designs in, 660–61
what-if analysis in, 661
Network planning process, 618–90
analysis in
  channel design in, 662–68
  conducting, 651–68
    auditing customer service levels in, 652–53
    benchmarking in, 655–56
    channel design in, 662–68
    integrated supply chain planning in, 668
    network configuration in, 656–62
  integrated supply chain planning in, 668
  models for, 644–50
    chart, compass, and ruler as, 644–45
    expert systems, 649–50
    heuristic, 646–47
    optimization, 647–49
    simulation, 645–46
  organizing, 653–55
  tools for, 644–51
    decision support systems as, 650–51
case studies on, 677–90
configuration problem in, 619–21
data in, 621–44
  checklist of, 621–22
  converting of, to information, 628–43
    facility capacities in, 640
    facility costs in, 638, 640, 641
    for-hire transport in, 630–32

future demand estimation in, 643
inventory-throughput relationships in, 641–43
mileage estimates in, 635–38, 639
order and shipment profiles in, 632–33
privately owned transport in, 629–30, 631
product grouping in, 628–29
sales aggregation in, 633–35
transport rate estimation in, 629
units of analysis in, 628
encoding of, 624–28
sources of, 622–24
location case study in, 669–73
missing information in, 643–44
Nodes, in network diagram, 41–42
Noninstantaneous resupply, 347–48

O

Obnoxious facilities, locating, 595
Ocean freight transportation rates, 205
Open-loop control systems, 730, 731
Operational planning, 38, 39
Optimization models, in network planning process, 647–49
Order assembly time, 98–99
Order batching, 146
Order condition standards, 102
Order constraints, 102
Order cycle time, 98–102
  adjustments to, 101–2
  delivery time in, 100

Reconsignment, of shipment, charges for, 205–6

Regional forecasting, prediction problems involving, 311

Regression analysis, multiple, in forecasting, 309

Regular demand, forecasting, 288, 289

Regular stock, in virtual inventories, 386

Released value transportation rates, 205

Reorder point inventory control
with demand and lead time uncertainty, 355–57
with known stockout costs, 353–54
with uncertain demand, 349–53
average inventory level in, 351–52
service level in, 352–53
total relevant cost in, 352

Repetitive order quantities, 344–48

Report(s)
accounting, in network planning process, 623
cost-service, 744–47
inventory status, 485
in logistics/supply chain control, 744–50
over, short, and damage, 485
productivity, 747–48

Response, in logistics/supply chain control system, 734–36

Resupply
instantaneous, 345–46
lead time for, 346–47
noninstantaneous, 347–48

Retail information system, 156–57, 158

Retail order processing, 138–39

Retail/service location analysis, 587–94

covering models in, 592
game theory in, 592
location-allocation models in, 592
regression analysis in, 591–92
spatial-interaction model of, 589–91
weighted checklist in, 587–89

Retrieval, stock, in warehouse management system, 149

Return on investment, in measuring supply chain strategy performance, 57

Return on logistics assets (ROLA), 28

Revenue, logistics and, 27–28

Reverse logistics channel, 7–8

Risk characteristics, of products, 74–75, 76

Risk pooling, in aggregate control of inventories, 378–82

ROLA. *See* Return on logistics assets (ROLA)

Route, transportation rates by, 204

Route sequencing, 246–48

Routing
ship, 249–52
in transportation management system, 151

S

Safety stock, in virtual inventories, 386–87

Sale(s)
aggregation of, in network planning, 633–35
relationship to service, 105–9
defining, 105–7
modeling, 107–9
service effects on, 102–4
terms of, 461

Satellite communication, in tracking shipments, 152

Savings, in measuring supply chain strategy performance, 57

Savings routing, 243–46

SC. *See* Supply chain (SC)

Scheduling
just-in-time distribution, 442–46
ship, 249–52
of shipments, in transportation management system, 151
supply, 427–46 (*See also* Supply scheduling)
vehicle routing and, 235–52 (*See also* Vehicle routing and scheduling (VRP))

SCM. *See* Supply chain management (SCM)

SCOR model. *See* Supply chain operations reference (SCOR) model

Sequencing
in order-picking layout, 488, 490
product, 541–42

Service improvement, as strategic objective, 36–37

Service industry, logistics/supply chain management in, 21–22

Service levels, benchmark, establishing, in network configuration, 656–59

Service targets, in logistics/supply chain control, 736

Shipment(s)
consolidation of, 146
preparation of, in warehouse management system, 149–50

scheduling of, in transportation management system, 151

size of, transportation rates by, 201–4

tracking of, in transportation management system, 151–52

Shipment profiles, in network planning, 632–33

Ship routing and scheduling, 249–52

Shopping products, 64

Simulation facility-location models, 569–72

Simulation models, in network planning process, 645–46

Single item control, in periodic review inventory control, 358–61

Single-order quantity, 342–44

Small-shipment transportation services, 179

Sourcing, 458–61
  fixed, 458–60
  flexible, 461

Space costs, 338

Space layout, 487–90
  for order picking, 488–90
  for storage, 488

Spatial demand, forecasting, 287–88

Specialty products, 64–65

Speculation, inventories for, 331

Square root rule, 380–81

Staff type of organization, 706–7

Standardization, in strategic planning, 53

Standardized normal distribution, areas under, 761–65

Start-up, prediction problems involving, 310

Stock availability, in order cycle time, 99–100

Stockout costs, known, reorder point inventory control with, 353–54

Stock retrieval, in warehouse management system, 149

Stock spotting, as public warehouse service, 483

Stock-to-demand system, of inventory control, 368

Stop-off privilege, charges for, 206–9

Storage
  facilities for (See Warehouses)
  space layout for, 488
  in transit, 485–86

Storage alternatives, 479–86
  leased space as, 485
  rented space as, 479–85
  space ownership as, 479
  storage in transit as, 485–86

Storage equipment choice, in materials handling, 490

Storage system, 469–549
  in coordination of supply and demand, 471
  costs and rates for, 493–96
  functions of, 472–79
    materials handling, 477–79
    storage, 472–77
  in marketing, 472
  need for, 470
  in production process, 472
  reasons for, 470–72
  in transportation-production cost reduction, 470–71
  See also Warehouses

Strategic planning, 38–39

Strategy, logistics/supply chain, 35–37
  See also Logistics/supply chain strategy

Substitutability, of products, 74, 75

Superorganization, 710–12

Supply
  coordination of demand with, storage in, 471
  inventory control driven by, 384–85

Supply chain management (SCM), 4–7
  See also Logistics/supply chain management

Supply chain operations reference (SCOR) model, 752–54

Supply chain (SC), 7–9
  channel design and, 53–57
  definition of, 5
  efficient, 53–55
  extended, 13
  integrated planning of, 668
  locating facilities in, 550–617 (See also Facility(ies), location of)
  requirements of, forecasting, 286–325 (See also Forecasting)
  responsive, 53–57

Supply channel
  coordination in, 425–27
  inventories in, 327 (See also Inventory(ies))
  physical, 7

Supply lines, lengthening and increased complexity of, 15–17

Supply scheduling, 427–46
  just-in-time, 428–42 (See also Just-in-time supply scheduling)

Supply-to-order channel strategy, 53–57

Supply-to-stock channel strategy, 53–55

Sweep routing, 241–43

Switching, charges for, 210

System breakdown, 119–23

T

Tactical planning, 38, 39
Tapering transportation rates,
191, 192
Temperature-controlled ware-
houses, 480
Temporal consolidation, 254
Temporal demand, forecast-
ing, 287–88
Threshold, in sales-service
relationship, 106
Time, transit, variability in,
transportation service
choice and, 168–68,
170
Time postponement, 50–51
TMS. *See* Transportation man-
agement system
(TMS)
TOFC. *See* Trailer on flatcar
(TOFC)
Total cost concept, 44–47
Total investment limit, in
aggregate control of
inventories, 383–84
Tracking shipments, in transportation manage-
ment system, 151–52
Trade-off analysis, 44
Trade zones, foreign,
181–83
Trailer on flatcar (TOFC)
transportation,
176–77
Transit, storage in, 485–86
Transit privileges, charges for,
206–9
Transit time and variability,
transportation service
choice and, 168–69,
170
Transportation, 12
costs of, reduction of, storage in, 470–71
decisions on, 219–85 (*See
also* Transport deci-
sions)
in system design, 41

for-hire, in network planning, 630–32
privately owned, in network
planning, 629–30, 631
Transportation management
system (TMS), 150–53
claims processing in, 151
freight bill payment and
auditing in, 152–53
freight consolidation in, 151
mode selection in, 151
routing in, 151
scheduling shipments in,
151
tracking shipments in,
151–52
Transportation method,
230–31
Transportation rate(s)
basic trade-offs in, 220–22,
223
blanket, 191, 192
common, 185–86
demand-related, 192–93
distance-related, 190–92
estimation of, in network
planning, 629
fixed, 185
joint, 185–86
line-haul, 185, 193–205
class, 195–200
contract, 200–201
cube, 204
deferred, 205
for diversion, 205–6
freight-all-kinds, 201
import/export, 204
incentive, 202–4
for interlining, 209
ocean freight, 205
by product, 194–201
for protection, 209
for reconsignment, 205–6
released value, 205
by route, 204
by shipment size, 201–4
for special services, 205–9
for transit privileges,
206–9

by mode, 187–89
profiles of, 190–93
proportional, 191, 192
tapered, facility location
and, 554–55
tapering, 191, 192
for terminal services,
210–11
uniform, 190, 191
variable, 185
volume-related, 190
Transportation system,
164–218
agents in, 178–79
company-controlled, 180
competition and, 165–66
cost characteristics of,
184–89 (*See also*
Transportation rate(s))
documentation for,
212–15
economies of scale and,
166
effective, importance of,
165–66
intermodal services in,
176–78
international, 180–84
agencies for, 183–84
physical plant for,
181–83
services in, 183–84
price reductions and, 166
private, costing of, 211–12
service choices in, 167–71,
220–25
basic cost trade-offs in,
220–22, 223
competitive considera-
tions in, 222, 224
loss and damage in, 169,
171
pricing in, 167–68
selection methods for,
appraisal of, 224–25
transit time and variability in, 168–69, 170
single-service choices in,
171–76

air as, 173–74, 176
pipeline as, 175, 176
rail as, 171–72, 176
truck as, 172–73, 176
water as, 174–75, 176
small-shipment services in, 179
special service charges in, 205–11
Transport decision(s)
case studies on, 267–85
on freight consolidation, 252–54
service selection as, 167–71, 220–22 (*See also* Transportation system, service choices in)
on vehicle routing, 225–52 (*See also* Vehicle routing)
Truck transportation, 172–73, 176
cost characteristics of, 188
Turnover ratios, in aggregate control of inventories, 376
Two-points method, of sales-service relationship modeling, 107–8

U

Uniform pricing, 79
Uniform transportation rates, 190, 191
Units of analysis, in network planning, 628
Unloading, as materials handling function, 477–78

V

Value, logistics and, 13, 18–19
Value-weight ratio, 73–74
Variable transportation costs, 185
Vehicle consolidation, 252

Vehicle routing, 225–52
for coincident origin and destination points, 232–35
with points not spatially related, 234–2325
with points spatially related, 233–34
for multiple origin and destination points, 230–31
and scheduling (VRP), 235–52
methods for, 240–46
implementation of, 248–49
principles for, 236–40, 241
route sequencing in, 246–48
"savings" method of, 243–46
"sweep" method of, 241–43
for separate and single origin and destination points, 225–30
shortest route method of, 225–30
Vendor-managed inventory (VMI), 157–59
Virtual inventories, 335, 385–89
Virtual warehousing, 496, 498
Visioning strategies, 34
VMI. *See* Vendor-managed inventory (VMI)
Volume-related transportation rates, 190
VRP. *See* Vehicle routing and scheduling (VRP)

W

Warehouse(s)
configuration of, 513–16
ceiling height in, 513
length versus width in, 513–16

design and operation of, planning for, 503–22
distribution, 474–75, 476, 477
dock design for, 520–22
rail, 520–21
truck, 521–22
financial space type for, selecting by, 509–12
location of, dynamic, 582–86
materials handling in (*See* Materials handling)
private, costs and rates for, 495–96, 497–98
product layout in, decisions on, 528, 530–41
activity profiling in, 537–38
stock arrangement in, 539–40
stock location in, 530–37
stock locator-identification methods in, 540–41
public
costs and rates for, 493–95
documentation and, 484–85
inherent advantages of, 480–81
legal considerations for, 484–85
services offered by, 481–84
bonding as, 483
field warehousing as, 483
inventory control as, 483
order tracking as, 483–84
stock spotting as, 483
types of, 480
site selection for, 502–3
sizing of, 503–9
method of, appraisal of, 508–9

READ THIS LICENSE CAREFULLY BEFORE OPENING THIS PACKAGE. BY OPENING THIS PACKAGE, YOU ARE AGREEING TO THE TERMS AND CONDITIONS OF THIS LICENSE. IF YOU DO NOT AGREE, DO NOT OPEN THE PACKAGE. PROMPTLY RETURN THE UNOPENED PACKAGE AND ALL ACCOMPANYING ITEMS TO THE PLACE YOU OBTAINED THEM [[FOR A FULL REFUND OF ANY SUMS YOU HAVE PAID FOR THE SOFTWARE]]. *THESE TERMS APPLY TO ALL LICENSED SOFTWARE ON THE DISK EXCEPT THAT THE TERMS FOR USE OF ANY SHAREWARE OR FREEWARE ON THE DISKETTES ARE AS SET FORTH IN THE ELECTRONIC LICENSE LOCATED ON THE DISK:*

1. GRANT OF LICENSE and OWNERSHIP: The enclosed computer programs and data ("Software") are licensed, not sold, to you by Pearson Education, Inc. publishing as Prentice-Hall, Inc. ("We" or the "Company") and in consideration your purchase or adoption of the accompanying Company textbooks and/or other materials, and your agreement to these terms. We reserve any rights not granted to you. You own only the disk(s) but we and/or our licensors own the Software itself. This license allows you to use and display your copy of the Software on a single computer (i.e., with a single CPU) at a single location for <u>academic</u> use only, so long as you comply with the terms of this Agreement. You may make one copy for back up, or transfer your copy to another CPU, provided that the Software is usable on only one computer.

2. RESTRICTIONS: You may <u>not</u> transfer or distribute the Software or documentation to anyone else. Except for backup, you may <u>not</u> copy the documentation or the Software. You may <u>not</u> network the Software or otherwise use it on more than one computer or computer terminal at the same time. You may <u>not</u> reverse engineer, disassemble, decompile, modify, adapt, translate, or create derivative works based on the Software or the Documentation. You may be held legally responsible for any copying or copyright infringement that is caused by your failure to abide by the terms of these restrictions.

3. TERMINATION: This license is effective until terminated. This license will terminate automatically without notice from the Company if you fail to comply with any provisions or limitations of this license. Upon termination, you shall destroy the Documentation and all copies of the Software. All provisions of this Agreement as to limitation and disclaimer of warranties, limitation of liability, remedies or damages, and our ownership rights shall survive termination.

4. LIMITED WARRANTY AND DISCLAIMER OF WARRANTY: Company warrants that for a period of 60 days from the date you purchase this SOFTWARE (or purchase or adopt the accompanying textbook), the Software, when properly installed and used in accordance with the Documentation, will operate in substantial conformity with the description of the Software set forth in the Documentation, and that for a period of 30 days the disk(s) on which the Software is delivered shall be free from defects in materials and workmanship under normal use. The Company does <u>not</u> warrant that the Software will meet your requirements or that the operation of the Software will be uninterrupted or error-free. Your only remedy and the Company's only obligation under these limited warranties is, at the Company's option, return of the disk for a refund of any amounts paid for it by you or replacement of the disk. THIS LIMITED WARRANTY IS THE ONLY WARRANTY PROVIDED BY THE COMPANY AND ITS LICENSORS, AND THE COMPANY AND ITS LICENSORS DISCLAIM ALL OTHER WARRANTIES, EXPRESS OR IMPLIED, INCLUDING WITHOUT LIMITATION, THE IMPLIED WARRANTIES OF MERCHANTABILITY AND FITNESS FOR A PARTICULAR PURPOSE. THE COMPANY DOES NOT WARRANT, GUARANTEE OR MAKE ANY REPRESENTATION REGARDING THE ACCURACY, RELIABILITY, CURRENTNESS, USE, OR RESULTS OF USE, OF THE SOFTWARE.

5. LIMITATION OF REMEDIES AND DAMAGES: IN NO EVENT, SHALL THE COMPANY OR ITS EMPLOYEES, AGENTS, LICENSORS, OR CONTRACTORS BE LIABLE FOR ANY INCIDENTAL, INDIRECT, SPECIAL, OR CONSEQUENTIAL DAMAGES ARISING OUT OF OR IN CONNECTION WITH THIS LICENSE OR THE SOFTWARE, INCLUDING FOR LOSS OF USE, LOSS OF DATA, LOSS OF INCOME OR PROFIT, OR OTHER LOSSES, SUSTAINED AS A RESULT OF INJURY TO ANY PERSON, OR LOSS OF OR DAMAGE TO PROPERTY, OR CLAIMS OF THIRD PARTIES, EVEN IF THE COMPANY OR AN AUTHORIZED REPRESENTATIVE OF THE COMPANY HAS BEEN ADVISED OF THE POSSIBILITY OF SUCH DAMAGES. IN NO EVENT SHALL THE LIABILITY OF THE COMPANY FOR DAMAGES WITH RESPECT TO THE SOFTWARE EXCEED THE AMOUNTS ACTUALLY PAID BY YOU, IF ANY, FOR THE SOFTWARE OR THE ACCOMPANYING TEXTBOOK. BECAUSE SOME JURISDICTIONS DO NOT ALLOW THE LIMITATION OF LIABILITY IN CERTAIN CIRCUMSTANCES, THE ABOVE LIMITATIONS MAY NOT ALWAYS APPLY TO YOU.

6. GENERAL: THIS AGREEMENT SHALL BE CONSTRUED IN ACCORDANCE WITH THE LAWS OF THE UNITED STATES OF AMERICA AND THE STATE OF NEW YORK, APPLICABLE TO CONTRACTS MADE IN NEW YORK, AND SHALL BENEFIT THE COMPANY, ITS AFFILIATES AND ASSIGNEES. HIS AGREEMENT IS THE COMPLETE AND EXCLUSIVE STATEMENT OF THE AGREEMENT BETWEEN YOU AND THE COMPANY AND SUPERSEDES ALL PROPOSALS OR PRIOR AGREEMENTS, ORAL, OR WRITTEN, AND ANY OTHER COMMUNICATIONS BETWEEN YOU AND THE COMPANY OR ANY REPRESENTATIVE OF THE COMPANY RELATING TO THE SUBJECT MATTER OF THIS AGREEMENT. If you are a U.S. Government user, this Software is licensed with "restricted rights" as set forth in subparagraphs (a)-(d) of the Commercial Computer-Restricted Rights clause at FAR 52.227-19 or in subparagraphs (c)(1)(ii) of the Rights in Technical Data and Computer Software clause at DFARS 252.227-7013, and similar clauses, as applicable.

Should you have any questions concerning this agreement or if you wish to contact the Company for any reason, please contact in writing:

Media Director
Prentice Hall Business Publishing, 1 Lake Street, Upper Saddle River NJ 07458